ALL AMERICAN
ALL THE WAY

ALL AMERICAN
ALL THE WAY

FROM SICILY TO NORMANDY

THE COMBAT HISTORY OF THE
82ND AIRBORNE DIVISION
IN WORLD WAR II

PHIL NORDYKE

ZENITH
PRESS

Dedicated to my wife Nancy
and my children Jason, Amy, and Robert

First published in 2005 by MBI Publishing Company LLC and Zenith Press, an imprint of MBI Publishing Company, 400 1st Avenue North, Suite 300, Minneapolis, MN 55401 USA.

Zenith Press titles are also available at discounts in bulk quantity for industrial or sales-promotional use. For details write to Special Sales Manager at MBI Publishing Company, 400 1st Avenue North, Suite 300, Minneapolis, MN 55401 USA.

Cover: Rochelle Schultz
Typography: Lynn Dragonette
Maps: Philip Schwartzberg, Meridian Mapping, Minneapolis

On the cover: The 2nd Battalion, 504th Parachute Infantry Regiment, June 5, 1944.
U.S. Army photograph courtesy of Julius Eisner

2009 softcover edition:
ISBN-13: 978-0-7603-3737-0

The Library of Congress has cataloged the one volume hardcover edition as follows:

Nordyke, Phil
All American, all the way : the combat history of the 82nd Airborne Division in World War II / Phil Nordyke.
p. cm.
ISBN-13: 978-0-7603-2201-7 (hardback)
ISBN-10: 0-7603-2201-5 (hardback)
1. United States. Army. Airborne Division, 82nd. 2. World War, 1939-1945--Regimental histories--United States. 3. World War, 1939-1945--Campaigns--Europe. I. Title.
D769.346 82nd .N67 2005
940.54/4973 22

2005541182

Printed in the United States of America

CONTENTS

MAPS

ACKNOWLEDGMENTS

Many people deserve my gratitude for contributing directly and indirectly to the completion of this work. First, I want to thank my family, beginning with my parents. My father, Zyra Jr., helped me to develop an interest in history and an appreciation for the U.S. military. I developed a love for reading and writing as a result of the efforts of my mother, Marjorie. My wife, Nancy, deserves special thanks for having faith in me when this project was just an idea and for putting up with me during the research, writing, and editing processes. She tirelessly supported the project by mailing almost two-thousand questionnaires, assisted in many of the videotaped interviews, traveled countless miles to museums and veterans' residences, and provided constructive feedback on the manuscript. My children, Jason, Amy, and Robert, also deserve thanks for their patience during the many side trips to battlefields of the 82nd Airborne Division while we vacationed in Europe. My elder son, Jason, provided tremendous assistance between semesters at college, locating and contacting many veterans using World War II company rosters and formulating some of the company-specific questionnaires. Amy took an interest in the project, providing much emotional support despite being away at college. Robert gave valuable help by using his computer skills and knowledge of Internet search engines to locate veterans.

Any work of this sort would not be possible without those great authors who came before. Cornelius Ryan pioneered the technique of using the words of the veterans to tell the stories in his two landmark works, *The Longest Day* and *A Bridge Too Far*. Mr. Ryan graciously donated his wealth of research material to Ohio University in Athens, Ohio, for others to utilize. Many thanks to Doug McCabe, Curator of Manuscripts, Robert E. and Jean R. Mahn Center for

Archives and Special Collections, the Alden Library, Ohio University, for providing the materials referenced in this book.

A second historian and author, Dr. Stephen E. Ambrose, has done more to educate the American public about the sacrifices of World War II combat veterans than probably any author. Dr. Ambrose established the National D-Day Museum and the Eisenhower Center in New Orleans, Louisiana, to preserve the oral histories and written accounts collected for his monumental works, *D-Day* and *Citizen Soldiers*. I owe a great debt to Martin K. A. Morgan, Research Historian, National D-Day Museum, and the curator of the Eisenhower Center World War II collection for the copies of oral histories and written accounts.

The 82nd Airborne Division War Memorial Museum at Fort Bragg, North Carolina, was the source of a great deal of the primary source material for this book. Dr. John Duvall, Museums Chief, and Betty Rucker, Collections Manager, gave me total access to the Ridgway–Gavin Archives at the museum. I am deeply in their debt.

I appreciate the photos, maps, and after-action reports obtained through the generous assistance of Joe Hays, Museum Director, at the Silent Wings Museum in Lubbock, Texas.

Many thanks go to Ericka L. Loze, Librarian, Donovan Research Library, Fort Benning, Georgia, for her tireless work in obtaining for me monographs of 82nd Airborne Division veterans from the library's massive collection.

I want to recognize and thank others who have provided research materials for this work. Guy LoFaro and Normand Thomas sent materials that I needed from the U.S. Army Military History Institute and the U.S. Army Center of Military History. Starlyn Jorgensen gave me access to her history of the 456th Parachute Field Artillery Battalion and Doc Hardie's account. Albert N. Parker gave me access to some of the key 507th veterans' accounts. Rick Erny graciously sent copies of World War II rosters of the 325th Glider Infantry Regiment. Bob Burns and Robert Slivatz provided the unit journal, contact information for veterans, and filled in the blanks regarding much of the action of the 80th Airborne Antiaircraft (Antitank) Battalion. Jan Bos, in the Netherlands, sent his history of the 376th Parachute Field Artillery Battalion.

The book publishing process was new to me, after spending my entire career in the high tech industry. My literary agent, Ms. Gayle Wurst, Princeton International Agency for the Arts, did a great job of representing my interests with and educating me about the publishing industry. Author and historian Ed Ruggero provided much appreciated counsel regarding the business aspects of book publishing.

I owe a great deal of thanks to Richard Kane, Editor, Zenith Press, who has been a pleasure to work with from the contract through the editing process to the final product. Bob Kane did a wonderful job with suggestions for improvement of the manuscript. The copyeditor, Tom Kailbourn, did a great job getting the manuscript ready for publication.

Special thanks to the cartographer, Phil Schwartzberg, Meridian Mapping, Minneapolis, Minnesota, for the fine maps he produced.

My greatest appreciation is for the contributions of the veterans of the 82nd Airborne Division. Space will not permit me to mention by name and thank all of the veterans that provided contributions for the book. I must begin by thanking General Jack Norton, Colonel Mark Alexander, and Colonel Ed Sayre for their support and for inspiring me to write this book. I owe an enormous debt to 82nd veteran Don Lassen and his *Static Line* magazine. The publication provided most of the contact information for the more than two-thousand veterans of the division. In each of the unit organizations I found key individuals who were instrumental in opening the door to their respective associations. Ray Fary was of immense assistance in providing material regarding the 80th AA Battalion. Al Nemeth gave me much information and contacts for the 307th Airborne Engineer Battalion. I received invaluable help from Wesley Ko and Wayne Pierce with 325th Glider Infantry Association in providing exposure through the *Tow Line* newsletter and for written accounts that Mr. Pierce had gathered during the research for his fine book, *Let's Go!* Ray Grossman and Tom Mattingly were of special help in providing contacts, accounts, and help with the 456th Parachute Field Artillery Battalion. T. Moffatt Burriss, Ed Dodd, Jim Megellas, and Ed Sims, all veterans of the 504th, were of great assistance. Jim Megellas, author of the great book *All The Way To Berlin*, gave me great advice about the publishing process and great contacts in the business. I am indebted to many veterans of the 505th RCT Association, particularly Frank Bilich, Chris Christensen, Robert Franco, Don McKeage, and Joe Tallett for having confidence in my abilities and for encouraging the membership to contribute their accounts. The late Jim Blue and O. B. Hill, along with Francis Lamoureux with the great 508th Association made available their personal material as well as contact information for the members. Doug Dillard with the 551st PIB Association was instrumental in getting accounts by the veterans of the unit for the book.

Finally, I owe the most gratitude to the more than nine-hundred veterans of the division and their families who contributed to the book. It is with regret that the size of the book didn't allow for each and every veteran's account to be included. They will, however, be included in future regimental histories and books about each of the campaigns.

PREFACE

"IN THEIR OWN WORDS"

This is the story of the 82nd Airborne Division during World War II, told in the words of those courageous men who fought in some of history's most critical battles. The names Sicily, Salerno, Anzio, Normandy, Market-Garden, and The Bulge rank as some of World War II's, and indeed modern history's, most pivotal battles and campaigns.

The World War II 82nd Airborne Division has legendary status in the honored fraternity of great American military units. It ranks with the greatest of military units in American history, such as Roger's Rangers, Robert E. Lee's Confederate Stonewall and Texas Brigades, the Iron and Irish Brigades of the Army of the Potomac, and Darby's and Rudder's Rangers.

The veterans of the World War II 82nd Airborne are held in awe not only by other members of the airborne fraternity, but by countless others in the US and British armies who fought beside them; the citizens of Sicily, Italy, France, Holland, and Belgium who were liberated by them; and the German soldiers who fought against them. Having the 82nd fighting alongside of your unit instilled confidence.

German Wehrmacht units, upon learning that they faced the 82nd, were gripped with fear. The diary of a dead German officer found at Anzio stated that "American parachutists—devils in baggy pants are less than one hundred yards from my outpost. I can't sleep at night; they pop up from nowhere and we never know when or how they will strike next. Seems like the black hearted devils are everywhere."

Many of the paratroopers and glider troopers of the 82nd were only eighteen or nineteen years old when they fought in some of history's greatest battles. Most had come right out of high school. As readers, it's hard to imagine ourselves (or in other cases our children) at that age fighting under the most difficult conditions against a tough, determined enemy that in almost all cases had numbers and firepower superior to the Americans. Time and again, in every battle, the elite young paratroopers and glidermen of the 82nd won against long odds.

From the officer ranks came great men such as Matthew B. Ridgway, who later commanded all United Nations forces during the Korean War and rose to become Chief of Staff of the US Army. James M. Gavin became the youngest brigadier general in the US Army since the Civil War at thirty-seven years of age and commanded the division for much of the war. Maxwell D. Taylor, the 82nd's artillery commander, was promoted shortly before the Normandy invasion to command the famed 101st Airborne "Screaming Eagles."

But this book is not about the generals. It is primarily the experiences of the enlisted men, NCOs, and junior officers who did most of the fighting and dying, who lived in foxholes, who endured terrible living conditions, that provide the perspective for this story. It is about the cutting edge of close combat through the eyes of the parachute and glider infantryman. Although in some cases I have made minor changes to some of the personal accounts to correct grammatical errors and spelling mistakes, to rearrange a quotation to put it in chronological order, to omit certain portions of long quotations that contain repetitive or irrelevant information, and to be consistent in references to unit designators, equipment, and other items, the quoted material is always true to the veterans' original words.

It is through the words of these veterans that the reader will come to know incredible bravery under fire, an undying devotion to duty and comrades, and some of the most incredible feats of arms ever achieved by any military unit. These are the men of the immortal 82nd Airborne "All-American" Division.

This is their story . . .

AUTHOR'S NOTE

As a first-time author I wondered if I would be able to find a publisher for my book recounting the valorous exploits of the 82nd Airborne Division in World War II. Then, when Zenith Press published my work under the title *All American, All the Way: The Combat History of the 82nd Airborne Division in World War II*, I wondered how the book would be accepted by the critics, by the marketplace, but most importantly by the surviving veterans themselves.

Fortunately, the response from all three has been excellent, more than I could have hoped for, so much so that the publisher has chosen to reissue it in a two-part softcover edition. This book, *All American, All the Way: From Sicily to Normandy*, takes you, the reader, on a journey that starts with the division's reactivation in early 1942 as an infantry outfit through its conversion to an airborne unit with two parachute regiments and one glider regiment.

Stateside training under the All Americans' legendary commander, Matthew Ridgway, was followed by deployment to North Africa in preparation for the invasion of Sicily, which would be the U.S. Army's first mass parachute assault with the July 1943 night drop of the 505th Regimental Combat Team under the command of another legendary commander, James Gavin. Heavy combat leading to the conquest of Sicily was followed by the invasion of mainland Italy at Salerno, where, when the American beachhead was threatened with being overrun, the All Americans were called on to parachute into battle to save the day.

Fierce fighting in the hills around Naples further demonstrated the hard-hitting versatility of the 82nd Airborne, so much so that when the division was withdrawn from the lines to go to England to prepare for Operation Overlord (the cross-channel invasion of France), Fifth Army commander General Mark Clark begged General Eisenhower that some of the All

Americans could remain behind to bolster his Fifth Army. The 504th Regimental Combat Team was detached from the division and fought its way through the rugged Italian mountains to a point just south of Monte Cassino, and later landed as part of the amphibious assault of Anzio, where its troopers acquired the nickname "devils in baggy pants" taken from a dead German officer's diary.

While the troopers of the 504th were fighting at Anzio, the division's other two regiments, the 505th Parachute Infantry and the 325th Glider Infantry, were joined by the newly arrived 507th and 508th Parachute Infantry Regiments for the parachute and glider-borne opening act of what is known simply as D-Day. Following the All Americans' linkup with the seaborne amphibious invasion forces, the division's troopers were used as shock troops in the vicious hedgerow fighting that characterized the Normandy campaign.

In a few months after the release of this book, Zenith Press will publish "the rest of the story" of these valiant American soldiers: *All American, All the Way: From Market Garden to Berlin*. I hope you will enjoy this book enough to seek out the other.

—Phil Nordyke, April 2009

CHAPTER 1

"FIERCE INDIVIDUALISTS"

"There can be no such animal as a typical parachutist. Every 82nd Airborne trooper is by the nature of his mode of warfare an individualist of the first rank. His deeds individually and collectively are legend in the annals of American courage and initiative. His personality is as unpredictable as his dependability in combat."[1]

The young men who became parachutists and glider troopers with the 82nd Airborne Division came from all walks of life. Many had volunteered to join the army after Pearl Harbor was attacked on December 7, 1941.

All of the paratroopers were volunteers. They underwent some of the most physically demanding training conducted by the US Army at that time. The men who graduated from jump school had all found the courage to jump from high towers, then from C-47 aircraft in order to earn their wings and jump boots. It takes a great deal of courage to jump off of a 34-foot tower with only the strap attached to your harness preventing a fatal plunge to earth, and even more to jump from an airplane, especially if you've never flown before.

The "glider riders" were also a special breed. Even though they weren't volunteers, they also underwent a selection process of sorts. When the men of the 325th Regiment were told that the 82nd Division, of which they were a part, was being converted from an infantry division to an airborne division, some men went AWOL (absent without leave). Others immediately requested a transfer to other units. Those who remained flew in canvas and plywood gliders where every landing was a controlled crash. The paratroopers who saw what happened to these glider men felt they had the safer mode of transportation.

The young men who volunteered for the airborne came from almost every imaginable background and had many different reasons for volunteering. Ross S. Carter, a college graduate from Duffield, Virginia, volunteered as an enlisted man and observed that "every level of society had its representation among us. Senators' sons rubbed shoulders with ex-cowboys. Steelworkers chummed up with tough guys from city slums. Farm boys, millionaires' spoiled brats, white-collar men, factory workers, ex-convicts, jailbirds, and hoboes joined for the thrill and adventure of parachute jumping. And so, the army's largest collection of adventurous men congregated in the parachute troops.

"The thing that distinguished us from most other soldiers was our willingness to take chances and risks in a branch of the Army that provided a great, new, almost unexplored frontier. In other days paratroopers would have been the type to sail with Columbus, or the first to seek out the West and fight the Indians."[2]

Russell McConnell of Rumford, Rhode Island was 22 years old when he heard the news of the attack on the US at Pearl Harbor. "I was in a barroom that we all went to, and a guy named Jackie Clark, one of our friends came in and said, 'Hey, they just bombed Pearl Harbor.'

"I said, 'Where the hell is Pearl Harbor?' I didn't even know where Pearl Harbor was.

"I was working in a textile mill and was on what they called a 'move gang,' moving big rolls of cloth to all the different places [in the mill]. I had been moving these things and they were big, heavy rolls. I said, 'It's easier to wear this stuff than move it around here.' So that's when I went down on March 10th and enlisted in the paratroops."[3]

Another man in Rhode Island that night was Otis L. Sampson. Sampson had been in the US Army earlier as a member of the horse cavalry. He had left the army eight years earlier, with his captain saying, "You'll be back."[4]

Sampson and his family were driving home to East Greenwich on Sunday night, December 7, 1941. " 'Extra! Extra!' a newsboy yelled, as we turned right on a lighted street corner. 'Pearl Harbor bombed!'

"By the light of a street lamp and my front headlights, I read the headlines. A strange, sensational feeling passed through my entire body, 'War!' My first thoughts, 'I have to get back in the service.' 'You'll be back,' rang in my ears. That was almost eight years before.

"It was a small article from a magazine that a neighbor had shown me, 'Join the Paratroopers' that had made up my mind as to what branch of service I would choose."[5]

Charles Miller of Youngstown, Ohio, grew up poor like most kids at the time. "It was right in the middle of the Depression, and things were rough. Nobody had it any rougher than we did. But, we survived as a family, and came out of it. During that time, I started boxing and got pretty good at it. It really helped me after I got into the service."[6]

Miller was too young to join the army. His parents would have to sign the papers to allow him to do so. "I remember my dad and I got my mother in a corner and lied to her, and told her that I was going into the Aviation Cadets. I would never see a German, I would never get shot, I'd be safe, and I'd be an officer. She said, 'OK,' so she signed the papers. I had already joined the airborne troops. I don't know if she's ever forgiven me, bless her heart."[7]

James Elmo Jones graduated from high school in Warrensville, North Carolina, at fifteen years of age. "And since my father had then had a heart attack, I left western North Carolina to go east to get a job to make a living for my mother, dad, two younger brothers, and a sister. I was talented enough to get a job with a country and western band that gave me approximately one hundred dollars a week, which was excellent money for that period of time.

"In making money in music, I had several friends, and one had been drafted into military service for a year. He came home and I saw him on December 7, 1941. We were both talking about the raid on Pearl Harbor and wondered where it was. I knew when we had been attacked by the Japanese that I would be volunteering to go into the service. I asked him what branch should I go into. He told me there was a new branch of the service called 'parachutists' and that they didn't have to march into battle, but jumped out of an airplane into battle. I said, 'It sounds extremely dangerous. Why would I want to go into that?'

"He said, 'Well, for two main reasons. The uniforms are simply loved by the women and they pay more money.' So, the two together made it seem logical for me to join the parachute troops."[8]

Arthur B. "Dutch" Schultz, whose father was a US Marine during the First World War, wanted to join the Marines. Schultz was underage and his mother would not sign the papers allowing him to do so. He was able to get his mother to sign the release form to join the army only after she talked to the recruiting sergeant, who told her that Dutch would be assigned to an antiaircraft unit. She felt that was safe, so she signed the papers to allow him to enlist in the army.

"I got very tired of this kind of war time duty, particularly since my father signed for my brother, who was a year younger than I, to enlist in the United States Marines. I felt very bad about this. I'm living a sort of 'life of Reilly' and my brother, of course was already on Guadalcanal. And to make a long story short, I decided that it was time for me to make a move and to get into combat. And so it was, I volunteered for the paratroopers."[9]

Other young men had a more simple motivation for volunteering for the airborne. Twenty-year-old Chet Harrington from Erie, Pennsylvania, a surgical technician in an army hospital, volunteered for the airborne because "I wanted to see some action. This looked like the way I could get it."[10]

W. A. "Arnold" Jones from Winnsboro, Texas, joined the army at age seventeen from the CCC (Civilian Conservation Corps) shortly after the attack on Pearl Harbor. Private Jones was stationed at Camp Roberts, California, after basic training when he saw something that caught his eye. "I was in the Day

Room one day and they had put some pictures of people jumping out of airplanes. I said, 'What's that?'

"The First Sergeant said, 'Paratroopers. That's a new organization. Do you want to join it?'

"I said, 'I don't know.'

"He said, 'Well, they pay $50 per month.'

"And that was more than I was making. I only made $20 a month. I said, 'Sure.' About two weeks later I was at Ft. Benning."[11]

Shortly after his eighteenth birthday, D. Zane Schlemmer from Canton, Ohio, enlisted and volunteered for the airborne. "I had been attending Northwestern University on a work study program. I joined the paratroops because I was attracted by the $50 per month jump pay, which would help pay for my postwar college. Also, I wanted to prove my capabilities, and I also wanted a pair of jump boots and jump wings. And then, a third reason that I joined was that being of German descent, we felt that we had to make a point, and prove our loyalty."[12]

William Katzenstein grew up a Jewish kid in Bad Langensalza, Germany. "As a child in Germany, I played soccer and other games with other children in my town. I had a normal childhood in the late '20s and early '30s. By the mid-30s things started to change when most of my friends began joining the Hitler Youth. At that time they started calling me a 'dirty Jew.' Only ten to twelve Jews lived in Bad Langensalza and everyone in town ostracized us. The insults soon escalated into violence, which included beatings. I remember many trips home from school that included bloody noses and broken glasses. I began to find different ways to go home, but that did not work.

"My father asked me if I wanted to take boxing or wrestling lessons so I could defend myself. I wanted both. A day or so later my father found a man named Ehrlich, who had been a professional boxer and wrestler. He was about thirty-five years old and a socialist. The Nazis banned him from all professional sports. To make a living he taught wrestling and boxing. Ehrlich taught me boxing, wrestling, and Judo. His lessons included stuff in the book and not in the book. I trained three afternoons a week for six months. Finally, he told me, 'You're ready.'

"One afternoon shortly after my last lesson, the same Hitler Youth gang that regularly assaulted me on the trip home from school, confronted me again. That day there were five or six boys taunting me. That day I felt prepared and confident. Recalling my lessons with Ehrlich, I was able to maneuver the fight to ground of my choosing. I chose a building that had a large brick wall and had my back to the wall to eliminate the possibility of being jumped from behind.

"When they confronted me I turned around, but didn't cringe or plead with them to let me go as I had in the past. They were surprised and shocked at my reaction. I pointed at the largest boy and said, 'Who's the first fatherland fighter to beat up on the dirty little Jew?' I told the largest boy to step forward and fight me one on one. As he moved forward, I kicked him as hard as I could in the groin. He crumpled forward in a great deal of pain. I grabbed him by the hair and swiftly and forcefully raised my knee to his face. As I pushed him back I gave him another kick in the belly and he landed flat on his back. I then said, 'Who's the next fatherland fighter to beat up on the dirty little Jew?' At that, the boys fled.

"A few months later we emigrated to New York. Our family had several relatives in the country at the time. However, immigration to the United States was very difficult. In order to immigrate legally to the United States, every sponsoring family had to have $5,000. It was a law so that no one would be a ward of the state. Once in New York, we opened a dairy store and worked long hours to get by.

"In March 1943, I was inducted into the US Army. I went to Camp Pickett, Virginia for basic training. Solicitation Boards arrived on base and I signed up for Intelligence School at Camp Ritchie, Maryland. There, I learned numerous ways to think on my feet. For example, I learned everything from how to drive a train to flying a Piper Cub airplane. I even learned how to make a crude map with just a pencil, string and a clipboard. I was then sent to Camp Grant, Illinois and I started practicing [interrogation] on Africa Korps POWs. Not long after my arrival, a Parachute Solicitation Board came to Camp Grant and I signed up."[13]

William R. "Rusty" Hays from Dallas, Texas, graduated from college in May 1942. "I received three pieces of paper—a degree in Forestry from Louisiana State University; a commission as a second lieutenant, infantry; and orders to report to Camp Wheeler in Georgia for active infantry duty.

"At the time, I had a decision to make. I learned to fly in college, and was a licensed pilot. I could go into the Army Air Corps for further pilot training, or I could stay in the infantry with the assurance that I would eventually be in infantry combat. I chose infantry combat—why, I'll never know. There is no one more unready for the job of leading men in infantry combat than a second lieutenant just out of college. Nothing he has experienced prepares him for that. Fortunately, the Army had a remedy for that inexperience—the Infantry School at Ft. Benning, Georgia: A thirteen week training course for inexperienced second lieutenants. We sometimes referred to it as 'The Benning School for Boys.'

"After Infantry School, I went back to Camp Wheeler. About that time the North African landings took place and I asked the regimental adjutant to send me to a unit that would be going overseas. At that time I naively thought going overseas meant going into combat. I felt I should be in combat. I had a friend killed in North Africa, and I felt strongly that if other men were risking their lives in combat, then I had a duty to serve in combat, too.

"The adjutant sent me to an outfit in North Carolina slated to go overseas soon—an Airfield Defense Battalion. I knew right away, that was not where I wanted to be. I also knew that if I was in combat, I wanted to be with the best combat unit in the Army and this Airfield Defense Battalion wasn't it. I did get in the best combat outfit in the Army, the 82nd Airborne.

"When I reported to the battalion commander, a colonel, the first question I asked was, 'Sir, how do I get out of this outfit?' I thought it would make him mad.

"But, he simply said, 'No officer wants to be here. If there was any way out, I'd be the first to go. But no one had been able to get a transfer.'

"I was the first officer to find a way out—I volunteered for the paratroops."[14]

In the spring of 1942 a college graduate and the son of an immigrant family from Greece, James Megellas had very much the same decision as Lieutenant Hays, but made a different choice. Like Lieutenant Hays, Megellas had a private pilot's license and was an ROTC student in college. "On the day of graduation, 28 May 1942, when I walked across the stage dressed in a black cap and gown, I was given a diploma in my left hand and an officer's commission in my right. I was a second lieutenant in the US Army. Only moments later, I received orders assigning me, along with six others, to report for duty on 8 June 1942 at Ft. Knox, Kentucky."[15]

One week after arriving at the Armored Forces Training Center at Fort Knox, Lieutenant Megellas was transferred to the Signal Corps at Fort Monmouth, New Jersey. This was not what Megellas wanted. He wanted to be in a combat unit. "Shortly after arriving at Fort Monmouth, I read in the *Army Times* that another new branch of the army, the glider pilot corps, was seeking volunteers. It was given top priority for officer recruitment. Among the several qualifications was a valid current pilot's license. Happy day! I immediately applied, then waited. I was hopeful that I might still see action if I became a glider pilot."[16]

On November 5, 1942, Lieutenant Megellas was accepted into the glider pilot training program. However, in March 1943 the glider pilot training program was discontinued due to a severe shortage of gliders. "On 13 March, a board of officers arrived from Washington to interview the officers and men in the glider pilot pool and reassign them to the appropriate branches of the service.

"At the conclusion of my interview, I asked one question of the board: 'What is the quickest way I can get into combat?'

"The answer was: 'Go to the parachute training school in Fort Benning, Georgia.'

"That was it. The sooner the better."[17]

Briand N. Beaudin was among the very few men in his peer group to volunteer for the airborne. "I spent four years in ROTC at Georgetown Medical School and was graduated as a physician and first lieutenant on May 25, 1942.

"I was inducted into the US Army as a first lieutenant and given orders to report to Carlisle Barracks in Pennsylvania for six weeks of military medical training to be followed by reporting to the 97th Infantry Division at Camp Swift in Bastrop, Texas. That unit was due for a transfer to Fort Lewis in Washington State, and then to the southwest Pacific. I did not like those orders at all.

"After four weeks at Carlisle Barracks, a paratroop medical officer with the rank of captain appeared at all our classes. As I remember, there was a total of about 1,600 medical officers on the base. He informed us that the parachute troops were looking for volunteers and invited us all to a meeting that night, where the concept of parachute troops would be explained, jump paraphernalia would be shown, as well as an up to date training film. About four hundred medics showed up that evening. After the talk and viewing of the equipment, about three hundred were left. After the film, only twelve were present. Of these twelve, after physical exams, I was one of four who were chosen.

"I had volunteered for three reasons. First, I had always had a serious fear of heights. Second, the extra hundred dollars a month sounded very good. Third, a matter of pride, and the knowledge that this training would cure me of my fears or kill me."[18]

Jump School at Fort Benning was designed to separate the "paratroopers from the men." It was divided into four one-week segments: "A" Stage, "B" Stage, "C" Stage, and "D" Stage. During jump school the instructors treated officers just like the enlisted men.

Upon his arrival at Fort Benning, Private James Elmo Jones knew immediately that this training was going to be serious. "It seemed all of the instructors were at least 6'2" or 6'3", and we were simply frightened to death of them. And me in particular, since I weighed one hundred thirty-five pounds and was 5'8" tall."[19]

Private W. A. Jones' first impression of the instructors was that "they were the meanest son of a guns in the world. I still think so. I was afraid of them.

"The first week, every time my left foot hit the ground I said, 'What in the hell am I doing here?' Because you ran everywhere you went, you didn't walk. They told you were going to forget how to walk. And you did. The first week was strictly physical training . . . eight, nine hours a day. Everywhere you went, you ran. You climbed ropes. You had to be able at the end of the week to climb a rope thirty-five feet high; climb up and then to hold it until they told you, and then come down. You had to be able to do a minimum of thirty pushups and a five-mile run. There were certain things you had to do. If you didn't, you were out.

"We had sawdust in the building where you climbed the ropes. This one guy spit in the sawdust. The instructors made him get down with his mouth and pick it up, and go outside and spit it out."[20]

Like all new volunteers at Parachute School, Private Jones did an endless number of pushups at the whims of the instructors. "I don't care what you did. 'Give me ten.' 'Give me twenty.' They could meet you on the street and not like the way you were walking."[21]

William Dunfee found that "A" Stage was "an all out effort to 'washout' all but the most determined. The regimen was constant physical exercise, calisthenics and double time. While in ranks you were at Attention, Parade Rest or Double Timing in place. Pushups were given as punishment at the slightest provocation. You had the added pressure of knowing an Instructor could wash you out at any time, and for any reason. Rope climbing and tumbling exercises were repeated over and over again. This was to build upper body strength and [it] taught body control on landing. During this week when you sat for instructions, which was rare, you sat upright as near as possible to Attention. When standing there were only two acceptable positions, at Attention or Parade Rest, you dared not lean on anything. Your hands were at your side or locked behind your back at all times. You did not wipe your brow or scratch your butt, without being instructed to do more pushups.

"In retrospect I realize the instructors had their orders to make it tough on us, but some seemed to take a sadistic joy in taking it out on the few guys that were having the most trouble. Our one pleasure in life was day dreaming about catching that bastard in town and teaching him some manners. It was July in Georgia, and very hot, we had men pass out in ranks from heat exhaustion. If you made an effort to help the fallen man, you were instructed to 'Leave him lay soldier, he ain't dead.'

"One instructor, 'Mr. Jab,' got his nickname while giving oral instructions in the parachute harness. Anytime in his conversation he would say 'JAB!' You were to immediately strike your breast with a clinched fist. Woe be it to the last man to comply. He stood at Attention while having his ass chewed out, and then dropped down for fifteen to twenty-five pushups. This all but eliminated dozing and day dreaming."[22]

Lieutenant William Hays' jump school experiences were typical. "The training was directed by specially trained sergeants. They all seemed to be glad for the chance to give orders to officers.

" 'A' Stage was designed to weed out the weaklings, those lacking stamina and character. The weeding out process was in pushing us physically beyond what we were capable of. The sergeants running this stage were in superb physical condition; much better condition than any of the trainees. For one week they pushed us beyond our physical capability, primarily with long runs. You could pass out from fatigue. But, if you quit, you were washed out. Only about fifty percent of the class that started 'A' Stage got their jump wings.

" 'B' Stage was the ground training stage. We kept up our physical activity, and began to learn how the parachute worked, how to exit the plane, how to control the chute in the air, and how to hit the ground without getting hurt.

"We learned that we would be wearing a main chute on our back and a reserve chute on our chest. Our main chute would be pulled open automatically when we jumped. As we went out the door, we were to begin counting 'one thousand and one, one thousand and two, one thousand and three.' If we reached 'one thousand and three' without our main chute opening, we were to open our reserve.

"The main chute opened like this: All planes rigged for parachute jumping had a steel cable running down the middle of the plane just above our heads.

Our main chute, which was strapped to our back, had a 12 foot long web strap (called a static line) which was tied to the top of our main chute canopy with a strong string. The other end of the static line was attached to a snap hook that we could hook over the cable, and as we moved to the door to jump, we pulled the snap hook along the cable.

"When we jumped, the static line would pull tight, pull the cover off the main chute, and pull the chute canopy out of the pack. When the static line was fully extended, the string that tied the top of the canopy to the static line would break, leaving the static line hooked to the cable in the plane, and leave us floating free.

"The men who jumped together, and who will follow each other out the door as fast as possible, were called a 'stick.' We needed to get the 'stick' out of the plane at the rate of about two per second. The faster we got out of the plane, the closer we would be when we hit the ground, and the quicker we could assemble and sooner we'd be ready to fight as a cohesive unit. Again and again, we practiced on a wooden mock-up plane getting the stick out of the door as fast as possible.

"We also learned a sequence of steps that got the stick ready to jump. We practiced the jump sequence again and again so we could do it under the duress of combat.

"As we approached the DZ (drop zone), the jumpmaster would shout, 'Stand up and hook up.' All of the troopers would hook their static line to the cable, and turn and face the door.

"The next command would be, 'Check your equipment.' Everyone would check his own equipment as best he could and then check the equipment of the man in front of him.

"The next command would be, 'Sound off for equipment check.'

"If the stick had thirteen men, the last man would shout, 'Thirteen OK.' and hit the man in front of him. The man in front would shout, 'Twelve OK.' and hit the man in front of him—and so on to the front of the stick.

"The stick would then wait for the green light located on a panel just above the door to come on and tell us when to jump.

" 'C' Stage—here we continued our physical training and our ground training of how to exit the plane, how to control our chute, and how to land. Now we began to learn to pack a parachute. Every trooper had to learn to pack a chute. As incentive to pay attention and learn, we would have to jump with the parachutes we had packed. Believe me, that's a real incentive."[23]

Tom W. Porcella of New York City understood the logic behind this requirement. "I always thought that the reason they let us pack our own chutes was because if they failed to open, well, you had nobody to complain to."[24]

The two other most significant things about "C" Stage that made a lasting impression on Lieutenant Hays were "the two hundred fifty foot towers and the thirty-four foot towers. The two hundred fifty foot towers were pretty easy.

We were harnessed into a chute, pulled up to the top of the tower and released. This gave us the experience of landing in a parachute, which is the most dangerous part of the jump. As we came down we had to turn our back to the wind, look at the horizon (never look at the ground), bend our knees, and as we land, do a right or left tumble to take up the shock of landing. We were told that the landing shock was equivalent to jumping from the second story of a house. The two hundred fifty foot towers were a snap.

"It was the thirty-four foot towers that washed so many guys out of the course. They had us climb to the top of the tower where there was a mock-up of the door of the C-47 airplane. There was a steel cable that went past the mock-up door and ended, one hundred feet away, just over a twenty foot pile of sawdust.

"We put on a parachute harness that was secured to fifteen foot straps with a snap hook at the other end. An instructor helped us into the harness and snapped the hook to a pulley on the cable. We had to jump out and take the proper exit position, which was head down, knees bent, and hands clasping the reserve chute on our chest. After we jumped, we would slide down the cable until we hit the sawdust pile.

"A lot of trainees could not force themselves to jump. I think it was because the ground was so close. Although they knew, theoretically, that the strap holding them to the cable would catch them just before they hit the ground, they just couldn't make themselves jump. Instead, they would have to get down by climbing down the ladder, which meant they were washed out of the course. Fortunately, as in the rest of the course, I did not have any trouble doing what I was asked to do."[25]

Private W. A. Jones was one of the many men who were afraid of the thirty-four foot towers. "I came very near quitting. I don't know what it was. But I was just scared to death of those towers, and I still am. I froze in the [mock-up] door, they had to 'help' me out the first two or three times. I wouldn't have gone out if the instructor, Sergeant Swetish hadn't pushed me."[26]

By the end of "C" Stage, Private William Dunfee had two overriding goals. "A critique was held daily by the Instructors to point out any real or imagined goofs we had made. We enjoyed these ass chewings, because as each day went by we were that much closer to graduating. We could dream that special dream of getting a particular Instructor in Columbus, Ga. and teaching him some manners."[27]

The fourth week, "D" Stage, would be the culmination of all of the hard training of the previous three weeks. Each man who would successfully make it through "D" Stage would have to overcome his particular fears: fear of heights, fear of falling to his death, fear of freezing at the door, and fear of failure. Private Charles Miller was no different. "All of us were scared on that first jump. I had never even been in an airplane in my life, let alone jumped out of one. But, we jumped."[28]

Lieutenant Hays and the other survivors of the previous three weeks of jump school at last were in sight of their goal. "Monday morning of 'D' Stage we were marched to the packing sheds to draw the chutes that we had so carefully packed the Friday before. We were then trucked to the airfield, where the C-47s were waiting. We were formed in sticks of twelve, and climbed aboard a plane—one stick per plane, and sat down on the bucket seats along each side of the plane.

"The plane circled for a while, then headed for the drop zone (DZ). The instructor-jumpmaster took us through the jump sequence we had practiced so often.

" 'Stand up and hook up.'

" 'Check your equipment.'

" 'Sound off for equipment check.'

"Then, 'Stand in the door.'

"Finally, when we were over the DZ, the jumpmaster shouted to the first man, 'Go' and out he went. As each man would come to the door the jumpmaster would shout, 'Go,' 'Go,' Go,' until we all had jumped. But that was the last time we jumped as individuals. Thereafter, when the first man jumped, the rest of the stick followed him as fast as possible—which was the way we would expect to jump in combat.

"Monday night everyone went to the packing shed to pack a chute for Tuesday's jump—all but the officers, who had to pack two, one for Tuesday's jump and one for Wednesday's jump. On Tuesday night, the officers took jumpmaster training while the enlisted men were packing a chute for Wednesday's jump. The jumpmaster, usually an officer, was in charge of the paratroops during the flight into the DZ and would be the first to jump, leading the stick out the door. Finally, Friday and the fifth jump, which qualified us as paratroopers, qualified to wear jump wings and parachute boots. We had received our parachute boots at the beginning of 'B' Stage, and immediately stepped into a wash tub of water and walked the boots dry. This was the quickest way to break them in and adapt them to our feet. After that, we shined them everyday. We had worn the boots during jump training; but until we made our fifth qualifying jump, we could not wear them out of the training area.

"Now we could blouse our pants legs at the top of our boots and wear them anywhere so that everyone would know we were paratroopers. You might say that our jump boots were our greatest reward for being a paratrooper, and our proudest possession. And, boy did we ever keep them shined."[29]

Private Charles Miller took great pride in the accomplishment of graduating from jump school. "I was so thrilled to walk up on that stage and get my wings; I've still got them."[30]

Every man who had endured the four-week test would not quit. Each had overcome extreme physical exhaustion, mental stress, and fear. This was going to be immensely important in combat when lives depend on men not quitting when the going gets rough.

• • •

Matthew Bunker Ridgway, born in 1895, had grown up the son of a West Point graduate and professional soldier. Ridgway was a strikingly handsome, physically fit, confident, charming, and well-mannered young man, who projected the intensity and charisma of a born leader. Following in his father's footsteps, Ridgway graduated from West Point in 1917, shortly after the US entered World War I.

Lieutenant Ridgway was assigned to the 3rd Infantry Regiment stationed near Eagle Pass, Texas, on the Mexican border, where he spent the first fifteen months after graduation. Ridgway wanted to be sent to France to fight with the US Expeditionary Force. Instead, in September 1918 he was ordered to report to West Point as an instructor of Romance languages.

To Ridgway, "this was the death knell of my military career. The last great war the world would ever see was drawing to an end and there would never be another. Once the Hun was beaten, the world would live in peace throughout my lifetime. And the soldier who had had no share in this last great victory of good over evil would be ruined. I did what I could, of course, to avoid this sorry fate. Immediately, I started trying to get my orders changed.

"There was only one person who might help me that I dared address a communication to—a lieutenant colonel in the Adjutant General's Office at Washington, a former 3rd Infantry man. I wrote him a long letter, pouring out my woes, protesting my assignment to a dull and dusty teaching job while a war was on.

"I heard nothing for quite a while. Then a telegram came. It was signed by some officer I'd never heard of, who had taken over the duties of my friend. Its tone was curt. It told me, in effect, to comply with orders at once and to keep my mouth shut in the future.

"I stayed at West Point for six years, first as language instructor, then as tactical officer, and later as faculty director of athletics, a job that was given me by Gen. [Douglas] MacArthur, then the Superintendent."[31]

"No duty lasts forever, even in the Army, so finally, after six years at West Point, orders came transferring me to Ft. Benning, to take the company officer's course. I was fairly rusty, having been away from troops for a long time, but the extra hours I'd spent teaching tactics at West Point had kept me pretty well abreast of new developments in that field, and I managed to finish fairly high in the class—second as I remember it now.

"From Benning I was sent to the 15th Infantry, then on duty in Tientsin [China]. There, for the first time I had the high privilege of serving under Gen. [George C.] Marshall, then the Lieutenant Colonel commanding the regiment, whose friendship and faith in me in later years were to have a profound effect on my career."[32]

Ridgway quickly rose through the ranks of a shrinking US Army officer corps after World War I. His leadership skills, dynamic personality, and intense desire to excel at everything caught the attention of his commanding officers and other senior officers with whom he served, particularly George Marshall, now a general.

By 1939, Ridgway was assigned to the War Plans Division of the War Department in Washington DC and General Marshall had risen to the highest position in the army, Chief of Staff, reporting to the Secretary of War, Henry Stimson. It was here that Lieutenant Colonel Ridgway and General Marshall developed a very close relationship. Due in part to his foreign language skills, he was assigned to a number of diplomatic missions in Latin America, where he excelled.

One of the officers that Lieutenant Colonel Ridgway brought into the department was Maxwell D. Taylor from Missouri, West Point class of 1922. Taylor was fluent in several foreign languages and a naturally gifted diplomat.

Four days after the December 7, 1941, attack on Pearl Harbor, Ridgway was promoted to full colonel. Near the end of January 1942, Marshall promoted Ridgway to brigadier general and assigned him as assistant division commander of the soon to be reactivated 82nd Infantry Division, reporting to General Omar Bradley. General Bradley called Ridgway "one of the most charismatic and able infantrymen in the army. He was absolutely delighted to be sprung from Washington; I was lucky to have him."[33]

General Ridgway was very familiar with the 82nd Division's proud history. "The 82nd had been one of the great fighting divisions of World War I, with a record of having spent more consecutive days in the line than any other American division in that conflict. Its battle streamers bore the names of fierce engagements that glow in the pages of military history—Lorraine, Saint-Mihiel, and the Meuse-Argonne. Its greatest hero was the sharp-shooting Presbyterian elder from Tennessee, Sergeant Alvin York, whose feats of arms in single-handedly breaking up an entire German battalion have never been duplicated in modern war.

"It was a proud division, but it was a name, a legend, a memory only, in February of 1942, when General Bradley and I reported to Camp Claiborne, Louisiana. It had been deactivated in 1918, and had gone out of existence. Now the German was on the march again, and it was our job to recreate it, from a cadre of professionals picked from the best units of the Regular Army. We had nothing on which to build, except this fine nucleus of trained regulars and the bright legend of the old 82nd. To both General Bradley and me it seemed vitally important to indoctrinate each new recruit with the proud spirit of the old division—to plant in each man's mind that valor endured from generation to generation; that the great deeds their fathers had performed could be repeated by the sons."[34]

To build esprit de corps, Bradley arranged a visit and an inspirational speech by Sergeant York, the man who had single-handedly killed over 20 Germans and captured 132 others during World War I and was a Congressional Medal of Honor recipient. It was a huge morale booster for the troops.

The 82nd Infantry Division was going to be built from new recruits and draftees, who would receive their basic and advanced training as part of the division. The expectation was that the division would be combat ready after only seventeen weeks of training, not very much time to turn raw civilians into infantrymen. However, Ridgway was grateful for the opportunity and wanted to show his gratitude to General Marshall by working to make the 82nd Infantry Division the most highly trained division in the army.

Ridgway devised a training regimen that was designed to transform every man in the division into peak physical condition, including General Bradley and his staff. There were daily calisthenics, long runs, and cross-country marches in the hot Louisiana sun. Each man was also required daily to run an obstacle course designed to exert every muscle in the body to the fullest extent. The training included instruction in the use of small arms and heavy weapons, tactics, hand-to-hand combat, and field problems requiring maneuver.

Bradley and Ridgway were doing such a superb job of training the 82nd that General Marshall decided to assign General Bradley to command the 28th Infantry Division, whose training and combat readiness were not progressing satisfactorily. Ridgway was promoted to major general and given command of the 82nd Infantry Division on June 26, 1942.

James Maurice Gavin was born in Brooklyn, New York, to poor Irish immigrants, who both died when he was very young. He grew up poor, being raised by foster parents, Martin and Mary Gavin, in the coal mining town of Mount Carmel, Pennsylvania. As a young schoolboy, Gavin sold newspapers in the morning and evenings to help support the family. By the time he was eleven years old he had two paper routes of his own and sold other out-of-town newspapers locally. When he was fifteen years old his foster parents made him drop out of school after the eighth grade to work full time to help support the family.

Young Gavin knew that the key to getting out of poverty was an education. When he turned seventeen he left Mount Carmel and traveled to New York City to pursue an education. While in New York City, Gavin found out that he could obtain an education while serving in the military. So, he lied about his age and joined the US Army as a private. Subsequently, he entered an army preparatory school to apply to the US Military Academy at West Point. He won an appointment and entered West Point at age eighteen in 1925.

Gavin was an avid reader and became very knowledgeable in military history. He graduated in 1929 and became an instructor at West Point. "In 1941 I had been a member of the Department of Tactics at the Military Academy at West Point. Normally, tactical officers concern themselves more with the discipline of the Corps of Cadets than with teaching. However, I became deeply interested in the Germans' conquest of Europe and their use of a new arm—parachute-glider troops—and I taught as many classes as possible in the new and evolving tactics that could be learned from the European war. I had access to many of the original documents relating to the German airborne operations in Holland. I also read avidly the reports from our military attaché in Cairo, Colonel Bonner Fellers, on the German parachute and glider operations in Crete. The whole concept of vertical envelopment was an exciting one, and it would seem to offer us a new dimension of tactics if we entered the war."[35]

Captain Gavin requested a transfer to the fledgling US Army airborne program, but was denied the transfer by the superintendent of West Point. However, Gavin was not one to be denied, and he used some connections in the War Department to obtain a transfer. He arrived at Fort Benning in August 1941 to take parachute training.

After graduating from jump school, Captain Gavin was assigned to command Company C of the 503rd Parachute Infantry Battalion, commanded by Colonel Robert F. Sink.

New army surgeon Lieutenant David Thomas from Clairton, Pennsylvania, was assigned to the 503rd at the same time. Lieutenant Thomas knew there was something special about Gavin. "I encountered Jimmy in August 1941 when I reported in to the 503rd PIB, Bourbon Bob Sink, commanding. Jimmy had C Company, the sharpest in a sharp outfit."[36]

When General Bradley toured Fort Benning in late 1941, he inspected the new paratroopers, whom he described as "a breed apart—the toughest, best trained infantry I had ever seen."[37]

Lieutenant Colonel Bill Lee, commanding the new airborne forces, quickly discovered the brilliant young Gavin and moved him up to his staff as plans and training officer. Gavin was assigned to write the very first manual of the US Army's airborne doctrine, entitled *The Employment of Airborne Forces.* "My new job, as Plans and Training Officer gave me an exciting opportunity to experiment and develop new techniques for large-scale parachute-gliders operations.

"The problems were without precedent. Individuals had to be capable of fighting at once against any opposition they met on landing. Although every effort was being made to develop the communications and techniques to permit battalions, companies, and platoons to organize promptly, we had to train our individuals to fight for hours and days, if necessary, without being part of a formal organization. Equipment had to be lightweight and readily transportable. Weapons had to be hand-carried. This meant that larger weapons had to be broken down into individual loads, such as mortars and parachute-dropped artillery. Finally, since entry into combat was to take place in the midst of the enemy, a new scheme for issuing combat orders and coordinating the efforts of all the troops had to be developed. All these problems brought into sharp focus the most important problem of all—how to train the individual paratrooper.

"We sought to train the paratroopers to the highest peak of individual pride and skill. It was at this time that the use of nameplates was adopted, the purpose being to emphasize the importance of an individual's personality and reputation. To the soldiers of another generation, it seemed to suggest too little discipline and too much initiative given to individual soldiers. We were willing to take a chance that this would not have a disrupting effect on larger formations.

"It did not. Aside from the impact of this type of training on the airborne formations themselves, it had tremendous significance to the army as a whole. The morale of the airborne units soared, especially after their first combat, when they could see for themselves the results of their training."[38]

In December 1941 Gavin was promoted to the rank of major and given the task to help sell the concept of an expanded role for airborne forces to General Marshall and his staff. "In the spring of 1942 Brigadier General William Lee and I, as his Plans and Training Officer, went to Washington to discuss the creation of our first airborne division. The Washington staff seemed rather skeptical about the whole idea.

"However, after some discussion it was agreed that we could start the organization of an airborne division provided certain stipulations were met. The division had to be one that had already completed basic training, and it could not be a regular Army or National Guard division; the States would not want the National Guard made airborne. It was also stipulated that the division should be one that was stationed where flying weather was generally good and near one or more airfields. The one division that met all these requirements was the 82nd Division at Camp Claiborne, Louisiana."[39]

Major Gavin's potential for higher command led newly promoted Brigadier General Bill Lee to arrange for Gavin to attend the army's prestigious Command and General Staff School. After graduation, newly promoted Lieutenant Colonel Gavin was assigned to the Airborne Command at Fort Bragg. In less than a year he had risen from captain to lieutenant colonel. Gavin was made for the role of leading elite soldiers in this new, experimental form of warfare.

On July 6, 1942, he took command of the newly formed 505th Parachute Infantry Regiment, which was activated on June 25, 1942. Gavin immediately set out to make the regiment the best in the army, with training "just about as tough and demanding as we could make it. The troopers responded well. However, despite the rigors of their training, they always seemed to have enough energy left to get into fights in Phenix City, Alabama, and its environs during time off."[40]

In the summer of 1942 physician Major David Thomas was sent overseas on a temporary assignment. "I spent six weeks with a small group in England comparing our methods with theirs, and resulting in changes in chute packing methods and landing techniques which markedly reduced opening shock and landing injuries to ankles and shoulders—a most productive TDY [temporary duty] trip. I returned a Major and found myself posted to the 505 PIR, commanded by Lieutenant Colonel soon to be Colonel Jimmy Gavin. Jimmy, from the start put his imprint on the 505. He was a soldier's soldier, always on top of the training and in the field with the troops every day. Soldiers could empathize with him. I can remember walking down a company street behind a couple of young troopers and Jimmy was ahead of us.

"One of these young guys said to the other one, 'I'd follow that guy through hell.' What he didn't know was, that was exactly where Jimmy was going to lead them!"[41]

Colonel Gavin expected the officers under his command to put their men first and lead by example. Captain Walter F. Winton, Jr., came to the 505th to take command of Headquarters Company, 1st Battalion. "I never forgot Colonel Gavin's welcoming remark, 'In this outfit an officer is the first man out of the airplane and the last man in the chow line.' "[42]

Private First Class Otis Sampson first met Gavin in August of 1942 at Fort Benning at the graduation ceremony of his jump class. "Colonel Gavin had a body of men on his hands that were of a different breed, and it took a man like the Colonel to understand them. Over the months of his leadership, he went to bat many times for various ones."[43]

New jump school graduates were sent to the 505th in an area south of Fort Benning for additional training. This location had been selected specifically for its densely wooded hills with heavy thickets, numerous streams, the Chattahoochee River, swamps, and blazing hot temperatures in the summer. This area had even acquired an intimidating name. Like other new paratroopers, Private First Class Otis Sampson had heard all about this training area prior to graduation from jump school: " 'Wait until they get you out in the "Frying Pan" area!' we were told by troopers who had previously been through the mill. 'That is where they will initiate you fellows.' I looked forward to this 'hell hole,' as it was described. I felt it would toughen us for the combat days ahead. And, as others before us, we too started our training in the 'Frying Pan.' A place well named when the burning sun bore down.

"One of our first training problems was a night compass course. In groups of four, we took off; a small light a good distance away was our destination. Shortly after the compass course we were given an endurance test with backpacks. Again we started out in groups, but this time we were each on our own. An obstacle course had been another challenge. Being short, I had to jump that much higher to catch the top of those high walls that had to be climbed over. I knew if I didn't make them the first time, my energy would be so much less on the second try. The fun some of the officers had while we enlisted men were crawling on our bellies through an obstacle course where live ammunition was used, to show us what it was like to be under fire. Explosions were also laid to go off at timed intervals. One had to keep his butt down or get it shot.

"Many times during leisure periods, while in the field or after retreat, a few of us would get together and wrestle. Some of the officers would join in, especially Lieutenant [Frank] Woosley. For a short fellow, he was quite active and strong. Lieutenant [Roper] Peddicord was another who liked to get into the fray."[44]

During the 505th's time at the Frying Pan there was continual shuffling of officers, as new paratroopers were added from each jump class. One day Company E platoon leader Lieutenant Frank Woosley was introduced to a young lieutenant newly assigned to the company. "When I met Lieutenant Wray, he said to me, 'My name is Waverly Wright Wray, but just call me Charlie.' He had a Mississippi drawl. We wondered a little about Charlie. He had a soft face, maybe a little heavy, read his Bible daily, and did not drink, smoke, or chase women. He was not quite our picture of a real paratroop hero.

"We were on a forced punishment march and the light machine gunners were complaining. There was no way to carry a light machine gun that it did not hurt. [They are] heavy and all sharp edges. Charlie said, 'John Brown,' which was his harshest expletive. He took both guns from the gunners in the platoon that he was in, and carried one on each shoulder until the next break. This seemed impossible. Then he walked up and down the road, where the platoon lay in the ditch during the break, with the guns still on his shoulders, and carried them until the following break. We did not wonder about Charlie anymore. We all knew we had a man among us."[45]

In late July 1942, as the 82nd Infantry Division was completing its last few weeks of training, General Ridgway received word that the division would be converted from an infantry to a motorized unit. Then, just a couple of weeks later, the designation was changed again to an airborne division. The 82nd would be the first of two new airborne divisions, the other being the 101st. The 82nd would provide the cadre of officers and men to form the 101st.

On August 15, 1942, after a dress parade, General Ridgway spoke to the assembled division over a public address system, announcing that the division would be split into two divisions and the three infantry regiments (325th, 326th, and 327th) would become four glider infantry regiments. The division was now officially designated the 82nd Airborne Division.

The troops were shocked by the announcement. Not only did they not want to be split up; they didn't want to be glider infantry. The next morning over 4,000 men of the 16,000 men in the division went AWOL (absent without leave). Most returned over the next few days. Some officers and men from these regiments requested transfer to other units.

General Ridgway had previously met in secret with General Bill Lee, who would command the other airborne division, the 101st, to divide up their staffs. Newly promoted Brigadier General Don Pratt, the 82nd's assistant division commander, was moved to the 101st in the same role. Bud Miley was promoted to brigadier general and named as the assistant division commander of the 82nd, replacing Pratt. Brigadier General Joe Swing remained as the commander of division artillery, and his executive officer, Anthony McAuliffe was promoted to brigadier general and assigned to command the 101st artillery. Ridgway's new chief of staff would be Colonel Maxwell Taylor. Despite the losses of great officers to fill the command positions with the 101st Airborne, Ridgway's 82nd Airborne staff remained very strong, filled with great officers destined for higher command.

A coin toss decided that the 82nd's 327th Regiment would transfer to the 101st, along with one battalion each from the 82nd's 325th and 326th Regiments to form the cadre for the 101st's second glider regiment, the 401st. The 82nd would get the 504th Parachute Infantry Regiment commanded by Colonel Theodore L. (Ted) Dunn, with Lieutenant Colonel Rueben H. Tucker, III, as the executive officer.

Lieutenant Colonel Tucker grew up in Ansonia, Connecticut, one of six children in a working class family. He worked briefly in a brass mill as an apprentice. Tucker determined that this sort of work was not what he wanted and decided to embark on a military career. Tucker overcame several setbacks and graduated from West Point in 1935. Tucker was described by a member of Ridgway's staff as "a wonderful athlete and soldier. Fearless. Dedicated. A gung-ho combat officer, exactly the kind of fellow you want when you go to war."[46]

On August 29, 1942, the 505th left the Frying Pan for the "Alabama Area," officially known as Camp Billy Mitchell, just across the Chattahoochee River from Fort Benning and the Frying Pan.

Private Ross Pippin, assigned to Company C, 504th, remembers his own unit's training in the Alabama Area as "intense and rugged. Some marches were over twenty miles or more in a single day. We were also given a lot of weapon training. We were taught how to operate our weapons in the dark. There were some times that I really thought I had made a mistake by joining the paratroopers, and then I would see some scrawny little guys who wouldn't quit and I thought to myself, 'If they can make it, so can I.' At the end of the training, I was beginning to appreciate it more and more."[47]

Private James Elmo Jones, with Company B, noticed that the training in the Alabama Area intensified, "particularly night jumps and hand-to-hand combat."[48] Maneuvers and war games were conducted against regular infantry units to simulate combat operations.

While in the Alabama Area, the young paratroopers of the 504th and 505th would go into the nearby towns when they were given passes. Private First Class Bill Bishop was an original member of Company G, 505th. "Invariably, we would have fist fights up there. [The] 2nd Armored Division, we tangled with them every time we went to town. There was a lot of jealousy. The regular troops envied us because of our boots, the money we made, and the prestige we had.

We were considered the elite of the whole Army. We were a cocky bunch of young fools."[49]

The paratroopers of the 504th and 505th also became acquainted with each other. Though some of the ways were not sanctioned by the commanders, according to Private William Blank, another member of Company G, 505th. "Phenix City, Alabama and Columbus, Georgia were two towns frequented by the two regiments. Phenix City was the most notorious, and you didn't go to this town alone, except at great risk. Often fights would occur between [troopers of] the two regiments.

"Boxing was promoted between the two regiments, and Company G and the 3rd Battalion produced two champions, one being Tommy Thompson."[50]

Boxing in the 130-pound weight class was Private First Class Otis Sampson, with Company E, 505th. "Whenever we would have our choice of sports, I would always go where the gloves were. I did sign up for the boxing tournament in the Alabama Area. I wanted to win the championship belt for my son, before leaving for overseas."[51]

After Sampson defeated every opponent in his weight class during the 505th qualifying rounds, his next opponent was the champion from the 504th. They were evenly matched and the hard fought bout ended with a late-round knockout and victory by the much older Sampson. The next time he checked the tournament match-ups for his next opponent, Sampson received quite a shock. "After knocking out Sailor Robertson, the pride of the 504th, then seeing my name up on the billboard to fight him again on the next card, I withdrew my name from the fight roster. I didn't think I had to lick any man more than once in any tournament. I was thirty-one years old and not quite as fast as I once was—experience and hard hitting had won the match.

"On one of our field trips, as I was resting on the ground, Colonel Gavin came to me and said, 'Stay as you are. I see you have taken your name off for boxing.'

" 'Yes sir,' I replied, 'I don't feel I have to fight a fellow twice in any one tournament for the championship and besides, I want to devote my time to the training of my men.

"He waited a while and then said, 'I wish you would change your mind. It would be nice to have a champion in our outfit when we get overseas.'

" 'I will think it over, sir. But I don't think I will change my mind.' I replied.

"I laid there thinking, when Lieutenant Peddicord came over to me and said, 'I would do as the Colonel asked, if it were me. You should feel proud to have the Colonel come over and talk to you as he did.'

"I liked Lieutenant Peddicord and I knew he meant every word he said. I also knew he was thinking of my interest, too. I had respect for our Colonel, for the fine job he was doing in the training of the men. He had asked me in a nice way and then left the decision to me. I thought, 'Why should I sign up again because a Colonel asked me to?' I felt it was nice of him to go out of his way and interested enough in our outfit to ask me."[52]

Sampson's withdrawal resulted in the title being awarded to Sailor Robertson of the 504th.

On October 1, 1942, the 82nd Airborne Division began moving from Camp Claiborne, Louisiana, to Fort Bragg, North Carolina. On October 14, 1942, the 504th Parachute Infantry Regiment and the 376th Parachute Field Artillery Battalion officially became a part of the 82nd Airborne Division. Shortly after the arrival of the 504th at Fort Bragg, an inspection was held for General Leslie McNair's Army Ground Forces staff in which two of the regiment's three battalions failed. General Ridgway relieved Colonel Dunn of command of the 504th for his "inability to achieve results." General Ridgway named young Lieutenant Colonel Tucker to replace Dunn as the CO of the 504th Parachute Infantry Regiment.

Shortly after arriving at Fort Bragg, Brigadier General Bud Miley left to take command of the yet to be formed 17th Airborne Division, and Brigadier General Joe Swing moved over to command the 11th Airborne Division. Ridgway filled Miley's assistant division commander role with Charles L. "Bull" Keerans, who had been the chief of staff for General Bill Lee. Colonel Maxwell Taylor, who for a short period had served as General Ridgway's chief of staff, was promoted to brigadier general and given command of division artillery, which suited Taylor's desire as well as his background.

In addition to the 376th Parachute Field Artillery (PFA) Battalion, the division's other two artillery battalions, the 319th and 320th, were converted to glider-borne units. This entailed adopting the smaller 75mm pack howitzer already in use by the 376th PFA Battalion. This gun could be disassembled into nine component parts, each of which could be dropped in a separate bundle by parachute, and was compact enough to be loaded on a glider. Each artillery battalion would consist of three batteries of four guns each, with the glider artillery battalions having a jeep to tow each gun. Each gun and jeep required a separate glider.

Meanwhile, at the Alabama Area, Gavin, who had been promoted to colonel in September, continued to hone the 505th to a razor's edge. Private William Blank recalls that the training was almost round the clock. "We were constantly undergoing extensive training and maneuvers. The 3rd Battalion had a daily retreat parade regardless of what training had been done that day. My first night jump was my 13th. We lost a couple of troopers who slipped out of their chutes over a blacktop road and were killed. They had mistaken the road for the Chattahoochee River, which was between us and Lawson Field at Fort Benning."[53]

In January 1943, General Marshall selected the 82nd Airborne Division over the 101st Airborne Division to participate in the planned invasion of Sicily, code named Operation Husky. The date for the invasion was set for July 10, 1943. This invasion would be the first time the US Army would conduct a large-scale airborne operation in support of amphibious landings. This gave Ridgway very little time to integrate the various elements of the division into a tightly knit unit and move the division to North Africa.

In late January the 505th received orders to move to Camp Hoffman, North Carolina, and on February 7, 1943, it left the Alabama Area by train for Camp Hoffman.

Major Bennie Zinn, S-4 (logistics and supply officer) of the 2nd Battalion, 325th Glider Infantry Regiment, was assigned to work out operational doctrine for the glider infantry, much as Gavin had done earlier for the paratroopers. "I had been promoted to the rank of major in February and was sent to special duty with division as assistant G-3 for the purpose of writing and conducting some division CPXs [command post exercises] and field exercises.

"As soon as that task was completed, I was sent as Brigadier General Keerans' G-3 to Maxton Airfield at Laurinburg, North Carolina. During the months of February and March 1943 we tried about everything that we could think of. We flew every type of equipment in every type of craft and tried every type of tactical principle."[54]

Due to an acute shortage of gliders to train pilots and infantry, another change was made to the airborne divisions. A parachute regiment would be substituted for one of the glider regiments in each division, resulting in the 82nd and 101st Airborne Divisions being composed of one glider and two parachute regiments.

On February 12, 1943, the 326th Glider Infantry Regiment was officially transferred to the newly forming 13th Airborne Division. Replacing the 326th was the 505th Parachute Infantry Regiment, commanded by Colonel James M. Gavin.

CHAPTER 2

"READY"

After seven months of grueling training under Colonel Gavin, the 505th was probably the best parachute regiment in the US Army. It had received the benefit of Gavin's intimate knowledge of airborne operations, his tough training regimen, his high expectations for the men, and the example he set by his leadership. Gavin's troopers were in superb physical condition, having spent months running extremely demanding obstacle courses, practicing jujitsu, and making long cross-country marches with full gear and weapons (including mortars, machine guns, and ammunition). The 505th had made a number of night jumps and had developed procedures for quick assembly. But most of all, extremely close bonds had developed between the enlisted men and their noncommissioned and commissioned officers. The men had seen Gavin every day, always in the field training along side of them and overseeing their progress. There was a fierce unit pride that rose above even the other parachute regiments. The 505ers were a tight-knit family, and Gavin was the patriarch. In fact, the 505 troopers had such a fierce loyalty to the 505 and to Gavin that the regiment had trouble fully integrating into the 82nd Airborne Division.

From February through early April 1943, Major Bennie Zinn, a member of the Division G-3 (Operations) staff, was busy making preparations for the division's deployment overseas. Zinn's wife and young son moved to Fayetteville to be with him. "I knew about the sailing schedule but could not tell [my wife] and I was about to go crazy. I had never fully realized how much my wife and boy meant to me before. Mental anguish is terrible and we all went through it in those days of March and April 1943. We all made plans for departure; made wills, fixed bank accounts, made new allotments, checked up on all insurance, etc. I had grown much since 1940, but now began to wonder how much I could take and keep coming back for more. I had stopped much of my cynical thinking and I had studied hard, but now as time for use of this knowledge came near, I was stunned. I cannot describe my feelings those last few weeks before sailing.

"On 19 March I was sent back to 325th Glider infantry as Regimental Executive Officer. Captain Ted Major and I planned the move to the [Port of Embarkation]. We managed to see our families for short periods, but it did not seem right at all. I have lived over many a time those last few weeks with [my wife] Neen and [son] Ben in the countryside home at Fayetteville, North Carolina. Gee how I hated to leave them."[1]

On March 30, 1943 the entire 505th Parachute Infantry Regiment made US Army history when they made the first mass parachute jump at Fort Jackson near Camden, South Carolina. The sky over the drop zone began to fill with over 2,000 parachutes. Private Mark Rupaner could only describe the sight as "awesome. It was like a canopy of parachutes coming down."[2]

In one of the Company A planes, Private Dave Bullington was jumping 17th, with the company medic, Private Kelly Byars jumping as the last man in the stick at number 19. As the green light came on, Bullington shuffled toward the door close behind the others in his stick. After he exited the plane, he felt the shock of his parachute opening. When Bullington looked up to check his canopy, he saw a C-47 and its propellers cutting a swath through a group of troopers. "One of the planes stalled and came down through a group of troopers. It was the most awful noise, the plane sounded like somebody beating on a tin roof with a 2x4, going down through that stick. It cut [Byars] parachute off. But, he opened his reserve."[3]

Private Mark Rupaner with Company B had just landed and looked up and saw that "men were hit by the airplane's propellers. There were pieces coming down."[4]

The bodies and body parts hit the ground with sickening thuds. Private Harvill Lazenby, also with Company B was horrified at the sight of "a jump boot complete with foot lying on the ground."[5]

Bullington landed a few seconds later, "right by the first sergeant of C Company. Of course, he was dead. I got out of my chute and went the other way. It killed three men. At that time they were slowing the planes to ninety knots [for the jump]. They decided [ninety knots] was a little slow and stalled [the plane]. Old Byars said, 'I'll never jump again.' But he did. He went all the way."[6]

Even though each paratrooper knew that parachuting from airplanes was dangerous, this horrible accident, witnessed by so many, brought home the grim reality of that danger. But it was too late for any of them to quit. Any refusal to jump after the fifth qualifying jump was a court-martial offense.

After landing on the drop zone, each company assembled and moved to designated objectives simulating capture of key bridges, crossroads, etc. Company

G had the mission to "hold" the bridge over the Catawba River. Private William Blank was assigned to one of the roadblocks. "We stopped all cars to search and asked if they had anything to drink. Most did, and this made for a nice night. We pooled our money and I hitched a ride to a Camden restaurant for sandwiches. When I arrived it seemed as though all of the regiment was there. I enjoyed the food and hitched a ride back."[7]

On April 17, 1943, the 82nd Airborne Division began to move by train from Fort Bragg to Camp Edwards, Massachusetts, as the first step in its journey overseas. This movement was made in strict secrecy, because the army didn't want the Germans to know that an elite airborne division was being deployed overseas. Private James Elmo Jones, with Company B, 505th, was told that everyone was to eliminate all items that would identify them as paratroopers. This included "removing patches and all identification from uniforms, hiding polished jump boots, using ordinary infantry leggings, much to everyone's disgust."[8] Jump wings couldn't be worn. Cameras and diaries were to be mailed home. Even the special chinstraps were to be tucked inside of their helmets. They were issued standard combat boots and leggings for the journey.

Major Bennie Zinn, now the S-3 of the 325th, drove to the train station with his wife and young son. "My train left at 18:00 after fifteen minutes with Neen and Ben on the highway. We had a very pleasant and interesting trip through the east to Massachusetts, arriving at Camp Edwards at 18:00 on 20 April. It was terribly cold but we had much to do and were restricted too. Supplies were taken on, CWS clothing was issued and shots were given for typhus.

"The division moved to the New York Port of Embarkation on 27–28 April and boarded the ships. We sailed before dawn on 29 April. We had seen the beauties of America and had seen the young and the old waving farewells to us as trains rolled by at thirty miles per hour. When Colonel [Harry L.] Lewis woke me up on the morning of 29 April, we were at sea and when I reached the deck, nothing was in sight except many ships. The 325th was aboard the *Santa Rosa*, which was a very capable ship. There were in the convoy, [the] Battleship *Texas*, six transports, three liners, one carrier, three tankers, six freighters and nine destroyers."[9]

Like most of the men, Private William Blank, with Company G, 505th, didn't know the destination of the convoy. "We eventually learned our destination was North Africa. On the way to Africa we were instructed on all of the do's and don't's of conduct when we were exposed to the Arabs and their customs."[10]

Major Zinn, with the 325th aboard the *Santa Rosa*, found plenty to do to pass the time. "We had 'abandon ship' drills and began to learn the navy language and customs. I bunked with [Lieutenant Colonel John H.] Swede Swenson and had a very fine bunk. The weather was fine all except for one day when it became pretty rough. We stood at the rail and watched fish, the foam and the other ships. We read, talked and sang. We even had movies at night. We had classes to learn to speak to the natives of North Africa.

"The escort was on alert at all times and we had several sub scares. The last Sunday at sea we had retired and at about 01:00, a huge explosion rocked the ship and the captain called 'prepare to abandon ship.' Boy was I scared stiff. It was cold and I could not swim much. I do remember that we shook on the deck for an hour just waiting. But then the *Texas* signaled 'all clear.'

"At 09:05 on 10 May 1943, the convoy was met by a large escort of British Corvettes and was split into two parts. It was indeed a pretty sight as the sun came up—ships as far as we could see. We continued on our course and the other part went through the Straits of Gibraltar to Oran. Our convoy sighted land at Casablanca at 05:30, 10 May 1943 and we pulled into the harbor at 13:00 the same day."[11]

The city did not make a favorable first impression with the 1st Battalion, 505th communications officer, Lieutenant Dean McCandless. "Casablanca could be smelled before it could be seen."[12]

Lieutenant T. Moffatt Burriss from South Carolina, a mortar platoon leader with Headquarters Company, 3rd Battalion, 504th, stood on the crowded deck of the ship as the Casablanca harbor came into view. "We could see the distant white buildings that gave the city its name. They appeared to be of fine, new marble. As we moved across the water and approached the dock, we looked down and saw the dark corpses of sunken French ships, resting on the bottom, their days of battle over.

"After what seemed like hours, we were given the order to disembark. For many of us, it was our first time on foreign soil. On the dock, I told my platoon to fall in. With full packs on our backs, we marched through Casablanca and saw the same white buildings at close range. They were bleached and mottled, worn smooth by time, the sun, and the wind. I remember the palmetto trees and the sand—sand that blew from the desert and made its way into our food, our shoes, our eyes, and our noses."[13]

Like most of the troopers of the 82nd Airborne Division, Major Zinn had never been overseas and he marveled at the exotic sights, sounds, and smells. "Our ship was unloaded by about 16:00 and we marched through the outskirts of Casablanca to Camp Don Passage, which was about five miles from town. My eyes really hurt with all the sights of the first foreign country. We saw soldiers of all nations and with all kinds of uniforms.

"We saw the people sleeping in the streets and on the walks. We saw the people tending to their toilet habits on the streets and in the roads. We saw the typical Arab dress, the sandals, the long baggy pants, the Harem Band working up a little business. We marveled at the tattoos of the Arabs and at the jewelry worn by them in ears and noses and on necks and wrists. The women were nearly all dressed in gaudy colored dresses with head cloths and no shoes. The men wore big seated pantaloons, sandals and head cloths of white or gaudy colors. The men rode small asses and the women walked. The men carried nothing and the women carried all sorts of boxes, baskets or bundles."[14]

Lieutenant Burriss, with Headquarters Company, 3rd Battalion, 504th, led his heavily laden 81mm mortar platoon from the docks through Casablanca. "After marching for seven or eight miles, we pitched our tents on the outskirts of the city. We listened to the wind blow and the grains of sand sweep over the canvas during the night. When we awoke in the morning, everything inside the tents was coated with sand.

"The Arabs swarmed all over us like roaches over food. They wanted to trade with us or, preferably, to steal. They were particularly interested in our sheets, mattress covers, cigarettes, and chocolate. For these things they offered trinkets and fresh food—dates, exotic bread, and meats of dubious origin.

"We were to post guards twenty-four hours a day in order to keep them from stealing everything we had. Theft was so common that we came to regard the Arabs with almost as much ill will as we did the Germans. When we shipped out, a sergeant exacted revenge for all of us. We had already boarded a train when an Arab came to the open window and offered to buy a mattress cover—anyone's mattress cover. A sergeant obliged. The Arab handed the money through the window and clutched the mattress cover, which was partially hanging out the window. At that moment, as the train started to move out, the Arab tried to pull out the cover. However, the sergeant had tied one end to the seat. When the train picked up speed, it dragged the Arab along with it. He turned a flip and let go of the cover. Scrambling to his feet, he chased the train for a few moments, shook his fist, and cursed in Arabic. Most of the soldiers laughed and jeered at him because Arabs had cheated or stolen from virtually all of them during their stay in Casablanca."[15]

On May 12, 1943, trains pulling a few passenger cars along with mostly 40 & 8s (boxcars that held forty men or eight horses) carrying part of the division left Casablanca. The destination was an area near the small town of Oujda, French Morocco, near the border with Spanish Morocco, over three hundred miles away. Truck convoys carried part of the division, while the lucky flew to Oujda in gliders and C-47s.

The boxcars were literally ovens, while riding in the back of the trucks took three days over rough roads, with the troopers eating the dust of the trucks ahead of them the whole way. Major Zinn, with the 325th, rode in one of the truck convoys. "After two days in Don Passage we made an overland trip to Oujda and Marnia. Enroute we saw bands of girls peddling their wares by dancing and singing. Others sent the little boys out to get Yanks for sister or mom. One band that we met was made up of ten girls, very gaudily dressed, equipped with castanets and tambourines and energetic and primitive in their mode of attack. In several places we would find many Arabs emerging from haystacks as we passed by. The children had learned to ask for 'bon bon.' Several times as we stopped for a brief rest, children would come to our trucks and ask for 'bon

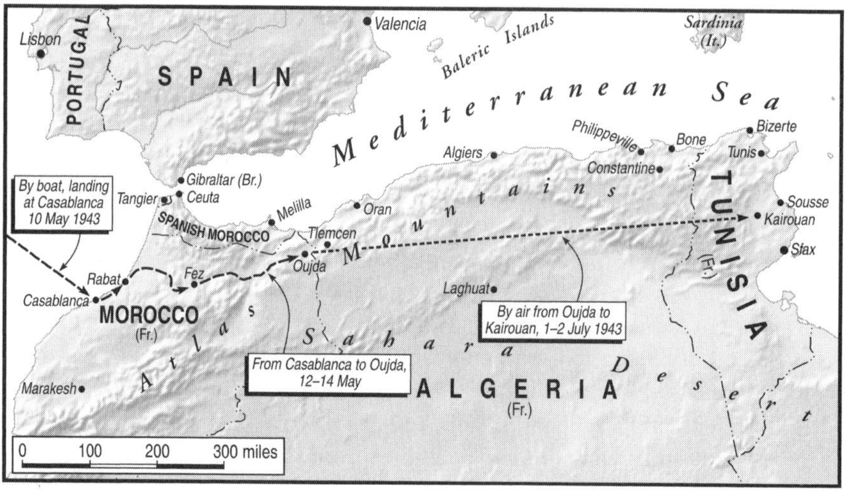

bon' and then help us to learn new words. But most of them were afraid to get too close to us, as they had been taught that we killed all Arabs. They had been kicked and beaten by the Germans and Italians, and were just afraid of all strangers. We went into some of the native huts; huts of paper, weeds, bushes and leaves. In the huts we often found a complete family of six to ten, an ass, several goats, many chickens, a dog, a camel and often a few supplies. The furnishings were very crude and very scanty. The huts are usually surrounded by briar fences and cactus fences. In some places we found small villages of these huts, but the more progressive settlements were rather attractive because the buildings are all of white stucco or adobe. Many of the ancient cities still had the old walls completely around the town.

"We found the Arabs very friendly as we progressed to the east; and very helpful. The old men would warn us of German mines and go out to show us where they were planted. We saw many families out gathering the cactus fruit with a long hook. They sat down on the ground and rubbed the thorns off with a little gadget, which looked like a handful of leaves. Some of them used a glove made of straw to rub the thorns off the fruit. We even found one family that showed us how to cut them open and eat the meat. This same family very reluctantly posed for a picture and showed us the house from front to back.

"On the trip to Oujda we passed through some of the most wonderful country imaginable. There were grain fields, olive orchards, citrus trees, vineyards, flowers, snow capped mountains, pretty rock formations and unique cities. We saw the antique methods of farming with plows made of scraps and pulled by oxen. Some of the plows were made of wood, which is very difficult to find anywhere in North Africa. All of the natives went to the fields very early and as they marched along with that slow gait of theirs they all chanted the religious music that they so well love. In several places we saw them harvesting the wheat by cutting it with hand made scythes and tying the bundles with the straw. The men cut and stacked the grain, and the women hauled it off to the rock where the thrashing was done. We watched the threshing several times, which was done by tromping on the grain, and the more prosperous Arabs used animals to tromp it. After the threshing was completed, the women beat the grain with clubs until it became flour, after which they buried it or hauled it off to the city. We visited several wineries and sampled some of the famous wines, but the places were so filthy that we almost became sick. We gathered some apricots, walnuts, peaches, grapes, lemons, limes, oranges, almonds, plums and dates and had a real feast along the route. We saw crude little French trains as they sped along at twenty m.p.h. We were much amused at the huge charcoal burning busses that hauled fifty or sixty passengers. Most of them broke down every few miles, but the people did not mind that at all. We saw the 'wadis' (creeks) running wild at the foot of the mountains as the melted snow came down in torrents.

"We passed by some of the olden castles and cities and soon got into the battle areas where we began to really see what a war does to a country. We began to see roadside graves marked with the fallen soldier's helmet or rifle. We passed a few neat cemeteries, which were kept up by the Arabs. We began to see the destroyed tanks, trucks and planes and other impedimenta. We were amazed at the amount of equipment that Jerry had deserted in his hasty retreat. The fields were covered with his supplies. Some of the cemeteries were almost beautiful, with ornamental walks and gadgets made by the soldiers. Our convoy spent the night in an open field with guards around it and completed our trip to Oujda at 17:00 the next day. We established new camps in order that we might start training for Sicily. The 325th was stationed at Marnia and the rest of the division was at Oujda."[16]

On May 15, one of the truck convoys stopped, and the order was given for the paratroopers to unload. Private William Blank, with Company G, 505th, and the other paratroopers had arrived at their new home near Oujda. Blank jumped out of the back of the 2½-ton truck and looked around at the flat, treeless desert. The ground was rock hard from the constant baking of the blazing sun. Sand was blowing across this barren landscape. There was not a tree in sight. It seemed as though nothing could survive in such a hostile environment. But insects abounded, as if to torment the troopers like some Biblical plague.

Blank and the other paratroopers "pitched our pup tents out in the middle of nowhere, dug slit trenches, and set up Lister bags. The weather was so hot during the day it kept down the extensive training to night problems. We used the mornings for physical conditioning exercises.

"The Arabs came every day to trade their wares with the GIs. They could carry more things under those long robes than can be imagined. They liked cigarettes (especially Camels), mattress covers and boots.

"Our kitchens were set up outdoors and the mess line was the same. Every day at meal time a dust storm would blow right down the mess line and the food would be full of dirt."[17]

Private W. A. "Arnold" Jones, with the 2nd Battalion, 505th, 81mm mortar platoon, had been in the CCC prior to the war and was used to eating food served outdoors from a mess line. But this was different. "You could hardly eat the dirt off of the 'C' rations." He heard some of his fellow troopers sarcastically say, "Well, it gave the 'C' rations a flavor."[18]

For troopers like Private Russell McConnell, with Company H, 505th, dirt in the food was only one of the miseries at chow time. "You take a bite of bread or anything, yellow jackets and hornets would land on it and you'd have to brush them off. They were almost in your mouth. It was absolute misery."[19]

Private William H. "Bill" Tucker was sent to North Africa to an EGB, the army's term for its replacement battalions. The 82nd Airborne Division had a replacement battalion assigned to it to fill the ranks when units lost men injured or killed in training and jump accidents, or from disease. Many jokingly said that EGB stood for "Excess Government Baggage." These EGBs were camped a couple of miles away from the 82nd bivouac near the 509th PIB, which was now attached to the 82nd Airborne Division.

Naturally, one of the things in short supply at Oujda was water. For most troopers, like Private Tucker, the taste of the water was just as bad as the food. "We got our water from fifty gallon Lister bags filled with chlorinated water standing in the sun. I never got a cool drink of water. We were allowed a half canteen per day per man to shave and wash. Many times during my stay at Oujda, I swore fervently I would give ten dollars for a glass of cold water, cold beer, or cold anything."[20]

General Ridgway had actually selected this location. "We had picked, on purpose, land that was not in use for grazing or agricultural purposes. We trained in a fiery furnace, where the hot wind carried a fine dust that clogged the nostrils, burned the eyes, and cut into the throat like an abrasive. We trained at first by day, until the men became lean and gaunt from their hard work in the sun. Then we trained at night, when it was cooler, but the troopers found it impossible to sleep in the savage heat of the African day.

"The wind and the terrain were our worst enemies. Even on the rare calm days, jumping was a hazard, for the ground was hard, and covered with loose boulders, from the size of a man's fist to the size of his head."[21]

Shortly after getting settled in the division's new bivouac near Oujda, Colonel Gavin was ordered to report to General Ridgway. "General Ridgway called myself and Colonel Tucker up to orient us on our probable combat task. It had been directed by the GHQ, and was to be known as 'Husky' and was to be executed July 10th. It contemplated the seizure of Sicily. The 505th CT was to spearhead the amphibious landing of the 1st or 45th Divisions. Our jump was to take place in moonlight the night of July 9th, 11:30 p.m. The exact mission was yet an issue.

From an analysis of the probable missions it was clear that the effort would be a very risky one and a costly one."[22]

When Colonel Rueben Tucker learned that his 504th Regimental Combat Team would be left out of the first mass combat jump in US Army history, he was furious. He felt his men had trained just as hard and that he and his staff had a regiment that was the equal of the 505th. It was a bitter pill for Tucker to swallow. "To make the situation worse, Ridgway had to steal one of my battalions and give it to Jim for the jump."[23]

Even though the 505th RCT would lead the assault, every unit in the division trained intensely for the invasion. As the Operations Officer for the 325th, Major Zinn was responsible for setting up the regiment's encampment. "As soon as all camps were established, we started an intensive schedule in preparation for the invasion of Sicily. We practiced the operation over and over again until we had it memorized. We had all sorts of training and firing exercises to care for any problem."[24]

Platoon Sergeant Harold Owens, with Company A, 325th, was one of the more experienced and highly respected NCOs in the regiment. Owens worked with his young troopers as they initially practiced small unit tactics, then graduated to larger unit maneuvers. "We had a lot of squad problems, platoon problems, battalion and regimental problems . . . simulated combat which we participated in."[25]

There were many new experiences for Zinn and the other officers and men of the division during this training. "Just about everything happened to us at Marnia and Oujda. We hit an Arab house with a mortar shell and killed the old man's wife, chicken and donkey. We paid him what he wanted which was $25 for the donkey, $2 for the chicken and $5 for his wife. He was happy for all except that he could not easily secure a new donkey. We caught thieves galore and even found our soldiers selling bed sacks at $20 each. We operated a 'cat house' in Oujda to fight venereal disease. We had parachute failures and had our first casualties from glider training, when two men were struck by an incoming glider and torn to bits. We found out what dysentery is like and how it hits a well man and pulls him down. We learned to barter with Arabs for eggs and a few fresh vegetables as we got tired of dehydrated foods. We learned how hot one hundred thirty degrees is and what it means to drop from one hundred thirty degrees at 17:00 to fifty degrees at 21:00. We learned how to keep water cool in the huge earthen jars that the Arab makes and sells. We learned how to make reconnaissance in a strange country. We saw our first bombings from a good comfortable distance and saw our bombers going out to Sicily and Italy."[26]

While training in Oujda, the 82nd Airborne Division would be under the command of the US Fifth Army, commanded by General Mark Clark. On May 19, a division review was conducted for Clark in Oujda. However, during the invasion of Sicily, the division would fight as part of the US Seventh Army, led by the already legendary General George S. Patton.

As the division trained and prepared for a night combat jump in a location known to only a few officers and men in the division, the 307th Airborne Medical Company was already at war. First malaria, then dysentery swept through the division. Private Bill Tucker had a most unfortunate experience. "It was compulsory to take Atabrine tablets [to prevent malaria]. An officer stood at the end of the chow line and watched while we each swallowed a pill. After I took the medicine a second time, I became violently ill. Life was at a low premium, so no one paid much attention to me. In my spasm and agony, I had to drag myself four hundred yards to the aid station.

"I was not alone. Two or three were there. We were taken to the hospital, and for approximately ten or twelve hours, I had steady dry heaves. I was told I had nearly died. There was nothing that could be done for me. I had a severe allergy, and I had to pull myself through. I rejoined my company a day or so later, but I never took another Atabrine tablet and wound up getting malaria."[27]

It seemed to Private Russell McConnell that everyone in his Company H, 505th, outfit was stricken. "I had dysentery; throwing up, urinating, everything all at once. Every one of us had dysentery. The Captain [John Norton] said, 'Well, you're not cleaning your mess gear. I haven't got it.' The next day he had it."[28]

Even with the cases of malaria occurring, the primary health problem remained, according to Captain Daniel B. "Doc" McIlvoy, Jr., the 3rd Battalion, 505th Surgeon, "diarrhea, which everyone had. This was not just an enlisted men's disease; we all had it."[29]

Each doctor who served in the 307th Airborne Medical Company was a paratrooper who had undergone the same grueling rigors as everyone else. Each had graduated from jump school; most of them had endured the Frying Pan and the Alabama Area, and were now living in the desert with the division. They wanted to be there.

For those reasons, young Captain McIlvoy admired his fellow physicians who chose this duty. "Doctor Zirkle already had two years of surgical training and could have stayed in Boston to finish. Doctor Stein was a Board Certified ear, nose, and throat specialist and could have stayed in a nice hospital setting. Doctor Scarborough was a psychiatrist and could have stayed on in a hospital setting. Doctor Savoy and Dr. Pete Suer, both dentists, could have practiced in a hospital setting. Doctor Stenhouse had had some Ob-Gyn training and he could have very well have remained in training as most doctors at that time were allowed to do. Doctor Lyle Putnam was a well-trained physician who already had a practice, and if he wanted, could very well have stayed home as an essential person. Doctor Lewis Smith, Dr. Carl Comstock, Dr. Ludwig Cebelli and others I knew from questioning, had no other reason to be in the parachute troops other than their sincere desire to volunteer for this hazardous duty."[30]

On May 26-27, Gavin made several important trips to attend meetings with the key commanders and their staffs for the upcoming operation, including General

Patton; General Omar Bradley, the II Corps commander; and General Terry Allen, the commander of the 1st Infantry Division. Concurrently, concentrated studies of enemy dispositions on the island of Sicily were taking place. On June 3, the division held a review for Generals Patton, Clark, and Bradley, as well as Lieutenant General Luis Orgaz, the high commissioner of Spanish Morocco, General Auguste Nogues of French Morocco, General Francisco Delgado Serrano of Spanish Morocco, and many other dignitaries. The review included a mass jump by paratroopers of the 1st Battalion, 505th, in full combat gear, while the remainder of the division conducted a parade.

On June 5, the 3rd Battalion, 505th, made a practice jump despite a 30-mile-an-hour wind. As the men touched down, they were pitched over by the strong surface winds. Some were thrown forward landing on the pockets of their jump suit pants, where many carried hand grenades, causing numerous injuries. Others were dragged by their parachute canopies, which reinflated upon landing. Still others landed hard on their sides. One of the troopers who participated in the jump that day was Private Pat Reid, with Company H, 505th. "There was a terrible downdraft and almost everyone came in hard and actually bounced when they hit the ground. I know that I came in and bounced several times. After I hit, I lay there a few moments feeling spots on my body to be sure I had no broken bones. After my examination I decided I was okay. I got up and started to assemble with my company. The first person I came to was one of my company's lieutenants. He was lying on the ground, I'm sure as much from disappointment as from hurting. He lay there, moaning and saying, 'I bent my collarbone. I bent my collarbone.'

"I looked at him and could see that his shoulder was sticking straight up. I said, 'Sir, it looks to me like you broke your collarbone.'

"He said, 'No, damn it. It's bent. I was in a car wreck in the States and had my right collarbone replaced with a silver one.' He was disappointed because he knew he would have to return to the States and he wanted to stay with his outfit."[31]

Private Howard Goodson, with Company I, 505th, had hand grenades in the front pockets of his jump suit pants. "As you got close to the ground, it was really windy. It took me, swung me up and slammed me down on the ground. I hit with those hand grenades in my pockets. I was purple and blue."[32]

Staff Sergeant Phillip O. Mattson, with Company G, 505th, broke both legs so severely that he was also sent back to the United States, as were a number of others. Taking the places of those sent home were men from the division's replacement battalion.

Doc McIlvoy tended to some of the casualties afterward. "Practically everybody had a bruised hip or leg and we hospitalized one hundred twenty."[33]

Tragically, two men were killed. One had a "streamer" in which his parachute failed to open, and the other trooper was dragged into a stone wall, striking his head, when his parachute reinflated.

The highlight of the day's events was a speech given by General Patton to the division. Colonel Gavin knew that Patton's "talks on such occasions were usually quite good. I was impressed. One thing he said always stuck with me, for it was contrary to what I believed up to that moment, but when I was in combat only a short while, I knew he was right. He said, 'Now, I want you to remember that no sonuvabitch ever won a war by dying for his country. He won it by making the other poor dumb sonuvabitch die for his country.'

"Patton went on to discuss the tactics we should employ in fighting the Germans and Italians, stressing the Italians. The point that he wanted to make was that we should avoid a direct assault on an enemy position, but seek to envelop his flanks. However, in doing so, the General used terms applicable to sexual relations. He did so in a very clever manner, emphasizing the point that when one arrived in the rear of one of their positions, the Italians would invariably quickly try to switch to a new position to protect themselves, and at that moment would become vulnerable to attack from the rear.

"It was not so much what he said as how he said it that caused us to remember the points he wanted to make—though I did feel somewhat embarrassed at times, and I sensed that some of the troops felt a bit embarrassed, too."[34]

The following week, arrangements were made for Gavin and a couple of his battalion commanders to fly with some RAF Mosquito bombers on a reconnaissance flight of the drop zones. Leaving from Oujda to fly first to Tunis, Gavin and the other officers "took off at 9:30, June 10th. Colonels Mitchell and Roberts of the 52nd Wing, Majors Kouns [CO, 3rd Battalion, 504th] and Krause [CO, 3rd Battalion, 505th] of the 82nd [were] in the party.

"This included about all of the people who would benefit most from this reconnaissance. There were others, but other duties precluded their attendance. We arrived at Tunis about noon. Our orders were to go to Headquarters NAAF [North Africa Air Force] at Carthage, which we proceeded to do. They never heard of us. Our mission was of such an extremely secret nature that we could not explain to anyone just what in the hell we were doing, where we were going, or what we were trying to accomplish. Everyone looked upon us as dangerous characters. We finally got a tip that sent us to Sousse, landing at Monastir airdrome at 4:00 p.m. We chiseled a ride to Headquarters at Sousse, arriving at 7:30 p.m. We slept in our ship at Monastir the night of the 10th and took off for an airdrome twenty miles south of Tripoli early the 11th. Here, we got clearance and briefing for Malta. All parachute identifications are to be removed.

"The route to Malta was very precisely defined, going to a town about sixty miles east of Tripoli at two hundred [miles per hour] and then turning directly to Malta. We arrived at Luqa, Malta at about 4:00. We finally made arrangements to fly into our DZs the night of the 11th at 10:30 p.m., [at] six hundred feet. I flew in one of the new Mosquito bombers as navigator. We found the DZs with no trouble shortly after leaving Malta. We flew over Lake Biviere, thence north, passing west of Niscemi, around Niscemi and then south over the checkpoint, the lake. Four searchlights tried to pick us up, but fortunately missed. We were not fired on. Two of the Battalion COs inadvertently flew over Ponte Olivo at three hundred feet and had six guns working on them. No one was hit. We all flew directly back to Malta. We were all pleased with the results of our reconnaissance. The DZ's were OK."[35]

The division continued to conduct most of its training at night. General Ridgway and his staff were always in the field with the men overseeing the training. Long cross-country marches with full combat loads, calisthenics, and hand-to-hand combat training were combined with assault rehearsals and field problems. The complexity of night field problems was increased. Nothing was left to chance; every activity associated with combat operations after a night jump was simulated in training exercises. Some of the many problems practiced included assembly of units at night after the drop; recovery of bundles containing crew-served weapons, ammunition, medical supplies, rations, etc.; establishment of communications among units and commanders; and night movements by compass.

The 1st Battalion, 505th, communications officer, Lieutenant Dean McCandless, described a typical night exercise: "We deployed everyone in a scattered fashion as we expected to be when we jumped in combat. At a predetermined time we rushed to our scattered equipment bundles, then to our positions on terrain selected to be similar to that of Sicily. My wire parties ran lines from our battalion switchboard to the telephone of each company. Once hooked up and able to communicate with the companies, I reported this to Lieutenant Colonel Gorham [the battalion commander]. On his telephone order, the companies were to launch their assault."[36]

With aerial reconnaissance photos of the objectives, Gavin had full-scale replicas constructed of the fortifications at each objective. Pillboxes, trenches, blockhouses, and barbed-wire obstacles were of the type and location of the same fortifications at each objective. Assaults were rehearsed repetitively against these fortifications using live ammunition. Private Dave Bullington, with Company A, 505th, took part in these mock assaults practiced at night in which "we did some live firing and going through barbed wire. We really couldn't see what we were shooting at. It's a wonder somebody didn't get shot."[37]

The 52nd Troop Carrier Wing, assigned to carry the 82nd Airborne into Sicily, received very little training in night operations despite the efforts of the commander, Brigadier General Hal Clark. The C-47 flight crews had not received training in the US in close-formation night flying prior to deployment to North Africa. The airfields around Oujda from which the 52nd Troop Carrier Wing would conduct practice drops with the 82nd had not been completed until May 25, 1943.

The 52nd was not ready for training operations with the 82nd Airborne Division until June 1. There just had not been enough time to conduct the training to prepare the troop carrier flight crews for the Sicily night jump. General

Hal Clark developed a combat formation for the Sicily drop of nine planes flying in a V-of-Vs configuration.

Nine planes would carry a company of paratroopers. Each V-of-V would fly one behind the next about a minute and a half apart. Four or five nine-plane formations would make up a serial. A serial would carry a parachute battalion. The serials would follow each other at 10-minute intervals. This formation would become standard in future airborne operations, although the intervals between serials would later be reduced.

During the time the 82nd Airborne Division was bivouacked at Oujda, only two practice night jumps were conducted, due to the delay in getting airfields built near Oujda and getting aircraft, flight crews, and ground crews in place. The practice jumps were primarily designed to give the C-47 crews of the 52nd Troop Carrier Wing some experience in close-formation flying and night navigation.

The first practice night jump while in Oujda involved the 505th. The paratroopers who would jump would be wearing full combat gear loads. Lieutenant James J. Coyle, an EGB, had only the five qualifying jumps to his credit. "Fortunately, I was picked to be part of a training operation as a test for the pilots and navigators of the C-47 airplanes at the airfield near our camp. Each plane was assigned one paratroop officer to jump after about a three hour flight in which the crew flew various assigned headings which eventually would bring them to our DZ. Each jumper was to plot his landing on a map and the results would indicate the accuracy of the aircrew's navigation.

"I must admit that I was a little nervous flying around alone in the back of the plane for hours. But when the crew chief came back and the red warning light came on, I acted as though I did this every night in the week, and nonchalantly said, 'So long' when the green light came on and I jumped out the door. The desert where I landed was full of rocks and I was lucky not to break a leg when I hit because there was no one around me if I were injured.

"After about twenty minutes of wandering in the desert in the dark, I heard a fellow wanderer nearby who turned out to be Lieutenant Bill Meddaugh. The battalion was supposed to be near the DZ when we dropped, but Bill and I were alone in a very silent desert, so we went to sleep for a few hours. At daybreak, we spotted parked trucks about two miles away and hiked over to them and located E Company nearby. The jumpers had been scattered all over the desert and landed everywhere but on the DZ This was pointed out to the aircrews very politely, but firmly by Colonel Gavin at the critique of the problem that afternoon."[38]

The second drop involved the 504th with two men from each plane jumping. It had somewhat improved results and was deemed a success.

By June 16, training in Oujda was completed, and on June 19, a parade was held for General Dwight Eisenhower and the brass.

On June 24, 1943, General Ridgway ordered the 82nd Airborne Division to move to its staging area for Operation Husky. "After six weeks in this dusty, wind-swept hell hole, we moved up to Kairouan, in central Tunisia, the jump-off point for Sicily. In Tunisia the men got a closer look at war, for here the desert was strewn with the wrecked trucks and tanks of Rommel's once proud Afrika Korps, beaten and destroyed by the armies of Anderson, Alexander, Patton, and Montgomery."[39]

Some of the division moved by train in 40 & 8 boxcars, with the rest moving by truck and C-47. Lieutenant Coyle, with Company E, 505th, was one of the lucky troopers to make the trip in a C-47. "We broke camp and flew to another unbearably hot area outside of the city of Kairouan in Tunisia. The crew chief on my plane said that the controller at the airfield told him it was 120° F on the field when we landed! We bivouacked in pup tents in this area and within a few days, briefings began for what we knew was a combat jump. We were never told exactly where we were going during the briefings, but the maps that were issued had Italian names on them."[40]

As if the misery in Oujda hadn't been bad enough, Kairouan's unrelenting heat and a logistics problem conspired to continue to make it almost unbearable for the division.

However, unlike Oujda, the bivouac areas General Ridgway selected for his men would offer at least some protection from the daily heat. "In the shade of the pear and almond trees, we took what refuge we could from the searing heat, but for those who had to work in the Quonset huts there was no escape. It was like living and working inside a stove. There was always a wind, at times the hot sirocco, blowing off the desert like the breath of hell, and at midday the thermometer sometimes stood at one hundred twenty-six degrees. For the first time our supply system broke down, and for one long stretch we lived almost exclusively on marmalade and Spam."[41]

However, some troopers like Private W. A. Jones thought Kairouan, even with the heat, was much better than Oujda. "That was a good move. They put us in a big olive grove. We were under some shade. That was just like moving into a nice hotel."[42] Plus, Kairouan was close enough to the Mediterranean Sea to get a relatively nice, cool breeze in the evenings.

Behind the scenes a feud had quietly developed between General Ridgway and British General Fredrick "Boy" Browning. It had been brewing since the 82nd Airborne Division's arrival in Oujda. The matter began somewhat innocently, but grew as Ridgway felt that his command was getting deprived of the resources needed to carry out the mission. "The British airborne at that time had a very distinguished soldier, Lt. Gen. 'Boy' Browning serving on Gen. Eisenhower's staff as his advisor on airborne matters. He was recognized, in his own service at least, as the senior authority in all matters pertaining to the use of airborne troops.

"It was only natural, I suppose, that he should seem to some of us to be a bit patronizing in his manner toward those who had had considerably less airborne experience than he. Some British officers, when we first began working together, made little effort to conceal the fact that they held no high opinion of the state of readiness of the American units, and of their combat know-how.

Naturally this made the hackles rise on the necks of the American commanders, who had great confidence in themselves and their military schooling, and who had great pride in their units.

"Such matters coming up during the planning period could be irritating as grains of sand in the eye. Practically all the troop carrier aircraft were United States, and we didn't have enough C-47 aircraft to fill the minimum needs of both the US and the British airborne forces who were to jump into Sicily. Every plane allotted the British, therefore, meant less combat strength my men could take into battle. A running argument developed with Gen. Browning as to how these planes were to be allotted between my division and the British 1st Airborne Division. I also began to feel that Gen. Browning, from his post at Supreme Headquarters, was in a position to exert an undue influence, both on the allocation of aircraft to American airborne troops and on their actual tactical employment.

"On one occasion, for example, one of my battalion commanders received a note that Gen. Browning was arriving to inspect his unit the following day. Naturally, I disliked that, for I had had no notice of such a visit. The note should not have gone to the subordinate commander in the first place. It should have come to me, in the form of a request, asking whether or not a visit to that particular commander at that particular time would be convenient.

"On another occasion I received a message from Gen. Browning telling me that he would be down to see my plans for the Sicily invasion. I sent back a rather blunt note to the effect that there were no plans for the Sicily invasion until such time as they had been approved by Gen. Patton, my commander. Until then they would not be available for inspection by anybody, except on Gen. Patton's orders.

"Patton liked that answer, and approved my sending it. Higher up the chain of command, though, it received quite a different reception. A few days later I was at Gen. Eisenhower's headquarters, in Algiers, and Bedell Smith, the Chief of Staff, read me a stern lecture, which I felt sure he had been directed to deliver by Gen. Eisenhower himself. The tenor of it was that the Supreme Commander had directed that there be the utmost cooperation between the British and American forces, and that any senior officer who in the slightest way transgressed that rule might as well start packing up, for he was going home.

"That disturbed me a little, for the issue as I saw it at the time was between standing up and fighting for the needs of my command, or allowing myself to be put upon in the name of harmony. I probably would have been sent home, or at least sternly rebuked, if Gen. Patton had not articulately and wholeheartedly approved my actions."[43]

General Eisenhower finally settled the matter of allocation of the troop carrier aircraft. He assigned 250 C-47s to the 82nd Airborne Division, and since the British 1st Airborne operation would be a glider assault, they would get 109 C-47s plus 30 Albermarle and Halifax bombers. Both the Americans and British felt cheated and thought General Eisenhower was favoring the other.

The 52nd Troop Carrier Wing had five groups that would carry the 505th Regimental Combat Team into Sicily. The 61st Group would carry the 3rd Battalion, 504th, and lead the other serials into Sicily; followed by the 314th Group carrying the 3rd Battalion, 505th; then the 313th Group with the 1st Battalion, 505th. The 316th Group would fly the 505th Headquarters, and the 64th Group would transport the 2nd Battalion, 505th.

The elements of the 505th Regimental Combat Team making the initial parachute assault would consist of the 505th Parachute Infantry Regiment, commanded by Colonel Gavin; the 3rd Battalion, 504th Parachute Infantry Regiment, commanded by Lieutenant Colonel Charles Kouns; the 456th Parachute Field Artillery Battalion, commanded by Lieutenant Colonel Harrison Harden; Company B, 307th Airborne Engineer Battalion, commanded by Captain William H. Johnson; a detachment of the 82nd Airborne Signal Company, commanded by Lieutenant Edward Kacyainski; and a detachment of the 307th Airborne Medical Company, commanded by Staff Sergeant Jack M. Bartley.

The 505th Regimental Combat Team's mission was to spearhead the invasion of Sicily. The regimental combat team would jump the night before the beach landings in an area east and northeast of Gela and south of Niscemi, to protect the landings of the US 1st Division and the US 45th Division.

The mission was to prevent enemy reserves from attacking the beaches by blocking key roads and disrupting enemy communications. The 3rd Battalion, 504th, would land on DZ "Q" on the northern end of the airhead and block the road south from Niscemi. The 1st and 2nd Battalions of the 505th and two batteries of the 456th PFA Battalion would jump on DZ "S" and capture Objective "Y," a key road junction. The 3rd Battalion less Company I, together with one battery of the 456th, would land on DZ "T" and capture the high ground to the south of Objective Y. Company I would land southeast of the 3rd Battalion drop zone to capture and block another road junction and light a bonfire to act as a beacon for the 1st Infantry Division's landing beach. A regimental demolition section would jump southeast of the main landings and blow the road and rail bridges over the Acate River. The 505th RCT would be attached to the 1st Infantry Division through D+1 and would assist with the capture of the airfield at Ponte Olivo. The second lift, 504th Regimental Combat Team, was alerted for movement to Sicily on the evening of D-Day or "in the event of negative instructions" for movement on the evening of D+1. The 504th Regimental Combat Team would consist of the 504th Parachute Infantry Regiment less the 3rd Battalion, commanded by Colonel Reuben H. Tucker; the 376th Parachute Field Artillery Battalion, commanded by Lieutenant Colonel Wilbur M. Griffith; and Company C, 307th Airborne Engineer Battalion, commanded by Captain Thomas M. Wight.

The third lift, Division Headquarters, would be ready to move by glider on the evening of D+1 or thereafter. Division Headquarters would consist of the

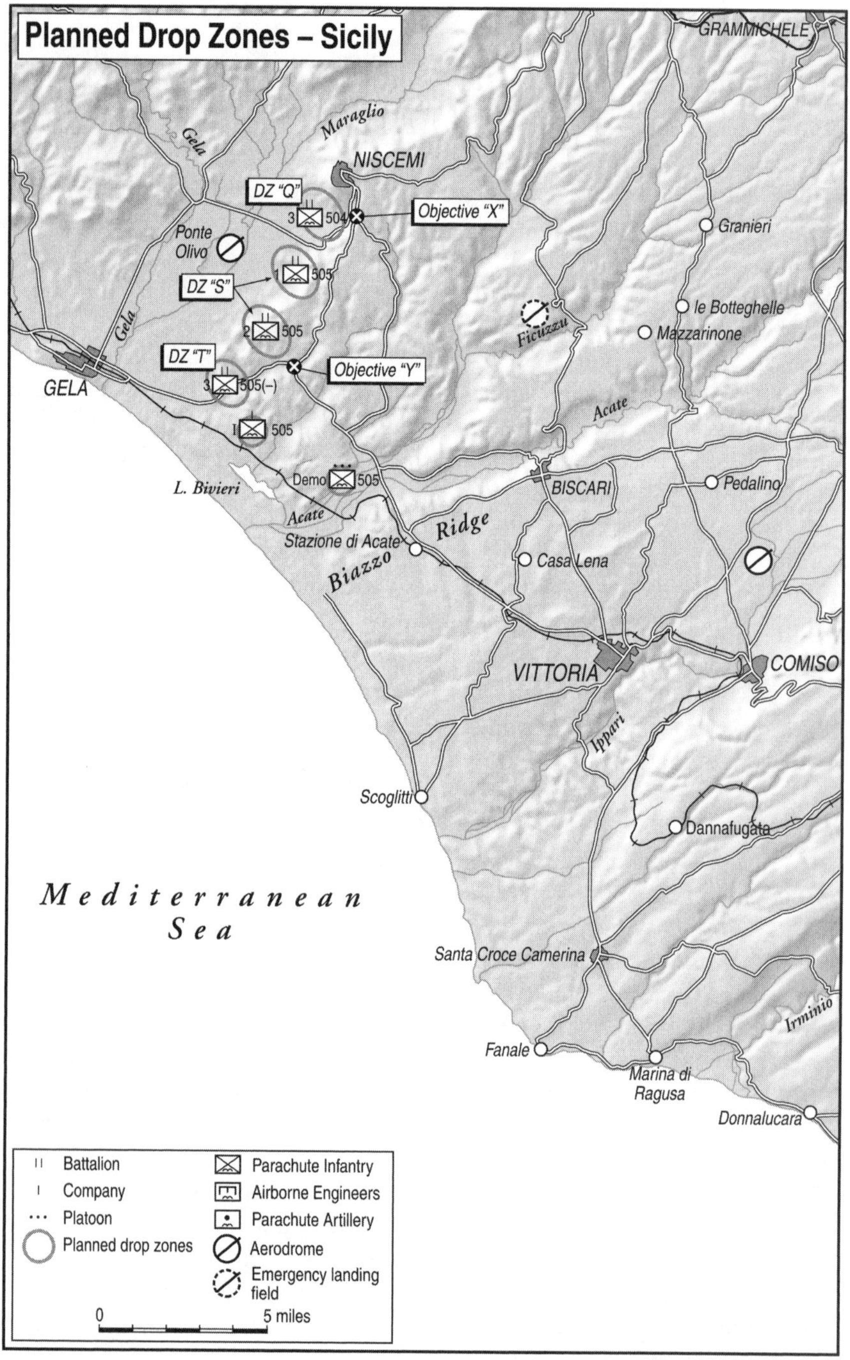
Planned Drop Zones – Sicily
GRAMMICHELE
Maraglio
Gela
NISCEMI
DZ "Q"
3 504
Objective "X"
Ponte Olivo
Granieri
DZ "S"
1 505
2 505
Ficuzzu
le Botteghelle
Mazzarinone
Gela
DZ "T"
3 505(–)
Objective "Y"
GELA
Acate
I 505
L. Bivieri
Demo 505
BISCARI
Pedalino
Acate
Stazione di Acate
Ridge
Biazzo
Casa Lena
VITTORIA
COMISO
Ippari
Scoglitti
Dannafugata
Mediterranean Sea
Santa Croce Camerina
Irminio
Fanale
Marina di Ragusa
Donnalucara
Battalion
Company
Platoon
Planned drop zones
Parachute Infantry
Airborne Engineers
Parachute Artillery
Aerodrome
Emergency landing field
0
5 miles

general and special staff sections; the Headquarters and Headquarters Battery of the Division Artillery; the Division Headquarters Company; the 82nd Airborne Signal Company; the 407th Quartermaster Company; the 307th Airborne Medical Company; the 782nd Ordnance Maintenance Company; and the 307th Airborne Engineer Battalion, all under the command of Lieutenant Colonel Robert Palmer, Division Engineer.

The fourth lift, the 325th Regimental Combat Team, commanded by Colonel Harry L. Lewis, and the 80th Airborne Antiaircraft Battalion, commanded by Major Raymond E. "Tex" Singleton, would follow as ordered. The 80th had been newly armed with the 57mm antitank gun to provide the division's antitank defense. Batteries A, B, and C had previously been armed with the far too small 37mm gun in an antitank role, while Batteries D, E, and F continued to perform the antiaircraft defense, armed with .50-caliber machine guns.

General Ridgway and his command staff would board the *Monrovia*, the Seventh Army command ship, and would land on D-Day at Gela by landing craft. Ridgway's accompanying staff would include Colonel Ralph P. Eaton, chief of staff; Lieutenant Colonel George E. Lynch, G-2; Lieutenant Colonel R. Klemm Boyd, G-3; Lieutenant Colonel Robert H. Wienecke, G-4; Lieutenant Colonel Frank Moorman, Signal Officer; Major Emory S. "Hank" Adams, Liaison Officer; Captain Don C. Faith, aide-de-camp; and eleven enlisted men from the staff sections.

After arriving in Kairouan, Major Mark Alexander, CO of the 2nd Battalion, 505th, met with commanders of the 64th Troop Carrier Group, Colonel John Cerny, the CO, and his XO (executive officer), Lieutenant Colonel Tommy Thompson. Major Alexander had just one request: "No matter where they dropped us, they would make every effort to drop us all together, that we would have the opportunity to organize and fight as a battalion."[44]

Captain Willard "Bill" Follmer, the commander of Company I, 505th, had just landed after the flight from Oujda with his company. "Somebody came to me as I got out of the plane and said that Krause wanted me and the other company commanders to come over to the area where they were doing the planning."[45] Captain Follmer was assigned the detached special mission of reducing a pillbox complex at a road junction and lighting a bonfire on a hill overlooking the landing beaches near the town of Gela that would act as a beacon for the 1st Infantry Division. The drop zone was near Lake Biviere, with a narrow valley and steep ridges running through the area. Follmer listened intently as he was briefed on the company's assignment. "There was a mission that [Major Krause] wanted me to do. There was an area where I was to go in just with my company alone, and the main thing he felt about the whole thing was to set this fire at two o'clock in the morning. Have somebody that I was sure would do it. That's why I got [Lieutenant George] Clark. [Krause] gave me two photographs that were rather blurred. It wasn't really totally effective, but it was good enough for me to make a guideline for where I'm going to go. I said, 'I'm going to look into this,' and he said, 'No, don't see the pilots.' I thought I shouldn't salute this guy, but I did and didn't say a word and walked off."[46]

Back at the Alabama Area, Follmer had been assigned to drop breakfast by parachute to the battalion, which was located in a small clearing in the middle of some tall pine trees. "It was that prior deal of putting the food on the ground at breakfast time for the battalion that alerted to me to all of the things you've got to look into. The pilots were new and not as well trained and I knew that they had dumped people in the wrong places. Recognizing that, I just said I'm waiting until dark."[47]

Shortly after dark, Follmer slipped out of his tent, moved through the olive grove where his company was bivouacked, crossed through a cactus hedge, and walked the considerable distance to the tents and planes of the Air Corps group that would carry the 3rd Battalion. On the way, he thought about Major Krause's order not to talk to the pilots. But Follmer was putting the mission ahead of his own well-being. "In the back of my mind, was when you go ahead and do something you're told not to do, it's a court martial possibility."[48]

Follmer was able to locate the tent of the lieutenant colonel commanding the group. "I said, 'I'm assigned to this position of going in first with a group of men at this area on this map. I would like to know [the pilot's] name and where he is, and I'd like to have permission to talk to him.' He turned me over to a sergeant. The sergeant gave me everything I wanted. The man's name he gave me was [Captain William R.] Bommar. He was more concerned about whether I was waking this guy up.

"When I got to the tent, I begged their pardon because three or four were lying down. I introduced myself to Bommar and he says, 'I heard you would probably see me.' That raised my imagination. 'Who said that to him?'

"He got out a flashlight and we looked at this thing and he had studied this. Apparently, the group leader had told him he going to have this special job. He was as well prepared as I was, plus he was just the right kind of guy.

"The first thing was so I wouldn't get tangled up with the rest of the four nine plane formations, I asked him, 'Can you please be the last group of nine planes in the serial?' "[49]

After studying the aerial photos and the map, Follmer determined that he would need to drop his company into a narrow valley to avoid his men being separated by the steep ridges on either side. The standard nine plane V-of-Vs formation would result in a wide drop pattern for the nine planes carrying Follmer's company. Part of the company would be dropped into the narrow valley and part on either side separated by the steep ridges that bordered both sides of the canyon. Follmer asked Bomar to fly in three, three-plane Vees, one behind the other.

"We looked up the coast on the map and we saw a river, I believe it was the Acate River, coming down to the water. That was significant on a half moon night. Then as you came along you would begin to see the beginning of a small inland lake almost running parallel with the coast, then a railroad and a road. They would be almost consecutive. If you would turn properly, where the Vee of the valley started to allow you inland, you could see all of those things."[50]

A white house, only visible from the right side of the cockpit when flying up the valley, would serve as the landmark for the drop. Follmer made a final request that Bomar sit on the right side of the cockpit. "The only little close scrap we had was when I asked him about that house on the side of the hill that we saw in the photograph.

"He says, 'Sir, I don't sit on the right side.'

"I said, 'Would you mind doing it for us, just this once? So you would be the man who would judge when you should give the dome light on, give us the green light, and that all of these guys be stacked up behind you and not over the ocean. Be sure they're inland.' I knew that white house was far enough inland that we would all land on the spot we were supposed to be.

"As soon as he studied this thing for a while and had thought it out, he said, 'Yes. sir.' "[51]

With the plan for the drop worked out to both men's satisfaction, Follmer thanked Bommar and left to return to his tent, convinced that whatever personal risk he ran, he had put the accomplishment of the mission above his own well-being.

On July 6, the 505 celebrated its first anniversary with a barbecue. Three steers were purchased from the Arabs, and someone in the 505 miraculously located and scrounged enough beer for each man in the regiment to have at least a canteen cup of the delicious liquid. This was as close to heaven as Sergeant Otis Sampson, with Company E, could get while in North Africa. "Some old steer who had lived through much of the past history of early Africa finally found himself barbecued as a special treat for the 505th. It was special. Not counting the real steaks, we also had beer and if the cards were played right, one was able to slip back into line now and again, which some of them did. It was a good party."[52]

Two days later, Sampson, who hadn't had a shower since arriving in North Africa was given his turn to clean up. "We were loaded in trucks and driven to an open area with showers. I walked under that pouring water with head up, mouth open, and clothes on, trying to absorb all I could of the cool pouring liquid. It was straight out of the ground."[53]

On July 7 and 8, briefings were conducted to inform each trooper of his company or platoon's mission. Private Howard Goodson, a member of the 2nd Platoon, Company I, 505th, was briefed by his platoon leader regarding their assignment, although the destination was not revealed. "Lieutenant [George] Clark took some of us down to an area where they had a sand table, told us exactly where we were supposed to jump and what we were supposed to do. We were supposed to go up this mountain at the western end of the lake and set a fire with whatever we could find . . . something that would really glow. The reason we did this was the 16th Infantry Regiment of the 1st Division was supposed to come through our area."[54]

Before dawn on the morning of the jump, Sergeant Bill Dunfee, with Company I, 505th, awoke the troopers in his squad. "July 9th started with an early breakfast, and we were then issued a basic combat load of ammo, grenades and rations. We were issued two items that were unique to the Sicily operation, being Mae West life preservers and gas masks."[55]

Each trooper was issued all of the equipment, weapons, ammunition, and food to be self-sufficient for several days. The typical combat load carried by each paratrooper included a main parachute, plus a reserve parachute. Each carried his personal weapon, ammunition, and grenades; typically an M1 rifle, 150 rounds of .30-caliber M1 ammunition, four fragmentation grenades, one smoke grenade, one Gammon grenade, plus a bayonet, trench knife, and switchblade jump knife. Along with their jumpsuit, each wore a helmet, gloves, silk escape map and compass sown inside their jumpsuit, wristwatch, combat harness, and carried a handkerchief. Extra clothes included two pairs of socks and one pair of under shorts. Each was issued a musette bag that held a mess kit, four 'K' rations, tooth brush, tooth powder, safety razor with five blades, one bar of soap, pencil, paper, ten packs of Camel cigarettes, matches, cigarette lighter, and Halazone tablets (for water purification). And finally, each load included a 30-foot rope, blanket, shelter half, gas mask, entrenching tool, two first aid kits, and a canteen filled with water. Most carried extra .30-caliber machine gun ammunition or other special items. Officers and NCOs carried a .45-caliber pistol with ammunition. Including the main and reserve parachutes, the average load would weigh around eighty to ninety pounds.

Crew-served weapons (60mm mortars, 81mm mortars, .30-caliber machine guns, bazookas, and 75mm pack howitzers) and ammunition, extra small arms ammunition, medical supplies, demolition materials (C4, fuses, blasting caps, detonators), and communications gear (radios, wire, switchboards) would be loaded in bundles attached underneath the fuselages of the C-47s. During the briefings, the paratroopers of the 505th and 504th were told that enemy opposition would consist of elements of the Italian army and a few German technicians. The Italian army had a poor reputation after being consistently defeated by the British and American forces in North Africa. So, the paratroopers were confident that they could easily handle anything that the Italians threw at them.

What no one in the 82nd Airborne Division knew was that the German Hermann Göring Fallschirm Panzer and 15th Panzer Grenadier Divisions were in Sicily. The detection of these two powerful German units was made as a result of the British "Ultra" machine that had been used to successfully break the German "Enigma" code, which the Germans felt was totally safe from enemy decoding. "Ultra" had decoded intercepted encrypted German communications traffic that confirmed the presence of these divisions in Sicily. But, because protecting the secrecy of the existence of "Ultra" was paramount to the Allies, the 82nd Airborne Division and other Allied units involved in the invasion of Sicily were not informed of the presence of these two German divisions.

To Company H, 505th, paratrooper Private Russell McConnell, it didn't matter where they jumped or who opposed them. "Africa was a living hell. We knew that Sicily couldn't be any worse. We were looking forward to it. By the time we were ready to go to Sicily, we were more than glad to go."[56]

General Ridgway was confident his paratroopers would make a good account of themselves in their first combat. "By the takeoff time for Sicily, the men were so lean and tough, so mean and mad, that they would have jumped into the fires of torment just to get out of Africa. Gavin had done a prodigious job preparing for that attack, and we were ready, right down to the last round of ammunition."[57]

CHAPTER 3

"DESTROY HIM WHEREVER FOUND"[1]

A couple of hours prior to takeoff, Colonel Gavin got on top of his jeep and spoke to his men. Private W. A. "Arnold" Jones, with Headquarters Company, 2nd Battalion, 505th, 81mm Mortar Platoon, heard him tell the assembled men: " 'Remember, you came over here to cause that SOB to die for his country, not to die for yours. He is no dummy; they're smart people. You've got to work just a little bit harder at staying alive than he does, if you want to go back home.' He told us, 'Look at the guy on your left. Look at the guy on your right. They're your friends. But, if you don't go in there saying, "I will take that so-and-so out. He's not going to get me." Then you're not coming back. Some of you are not going to be with me tomorrow.' "[2]

Sergeant Bill Dunfee, with Company I, 505th, had waited through the interminable heat of the long North African day with the same type of anxious tension as athletes develop before a big game. "We had an early supper and at 16:00 hours trucks carried each group to their C-47s that were manned by the 52nd Troop Carrier Wing. After the equipment bundles were checked and loaded, we crawled under the wing, in the shade and relaxed. At this time we were given the password, being 'George-Marshall' and told our destination by a mimeographed note given to each of us from Gavin."[3]

Soldiers Of The 505th Combat Team

Tonight you embark upon a combat mission for which our people and the free people of the world have been waiting for two years. You will spearhead the landing of the American Force upon the island of Sicily. Every preparation has been made to eliminate the element of chance. You have been given the means to do the job and you are backed by the largest assemblage of air power in the world's history.

The eyes of the world are upon you. The hopes and prayers of every American go with you.

Since it is our first fight at night you must use the countersign and avoid firing on each other. The bayonet is the night fighter's best weapon. Conserve your water and ammunition.

The term American Parachutist has become synonymous with courage of a high order. Let us carry the fight to the enemy and make the American Parachutist feared and respected through all his ranks. Attack violently. Destroy him wherever found.

Good landing, good fight, and good luck.

Colonel Gavin
Commanding

Not even Gavin knew that powerful German armored forces awaited the landings of his men in Sicily. General Omar Bradley, one of the few US generals with the security clearance to know of the existence of Ultra and its information, was disturbed by the knowledge he had of the German presence in Sicily. "Owing to the extreme secrecy of Ultra, we were not allowed to pass this information on to the lower echelons or include it in our circulated intelligence summaries. If we were asked if there were Germans on the island, we had to lie and say, 'There may be a few technicians.' This was a cruel deception on our own forces, but necessary in order to protect the secrets of Ultra."[4]

The Hermann Göring Fallschirm Division was a Luftwaffe unit made up of paratroopers (Fallschirmjägers) that was in the process of evolving into a panzer division. Although it was understrength, the division had significant armored elements, with over 131 tanks and assault guns (including a company of seventeen Mark VI Tiger I tanks), armored artillery, and reconnaissance units with many half-tracks and flak-wagons. Most dangerous of all, the division was deployed just north of the 82nd's drop zones and the landing beaches. It was in a perfect position to drive the American units back into the Mediterranean Sea.

As Private Russell McConnell, with Company H, 505th, sat with the rest of his stick in their assigned C-47 waiting for takeoff, he was glad to be leaving North Africa and going to Sicily regardless of what awaited them in combat.

The C-47 carrying Captain Ed Sayre, who was commanding Company A, 505th, waited its turn to take off. "At 19:30 hours 9 July 1943, the first of two hundred and twenty six planes carrying the paratroops began taking off from the dispersal airdromes."[5] After what seemed like an eternity, Sayre's plane began to taxi out onto the dirt runway, then revved both engines as the pilot applied the brake, and finally began rolling down the rough airstrip. Sayre could see other planes in the distance lifting off from other runways in the Kairouan area, joining the planes already in the air.

Planned Air Route of the 505th RCT from Kairouan to Sicily, 9 July 1943

After takeoff, Sergeant Otis Sampson commanding the 60mm mortar squad of the 1st Platoon, Company E, 505th, looked out of the door of his C-47. "The sunset was beautiful as we climbed in a wide circle to gain altitude; below the shadows had lengthened and turned to darkness. In flock formation of three, we had joined the long line of planes and disappeared into the night out over a darkening sea. The troopers had settled down and I supposed their thoughts were much the same as mine. There was much of my past life I wanted to think over and put in place; it would be a long four hours, the time we were told it took before crossing the Sicilian coast over our destination. 'Plenty of time to reminisce,' I thought."[6]

What Sergeant Bill Dunfee, with Company I, 505th, would later learn was that "a gale of thirty-five miles per hour [had] developed over the Mediterranean. The Air Corps was ordered to fly the mission two hundred feet above the water to avoid detection by enemy radio directional finders. The pilots were as green as ourselves, and navigation at the time was pretty primitive. They established a heading and flew it for X number of minutes and made their turns as indicated to another heading. This did not take into account the thirty-five miles per hour gale we were experiencing. Consequently the flights became separated and many missed the checkpoints of the small island of Linosa and the larger island of Malta."[7]

Standing in the door of his plane, Captain Sayre glanced at his watch and noticed that something was amiss. "The first thought that all was not going just as planned came when the Island of Malta was not sighted on schedule. At about the time the planes should have passed over Malta, the formation ran into heavy headwinds and then began breaking up into small groups. The nine plane formation carrying the Battalion Commander's group and the 1st and 2nd Platoons and Company Headquarters of Company A managed to stay together."[8]

The first serial into Sicily consisted of the 3rd Battalion, 504th, commanded by Lieutenant Colonel Charles Kouns. From the door on the left side of the aircraft, Lieutenant Roy M. Hanna, commanding the Headquarters Company Machine Gun Platoon, could see the coastline of Sicily and the Mediterranean Sea a short distance out from his plane. "The pilot turned on the red light designating to me that we had five minutes before the jump. We stood up, had our equipment check procedure, and I was standing in the door as we approached the town of Gela. I would guess that our altitude was about eight hundred feet, because the scheduled jump height was five hundred feet. Suddenly we were in the center of what could best be described as a large Fourth of July fireworks celebration. Puffs of smoke and fireballs began to appear near our plane, and tracers could be seen headed our way.

"Our pilot must have decided that it was time to get out of there because he put the plane in a bank and steep climb mode that was so severe that I had to hang on to the sides of the open doorway to keep from falling down or out.

"Very shortly thereafter, the green light came on over the doorway indicating that it was time to jump. Before leaving North Africa I had been given a landmark of a small lake [Lake Biviere] that was to indicate that we were near our jump area. I could not locate the lake, but decided that the pilot was better oriented than I, and so, out we went.

"Our machine guns and ammunition were packed in bundles and fastened to the carriage underneath the C-47. The bundles each weighed three hundred fifty pounds and were carried by a twenty-four foot parachute, compared to our twenty-eight foot chute that supported a man and equipment of about two hundred fifty pounds. These bundles were released by the C-47's crew chief shortly after we started jumping.

"This was the highest jump I ever made—must have been up at least 2,000 feet. My chute opened and I was drifting in a bright moonlit sky. As I drifted in the breeze like a feather, I tried to keep track of our equipment that was dropping very rapidly straight down. I made my first tree landing in an olive tree. I didn't know how high I was off the ground. But after cutting off a few parachute suspension lines with my switchblade, my one foot touched the ground, indicating that I was only a couple of feet off of the ground. I unhooked myself from the parachute harness and stood there listening. The night was completely silent except for some dog barking some distance away. I started walking in the direction of where I assumed my men were.

"Suddenly, I was halted with our password, 'George.'

"I replied, 'Marshall.'

"After I identified myself, the rifleman said, 'I'm sure glad you are friendly because I can't get this M1 assembled. I didn't recognize this soldier, but found out after questioning him that he had just been assigned to H Company a few weeks before as a replacement. I put the man's M1 together, loaded it, and sent him in the direction of where I thought my men should be. I went in search of our machine guns. I searched for our machine guns for what seemed to be a long time and finding nothing went in search of my platoon. During the next several hours I collected a total of seven of my platoon. And so, the eight of us walked up to the top of a small hill, rested and waited for daylight. I knew we were in Sicily, but had no idea where."[9]

Only a few small groups of paratroopers from the 3rd Battalion, 504th, landed near their intended drop zone, "Q," south of Niscemi. They would be some of the first to oppose the drive by the Western Kampfgruppe of the Hermann Göring Panzer Division moving toward the beaches to drive the US Army's seaborne forces into the Mediterranean Sea.

Private First Class Shelby Hord, a machine gunner with Company H, 504th, came down near an ancient chateau-like building that sat on high ground overlooking a road running southeast from the main Niscemi–Gela highway. The locals referred to the stone fortress as the Castle Nocera. Hord landed like a ton of bricks in the darkness. "I hit a big stone pile that the farmer had put on the side of the hill and knocked myself out cold. I had three brand new men that had just come from the United States as replacements. I had only had them [in my machine gun squad] for a few days. These three men kept asking me what was the password. They patted me on the face. I was out cold, then when I finally realized what they were saying . . . When I woke up enough, I said, 'What are you carrying your parachute for? One of you is dragging one. You go and you bury them right now.'

"They came back and I saw that all of the company's equipment had landed on the side of this hill. The four of us brought all of that stuff, put it around that wall of that home that was up there. It was the closest place and was the highest place, to protect ourselves. In front of the house, I dug in the machine gun overlooking the hill and then one over by the rocks. We knocked on the door and told the people to leave. To the left of the door they had a beautiful flower garden. We put the eight 60mm mortars in the flower garden. Finally Lieutenant Ferrill came."[10]

Arriving with another seventeen men, Lieutenant Willis Ferrill began to get the force organized, and "by 09:00, had assembled twenty-four enlisted men. A strong position was set up on the high ground at Castle Nocera, three miles southeast of Niscemi. A patrol sent out to contact the rest of the battalion, encountered a German antiaircraft company. In the engagement two Germans were killed and two captured, but the patrol was forced to withdraw to the defensive position."[11]

One group of troopers landed about a mile and a half from the 3rd Battalion's objective, a road intersection code named "X." Lieutenant James C. Ott assembled a group of fifteen men, including some jump-injured troopers. He assumed the battalion had landed on the drop zone and set out to cover the right flank. Ott led his men "north towards a house, found that the occupants were friendly, and left four injured troopers there. [I] then oriented [myself] in relation to Niscemi by questioning the Italians. From about 02:00 of 10 July, [we] patrolled the area to the east and got exact bearings for the road to Niscemi."[12]

Lieutenant Colonel Charles W. Kouns landed about three miles southeast of Niscemi, near an east-west secondary road that led to the town, where he assembled nine men and positioned the force on a nearby hill. Kouns then waited for either other paratroopers or the enemy. "Early on the morning of 10 July, Lieutenant Ott working east, joined his group to [mine]. In position, [we] saw a column of German infantry, estimated as one regiment of the Hermann Göring Division, moving along the road toward Niscemi and turning left on the bypass toward Gela.

"[I] asked Lieutenant Ott to go to the road and observe. Lieutenant Ott, with nine enlisted men, including a rocket launcher team, proceeded toward the road, a distance of five hundred to seven hundred yards, covered by the rifles of the remaining men. This was accomplished without observation by the enemy, although they had machine guns in position dominating the zone.

"Lieutenant Ott reached a cactus hedge and through an opening observed that the enemy was taking a break and their men were somewhat scattered. Lieutenant Ott was seen by a German officer, so he shot him and took a rocket launcher from one of his men and blew a German car to bits, killing three officers and the driver. German trucks and riflemen opened fire. [I] directed a covering fire against the enemy as Lieutenant Ott's group withdrew by taking quick cover in bamboo and running or crawling back through a vineyard, getting to a house with three of his men."[13]

Landing within a mile and a half of Niscemi, Lieutenant George J. Watts, with Company G, 504th, "had assembled fifteen men by 08:30, and had moved to a strategic hill and set up all round defensive positions which were maintained July 10-11."[14]

However, most of the 3rd Battalion, 504th, serial was dropped far to the southeast of DZ "Q." Lieutenant Peter J. Eaton, commanding the 3rd Battalion, Headquarters Company Mortar Platoon, landed a couple of miles northwest of

Biscari. He took charge of three planeloads of troopers that had landed in the same vicinity, and by sunrise had gathered all of the equipment and men he could find and started moving west toward Niscemi.

The 3rd Battalion Executive Officer, Major William R. Beall found himself "with one Medical Officer (Captain William W. Kitchin) after jumping beside an Italian garrison. Surrounded by enemy who were hunting us in the dark, we withdrew to a vineyard to figure our location and attempt to round up more men. About 02:00 10 July, we heard machine gun fire about 200 yards away and carbine return fire intermittently for one hour, and knew other troopers were in the vicinity."[15]

The second serial carried Major Edward "Cannonball" Krause's 3rd Battalion, 505th. Most of the battalion landed far to the southeast of their intended drop zone, between the towns of Scoglitti and Vittoria. Flying at the rear of the serial was Company I in three trailing three-plane Vs, as Captain Follmer and Captain Bommar had agreed. Sergeant Bill Dunfee was the assistant jumpmaster of the stick. "Since my squad was jumping from Captain Follmer's plane, I was put at the end of the line, being the last man out. I was concerned when Follmer put one of the new men between me and the rest of my squad. We had a direct order from Major Krause to shoot any man that refused to jump. This presented an interesting problem, since had it occurred, my M1 was in a canvas container under my reserve chute. During most of the flight Captain Follmer was spending his time up front with the pilot. I recall asking him if he had them headed in the right direction, he grinned and nodded yes.

"As we approached Sicily and for reasons unknown to this day, the rest of the 3rd Battalion flight turned back out to sea, subsequently returning to be dropped on the wrong DZ. Pilot Bommar and Captain Follmer seeing the Acate River in the distance were satisfied we were on a proper course and the I Company flight proceeded toward Sicily. As we crossed the coastline Follmer told me to pass the word back to 'Stand up, hook up and check equipment.' This done, we sounded off equipment check, starting with me and moving toward the door. At about this time we were over Lake Biviere, Captain Follmer moving by me said, 'About five minutes,' and moved on back to his position at the door. Being crowded when we stood up and hooked up, it was necessary for me to step through the bulkhead into the Radio Operator's area.

"At this point I noticed the new man in front of me had sat down. I told him to stand up and he started giving me conversation and I made it very clear to him in four-letter words that he damned well better stand back up. I had noticed the green light had been on for some time when Captain Follmer yelled, 'Let's Go!' and we started moving toward the door. For whatever reason the man in front of me went past the door into the tail section of the plane. I grabbed his backpack and pulled him back to the door. He started to back off again, so I grabbed the sides of the door opening and pulled us both out. I had no more than felt the shock of the parachute opening, when I was going through pine trees, hitting the ground going downhill. Getting down so fast, my thought was as I hit the ground, I've had a malfunction (partial opening) but I was able to get up, get rid of the parachute harness, getting my equipment together and moved out. Being unable to find the man who went out ahead of me, I assumed he hit the ground ahead of me and could be dead. Starting back the way we flew in to 'roll up the stick,' I couldn't find anyone and spent the night searching for my company. Since I had no idea how far the plane had traveled during the mix-up at the door, my assumption was that I had landed over the crest of a mountain beyond the valley we were to land in."[16]

As Follmer's chute deployed, a strong wind caught him. "I saw the other side of the valley coming up . . . before I could get anything flat to land on. I thought I'd be smart and lower my right leg so I could take [the side of the ridge] on a tilt. The right leg just snapped right away. Then I started crawling, trying to find somebody. There was quite a bit of crawling down the hill. I heard a rustle in some bushes down by the roadside. I was down by the road by then. I yelled, 'George.'

"There was a, 'Marshall.' Out comes John [Scotty] Hough.

"We went on and gradually picked up more men, while I'm riding on John's back. We're heading for where I told the men that my headquarters would be . . . up on this hill near Gela . . . if they needed anything that was where to go, and where to bring prisoners.

"I said, 'I think I can get up and walk.'

"And John says, 'You better not.'

"I start [to stand] up a little bit and slide, and he promptly picks me up and carries me up that hill that would rise to where we put the headquarters. The headquarters group went up ahead of me, to this farmhouse where John Hough had told them there was a mule. John wanted to get some relief [from carrying Follmer with a full equipment load on his back]. One guy banged against the front door with the butt of his rifle and said, 'American . . . American.'

"All of the lights came on and the farmer came out. The men said, 'We want your mule.' They brought him out and John hoisted me aboard practically by himself.

"We went on up that road and started to go up the hill again. By the time we got to the top of the hill, all of the men were there and they circled me and I said, 'Let's not get so close here.'

"I began to hear some firing coming from what looked like a pillbox, but later turned out to be a bathroom for the Italians that were supposed to defend that place. The officer who got there first, Lieutenant [Joseph W.] Vandevegt, tried to rouse all of those Italians and get them out of there. They all tried to hide behind a shower curtain and didn't realize that their legs showed. One guy let go with a tommy gun and put a couple of rows of shots down there. And they came out in a hurry. We had quite a few prisoners to take care of.

"I recall two pillboxes at the crossroads. I had a man drop on top of one of them, and the Italians came out. And there wasn't anyone in the other pillbox."[17]

After landing, Company I trooper Private Howard "Goody" Goodson found the trooper who had jumped behind him, Private Joe Patrick. Goodson and his buddy began to climb the hill overlooking the 1st Division landing beach. "We knew what our mission was. Joe was with Lieutenant Clark's platoon. We eventually wound our way up this mountain and ran into different guys and ended up with a group of seven or eight of us. We found this farmhouse right at the western end of this lake, and we set the barn and the haystacks on fire."[18]

By 2:00 a.m., Company I, 505th, had accomplished all of its initial objectives: eliminating the opposition at the pillboxes at the crossroads, setting up a perimeter defense of the crossroads, and lighting a bonfire to mark the landing beach for the 1st Infantry Division landings. Due to brilliant planning and cooperation between Captains Follmer and Bommar, and flawless execution, Company I was the only company in the 505 Regimental Combat Team to land largely on the intended drop zone. The only exception was one planeload jumped by Lieutenant Walter B. Kroener, which landed far inland.

Ten minutes behind the 3rd Battalion, 505th, serial was Lieutenant Colonel Arthur "Hardnose" Gorham's 1st Battalion, 505th. The only significant portion of the battalion to land near the planned drop zone were the nine planes carrying Captain Ed Sayre and his Company A, 505th, paratroopers. However, Sayre knew something wasn't right. "At the time when the planes were supposed to be nearing the drop zone, antiaircraft fire could be seen coming up on the left side of the planes. This could only mean one thing: the planes were coming in on the wrong side of the island. The Flight Commander realized this and the formation was turned back out to sea in order to make another attempt to find the correct drop zone. After about an hour, a lake, which was the final checkpoint, was sighted. The planes turned over the lake in the direction to bring them over the drop zone in about two minutes. After proceeding about one minute and a half, the formation met heavy antiaircraft fire and began breaking up. One minute later the green 'go' light was given and the parachutists left the planes.

"I led my group out and a few seconds later disentangled myself from my parachute in a vineyard on the side of a very steep hill. Because of losing so much time in trying to find the drop zone, it was now very dark and no one could see over a few feet. About six machine guns which had been firing on the planes as the men jumped, had now lowered their fire and were traversing back and forth over the area in which the troops had landed. Due to the rough terrain and the fact that the guns were firing tracer ammunition, which could be seen coming, the fire caused the troops very little trouble."[19]

Private Dave Bullington was a scout/sniper with Company A, and had slept on the flight over. "The .03-A3 Springfield rifle was jumped in a bundle. I jumped the sight in the musette bag and I was also armed with folding-stock carbine. The fellow in front of me, a buddy of mine, Orval Hartman from Texas, he fixed his [belly] band on his M1 rifle. He didn't put it in a Griswold container like he was supposed to. He fixed the bayonet and went out the door with his rifle at high port and you know what happened . . . he lost that rifle.

"When I went out the door it was lit up like the Fourth of July. The red tracers looked like it was a couple or three miles down near the beach. They didn't even come close to the plane I was in. Somebody was sure shooting at something. We must have jumped at about three or four hundred feet, because I stepped out of the plane and it seemed like I oscillated a couple of times and I was on the ground. I know there were three planeloads that jumped there, because I could see three planes going across the top of the hill in a Vee.

"I went about a hundred or two yards back the direction we came in and found the bundle easily. I got my .03 out, and about that time Hartman came up and said he lost his rifle, and I gave him my carbine and some of the ammunition I had."[20]

Behind the 1st Battalion serial was the 505th Regimental Headquarters serial. Sergeant Bob Gillette was assigned to the stick that included Colonel Gavin and Major Benjamin H. Vandervoort, the Regimental S-3. As Sergeant Gillette followed Gavin out of the door, he felt a terrific opening shock as his parachute deployed. Then Gillette noticed something else wasn't right. "It seemed to me that we were dropped much higher than expected and at a much higher speed than we wanted. While descending, in the light of flares fired from the ground, I could see many other chutes in the air. Once on the ground, they all seemed to have disappeared, and there was nothing but silence and aloneness until one by one, contact was made over what seemed to be a long, long time.

"I was in the early group assembled with Colonel Gavin. It wasn't until [we were] on the ground and partially assembled that we knew we had been seriously misdropped. At one time, an hour or two after landing there were possibly thirty to forty of us together."[21]

The small group moved silently through the darkness when Gillette was suddenly given a hand signal from the trooper in front of him to stop. "Under a regime of silence, we rested at the side of the trail while the leaders were trying to determine our location. When the front of the column restarted, there was a break in the chain of contact, and the remainder of the group, of which I was a part, was not alerted. This was just one of our early learning experiences."[22]

The regimental headquarters group that had left Gillette and the others behind in the darkness consisted of Colonel Gavin; Captain Al Ireland, the 505 S-1; Major Ben Vandervoort, the S-3; and about twenty men.

The final serial contained the 2nd Battalion, 505th. Major Mark Alexander, the CO, was standing in the door looking at the beautiful blue Mediterranean water below, which shone in the moonlight as the armada approached the coast of Sicily. "The red light came on, we hooked up and prepared to jump. The green light came on and I was still looking down at the Mediterranean. Of course, the men tried to push me out the door and after fighting them off; I went forward and cussed out [Tommy] Thompson. His reply was simply that the copilot was nervous and had gotten in too much of a hurry.

"We received considerable tracer fire as we finally crossed the coast. We were to have dropped on a ground elevation of one hundred twenty meters, but instead, were dropped on an elevation of two hundred to two hundred fifty meters."[23]

As Major Alexander and his troopers landed, they received immediate heavy fire from very close range. "Our Battalion Headquarters Company dropped on a concentration of five pillboxes and wire. Lieutenant (Dr.) [Kurt B. Klee] Clee [*sic*] unfortunately landed in the wire to the east of the larger pillbox and was killed immediately. Corporal Fred Freeland [Company D] got hung up in the same area and played dead until we took the pillbox later in the morning. My Battalion XO, Captain John Norton had an interesting experience. 'George'-'Marshall' was our sign and countersign. In the dark of early D-Day, in trying to locate other members of the battalion, he approached what appeared to be a house, heard low voices, called out, 'George' and some Italian voice called back, 'George, hell!' and nearly shot his head off with a machine gun. Norton later learned that he had approached one of the pillboxes."[24]

After landing, Captain Sayre began getting his Company A, 505th, troopers assembled. "My group seemed to be scattered over an area of several hundred yards. About an hour was consumed in getting this group and their equipment together. During this time, none of the other planes which were supposed to land in the same area as Company A had landed, so the 536 radios were opened in an attempt to contact other elements of Company A. The 1st and 2nd Platoon leaders were soon contacted, but they did not know where they were in relation to my position. They were told to listen for three rapid shots from an M1 rifle and tell us if they heard them. They did hear the shots. They were given orders to make every effort to recover their crew served weapons and ammunition from the bundles dropped by the planes and then to assemble at my position.

"About 02:30, I went on a reconnaissance to see if I could determine the exact positions of the machine guns which had continued firing from the time the troops had jumped. The positions of the guns were easily located because of the tracers being fired. During the reconnaissance, the Battalion Executive Officer [Major Walter Winton] was contacted. I requested permission to attack the machine guns and it was given.

"While the communications sergeant waited at the spot on which the platoon was to assemble, I took twelve men and moved out to attack the machine guns. The men were divided into two-man teams. Each team was to crawl as far as possible to their assigned gun and pull the pin on their hand grenades. When

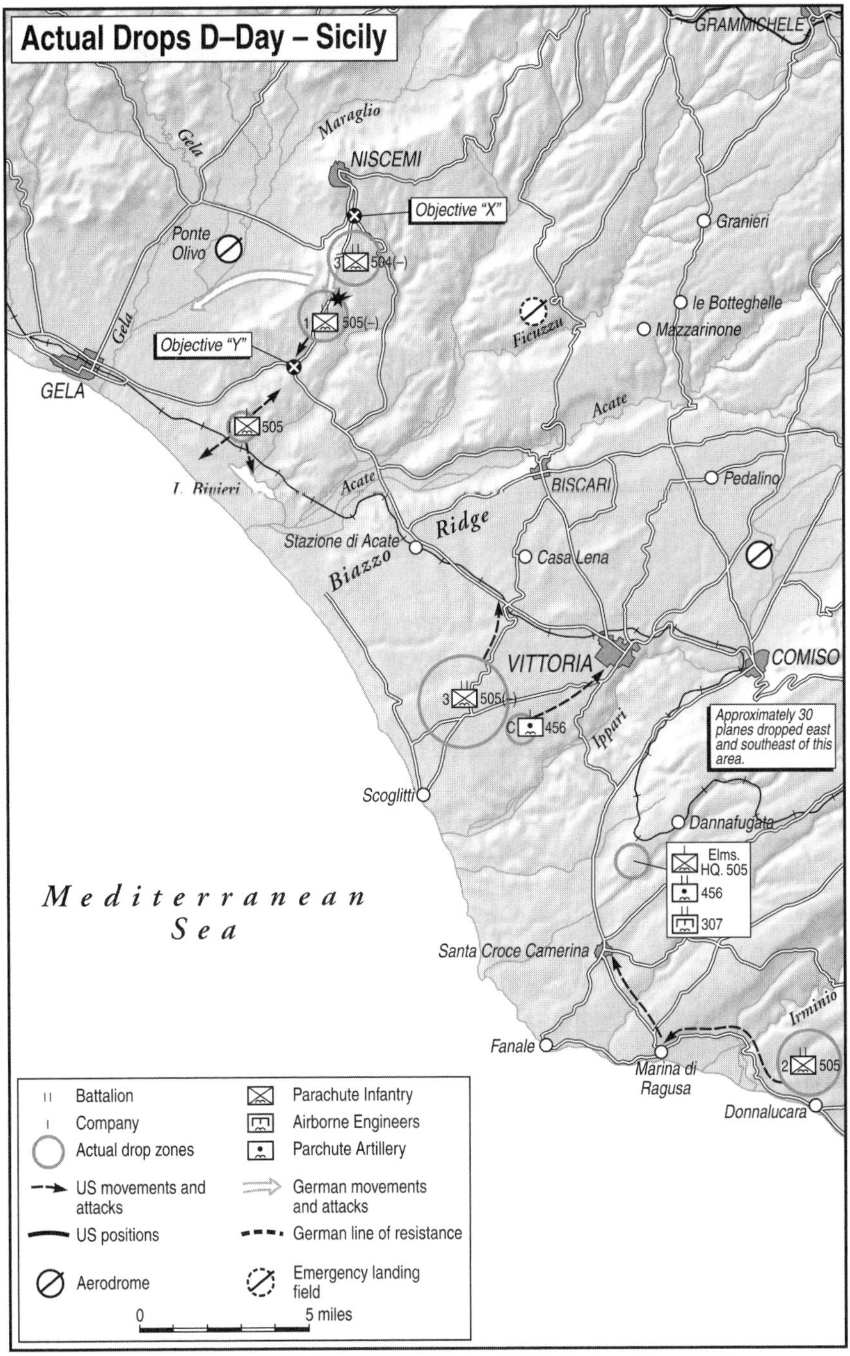
Actual Drops D-Day – Sicily
GRAMMICHELE
Maraglio
Gela
NISCEMI
Objective "X"
Granieri
Ponte Olivo
3 504(–)
le Botteghelle
Mazzarinone
1 505(–)
Ficuzza
Gela
Objective "Y"
GELA
Acate
1 505
Pedalino
L. Biviere
Acate
BISCARI
Ridge
Stazione di Acate
Casa Lena
Biazzo
VITTORIA
COMISO
3 505(–)
C 456
Ippari
Approximately 30 planes dropped east and southeast of this area.
Scoglitti
Dannafugata
Elms. HQ. 505
456
307
Mediterranean Sea
Santa Croce Camerina
Irminio
Fanale
Marina di Ragusa
2 505
Donnalucara
Battalion
Company
Actual drop zones
US movements and attacks
US positions
Aerodrome
Parachute Infantry
Airborne Engineers
Parchute Artillery
German movements and attacks
German line of resistance
Emergency landing field
0
5 miles

I threw my grenade, all other teams were to throw at the same time. If, after the grenades exploded, it looked as if there were too many enemy for the men to overcome, they were to immediately withdraw to a rendezvous point in an unoccupied trench about one hundred yards from the machine gun positions.

"With the pop of the fuse on the first grenade, the teams threw their grenades. By the light of the grenades thrown and by about twenty [grenades] that the enemy threw back, it could be seen that the troops were attacking not dug in machine guns as supposed, but heavy concrete and stone pillboxes. A very hasty withdrawal to the rendezvous point was made. One man was slightly wounded, but none lost.

"The group then returned to the company assembly point. By 05:00 hours, about forty-five men from the 1st and 2nd Platoons had assembled. They had been able to recover two 60mm mortars with fifty rounds of ammunition and three light machine guns with 2,000 rounds for each gun."[25]

At sunrise Sergeant Bob Gillette, the regimental communications NCO, found himself "in a group of about fifteen along with Captain Johnson of the 307 Engineers. We later connected with a small group led by Lieutenant [Harold] Swingler at a crossroads pillbox, (by then abandoned) where Swingler conducted a brief service while we buried (temporarily) three Regimental Headquarters Company men KIA, probably during the night in front of that pillbox. Those three were [Private David J. Jr.] McKeown, [Private First Class Thomas D.] Adams, and [Private William J.] Kerrigan. This was south of Vittoria, probably in the vicinity of Santa Croce Camerina."[26]

As the first rays of sunlight began to appear, Captain Ed Sayre, commanding Company A, 505th, was able to assess what he and his small group of paratroopers faced. "It could now be seen that the pillboxes attacked during the night were surrounding a large two story stone house which had been converted into a garrison. It was decided to reattack the position immediately in order that it might be taken before the enemy could bring up reinforcements.

"The plan of attack was for the 1st Platoon and Company Headquarters to attack from the front and the 2nd Platoon to attack from the right flank. All rifle grenadiers and the rocket launcher would accompany me. The two mortars were to take up positions in battery some four hundred yards from the pillboxes. They were to be controlled by relayed voice commands. The mortars were to fire first on the pillboxes and, on order, shift to the stone house. The 2nd Platoon was to place heavy fire on the pillboxes keeping the vents covered until they could be assaulted by the 1st Platoon with the rifle grenadiers and rocket launcher.

"All troops were able to get within one hundred yards of positions due to the unoccupied trenches which led almost up to the pillboxes. At 05:30 hours, the 1st Platoon and Company Headquarters were able to bring effective fire with the rifle grenades and rocket launcher on the pillboxes, which were then assaulted with hand grenades and taken."[27]

Private Dave Bullington and "a fellow by the name of Anderson worked our way around to the back of the house. We could hear machine guns firing there. There were two out buildings behind the house, and right behind them the ground sloped off rather abruptly . . . three or four feet. We could crawl on our hands and knees and not be seen. We got around to the back where we could look between those buildings and see the back door of the house. About the time we stuck our heads up, a grenade landed right in front of me, I saw it coming . . . I ducked but didn't duck soon enough. A little piece got me in the neck. The next one went way over me. I thought, 'That old boy has got a pretty good arm.' Later, I found it wasn't his arm at all, he had a grenade launcher in the back door of that house. I went back the way I came. I heard Captain Sayre say, 'Fix bayonets. Give me five more rounds on that mortar and we're going in.' That was the first thing I heard him say. I didn't even know he was there. It was the second try before I got [the bayonet] on [the rifle]. I guess I was a little shaky after being hit by that grenade."[28]

Captain Sayre led his men forward as they assaulted the stone house. "The machine guns in the pillboxes were now turned on the enemy troops who were firing from the first and second story of the garrison. Under cover of this heavy fire, the 1st Platoon gained the side of the building and began tossing grenades in the windows. The heavy doors on the building were blown down with rocket launcher fire and more grenades were tossed in."[29]

Bullington "went straight up over that bank [of dirt] toward one the outbuildings, and Captain Sayre came in from the other direction and we met there at the corner. He told me to put a grenade into the outbuilding right across from him. It wasn't but about fifteen feet. The opening wasn't very big, and [the grenade] kind of hung up on the roof, and when it did [go in] I got out of there fast. I ducked around the building."[30]

After the grenades thrown through the windows had exploded, Sayre heard the enemy "yelling that they would surrender. The ones able to walk were rounded up. They included about forty Italians and ten Germans. During the attack, four of the parachutists had been wounded, one seriously and three slightly."[31] Sayre and his men had killed fifteen enemy soldiers during the assault.

Meanwhile, Bullington, at the back of the house, decided to go in and clear the building. "The back door of that house was open. As soon as you went in the door, there was a room off to the right that had a bench running along the wall. There were about a half a dozen Italians in there, sitting and laying down. I guess some mortar fragments got them, it looked like they were wounded and bleeding. I knew there were some people up stairs, because they had fired. I went on up stairs and thought that Sayre was behind me, but it was 'Wild' Bill Harris. We got several of them out of a room."[32]

After a couple of his men interrogated the prisoners, Sayre learned "that the Germans were an outpost from a combat team of the Hermann Göring Panzer Division, which was only about two miles away. An attack was expected very soon, so a hasty reorganization was made and all around defense was set up. The garrison contained nearly 500,000 rounds of machine gun ammunition and twenty machine guns. All of these were utilized in the defense. While the organization for the defense was going on, the battalion commander, Lieutenant Colonel [Arthur] Gorham came in with about thirty men, including the two battalion surgeons. They were carrying several men who had been seriously wounded.

"Colonel Gorham ordered the troops to continue to consolidate the position, since it commanded the road leading from Niscemi to the beaches. He also ordered a patrol to be sent to the drop zone to obtain information as to the strength of enemy there as well as in fortifications around the road, which it was our mission to capture.

"At 07:00 hours, a German armored column was seen about 4,000 yards away coming from Niscemi. It was preceded by a point of two motorcycles and a Volkswagen. The point was allowed to get into the position and was fired on. All of its personnel were killed or captured. The armored column stopped when they heard the firing.

"Within about thirty minutes, two companies of enemy troops were seen moving across the open ground to the front toward our position. When they were within about two hundred yards of the positions, they were fired on by all of the twenty machine guns. Most of the enemy were pinned down and killed. But the few who did manage to escape evidently informed the German armored unit of our positions, for shortly thereafter a mobile 88 moved to a position on a hill just out of range of any weapon the parachutists had and began shelling the position.

"The patrol sent out to reconnoiter the drop zone had now returned with the news that there were no enemy there. But, about twenty Italians armed with heavy machine guns were holding a fortified position, surrounded by several rows of barbed wire, around the road junction [that] it was our mission to capture.

"Colonel Gorham moved the troops toward the drop zone with the prisoners carrying the wounded, leaving one officer and a squad of men to cover the withdrawal. When the troops had reached the next terrain feature to the rear, the squad withdrew under covering fire. As the troops continued to move to the drop zone area, German tanks could be heard coming around our right flank. Shortly after the tanks were heard, the troops also heard several rounds of rocket launcher fire."[33]

The paratroopers firing at those tanks were a squad from Company A, led by Sergeant Tim Dyas. "As the sounds of battle were nearby, I headed my group towards them for this is why we jumped. A small hill appeared in front of us so I headed my group that way. The bazooka team of Pat Sheridan and John Wroblewski went around the hill to be on the roadside. As we came atop the hill a German tank roared up the side of it as we ran down the side of the hill near the road. Training paid off for we were able to avoid any tank fire.

"As we hugged the side of the almost vertical hill Sergeant John Dixon reported to me that the bazooka team had knocked out the two German tanks we could see on the road to our left. He told me that the first bazooka shot hit the turret of the first tank, killing the officer who was looking ahead not aware of the presence of our group.

"Shortly after the tanks were knocked out, German hand grenades came over the crest of the hill, as I ordered our men to throw our grenades up over the crest at the Germans. This type of warfare went on for about two to three hours before a German tank bypassed the two burning ones and turned its [75mm] gun on us. As soon as I saw this I knew we had no chance, so I ordered our men to surrender as I threw down my weapon. This has haunted me all my life, but intellectually I knew I was right.

"As we came down from the hill, German grenadiers approached with fingers on the triggers of their weapons and I fully expected we'd be shot. Fortunately for us they were good soldiers and a good soldier does not kill an unarmed enemy. We were then moved off and eventually up to Germany as POWs for some twenty-three months. I returned home weighing eighty-five pounds."[34]

As the morning drew on, Colonel Gavin, Captain Ireland, Major Vandervoort, and three other troopers continued across the Sicilian countryside. Following a trooper who was acting as lead scout, Gavin led his small group in the direction he believed would take them to their objective. "Suddenly, as we came over the crest of high ground, there was a burst of small arms fire. We hit the ground. There was a sickening thud of near misses kicking up dirt in my face. I reacted instinctively as I had been taught in the infiltration course by hugging closely to the ground. In no time I realized that I would not continue to live doing that; I had to shoot back. I started firing my carbine, and it jammed. I looked to Vandervoort about six feet to my left; he was having the same trouble."[35]

As he was working to get his jammed carbine working, Gavin suddenly saw an Italian officer appear only fifty feet away, looking at him through the branches of an olive tree. "Captain Ireland gave him the first squirt from his tommy gun, and he went down like a rag doll. I began to fire my carbine single-shot. The leading trooper, who had gone down in the first fusillade, writhed and rolled over. He appeared to be dead, practically in the enemy position. Their fire increased, and there was a loud explosion like that of a mortar shell. I decided that there was at least a platoon of enemy and that our best prospects were to try to work around it. I yelled to Vandervoort, Ireland, and the troopers to start moving back while I covered. It worked. We had a close call and nothing to show for it but casualties, and our prospects were not very bright."[36]

During the predawn darkness of July 10, Lieutenant Dean McCandless, the 1st Battalion, 505th communications officer, had managed to find only one of his men, Sergeant Otto J. "Ott" Carpenter. They had climbed to the top of a hill and had dug in. As the sun came up, Lieutenant McCandless looked out through a hedge next to the road where they had dug in. McCandless could see the "invasion fleet several miles east of us, a beautiful sight."[37]

A short time later McCandless heard a strange, low, roaring sound that grew louder and louder. It was "our own Navy shooting over our heads—those big shells sounding almost like a freight train going over!"[38]

Early that morning, a landing craft brought General Ridgway and his aide, Captain Don Faith ashore on the 1st Infantry Division's beach. Together they immediately set out for the command post (CP) of General Terry Allen, the commanding officer of the 1st Division. There, Ridgway learned from Allen, that reconnaissance elements of the 1st Division moving inland had reported that they had not found any paratroopers, nor were his communications sections successful in reaching any paratroopers via radio. It was very disturbing, and Ridgway decided to set out on foot with Faith and a couple of bodyguards that Allen insisted he take along, to try to find his paratroopers on his own.

Just before dawn, after landing in the British zone, Private First Class Elmo Bell, with Company C, 505th, heard a trooper begging for help. "I just slew my rifle and started walking in the direction of the voice. I walked down to the person, and it turned out to be a member of my platoon, an Italian boy named [Private First Class Michael A.] Scambelluri. Scambelluri was fully conscious and very lucid. He described in detail how he had landed in the courtyard of a small Italian Army garrison, and he had been captured before he got out of his chute. And the captors carried him into the garrison commander, and the commander was interrogating him. And in the course of the interrogation, Mike started answering in Italian. Mike was born in Italy and came over to the states as a small child. The garrison commander was highly incensed when he found Scambelluri was a native Italian, and he accused him of being a traitor to his homeland, and he directed the two enlisted men who had brought him in, to take him out in the courtyard, shoot him, and bury him.

"And they carried him out and backed him against the wall, and one of them emptied a little Beretta .32-caliber pistol into his stomach area, and Mike slumped down by the wall. Then they took his hand grenades and got on the other side of the wall and tossed his hand grenades over, and one of his grenades rolled up in his crotch and exploded. As soon as Mike explained what happened, and I saw the nature of his wounds, the bullet holes in his belly and everything, I gave him a shot of morphine. I didn't realize that Scambelluri had already injected himself, and he wasn't feeling a lot of pain. That's the reason he was perfectly conscious and cognizant of everything that had happened."[39]

About that time, four or five other troopers that had been hiding in some nearby bushes joined Bell. Together they rigged a litter from a piece of a parachute that Bell had cut from an equipment bundle and two poles. They carried Scambelluri back to an olive orchard as it was getting daylight. As he was attending to the badly wounded trooper, Bell noticed a small group approaching. "Two troopers came in with an Italian POW, and they asked Scambelluri if he had seen this one at the garrison. Scambelluri indicated that he was one of the two that carried him out and shot him. He said he was the one who shot him in the belly with a pistol. So they carried this Italian soldier out and had him dig a grave and shot him and buried him. And then a half hour later, I guess someone came in with another one. And Scam identified him as being the second of the two enlisted men, and they asked if he had anything to do with his being wounded.

"Scambelluri didn't know of any, said, 'He didn't shoot the gun.' He didn't know who threw the grenades, but he wasn't involved unless he threw the grenades.

"And they said, 'Well, did he do anything to stop the other one?'

"And he said, 'No, he didn't.'

"So they carried him out and shot him, too.

"We covered [Scambelluri] with this piece of parachute to protect him from the flies, and he could reach down in his crotch and just get a handful of, like, hamburger meat and throw it aside. And it became obvious that if he didn't get medical attention soon, that he couldn't possibly make it. And the only medical attention that I could think of was on the beach."[40]

Bell got Scambelluri evacuated to a British floating hospital ship. A couple of days later, the ship was hit and sunk by German aircraft. Scambelluri miraculously escaped and wound up in a hospital in Tripoli. *The Stars and Stripes* got word of this story and dubbed Scambelluri "Iron Mike." Because of the terrible damage done to his digestive system by the wounds, Iron Mike slowly dropped from his normal weight of one hundred eighty pounds to eighty-seven pounds at the time of his death a few months later. His death made three-inch headlines in *The Stars and Stripes*, "Iron Mike Dies."

Despite being horribly misdropped, paratroopers individually and in small groups, though badly outnumbered, were wreaking havoc on the Italian and German reinforcements moving toward the beach landings. They laid impromptu ambushes and formed roadblocks, which held up the counterattacking forces during the critical first hours when beach landings are always most vulnerable.

Moving west toward Niscemi, Lieutenant Peter J. Eaton, with Headquarters Company, 3rd Battalion, 504th, was leading about forty-five men when around noon his "scouts encountered two Italian cars towing 47mm antitank guns. They killed the occupants and took the guns. With this added equipment, positions were set up, and manned, with [the captured antitank] guns covering the roads toward Biscari. About 12:30, a column of Italian motorized infantry, with an eleven ton Italian tankette in the lead (estimated at a battalion because it occupied about 2,200 yards on the Niscemi-Biscari highway) [approached]. Sergeant Suggs of Headquarters Company and seven other men of that company manned these guns, of which they had no knowledge. Bore-sighting them, they fired them like veterans. Sergeant Suggs and his men knocked out the tankette with their

Italian 47mm antitank guns and so disorganized the foe with their fire, backed by our 81mm mortars, that they retreated in confusion.

"Believing that the enemy force, after reorganization, would be too large and possess too much firepower for our own weapons, which were carbines, [we] destroyed the enemy equipment and withdrew to the south."[41]

The 3rd Battalion, 504th executive officer, Major William Beall, and his battalion surgeon had landed in the British sector and been forced to hide from Italian troops who were systematically hunting them. Beall was determined to attack the Italians as soon as he could get some help. "About 07:30, 10 July, an advance patrol of Canadians came up. They gave me their positions. . . . I asked for help to attack the Italian garrison, but was not able to secure it, because the Canadians had another mission, that of establishing and protecting the beachheads in another zone. I worked back to the beach and got assistance. The garrison was taken with Canadian assistance a little later. One Italian officer and twenty enlisted men were captured, and six paratroopers were released, having been imprisoned by the Italians. I continued my search for more men, and with what I rounded up, went back to the beach."[42]

About noon, from his position dug in on a hill, Lieutenant Dean McCandless, with the 1st Battalion, 505th, heard the low rumble of engines and the squeaking sound of bogey wheels and tank treads. "Several German tanks came clanking up our road and stopped just opposite us. I was peeking up at the German tank commander as he looked across toward our invasion fleet. Thank God, he never looked down and they soon clanked on."[43]

The tanks were part of the Western Kampfgruppe of the Hermann Göring Panzer Division. It consisted of two panzer battalions: approximately ninety Mark III (23 tons) and Mark IV tanks (25 tons, with a high velocity, long barrel 75mm main gun), two armored artillery battalions, one armored reconnaissance battalion (less one company), and one armored engineer battalion (less one company). The lead elements of this powerful German armored force had tangled with Captain Sayre's two Company A platoons. Then two of their tanks had been knocked out and the force held up for several hours by Sergeant Tim Dyas' Company A troopers when it attempted to move around the flank of Sayre's position. After overwhelming Dyas and his men, the kampfgruppe continued to move south toward the beaches.

The heroic fight by Dyas and his squad against the tanks had enabled Sayre and his men to continue to move toward Objective "Y." As Sayre led his men south, he kept hearing tanks in the distance to the west. "When the drop zone was reached, the troops could see heavy naval gunfire landing about two hundred yards in front of the enemy fortified position. This fire was apparently being directed by a naval plane, which was circling overhead. At this time, a German fighter plane appeared and shot down the naval plane. However, the fire continued to land in front of the enemy positions. The fire could not be brought directly onto the positions because of high ground protecting them.

"Company A took up positions about one thousand yards from the pillboxes, and we told one of the prisoners to go to the pillboxes to tell them that the paratroops were controlling the heavy gunfire and if they did not immediately surrender, the fire would be placed on them. The prisoner was evidently an eloquent speaker, for in a very few minutes after he entered the first pillbox, all occupants of the three pillboxes in the area came out with their hands up.

"Company A took over the pillboxes at 10:45 hours, and none too soon, for within a few minutes four German tanks approached from the north. When the troopers in the pillboxes fired on them with machine guns, they withdrew. At 11:30 hours, scouts from the 2nd Battalion of the 16th Infantry, 1st Division contacted the troopers. The prisoners and wounded were evacuated through the 1st Division, and I, through the 1st Division communication channels, was able to inform General Ridgway of our position and actions."[44]

This was the first communication that Ridgway had with any of his paratroopers since the operation commenced. It was a huge relief, but still didn't calm his concern that the bulk of Gavin's troopers had been wiped out, or badly misdropped, or both.

After notifying Ridgway of the capture of Objective "Y," Sayre met with the battalion commander whose men had linked up with his force earlier. "The two platoons from Company A and the battalion command group were now attached to the 2nd Battalion of the 16th Infantry, commanded by Lieutenant Colonel Crawford. We started forward against the enemy who had been pursuing us. Colonel Crawford was very apprehensive of the attack because he had only one 57mm gun for defense against the German armor, which seemed to be concentrating to the front. The battalion was able to advance only one mile in the face of light resistance before being given orders to dig in for the night.

"About half of the [2nd] battalion [16th Infantry] was made up of new replacements who had joined the battalion only a few weeks before to replace casualties suffered in the African campaign. The noncommissioned officers did a wonderful job at all times in keeping them down when under fire and getting them on the move again as the attack continued."[45]

For his courage and exceptional leadership in capturing the regimental objective that morning with fewer than one hundred men, Captain Ed Sayre was later awarded the Distinguished Service Cross, the country's second highest decoration for valor.

Through the darkness and into the dawn's light, Major Mark Alexander and his 2nd Battalion, 505th, worked to knock out the pillbox complex that he and his men had landed among. "We had a good fight in the early hours of the morning. The two large pillboxes gave us considerable resistance. With Lieutenant Wilson directing the fire of his light machine guns into the apertures and Lieutenant Connell directing mortar fire, we attacked and cleared out the large domed pillbox of about forty feet in diameter. In the meantime, we were receiving heavy fire from the smaller, two story pillbox. Lieutenant [John D.]

Sprinkle [the executive officer of Company D, 505th] led the gallant attack on this pillbox later in the morning."[46]

As the Italians in the pillbox fired at Sprinkle and his men with machine guns, they worked their way through the barbed wire entanglements surrounding the pillbox. Individual troopers would jump up and run a few yards and hit the ground again as the other troopers fired at the apertures of the pillbox. As they got closer they began receiving machine gun fire from another pillbox that had a mutually supporting field of fire covering the approaches to the pillbox that Sprinkle and his men were assaulting.

The troopers crawled closer and closer to the pillbox, despite the fire coming from both pillboxes. Lieutenant Sprinkle and three of his troopers were killed by this crossfire, but that didn't stop the assault.[47] Major Alexander watched his men knock out the pillbox "by throwing grenades through the fire ports and a door at ground level.

"By about 10:00 a.m. we had cleared out the five pillboxes and were pretty well organized. I could see some enemy armor and trucks on a road about one half mile north of us, but they chose not to attack. I was faced with the decision of whether to stay there and fight or move toward the regimental objective.

"In the early morning we had accounted for about four hundred men, by 10:00 a.m. we had assembled about four hundred seventy-five men. By 11:00 a.m. we had most of the battalion, plus twenty-one men from the 456th Parachute Field Artillery with Lieutenant Colonel Harrison Harden, Jr., and one 75mm howitzer and thirty rounds of ammunition. My adjutant, Lieutenant Clyde Russell, gave me a strength report at about 12:00 on D-Day, and our total strength was five hundred thirty-six men inclusive of the twenty-one from the 456th.

"On the coast and one half mile south of our landing area, we had spotted an extensive coastal artillery fortification, at the village of Marina di Ragusa. We attacked from the north and rear. We placed a few rounds of 75mm howitzer into the fortification and without much trouble, captured most of the artillery company defending the fortification. We disabled the guns by throwing the breach blocks and other weapons into the sea. By this time it was late in the day and we took a perimeter defense position to the north and west of Marina di Ragusa."[48]

Landing near Vittoria, Lieutenant Ray Grossman, with Battery C, 456th PFA Battalion, quickly found most of the battery. "We were a three gun battery because our fourth section plane ditched offshore and the crew came in by rubber dinghy. I think we had most of the battery together by early morning. The guns were moved by hand, using the harnesses for the gunners. We had three howitzers. We went into the town of Vittoria. No opposition except one sniper and we fired a 75mm into the bell tower and silenced him. Then we started for Gela. We had picked up two small Italian personnel carriers and a couple of donkeys to help pull the guns. It was a ragtag looking outfit going down the road."[49]

About three miles southeast of Niscemi, Lieutenant Willis J. Ferrill and twenty-four enlisted men, mostly from Company H and Company I, 504th, had gathered at an ancient stone chateau-like structure called the Castle Nocera that stood on some high ground overlooking the road that ran south from Niscemi. Leaving his dug-in machine gun position around 2:00 p.m., as everyone was eating lunch, Private First Class Shelby Hord went down to a nearby creek to get some water. "A battle started and there were about forty to forty-eight men, Italians, firing at us. There were three machine guns.

"They were good soldiers. I watched them move from a position that was about fifty yards from me . . . move up this little ridge that was a little higher than the house was, about two to three hundred yards from that house. This one group, [consisting] of a machine gunner, the assistant, and a rifleman came running [toward me]. The farmer had made a big high dirt furrow around one of the trees that wasn't far from me. They ran [and took cover behind the furrow] and were maybe twenty-five feet away from me. I just picked up my hand grenade and threw it in there. I waited a few moments and I slowly walked by and I realized they were dead. Then I went to this next terrace where the farmer had a road going up to the next terrace where there was an olive orchard."[50]

With his carbine in one hand, Hord made a couple of attempts to climb the steep terrace wall, before finally getting to the top. While doing this, he had accidentally put his carbine in the dirt as he used that hand for leverage to climb the steep dirt wall. As he climbed over the top of the terrace ledge, he came face to face with an Italian officer, just yards away.

The officer was shocked to see an enemy paratrooper in the midst of his force and momentarily froze. Hord raised his carbine and pulled the trigger. Nothing . . . it was jammed . . . fouled by dirt from the climb up the ledge. With quick thinking and lightning speed, Hord pulled back the slide on the top of the chamber of his carbine, grabbed a loose round from his jump pants pocket, shoved it into the chamber of his carbine, pushed the slide forward, aimed and fired at the officer. The officer was hit with the armor-piercing round, but didn't fall. Immediately, Hord repeated the process. After he fired a second time the officer was still standing. Again, he shoved another round in the carbine. "I shot him three times before he fell."[51]

The firing cleared the jam in Hord's weapon, and he continued his one-man assault on the Italian force. "By the time I got up on the next terrace, [there was] a young man with his feet just a foot or two from me. It was a rifleman protecting the flank of the two machine guns. I was on my knees and I put my gun up and I started shooting him. The poor man turned over and he put his hands up in prayer. I had no recourse . . . I shot and killed him. And then I started shooting where I could see the machine guns."[52]

Hord relentlessly fired at the Italians manning the machine guns and at the riflemen who were supposed to be protecting them. Simultaneously, Company I, 504th trooper Private Thomas E. Lane killed an additional four Italian riflemen who were protecting the machine guns, during the four-hour firefight.

Hord fired clip after clip of ammunition into the Italian positions. "Then all at once, their machine guns stopped. They just picked up their dying and wounded. They were good soldiers; they didn't drop one gun, except their machine guns and the machine gun ammunition. They took what they had to, and took care of their wounded. They went over the side of this hill, which was the top part of it, and were gone.

"We came and took those three [Italian] machine guns and placed them in the right side in the back of the castle. We put enough ammunition there that no one would have to worry about anything for about three days. No one would have to bring anything to them. We dug them in just below the crest."[53]

For his initiative and extreme courage in the face of a numerically superior force, Private First Class Shelby R. Hord would later be awarded the Distinguished Service Cross.

By the afternoon of July 10, the Eastern Kampfgruppe of the Hermann Göring Panzer Division had begun to move south toward the left and right flanks of the US 45th Infantry Division's beachhead. This powerful armored force consisted of the 1st Panzer Grenadier Regiment, one armored artillery battalion, and one heavy panzer company, consisting of seventeen Mark VI Tiger I tanks each weighing sixty tons and mounting an 88mm main gun.

Late on the afternoon of July 10, General Ridgway found his first paratroopers. Captain Bill Follmer was sitting on the edge of his foxhole, trying to alleviate the pain of his badly broken ankle as Ridgway approached. Follmer struggled to his feet and saluted. "[General Ridgway] had a talk with me and he said, 'Well you've got to get up and get around.'

"I said, 'Yes I do.'

"He was mainly interested in, 'Where is everybody else?' Luckily my men that I had sent out had found remnants of different organizations on both sides [of our positions].

"He was headed toward where Sayre and 'Hardnose' [Gorham] were around the airport. That's the afternoon on which they gave the order to bring more planes and parachutists up that direction. That's the first time I knew they were up there."[54]

At dusk Captain Sayre, approached the commander of the 2nd Battalion, 16th Infantry Regiment, to whom his company was temporarily attached. "I asked for and received permission to take a patrol to the front to see if any wounded paratroopers in the area could be picked up. The patrol moved out just after dark with eight men. When we had advanced about one half mile in front of the battalion's positions, we were met by heavy machine gun fire which stopped our advance and forced us to crawl several hundred yards to reach cover in an old dry stream bed about five feet deep. As the men were sitting in the stream bed catching their breath, an enemy patrol jumped in with us. The enemy were as surprised as the paratroops. I had picked up an extra pistol from one of my officers who had been killed, and now started firing at the enemy not actually struggling with my own men, with two guns. The superior ability of the American parachutists was now in its best element, and the enemy who came in hand-to-hand combat with us were soon on the ground. Three were captured, one killed, and the other six men of the patrol escaped in the darkness. When the patrol arrived back at the 2nd Battalion CP with our prisoners, we were told to prepare for a dawn attack on Hill 41 about one half mile to the front.

"The attack jumped off shortly after daylight with the parachutists leading. The battalion was on the objective within an hour after meeting only light enemy resistance. We had been on the hill for about an hour when we were hit by a heavy German tank attack. Six tanks were coming directly toward the battalion positions and about twenty more hitting the 26th Infantry about four hundred yards to the battalion's rear and left flank. The rawness of the replacements of the 2nd Battalion now became evident for the first time. When most of them saw the tanks coming, they jumped from their foxholes and started running to the rear. About one-third of that battalion and all of the parachutists stuck to their positions. The tanks were soon on top of the battalion positions. The troops were fighting back desperately with rocket launchers, rifle grenades, machine guns, rifles, pistols, and throwing hand grenades. One of the tanks was knocked out by Colonel Gorham with a rocket launcher. Two officers of the 2nd Battalion managed to get a 57mm gun, which had been deserted by its crew, into action. They also knocked out a tank. When this tank was knocked out, the remaining tanks withdrew to the battalion's left flank. The desperate fighting of the American troops denied them the only covered route of approach to the beaches of the 1st Division. As the tanks could not take the covered route, they continued to the left flank and pushed on toward the beaches.

"In order to get to the beaches, the tanks were forced to cross a wide open flat piece of terrain about three miles from the beaches. As the tanks started across this open ground, they were taken under fire by US Navy destroyers in the landing area of the 1st Division. When the smoke cleared away, more than fifteen of the enemy's heavy tanks had been knocked out and the others forced to withdraw.

"Because the 2nd Battalion now only had about two hundred men, Colonel Crawford decided to withdraw to a hill about five hundred yards to the rear. This hill was almost inaccessible to tanks and gave the battalion a chance to round up their men and reorganize. Many of the men who ran had abandoned crew-served weapons and these all had to be redistributed. The parachutists had picked up six Browning Automatic Rifles and were happy to have them."[55]

By the morning of July 11, the number of paratroopers defending the stone chateau, known as Castle Nocera, that overlooked the Niscemi-Gela highway had grown to almost sixty, as men had drifted in during the previous day and night. Likewise, another force under the command of Lieutenant George Watts, with Company G, 504th, had grown to almost sixty troopers. At around 1:00 p.m. Lieutenant Willis J. Ferrill, commanding the force at Castle Nocera, was able to contact Lieutenant Watts by radio, and Watts led his men to the chateau to join Lieutenant Ferrill's force.

Private First Class Shelby Hord had put twelve Hawkins mines in the road around a curve, in order to at least slow down any armor that approached the chateau. Hord had not had any sleep since the night of July 8. "That morning about 10:00 Lieutenant Ferrill said, 'Shelby, you have not had any sleep in three days. They've got nice bedrooms up there. You go up there on that second floor and you get in bed and get some rest. Get in one of those nice beds.' There was a nice bathroom next to me, bathtub and everything . . . just like you'd find in a nice hotel. I turned the covers back, then I went and looked out of the window, and just looked down that valley that was in the rear of the building. All at once I could see one of those Mark VI [tanks] coming up the road around the bend. I watched two more Mark IVs come, and I went running down and I got a hold of Lieutenant Ferrill.

"Lieutenant Ferrill said, 'Shelby, I'll go into the flower garden and I'll tell those men to fire [the mortars] almost as quickly as they can simultaneously, and you go around and you tell those men [on the line] what's going to happen. When they hear the puff of those mortars to open fire on them.' "[56]

Accompanying the three tanks was an estimated battalion of German infantry. The force was moving north, retreating after their attack on the beach area. Suddenly the German infantry column stopped. As Hord moved from man to man he kept an eye on the German infantry on the road. Then he saw something that astonished him. Hord could hardly believe this stroke of good fortune. "They had taken a break right in front of us! The tanks had gone way up and around this hill and were gone. So we opened up at the same time the mortars opened up. We fought about two or three hours."[57]

As the ferocious firefight escalated in intensity, Hord suddenly saw the German tanks returning. "One of those Mark IVs came and I called the bazooka man over and I said, 'Now I want you to try and shoot that damned tank.' And damned, his first round hit and knocked everything off the back where they put all of the baggage. I guess [the tank commander] thought there was more power over here, so he moved [the tank] out of the way. Then he came back, and in the bushes you could see him under the trees, with his glasses trying to estimate what was going on. Then he and another tank that had come hit a couple of machine gunners in the holes. I know we lost those men. They lobbed a couple of shells into the center of the house and they came down into the stairwell. There was a wounded man there that got wounded in the face, and we didn't have a medic. I don't know why we didn't carry him down into the wine cellar, but we didn't.

"Lieutenant Ferrill was in the deep cellar trying to get help for us. We had a big radio, and we were trying to [contact] whoever was coming our way, hopefully it would be the 'Big Red One.' I tried to watch the front [of the chateau]. I'd run down and tell him what was going on, then I would run back and take care of my job. Then a couple of [German] officers came up with white flags and asked us to surrender. This soldier said, 'Like hell we are,' and he shot both of them dead. Then the battle really started and went on for the rest of the day, all the way until dark and then everybody stopped shooting."[58]

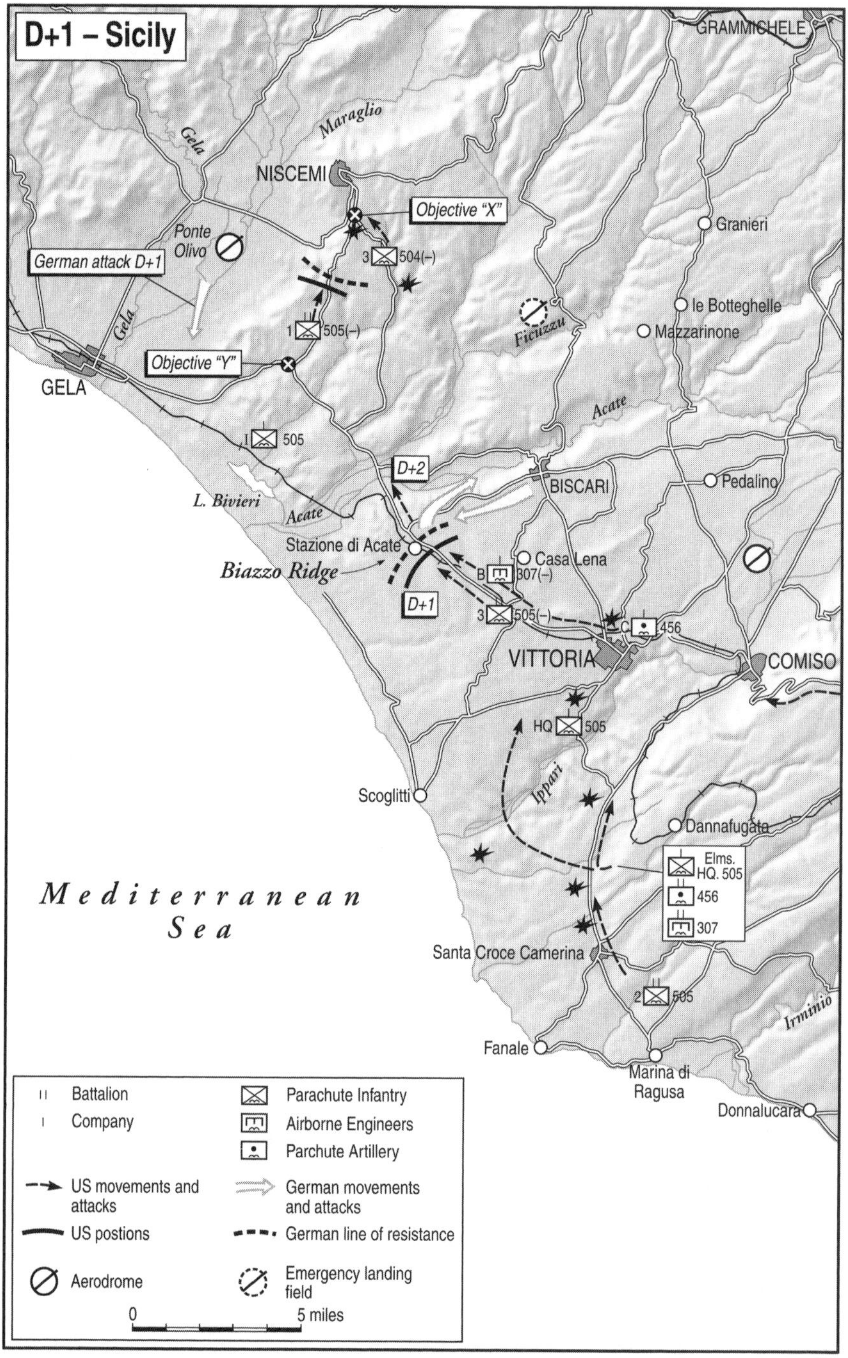
D+1 – Sicily
GRAMMICHELE
Maraglio
Gela
NISCEMI
Objective "X"
Ponte Olivo
German attack D+1
3 504(–)
Granieri
le Botteghelle
Mazzarinone
Ficuzzu
1 505(–)
Gela
Objective "Y"
GELA
Acate
I 505
D+2
BISCARI
Pedalino
L. Bivieri
Acate
Stazione di Acate
Casa Lena
Biazzo Ridge
B 307(–)
D+1
3 505(–)
C 456
VITTORIA
COMISO
HQ 505
Ippari
Scoglitti
Dannafugata
Elms. HQ. 505
456
307
Mediterranean Sea
Santa Croce Camerina
2 505
Irminio
Fanale
Marina di Ragusa
Donnalucara
Battalion
Company
Parachute Infantry
Airborne Engineers
Parchute Artillery
US movements and attacks
German movements and attacks
US postions
German line of resistance
Aerodrome
Emergency landing field
0
5 miles

CHAPTER 4

"WE HAD A LONG WAY TO GO YET, AND SOME OF THE MEN WOULD ACCOMPANY US NO MORE"[1]

By dawn on July 11, southeast of the fighting that was taking place around Gela and Niscemi, Colonel Gavin and his small group had made it to Vittoria after moving all night. There, Gavin borrowed a jeep and together with Major Ben Vandervoort and Captain Al Ireland drove west, determined to find the regiment. A couple of miles west of town, Gavin found Major Krause and a couple of hundred of his men sitting on the edges of their foxholes in a tomato field beside the road. Gavin asked Krause what his battalion was doing, and Krause said he was getting the battalion reorganized. Gavin ordered him to immediately get his battalion moving west toward Gela.

Gavin, Vandervoort, and Ireland then left, driving west along the road to Gela. About two miles down the road Gavin found "a group of forty men of L Company, 180th Infantry and twenty parachutists."[2]

Gavin ordered the paratroopers, engineers from the 307th Airborne Engineer Battalion under the command of Lieutenant Ben Wechsler, to move west as well. Gavin drove a little less than a mile west "to the railroad station one mile east of Biazzo Ridge where a point reconnaissance was made. At this point a German officer and private suddenly came around the corner in a motorcycle and were captured. They made no effort to resist capture and appeared to be quite disgusted with the lack of resistance being offered by the Italian troops, but refused to give any information regarding their own troops."[3]

Gavin then sent Vandervoort back down the road to expedite the arrival of Krause and his battalion, then to find the 45th Division CP to get a message to the 1st and 82nd Divisions of his plan to advance west toward Gela. Meanwhile, Gavin awaited the arrival of the twenty paratroopers that he had found a mile or so back. "Just ahead was a ridge, about half a mile away and perhaps a hundred feet high. The slope to the top was gradual. On both sides of the road were olive trees and beneath them tall brown and yellow grass, burnt by the hot Sicilian summer sun. The firing from the ridge increased. I told Lieutenant Wechsler to deploy his platoon on the right and to move on to seize the ridge.

"We moved forward. I was with Wechsler, and in a few hundred yards the fire became intense. As we neared the top of the ridge, there was a rain of leaves and branches as bullets tore through the trees, and there was a buzzing like the sound of swarms of bees. A few moments later Wechsler was hit and fell. Some troopers were hit; others continued to crawl forward. Soon we were pinned down by heavy small arms fire, but so far nothing else.

"I made my way back to the railroad crossing, and in about twenty minutes Major Hagan joined me. He was the Battalion Executive Officer for the 3rd Battalion. He said the battalion was coming up. I asked where Cannonball [Krause] was, and he said that he had gone back to the 45th Division to tell them what was going on. I ordered Hagan to have the troops drop their packs and get ready to attack the Germans on the ridge as soon as they came up. By that time we had picked up a platoon of the 45th Division that happened to be there, part of a company from the 180th Infantry. There was also a sailor or two who had come ashore in the amphibious landings. We grabbed them also."[4]

Gavin was unaware at the time that a powerful German force was fighting the 180th Infantry Regiment west of the ridge and south of the highway and had deployed a screening force of infantry on the ridge as flank protection. His small force was unknowingly attacking the flank of powerful elements of the Eastern Kampfgruppe of the Hermann Göring Division.

As Company G, 505th, leading the 3rd Battalion, swept across the ground in front of the ridge, pinned-down engineers and headquarters troopers jumped to their feet and joined them in the assault up the eastern slope. Sergeant Bill Bishop, a Company G trooper, saw the Germans pulling back from the crest as they came up the eastern slope of Biazzo Ridge. "It didn't take too long to capture it."[5]

As his paratroopers reached the top of the ridge, Gavin stopped to direct the deployment of 3rd Battalion troopers who were coming up the road from the east. "The attack went off as planned, and the infantry reached the top of the ridge and continued to attack down the far side. As they went over the top of the ridge, the fire became intense. We were going to have a very serious situation on our hands. This was not a patrol or platoon action. Mortar and artillery fire began to fall on the ridge, and there was considerable machine gun fire."[6]

But immediately afterward, German infantry counterattacked and pushed the thin line of paratroopers back over the crest of the ridge. Just as the Germans reached the crest, Sergeant Bishop saw Company H coming up the ridge behind him. The Germans "were at the crest of this hill. It amounted to a bayonet fight. They ordered us to fix bayonets and I said, 'Oh Lord, help me.' "[7]

Private Russell McConnell, with Company H, heard the order to fix bayonets. As he seated his bayonet on his M1, McConnell could hear the click of other razor sharp bayonets being seated on rifle barrels around him. "You could hear the German tanks milling about. All of a sudden they told us to charge up and we all started running up over the ridge."[8]

As Sergeant Bishop was waiting for the command to charge up and over the crest, "H Company came through us, since we had fought up to the crest of the hill, and they went over and engaged in a bayonet fight . . . and that was a bloody, terrible looking sight. I didn't see it, but we could hear it. We saw it when we followed H Company . . . just mangled up bodies. [The Germans] had quite a few killed, and they pulled out."[9]

For McConnell and the Company H troopers, the hand-to-hand combat was terrifying and bloody, but thankfully brief. "The whole fight didn't seem to last too long until we drove them off. They were shooting at us and we were shooting back at them. I saw dead Germans, but I don't know whether I hit anyone. And then everything quieted down.

"One of the sergeants said, 'Grab that pair of binoculars.' This German had been shot dead. They caught on the back of his helmet and I'm pulling them off and I finally got them away from him."[10]

The 3rd Battalion kept pursuing the German survivors down the western slope of Biazzo Ridge. As they reached the bottom of the ridge, other German infantry was getting ready to launch another counterattack; this time with tanks. As Lieutenant Bob Fielder, the 505th Regimental Headquarters communications officer, came over the ridge, he looked down and "saw one of our troopers draped over the limb of a tree, quite dead. Suddenly it started . . . unmistakable ripping noises that were bursts from a rapid fire German machine gun. Having never heard the sound of 1,200 rounds per minute, I thought, 'What was that?' But it took only a minute or two to figure it out. It was impossible to distinguish a single burst.

"Running down the embankment from the ridge with the others, I lay prone there most of the day. Initially the Germans fired [white] phosphorous shells that started to burn the foliage and grass, but proved ineffectual."[11]

When those white phosphorous mortar rounds began hitting, Private First Class Cloid Wigle, with Company H, tried to dig in. "This ridge was a hard place to dig a foxhole and I finally dug a slit trench. It was hard shale and with extra hard work I finally got it about twenty inches deep, when I saw the tank."[12]

It was the most terrifying thing Wigle had ever seen, a German Mark VI Tiger I tank. "We had no idea the Germans had tanks, let alone Tiger tanks. I saw the tank rotate its gun towards me and I jumped into the hole."[13]

The tank's 88mm main gun fired at Wigle. The shell hit an oak tree about twelve feet behind him, obliterating it and blowing Wigle out of his shallow trench as shrapnel buzzed overhead, with splinters and pieces of jagged wood raining down all around him. Wigle jumped back into his slit trench and hugged the bottom as the Tiger tank came up the slope toward his hole. "It ran over [the top of] me and twisted [its treads] over the hole. I think I lost consciousness for a short period. I was completely covered with dirt."[14]

Sergeant Bill Bishop, with Company G, hadn't had enough time to dig a slit trench when one of the Mark VI tanks came up the gentle slope toward him, suddenly stopping close by. "Me and a fellow named Duke Boswell were laying within two or three feet of the tank treads in a small ditch. They would shoot at a single man with the 88s they had on those tanks. They killed a bunch of people with that 88. They ran over one man's legs. Of course he died from shock. His name was [Sergeant] Gerald Ludlam.

"We had two bazooka men [Earl Wright and Kenny Harris] and they knocked the track off the first tank that pulled out of this little village. The second tank came around the disabled tank and luckily he jammed the turret and so he withdrew. The third tank saw what was happening and he too withdrew. Bazooka men were in great peril because that's the first thing they would try to knock out was the bazooka men."[15]

Private McConnell watched the Company H bazooka team of Private Leland "Chief" Laye and Corporal Warren "Pappy" Lyons, the oldest guy in the company, out in front of the line stalking the tanks. Then, suddenly McConnell saw the turret of the tank rotate toward the bazooka team. "They just turned that 88 on them and blew them to hell. These two guys both got killed. They never had a chance."[16]

Another H Company trooper, Private Richard E. "Pat" Reid, was with another Company H bazooka team out in front, crawling up and trying to get into position to get a good shot at one of the tanks. "[Private James D.] J. D. Long and I were together. He was packing a bazooka. We spotted a German tank and believing everything you were told in training, we thought we would be able to disable the tank with what equipment we were carrying.

"J. D. [was] to the left with his bazooka and I to the right with my two pound Gammon grenade to try and blow its tracks off. As we were running toward the tank, the turret swung around and they fired at J. D. They hit him dead center. They then started turning the turret in my direction. I dove behind a tree, its trunk at least two and one half feet in diameter. When they fired, they hit the tree about three feet above the ground, cutting it completely in two. The next thing I remember is trying to stop the flow of blood from my right arm or shoulder. I couldn't do it, so I thought it best if I could get to the aid station on my own. I knew where it was because we had come by it when we first got to Biazzo ridge."[17]

A machine gunner in one of the Tiger tanks spotted Lieutenant Bob Fielder, with the 505th Regimental Headquarters, lying as flat as he could get in the grass. "The Tiger tank got me in its sights, traversed its machine gun, fired a burst, then traversed three or four clicks and fired another burst. The first burst stitched up the ground inches from me on one side, while the next burst stitched up the ground inches from me on the other side. Any lesser clicks, traversing from left to right would have cut me in two."[18]

As the Mark VI tanks ran low on ammunition they would back up and return to their ammunition carriers in the distance and then come back to continue to inflict their terror on the all but helpless troopers.

As the tank that had tried to crush him pulled back, Private First Class Cloid Wigle, with Company H, still covered with dirt in the bottom of his shallow slit trench, heard the voices of some of his buddies coming closer as they crawled up to check on him. "When the other guys found me I was kind of out of my head and had blood in my ears. My mouth and nose were full of dirt. I sure thought my war was going to be a short one when I saw that tank. If I hadn't been persistent in digging in that shale, I probably would have had it."[19]

With all of Krause's available infantry fighting on the ridge, Colonel Gavin had no ready reserve, and he was justifiably concerned about the next move the Germans might make. "I was worried about being enveloped on the right; some of the 45th Infantry Division should have been down on the left toward the beaches, but the right was wide open, and so far I had no one I could send out to protect that flank. If the German column was coming from Biscari, the tactical logic would have suggested that they bypass me on the right and attack me from the rear. At that time I had a few engineers I kept in reserve, and two 81mm mortars."[20]

Gavin was unaware that a group of about 65 troopers led by Captain James E. McGinity, the Company G, 505th commander, were occupying a hill about a mile north of Biazzo Ridge, which discouraged a German attack around his right flank. Nevertheless, the situation remained very precarious.

As Gavin worked on trying to scrape out a hole for protection against mortar fire in the rock hard shale, "the first wounded began to crawl back over the ridge. They all told the same story. They fired their bazookas at the front plate of German tanks, and then the tanks swiveled their huge 88mm guns at them and fired at individual infantrymen. By this time the tanks could be heard, although I could not see any because of the smoke and dust and the cover of vegetation. [Major] Hagan came in, walking and holding his thigh, which had been badly torn by fire. Cannonball had gone forward to command the attack. It did not seem to be getting anywhere, however, as the German fire increased in intensity and our wounded were coming back in greater numbers. The first German prisoners also came back. They said they were from the Hermann Göring Parachute Panzer Division. I remember one of them asking if we had fought the Japanese in the Pacific; he said he asked because the paratroopers had fought so hard."[21]

The battle was reaching a critical stage, and Gavin fed troops into the thin line as they arrived in small groups. Lieutenant Harvey Zeigler, with Service Company, 505th, arrived during the late morning with about fifty desperately needed troopers. Gavin didn't have much in the way of heavy weapons to stop a determined attack by the Germans. "I went back a few hundred yards to check the 81mm mortars and to see what other troopers had joined us. A few had. Lieutenant [Robert] May had been hit by mortar fragments. I talked to the crews of the two pack 75mm artillery pieces and told them we were going to stay on the ridge no matter what happened. We agreed that they should stay concealed and engage the less heavily armored underbellies of the tanks when they appeared at the top of the rise. It was a dangerous tactic, but the only thing we could do, and tanks are vulnerable in that position. I was determined that if the tanks overran us we would stay and fight the infantry."[22]

Captain Al Ireland, the 505 S-1, told Gavin that someone ought to go get some help from the 45th Division. Gavin thought it was a great idea and sent Ireland off to get that help. Ireland took off on foot, but later commandeered a bicycle and rode east on the road toward Vittoria looking for the 45th Division CP. Meanwhile, the German tanks were continuing to pound Gavin's troopers.

Lieutenant Ray Grossman, with Battery C, 456th PFA Battalion, was hearing from the wounded troopers coming back over the east side of the ridge "that a Tiger tank was in the area and kicking the hell out of our troopers. I was next to the 2nd Section, so Sergeant Thomas, the section crew and I rolled the gun up to the top of the ridge. I don't think it was over seventy-five feet high and some thirty-five feet across the top. Captain [Raymond] Crossman [the battery commander] had his glasses on the target."[23]

Gavin watched the crew get the gun set up. "The crew of our 75mm [commanded by Lieutenant Loren and Sergeant Thomas] were on their knees and lying down, with the gun loaded and ready to fire. Suddenly there was a tremendous explosion in front of the gun. The tank had fired and hit the ground just in front of the gun, knocking the troopers like tenpins in all directions. I was standing just to the left rear, watching the action, and I was knocked down, too. . . . The troopers got up and ran off like startled quail. A second later they realized, to their embarrassment, what they were doing, and they ran back to the gun."[24]

Looking through his binoculars, Lieutenant Grossman had a perfect view of what was about to occur. "Captain Crossman was beside the gun to direct fire. My first look across the smoky valley through the tops of a few trees showed a big tank. I watched the first round, which looked low to me. I was right behind the gun, so [I was] following the projectile with my glasses. It looked real slow, around 1,050 feet per second. In the haste and excitement nobody rode the trail of the gun, so it had a long recoil. The wheel hit the gunner in the chest and he did a somersault. He came up like a cat and scratched his way back to the gun. The next round, a crewmember rode the trail so [there was] not much recoil.

"I busied myself checking ammo, crewman on the trail, etc. and didn't follow the rest of the rounds through my glasses. About this time, I caught the white flash of an exploding shell just to our left and behind us. I assume it came from the tank and just missed us. Smoke started coming up around the tank and we got off the ridge. It didn't take long and I can't say how many rounds were expended. Lots of adrenaline was flowing and [we were] cheering like we had just scored a touchdown. If machine gun fire was coming in our direction, I don't remember, although we were sure exposed."[25]

In the distance, Gavin looked for signs of the Mark VI tank. "In the smoke and dust the tank backed out of sight. That was the last we saw of it. To my amazement, none of the gun crew was hurt. Tanks began to work their way forward off to our left, coming directly up through the vineyard. Although the tank we fired at had backed up, I got the impression that the tank activity was increasing and that we were facing a pretty heavy attack that would come over the ridge at any moment. . . .

"Two troopers came from my left rear in an Italian [tracked] personnel carrier. They were equipped with rifles and wanted to go over the top of the ridge to engage the Germans. I suggested that they not do it, warning them they would be knocked out, but they insisted they could take care of themselves. They added that they wanted to 'scare the Krauts' into thinking that we too had armor.

"They had hardly gotten over the top of the ridge when a direct hit exploded the vehicle in flames. All the next day it was still there, smoking, with two skeletons in the front seat, one of them with a direct hit through his body, the trooper on the driver's side."[26]

Private First Class Murray Goldman, a medic with 3rd Battalion, 505th, arrived at the aid station on the reverse slope of Biazzo Ridge in the middle of heavy fighting. "I found the entire area under intense mortar, small arms, and high velocity artillery fire. However, the aid station was functioning and about twenty to thirty wounded were collected and being treated in a defiladed area in an olive orchard. Captain McIlvoy [3rd Battalion Surgeon] was present and had procured an Italian truck, which was marked with a Geneva cross.

"A runner appeared and excitedly reported that there were very many wounded up ahead, and exposed to enemy fire. The captain never hesitated. He jumped into the driver's seat of the vehicle and asked for two volunteers to accompany him, as he knew the mission was extremely hazardous. Private First Class Marvin L. Crosley and I were the first aboard and we were off.

"We drove into the fire swept area searching the fields on both sides of the road for our wounded. Making a turn in the road, we came face to face with a German Mark VI tank."[27]

Captain McIlvoy attempted to turn the truck around, but instead drove it off the road and into the ditch. "It was a right hand drive truck. They shot out the windshield with a machine gun. One of the boys got off and ran back to the aid station. [Private First Class Murray] Goldman stayed with me. I got my foot caught between the brake and the clutch trying to get out, and he actually got me released."[28]

Goldman took cover behind a concrete road marker. "We were immediately machine gunned by fire from the tank and several other positions on our flank.

The concrete road marker that I was lying behind received a direct hit and [the] concussion stunned me. I looked up and saw the captain and cried out that I had been hit.

"The captain started toward me and was himself hit in the back by a mortar fragment. Nevertheless, he helped me to my feet and we both started back. We had proceeded about twenty yards when the truck we had used was blown to bits by a direct hit by cannon fire from the tank.

"The captain helped me back to the aid station and continued throughout the day and far into the night to supervise the collection, treatment, and evacuation of every wounded man in that entire area.

"We had no transportation, our medical supplies were only what we brought in by air and carried for the most part on our persons; yet no wounded man failed to be evacuated to the rear within a short time after being wounded."[29]

Still pinned down on the western slope of Biazzo Ridge, as the word was passed from man to man, Lieutenant Bob Fielder, with 505th Regimental Headquarters, was told to pull back. "We were told to come back to the top of the ridge. There we saw 'Cannonball' Krause fire a bazooka, the shell bouncing off the tank harmlessly."[30]

It looked as though the German tanks and supporting infantry might break through the thinly spread line of grimy, dirty, thirsty paratroopers. Gavin expected the German tanks to crest the ridge at any moment. "By this time all of the [rocket] launchers except three had been destroyed and the tanks were within fifty yards of the Combat Team Command Post."[31]

Just as it appeared the Germans might overrun their positions, Gavin saw a group of men coming up the eastern slope of the ridge. It was Captain Ireland, who brought with him forward observer liaison teams for a battalion of 155mm guns from the 45th Division and for Navy destroyers. Gavin quickly briefed the officers and together they tried to get a fix on just where they were located, so that they wouldn't have rounds from heavy artillery and five-inch naval guns landing on Gavin and his men, instead of the enemy. The Navy ensign used the intersection of the railroad and the Vittoria-Gela road to get a fix on their position and then asked for a smoke round, which came in momentarily and impacted near the buildings that the Tiger tank had been positioned behind. He then ordered the destroyers to fire for effect. The liaison officer for the 155mm battalion also called in a barrage on the same grid coordinates.

For the first time since the fighting began that morning, Gavin could breathe a little easier. Gavin was grateful to Captain Ireland and the two liaison teams. "They did splendid work and about three o'clock were firing upon known German assembly areas and positions. The 45th Division also sent up two 57mm antitank guns. The attacking forces withdrew and appeared to be regrouping and reorganizing about one thousand yards to a mile in front of the ridge."[32]

Gavin now had enough heavy firepower to make it an even fight. But soon, troopers who had "marched to the sound of the guns" were arriving, giving Gavin the manpower he needed to contemplate a counterattack to drive the Germans from the field. "In about an hour I heard that more troopers were coming, and at six o'clock I heard that Lieutenant Harold H. Swingler and quite a few troopers from Regimental Headquarters Company were on the road. Swingler had been a former intercollegiate boxing champion; he was a tough combat soldier. He arrived about seven o'clock. In his wake appeared half a dozen of our own Sherman tanks. All the troopers cheered loud and long; it was a very dramatic moment. The Germans must have heard the cheering, although they did not know then what it was about. They soon found out.

"By now no more wounded were coming back. A heavy pall of dust and acrid smoke covered the battlefield. I decided it was time to counterattack. I wanted to destroy the German force in front of us and to recover our dead and wounded. I felt that if I could do this and at the same time secure the ridge, I would be in good shape for whatever came next—probably a German attack against our defenses at daylight, with us having the advantage of holding the ridge. Our attack jumped off on schedule; regimental clerks, cooks, truck drivers, everyone who could carry a rifle or carbine was in the attack."[33]

Just before the scheduled attack at 8:30 p.m., T/5 Jerry Huth, a member of the 505 Regimental Communications section, could see a Mark VI Tiger I tank down the hill in front of him. "The tank had come up the road through a little cut. He had a command of the whole field. We were ordered to make an attack down the hill just before sunset. We made a line across the top of the hill. I remember we all hesitated a moment."[34]

Sergeant Frank M. Miale, with Company B, 307th Engineer Battalion, who had somehow survived the initial assault, the German counterattacks, the constant shelling, and the terrifying Tiger tanks, now rose up with the other surviving troopers and began to "walk into a blazing hell of mortar, artillery, and small arms fire. We could hardly see one another for the dust and smoke."[35]

Huth also jumped to his feet and started forward. "[Jack] Ospital and I went down the hill together. Two radio guys, [T/5] George Banta and [Private First Class] Dick Symonds, got a hold of a bazooka. They were on the left side and I was on the right side. They crept up to within twenty yards [of the Tiger tank] and they fired the bazooka and took out the right track. They were both awarded the Bronze Star."

After Banta and Symonds disabled the tank, the German crew remained in the tank, hosing down anything that moved. Huth and the other troopers nearby could only stay low and hope that the tank didn't spot them. "I was under a grapevine. There was concealment, but no cover. The Tiger kept spraying machine gun bullets over our heads. He either didn't know we were there or couldn't depress his gun because of the position of the tank."[36]

Drawn by the sounds of the firing and explosions, Lieutenant Jim Rightley and another group from Company B, 307th Engineer Battalion, arrived on the eastern side of Biazzo Ridge as the paratroopers made their assault down the western slope. "My group and I were told to drop what packs we had and join in the attack. Saw my first trooper killed; he was right next to me . . . his head was nearly blown off. There were at least three engineer officers on the ridge that day . . . Lieutenant Wechsler; 2nd Lieutenant Warren Riffle, killed on the ridge . . . he was my assistant platoon commander; and I."[37]

Lieutenant Harold "Swede" Swingler moved down the western side of the ridge near the road, where he saw an incredible sight: the crew of one of the Mark VI Tiger tanks standing outside of their tank, between it and a dirt embankment at the side of the road. They were talking among themselves as if they were participating in a field exercise. Swingler slipped quietly to a position a few yards away and then pulled the pin on a fragmentation grenade and tossed it into the middle of the crew, killing all of them. He had single-handedly captured the division's first Tiger tank.

Despite the storm of lead and shrapnel from German machine guns, small arms, mortars, and the main guns of the Tiger tanks, the thin line of dirty, sweating, tired, paratroopers relentlessly drove the German infantry back, overrunning their machine gun squads and mortar crews. As darkness fell, Gavin's troopers had finally driven elements of the numerically superior Hermann Göring Division from the field after a vicious, day-long struggle.

Gavin could see the Germans withdrawing "in apparent confusion, leaving many dead and wounded and considerable equipment of all types. Four tanks were believed to have been knocked out, although all but one were recovered by the Germans during the night."[38]

After the assault, an exhausted Sergeant Frank Miale, with Company B, 307th Engineer Battalion, sat down and reflected on what had happened that day. "We had triumphed, but there were no pats on the back; we had a long way to go yet and some of the men would accompany us no more."[39]

On the evening of July 11, Lieutenant McCandless and Sergeant Ott Carpenter found their way to the 1st Battalion, 505th command post near Objective X. Lieutenant McCandless was expecting to get chewed out by Lieutenant Colonel Gorham for showing up so late. "Instead, Colonel Gorham greeted me like a long lost son!

"That evening he asked me if I could establish an outpost. I was pleased to be asked and assured him that I'd been in the Infantry longer than Communications. He gave me a bazooka team and machine gun squad. We established the outpost a hundred yards or so on our right flank, and took turns keeping watch, uneventfully throughout the night."[40]

On the same night, the 52nd Troop Carrier Wing, carrying the 504th RCT in 144 C-47s, flew a similar route as the 505th RCT two nights before. The drop zone was the Farello airport behind the 1st Infantry Division's positions.

Captain John S. Thompson, a platoon leader with Company E, 504th, stood in the door of his C-47 as it flew toward Sicily. "The 2nd Battalion was flying in a tight V-of-Vs as we flew over a calm Mediterranean Sea. As we neared the island of Malta we could see a long convoy of ships edging their way toward the coast of Sicily."[41]

Captain Willard E. Harrison, commanding Company A, 504th, was the jumpmaster in his plane. "I flew in the leading plane of the first serial and reached the coast of Sicily near Punta Socca at approximately 22:30 hours, thence flew in a northwesterly direction along the coast toward Gela. The left wing plane flew just over the water line, and the squadron of nine planes continued perfect formation up the coast at an altitude of approximately nine hundred feet. We encountered no fire of any kind until the lead plane reached Lake Biviere when one .50-caliber machine gun, situated in the sand dunes several hundred yards from the shore, opened fire. As soon as this firing began, guns along the coast as far as we could see toward Punta Socca opened fire and the naval craft lying offshore, both towards Punta Socca and toward Gela began firing antiaircraft guns."[42]

Farther back in the formation, the pilot of one of the C-47s struggled to keep his plane in the air as it was hit by antiaircraft fire. "A shell smashed into the starboard side of the fuselage and knocked out a hole about four by six feet, while a fragment from the shell split the aluminum and every rib from hole to rudder. Passing through the plane the fragment ripped off a door as a second ack-ack blast carried away a portion of the left stabilizer.

"The airplane spun at a right angle and nearly pulled the controls from my grasp. For a second I didn't realize what had happened, then finding myself out of formation I began violent evasive action. I saw three planes burning on the ground and red tracers everywhere as machine gunners sprayed us as if spotting a flight of ducks.

"Meanwhile, I had cut into a less dangerous spot to give the parachutists a fighting chance to reach the ground. But I've got to hand it to those boys; one who had been pretty badly hit by shrapnel insisted on leaping with the others, although he had been ordered to remain in the plane."[43]

Private Keith K. Scott, with 1st Battalion, Headquarters Company, 504th, had just received the order to stand up and hook up when "just over the beach we ran into AA fire. Our plane kept diving and banking. The pilot passed the word down the line to jump on the red light. At the time the word reached Lieutenant [Richard] Mills the red light flashed on. We started out. Just as I got to the door our plane was hit. I was knocked back against the opposite side of the ship. I finally got out."[44]

As the 2nd Battalion serial flew along the coastline, Captain John Thompson, with Company E, was incredulous as "a sea of red tracers wound their way up through our formation and we wondered why and of what origin they came. Some of the planes had been hit and the formation scattered in many directions as we flew over the coast. We were flying very low now and one plane on our left went down in flames. Looking out of the door, I found that there were no other planes in sight and we were all alone in the air.

"The pilot sent back word that he thought we had just flown over our DZ and wanted to know if we should return by circling around and coming in from the water over the east coast. I told him to circle around and as soon as we hit the coastline to give us the green light. As soon as we were over land again the green light went on. Picking out what I thought was a good jump field, out we went."[45]

Major Mark Alexander witnessed the whole tragic incident. "We of the 2nd Battalion saw from our strung out position along the coastal road, two German bombers come in and bomb the naval fleet. About two minutes later at the same altitude and from the same direction the 504th came in over the naval fleet. The Navy gunners just continued shooting and downed twenty-three of our C-47s carrying the 504th Parachute Infantry Regiment [Combat Team, less the 3rd Battalion]. From where we were on the coastal road, we could see the Allied white markings on our C-47s. Even the 45th Division got in on the shooting."[46] The soldiers of the 45th Infantry Division, new to combat, thought the planes were carrying German paratroopers.

Standing in the door of his plane, Lieutenant Edward J. Sims, a platoon leader with Company F, 504th, watched helplessly as "a gradual build-up of fire red tracers from below were engulfing our formation. I felt a shimmy go through our plane and then pandemonium reigned as antiaircraft guns of our own forces, at sea and on the beaches, were blasting our slow flying aircraft. As my plane flew through the heavy flak, I could hear the hits as they penetrated. From my door position, I scanned the sky for other planes, but could see only those going down in flames.

"My plane developed a distinct shudder and banked away from the flak with one engine starting to sputter. I had my men stand up and hook up then, before going forward to talk with the pilot. I instructed my platoon sergeant to get the men out fast if the plane started to go down before I returned.

"From the pilot I learned he had lost the formation and had a damaged starboard engine. We decided since there was land below, that he would stay our present course and allow me a few seconds to return to the door, then turn on the green light. We both realized that with the heavy load he had, it would be difficult for him to fly back to North Africa. I rushed back to the door yelling to my men to get ready to jump. As I arrived, the red light came on, followed within seconds by the green light just as I hooked up. I immediately released the equipment bundles from under the plane, then jumped into darkness with my men following."[47]

The plane carrying Lieutenant A. C. Drew and his stick of Company F, 504th troopers was badly damaged by antiaircraft fire. "The pilot of my plane gave me the warning twenty minutes out from the DZ. After the red light came on, he had to give me the green light in about one minute, due to the plane being on fire.

"We jumped into a steady stream of antiaircraft fire, and not knowing that they were friendly troops. About seventy-five yards from where I landed, plane No. 915 was hit and burned. To my knowledge, only the pilot and three men got out. The pilot was thrown through the window. Another plane was shot down on the beach and another plane was down burning about one thousand yards to my front.

"There were four men killed and four wounded from my platoon. Three of these men were hit coming down and one was killed on the ground because he had the wrong password. After landing, we found out this had been changed to 'Think'-'Quickly'. The antiaircraft fire we jumped into was the 180th Infantry of the 45th Division. They also were not told we were coming.

"We tried to reorganize, but found we didn't have but forty-four men, including three officers. We searched all night for the rest of the men. After accounting for them we took care of the dead and wounded and started toward our objective. We arrived at the 504th CP at 2:00, July 12, 1943."[48]

Approximately sixty of the one hundred forty-four planes carrying Colonel Reuben H. Tucker's 504th Regimental Combat Team were damaged. In seventeen of the twenty-three planes shot down, the paratroopers were able to jump. Some of the paratroopers who jumped were killed in the air, and still others shot upon landing. Six of the planes went down before their paratroopers could jump. One plane contained five officers and fifteen men from the 504th Headquarters and Headquarters Company. Fifteen of the twenty on board survived, including Lieutenant Colonel Leslie Freeman, XO of the 504th, along with two other officers and twelve men. Eleven of the fifteen survivors were wounded.

Another plane carrying three officers and fifteen men of Headquarters Company, 2nd Battalion, 504th, crashed with the jumpmaster, Lieutenant M. C. Shelly, standing in the door. Shelly was thrown clear of the wreckage and miraculously survived. All of the other occupants of his plane were killed.

Four of the planes carried one officer and thirty-two troopers from Battery C, 376th Parachute Field Artillery Battalion. One of the four crashed into the sea with nine troopers aboard. From the other three planes, five men deployed their reserve chutes and survived. Two additional survivors crawled out of the wreckage of their plane. Three men were thrown clear as their planes crashed.

A C-47 crashed carrying the 82nd Airborne Division's assistant division commander, Brigadier General Charles L. "Bull" Keerans, Jr. He had flown with the 504th to observe the jump. His body was never found.

Other planes returned to Tunisia with four dead and six wounded paratroopers aboard. Eight planes returned without giving their troopers the opportunity to jump.

The disastrous friendly fire incident had cost the 504th RCT eighty-one killed, sixteen missing, and one hundred and thirty-two wounded. An estimated sixty aircrew of the 52nd Troop Carrier Wing were killed and another thirty wounded.

Private Keith K. Scott, with 1st Battalion, Headquarters Company, 504th, landed near a couple of burning enemy pillboxes. "We started to assemble in an orchard when the artillery opened up on us. That didn't last long. We assembled and found out that one man, Corporal Len, had broken his leg. We wrapped him in a chute and hid him in a vine patch. We left him with two riggers.

"Lieutenant [Richard] Mills got his bearings and told us what the score was. We had dropped fifteen miles from the right DZ, in enemy territory. We got our weapons and marched down the road. We heard somebody yelling and a whirring sound like an auto stuck in the mud. I don't know why, but we marched right into them. We walked across a bridge. As we reached the end [of the bridge] we heard someone yell, 'Halt!' It was the Heinies.

"Lieutenant Mills said, 'Ground equipment and jump over the bridge.' He no sooner said that than they opened fire on us. We ran into a vine patch and hid. They shot flares in the air and tried to pick us off. They tossed grenades and fired their guns into the patch. Privates Boggs, Wright and I were cut off from the rest. We started to run and were chased and fired on. We lost Wright somewhere. Boggs and I hid in a cane break for an hour or two."[49]

After landing, Lieutenant Edward Sims, a platoon leader with Company F, 504th, assembled his men. "I sent patrols in opposite directions on a nearby road to look for signs and landmarks. One patrol located a road sign indicating that Augusta was forty kilometers. This was sufficient to allow me to locate our general position on the map as being southwest of Augusta, Sicily and about twenty-five miles from where we planned to land in the vicinity of Gela. Also, we were several miles behind the Axis forces opposing the beach landing of the US 45th Division. I had 14 men with me, so we moved in a southwesterly direction, on roads and cross-country, toward Gela. At one point, we had a short firefight with a small German force, but they soon fled. Later, we spotted a company size German force moving north, but since they did not see us, we held our fire and let them pass. Our next contact was with advance elements of the US 45th Division. They opened fire on us and for a few moments the situation was dangerous. We had a tough job trying to convince them that we were US paratroopers."[50]

One stick of Company E, 504th troopers, led by Lieutenant John Thompson, landed on the southeastern coast of Sicily. "We hit the ground very quickly, and with no casualties, assembled and immediately sent out three groups of four men each in different directions to gain information and find out where we were. Two hours later, the three groups had returned. One group had six German prisoners. These prisoners were part of thirteen Germans who were surprised down near the shore and seven had been killed in resisting. With no one able to speak German, we decided to take them along with us. Knowing that we were on the eastern part of the island, and knowing that our objective, in the vicinity of Gela, was on the central part of the island, we decided to head west along the coast, moving at night and resting in the daytime. Traveling was difficult, having to climb over one stone wall after another, and the terrain was mountainous."[51]

At 2:00 a.m. on the morning of July 12, Captain Ed Sayre, with Company A, 505th, reported to the CP of the 2nd Battalion, 16th Infantry Regiment, 1st Infantry Division, to which his company was still attached. "Orders were received to retake Hill 41 immediately. Colonel Crawford issued the order of attack to jump off at 03:00 hours. The battalion would attack in a column of companies with the paratroopers leading. The column of companies formation was necessary because of the difficulty of control in the extreme darkness. Direction in the attack was to be maintained by following an old German wire line, which led to Hill 41. I picked up the wire and moved out with a platoon to my right and left in platoon column. The Heavy Weapons Company and battalion commander followed closely behind. No fire was received until the parachutists were almost on top of the hill. Machine guns then opened up on us. Due to the steepness of the hill, none of the machine gun fire was hitting A Company, but the Heavy Weapons Company was receiving heavy casualties. Colonel Crawford was also hit and had to be evacuated. The two machine guns of the enemy on top of the hill were soon knocked out and the battalion began to reorganize on the hill. There were many enemy trenches and emplacements and these were utilized to the fullest extent in the defense.

"At dawn that morning it could be seen that the 2nd Battalion was in a very bad position. During the night, Germans tanks had moved between us and the rear leaving us completely surrounded.

"At 07:00 hours the first tank attack came. Several Mark IVs and one Mark VI were heading toward the battalion's position with the Mark VI leading."[52]

As the German armored attack hit Hill 41, a group of 1st Battalion Headquarters personnel led by Colonel Gorham arrived on the hill to the left of Sayre's position. Lieutenant Dean McCandless, the 1st Battalion communications officer, had been on outpost during the previous night. "At dawn Colonel Gorham recalled us. Later that morning he decided to reconnoiter the forward areas and asked me, Lieutenant [Carl R.] Comstock (assistant battalion surgeon), Corporal [Thomas] Higgins, and Private [Bernard] Williams to join him. We were climbing a small hill when all of a sudden there was a lot of shooting in front and to our right. A few paces later, we could see over the crest of the hill and there was a German Tiger tank in the valley to our right, some two hundred yards away. We were all prone in a second! It seemed like everyone was shooting at that tank and that it had been disabled somehow. Colonel Gorham motioned us to keep down while he crept ahead.

"He was either on the crest of the hill or a bit on the forward slope when he knelt and raised the bazooka that he was carrying. Within seconds there was a tremendous explosion right there and Colonel Gorham was down. Lieutenant Comstock jumped up and ran to his side. There was a second tremendous explosion and Lieutenant Comstock was down. I then ran to them. The Tiger tank did not fire at us again.

"At first, I thought they were dead. Colonel Gorham had no pulse, was not breathing, and had a large triangular hole in the center of his forehead. He was dead.

"Lieutenant Comstock had a terrible long gash obliquely across his face, so that his nose and lips were lying on one side of his face. But, he was alive, but in great distress.

"I asked Corporal Higgins to go get a jeep in a hurry, even if he had to steal it. In the meantime, I gave Lieutenant Comstock a syrette of morphine, even though he tried to protest through his shattered face.

"In a very short time Higgins was back with a jeep. (I never asked where he got it.) We all loaded Comstock onto the jeep and rushed him back to the hospital on the beach. Higgins and Williams then returned with the jeep and recovered Colonel Gorham's body.

"Why Colonel Gorham took the chances he took we'll never know. I'd never seen him fire a bazooka and he did not fire it that day. We were well out of bazooka range at any rate. He was a brave and aggressive leader. Such leaders get right up close to the action and take chances."[53]

Captain Sayre, unaware of Lieutenant Colonel Gorham's death, could see the German tanks moving relentlessly toward his positions. "It was almost exactly like the attack in the same spot on the previous morning except for one very important factor: the 2nd Battalion had a battalion of 155s supporting us. The forward observer called for fire. The first salvo landed on the Mark VI Tiger tank, fifty yards from the main line of resistance. The fire then began to land among the other tanks and they were forced to withdraw.

"In the meantime, elements of the 2nd Armored Division were in direct contact with the German armor between the 2nd Battalion and our rear. Our troops were treated to a grandstand spectacle of German and American armor fighting it out in the valley below. While the Germans were engaged to the front, a section of Sherman tanks managed to get directly on their flank and opened fire before they were observed. Several German tanks were knocked out and the others forced to withdraw. Three times during the day the German tanks started toward the position of the 2nd Battalion, but each time were driven back by artillery fire."[54]

Shortly after dawn on July 12, at the Castle Nocera southeast of Niscemi, Private First Class Shelby R. Hord could see that the Germans had pulled out during the night, after the savage fighting of the previous day. So he went down the hill to take a look around. "The poor Germans were dead in that field as far as I could see, and then on the other side of the road there were dead Germans, and then on the hill across from us there were dead.

"In the distance I could see the 'Red One' that stands out on a man's shoulder, you could see it was a 1st Division combat patrol. They came and talked with me and said, 'Do you realize that you guys have killed almost four hundred men?' One of the men told me it was three hundred eighty-six dead [Germans] that they had already counted and they haven't counted some of the ones up closer [to the chateau]."[55]

As of daybreak on July 12, General Ridgway had not been able to contact Colonel Gavin or the 505th Command Post since coming ashore at 7:30 a.m. on July 10. He had only been able to make contact with Company I, 505th, in person and with Company A, 505th, by radio using the 1st Infantry Division's radio net. Ridgway's landing party set up a Division CP three miles southeast of Gela, about a mile from the coast. At 7:15 a.m. that morning Colonel Tucker arrived at Ridgway's CP. Ridgway sent a report at 7:55 a.m. to Seventh Army Headquarters that stated, "No formed element of Combat Team 505 under my control. Expect some today based on 1st Division reports. Elements of Combat Team 504 dribbling in. At present one battery 75 pack howitzer and equivalent of one infantry company available for use . . . Am concentrating all efforts on reorganization."[56]

By the morning of July 12, German prisoners captured at Biazzo Ridge were digging graves for burial of the 505th's dead as a result of the previous day's fighting. As Sergeant Fredrick W. Randall, with Company H, 505th, moved out west on the highway toward Gela with the other survivors of the fighting at Biazzo Ridge, he saw graves being dug in the orchard to the right of the road. "Sergeant [Tony] Castillo, 1st Sergeant of G Company, was in charge of the burial detail. He was a Pueblo Indian from Colorado. German POWs were digging graves and Castillo gave them a rough time."[57]

In the Company H column, Private Russell McConnell could see the fresh graves and the covered bodies where so many of his buddies were now being buried. "When we marched past where their graves were, that's when it really hit. We had lost some of our closest friends."[58]

Lieutenant Bob Fielder, Communications Platoon leader with the 505th Regimental Headquarters, was one of the lucky troopers who rode in a jeep with Colonel Gavin's staff because he and his men carried and operated the radios for the regimental staff. Fielder's jeepload of men and equipment left Biazzo Ridge, "drove around the bend, and up the road for a short distance, to be greeted by the very grim sight of dead paratroopers hanging from trees. A part of a stick of troopers [from the 504th] had been dropped the night before along the road on top of elements of Germans who cut them down."[59]

Major William Beall, the 3rd Battalion, 504th executive officer, who had rounded up some paratroopers that had landed in the British zone, had spent the night of July 11 on the beach. On the morning of July 12, together with nineteen troopers, Beall "left by RAF crash boat to rejoin the unit, and stopped enroute at coast towns to pick up United States paratroopers."[60]

Lieutenant Thompson, with Company E, 504th, had been badly misdropped the previous night during the friendly fire disaster. Thompson led the men from his stick and their six German prisoners west across southern Sicily, trying to find friendly forces. "In our two days of walking we observed many more enemy troops, at a distance, moving north. On the third day we came across a field strewn with parachutes. These parachutes had been used by members of the 505th CT and some men were lying quite still in their harnesses, evidently not having a chance to get out of them.

"Upon coming to a crossroad, we saw three pillboxes commanding all the road entrances. There had evidently been a stiff fight there, for there were about twenty bodies of paratroopers in the vicinity of the pillboxes, also many enemy dead.

"Later in the afternoon we came upon a battalion CP and were informed that it belonged to the 45th Division. Here we turned over our prisoners for interrogation. We found that these Germans were part of a force who had the mission of laying mines along the coast. At this CP we were able to find that we were fifteen miles southeast of Ragusa, which was on our way to Gela.

"Later that night we arrived at Ragusa and met several paratroopers from the 504th CT who were on their way to Vittoria, where the 2nd Battalion was assembling. We took these men along with us, and early the next morning we arrived at the 2nd Battalion CP, where we met [Major William P.] Yarborough [the 2nd Battalion, 504th, CO] and Jack Thompson of the Chicago Tribune. They informed me that only one third of the battalion had reported in so far and it was believed that the rest of the regiment had landed on their designated DZ at Gela."[61]

At about 5:00 p.m. on July 12, Captain Ed Sayre was once again ordered to lead Company A, 505th, forward in yet another attack. "The battalion received orders from regimental headquarters to prepare to attack a ridge three thousand yards to our front. We were to be supported by a platoon of Sherman tanks. The battalion was to move forward to a line of departure three hundred yards to our front and move out as soon as the tanks arrived.

"All but one of the tanks were knocked out by long range 88 fire before they reached the line of departure, so the attack was delayed until the next morning.

"The captain who was now commanding the 2nd Battalion, pulled the parachutists out of the line and brought us back to the battalion CP, where we were allowed to get our first real rest since we had jumped three nights before. With artillery fire landing around them all night, the men slept like they were home in a nice warm bed until awakened at 04:00 hours the next morning to prepare for the attack on the ridge to our front. With a heavy artillery barrage preceding us, the battalion moved out, two companies on line, parachutists and the Heavy Weapons Company on their open right flank and the reserve company following the left company and protecting that flank. Machine gun fire, which had been coming from the ridge, stopped as the artillery fire began landing on the ridge. The battalion moved to the ridge, receiving no fire from there, but a few scattered sniper rounds from a ridge farther to the front.

"When the battalion reached the ridge, the enemy had pulled out leaving behind a mobile 88 and several of its crew dead nearby. Regimental headquarters was notified that the ridge was taken. The battalion was given orders to pursue the enemy closely and to take the town of Niscemi if possible.

"The battalion moved forward without resistance, except for long range sniper fire until we reached the hill overlooking the town. The battalion commander now called for five men from each company to volunteer for a twenty-man patrol to enter the town. No volunteers were found.

"The paratroopers were much fresher than the other men of the battalion due to our good rest the night before, so we were ordered to enter the town. There was one machine gun firing from long range as we entered the outskirts of the town, but it withdrew as soon as fired upon. The parachutists now stopped and the battalion passed through us to take up defensive positions on the other side of town. At this time we received orders from Headquarters, 16th Infantry, that we were relieved from the 16th Infantry and would be returning to an area near Gela where the 505th Parachute Infantry was reassembling."[62]

On July 13, Major William Beall, the executive officer with the 3rd Battalion, 504th, and a number of paratroopers that had been misdropped in the British sector and shuttled to the American sector by an RAF boat, landed at Scoglitti. Beall "reported to bivouac area west of Vittoria (505th Combat Team CP) with Captain [William] Kitchin, one other officer, and forty-eight enlisted men from various organizations. At Vittoria, I was told that Lieutenant Colonel Kouns, the Battalion Commanding Officer had been captured and I was in command. I proceeded to organize the remainder of the battalion preparatory to continuing operations. We assembled a total of four officers and ninety enlisted men."[63]

At 9:00 a.m. on July 13, Colonel Gavin reached the Division CP and told General Ridgway that he had about 1,200 men under his command. The 504th and 505th Regimental Combat Teams began the process of reorganization. The 3rd Battalion, 504th, was returned to control of the 504th RCT. They were able to collect 3,790 men by midnight on July 14, out of a total of 5,307 that had parachuted into Sicily. Only 93 more men would find their way to the division by July 17. Virtually all of the remaining 1,424 paratroopers had been killed, wounded, or captured.

On July 15, Ridgway requested a daylight operation protected by allied fighters for the third lift, consisting of 426 officers and men with division headquarters to be landed by glider, which was executed without incident the following day. In preparation for further combat operations, Ridgway acquired limited transport and a basic combat load of ammunition for his two regimental combat teams. That same day, orders were received from Seventh Army for the division to move to the Palma di Montechiaro area to relieve the 3rd Infantry Division by the night of July 19. Afterward the division would advance west to the Verdura River, turning north and driving to Palermo with a five- to ten-mile zone of responsibility, with the coast on the left and the 3rd Division on the right. The main transportation route would be Highway 115.

The move from the Gela assembly area began at 6:00 a.m. on July 17. At 3:00 a.m. on July 19, the 504th RCT, led by the 2nd Battalion, with the 82nd Armored Field Artillery Battalion and Batteries A and B of the 83rd Chemical Mortar Battalion attached, moved west from Realmonte to Montallegro. By nightfall the 504th RCT was stopped by an order from corps at a phase line about halfway to the town of Sciacca. The major obstacle was a blown bridge at the Canne River. A detachment of the 307th Airborne Engineer Battalion commanded by Lieutenant Colonel Robert S. Palmer solved this with the rapid construction of a temporary bridge strong enough to support heavy vehicles, completing it early on the morning of July 19.

At 6:00 a.m. on July 20, the 2nd Battalion, 504th, continued to lead the regimental combat team in the advance to Sciacca. As Lieutenant Edward Sims led his Company F, 504th platoon up the road toward Sciacca they were strafed by German fighter aircraft. "We did take up dispersed positions and opened fire, but all of the planes continued to fly south. As we approached Sciacca, I was leading with my platoon when I noticed smoke rising from the road ahead, so I dispersed my platoon into firing positions and went forward to check out the smoke. The road had been mined with antitank mines and a two-wheeled cart, driven by an old man with a young child, had set off one mine, killing both of them and the mule that was pulling the cart. To our left on the crest of a small rise were a number of pillboxes with white flags being waved from the gun ports. We advanced cautiously and flushed out a large group (about one hundred) of Italian soldiers who wanted to surrender. After disarming them, they were sent, under guard, to our rear. We cleared Sciacca, then headed for Marsala."[64] The day ended with a total of approximately 1,000 prisoners taken at the cost of only two casualties during the advance.

On July 21, with Lieutenant Sims and Company F, 504th, once again in the lead, Italian infantry supported by a battery of 75mm guns and two 90mm guns ambushed the paratroopers. "In an area called Tumminello Pass, we were forced to make a frontal assault when a strong [Italian] force caught us by surprise and opened fire on our column. This turned into a long hard firefight, with a number of casualties on both sides."[65] As Company F assaulted the Italian positions frontally, a flanking movement was undertaken, resulting in the surrender of all of the Italian personnel and weapons. Company F suffered six men killed and eight wounded in the attack.

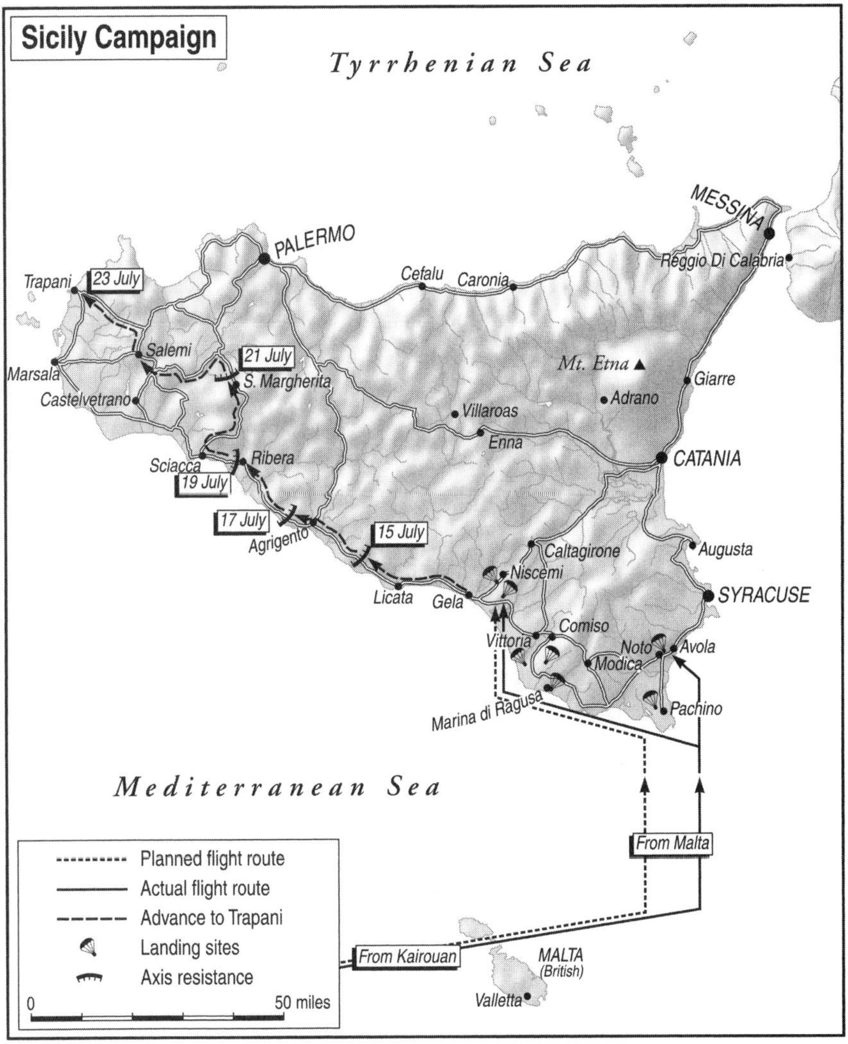

At 9:30 a.m., the 505th RCT took up the lead as the 2nd Battalion, 505th, passed through the 2nd Battalion, 504th, and marched to Santa Margherita, occupying it by 11:40 a.m., then pushed on to capture Bellice by 3:00 p.m. By the end of the day, the 2nd Battalion, 505th, had marched 23 miles without food or a resupply of water.

A platoon from Company G, 505th, was assigned to march west to take the town of Montevago, while Company I, 505th, was ordered to move east from Santa Margherita to capture Sambuca. Sergeant Bill Dunfee was a squad leader with Company I. "The combat team moved up the west coast of Sicily. This was accomplished by leap-frogging the battalions, first one then another leading the way. Although I Company had accomplished its mission with dispatch, we were on Krause's shit list, since we had not participated at Biazzo Ridge. Consequently, when the 3rd Battalion was in the lead position, I Company was out in front. In fairness, I'm sure at that time I Company had the fewest casualties. I'm sure it was obvious to those on high that the Germans were sacrificing the Italian Army to fight a delaying action. This allowed them to evacuate most of their units across the Strait of Messina into Italy. The Germans did have to abandon huge quantities of materiel. The Italians were something less than enthused about fighting, and gave up after a token effort of defense. This was of little comfort to our wounded, and frustrating to those of us that had to take them prisoner."[66] During the 15-mile advance on July 21, 1,515 enemy soldiers were added to the POW cages, while the division suffered a total of fourteen casualties, all from Company F, 504th.

The next day the division was placed in corps reserve, but maintained the positions from the previous day, while patrolling to the north and east. On the morning of the 23rd of July, the 82nd was ordered to move immediately to seize Trapani, which lay on the northwest coast of Sicily.

The 3rd Battalion, 505th, moved from Montevago by truck at 11:30 a.m. and drove through territory that no Allied troops had moved through previously. As the convoy rolled through the towns of Partanna, Santa Ninfa, and Salemi, the citizenry lined the road, welcoming the troopers as liberators and throwing such delicacies as fruit, bread, and chocolate to the passing truck-borne troopers. It seemed that the locals had appropriated food stocks left behind by the retreating Italian Army.

Once again, Company I, 505th, was in the lead. Sergeant Dunfee enjoyed the ride and the hospitality from the civilians along the way after marching so many miles during the last week. Outside of Trapani the convoy halted and Dunfee ordered his squad out of the back of the truck. Dunfee could see in the distance to the west enemy roadblocks and minefields in the road leading into Trapani. "It was an Italian Naval and Marine base, and we were not real sure of the number of defenders to expect. We had formed up at the edge of an olive grove looking out on a plain that was about a mile to the foothills overlooking the harbor."[67]

Following Company I, the rest of the 3rd Battalion arrived. Sergeant Bill Blank, a squad leader with Company G, got his squad deployed. "Just outside of town we unloaded for the assault on the town and they fired a few rounds of artillery at us without too much effect. We fixed bayonets and went toward the town. We crossed an open area used for an airport and expected the worst, since there was no cover."[68]

Simultaneously, Sergeant Dunfee and his squad crossed the open ground as "I Company moved out of the cover of the olive grove and immediately drew artillery fire. On hearing incoming mail we would hit the deck and move forward after the explosions. Hearing incoming rounds, we had just hit the deck, when Major Krause drove up in his jeep. He had not heard the incoming rounds and started giving us hell. As luck would have it, at this very moment two rounds bracketed his jeep, and to quote from that era: 'He hauled ass out of there.' We continued forward under constant but moderate artillery fire. When we started up the hill the artillery ceased, and mortar rounds took over. Small arms fire was quite intense, but we had ample cover in the form of large rock formations. As we neared the crest we were ordered to fix bayonets. We continued our advance and the mortar fire became only an occasional round and the rifle fire diminished. In short order white flags appeared and for these Italians the war was over. I had observed two Italian soldiers disappear into what appeared to be a hole in the ground. Being so close to Trapani, it was probably a homemade air raid shelter. I called [Corporal Harry] Buffone forward, knowing he spoke Italian and told him to tell the ten people in the cave to come out, or we were coming in shooting. About this time one of the men came up with the pin pulled on a fragmentation grenade. Having heard women and children crying in the cave, I told him not to use it. What was funny to me at the time was, he had discarded the pin and couldn't find it. I told Buff, 'Let's get the hell out of here before he drops the damned thing.' The balance of our stay on Sicily was spent rounding up and guarding POWs."[69]

Miraculously, the 3rd Battalion, 505th, captured the town with only one casualty, a bazooka loader who was accidentally burned by the back blast from the bazooka as it was fired.

General Ridgway arrived in town and met with the Italian commander for the Trapani district, Admiral Alberto Manfredi. Ridgway dictated a surrender document requiring that all resistance cease immediately; that all Italian military stocks of food, ammunition, and supplies be preserved; and that his troopers be permitted to post guards on all military property.

That same afternoon, Colonel Tucker led his 504th Reconnaissance Platoon into Castellammare del Golfo, with the rest of his combat team arriving the following day, as trucks were obtained after the 505th advance on Trapani.

Also on July 23, the promotion of Major Mark Alexander, the CO of the 2nd Battalion, 505th, to lieutenant colonel was approved.

The 82nd Airborne Division had conducted the first regimental sized combat jump conducted by the US Army. Although the drops of both the 505th and 504th were badly scattered, the paratroopers engaged elements of the elite German Hermann Göring and 15th Panzer Divisions, and the Italian 4th Livorno, 54th Napoli, and 206th Coastal Divisions. The aggressive fighting by small isolated groups of paratroopers cleared defenders from the beach areas, delayed counterattacking armored and motorized forces, and caused the Germans and Italians to estimate their numbers to be far in excess of the actual size of the forces.

No less an authority than General Kurt Student, commander of all German parachute forces, said, "The Allied airborne operation in Sicily was decisive despite widely scattered drops, which must be expected in a night landing. It is my opinion that if it had not been for the airborne forces blocking the Hermann Göring Panzer Division from reaching the beachhead, that division would have driven the initial seaborne forces back into the sea. I attribute the entire success of the Allied Sicilian Operation to the delaying of German reserves until sufficient forces had been landed by sea to resist the counterattacks by our defending forces."[70]

CHAPTER 5

"RETREAT HELL!— SEND ME MY 3RD BATTALION!"[1]

On July 29, 1943, General Ridgway was informed that the 82nd Airborne Division would conduct an airborne operation as part of an amphibious landing scheduled for September 9 in the Bay of Salerno on the western coast above the toe of the Italian boot. On August 2, Ridgway and some of the division staff flew to Fifth Army Headquarters to discuss the operational plan. General Clark's new airborne planner was Major William P. Yarborough, who had commanded the 2nd Battalion, 504th, in Sicily and whom Ridgway had relieved shortly after the Sicily campaign for allowing his men to be ambushed at the Tumminello Pass.

Yarborough's plan called for Ridgway's two parachute regiments to drop on the north side of the Sorrento Mountains, to block the north end of the mountain passes, and prevent two German panzer divisions in the Naples area from reinforcing German forces defending the Salerno Bay area. The 325th Glider Infantry Regiment would make an amphibious landing at the town of Maiori to forge a quick link-up with the parachute forces. This plan was fraught with risks and problems. Ridgway got Clark's assurance that he would get at least three weeks of training for the 504th and 505th to work with the troop carrier forces and for amphibious training for the 325th. After the meeting, Ridgway assigned Brigadier General Maxwell Taylor, division artillery commander, as a liaison to General Eisenhower's Headquarters in Algiers, in order to keep an eye on Yarborough.

There wasn't much time to take the lessons learned from the Sicily jump and make improvements. Due to the badly scattered drops in Sicily, there was a critical need to dramatically improve the accuracy of night parachute drops. A pathfinder concept was conceived, whereby a small group of paratroopers would jump twenty to thirty minutes before the main forces and employ newly developed electronic gear to guide the main forces to the drop zones and special light beacons to mark the drop zones. The initial training was conducted at the airfield at Comiso, Sicily.

The primary electronic gear consisted of a transmitter device, called a Rebecca, mounted in 16 special pathfinder C-47s, and a responder homing beacon, called a Eureka, used by the pathfinders on the ground. Communications specialists from the 504th, 505th, and the attached 2nd Battalion, 509th, were selected for Rebecca-Eureka training, thus becoming the original US Army pathfinders. One of those selected was T/5 Jerry Huth, with the 505th Regimental Headquarters Company. "They selected half a dozen guys, Lieutenant [Albert V.] Konar headed it up. The Eureka was a set which all pathfinders used. You set up a beam on the ground. The aircraft were tuned to that frequency and they followed the beam. [There] was only about five days [that] we had to do the training. We were put at a separate airport. There was a British sergeant and an officer, I believe they came out of the UK to train us. The burly British sergeant did all of the training on the Rebecca-Eureka."[2]

Because Ridgway's parachute forces were still in Sicily performing occupation duties and the troop carrier forces were located in the Kairouan, Tunisia, area, no joint training could take place until the parachute elements of Ridgway's forces could be returned to Kairouan. The 504th and 505th Regimental Combat Teams also had to integrate around 1,000 replacements to compensate for the casualties incurred during the Sicily campaign. After training in Kairouan, the plan was for the troop carrier forces and Ridgway's parachute elements to move to the closer airfields in Sicily a few days prior to the operation.

On August 18, formal orders arrived for the operation, code-named Giant I, that by this time had become even more ambitious. The plan now called for the 504th and 505th RCTs to jump northwest of Naples near the Volturno River, even farther away from the landings at Salerno. The amphibious operation by the 325th RCT would also change to a landing at the mouth of the Volturno River. There was precious little time to prepare. Having only twenty-four trucks available, the division's troops, weapons, and equipment were moved by shuttles to airfields and returned to Kairouan, Tunisia on August 19 and 20.

With the division back in Kairouan, training began immediately. When Lieutenant Colonel Mark Alexander, CO of the 2nd Battalion, 505th, attended the briefing for Giant I, he had grave concerns about dropping "northwest of Naples and approximately forty miles from the nearest proposed Allied beach landing, south of Naples in the vicinity of Salerno. My 2nd Battalion was to have jumped on the banks of the Volturno River near the villages of Arnone and Conchello. Relief of airborne units by ground force elements of the Fifth Army could not be expected for several days."[3]

On the night of August 28–29, a test was conducted using the new electronic equipment and lights planned for pathfinder operations. The equipment was set up at a location near the town of Enfidaville, Tunisia. Specially selected and trained aircrews flying the sixteen C-47 pathfinder aircraft outfitted with Rebeccas were able to pick up the Eureka beacon about twenty miles out and were effectively guided to the location of the equipment. A high-frequency radio beacon called 5G that was susceptible to jamming was also tested and was not as effective as the Rebecca-Eureka gear. Aldis lamps and Krypton lights were used to mark the location and were supposedly capable of being visible from twenty-five miles away. The lights were deemed to be satisfactory in the test. Based upon the results of the test, on August 30 a second test was conducted, this time using a small number of paratroopers to actually jump on the drop zone location of the equipment. The test resulted in an extrapolation that if a mass jump had been executed, over ninety percent of the paratroopers would have landed within a mile of the drop zone, a huge improvement over the Sicily jump.

As the preparations for Operation Giant I proceeded at a frenzied pace, the 325th RCT was ordered to move to Bizerte, Tunisia, for amphibious training to support the parachute landings. The regiment moved to Bizerte on August 25, but no landing craft were available for training upon their arrival. When the landing craft did become available, only a few days of training was possible before they were to be ready to sail on September 3.

Major Bennie Zinn, the S-4 of the 325th, and most of the regimental staff had attended an amphibious school the week before so that they could train the regiment in Bizerte before departing. "We taught our men how to load the various types of landing craft, how to fight from them, and how to waterproof all equipment. We got all ready and even had time to get some new 57mm anti-tank guns and zero them in. We practiced day and night and then began to load the 325th Combat Team. The night that our ships were loaded and all set to go, Jerry came in to bomb Bizerte Harbor. It was thrilling, even if it was nerve-racking on us. The searchlights went after the planes and flak tore at them from all directions. Finally two were knocked down and not a ship was hit in the harbor."[4]

General Ridgway and most of the division staff planned to board the ships carrying the 325th. Because he would be aboard ship and Brigadier General Keerans was missing and presumed dead, General Ridgway decided to put Colonel Gavin in charge of the parachute force for the upcoming operation.

Unknown to anyone in the division, General Eisenhower had been conducting top secret talks with an emissary of the Italian king since shortly after the overthrow and arrest of the Italian dictator, Benito Mussolini, on July 25. The new Italian government was prepared to sign a separate surrender and join the Allies in fighting the Germans. Eisenhower demanded that the Italian government announce the surrender before the Allies invaded Italy and that Italian forces would be ordered to not fire on Allied forces once the landings began. The Italian government wanted an Allied airborne landing near

Rome, to protect the government from German retribution once the surrender was announced.

The emissary told Eisenhower that Italian troops could protect three airfields around Rome so that additional forces could be air landed, would provide transportation for the Allied forces, and would help fight German forces that would surely be sent to take over Rome. Eisenhower was suspicious of the emissary and of the commitment of the Italian government to stick to any deal that was negotiated. Nevertheless, on September 2, Eisenhower decided to take the 82nd Airborne Division away from General Clark's Salerno invasion force for the airborne operation near Rome. The new plan, code-named Giant II, entailed parachuting the 504th and 505th on to Italian-held airfields on the night of September 8 and air landing the remainder of the division, including the 325th RCT, at the airfields held by the paratroopers and the Italian forces. The 325th RCT, already loaded on its assigned LSTs in Bizerte, was ordered to disembark.

On September 3, the Italian government's emissary, Giuseppe Castellano, signed an armistice, with a commitment stipulated in the agreement for the Allies to land forces near Rome to protect the Italian government. That same night, Ridgway, Taylor, and numerous other officers met with Castellano to discuss the planned airborne operation. Already skeptical, Ridgway and Taylor became convinced during the discussions that the Italians could not be relied upon to take on the Germans, which would mean certain destruction of the division.

Ridgway argued and succeeded in getting the scale of the initial parachute jump reduced to a regimental combat team, less one battalion for the initial drop. If the drop went well, it would be reinforced on the following nights.

He also argued for a secret mission to Rome to determine the capability and commitment of the Italian government and military forces before the operation was executed. The mission was approved with one condition—the mission could not commence until 24 hours before the operation so that if the emissaries were captured, the Germans would not have time to extract details of the plan and implement actions in time to counter the drop. General Maxwell Taylor and Colonel William Gardiner, an intelligence officer with the 51st Troop Carrier Wing, volunteered for this very dangerous assignment.

On September 4, Ridgway flew to his advanced CP at Bizerte to work on planning of the operation. He chose Colonel Tucker's 504th RCT, less the 3rd Battalion, for the initial drop. Shortly afterward, the division was issued new orders. Lieutenant Colonel Alexander attended another secret briefing that began with the news that Operation Giant I had been cancelled. "The proposal had many problems and we battalion commanders of the 505th Parachute Regiment were relieved when the plan was cancelled. We had not had time for adequate training, and the transport of supplies by air and ground forces would not be adequate for days or weeks of defense of the proposed objective. After a great deal of preparation, the show was cancelled and replaced with a plan for airborne operations in the Rome area, Giant II. The revision called for a drop by the 82nd Airborne Division near, and on three airfields east and north of Rome in conjunction with Italian forces in the area."[5]

On September 6, the 319th Glider Field Artillery (GFA) Battalion; Company H, 504th; D, E, and F Batteries, Headquarters Battery and the Medical Detachment of the 80th AA Battalion; the 2nd Platoon of Company A, 307th Airborne Engineer Battalion; and two platoons of the 813th Tank Destroyer (TD) Battalion loaded on one LST and three LCIs at Bizerte. The amphibious force sailed the next day for the Tiber River with the mission of sailing up the river and linking up with the airborne forces near Rome.

At 4:00 a.m. on September 7, General Taylor and Colonel Gardiner left Palermo, Sicily, aboard a British PT boat for the small island of Ustica, forty miles northwest of Sicily. There, they were transferred to an Italian corvette, which took them to the Italian mainland. They both decided to wear their uniforms and carry their pistols so that if the Germans caught them they technically would not be considered spies. At about 6:30 p.m. they landed at Gaeta on the western coast, about seventy-five miles from Rome. Before disembarking from the ship, they took off their caps, ruffled their hair, and disheveled their uniforms. Armed Italian guards were placed around them to give them the appearance of being POWs to anyone observing them leaving the ship. General Taylor "knew the kind of treatment we'd get if the Germans did nab us. It had been arranged that if any questions were asked when we were first taken ashore, we were to be described as American aviators who had been shot down in the Mediterranean, and picked up by the corvette as prisoners."[6]

They were put into a waiting car and driven to a small side road outside of town and transferred to a Red Cross ambulance with frosted glass windows, which allowed them to look out but prevented anyone from being able to see into the back of the vehicle. They passed through six roadblocks and only saw four German soldiers during their drive into Rome. They arrived in Rome around nightfall and were taken to a building across the street from the War Office. They used their trench coats to cover their uniforms as they moved quickly from the back of the truck into the building. They were taken to their rooms in a wing of the building that had been entirely blocked off, and armed guards were posted at each end of the corridor where their rooms were located. They were treated to a superb dinner a short time later with Colonel Salbi, the Chief of Staff to General Carboni, commander of the Italian Army corps in the Rome area. The Italians were totally unaware of the impending airborne operation and were planning to take the emissaries to meet with General Carboni the next morning. After dinner, Taylor and Gardiner insisted on seeing General Carboni immediately, which was hastily arranged. Carboni arrived at about 9:30 p.m. for the meeting.

Taylor's patience was tested as the Italian general "launched upon an expose of his views of the military situation in the Rome area. Since the fall of Mussolini (he said), the Germans had been bringing in men and supplies through the Brenner Pass and also through Resia and Tarvisio, with the result that their forces near Rome had greatly increased. There were now 12,000 Germans, principally parachutists in the valley of the Tiber who have heavy equipment including one hundred pieces of artillery, principally 88mm. The Panzer Grenadier Division had been raised to an effective strength of 24,000 men with fifty light and one hundred fifty heavy tanks. In the meantime, the Germans had ceased to supply the Italians with gas and munitions so that their divisions were virtually immobilized and had only enough ammunition for a few hours of combat. General Carboni's estimate of the situation was as follows:

"If the Italians declare an armistice, the Germans will occupy Rome, and the Italians can do little to prevent it. The simultaneous arrival of US airborne troops would only provoke the Germans to more drastic action. Furthermore, the Italians would be unable to secure the airfields, cover the assembly and provide the desired logistical aid to the airborne troops. If it must be assumed that an Allied seaborne landing is impossible north of Rome, then the only hope of saving the capital is to avoid overt acts against the Germans and await the effects of the Allied attacks in the south. He stated that he knew that the Allied landings would be at Salerno, which was too far away to aid directly in the defense of Rome. He stated that General Reatta shared his views.

"It was apparent that regardless of the soundness of General Carboni's information and views, he displayed an alarming pessimism certain to affect his conduct of operations in connection with Giant II."[7]

Taylor and Gardiner asked for an immediate meeting with Marshall Pietro Badoglio, the Italian head of state, and were taken by General Carboni to the marshall's private villa, arriving around midnight. They waited while Carboni met privately with Badoglio and about fifteen minutes later were taken in to meet with the marshall, where they were warmly greeted.

Taylor asked, "Was Marshall Badoglio in accord with General Carboni in considering an immediate armistice and the reception of airborne troops impossible of execution? The Marshall replied that he agreed with Carboni and repeated much the same arguments. I asked if he realized how deeply his government was committed by the agreements entered into by the Castellano mission. He replied that the situation had changed and that General Castellano had not known all the facts."[8]

After some more discussion in which General Taylor emphasized the seriousness of the situation for the Italian government, Taylor agreed to send a statement of the Italian views signed by Marshall Badoglio to Eisenhower's Headquarters in Algiers along with his own message recommending cancellation of Giant II. Badoglio agreed, and with the message in hand, the group returned to the quarters in Rome, where General Carboni arranged for immediate transmission of the two messages. At 8:00 a.m. the morning of September 8, word was received by Taylor and Gardiner that the messages had been received in Algiers.

Taylor waited most of the morning for a reply. "At 11:35, as no acknowledgement of the message recommending the cancellation of Giant II had been received, the code phrase 'Situation Innocuous' was sent off. This had not been sent initially as its use had been reserved for the case of an Italian refusal to transmit a request for cancellation. It was used in this instance to save time as the encoding of longer messages was taking as much as three hours."[9]

By September 8, the division's parachute and glider forces had been flown from Kairouan to several airfields in Sicily and were prepared for the operation, with Colonel Tucker's Regimental Combat Team less the 3rd Battalion to begin taking off at 5:45 p.m. Private Joe Watts, with Company F, 504th, was at the airfield near Trapani, Sicily, loaded in his plane with the 2nd Battalion troopers ready for takeoff. "Our 1st Battalion aircraft were in the air and forming up to fly to Italy when jeeps came screaming onto the tarmac among the 2nd Battalion taxiing aircraft. Bagdoglio had renounced the armistice terms—he needed more time. The Rome operation was cancelled."[10]

Like everyone in the division, Lieutenant Colonel Mark Alexander was relieved when he heard that the mission was cancelled. "Several of us knowing the background, by this time had no confidence in the airborne planners at Fifth Army. It would have been a suicide operation with three German armored divisions within twenty miles of Rome."[11]

A message arrived about 3:00 p.m. ordering Taylor and Gardiner back to Tunis. They traveled by ambulance to an airfield near Rome, where they boarded an Italian bomber and were flown straight to El Alonia, Tunis, then driven to Algiers, where they reported to General Eisenhower.

Their mission had, by the slimmest of margins, avoided what would have been a disaster for the 82nd Airborne Division, particularly Colonel Tucker and his men. With the cancellation of the operation, the seaborne force that had been ordered to sail up the Tiber River to link up with the airborne forces was diverted to Maiori, Italy.

Lieutenant Edward J. Sims, now a platoon leader with Company H, 504th (after leading a platoon of Company F, 504th, in Sicily), was aboard one of the Navy LCIs and was briefed on the change in plans for the seaborne force. "Company H was given a new mission to land at Maiori, Italy. We had to coordinate, by radio, with the US Rangers who would land in the same area on September 9, 1943."[12]

The next morning, September 9, at 3:30 a.m. the Fifth Army, under General Mark Clark, began amphibious landings near Salerno, Italy. The landings were made over a wide area, with a gap of seven miles between the British X Corps landing on the left and the American VI Corps landing on the right. The German 16th Panzer Division was waiting. They had ringed the bay with artillery and mortars, had placed mines and barbed wire entanglements on the beaches, had sighted machine guns to cover the beaches, and had a mobile force of tanks to attack any landing site. The new US 36th Division met heavy resistance during the beach landing. Then, about 7:00 a.m. the Germans attacked all landing beaches with tanks and infantry. The German armored attack was thrown back only through the employment of every weapon available to the landing forces. However, by the end of the day the American and British forces had driven inland between three and five miles. Only on the extreme right flank of the 36th Division was the situation precarious.

While the invasion of Italy was commencing, the 82nd wasted no time in getting in whatever training they could before their next operation. For the next several days, the 505th's S-3, Captain John Norton, whom everyone called Jack, was assigned to organize, train, and prepare the three newly formed pathfinder teams at the airfield at Agrigento, Sicily. The teams, one each for the 504th, 505th, and attached 2nd Battalion, 509th, would be under the command of Lieutenant Colonel Charles Billingslea, an airborne adviser to General Mark Clark. Norton spent the next week "further familiarizing the teams with the equipment: nomenclature, operation, and method of wearing same. Men actually became proficient at setting up the equipment blindfolded in a few minutes.

"Each [Eureka] set weighed about fifty-one pounds fitted into a compact container known as a leg pack, jumped on one man. Two men were required to work each set; one to jump with the equipment, and the other to assist in setting up and provide a safety factor for operation."[13]

On September 10, the Allied beachhead was expanded, while the Hermann Göring Panzer Division arrived to reinforce the 16th Panzer Division. That evening Lieutenant Ed Sims, with Company H, 504th, went ashore with the 82nd Airborne Division's seaborne force. "We landed unopposed on the narrow stone coastal area near Maiori, which is nine miles west of Salerno and part of the Sorrentine Peninsula. After landing, we moved inland and went to the mountains where we seized some high ground near the Chiunzi Pass area, including a vital tunnel. Two battalions of US Rangers moved north to positions that commanded the Pagni-Nocera Pass. Another battalion moved into the Amalfi area.

"My platoon occupied positions at the tunnel on the right flank of the company. The company commander borrowed a truck from a local citizen to use for mobility in order to cover the wide area (about five miles) we had to defend. Our company strength at that time was about one hundred twenty men. This rugged mountain area was not difficult to defend because the heavy equipment of the Germans was restricted to road use. There were two roads that had to be considered—one from Gragniano through the tunnel and the other through Sorrento and Amalfi. It was our job to prevent German forces from using these roads to get through to Salerno."[14]

The following day, September 11, the US 36th Infantry Division pushed into the hills overlooking the beaches, moving east through Altavilla, occupying the strategic Hill 424 east of the town, and capturing Albanella to the south. The US 45th Infantry Division's 179th RCT to the left of the 36th Division drove east from Persano toward Ponte Sele that lay in the hills.

By the evening of September 11, a dangerous situation existed along the boundary between the US and British forces, where a gap appeared as the American left flank advanced east and the British right turned northeast. Also by that evening, the German 26th Panzer Division, 29th Panzer Grenadier Division, and elements of the 15th Panzer Grenadier Division arrived to strengthen the German defenses, now totaling five powerful armored and armored infantry divisions ready to drive the Allied forces into the sea.

During the night, the Germans infiltrated around Hill 424 near the town of Altavilla, in the 36th Division sector. At dawn on September 12, German infantry and tanks struck Hill 424 from three sides and finally from the rear. The Germans broke through to take Altavilla, cutting the 1st Battalion, 142nd Infantry in two, and surrounded Company K, 143rd Infantry Regiment.

With the British hard pressed on the left and unable to protect the 45th Division's left flank, the Germans drove down the highway north of Persano with eight tanks leading a battalion of infantry. This powerful force struck the rear area and attached units of the 179th RCT, then turning northeast, hit the rifle companies from behind, forcing the regiment into a perimeter defense, as it was now virtually surrounded. Other strong forces overran British forces in Battipaglia. The Germans were now in a position for a concerted push the following morning west from Altavilla and south from Presano across the Salerno plain, with the goal to meet at the Sele River and drive toward the beaches.

To relieve the pressure on the beachhead and cut off German reinforcements, Fifth Army directed the 82nd to execute the previously cancelled operation, Giant I, with a jump northwest of Naples. Ridgway also received an order to drop the 2nd Battalion, 509th Parachute Infantry Regiment (still attached to the division) near Avellino, Italy, to block the mountain pass there. The orders stipulated that the jumps were to take place that night. Ridgway replied that the Avellino drop could be made on the night of September 15–16 and that the Giant I operation could not take place until the night of September 14–15. Ridgway also indicated that because no suitable drop zones were available northwest of Naples, the operation could be executed at Capua, northeast of Naples.

On the morning of September 13, the 325th Glider Infantry Regiment and the 3rd Battalion, 504th, less Company H, were loaded aboard nine LCIs at Licata, Sicily. The seaborne force began the voyage to the mouth of the Volturno River northwest of Naples to land and quickly link up with the parachute elements.

Ominously, that same morning the Germans unleashed a combined arms attack that struck the 36th and 45th Divisions with massive sledgehammer blows that sent both divisions reeling back toward the beaches. The situation quickly became critical as German tanks and infantry hit several rifle companies from the rear and surrounded the headquarters of the 1st Battalion, 157th

Infantry Regiment. The German forces pushed hard and penetrated precariously close to the beaches.

General Clark ordered his chief of staff to prepare a plan for evacuating the beachhead. The US and Royal Navy ships offshore fired salvo after salvo into the oncoming German armor and infantry with devastating effect. On shore every man and weapon available were thrown into the fight against the relentless German advance.

Clark needed help desperately, and he had already committed his floating reserve, the 45th Division's 180th Regimental Combat Team. He turned to the 82nd Airborne Division for help. Around noon, Clark wrote a letter to General Ridgway and gave it to a pilot with a reconnaissance squadron, which was operating from a dirt airstrip near Paestum, telling him to personally give the letter to General Ridgway and nobody else. The pilot immediately returned to his P-38 and took off for Sicily with the letter.

At around 1:30 p.m. Colonel Gavin was working at division headquarters at the Licata airfield when the P-38 landed. Gavin met with the pilot, who asked to see General Ridgway. "He had an urgent message for the division commander and refused to give it to anyone else. I talked to him on the field, but finally had the Chief of Staff radio General Ridgway, who had taken off for Termini."[15]

Ridgway was making "an inspection swing over the 82nd's bivouac areas. About fifteen minutes out, the navigator of my C-47 came back and told me that there was an urgent message for me back at Licata. He had no information as to who the sender was, nor what the nature of the message might be. This presented quite a problem of decision, for I was on fairly urgent business of my own. However, some sixth sense must have told me that this thing was important, for I gave orders to return. We landed at Licata about 2:00, and there I found a tired, begrimed P-38 pilot bearing a personal letter from Mark Clark.

"Even through the formal official phrases I could read my old friend's deep concern. The gist of the message was that unless we could get help to him and get it there fast, the landing in Italy might be turned into another Dunkirk. It was absolutely essential, he wrote, that we drop strong forces within the beachhead area that night.

"Word was sent at once to Troop Carrier Command, and I took off immediately for south central Sicily, where Reuben Tucker's fine 504th was in bivouac. To Tucker and his staff I quickly outlined the plan. Within two hours the men were assembling at their aircraft in full combat gear. Maps were spread over the tail surfaces of the C-47s, and there on the field the units of the regiment were given their missions. Plans for lighting the drop zone came with Clark's letter. The troops on the ground were to fill oil cans with sand soaked with gasoline, arrange the cans in a big 'T,' and as the first drop plane drew near, the 'T' would be lighted. Every plane would spill its stick to fall on this flaming beacon. We also had Clark's assurance that along the corridor we would fly, not a gun on the ground would fire. Eight hours after the pilot had handed me

General Clark's letter, planes of the 52nd Troop Carrier were lifting from the Sicilian fields, carrying the 504th Regiment, plus Company C of the 307th Airborne Engineers."[16]

Dropping ahead of Tucker's paratroopers to guide the planes to the drop zone would be the 504th Pathfinder Team, the first pathfinder team to be used in a combat jump. Behind the pathfinder team, the main force serials took off from several airfields in Sicily. Lieutenant Chester Garrison, the S-1 of the 2nd Battalion, 504th, was the jumpmaster on his plane. "The course was along the north Sicilian coast to Italy, up the west Italian coast to the designated drop zone at Paestum."[17]

In the three-quarter moonlit night, soldiers of the 36th and 45th Divisions stood up in their foxholes and cheered as first they heard the low roar of C-47s, then saw the dark silhouettes of C-47s in the distance as parachutes filled the night sky.

As his plane came in low over the mountains, Garrison could see the drop zone marked with the flaming gasoline drums. "A 'T' designated the field clearly. We jumped at 23:35, assembled on the blinker, and moved to the road where trucks were waiting. We were the first elements of the regiment to arrive with the exception of the pathfinder group, which we met on the field."[18]

The 1st Battalion, 504th serial dropped shortly after the 2nd Battalion. Lieutenant Reneau Breard, an assistant platoon leader with Company A, 504th, was concerned about a repeat of the friendly fire disaster that had occurred over Sicily. "We didn't fly over the Navy at all. We came up from the south. We stayed over the sea. The south end of the Bay of Salerno juts out, so we flew over that; and when we came over that we could see the drop zone. We dropped between six and eight hundred feet."[19]

After landing, Colonel Tucker was taken to a house a few hundred yards from the drop zone, where he, his regimental staff, and his battalion commanders were briefed on the situation. Lieutenant Colonel Warren R. Williams, CO of the 1st Battalion, told his S-3, Lieutenant John S. Lekson, to accompany him to the briefing. Shortly after Lekson arrived at the house, "a Lieutenant Colonel [Wiley O'Mohundro] of VI Corps began to review the situation in the VI Corps sector. He told of the troops that had been cut off at Altavilla, and of a gap that existed in the VI Corps line into which the regiment, led by Corps guides, would move. The regiment would 'hold to the last man and last round.' Troops were to be warned that men of the 36th Division would undoubtedly be drifting through the lines.

"Then Colonel Tucker made his assignments. The 2nd Battalion would defend the left sector; the 1st Battalion, the right, extending up the slope of Mt. Soprano."[20]

Within an hour Colonel Tucker's regimental headquarters; 1st Battalion, 504th; 2nd Battalion, 504th; Company C, 307th Airborne Engineer Battalion; a detachment of the 307th Medical Company; and a detachment of the 82nd

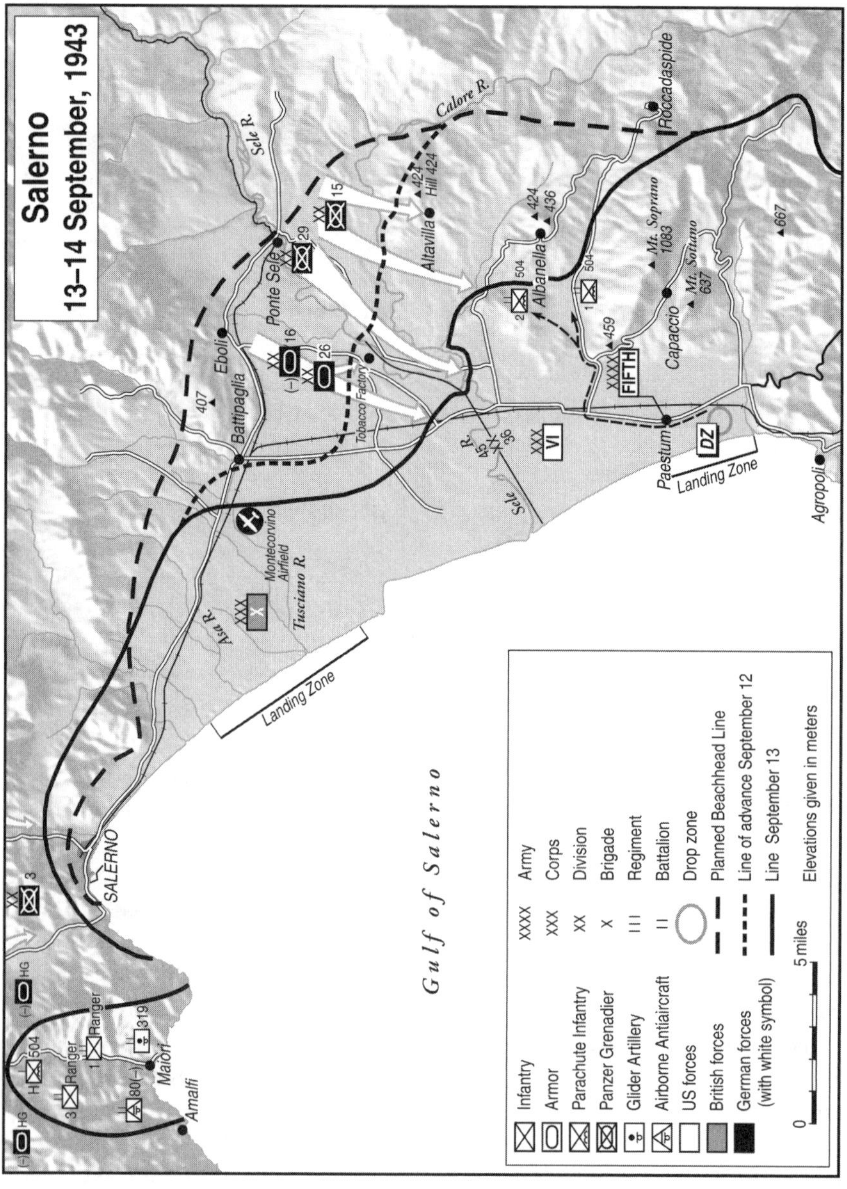
Salerno
13–14 September, 1943
Gulf of Salerno
Landing Zone
Landing Zone
SALERNO
Amalfi
Maiori
Ranger
504
319
80(-)
HG
Battipaglia
Eboli
Ponte Sele
Tobacco Factory
Montecorvino Airfield
Tusciano R.
Asa R.
Sele R.
Calore R.
Altavilla
Hill 424
Albanella
Roccadaspide
Capaccio
Mt. Soprano 1083
Mt. Sottano 637
Paestum
Agropoli
FIFTH
VI
X
DZ
Infantry
Armor
Parachute Infantry
Panzer Grenadier
Glider Artillery
Airborne Antiaircraft
US forces
British forces
German forces (with white symbol)
XXXX Army
XXX Corps
XX Division
X Brigade
III Regiment
II Battalion
Drop zone
Planned Beachhead Line
Line of advance September 12
Line September 13
Elevations given in meters
0
5 miles

Reconnaissance Platoon were assembled. One plane from 2nd Battalion, Headquarters Company and one from D Company were missing from the 2nd Battalion, while five plane loads of troopers from Company B were missing from the 1st Battalion serial. After the briefing, Tucker was met by General Clark, who told him, "As soon as assembled you are to be placed in the front lines."[21]

Colonel Tucker replied, "Sir, we are assembled and ready now."[22]

Lekson returned and boarded one of the waiting trucks. "Then came an order to move out. North and then east toward Mt. Soprano went the convoy until some eight miles from the drop zone, it halted. The position to be defended was a flat valley floor and the north slopes of Mt. Soprano."[23]

Tucker's men unloaded from their trucks, then marched up to the assigned area, and were dug in by 3:00 a.m. Company A was assigned the right flank on the northern slope of Mt. Soprano facing east, their line running down to the valley floor to an east-west road that was the boundary with Company C. The valley floor, that Company C was responsible for, was a very poor defensive position with virtually no natural terrain obstacles to an enemy advance. The Company C position tied in with 2nd Battalion on its left that occupied a hill called Tempone Di San Paolo. The 2nd Battalion's line extended north from Tempone Di San Paolo where it tied in with the 45th Division. At dawn, the two battalion commanders made a personal reconnaissance of their respective battalion lines in order to make adjustments as necessary.

Tucker's troopers now occupied the gap that the Germans had torn in the 36th Division line. It was logical, therefore, that the Germans would exploit this gap. Word was passed to expect an attack later that morning. In the predawn darkness, the two battalions put out listening posts and patrols toward Albanella in order to gain advanced warning of any German assaults.

Mid-morning of the 14th, the missing troopers from Company B arrived in the 1st Battalion CP area. Two of the company's planes had experienced problems on the ground prior to takeoff. With no spare planes, they were forced to distribute the troopers among the planes still on the ground. As Lieutenant Lekson was getting some administrative work done, he heard that the five Company B planes had taken off about an hour after the 1st Battalion serial. "Probably due to an insufficient briefing, the pilot of the lead plane gave B Company a green light over the mountains some six miles south of the drop zone. Upon landing Captain Charles W. Duncan failed to recognize any landmarks and decided to form a perimeter with his group of four officers and eighty men. When dawn came this group could see the Paestum beaches to their north. At once, they moved off toward the beaches. Near the regimental drop zone they were able to obtain truck transportation and a guide who led them to the battalion defense position.

"With the coming of B Company, C Company moved to the north and B Company filled in the center of the battalion sector, astride the road, tying in with A Company on the right."[24]

The missing D Company planeload also reported into the 2nd Battalion during the morning. So other than about seventy-five jump injured troopers, the two battalions were at full strength. As the morning progressed, the Germans began concentrating some strength for an attack against the 2nd Battalion, 504th sector.

Lieutenant Chester Garrison, the 2nd Battalion's S-1, responsible for maintaining the battalion's unit journal, kept apprised of reports coming into the battalion CP during the day. "Fifteen tanks have been sighted to our front . . . six have been knocked out by artillery."[25] The Germans continued to probe the 504th line afterward, but the artillery barrage evidently discouraged German plans for an attack in the 504th sector that day. During the night of the 14th, Tucker's two battalions and the attached units continued to patrol aggressively, as much as three miles forward of their lines.

Back in Sicily, the 505th RCT and 2nd Battalion, 509th, prepared for their missions. The 2nd Battalion, 509th, had been ordered by Fifth Army Headquarters to make the jump at Avellino to block the mountain pass there and cut off German reinforcements coming down from Rome and northern Italy, and the 505th would jump at Paestum to reinforce the Salerno beachhead.

Three C-47 aircraft would carry the 505th Pathfinder team ahead of the main force. The first plane's stick would consist of Colonel Gavin, jumpmaster; Lieutenant Colonel Billingslea, Pathfinder Commander; Lieutenant Albert Konar, 505th team leader with the Eureka set; Corporal George F. Huston, assistant Eureka operator; Corporal Joseph Fitzgerald, 505th Regimental Headquarters Company; two men equipped with flashlights to mark the drop zone if needed; and two riflemen with Company B, 307th Airborne Engineer Battalion.

The jumpmaster of the second plane was Lieutenant Patrick D. Mulcahy, 505th Regimental Headquarters Company; T/5 Jerome V. "Jerry" Huth, Eureka operator with backup set; Corporal Leo T. Girodo, assistant Eureka operator with 505th Regimental Headquarters Company; and the same light and security teams as the first plane.

The jumpmaster on the third plane was Captain Jack Norton; Lieutenant Claiborne Cooperider, with the 505th Service Company in charge of the light teams; and the same light and security teams as the other two planes.

At 9:00 p.m., Norton climbed aboard his plane, and a short time later it began rolling down the runway at the Agrigento airfield. Norton could feel the nose lift up, then the wheels, and finally the plane was airborne. "Our planes flew in a close 'V' formation at an altitude from 6,000 to 7,000 feet along the prescribed course until a few miles off the coast of Italy. It was evident at the time that the navigation of the lead plane would largely govern the results of the pathfinder work. We crossed the coastline at about one thousand feet and jumped at seven hundred feet. There wasn't any wind. The chutes came straight down near the center of the DZ. Groups assembled without difficulty and without casualty. In three minutes Lieutenant Konar's set was in operation. Corporal [T/5] Huth, standing by, had his set ready for operation. The flashlights were not needed as the gasoline sand fire signals were operating in good order."[26]

The 36 planes carrying the 3rd Battalion took off late at 10:40 p.m. from Castelvetrano, Sicily. The nine planes of the Regimental Headquarters and Headquarters Company serial followed the 3rd Battalion, leaving from Castelvetrano. The 36-plane 2nd Battalion serial was airborne at 11:20 p.m. from Comiso, Sicily, while nine planes transporting Company B, 307th Eng. Battalion, left the airfield at Barizzo, Sicily, at 11:30 p.m. The 1st Battalion serial of 36 C-47s was the last serial, lifting off at 1:00 a.m. from Barizzo.

At 1:10 a.m. the 3rd Battalion serial appeared overhead near Paestum and started dropping, followed by Regimental Headquarters and Headquarters Company at 1:20 a.m., the 2nd Battalion at 1:30 a.m., Company B, 307th Engineer Battalion at 1:40 a.m., and the 1st Battalion at 2:55 a.m. The work of the pathfinder teams had paid huge dividends. Captain Norton couldn't have asked for a better operation. "The battalion jump patterns were extremely small and all personnel and equipment were assembled in a remarkably short period of time . . . no battalion taking more than sixty minutes to assemble. Jump casualties were extremely light.

"The marking of the DZ was satisfactory from the standpoint of results achieved and the situation of jumping behind our own lines. It is believed, however, that under normal circumstances Krypton Lights or Aldis Lamps would be more practical from the security viewpoint. Smoke Pots as used consisted of gasoline and sand, and threw off a considerable flame.

"Plane recognition was accomplished with amber lights on the underside of the wings. The lights were easily visible from the ground. Plane formations flew directly over friendly ships in the harbor at Paestum, and also over shore installations. Previous instructions with the additional aid of amber recognition lights were most necessary and no doubt helped prevent a reoccurrence of the disaster, which met the second lift in the Sicilian operation two months previous."[27]

One plane, carrying jumpmaster Lieutenant Jack Tallerday's stick of Company C troopers, had one of its engines hit by antiaircraft fire. The paratroopers and the C-47's crew all bailed out safely and landed in the British zone, near the town of Battipaglia. Because of a problem, two other planes never took off and four others became separated from their formations and returned to Sicily with their paratroopers still aboard.

After the regiment was assembled, it loaded on trucks and was driven to the Mt. Soprano area and placed in corps reserve behind the frontline. That same night, the 2nd Battalion, 509th Parachute Infantry Regiment, still attached to the 82nd Airborne Division, dropped south of the mountain pass town of Avellino, Italy, twenty miles north of Salerno in the Sorrento Mountains. The 509th Pathfinder team, consisting of one eleven-man stick, dropped with a 5G radio beacon and a couple of Aldis lamps, but didn't take a Eureka, because the planes carrying the 2nd Battalion, 509th, weren't yet equipped with Rebeccas. The pathfinders were dropped about a mile south of the intended DZ, and the serial carrying the battalion was only ten minutes behind. Therefore, rather than try to find the DZ, the pathfinders set up the 5G radio beacon and two lights where they landed. The 5G proved to be almost useless in the terrain surrounded by tall mountains on almost all sides. The lights couldn't be seen in time by the pilots coming in a few minutes later and weren't much help.

The result was a widely scattered drop, with some sticks being dropped as much as 25 miles from the DZ. Slightly less than half of the battalion landed near the DZ. Unfortunately, a German armored force maintained a large bivouac just north of Avellino. Some troopers dropped right into the middle of the Germans and were machine gunned in the air or after they hit the ground, still helpless in their harnesses. The lucky ones slipped away in the darkness and hid out until they found other troopers.

Still, about thirty others assembled south of the DZ with Major Doyle Yardley, the CO. An Italian offered to take them to a German truck park, where he said there were 250 trucks. Instead, they walked into a German ambush and were pinned down by machine gun fire and then shelled mercilessly. Major Yardley was severely wounded and taken prisoner. Staff Sergeant William Sullivan, with Headquarters Company, was all alone in a cornfield. "Not long after the jump, it seemed like the whole German Army moved into the area and they were hunting for us—they were hunting us like rabbits. That scared the hell out of me. They were going up and down the rows of corn and shooting anything that moved. The idea of fighting back is one thing—you take a rifle and here comes the enemy. But the idea you were being hunted, there's nothing you can do, you have to hide."[28] Other troopers ambushed the Germans, while others, figuring out that they were far from the drop zone, hid out during the day and moved south by night in an effort to find friendly forces.

On the morning of September 15, Ridgway arrived at the Salerno beachhead aboard an LST, then found his way to Tucker's and Gavin's regimental CPs. After the defeat of their counteroffensive, the Germans continued an active defense, using the hilly and mountainous terrain to its advantage, with its tanks and infantry making localized counterattacks against any ground gained by Allied infantry.

At 11:00 p.m. that evening, the LCIs transporting the 325th RCT and the 3rd Battalion, 504th (less Company H), arrived on Red Beach in the 36th Division sector and began unloading their men and equipment. Most of the men had to wade ashore, such as Sergeant Mike Colella, with Company E, 325th. "The LCI bearing Company E ran aground on a sandbar approximately three hundred yards from the shore. Company E disembarked and waded through waist deep water to the beach, cleared the dune line and waited for daylight and further instructions."[29]

Shortly afterward, Platoon Sergeant George Speakman, with the Heavy Weapons Platoon of Company E, 325th, heard the sound of approaching fighter aircraft. "We were strafed by two Jerry planes . . . no one was hit."[30]

At sunrise on September 16, Captain Robert L. Dickerson, CO of Company E, 325th, got his men ready to move out. "From the bivouac area near the beach, the 325th Combat Team moved to Highway 18, and north along that road to Stazione di Cappucio, on the outskirts of Paestum. The combat team occupied an assembly area one thousand yards northeast of this railroad station."[31]

Later that morning, Dickerson was present when Colonel Harry L. Lewis, the CO of the 325th RCT, approached the 2nd Battalion CO, Major John H. "Swede" Swenson, and gave him verbal orders for his battalion: " 'I have a job for you. Go to the beach. There you will find three LCIs. Get on them with your battalion, less Company G. They will take you up the coast, I believe to a place called Maiori, but I couldn't get much out of Army. When you get ashore, contact a Colonel [William] Darby. He has grabbed off a toehold. They want him to get out, but he isn't the kind to get [out]. He says he is going to stay, but he needs help. You will get detailed orders from him. Are there any questions?'

" 'My mission, then, is to reinforce Colonel Darby?'

" 'Right . . .'

" 'You indicated that I could get detailed orders from Colonel Darby. What am I to do if I can't contact him?'

" 'You'd better make sure that the boats don't leave until you have determined the situation on the beach.'

" 'Will the beach be defended when we arrive?'

" 'There's no way of telling. Darby seems to be hard pressed. You had better assume that it will be. Then, if you run into fire, there will be no surprise.'

" 'Where can I get detailed information on which to plan?'

" 'You have all that I was able to get.'

" 'What about maps?'

" 'Just what you have already.'

" 'On what beach are these LCIs located?'

" 'Damned if I know. You'll just have to hunt for them. When you find them, send me word, I might have more information before you sail.'

" 'Very well, Sir.' "[32]

Dickerson was told that "orders were issued attaching Company G to Fifth Army Headquarters, with the mission of occupying the island of Ischia, in the Bay of Naples."[33]

With his new orders, Dickerson got Company E "loaded on trucks and taken to the beaches near Paestum where the convoy of vehicles was strafed by one German fighter aircraft. This action resulted in loss of time, little confusion, and no casualties.

"The three LCIs were located without difficulty on the beaches. One LCI had become mired in the mud, but after some tugging by her sister ships, and another strafing by the same German fighter aircraft, the LCI was floated and the convoy stood out to sea at about 15:00 hours."[34]

In the 504th sector, Colonel Tucker called an 11:00 a.m. meeting with his 1st and 2nd Battalion commanders and their company commanders. Tucker briefed them on an attack that was to begin at 3:00 p.m.; the 1st Battalion objective was Hill 424 east of Altavilla, while the 2nd Battalion was assigned to capture Hill 344 and another, known as the unnumbered hill east of the town of Albanella. The 1st Battalion of the 505th would screen the regiment's right flank.

Around noon on the 16th, the S-3 of the 2nd Battalion, 504th, Lieutenant John Lekson, received reports relayed from a couple of patrols that had returned after daybreak. "While C Company prepared to move, its combat patrol returned. They had much to report. They had engaged in three firefights. Considerable enemy artillery and mortar fire had fallen on them. However, the resistance seemed so scattered that it was deemed unimportant. A regimental patrol reported that some forty enemy tanks were located on the reverse slope of a hill about a mile and a half southeast of Altavilla."[35]

In the short time he had been at the Salerno beachhead, Lieutenant Lekson had learned from 36th Division officers how the Germans were taking full advantage of the terrain features in the hills. "On the slopes of the hills were intermittent streams, dry now, that had cut deep gullies into the slopes. Numerous additional erosion features such as dips and gullies marred the hillsides. Many of these had steep sides and narrow bottoms. Trails that went from Albanella to Altavilla followed north on noses jutting from the hill mass. These trails dipped through draws and gullies and often formed defiles as they did so. Lining the trails were trees and stone walls. In places the trails moved along terraced levels with drops on one side and walls on the other. A profusion of minor footpaths and trails joined the main trail.

"Cognizant of the terrain and affected by the heavy American artillery, the Germans had adopted a set of peculiar tactics to hold the hills. Occupying only certain features with outposts and observation parties, the enemy would be alerted as American troops entered the hill mass. From their covered positions would come the enemy main force which, after locating the American forces, would maneuver through gullies and ditches to hit the American forces from all directions. Often they were not detected until they were on the positions. With these tactics the enemy had driven out the previous 36th Division attackers."[36]

Just before 3:00 p.m., Tucker's two battalions marched east in a column of companies, with each company in a tactical column of twos. Lieutenant Chester Garrison, the 2nd Battalion S-1, moved out with headquarters company. "The march went across country, ploughed fields, and up a very steep hill. The terrific heat of the day and the stiffness of the walk, together with the excessive weight of the equipment, were too much for the men. They could not keep up with the rate of the march, particularly the [81mm] mortar platoon, several of whom passed out along the way."[37]

Otto W. Huebner was the Company A, 504th, Operations Sergeant. "The march to the objective was long, hard, and tiresome. The winding trails were narrow and rocky, with overhanging brush in many places, which made it difficult to follow. From the last positions on Mt. Soprano to Albanella, the distance was four miles and yet that was only about half the way to the company's objective. Near Albanella, enemy artillery shells began to drop on the column. It was more harassing than harmful, but it slowed the column down considerably. Gaps began to show between men, and it became very difficult to keep contact. The company commander, Captain Willard J. Harrison, told the point to move faster because the column was behind schedule."[38]

At about the same time as the 504th had moved east, the 2nd Battalion, 325th, started for Maiori aboard three LCIs. Because they were moving in daylight, Captain Robert Dickerson, the commander of Company E, was concerned about a German bombing attack. But, "the movement to Maiori was made without incident, and at approximately 22:00 hours, 16 September 1943, the convoy slipped into the cove at Maiori. The ramps were lowered and the troops ran ashore. Since Major Swenson had passed on the information regarding the uncertainty of the beach being secure, the battalion wasted no time in occupying the slopes surrounding the cove. In the meantime, Major Swenson searched for Colonel Darby, while Captain [Roscoe] Roy, Battalion Executive Officer, was left in charge of the battalion, who moved the troops to a bivouac area in a lemon grove near the town square of Maiori, where the night of 16–17 September 1943 was spent."[39]

The 1st Battalion, 504th, found Albanella undefended and moved on toward their objective, with Company A in the lead, followed by Company C, then Company B, with Headquarters Company bringing up the rear. As Company A turned north toward Altavilla and Hill 424, Sergeant Huebner suddenly heard and saw firing up ahead. "As the 1st Platoon reached a creek just north of Albanella, two enemy machine guns opened fire on the point, without inflicting a casualty, but caused the front of the column to take cover. It was easy to observe the fire, for the enemy was using tracer ammunition and the fire was about five feet off the ground. The 1st Platoon leader, Lieutenant Horton put his 60mm mortar into action and knocked out the machine guns in quick order.

"After this short action, the column continued to move again, but at a much slower pace. The men were very tired and began to lag. About this time the enemy artillery began to fall with greater intensity and accuracy. Calls for medics from wounded men in the column could be heard frequently.

"The officers and NCOs had to move up and down the column to get the men to their feet and keep them moving. The men had a tendency to lie down when the artillery came close and not watch the individual in front of him, thereby losing contact. The battalion commander, Lieutenant Colonel Warren R. Williams and Captain Harrison, the company commander, came up to the point many times and directed the route. About 22:00, word came up the column to the company commander that most of Company C and all of Company B had lost contact. Lieutenant Colonel Williams, who was still with Company A, gave the order to Captain Harrison to move anyway to the objective."[40]

At his newly established forward CP in Albanella, Colonel Tucker tried without success to reach his two battalions by radio. Frustrated, Tucker set out to find them in the dark. Tucker had with him his command group, 14 engineers from Company C, 307th Airborne Engineer Battalion, and about 20 troopers of the 505th who had been picked up during the advance into Albanella. As they moved through the darkness, the group was subjected to shelling by German artillery. Journalists Richard Tregaskis, Cy Korman, and Reynolds Packard, along with photographer Bob Capa, caught up with Tucker's group strung out along a drainage ditch next to a farmer's field on one of the trails. It seemed that the Germans had a spotter nearby, because the German artillery fire bracketed the group. Tregaskis heard Tucker say, "We better get out of here. They're getting the range. Let's go." Tregaskis followed the colonel's lead. "We jumped up the bank and sprinted across the field and up a hillside. With the motion of our running we saw a farmhouse bouncing in the moonlight; that would be our immediate objective. We saw another ditch, as the bouncing image of the farmhouse grew larger. We scrambled into the ditch, panting. We were just in time. The shells came again and exploded between this trench and the ditch we had just left.

"The firing lulled, and in a few seconds when thought comes back again, and motion, when the concussion has done its work and gone, Lieutenant Colonel [Leslie G.] Freeman, the regimental executive, and Major [Don B.] Dunham, came clumping over the no-man's land between the two ditches. They had stayed behind to care for Captain Tom Wight [CO of Company C, 307th Airborne Engineer Battalion], who had been hit by the last shell. He was beyond care. A fragment had struck him squarely in the back."[41] Shortly afterward, Tucker and his group moved out again searching for the two battalions.

After the break in the column, the 1st Battalion staff was trying to assist the company commanders in reestablishing a cohesive force in the darkness. Lieutenant Lekson, the S-3, together with Captain Duncan, the CO of Company B, found the break in the column. Lekson listened as the executive officer and the 3rd Platoon leader of Company C explained what had happened. "Their story was brief. Men had fallen asleep. A man looking up saw that the man who had been before him was no longer there. As he called back, he frantically tried to find the column in front of him with no success. The platoon

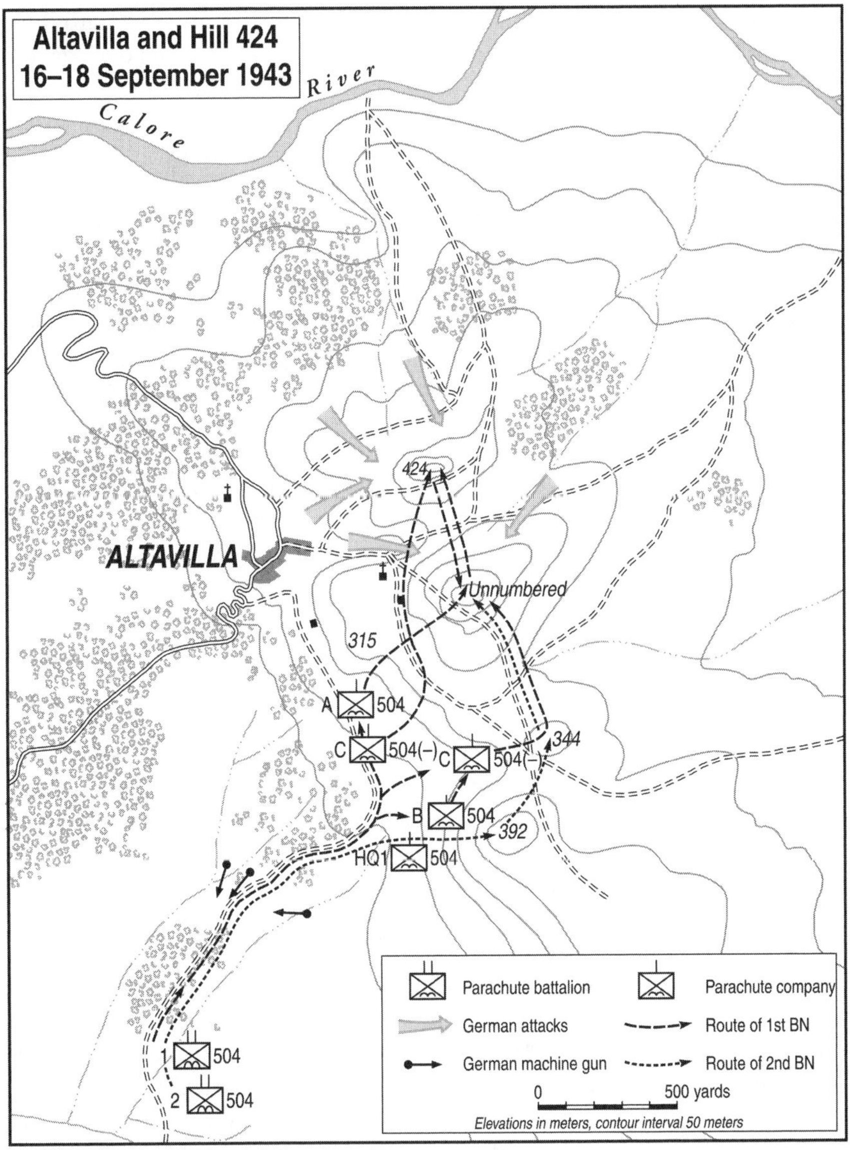

leader, upon hearing the commotion, had sent out a two man patrol north on the trail and had reported the break to the C Company Executive Officer, who was marching at the rear of C Company.

"As I awaited word from the contact patrol, a quick check was made of the forces. The 3rd Platoon of Company C was still on the trail; tied in behind it was B Company, followed by Headquarters Company. Ahead somewhere was A Company and C Company with the battalion commander.

"Soon the contact patrol was back. They had gone north on the trail a short distance but had neither seen nor heard anything. It was decided that I would command this force until contact had been established. The 3rd Platoon of C Company would furnish the point. The march was resumed and the point had gone several hundred yards when machine pistol fire from the left of the trail stopped it. My orders to the point commander were to swing off to the right toward the high ground; bypass the Germans; and when the point got on the hill, halt, and the column would close in.

"The point swung off to the right of the trail and to the east without returning the fire of the machine pistols. It dropped down into a steep gully and then climbed up the fairly steep slopes of the hill. When it reached the top, I ordered the point commander to guard the north side of the hill. As B Company came up it was swung to the west and south [sides] of the hill. Headquarters Company was routed to the east and southeast. As Headquarters Company moved in it was found that the 81mm mortar platoon was completely missing. When we met to discuss the situation over the only map, Captain [Charles W.] Duncan's, it was decided that Hill 424 was farther to the north. The march would be resumed again."[42]

The two platoons and headquarters group of Company C led by Captain Albert E. "Ernie" Milloy had lost contact with Company A during the long halt. Captain Milloy decided to try to regain contact, leading his men east off of the trail and then north along the western slopes of the hills and valleys looking for Hill 424. At approximately 11:00 p.m., they found a well on the northwestern slope of the unnumbered hill, south of Hill 424. While his men filled their canteens, Milloy sent a patrol led by Lieutenant James Dunn across the dark valley below to the north to reconnoiter Hill 424. While Captain Milloy was waiting for the patrol to return, Colonel Tucker and his group found Milloy and his men.

The patrol returned and informed Milloy and Tucker that Company A was not on the hill and that only a few Germans held it. Dunn and his men had also found a route to the top of hill that avoided the Germans occupying it. Tucker decided to take the hill with the force he had, fully expecting the remainder of the 1st Battalion to arrive on Hill 424 shortly afterward.

The two platoons of Company C and Tucker's group moved out around midnight and found the hill undefended. They immediately formed a perimeter defense and began to dig in. As this was in progress, a German patrol walked into their perimeter. The situation in the dark was confusing, with both sides not wanting to shoot their own men, yet having to react to the split-second movements of their enemies. Richard Tregaskis, the journalist, was caught in the middle of the confusing cat-and-mouse, life-and-death game being played out in the dark. Tregaskis heard somebody shout, "'Keep you hands up—high!' Turning fast, I saw Major Dunham at a nervous crouch leveling his .45 at three Germans, who had their hands up. They had thrown their guns on the ground.

I helped to frisk them. They were sturdy, muscular men, wearing the usual square-visored khaki caps of the German infantryman. The prisoners were taken over to the center of the open spot atop the hill, and told to sit down on the open ground.

"From the opposite side of the hill, behind us, we heard the rapid, 'Brrdddt-t-t-t, brrdddt-t-t-t, brrdddt-t-t-t' of a German Schmeisser machine pistol, firing in short bursts. Lines of white tracers blinked across the sky. Then we heard the heavier-toned, slower-paced firing of our own automatic weapons, and a few rifle shots.

"[Major] Dunham, dragging his tommy gun, crawled up the slope to the bare crown of the hill. He kept low, for somewhere on the other side of the hill, very close, according to the sound, snipers lurked. Don was looking for human game, and he moved like a practiced hunter. I watched his feet, and the one knee bending and unbending like the rocker arm of an old side-wheeler, disappear over the crown of the slope.

"A trooper crawled back, and reported, 'Freeman and Richter got hit.' But they had not been badly wounded. It had begun to look like we were cut off on three sides."[43]

Tucker's attempts to contact both battalions by radio continued to be unsuccessful. Two messengers were sent out to find them, but both were killed a short time later.

After discovering the break in the column, Sergeant Otto Huebner helped get Company A moving again. "After proceeding a short distance we came directly into a German occupied position, which surprised us as well as the Germans. The small detachment of Germans gave up without a fight. By this time the company knew we were getting deep into enemy territory. As the point came to a small hill, three or four enemy machine guns opened fire. Everybody hit the ground and it looked as if we were going to have a rough firefight. As the men lay on the ground, word came down the column to fix bayonets and get prepared to charge the enemy positions, which were only about fifty yards to the front. The only real concealment one had was the deep darkness of the night. The squad leaders managed to get their squads into a skirmish line.

"Then a voice rang out along the line, 'Let's Go!' The men got on their feet and took off hooting and yelling like a tribe of Indians on the warpath. The Germans took off on the double without a shot fired on either side. Total captured: one small, skinny medic, and he was too scared to run.

"After the company reorganized, we moved on toward the objective and shortly thereafter came to a hill. The company commander, with a small party, reconnoitered the hill, and on his return summoned the platoon leaders. He told them this was the objective and then gave the company defense orders. He ordered the platoon leaders to prepare an all-round defense, close to the crest of the hill with the 1st Platoon on the forward slope, 2nd on the left, 3rd on the right, tying in all the way around. This was about 02:00 hours, 17 September."[44]

When Lieutenant Lekson found out that his force was on the wrong hill, he and the other officers pulled in their outposts, awakened others, got everyone on their feet, and started north trying to find Hill 424. Lekson put the force in single file, with Company B leading, and moved toward the hill to the north, some five hundred yards away. After reaching the hill to the north, he sent a patrol to the east and one to the north with instructions to find Lieutenant Colonel Williams while and he and Captain Duncan reconnoitered to the north. When Lekson returned to the hill, the 2nd Battalion CO, Major Daniel W. Danielson, had arrived and informed him that they were standing on the unnumbered hill that was his battalion's objective, and his battalion would arrive on the hill shortly.

At about 1:00 a.m., as Lekson was getting his force ready to move north, the patrol from Company B that had reconnoitered the trail to the north returned. "Its leader, Sergeant Gerald Murphy, reported that he had contacted Colonel Tucker near a well on the next hill north. Colonel Tucker's message was, 'Bring the battalion down here at once.' As rapidly as the column could, it moved out with Sergeant Murphy leading the point. Somewhere, after the column started, a platoon of Company C, 307th Airborne Engineer Battalion, had tied in behind Headquarters Company. In addition, some twenty men of B Company, 505th Parachute Infantry, the flank security had joined the column. At 02:00 he halted at a well below the hill and said that this was where Colonel Tucker had been. The S-2 and I, reconnoitering along the trail ran into Lieutenant Colonel Williams, who had just left A Company as it moved up the hill."[45]

After conferring with Williams, Lekson led his force up the hill and joined the defense with Company A. While the men who had been with Lieutenant Lekson dug in, a patrol was sent out to find the 81mm mortar platoon that was still missing.

As the 1st Battalion was trying to find Hill 424, Lieutenant Chester Garrison moved with 2nd Battalion Headquarters Company through the darkness toward the battalion's objectives, the unnumbered hill and Hill 344. "About 21:00, we moved slowly to our high ground objective which we reached about 02:00, after numerous stops. Artillery fire was directed at our column throughout the night. The battalion dug in on the high ground assigned to us. The 1st Battalion was to the hill north of us. F Company and most of the 81mm mortar platoon became detached from us in the dark and were somewhere to our rear."[46]

As of 4:00 a.m. on September 17, Colonel Tucker, on Hill 424 with his regimental headquarters command group and part of Company C, was still not able to make contact with either of his battalions. Even though two men sent earlier had both been killed, the regimental S-3, Major Don B. Dunham, and the operations sergeant, Jack Furst, volunteered to try to find the 1st Battalion.

About five minutes after they left, German burp gun fire was heard. Approximately ten minutes later, Furst made it back to the perimeter and reported to Colonel Tucker that Dunham had been killed.

At dawn, Company C trooper Corporal Ross Carter got his first look at the scene of heavy fighting earlier between the 36th Division and the Germans. "Cadavers lay everywhere. Having seen only a few corpses in Sicily, it was a horrible experience for us to see dead men, purpled and blackened by the intense heat, lying scattered all over the hill. The body of a huge man, eyes bloated out of their sockets, who lay dead about twenty yards from me, had swollen and burst. First lieutenant's bars were on his shoulders. His pistol belt with open compass case and empty binocular case bore witness to the quality of our equipment: the Krauts had looted them. A broken carbine lay by the body."[47]

As Carter surveyed the carnage around him, Captain Milloy, the Company C commander, sent a patrol from Hill 424 toward Altavilla to the west. At the base of the hill the patrol spotted a German self-propelled gun and light tank. The patrol returned and asked for a bazooka to take back down the hill and try to knock out the German armor. After obtaining the bazooka, the patrol was moving down the hill once more when it encountered a German combat patrol, which drove them back up the hill.

A second patrol sent by Milloy to the north ran into a large number of German infantry advancing toward the hill. A firefight broke out as the patrol attempted to make it back up the northern slope of Hill 424, killing one trooper before they were able to get back to the perimeter.

A short time later the German tank and self-propelled gun west of Hill 424 opened fire on the Company C foxholes on the western slope. The Company C troopers could hear German infantry moving toward them up the slope. When the Germans got about 75 yards away, the troopers opened up simultaneously with deadly accuracy, decimating the German infantry before they could take cover or maneuver. Corporal Ross Carter took careful aim with his Tommy gun, making sure each burst found its mark. "Since only a few of our machine guns and automatic rifles had reached us, it was up to the riflemen and Tommy gunners to hold off the assault. The boys lay in their holes around the top of the hill and calmly squeezed off shots. American riflemen were always among the best in the world, and our Legion riflemen were among the best in the Army. In about thirty minutes the attack was broken up."[48]

The survivors withdrew down the hill as the two German armored vehicles increased their fire. After pulling back, the Germans fired on the troopers' positions on the hill from three sides with small arms and machine guns in an effort to pin them down and inflict casualties.

Shortly after sunup, seeing troop movement on the hill to the north and believing that they might be friendly troops, the 1st Platoon of Company A was ordered to investigate. From his foxhole, Sergeant Otto Huebner, with Company A, observed the scouts leave the perimeter defenses ahead of the platoon.

"As the lead scout, Private First Class Ralph R. Young went down the crest about two hundred yards, he spotted troops to his front. Thinking they were friendly troops he did not take cover and was fired upon and killed. The platoon leader, Lieutenant Duvall went out to help him and was hit in the legs with shrapnel from a mortar shell."[49]

Lieutenant Lekson instinctively moved over the crest of the hill, where he saw the two men lying below. "Captain Harrison [Company A, CO] ordered the 1st Platoon back into their foxholes. As they covered him, he ran out and brought back the platoon leader [Lieutenant Duvall], under both friendly and enemy fire.

"Shortly after 08:00, we observed enemy troops moving from the edge of Altavilla into the valley toward us. As Lieutenant Colonel Williams and I watched this force of some seventy-five to one hundred Germans moving, another smaller enemy force appeared from the south edge of Altavilla and swung around Hill 315. As the Germans approached within three hundred yards of B Company, our men opened fire. The Germans broke into small groups that moved forward from bush to bush and terrace to terrace.

"Lieutenant Colonel Williams ordered troops on the east edge of the perimeter into position facing [west toward] Altavilla. Enemy artillery began to fall on B Company and into the [perimeter].

"By this time, some fifty men including about six automatic riflemen were firing at the enemy. As the Germans sought cover, the 60mm mortar of the 2nd Platoon of B Company drove them out into the open. The 60mm mortar squad leader, Sergeant Douglas Morehead, was directing the mortar fire from the crest. His mortar crew was some fifteen feet behind him. From down on the forward slope Lieutenant William Meerman, 3rd Platoon leader, B Company, was calling out targets to Morehead. As the German attack slowed down and then dropped back, Lieutenant Colonel Williams ordered the mortar to stop firing. It had expended much of its ammunition and resupply was not certain.

"Enemy artillery concentrations of thirty to forty rounds each and mortar fire hit the slopes of the hill. Then a mist began to gather in the valley obscuring Altavilla and parts of Hill 424. The battalion waited.

"Though the mist did not last more than a half hour, it seemed much longer. The troops on the forward slope were tense and word was being passed back and forth to watch for enemy infiltrations.

"When the mist thinned, an enemy tank opened fire on the hill. At the northeastern edge of Altavilla, on the road that ran east along Hill 424 could be seen three German tanks. All three tanks soon began to fire into foxhole after foxhole along the northwest slope on the hill. The tanks first fired on the foxholes on the western edge of A Company, then along the 2nd and 3rd Platoons of B Company.

"A direct hit on a bazooka position of the 2nd Platoon, B Company blasted two men out of the position. The platoon leader of the 2nd Platoon of A Company and his aid man ran down. They were joined by the 1st Platoon leader and his platoon sergeant. Another shell burst wounded the A Company platoon leader before the bazooka team could be evacuated. On the right flank of the 2nd Platoon, B Company, was a company strongpoint dug in among a cluster of trees. Two shell bursts killed six men there.

"As the tanks fired, a German attack was launched from the northwest along the draw against the 1st Platoon of A Company. In a short firefight the German force was driven back with some loss. Though the German tank support had hit the battalion ['s] northwest perimeter hard, the 1st and 3rd Platoons of A Company had not been affected by the tank fire.

"While the tanks had been active, the artillery observer had gained radio contact. Soon, VI Corps artillery was firing on Altavilla and on the tanks. As the German tanks and infantry withdrew, enemy artillery began to pound the hill.

"I, with a command post detail, moved to the aid station to collect ammunition from the wounded. Some of the troops had reached a critical low in small arms [ammunition]. In the aid station were some twenty wounded. About ten had been killed so far in the morning's action."[50]

Two hills to the south of Hill 424, Lieutenant Chester Garrison, the 2nd Battalion, S-1, saw a plane coming toward the hill from the west. "About 08:30 a P-38 flew over, dropping two bombs in the D Company area, killing five men . . . Private First Class John Di Rienso, Private James E. Lechner, Private First Class John C. Le Count, Private John J. Monti, and Private James H. King, Jr."[51]

Still unable to contact the two battalions, and seeing movement that appeared to be friendly troops on the unnumbered hill, Colonel Tucker decided to withdraw to the unnumbered hill to the south about 9:30 a.m.

Shortly after the attack on the unnumbered hill was broken up, Tucker with the two platoons of Company C and Regimental Headquarters began coming into the perimeter of the 1st Battalion. After a conference with Lieutenant Colonel Williams, Tucker ordered Hill 424 retaken. Company A would lead the assault, with Company C following, and Company B would take over the defense of the unnumbered hill. At the same time, Tucker sent a radio message to the 2nd Battalion, which was occupying the hill to the south, to move to occupy the hill that was the present 1st Battalion position.

About 10:30 a.m. Sergeant Otto Huebner moved out with Company A, led by the 2nd Platoon. "They passed down the gully and started up Hill 424, when a machine gun opened fire, killing three men instantly. The 3rd Platoon, which was in the rear of the column, moved around the west side of the hill in a flanking movement, attacked the [enemy] position and eliminated it quickly.

"The 3rd and 2nd Platoons abreast moved up to the top of the hill at once, with the 1st Platoon following. As the platoons reached the top of the hill, Captain Harrison ordered the 2nd Platoon to move to the right, 3rd to the front, and 1st to the left."[52]

Lieutenant Reneau Breard, the assistant platoon leader of the 1st Platoon of Company A, quickly advanced toward the top of Hill 424. "We went up there and it was unoccupied, the place was full of dead 36th Division people. As we went over the hill, we found the Germans coming up to reoccupy it."[53]

Sergeant Huebner helped to get the company deployed. "Just as the platoons were moving to the crest in their sector, a strong force of Germans started moving over the crest on the opposite side. Company A immediately set up a hasty defense.

"One advantage the company had was the fact that we were on the hill while the main German force was still climbing. As for surprise, both were stunned, but the Germans threw the first punch.

"Every man hit the ground and scuffled about seeking any kind of cover or concealment. After a few seconds elapsed and men gathered their wits, each man who could bring fire to bear on the enemy opened up without being told. This caused the enemy to hunt for cover and as the men noticed how effective their fire was, they seemed to gain confidence and the company's firepower really increased. For the first ten minutes it was each man for himself; but after a short time the men began to coordinate and give each other a little mutual [fire] support. By this time, the officers and NCOs began coordinating the company's fires.

"Finally, the 1st Platoon drove the Germans back over the crest and closed in fast, taking up positions along the crest. The 1st Platoon then swung part of its fire to the right in front of the 3rd Platoon, causing the Germans to withdraw in that sector. Every step the Germans would take backward, the company would take forward, using every possible means of cover. Finally, the company with all three platoons abreast held the entire crest of the hill. The fires soon ceased; the attack was repelled, but the company suffered eight casualties, though the enemy suffered many times more.

"Immediately, the company commander ordered a hasty defense set up in a moon shape design with the 1st Platoon on the west overlooking Altavilla, the 3rd Platoon to the north, and the 2nd Platoon to the east, all tying in. Company headquarters [was] to the rear and center of the company, and a couple of small security positions [were] to the rear facing the unnumbered hill for rear security."[54]

For the first time since arriving on Hill 424, Company A trooper, Private Albert B. Clark, took time to notice the view to the west. "We found out why the Germans wanted this hill so badly. It had a perfect view of the beachhead and they could see everything that went on down there. There was a small airfield that fighter planes were using. When one started to take off, they would send a couple of shells."[55]

While the officers and noncoms got the company reorganized, Sergeant Huebner scrounged what he could from the scene of devastation around him. "The sight on the hill was an unpleasant one. This was the same place that the 1st Battalion of the 142nd Infantry, 36th Division four days previously was finally forced to withdraw after great losses were inflicted on both sides.

"The hill was infested with scattered dead Germans and American soldiers, supplies, and ammunition. There were machine guns still in their original emplacements, rifles, packs, clothing, ammunition belts, machine gun [ammunition] boxes, and stacks of 60mm mortar shells scattered all over the hill.

"The ammunition was gathered up and distributed through the company as soon as possible. The platoons began digging positions in their sectors. Foxholes dug by the 142nd Infantry were improved and used in many cases. Slit trenches were also used in many instances instead of foxholes, because the hard ground made digging difficult.

"The officers and NCOs directed the exact spots of positions. We tried to arrange them to cover the most likely enemy approaches, have each position give mutual support to the one on the right and left, with observation, fire, and depth in that order of priority. To add firepower, the machine guns that were left on the hill by the 142nd, were put in the platoon positions.

"It was about 11:00 now and the men were still digging their positions, when enemy tanks began to shell the hill. One could hear the tank fire; about a second later the shell would burst. The men dug deeper because the fire was extremely accurate, causing many casualties.

"The tank fire continued on without a let up. The men were quite hungry about this time, for they had not had any rations since the day before. A few were lucky enough to find a little bread and jam in the dead Germans' packs. Water was also scarce. There was a well down the draw to northwest, about two hundred yards, but every time anyone would go for water, they would either get in a firefight or be shelled.

"The company radio operator had finally gotten through to battalion on the unnumbered hill. Lieutenant Colonel Williams, the battalion commander, told Captain Harrison, the company commander, that Company C would be on their way to help.

"It was impossible at this time to evacuate the wounded, but the company medical personnel were doing a fine job of taking care of them. Their greatest assistant was the little morphine syringe.

"The shelling increased with mortar and heavy artillery falling and everyone stayed low in his hole. At noon the shelling became almost unbearable. It was so bad that the sides of the foxholes began caving in. The air was thick with smoke and dust from the bursting shells, and then—all quiet.

"The quiet period continued for only a minute, as heavy enemy machine guns began blasting away from the front of the 1st and 3rd Platoon areas, supporting a German assault force approaching the positions.

"The men ducked their heads in the foxholes to escape the machine gun fire. A couple of alert squad leaders immediately noticed the machine gun fire, approximately two feet off the ground in most places, and yelled to the men to get their heads up and start firing—which they did. The platoons laid down a heavy base of fire with every possible weapon being fired. The 60mm mortars were employed singly with each platoon. The 1st and 3rd Platoon mortars began laying down fire within a hundred yards of the front line positions traversing back and forth.

"The company radio operator finally managed to communicate with battalion again on the unnumbered hill and the company commander requested artillery support."[56]

Lieutenant Lekson was at the 1st Battalion CP on the unnumbered hill when a radio transmission from Company A on Hill 424 was received. "Captain Harrison radioed a request for artillery to Lieutenant Colonel Williams. He had spotted two tanks in the churchyard north of Altavilla. Relaying the message to the forward observer, Lieutenant Colonel Williams asked if Captain Harrison could adjust."[57]

As the assaulting German infantry climbed the slope of Hill 424, Sergeant Huebner hoped that the VI Corps Artillery fire would not be too late. "When the company opened up its final protective fire, it momentarily stopped the assault. After a few minutes of hesitation, the Germans began rushing the positions in groups, while another group would support by fire, but for some reason their fire was inaccurate.

"In the 1st platoon, a Private [First Class Peter] Schneider, of German [birth] and who spoke German well, began shouting orders to the Germans in their native tongue [and] caused a considerable amount of confusion, making it possible for his platoon to pick them off. This still did not take away their aggressiveness, for they continued the firefight and moved forward by leaps and bounds.

"Soon, the hand grenades flew like snowballs from both sides, but for every shot or grenade from the Germans on the 1st and 3rd Platoon positions, they received two back. The officers and NCOs were up in the front foxholes firing with the men. Heavy artillery began falling on the hill, only this time it was falling in the middle of the enemy position, which was deeply appreciated by the company, because shortly after, the attack seemed to become disorganized and easier to control by fire. Before long the Germans began to withdraw down the crest. Once the 2nd Platoon leader had to yell at a couple of men to get back in their foxholes, for they began to pursue the enemy. The company had killed approximately 50 Germans, but had suffered almost half that number in casualties.

"The squad leaders now checked on their men, redistributed ammunition and reported in detail to the platoon leader. The platoon leaders did the same and reported to the company commander. Evacuation of the wounded was still impossible and the best place for them was in their foxholes.

"For the next few minutes everyone on the hill thought the attack started all over again due to the fact that in the 2nd Platoon area on the east, a small arms firefight began. We didn't know if the Germans were getting aggressive again or not, but it was only a five or six man patrol trying to penetrate the lines. They were repelled without much trouble.

"Shortly after this small firefight, the enemy started shelling the hill again. Much to our delight, Company C had just come up the hill to help. The battalion commander and his CP group were with them, including the battalion medical officer. The medical officer was needed greatly and performed miracles, including two amputations, with his meager stock of medical supplies.

"The battalion aid station was set up in a gully near the battalion CP. Evacuation of the wounded was still impossible, and to add to the evacuation problem a heavy concentration began falling on the hill, including air bursts, which caused many additional casualties."[58] Two of the Company A dead were Lieutenant Ed Wall, the executive officer, and First Sergeant Edwin L. Rouse, both killed by one of the air bursts.

Late that morning, radio contact was finally established between Tucker's CP on hill 424 and the 2nd Battalion, and Tucker ordered the battalion to move north one hill.

Lieutenant Garrison helped get the CP ready to move. "At 13:00 the battalion began to move forward to the hill originally assigned to them, but which had been held by the 1st Battalion. We moved out with E Company in the lead, F Company, Battalion CP, Headquarters Company, and D Company. Another climb; it took at least three hours to get everybody there."[59]

After arriving, the 1st Battalion command group organized an all-around defense of Hill 424. Company A was shifted to cover the west and northwest side of the hill, while Lieutenant Lekson assisted in getting Company C deployed. "C Company was placed in position along the north side of Hill 424, tying in with A Company on its left.

"The next German attack, about 15:00 hours, struck against A Company from the west slope of Hill 424 and against C Company from the northwest. The attack was preceded by a heavy artillery and mortar preparation that lasted almost an hour. Again, enemy machine guns covered the advance of an estimated two German companies. The Germans coming up the slopes could be seen as they got within three hundred yards of the riflemen's positions."[60]

Sergeant Otto Huebner, with Company A, waited in his foxhole on the western slope as German panzer grenadiers moved relentlessly up the hill. "The Germans began advancing by fire and movement, taking advantage of the cover afforded by the good approaches. They were hitting all three platoons of Company A with the main force coming up the west slope.

"Due to the shape of the hill mass, it was impossible to lay down a good final protective line. The field of fire was very limited, in places only 50 yards. One outpost was cut off and later eliminated, while the other fought its way back, giving the company very little notice of the attack. With the large volume of fire the enemy was laying down, it sounded as if the entire German Army was attacking.

"Mortar targets were picked and fired upon as close as 50 yards in front of the troops. Its fire was very effective and most valuable in disorganizing assaults.

"In one squad of the 3rd Platoon, the BAR team was killed and four or five Germans penetrated that area. Fast thinking NCOs grabbed a couple of men from the two-man foxholes, charged the penetration area, killing all the Germans. The platoon sergeant jumped in the BAR position and took over command.

"Frequently, potato masher grenades would be thrown, but unless they went off in the foxhole, they had little or no effect. One dropped in a foxhole with a man, but he jumped out and when the grenade went off, he jumped back."[61]

Lieutenant Reneau Breard was now leading the 1st Platoon of Company A, after the platoon leader, Lieutenant Whitman, was wounded by mortar fire. Breard and his men poured fire down on the German infantry at close range with devastating effectiveness. "It was just a good old infantry fight. We were on top looking down."[62]

For a few moments it appeared to Sergeant Huebner that the hill might get overrun if they couldn't get artillery support and get it soon. "The company commander kept calling back to battalion for artillery fire. The [battalion] commander said the only kind he could get was from the naval boats off the beaches, and it was very dangerous to fire so close to friendly troops. The company commander said he had to take the chance and the battalion commander agreed.

"The firefight continued on, and in its second hour casualties began mounting on both sides. The word was passed along for the men to get deep down in their holes as the Navy began firing.

"The shell bursts, landing on the northwest slope, seemed to rock the entire hill. The foxholes cracked like glass, and the topsoil around [them] sprinkled into the foxholes with every burst. One could hear terror-stricken screams coming from the Germans along the slope of the hill, which made one's backbone quiver."[63]

Lieutenant Breard and his platoon were positioned on the northwest slope, closest to where the naval rounds were impacting. "I thought they were going to cave my hole in."[64]

As Sergeant Huebner took a peek over the lip of his foxhole, he could see the German infantry getting pounded mercilessly. "A few Germans still tried to come forward, but the bombardment disorganized them completely, and before long the enemy withdrew. The hill was still ours, although Company A suffered twenty more casualties during that attack. The Germans suffered many, many more."[65]

When the 2nd Battalion arrived on the unnumbered hill, Company B was relieved and it moved out to rejoin the 1st Battalion while the fighting was still raging for Hill 424. From the crest of Hill 424, Lieutenant Lekson watched Company B cross the saddle between the two hills. "As it started to cross along the east slope of the saddle, several rounds of enemy artillery fell along the column. As men lay in a narrow sunken trail, some one hundred rounds fell. Before a lull in the firing allowed the group to cross the saddle, two officers had been wounded and some fifteen men killed or wounded. The company commander estimated that some forty or fifty tanks, between one thousand and two thousand yards away had shelled his company. Most of the rounds that fell seemed to be armor piercing."

After arriving on the unnumbered hill, Lieutenant Garrison helped to get the 2nd Battalion CP set up. "The artillery became particularly stiff about 17:00. One barrage was constant for two minutes. Colonel Tucker set up in our Battalion CP area . . . many of the regimental staff were casualties. About 17:30 a messenger came through with information that we were to return to Albanella. This was much to our disgust as we have the hill and are not suffering undue casualties."[66]

General Mike Dawley, commander of the US VI Corps, had received no information regarding Tucker's two battalions all day. Fearing the worst, and correctly believing that Tucker and his men were now surrounded, Dawley had sent a runner to Tucker with a message instructing him to try to break out while he could still do so.

Colonel Tucker ignored the order to retreat to Albanella; his troopers had captured the two hills and they were going to keep them. That night, a sound-powered phone line was run to Tucker's CP. When General Dawley was patched through, Tucker explained the situation. When Dawley suggested to Tucker that his two battalions retreat because they were cut off from other friendly forces, Colonel Tucker replied, "Retreat hell! Send me my 3rd Battalion!"[67]

CHAPTER 6

"WAIT UNTIL A TRIUMPHANT ENTRY IS ORGANIZED"[1]

Colonel Tucker got what he wanted. At 12:01 a.m. on September 18, his 3rd Battalion was relieved from attachment to the 325th RCT. Small-scale German attacks continued during the night against the rest of the 504th holding the hills east of Altavilla. About 3:00 a.m. the 3rd Battalion, 504th, supported by the 1st Battalion, 325th, broke through German resistance to occupy Hill 344 and contact the 2nd Battalion, 504th, on the unnumbered hill northeast of Albanella. At dawn, a combat patrol from Company A moved out from Hill 424 to contact the enemy. They moved through the ruins of Altavilla and then about a mile north, returning two hours later without finding any Germans. A second combat patrol was then sent north to gain contact with the Germans. A mule train carrying supplies arrived early that morning, providing the first meal for most of them in the last forty-eight hours. During the afternoon, the second combat patrol returned without contacting the enemy. After establishing outpost security, most of the men were finally able to get their first real sleep in almost 72 hours. For his leadership and heroism during the capture and subsequent fighting for Hill 424 and the surrounding area, Colonel Rueben Tucker was later awarded the Distinguished Service Cross.

Shortly after dawn on the 18th, Company E, 325th, finished relieving the 1st Ranger Battalion on Mt. San Angelo, west of Maiori. The previous day, as his men were making the long march up from the beach area, Captain Robert Dickerson had made a personal reconnaissance and met with Captain Frederick I. Saam, the S-3 of the 1st Ranger Battalion, at their CP to formulate a plan for the relief. Captain Saam told Dickerson, "The Germans have been hitting us in small groups every morning about dawn and in the late afternoon about twilight. We have beaten them off every time, except one, when they shelled us off this hill, and we had to attack and retake it. They usually come up on the north side of the point, through those woods. They work in pairs and get in close as hell before we spot them. Most of them are big young guys out of the 16th Panzer Engineer Battalion, although we found one the other day from the Hermann Göring Division. Watch that hospital down in Nocera. I think it is a Kraut headquarters, because I have never seen an ambulance go in there. Other vehicles of all types have been going in and out of that place at all hours of the day and night. I haven't fired on it yet. We will be going down there soon, now that you people are here. We will let you know what the score is, and you can direct the fire on it, if my suspicions are confirmed. About the relief—send your people on up here. There are enough holes for one company in my area. The 1st Rangers will stay until morning and show your people the ropes. We will pull out in the morning. By the way, stay off the Point. We will leave all of our small arms ammunition and telephones on position, as your people will need these items."[2]

Dickerson then made a reconnaissance of the 3,700-foot mountain. "From its summit could be seen the hotly contested Nocera-Pagani Pass, the narrow valley through which ran Highway 18 and the double tracked railway from Rome to Battipaglia, and of course, any movement by the enemy in that area. From its south slopes could be seen the secondary road coming north from Maiori, and Chiunzi Pass. From the Point, the approaches to the town of Cava and the village of Camarelle could be observed.

"The mountain itself contained several terrain features. On the eastern edge, the cliff side, it was almost vertical. No vegetation of any kind grew here. The southern slope was bare in spots while sparsely wooded with scrub oak in other areas. The grade of the southern slope was approximately forty-five degrees. The north slope was bare in spots, while in others it was heavily wooded. Inside these woods were entangling vines and thorn bushes. This factor alone materially affected fields of fire and observation for the crew served weapons."[3]

About 11:00 p.m. Dickerson heard his men beginning to arrive at the Ranger CP. "They were exhausted, water was low, and they were in general, disorganized. Base plates of mortars were clanging against the rocks, muttered curses could be heard, but no infractions of light discipline could be seen. Platoons were reorganized as quickly as they assembled. Stragglers were collected. Platoon leaders were briefed as they arrived."[4]

Sergeant Mike Colella helped to get his men in position. "The men were very tired, but some new emplacements and foxholes had to be dug. This proved to be nearly impossible because of the granite, which lay just beneath the loose volcanic topsoil. The balance of the night was spent digging in or emplacing the crew served weapons and dispersing the troops to their positions. Very little sleeping was done."[5]

After moving his 1st Platoon, the Weapons Platoon, and Company Headquarters into position, Captain Saam, the Ranger S-3, requested that Dickerson not move his 2nd Platoon into position because he was concerned that his Rangers might fire on them by mistake as they moved into their positions. Dickerson agreed, and the 2nd Platoon spent the rest of the night at the Ranger Observation Post.

As dawn approached, Captain Dickerson prepared to deploy his 2nd Platoon. "At approximately 07:00, at first light, 18 September 1943, the enemy began a shelling of the position held jointly by the 1st Ranger Battalion and Company E, 325th Glider Infantry. This artillery fire lasted until 07:15, approximately. Three Rangers were wounded, while Company E, 325th Glider Infantry had one killed and four wounded.

"The relief was carried out in great haste after the fires ceased. By 08:00, the Ranger force had evacuated the position, and command had passed to Major Swenson, who now had the responsibility for Mt. San Angelo.

"There was no further enemy activity for the day. Company E spent the day improving the position. The two-man foxholes were dug deeper, and 'undercuts' were dug in these holes. These undercuts were simply recesses dug away from the center of the hole and parallel with the surface of the ground. They furnished cover from tree [and air] bursts. Overhead cover for the foxholes was also fashioned by cutting trunks of trees which had been felled by artillery fire, and placing a layer of these logs over about one-half the opening of the foxholes. During the day, the defensive fires, which were planned by me the day before, were registered and range cards were made. All fires were observed except those designed to meet the enemy threat from the east, or cliff side, beneath the Point. These fires could not be observed because of enemy fire on the Point when the slightest movement was detected."[6]

Company F, 325th, relieved the 3rd Ranger Battalion on Mt. di Chiunzi. Corporal Daniel Clark, an assistant squad leader with Company F, had made the long climb to the top of the mountain during the previous day and most of the night. "We took up positions on a line just before the top of the mountain. The scrub trees made vision difficult. Our supplies and water came up to us by horse or mule."[7]

Supplying the troopers defending Mt. San Angelo and Mt. di Chiunzi was a difficult logistical problem. While positioned on Mt. di Chiunzi, Private First Class Andrew A. Devorak, with Company F, 325th, was most concerned with the shortage of water. "We had to send patrols down to get water each day. You only got one canteen cup of water daily. That was the only time you could eat. In time, we looked like 'Willie and Joe' in Stars and Stripes. We developed sores about the size of a nickel with a grayish crust. I suspect it was scurvy."[8]

Private First Class Darrell C. Dilley, with Company F, 325th, was an ammo bearer for his BAR team and had experienced a difficult climb up Mt. di Chiunzi with his heavy load. When he was hit by shrapnel during a German shelling shortly after arriving, Dilley and the medic "just fixed it up the best we could, as I didn't want to go down the mountain and then back up."[9]

During the previous eight days Company H, 504th, attached to the Ranger Force, had held the railroad tunnel and Chiunzi Pass against almost daily German attacks. During that time the German force was estimated to outnumber the Ranger Force by as much as eight to one. Providing invaluable support to Company H and the Rangers in repulsing the attacks was the 319th Glider Field Artillery Battalion, while the D, E, F, and Headquarters Batteries of the 80th Airborne Antiaircraft Battalion protected Maiori and relieved the Rangers on outpost duty.

There was little activity on September 19th in the 325th RCT or 504th RCT sectors. The 504th was relieved in the morning by the 36th Infantry Division; the 2nd Battalion, 325th, continued to hold Mt. San Angelo and Mt. di Chiunzi; while Company H, 504th, continued to hold the Chiunzi Pass.

At dawn that day, when his movement was unlikely to be detected by German artillery spotters, Captain Dickerson left his CP to check on his Company E, 325th troopers. "The southern slopes of Mt. San Angelo were covered by a cold clammy fog bank from the valley. The wind, which blew from the northwest, dispersed this fog when it was within fifty yards of the crest. I was awakened at first light by the tinkling of many bells and could make out a herd of sheep approaching the position from the south. Exactly at 06:00 hours a hostile mortar barrage smothered our position while the sheep continued their slow climb toward our position. One of our mortar observers heard the bells begin to tinkle out of rhythm and alerted the machine guns. Four light machine guns and two heavies were trained on the sheep. As one of the clouds was dissolved by the wind blowing from the west, a force of Germans was seen on the south slope directly in the rear of the 1st Platoon's position. The Germans, who had come up the hill crawling with the sheep, jumped to their feet at twenty-five yards from the 1st Platoon and charged the 1st Platoon. The [machine gun] section leader and I were both so amazed and dumbfounded, not to mention being frightened, that, for a second, neither acted.

"As this machine gunner's dream was realized, the section leader, Corporal [Donald T.] Harmon, fired a belt of continuous fire at the stricken Germans. Our machine guns and the 1st Platoon killed all but a few, who escaped to the north cliff. Though surprised, the Germans retired well under the circumstances, leaving only a few of their wounded, but most of their dead. This force was later estimated at one hundred fifty men by various observers near the company CP.

"This action was reported to the battalion commander [Major Swenson], who ordered a search made of the enemy dead and wounded to establish the identity of the unit engaged.

"Before this order could be transmitted to a searching detail, the enemy artillery located in the Pagani-Nocera valley began a merciless shelling of the position which lasted from 07:00 to 08:00.

"At 08:00, approximately, the shelling abated in fury, and the wounded and dead were evacuated. This operation was completed at about 08:15. The 1st Platoon had approximately twenty effectives at this time.

"At approximately 08:20, a messenger from the 1st Platoon reported to me that the enemy were seen coming up the cliff on the northeast side of the position toward the Point. He stated that their number was unknown, but that they were armed with one large mortar and two machine guns. The fires of the 81mm and 60mm mortars were placed on this group of the enemy, but the fires failed to stop the enemy's advance.

"The enemy shelling increased at 08:35, which restricted movement considerably. Tree bursts were harassing the 1st Platoon, but they were bearing up under this ordeal very well because of the undercuts they had made in their foxholes the day before. Lieutenant [Jim A.] Gayley, 1st Platoon leader, transmitted a radio message at 08:40, which could barely be heard, stating that he needed help to hold the position, for the enemy had worked to within grenade throwing distance of his 1st Squad near the Point. He was told to hold the position, and that final protective fires would be fired for two minutes. This message was transmitted to the weapons supporting Company E, and the fires were brought down, with the exception of the machine guns on the left, or north flank. Repeated messages were sent to the section leader of this section, and finally, two or three timid bursts were fired. Battalion was notified of the situation at this time."[10]

The shelling was intense, and this was the first combat for these troopers. Word was passed from the 1st Platoon to medic Private First Class Tad Lainhart "that a sergeant in one of the front line foxholes was suffering from combat fatigue. I moved forward along the row of foxholes looking for this man when a fierce firefight broke out. I yelled to a private and asked where was the sergeant. The private rolled a grenade down the side of the mountain and without looking back said, 'I don't know, and besides, I've got troubles of my own,' then picked up his rifle and started firing.

"I finally located the sergeant. He was suffering from combat fatigue and mumbling incoherently, 'Get down, get down.' I finally convinced him that I would take him to safety; so he crawled out of the foxhole and we moved back."[11]

The mountain crest precluded the use of naval guns and the 319th Glider Field Artillery because the trajectories could not hit the Germans, who had worked their way to just below the crest of the mountain. All that Captain Dickerson had were mortars to put high explosive fire on the enemy. "The 81mm mortar section [led by Lieutenant Joe Shealy, Headquarters Company, 2nd Battalion], which had been the most effective weapon against the enemy, reported a total of fifty rounds on position. Since the mortars were firing an average of five rounds per minute, it was rapidly deduced that this supply would not be sufficient. Again, the battalion commander was called and notified. He assured me that the supply was to be replenished momentarily, for the supply train was just passing the battalion CP, headed in the direction of Company E. He further stated that they had about twenty cloverleaves of 81mm HE [high explosive] Medium ammunition. This was welcome news, but luck was still with the enemy, as all of this ammunition was faulty, and failed to detonate. The battalion commander was again notified of the urgency of the situation. He gathered all the personnel around the battalion CP, and dispatched them to the ammunition supply point at the base of the mountain after a supply of 81mm HE Light ammunition. In the meantime, the mortar section firing in support of Company E, was rationed to an average of one round per minute, which exhausted the supply in approximately twenty-five minutes. The only mortar support available to Company E was the 60mm mortar section, which was doing yeoman service, which had enough ammunition to keep up the fire for a short period. The fires of these weapons were placed on the cliff over the Point.

"The Germans, seeming to notice that no machine gun or heavy mortar fire was being delivered on the left or north flank, infiltrated a small group through the heavily wooded area near the Point, and assaulted the 1st Squad of the 1st Platoon, which held the terrain nearest the Point. In the hand-to-hand fighting which ensued, the Germans succeeded in eliminating the 1st Squad and occupying the squad position and the Point. This was the situation at approximately 09:20.

"At this time I notified the battalion commander of the situation and was told to hold the position somehow until the reserve could be committed. The battalion reserve consisted of one platoon, called the 'Commando Platoon,' which was a special unit made up from volunteers in the battalion who did patrolling and other special tasks as desired by the battalion commander. This platoon was led by Lieutenant Wade H. Meintzer. In the meantime, the fires of the 60mm mortars were placed on the Point and the position occupied by the enemy.

"At approximately 09:30, the Commando Platoon passed through the 2nd Platoon of Company E, and assaulted the Germans on the Point, when the 60mm mortar fire was lifted. They were successful in ejecting the enemy and restoring the MLR [main line of resistance].

"After the Germans were ejected from the Point, I ordered the 1st Platoon to reorganize. The Commando Platoon, under Lieutenant Meintzer, was attached to the company as reinforcement, and assigned an area in the western half of the 1st Platoon's position. The positions near the Point were reoccupied. The time was approximately noon.

"Ammunition was needed, as was water, food, and first aid packets. At 13:00 the needed supplies were on their way up the mountain by carrying parties under Sergeant [Louis E.] Famigletti [Company E supply sergeant].

"At approximately 14:00, while this reorganization was in progress, the enemy attacked the south slopes near the position held by the machine gun section of the Weapons Platoon. This attack was beaten off by the 2nd Platoon using rifle grenades, hand grenades, and rifle fire. The Germans did succeed in working a small group up the deep gorge to the right or to the south of, the 1st Squad, 2nd Platoon. None of the fires of the platoon, or of the machine guns, could be brought to bear on the enemy in this situation. I ordered the 60mm mortars to fire a round on the south slope of the mountain near the Point, record the range and elevation, then to decrease the range twenty-five yards each time a round was fired until the mortar fire was falling in the gorge, which was approximately fifty yards in front, or to the east, of the 1st Squad of the 2nd Platoon. This was accomplished in approximately five rounds, and the enemy group in the gorge, numbering three men, was destroyed. At 16:00, the enemy had apparently disengaged, for no more firing of small arms was heard."[12]

That same day, the 325th RCT (less the 2nd Battalion) and the 3rd Battalion, 504th (less Company H) were trucked to the beach near Paestum, then at 3:00 p.m. the following day boarded LCIs and LSTs and sailed to Maiori, landing about 6:30 p.m. The 3rd Battalion, 504th, made the long, hard climb up to the Chiunzi Pass to relieve their own Company H troopers who had been holding the pass and the key railroad tunnel against German attacks since arriving there on the night of the 10th of September.

Lieutenant Edward Sims and his Company H platoon had defended the key tunnel that could have allowed German forces to pass south through the mountains. "During the ten days we defended in this area, the Germans made a number of attempts to get through, but were repulsed. They did get a few small patrols into our position and on one occasion, took two of my men prisoner. During part of the time in this position, we received supporting fire from a 4.2" Chemical Mortar unit and from the 319th Glider Field Artillery Battalion."[13]

As part of the Ranger Force, Company H, 504th; the 2nd Platoon, Company C of the 307th Airborne Engineer Battalion; the 319th GFA Battalion; D, E, and F Batteries, and Headquarters Battery and the Medical Detachment of the 80th AA Battalion were later awarded the Presidential Unit Citation for this action. This was the first of many awarded to units of the 82nd Airborne Division during World War II.

While still holding Mt. San Angelo, Company E, 325th, received an unexpected visit from General Ridgway. Captain Robert Dickerson had not prepared for an inspection. "My company had been engaged with elements of the Hermann Göring Division for several days. We were very short of ammunition, food, and water. I had not shaved in about ten days because of the water shortage and I did not insist that my men do so. Who appears from the valley below but General Ridgway. His first question was, 'Why aren't you shaved?' He would not accept the excuse about water, but pointed out that I was the senior officer on the mountain and expected to set the example and that I should shave immediately, then require my men to do so. Then he asked how many casualties we had suffered, complimented me on the performance of Company E, and approved all my weapons and troop dispositions. His last words were, 'You and your soldiers have done a fine job.'

"I thought there was no way General Ridgway could be a better division commander. He was most respected but not feared. We welcomed his visits. He never talked down to us, but spoke as though we were on his level. He never used a profane or vulgar word and his tone was always conversational. He could be ruthless but never cruel. He gained the respect of my people by pointing out our mistakes in a gentlemanly, but firm manner, and he therefore secured instant compliance."[14]

The 376th Parachute Field Artillery Battalion and the 320th Glider Field Artillery Battalion landed by ship on September 23. The 456th PFA Battalion, which had returned from Sicily to North Africa, would not catch up to the division until later.

Major William R. Beall, the 3rd Battalion, 504th executive officer, was acting as the battalion commander while Major Emory S. "Hank" Adams recovered from malaria. Sergeant Robert Tallon, with Headquarters Company, 3rd Battalion, 504th, was digging his foxhole on a hillside when Beall and his aide approached. "Beall had his orderly construct the major's foxhole into the side of a terrace with about four feet of soil on top of it. This would prevent shrapnel from hitting him when we were attacked with aerial artillery [bursts].

"About 22:30, a shell hit about thirty feet from me. Moments later a runner from one of the line companies, lost in the dark, fell into my foxhole, saying he had a message for Major Beall. I said, 'He's just a few feet away' and then I called in a low voice, 'Major Beall?' No answer . . . Then I called again . . . No answer. Suddenly my heart seemed to jump into my throat as I thought about the dirt on top of the major's foxhole.

"As quickly as I could, I scrambled over to his foxhole. It had caved in and buried him under four feet of dirt. I called for help and medics. We dug as fast as we could with hands and helmets."[15]

Lieutenant Moffatt Burriss, the 3rd Battalion S-2, was nearby. "I was one of those who started digging with his hands as I tried to reach the major in time."[16]

After digging frantically in the darkness, they uncovered Major Beall. Tallon could tell that they were too late. "When we reached his body, we didn't need the medic to tell us that he was dead."[17]

Burriss could sense the sadness that the battalion felt as the news spread of Beall's suffocation. "His death was a great loss to our unit. He was an outstanding soldier—a leader whom we had confidently followed into battle."[18]

On the morning of September 25, Company B, 325th, moved up the supply trail to relieve Company E, while Company A, 325th, was ordered to clear German infantry that had dug in near the top of the northern slope of Mt. San Angelo. Lieutenant James Helmer, the 1st Battalion communications officer, and a couple of his men accompanied the assault troops. "The Germans had machine gun nests around the top of the mountain. As we got half way up the mountain the slope became so steep it was a great effort with full pack, weapons and ammunition just to climb the hill. Our men were using hand grenades to clear out the machine gun nests and some of the Germans jumped out of their nests and fled down the other side of the mountain. I had two of my men with me with phone line reels and I kept reporting our progress to battalion command. Then I think we were at least three-fourths of the way up the mountain when it appeared that I was the only officer left in the area. I just kept urging the men forward and keeping in touch with the colonel. Finally, it appeared that a few men ahead of me cleaned out the last machine gun nest and we were on top of the hill."[19]

After reaching the top of the northern slope of Mt. San Angelo, Company A relieved the Commando Platoon attached to Company E. After being relieved by Company B, 325th, Company E was ordered to relieve Company F, 325th, on Mt. di Chiunzi, which they did that afternoon.

On September 26, Company B, 325th, and one platoon of Company A were ordered to attack and clear the Germans from the southern slope of Mt. San Angelo and push southeast and link up with the British 46th Division. As the Company B runner, Private First Class Clinton Riddle had the difficult task of carrying messages up and down the mountain under fire. "We gathered our forces together and made an attack on the German positions at noon. We caught the Germans eating. The mortars were heavy on the fire on the enemy. It held most of them down in their holes. Our company commander [Lieutenant Richard Gibson] and a lieutenant [Herbert R. Dew] were shot. Two of our boys in Company B were killed and several wounded. Part of the Jerries were killed, others captured, and some escaped down the mountain where the English finished them off."[20]

The 3rd Battalion, 505th, was trucked to the Chiunzi Pass area on September 27. There, the battalion dismounted and moved through the frontline positions of the Rangers and the 3rd Battalion, 504th, shortly before nightfall and began a push through the mountains toward the open plain south of Naples, twenty miles to the northwest. On the right flank, the VI Corps advanced toward Avellino, which the US 34th Infantry Division captured on September 30. It was during this advance that the 2nd Battalion, 509th paratroopers dropped around Avellino began to filter in to link up with the American forces driving north. After hiding out from the Germans for almost two weeks, over 500 of the 640 troopers of the battalion would eventually be picked up.

The rest of the 505th RCT moved by LCI to Maiori on September 28 and were driven by truck to catch the 3rd Battalion, 505th. With the 3rd Battalion, 505th, still in the lead, the 505th, 504th, and 325th RCTs moved across the plains toward Naples, fighting German rear-guard delaying actions and occupying Castellammare di Stabia on the evening of September 29.

The 3rd Battalion, 505th, continued to lead the swift advance past Pompeii and Mount Vesuvius the following day against token resistance. That evening, the 505th was attached to the British 23rd Mechanized Brigade for the final push into Naples the next day.

On October 1, 1943, the 505th RCT and the British 23rd Armoured Brigade approached the outskirts of Naples, where they were ordered to halt while the British made a reconnaissance of the city. Colonel Gavin was up front with the lead elements of the 505th. "I was standing with the advance guard, discussing the situation, when the Regimental S-3, Major Jack Norton approached.

" 'Colonel,' he said, 'We are to wait until a triumphant entry is organized.'

" 'A triumphant entry!' I exclaimed. 'How in the world can we organize such a thing? It takes participation of the natives.' I had never put anything like that together in my life, and visions crossed my mind of Napoleon's colorfully clad soldiers entering European capitals that had just capitulated, beautiful nubile women leaning over the balconies tossing flowers, much waving of handkerchiefs, and bands playing. And I recalled the entry of Allenby into Jerusalem—and here I was told to organize a triumphant entry.

"Word came down that General Clark was going to come to the head of the column and that he would lead the triumphant march into the city. Then word arrived that we were to lead them to Garibaldi Square. I found it on the map; it was in front of the railroad station. But suppose instead of people tossing flowers there were Germans tossing grenades from the rooftops. And in any event, the masses of people milling around in the streets and throwing candy and offering bottles of wine to the troops all had to be dealt with."[21]

General Mark Clark wanted army and civilian press photographers, newsreel cameramen, and reporters to see him entering Naples as the conquering hero, at the head of his men. This was to be one of many such publicity events that he staged.

General Ridgway foresaw the potential problem and had a solution: "I halted the whole division some five or six miles from Naples and sent for the Chief of Police. He arrived within a couple of hours, and I gave him explicit instructions. I told him I wanted the streets of Naples cleared completely, because when we came in we were coming fast, and anybody in our path, either German or Italian, was to get hurt. We gave him time to get back to town and carry out this order, and then we went in."[22]

Gavin decided that he would lead the procession into Naples in a jeep to act as a guide for the column, followed by Clark and Ridgway riding in a half-track, with the 3rd Battalion in trucks following immediately behind. Gavin then briefed his staff of the plan. "It was mid-afternoon before we were fully organized and Generals Clark and Ridgway took their places in the column. Finding my way in was not so difficult as I had anticipated, and the streets were ominously empty. The map took us right to Garibaldi Square, and as we pulled up into it, there was hardly a soul in sight.

"Later I learned that thousands of people had massed at the Plaza Plebiscito about a mile away in another part of the city. It was here that the conquerors traditionally had been received, and the people had assumed that that was where the Allied generals would make their triumphant appearance."[23]

As the column of trucks carrying the 3rd Battalion, 505th moved into the city Sergeant William Blank, with Company G, heard firing in the distance. "We moved into Naples without too much difficulty and set up a defensive perimeter at Garibaldi Square. We closed off the square to prevent a congregation of civilians. There was spasmodic shooting from the rooftops by what the civilians said were diehard Fascists. Thousands of people came to the square. Most of them had weapons, which they promptly turned in. We broke the rifles in half and made a pile of them.

"The town was pretty much destroyed, including the public water system and everything useful. This was done by the Germans on their way out of town. G Company spent the night in a bombed out railroad station. The next day we moved to a bombed out theater where we were organized into patrol groups. My group was assigned to the area near the docks, which by this time was beginning to unload supplies. Our biggest problem was controlling the bread lines at bakeries, where there was a limited amount of bread being produced due to the limited supplies."[24]

Shortly after entering Naples, Major Edward "Cannonball" Krause, the CO of the 3rd Battalion, 505th, took the American flag he carried with him to the post office, where on behalf of the 82nd Airborne Division, he raised the Stars and Stripes over the first major city liberated in Europe. A couple of hours later, Krause was told that the Germans were planning to blow up a reservoir that supplied much of the city's drinking water. Krause ordered Lieutenant Harvey J. Zeigler, the executive officer of Company H, 505th, to take a platoon and move to the reservoir without delay. Upon arrival at the reservoir, Zeigler found it to be already destroyed. Local citizens told them of another reservoir close by, and Lieutenant Zeigler led his platoon to the second reservoir, which he found to be intact. He immediately deployed his platoon to guard the reservoir. A short time later, Zeigler received word from other local citizens that the German engineers had mined a bridge on the only road leading north out of Naples. Taking four troopers with him, Zeigler moved two miles through an area not yet cleared of the enemy and found the bridge, which was guarded by a few Germans and a Mark IV tank. Zeigler and his small group drove off the enemy force and the tank guarding the bridge and established a defensive perimeter on the far side. He sent one man to get help from the 307th Airborne Engineer Battalion to deal with the demolition charge wired to the bridge supports. Zeigler and his men held the small bridgehead during the night while the engineers removed the explosives, thus saving the bridge.

Because much of the water system was destroyed by the retreating Germans, disease began to spread through both the Italian civilian population and the US and British Army soldiers in Naples. Sergeant Blank was of one the many unfortunate victims. "After several days I was taken sick with malaria and jaundice.

After a few days at the evacuation hospital, I was sent to the 3rd Convalescent Hospital just outside the city in an area that was designed for a World's Fair. It was a tent hospital, which had just arrived from the States.

"While there, we were bombed for three nights in a row. The first night we lost a number of men, some from the 82nd. My row of tents took two direct hits and we counted fourteen dead at that spot. The hospital had not been properly marked and the Germans probably thought it was a supply depot."[25]

Lieutenant Colonel Mark Alexander received orders on the morning of October 4 that his 2nd Battalion, 505th, would be attached to the British 23rd Armoured Brigade. "The 2nd Battalion was trucked to a position about halfway between Naples and the Volturno River, just short of the area held by the Germans. We arrived at about 18:00 hours with the mission to drive to the Volturno River, about fifteen miles to the northwest, to save five canal bridges in route to the Volturno River and the village of Arnone on the southwest bank of the river. The bridges were essential to the movement of the armored brigade and eventual crossing of the Volturno River.

"Rather than wait until morning, I directed two platoons of about twenty-four men each to move out as fast as possible in the dark to take the first two bridges. Each platoon had a light machine gun and a bazooka team. The battalion followed in column on both sides of the road."[26]

Company F led the battalion as it approached the first bridge, which was taken without incident. Spencer Wurst had been busted from sergeant to private in Sicily when an empty wine bottle was tossed into his slit trench while he was away, and the commanding officer assumed Wurst had drunk the wine. Private Wurst and his platoon were following the two lead platoons toward the second bridge. "We approached the bridge, which was already partially destroyed, sometime towards midnight. At least two and maybe three German machine guns from across the canal took us under fire. Very fortunately for us they were shooting high, but from the first slug that went over our heads, it wasn't a split second before everyone was in the ditch. I can still see the tracers whizzing two or three feet above us. I am thankful to this day that the Germans didn't have guns covering the ditches. The guns were positioned forward, from twenty-five to fifty yards off to the left and right of the road, and they really poured it onto us."[27]

Lieutenant Colonel Alexander was walking along the road with the battalion, just behind Company F. "The leading platoons had alerted the Germans as we heard fire fighting ahead of us. As we marched along on this very dark night the Germans let loose on the battalion, with tracer machine gun fire skipping down the concrete road ahead of us. Of course, both columns of men on both sides of the road took a dive into the ditches on the roadside. It was so dark that we did not know there was a five foot concrete ditch on the right side of the road. First, I heard thuds and banging as the men on the right side of the road hit the concrete bottom; then moans and curses. When daylight came

I could see cut and bruised faces from the dive to the bottom of the concrete lined ditch on the right."[28]

Up ahead, Private Wurst just stayed down in the ditch while the German machine guns continued to fire in the darkness. "We didn't return much fire. We remained in the ditch waiting for orders, and the MGs finally stopped. The orders were that we would go into defensive positions and start attacking at first light. The 1st Platoon, the point, dug in on the south side of the bridge. The 2nd and 3rd Platoons went into all-around circular positions and dug in, the 2nd Platoon moving off to the left of the road, and the 3rd Platoon, which was mine, moving to the right. We had to string out and dig individual foxholes.

"We remained in these positions throughout the night in a high state of alert, because we were in such close contact with the enemy. Usually, we tried to pair up, two men to a fighting position, digging two-man holes whenever the situation allowed. People performed much better when they had someone with them. With two men to a hole, when we were not in battle, we could also take turns staying on the alert and sleeping or resting. That night, however, no one got any sleep. The unit's defense area was just too large to permit us to pair up. I remember it was very cold. With jaundice and malaria coming on, and a very empty stomach, I spent an entirely miserable night.

"At first break of light on October 5th, a tremendous firefight broke out in the 1st Platoon's area, a position close to the road, by the partially destroyed bridge. The canal was about twenty feet across, and the Germans were still in position on the other side, or had moved back in through the night undetected. The 1st Platoon lost a number of men, and so did the Germans, although they didn't hold us up too long."[29]

Lieutenant Colonel Alexander got his battalion moving a short time later. "We drove on ahead to the third bridge. The Germans had blown about half of the bridge, but other than for intermittent German machine gun fire from a farmhouse about one hundred yards to the right, we could cross between bursts of fire and I led my men across. About this time D Company, which I had moving parallel to the road about one hundred yards to our right flank, took the farmhouse and silenced the machine gun.

"Ahead of us about one-third mile I could see Germans retreating north on the road. I brought forward an 81mm mortar and they had a good shoot, very accurate as they could see their targets. The Germans moved out fast ahead of us and left a horse drawn wagonload of ammunition and guns, plus a 35mm antitank gun. We drove forward rapidly, took the fourth and fifth canal bridges and set down for the night to attacking the village of Arnone and the railroad yard the next morning.

"A Company of the 1st Battalion under command of Captain Ed Sayre had been attached to my 2nd Battalion in our advance. Captain Sayre had tripped a wired mine and was severely injured. A Company was still held back in reserve.

"The last three miles of our drive we had straddled the road, with the railroad running along parallel and about one hundred yards to our left; the railroad and road converging at Arnone."[30]

As Company F moved into Arnone, they were hit with artillery fire and then with a counterattack. Private Wurst and the 3rd Platoon were south of the town: "We could tell by the amount of incoming artillery and small arms fire that the 1st and 2nd Platoons were having quite a fight in town. Eventually, we received orders to move forward. We moved on the double to help our comrades, going from one covered position to the next. We got into town and deployed to the left of the company position, where it was reported that the Germans were attempting to counterattack. We had our hands full in our portion of town. We moved quickly through Arnone, passing the Company CP. The scene that sticks in my mind, because the CP area was like a shed with an open side, and this served as a collection point for the wounded and the dead. We saw them lying there as we passed through; I think most of the fatalities and wounds were caused by the heavy artillery fire we had been receiving. It turned out that after the artillery barrages, an enemy company had hit the 1st and 2nd Platoons from the west, and a German battalion from across the river had joined them in the attack."[31]

As Company F was being hit, Company E moved into the railroad yard to clear the enemy from F Company's flank, with the 1st Platoon led by Lieutenant David L. Packard at the point. Julius Axman was the acting platoon sergeant. "The 1st Platoon advanced to the railroad yard on the right bank, climbing the twelve foot elevation to the yard's level. We had scouts out—[Private First Class Ben N.] Popilsky, [Private Thomas] Burke, and [Corporal Edward] Carpus; [Private Alvin E.] Hart was also a lead man. Lieutenant Packard led the main body up the right side. I was directly behind Lieutenant Packard. The 1st Platoon squad leader, Sergeant [Edward G.] Bartunek, was on the left flank, Corporal Carpus had the 1st Squad, but was also acting as scout.

"When we reached the rear of the second railroad car, the Krauts opened up on us from both sides and the front. We all hit the dirt and when I looked up, Lieutenant Packard was in a standing position and firing his Thompson. I yelled for him to get down, which he did. He gave me an order to take five men and circle around to the left; the fire was intense as I moved to the rear."[32]

As the Germans hit the point of the platoon from three sides, Corporal Carpus glanced over as the two scouts, "Ben Popilsky and Tom Burke dashed to my right." Carpus then heard Packard say "something like, 'Let me get them!' He stepped out to the front of a car and took a burst of burp gun fire. As he fell he said to me, 'Put me under the car!' No luck, he was already dead."[33]

As the burst hit Lieutenant Packard, Private Earl W. Boling dove for cover between a set of tracks. "As I hit the dirt I called, 'Medic!' to try to get medical aid for the lieutenant. As I was lying between the rails of one set of tracks, I rolled over to get between two sets of tracks where I was not quite as exposed to enemy fire. Every time I attempted to move I was coming under automatic weapons fire with tracers and other bullets hitting the rails a few inches from my face. I finally spotted the gunner on a railroad signal tower and returned fire until he fell from the tower."[34]

Once behind cover, Private John Keller tried to figure out what to do next. "[Corporal] Jack Francis was in a shell hole about twenty feet northeast of where I was positioned. I could hear him trying to raise E Company to our rear. He was saying, 'E Company, can you hear me?!' and repeated it several times, then commented, 'Damn the batteries must be dead.' "[35]

As Sergeant Axman and five men began moving toward the rear to hit the flank of the Germans, he ran into the assistant platoon leader, who ordered him to cover the right flank instead. "We were quite fortunate to have a little cover, as railroad ties were piled up along the bank about twelve inches high in places. I crawled to a position where I could observe a bunker and alternate positions where heavy fire was coming from. Captain [Talton W. "Woody"] Long and the rest of the company was completely cut off from us."[36]

Sergeant Otis Sampson and his mortar squad were bringing up the rear of the 1st Platoon column, hauling their heavy load of a 60mm mortar and ammunition. "The sound of machine gun and rifle fire broke out forward of us; freight cars obstructed our view. I brought the squad to a halt and gave the signal to, 'Get down!'

" 'Nothing unusual about running into opposition . . . knock it out and continue on,' were my thoughts as I lazily lay there taking advantage of the rest.

"[Private] Jack Hill, Captain [Talton] Long's runner, came running around the back of a freight car that sat just to the left of us. There was a serious expression on his face as he said, 'Hey, Sarg, Lieutenant Packard has been killed and the platoon is pinned down! And nothing is being done!'

"My first thought, 'I've got to get to the front!'

"Turning to [Private First Class Harry G.] Pickels, I said, 'Take over!'

" 'Let's get the hell up front. Jack, lead the way!'

"Hill took off at a run and I followed. We worked our way to the left of the yard and ended up at the left front of a freight car. Dense foliage was on our left. 'Jerry' was in control and I knew something had to be done and fast.

" 'Cover my back!' I quickly said to Hill, and I saw his long legs take off for the rear to position himself.

" 'If I can only hold them up long enough for the platoon to get organized,' I thought, and dashed forward, well out in front along the tracks that were barren of cars and went down firing at two helmeted Germans that were sighting in on me. The bullets were whizzing by. . . . My helmet interfered with my sighting. With one sweep of my right hand I knocked it off.

"I tried my best to get one or two shots off at a time to save ammunition and to have more control of the Tommy [gun]. I know I wasn't short on targets as I silenced one gun after another. With no more action from the front, I moved to the left bank, near a switch box.

"A burst of burp gun fire shattered the branches just forward of my head. About a five foot bank ran at left angle to the higher railroad yard and continued on out into the flat lands for a couple of hundred yards or more, starting just forward of me. I saw the heads and shoulders of two helmeted soldiers using the bank's top to support their machine pistols. I was zeroed in at a range of about fifty feet at eleven o'clock. Picking the one on the right, I figured he was the one that had missed me. I knew I wouldn't have a second chance and I made sure of my first; his face just disappeared. On his right, the soldier had ducked down, but came right back up and got the first burst in, which again just cleared my head. A couple of quick shots and he too picked up some .45 slugs; his face just disappeared too. A third one appeared just to the right side of the last, a quick burst sent him to the protection of the bank; I doubted if I had hit him.

"I checked my inserted clip to see if I had enough rounds in it for another possible shoot-out. I counted eight, and reached for another [clip]. There wasn't any! Frantically, I searched with the thought, 'I couldn't be out of them!' I scanned the area thinking, 'I must have lost them in the commotion I had gone through,' but I saw no full ones. A feeling of panic seized me. I had gone through most all of my ammunition; I must have been fighting longer than I thought. Time had stood still.

"I hadn't thought of myself. I just happened to be in the right place at the right time; the enemy's control over the front had to be stopped. How I accomplished the job is simple. I just wasn't hit. Now I had little to fight back with if more Jerries popped up. I was licked. . . . I needed help! 'Mortar fire!' I yelled, repeating the command and giving the short range and direction to get mortar fire behind that bank.

"A Jerry crawled the near bank and tried to take me out with a concussion grenade. It landed a little to my right rear. I glanced its way when it hit and saw a funnel shaped form shoot upward from the explosion. Just glad it had not been a potato masher.

"Like a prayer answered from heaven, a mortar shell exploded about twenty feet back of the bank where the two Germans had been killed . . . a perfect round. I looked around, amazed at the short time it took to put the mortar in action. The sight that met my eyes will go to my grave with me, for there was [Corporal] Pickels and [Private] Watts right out in the open at about four o'clock from where I lay, facing north with the side of the freight car for a background. Pickels had a squinted face as he sighted in the M4 sights with a look of expecting to feel the impact of bullets. But it didn't interfere with the work cut out for him. Watts sat on the ground, his legs crossed under him to the right of the mortar, a shell in hand, ready to feed another to the tube as soon as he received the command. The mortar tube looked almost vertical; utility wires dominated the area above. It was a worry that some may be hit. I felt proud of those two men. I did not intend for them to come forward as they did, but to set up in a protected position. They knew there was only one way to get the job done quickly. My voice must have told them I was in trouble. They were willing to sacrifice their lives to help me and the rest of the platoon when help was so badly needed.

"A large German soldier, in a lumbering run, tried to escape to the rear of the five foot bank to get away from the bursting shells. Carefully I took aim to be sure of preserving my precious last rounds. I let one off. . . . As if hit in the head by a sledgehammer, he went down. I put another one into him to be sure. Another tried his luck, but with the same results. A third started, but changed his mind, knowing the fate of the first two. They were trying for the protective coverage of the foliage to their rear along the railroad bank.

"I had but a few rounds left when [Private] John Burdge came running up from the rear between a freight car and the foliage, his long BAR in his hands. 'Where are they?' he excitedly asked, ready to do battle."[37]

The action by Sergeant Sampson was instrumental in knocking out several German positions on the left or west side of the railroad yard. Private Tom Burke had crawled between the railroad tracks under intense automatic weapons fire and killed a German machine gun crew with grenades. Individual acts such as these began to turn the tide.

Finally, Corporal Jack Francis got the radio working again. "I was trying to get Captain Long on the radio to relay a range for the British artillery that was backing us up."[38]

Captain Long received the call for help from his 1st Platoon. "I was south of the railroad station and east of the railroad a bit. I double-timed the reserve platoon (2nd Platoon) up to the railroad station. I jumped a ditch, moving to the east a little to use the station building as cover. [Private] Dave Comly, a runner, who was second behind me, was hit while in the air jumping the ditch; his death was instant. I always thought the shot came from a sniper in the station building."[39]

Sergeant Sampson was still near the embankment west of the railroad tracks when the 2nd Platoon arrived. "I heard [Private Dennis] O'Loughlin's voice behind me.

" 'Do you want some mortar fire up there?'

"Looking back down I saw him, loaded down with the mortar and a bag of ammunition, not counting the rest of his equipment.

" 'Where in the hell did you come from?' I asked, wondering at the time what a 2nd Platoon man was doing up with the First.

" 'Captain Long sent me up. I've lost my men and the lieutenant trying to get through, but I've got the mortar and some ammunition.'

" 'Yes, let's give them a few rounds.'

"O'Loughlin's mortar fire itself helped to keep Jerry held down. He was set up at the bottom of the V-shaped ditch just to my rear. O'Loughlin was a good man to have around, cool and steady. It was the first time I had worked with him in action. . . . It wouldn't be the last."[40]

After getting pinned down for a short time, Captain Long arrived with the rest of the 2nd Platoon. "I next recall being up in the station area and to the left (west) of some railroad cars. There was some machine gun and rifle fire coming from the left front, it seemed to be coming from a grown up area of foliage just west of the railroad tracks. I recall calling for artillery fire and trying to adjust by reference to pre-designated concentrations. I don't think the salvo did much good except scare them off. I know I was pretty upset when I was told that we had used up our allocation."[41]

The German force around the railroad yard and west of Arnone was of company strength, supported by an additional battalion just across the Volturno River. The short British artillery barrage caused the German company to withdraw across the river over a foot bridge that was still intact.

As darkness closed in, Lieutenant Colonel Alexander, the 2nd Battalion, 505th CO, decided to pull Company E and F back to better defensive positions in anticipation of a possible counterattack by the German battalion just across the river. Alexander moved Company A, 505th, up on the left of Company E and had them dig in for the night. Both companies had evacuated their wounded to a forward aid station.

Alexander called back to his headquarters to get a doctor to attend to the wounded. "We had twenty-four or twenty-five wounded and sheltered under a culvert, but no doctor. I got on the field telephone and told one of our doctors that we needed him at the forward aid station. He insisted that I should take [the wounded] back to him at the rear CP. I told him we had no transportation and also that the road had not been cleared of mines. [The doctor] argued and I told him to come forward or I would come back there and kick his ass all the way forward.

"He did not arrive, so I headed back to the rear to get him. I looked down the road and there he comes, medical bag across his shoulder, a white bandage around his head (helmet on top), and limping. I said, 'What happened to you?'

"He said, 'You go to hell!' and continued to walk toward the forward aid station and the wounded.

"I said, 'OK.' He was going in the right direction, so what more could I say?

"I went down the road a little farther and met Dr. Franco [another of the battalion's doctors] and asked him what happened. [Franco] said he was watching the ambulance head toward our forward positions when it hit a mine and blew up in the air, coming down in a pile of junk. He then said he ran to the site. He was standing there looking at what was left of the ambulance when a voice called out, 'Don't just stand there you dummy! Get me out from under here!' Franco said he pulled [the doctor] out, bandaged his head and off he went, headed for the front. The ambulance driver had been killed."[42]

Alexander's troopers had captured all five bridges as ordered. The next morning he drove to the headquarters of the British 23rd Armoured Brigade and reported to General H. R. Arkwright, informing him that his 2nd Battalion, 505th troopers had captured all of their objectives.

One of the 505th chaplains, Captain George B. Wood, took a few volunteers with him into Arnone and the railroad yard and recovered the bodies of

Lieutenant Packard and the others killed the previous day that had not been evacuated. The night of October 7, the 2nd Battalion, 505th, and the attached 1st Battalion, 505th, were relieved by the British and trucked the next day back to Naples to continue occupation duty.

Back in Naples on the 7th, a huge time bomb left behind a false wall in the main post office building by the retreating Germans, exploded, killing or wounding upward of one hundred people, primarily civilians. The 307th Airborne Engineer Battalion was immediately assigned the job of searching for, finding, and disarming any other time bombs that might have been left behind.

The following Sunday morning, October 10, many of the troopers were sleeping late in various public buildings in Naples in which they had been billeted. While General Ridgway was attending church services he heard the low rumbling sound of a huge explosion in the distance. "We left at once, to find the barracks where the engineer battalion had been quartered had blown up. I will never forget the tragic sight. Arms and legs of American soldiers, killed in their sleep, were sticking pitifully out of the rubble on the second floor. We were never able to establish definitely whether some of the engineers' own demolitions went off by accident. I still believe, though, that it was the result of a German booby trap."[43]

Lieutenant James Rightley, the platoon leader of the 1st Platoon, Company B, 307th Airborne Engineer Battalion, was away from the barracks when it exploded. "I had been ordered to take some men and check out a building for explosives. We were doing this when the blast occurred. The 1st Platoon was hit hard by the explosion."[44] Although Rightley lost 23 of his men killed, three miraculously survived, though severely wounded.

Sergeant Frank M. Miale had lost many of his friends in the explosion. "The irony of it all was that some of the men were out looking for demolitions under other buildings, while ours was the one to suffer the fate that we wanted to prevent in others. The loss of these men can never be replaced, nor can the memory of the men who died there ever be forgotten by we who knew and cherished their friendship."[45]

When word spread of what had happened to the engineers, Lieutenant Reneau Breard, a platoon leader with Company A, 504th, and others in his building took action to prevent the same thing. "We went down in our cellar and we cut off every wire we could find, trying to make the building safe."[46]

That same day, several promotions and changes of responsibility were made. Brigadier General Maxwell Taylor had been the temporary assistant division commander after the death of General Keerans. But General Eisenhower had assigned Taylor as the liaison with the Italian government representatives at Eisenhower's headquarters. As a result, Gavin was promoted to brigadier general and named as assistant division commander. "I hated to leave the 505th, since I had been through so much combat with it, but it would still be in the division with me. General Ridgway arranged for a brief star-pinning ceremony in front of the Questura, the city police station, which we had been using as headquarters."[47]

The 505 executive officer, Lieutenant Colonel Herbert Batcheller, was given command of the 505, while Lieutenant Colonel Alexander moved from CO of the 2nd Battalion to 505 regimental executive officer, and Major Benjamin H. Vandervoort took command of the 2nd Battalion.

General Mark Clark wanted to keep the 82nd Airborne Division as part of his Fifth Army for the drive north to Rome and beyond. However, Eisenhower had decided to use the division to spearhead the cross-channel invasion the following spring. Clark asked for and received permission to retain the 504th RCT on a temporary basis, promising to return them to the division in time to participate in the cross-channel invasion. Ridgway, bitterly disappointed that the 504th would not be accompanying the rest of the division, sent a letter to Clark in which he stated that the division would be leaving a major part of itself in Italy. Clark responded in a letter, assuring him that he would take care of the 504th RCT. Ridgway directed Taylor to keep pressure on Clark to expedite the return of the 504th to the division.

Clark immediately put Tucker's tough veterans to work. The 504th was attached to the US 34th Infantry Division and on October 27, 1943, was moved by truck from Naples to Alife, in the Apennine Mountains.

Lieutenant Ed Sims, a platoon leader with Company H, 504th, was briefed on the combat team's mission after arriving at Alife. "Our job was to protect the right flank of the US Fifth Army and to maintain contact with the British Eighth Army on our right. We were restricted to movement by foot and had to carry our equipment and ammunition. The few mules we had were a big help, but progress was slow in these treacherous mountains. The numerous booby traps and destruction of trails made it more difficult. German resistance was sporadic."[48]

The Germans were using delaying tactics and minefields to slow the advance, while waiting for winter weather and the completion of the Gustav Line behind them. The weather in the mountains had turned bad, with cold temperatures, overcast skies, intermittent rain, and mist as the 2nd Battalion, 504th, approached Gallo. On the night of October 30, a four-man patrol led by Italian-speaking Private Robert Finizio, with Company E, went into the town of Gallo to contact the local priest. Lieutenant Chester Garrison, the 2nd Battalion S-1, was at the CP, located a short distance down the valley in the town of Latino, when the patrol returned. "[Finizio] gained the information that the German vehicles had left town as it had grown dark; also, that a fifteen man machine gun squad was believed to be in the hills. An engineer patrol [had] set up mines on a small bridge on the road leading out [of] the opposite side of town."[49]

The following morning at 5:00, the 2nd Battalion's S-2, Lieutenant Virgil Carmichael, led a patrol into Gallo to check out the town. At 8:30 a.m. the 2nd

Battalion advanced into the town with Company D on the left and Company F on the right in a skirmish line. No enemy resistance was encountered until the forward elements reached the far side of the town and began to receive machine gun fire, wounding one man.

For the next twelve days, the 504th RCT moved through the rugged hills and mountains and north along the Volturno River valley. The terrain was so rugged that mules were used almost exclusively to carry ammunition, rations, water, and other essentials to Tucker's troopers. Patrols were sent deep into enemy-held territory as the combat team moved north, clearing the towns of Monteroduni, Sant Agipato, Macchia, Fornelli, Cerro, Scapoli, and Rocchetta as they moved up the valley.

After capturing the town of Colli, the 3rd Battalion was ordered on November 12, to seize Hill 1017. This objective dominated Hill 710 to the south and had to be captured before the 168th Infantry Regiment of the 34th Division could move to take Hill 710. The following morning, before dawn, Lieutenant Ed Sims led his Company H platoon out of the valley far below, to begin an assault to capture Hill 1017. "The attack started by forging a raging stream, then up the south slope of the hill. Resistance was moderate, but the entire area had been heavily mined with personnel mines (S-mines). The first casualty was the company commander [Captain Fred Thomas] who had his heel blown off."[50]

Company H trooper, Corporal Shelby Hord, saw it happen. "The radioman we had at the time for the company was injured badly and so was Captain Thomas. He never came back to us."[51]

The executive officer took command, but only lasted a few minutes, falling from a cliff and breaking his leg while trying to avoid enemy artillery fire. Sims then took command of Company H and kept the attack going. "Due to enemy fire and personnel mines, we had to proceed slowly and cautiously. While doing so, many S-mines were activated causing a number of casualties."[52]

That morning, Francis W. "Mac" McLane, with Company I, had watched the long line of shadowy figures pass, trudging through the mud as they wound their way out of the valley. "Before daylight H Company moved out to lead the attack on Hill 1017. The donkey cart trail was mined, and it was too dark for the men to see where they were stepping. They lost a lot of men. My company was then sent in. It was light enough by then, and we fared better. There was a nice spring on one side of the trail and a brick wall on the other. A [German] machine gun was [firing] on the trail above where the mountain started, making it impossible to go any farther up the trail. I had been so involved that when the gun stopped firing, I found myself practically alone.

"The rest of I Company was way out in a plowed field, circling around a machine gun that was [positioned] in an upthrust of rock. This gun was not firing, so I decided to cut across to the wooded hillside. . . .

"I found myself in a minefield. The morning sun made the trip wires shine, so I had little trouble getting through. I Company was heavily involved with

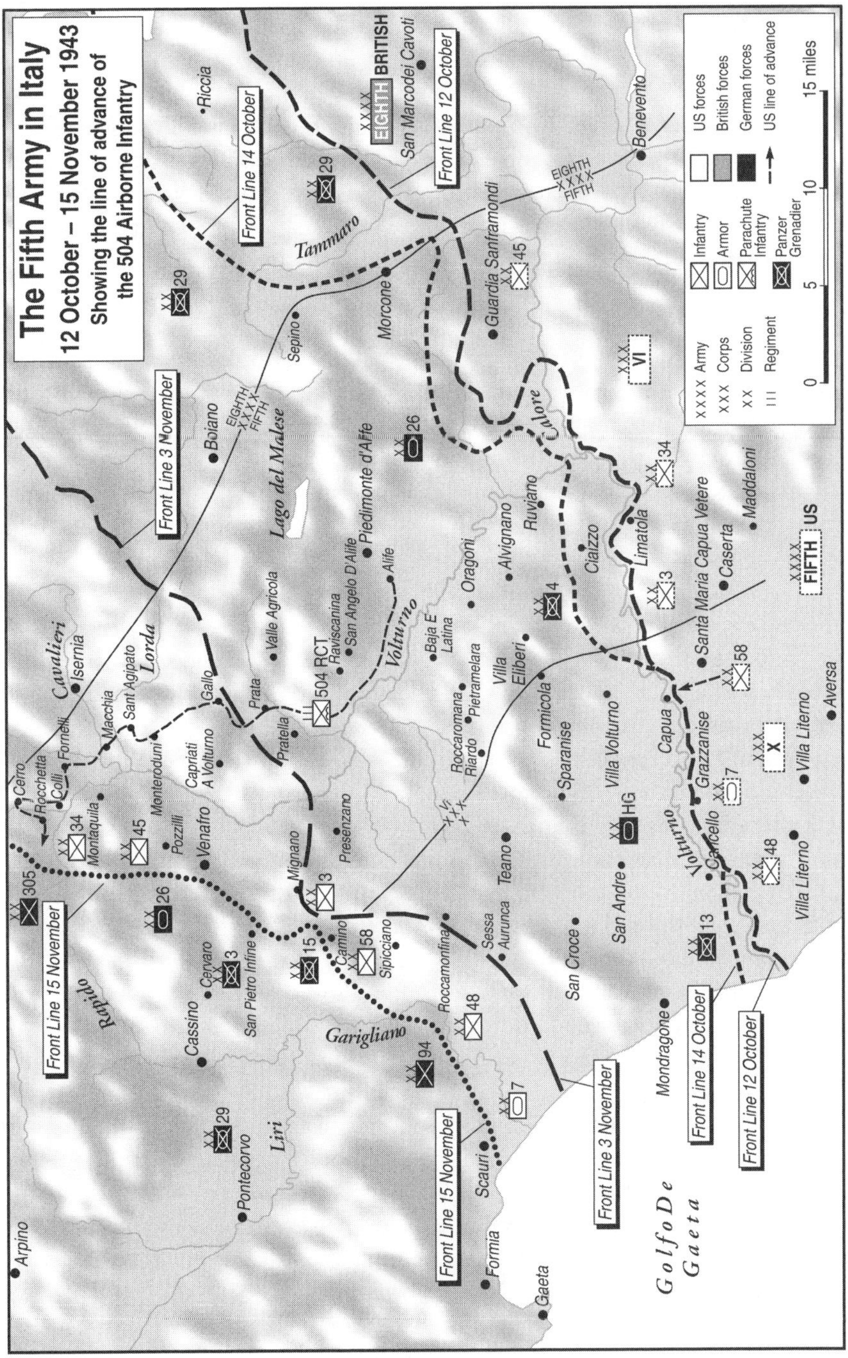
The Fifth Army in Italy
12 October – 15 November 1943
Showing the line of advance of
the 504 Airborne Infantry
US forces
British forces
German forces
US line of advance
Infantry
Armor
Parachute Infantry
Panzer Grenadier
Army
Corps
Division
Regiment
0
5
10
15 miles
Front Line 12 October
Front Line 14 October
Front Line 3 November
Front Line 15 November
EIGHTH
BRITISH
FIFTH
US
504 RCT
Volturno
Calore
Tammaro
Lago del Malese
Garigliano
Rapido
Liri
Cavalieri
Lorda
Golfo De Gaeta
Benevento
San Marco dei Cavoti
Riccia
Morcone
Sepino
Guardia Sanframondi
Boiano
Isernia
Piedimonte d'Alife
Alife
Valle Agricola
Raviscanina
San Angelo D'Alife
Prata
Pratella
Sant Agipato
Macchia
Gallo
Fornelli
Colli
Rocchetta
Cerro
Montaquila
Monteroduni
Capriati A Volturno
Pozzilli
Venafro
Mignano
Presenzano
Roccaromana
Riardo
Pietramelara
Baja E Latina
Oragoni
Alvignano
Ruviano
Cialzzo
Limatola
Caserta
Maddaloni
Santa Maria Capua Vetere
Capua
Grazzanise
Villa Volturno
Formicola
Villa Eliberi
Sparanise
Teano
San Andre
Cancello
Villa Literno
Aversa
Sessa Aurunca
Roccamonfina
Camino
Sipicciano
San Pietro Infine
Cervaro
Cassino
San Croce
Mondragone
Pontecorvo
Arpino
Scauri
Formia
Gaeta
HG

machine guns farther along the hillside, and I felt I could be more effective if I tried to gain the top of the hill. I ran into Sergeant Engebritzen, who had made the same decision. We stayed off the trail and kept to the shadows as much as possible. We soon noticed a group of our people going up a gully below and parallel to us."[53]

As Lieutenant Sims led Company H through the minefields as they moved up Hill 1017, he stepped on three mines. "Of the three mines I stepped on, the first one angled up under a mule in front of me and demolished his rear end. The second one while I was carrying a wounded man, exploded in the ground when it failed to bounce up. And the third mine bounced up but failed to explode."[54]

After negotiating the minefield near the bottom of the hill, Private McLane reached the crest of Hill 1017. "When we got to the top of the mountain, we saw a very pretty meadow, a tent, and a large supply dump with stacks of boxes of food and ammunition. Engebritzen covered me while I crossed the meadow looking for a good spot for a defensive position. I was halfway across when I came face to face with a Jerry who was running toward me. I fired without a thought, just a reaction. He called, 'Nicht schiessen,' but it was too late. I didn't have to shoot him, but I couldn't think fast enough to avoid it. I think he had been manning the machine gun at the head of the gully and was coming for more ammunition.

"The men from the gully came up and joined us. They were, Lieutenant [Henry B.] Keep, Lieutenant [Bob] Blankenship, and Corporal Evenson. We had found a round depression edged by small trees—a perfect spot for defense. A column of Krauts came up to, and around our position. They didn't see us, but we couldn't engage them because they held one of our boys prisoner. He had a strong Arkansas accent and, for our benefit I'm sure, talked very loudly all the time. They headed down the hill and were taken care of there. We waited until we collected ten more people. It was getting late in the day, so we headed for the peak at the end of the ridge that we were on. The fifteen of us got credit for the capture of Hill 1017."[55]

Company H arrived late that afternoon followed by the rest of Company I after dark. Sims positioned his men to defend the hill, then, "I ordered everyone to stay in place until I could get our engineers up to clear the mines from the area."[56]

After taking Hill 1017, Companies H and I remained there, while being shelled mercilessly by German artillery and mortars. Private McLane and the other men holding the hill were in bad shape. "We had been without food or water for several days. We spread out shelter halves to try to catch rainwater. We could only catch a sip or two. The hunger subsided, but the thirst was unbearable."[57]

Three days after Hill 1017 had been captured, Company C moved up to relieve them in a torrential rain. When Corporal Ross Carter, struggling through the mud, reached the Volturno River, he couldn't believe what he saw: "A crude bridge consisting of two Manila ropes with planks tied between. There were no wires or ropes to cling to. The Volturno churned through the gorge as if speeded by hydraulic pressures. If a man tumbled into that angry stream, nothing could save him from drowning.

"We had to stick to the center of the path because the S-mines were still planted on the sides. When we rested, we had to sit in the center, down which a fair-sized stream of water was pouring, or else run the risk of springing a mine. The rain trickled down our necks and into our boots. We didn't mind the rain though as much as usual since our tails were continuously wet anyhow from siting [sic] in a brook."[58]

After Company C relieved them, Companies H and I moved down Hill 1017 to a rear-area encampment. But by the time McLane's group reached the crossing on the Volturno River, the continuous rains had greatly swollen the river, making it impassable. "So we had to make a wide detour to get back to Colli. We headed north across a plowed field. Every step [we] sank into mud halfway up to our knees. It was getting dark and we were exhausted from the effort.

"When we found a big barn, we made the most of it. We covered the windows with blankets and built a fire in the middle of the floor. It was like heaven. We were in enemy territory, but it was worth the risk."[59]

Meanwhile, up on Hill 1017, Corporal Carter spent a miserable night. "At three in the morning my platoon was ordered to take up positions near the crest of the hill. At four it began to rain. We rigged up a crude tent in the dark and crawled into it. By this time the water had soaked through even our epidermis.

"Wild Bill [Murray] started to cuss. He was seldom moved to blasphemy and invective, but when he got going his artistry made the best of us take off our hats in admiring astonishment."[60]

At dawn the next morning in the valley, Private McLane continued the journey. "We found a main road and traveled in the direction we wanted to go. There were German oil bottles and assorted trash along the sides of the road—all the labels were in German. We came to a group of small buildings, obviously having been recently occupied by the Krauts. Lieutenant Blankenship asked me to take a patrol out to the north to find out where the Krauts were. He said, 'Don't try to contact them, just get as much information as you can, and above all, try to scrounge a meal for us somewhere.'

"We hadn't eaten in four days."[61]

On November 18, Corporal Carter was ordered to take a man and go to the bottom of Hill 1017 and get some water. On the way back, they could hear Hill 1017 being pounded by German artillery. As they continued up the trail, Carter and the other man were caught in a barrage, shrapnel breaking their water jug. Carter wearily reached the top of the mountain where "bad news awaited us. A captain and two radio operators from the 376th Parachute Field Artillery Battalion were on top of the mountain observing for their guns. Since Krautheads were not firing at the mountaintop, the captain is reported to have said, 'Hell, I'll give them a target so I can find out where their guns are.' He stepped out into an open space where the Krautheads could see him. They dropped a mortar barrage that killed the captain, Lieutenant [Lyle] Nightingale, our first sergeant [Albert Henry, Jr.], one radio operator [Sergeant William C. Jones], and severely wounded three other men.

"Next afternoon, donkeys were brought up on the mountain to carry off the dead men. The wounded had been carried down the night before. Ernie Pyle wrote about the beloved captain who came down the mountain on a donkey with his men hating to see him go.

"First Sergeant Henry, the last to be carried down, was one of the best men who ever served his country. We stood looking at Henry, whose short, black, curly-haired blood-matted head hung on one side of the donkey and his shrapnel-mangled legs on the other. More than one man had tears in his eyes as Henry disappeared around a bend."[62]

In mid-November 1943, responding to a request from General Eisenhower, Brigadier General Jim Gavin was temporarily detached from duty with the 82nd Airborne Division to become the senior airborne advisor to the COSSAC (Chief Of Staff, Supreme Allied Command) organization, which was established to plan the cross-channel invasion of France. The code name for the invasion was Operation Overlord. Gavin was briefed by Ridgway on the mission prior to his departure to England and given the general aspects of the mission. Ridgway assured Gavin that he would be returned to the division in time to participate in the operation.

Then just before leaving, Gavin was told to be careful when working with British General Frederick E. "Boy" Browning. "General Ridgway warned me of the machinations of Major General Browning, stating that he was intelligent, charming, and very close to Mr. Churchill. Further that he was unprincipled and ruthless in his efforts to align every operation and every piece of equipment to the complete benefit of the British Empire, at our expense. This is just about entirely true and Browning must be handled cautiously but firmly."[63]

Sergeant William Blank, with Company G, 505th, had been released from the hospital outside Naples after contracting malaria and yellow jaundice. "I was sent from the hospital to a replacement depot, where I heard the 505 was moving out. I didn't want to be left behind, so I jumped on a truck headed for Naples and got there just in time to move to the dock and boarded a ship for Ireland."[64]

The 456th Parachute Field Artillery Battalion, less Batteries C and D, left North Africa on November 17, to join the 504th RCT for combat in Italy. Batteries C and D left by ship eleven days later and would rendezvous with the 82nd Airborne Division enroute to Northern Ireland.

On November 18, 1943, the 82nd Airborne Division sailed from Naples for Northern Ireland, but without the 504th RCT. Colonel Tucker's fierce warriors, the trusted companions of the 505th and 325th RCTs, would stay behind in Italy.

On the morning of his first day in London, November 19, General Gavin reported to Major General Ray Barker, the American deputy chief of staff of COSSAC, at his office, and then visited General Omar Bradley. "I talked with him for about an hour on the coming operation; he has some sound ideas."[65]

At 10:00 a.m. the following day, Gavin returned to General Barker's office. "He took me into see General Morgan, there I met General Browning. I talked to him quite a while. He is as smooth as ever. Afterwards, General Barker said, referring to him, 'Oh yes, he is an empire builder.' "[66]

Lieutenant Ed Sims, who had taken command of Company H, 504th, after the company commander and the executive officer were wounded during the assault on Hill 1017, was thankful when he got the news that the 504th RCT was going to be relieved. "On November 23, 1943 the entire regiment was replaced by the 133rd Infantry and went into two weeks reserve near Ciorlano. During the period we had an exceptional Thanksgiving dinner."[67] It was to be a short-lived rest.

CHAPTER 7

"DEVILS IN BAGGY PANTS"

On December 9, 1943, the same day the 82nd Airborne Division arrived in Belfast, Northern Ireland, the 504th RCT was ordered to get ready to move. Corporal Ross Carter was hopeful at the news. "Since we hadn't been re-equipped we thought, and rumor confirmed it, that our mission in Italy was completed and that we were going to England to rejoin the 82nd. Rumor was wrong as usual. Although we didn't all have entrenching tools, and our shelter halves were worn out, and some of our guns were in bad shape, we got into some trucks and went driving through the rain. It always rained when we went anywhere. If the Legion would drive through the Sahara in the driest season, I bet a cloudburst would fall on it. We got off the trucks under the rocky slopes of the biggest mountain we ever saw in Italy and set up a bivouac in some olive trees. Dozens of 105[mm] howitzers and 155[mm] long toms and other breeds of howitzers were all around us. They fired day and night. A man had to be stone deaf to get any sleep. Plenty of tanks were all around. It looked like something big was going on, something bigger than anything we'd seen so far."[1]

The regimental CP was set up in the town of Venafro on December 10. That night, Lieutenant James Megellas arrived as one of the group of replacements that reported to the 504th regimental headquarters in the cellar of a house in the town. "We reported to the regimental commander, Colonel Reuben Tucker, who was seated behind a desk in a dimly lit room. He was an impressive looking man who had a deep voice and wasn't given to small talk. As he welcomed us, he talked about what we would be up against: rugged terrain and a determined enemy giving up ground only grudgingly and at a high price. The sounds of incoming and outgoing artillery permeating the air made the briefing short.

For me, I had found a home after eighteen months of frustration trying to become part of a combat unit. I could not have been assigned to a better fighting unit than the 504th Parachute Regiment."[2]

Megellas and Lieutenants Richard G. LaRiviere and Peter Gerle were assigned to Company H. Megellas "was sent to the 3rd Platoon, then being led by Staff Sergeant Michael 'Mike' Kogut, who reverted to platoon sergeant. Mike was an original member of the 504th, a combat veteran of the jump in Sicily; the landings at Salerno, Maiori, Chiunzi Pass, and Naples; and the crossing of the Volturno River. It was my good fortune to be with him during my baptism of fire. I learned from him some of the tricks of staying alive and how to lead men, not command them. At six foot three Mike was an impressive figure, but his stature was based on the respect his men had for him more than his physique. As a replacement officer in combat for the first time with a lot to learn, I relied heavily on Mike's advice and assistance. Being an officer and a platoon leader did not automatically command the respect of the men. It had to be earned, and that could be done only by leading."[3]

The next day the 3rd Battalion, 504th, was ordered to relieve the 3rd Ranger Battalion, which had suffered 50 percent casualties and was still fighting on Hill 950. The 2nd Battalion, 504th, was to reinforce the 1st Battalion of the 143rd Infantry on Mt. Sammucro, designated on the combat maps as Hill 1205. Private "Mac" McLane, with Company I, gathered his gear and began the long walk to the top of Hill 950. "We walked through a narrow pass into a moonscape—a bowl of a mountain in front of us, covered with boulders and rocks. There was not a speck of anything green and growing. Artillery had pounded the life out of it. On our right was a peak shaped like an upside down ice cream cone. The whole area was echoing with the screech and explosions of hundreds of shells. It was obvious that this was not a neighborhood in which to raise children. The ice cream cone was to be ours—Hill 950. The bursting flowers of flame could be nothing but hand grenades, which meant very close contact with the enemy. We started up. My old friend, Engebritzen was waiting for me, but we hadn't gone far when a grenade exploded next to his thigh, giving him a very nasty wound. After calling for a medic, I moved on. It was so steep that you had to use your hands as well as your feet."[4]

At 5:30 p.m. the 2nd Battalion, 504th, began their approach march to Hill 1205, the highest elevation facing the German Gustav Line, with a clear view across the valley of the abbey on Monte Cassino. The mountain overlooked the town of San Pietro that would be the scene of fierce fighting in the days to come. At about 6:45 p.m. Lieutenant Chester Garrison, the battalion's S-1, left the road and began the climb up "a long, muddy torturous trail. The night was as black as could be, with a mist setting in early and turning to rain. When at 03:00 a place was reached where the ascent was possible only by pulling oneself up by a long rope, the battalion stopped for a few hours' sleep. Loose and rolling rocks also hampered the climb. In the dark, it was almost impossible to find a nook or cranny large enough to lay down on a level. Most of the men slept where they were able to sit and still keep from sliding down the mountainside."[5]

As the 1st Battalion followed the 2nd up Hill 1205, Lieutenant Reneau Breard, a platoon leader with Company A, heard an explosion ahead of him in the column. "Somebody ahead of me had a grenade go off in his pants pocket. I thought it blew his leg off. But, he survived. . . . I don't know how in the hell he did. We had a Cajun medic from south Louisiana named Polette and he took care of him and got him evacuated. He never did come back to the unit."[6]

After a very long and difficult climb, Private McLane reached the crest of Hill 950. "I got to the top where my squad was digging in. How do you dig in on a forty-five degree slope of solid rock?

"[Leonard] Muri, [Bill] Leonard, [George] Leoleis and Goodwin had found spots, but before I got located, Evenson found me and said that Blankenship wanted to see me on top. I thought we were on top, but there was a shelf on the other side that furnished positions for twelve to fourteen men."[7]

As McLane approached the position it was under attack from Germans just below. "The Krauts were throwing 'egg' grenades in such numbers that we were holding our rifles in a way that we could bat them off—like you bunt a ball in baseball. As if the Krauts didn't pose enough trouble, Lieutenant Blankenship was suffering from an attack of malaria. The enemy had a 170mm gun in the valley below us, and between attacks, would shell us. Evenson and I found a position behind a boulder that was close to the officers, but gave us a good field of fire."[8]

That night, a heavy German counterattack to capture Hill 1205 fell on the 1st Battalion of the 143rd Infantry, but was repulsed. The 1st and 2nd Battalions of the 504th arrived to take over the northern half of Hill 1205 before dawn. When Lieutenant Breard, with Company A, arrived at the top of the mountain, he found a barren, boulder-strewn surface. "You couldn't dig a hole, there was nothing but rock. You just had to build rocks around you."[9]

On Hill 950, German infantry maintained harassing fire all night, until they attacked at 4:00 a.m. Private McLane, with Company I, helped to fight the German assault to a standstill. "All night I took very careful aim at the muzzle blast of their automatic weapons. The distance was like one hundred yards, or less. They set up a machine gun in front of us and Evenson knocked it out with a rifle grenade. Toward morning, he got hit in the face and had to leave. He had been like a rock and I sorely missed him.

"Near dawn there was a lull in the firing, and I must have dozed off, when I heard several excited voices saying that the Krauts were flanking us. It took a while for my eyes to adjust to the light. I counted five helmet tops moving above a niche in the rocks. I had no way of knowing how many had already passed. The captain told me to get some help and stop them. I had to start from the extreme right of our position and go to the extreme left, maybe one hundred feet distance. On the way, I tried to enlist help, but didn't have any success. I asked a very young, white-faced kid to give me some covering fire.

"His reply was, 'I was told to face that way.' (Not in my direction.) I had no time for extended debate. I ran to a bald slope and hit the ground in the prone position. This was the saddle that gave access to both the front and rear of our position . . . the most vulnerable part of our defense. The first Jerry started to run up the slope toward me; his gaze was riveted above me. This guy looked exactly like my brother! I was completely shaken. What the hell was he doing here? The Jerry didn't have my type of problem. He dropped his gaze and saw me. He snap fired his P-38 [pistol]. The bullet hit the dirt about a foot from my head. Brotherly love notwithstanding, I had to consider my priorities and I shot him. The other Krauts were trying to shoot, but I shot them before they could pull a trigger. They tried to do a 'jumping jack' (popping up from dispersed positions). This exaggerated popping up gave me time to hit each one as he showed himself. They gave up trying to outshoot me and tried the same tactic with grenades. This was even more futile as they were exposed longer, I had no idea how many there were, but the last three gave it up and tried to run back to their positions. I ran parallel to them and got all three before they made it. This turned out to be a very messy business, as I couldn't shoot accurately while running over rough ground. I won't go into detail, as it was not a matter of which to look back upon with pride. I couldn't be sure, but I think the rest of the Jerries just watched. I don't believe anyone even shot at me. After this, the Jerries seemed to have lost heart. I could see helmet tops moving around aimlessly and I tried to get in a shot.

"The Germans and we were exhausted. They had quit firing and prisoners were coming in. Private First Class [John] Schultz, the BAR man, had performed extremely well all through this battle. His position had been about five yards below and to the left of me. He spoke German and interrogated the prisoners who came in.

"These men had been on the Russian front and had been sent to Italy as sort of a rest area. It wasn't what they expected. They were terrified by our marksmanship. Many of their dead had been shot squarely between the eyes; our firepower was too much for them to cope with. This seemed strange to me, because the whole German system was always based on firepower—more automatic weapons, higher rates of fire. Their weakness may have been that these fast-firing weapons climbed too much, and much of their power was wasted. The estimate of German loss of men was one hundred fifty killed—our loss around forty-five."[10]

From December 12–14, the Germans subjected both Hill 950 and Hill 1205 to intense artillery and mortar fire, while snipers infiltrated at night to hidden positions among the boulder strewn ridges and took a deadly toll. Anyone appearing to be an officer or NCO was targeted. On December 12, Captain George Watts and Lieutenant James Kierstead, both with Company G, and Lieutenant Frank Gilson, with Company I, were all killed. Artillery and mortar fire was directed on the suspected positions of the enemy snipers. Patrols were also sent out to hunt these snipers, often resulting in the elimination of the snipers, but usually at the cost of more men. On December 14, Lieutenant James Breathwit, with Company G, took a patrol out to clear snipers from the saddle between Hill 950 and Hill 1205. The German snipers, hidden among the rocks, waited as the patrol got close and then opened fire, killing Lieutenant Breathwit, who was said to be wearing second lieutenant bars on his shoulders and had a gold stripe on the back of his helmet, indicating his rank.

Lieutenant Joseph W. Lyons, with Battery B, 456th Parachute Field Artillery Battalion, was sent up Hill 1205 to act as a forward observer and would stay up there for around two weeks. "The guns were always in the valleys, and the OPs [observation posts] on high ground. These actions were the classrooms for the 456. The outfit molded into an outstanding battalion. We all looked like 'Willie and Joe.' "[11]

As part of the effort by the 36th Division to put pressure on the Germans holding San Pietro, the 504th was ordered on December 14 to assist in seizing the high ground overlooking the valley behind the town. Specifically, the 2nd Battalion, 504th, on Hill 1205 would attack across a deep saddle and capture Hill 687 to the west, while the 3rd Battalion, 504th, would send a strong patrol from Hill 950 to the northeast to grab Hill 954.

On the night of December 14, Lieutenant Chester Garrison went down to meet some replacements and bring them up to Hill 1205, while "the battalion moved forward in column at 20:15 with E Company in the lead. The head of the column went down the far side of the mountain reaching its objective. Contact between E and D Companies was lost and E Company proceeded alone without knowledge of the loss of the rest of the battalion. The battalion CP group never cleared the ridge. When they got into a firefight and realized their loss of contact, Lieutenant [Walter S.] VanPoyck gave the company orders to return to their starting position on the ridge. They did not discover any of the rest of the battalion until they reached this position, as Major [Daniel W.] Danielson had given the battalion orders to return there. The battalion stayed in this position for the remainder of the night. The 1st Battalion moved into the area which the 2nd Battalion had used, putting their CP in the locality of the 2nd Battalion CP.

"The [2nd] Battalion remained along the ridge [of Hill 1205] all day in preparation of a night attack. It moved out at 18:45 in the same order of march, in column with E Company in the lead. It was again pinned down by fire on the northwest side of the mountain. Heavy casualties [resulted] from artillery, machine gun, mortar, small arms, and grenade fire."[12]

Caught in the rocky low ground in front of Hill 687 with little cover and no way to dig in, the 2nd Battalion, 504th, was once again forced to withdraw before dawn back to Hill 1205. They had suffered 15 killed and 75 wounded in the two attacks.

Lieutenant Garrison once again made the trip to the bottom of Hill 1205 and brought more replacements up the mountain. "Additional rations and ammunition were picked up by each man at the supply dump at the end of the mule trail, only half way up."[13]

The next morning, December 16, on top of Hill 1205, Captain Delbert Kuehl, one of the regimental chaplains, overheard a conversation in which a trooper mentioned that there were some wounded 2nd Battalion troopers in no-man's-land on the other side of the ridge from the previous night attack. Chaplain Kuehl talked with the medics, and they agreed that they couldn't leave the wounded out there to die. Kuehl and the battalion surgeons and medics decided to go get them in broad daylight. "We found in the medics' supplies a tattered Red Cross flag, put it on a stick, took some folding litters, and started over the mountain to the German side.

"We all knew that if the German troops were from the fanatical SS, or if they couldn't figure out our purpose, we wouldn't be coming back.

"As we started down the open slope, a machine gun opened up, with bullets hitting beside us and spraying us with bits of rock. We thought, 'This is it.' All they had to do was traverse that gun slightly and we would have been wiped out. Then the firing stopped.

"We found a number of our wounded men. We put some on litters and dragged others across our shoulders, and struggled back over the rugged slope—back to our side of the mountain."[14]

That same morning Lieutenant Garrison put the replacements to work hauling more supplies instead of assigning them to rifle companies. "They far excelled any expectations in their willingness and stamina to do their utmost to aid the battalion on the forward slope. The climbing and re-climbing with loads of supplies on their backs is extremely exhausting. Captain [Robert N.] Johnson [CO of Headquarters Company, 2nd Battalion] with an enlisted man made his way back safely over the exposed rocky mountainside to get some water for the men. They returned to the forward position without drawing any fire by 09:00. Captain Johnson was shortly afterwards killed in his foxhole by an almost direct hit of enemy artillery. A terrific barrage was laid down on the battalion lasting about two hours and forcing the personnel to seek refuge and slight protection of the saddle to the rear of their prepared positions. Numerous casualties were inflicted [on the battalion]."[15]

On December 17, Lieutenant Peter Gerle, one of three replacement officers assigned to Company H, was killed by a sniper. Later that day, another of the replacement officers assigned to Company H, Lieutenant Jim Megellas, was ordered to take his platoon and capture Hill 610, about 300 yards to the front, which was being used as a base by German snipers and forward observers. Megellas led his men down the trail, watching for mines as he went. "We reached the base of Hill 610 and started climbing to the crest. At about the halfway point, an explosion and a flash appeared in the center of the column. The call went out: 'Mines,' then 'Scannell; is hit!' The platoon froze in place."[16]

They were caught in a minefield on open ground in front of Hill 610. They were incredibly lucky that the Germans had withdrawn the previous night, or it could have been a bloodbath. The platoon moved forward very slowly, with each man stepping on the same ground as the man ahead, all the while carefully looking for the telltale signs of mines: tripwires and disturbed ground.

Megellas got his men to the top of the hill without incurring additional casualties. "Before we took up defensive positions, we made a fine-toothed comb search for enemy mines left behind. I learned to look for and trace a trip wire, often concealed, to an armed and activated mine, but more importantly I learned how to disarm and render it ineffective. On Hill 610 I developed a healthy respect for German antipersonnel mines, the silent killers.

"Scannell's body was left where he fell. After dark, the mules coming up with water and rations would take his body back to Graves Registration. I had joined the company only a short while before and was not familiar with most of the men, but I will always remember Private [John R.] Scannell, the first man killed in a platoon I led. He would not be the last."[17]

The 1st Battalion, 504th, relieved the 2nd Battalion on the evening of December 17. After reaching the summit of Hill 1205, Captain Albert E. "Ernie" Milloy, the CO of Company C, was ordered to report to Major Warren Williams, the 1st Battalion commander. Milloy was ordered to take his company forward about 1,000 yards to establish a line of outposts. "The position may have looked good on a higher headquarters situation map, but on the ground it was nearly untenable. The ground was barren and too rocky to dig in, and we were literally under the gun muzzles of the Germans. Any movement on our part immediately drew heavy fire."[18]

That following night, Company A succeeded in capturing Hill 687. Lieutenant Reneau Breard spent a restless night with his platoon waiting for the inevitable counterattack. A strong German force hit Breard and his men at around dawn the next morning. "The Germans came up [the slope] and we held them off."[19]

The 504th held on to the hard won hills for another two weeks. The weather and enemy artillery continued to take their tolls. The morning report for the 2nd Battalion on December 20 indicated 3 officers and 24 enlisted men in Company D, while Company E had 4 officers and only 10 enlisted men, and Company F only 2 officers and 28 enlisted men. Even the 2nd Battalion Headquarters Company reflected the attrition: 8 officers, but only 69 enlisted men. Lieutenant Breard saw the strength of Company A slowly dwindle over those bitterly cold days and nights. "It was so damned cold, people just had to quit . . . it was exposure. I think we got down to about fourteen men in the company. I think that on Christmas Day they gave us these tankers' uniforms. I threw away my wet blanket."[20]

Private Russell Long, a radio operator with Headquarters Battery, 376th Parachute Field Artillery, spent a couple of weeks on Hill 1025 as part of a forward observation team. "I spent Christmas Day on Hill 1205 and although we did have a field day at Jerry's expense, who wants to be killing even the enemy on such a day."[21]

Even after the 504th was officially relieved on the 27th of December, it took a few days before the rifle companies were able to leave their positions. Lieutenant Breard and what was left of Company A were occupying Hill 687 out in front on Hill 1205 and were some of the last to be relieved. "We came off of that mountain on the 31st. When we pulled out of there, I decided I'd go back over the mountain, 1205 and get my [60mm] mortar . . . we had left it up there. [Sergeant Bernard] Karnap, one other person, and I went; and we got up there and got that mortar. We were so damned tired . . . it was dark and everything . . . we were just worn out. So we said to hell with the mortar. I just left it up there.

"We went down the mountain and found a little ration dump with ten-in-one rations. We built a fire and we had bacon, chopped eggs and I don't know what all in there. It was good! Then we took a nap and started off again, and got down to the bottom and passed a kitchen on the road. It was an artillery unit down there and they were frying pork chops. They gave us pork chop sandwiches. They let us sleep in their beds, until the damned one-five-five's went off on a fire mission. We got up and got the hell out of there.

"It was the morning of the 1st of January when we got back. I think we were about the last to get back. Somebody saw us and gave us a ride. We caught up with the regiment and came on back to Naples."[22]

Since the 11th of December, the 504th Parachute Infantry Regiment had suffered 58 killed; Company C, 307th Airborne Engineer Battalion had two men killed; and the 376th Parachute Field Artillery lost three men killed. The 504th Parachute Infantry had 226 wounded and many more evacuated for illness and injuries.

An exhausted and depleted 504th RCT moved to the town of Pignatoro, about twenty miles south of Venafro. It was welcome relief for men like Corporal Shelby Hord, with Company H, 504th. "They gave us a bath, sprayed us with DDT, and gave us clean clothes."[23]

Back in the United States in December 1943 the 2nd Parachute Brigade, consisting of the 507th and 508th regiments, sailed from the United States to Northern Ireland. The 507th sailed on December 3, arriving in late December. The 508th at Camp Shanks in New York left a few weeks later. The strict secrecy that had accompanied all of the deployment of airborne units overseas was in force. Before leaving for Camp Shanks, Harry Reisenleiter, with Company B, 508th, had been told that "we had to strip ourselves of all identification as paratroopers. Nothing to identify us as airborne. This was supposed to be done so that nobody would know who we were and think that we were just another regular infantry unit that was getting ready to ship out.

"I was able to see New York for a few hours on Christmas Eve, and I had dinner with some buddies. Some of the folks that had people in the service felt that they would like to purchase our dinner for us, which was greatly appreciated. We had a very enjoyable time.

"We pulled out of New York Harbor on the 28th of December, 1943 on the USS *James Parker*. We were aboard ship for eleven days, after which we landed in Belfast, Northern Ireland. When we landed in Ireland, the 'Berlin Bitch' not only identified us as our unit, but she also knew what days were going to be payday, so we really didn't fool anybody."[24]

In England, Brigadier General Gavin, the airborne advisor for COSSAC, worked throughout December with the invasion planners to develop an airborne plan to support the cross-channel landings. "Our planning had to begin with a determination of an objective for the amphibious assault. Early in our planning we were told that our first objective was to establish a firm lodgment from which we could not be driven by the German forces known to be nearby. Our next objective was to seize Cherbourg as rapidly as possible, and finally, to achieve a build-up in the lodgment area and a breakout with a subsequent defeat of the major German commands opposing us.

"The airborne landing areas had to be selected so as to contribute directly to the success of the amphibious landings, both by blocking enemy troop movements toward the beaches and by helping open avenues of approach from the beaches to the interior.

"Late in December General Bradley called me to his office to discuss the landing areas for the US airborne divisions. He was beginning to think of landing the airborne divisions on the Cherbourg peninsula. We discussed the German troop dispositions and the layout of the land. He had some excellent photographs. One of the most reassuring things about them was that the Germans were beginning to flood the area—a clear indication that they did not intend to fight an offensive battle or use large amounts of armor. We would be at our best under those conditions, where we would be engaging their infantry with little armor."[25]

Back in Italy on New Year's Day, the men of the 504th RCT were fed a special dinner. Christmas packages and mail from back home were passed out and opened. On January 4, 1944, the 504th RCT once again moved to the suburbs north of Naples, where they continued to rest, refit, take on replacements, and get troopers back from various hospitals.

After another two weeks, the 504th RCT prepared to once more return to combat. The initial plan was to use the 504th RCT to make a parachute jump to support amphibious landings at Anzio on the western coast of Italy about fifteen miles southwest of Rome. The landings were code-named Operation Shingle and were designed to draw German reserves away from the Gustav Line, which was proving to be a tough and costly obstacle in the Fifth Army's drive toward Rome.

Concerns about a parachute landing alerting German forces to the amphibious landings caused the planners to decide to bring in the 504th RCT with the seaborne forces. Briefings were held on January 20 for 504th troopers regarding the amphibious landings.

Immediately upon their arrival in Northern Ireland the 507th and 508th began training for the upcoming invasion of Europe. Sergeant Zane Schlemmer, with Headquarters Company, 2nd Battalion, 508th, was a forward observer for the 81mm mortar platoon. "In the airborne, all being volunteers, from the generals down to the privates, we all jumped together, and shared the same experiences. In the field, there was unusual camaraderie and mutual respect between the officers of all ranks, many of whom were West Pointers, and the enlisted men.

"We spent most of the pre-invasion months in England, doing many tactical combat exercises for which we had been trained. Most of our training involved jumps, or mock jumps, then assembling and setting up hillside defensive positions. All this constant training triggered a great deal of speculation on which country we would be invading. The conjecture and the rumors ranged all the way from Norway to the Pyrenees Mountains. We were looking forward to our first combat jump."[26]

After several meetings, General Ridgway convinced General Omar Bradley that an increase in the authorized strength of the 82nd and 101st was necessary in order for these airborne divisions to carry out the missions being planned as part of Operation Overlord. With Bradley's support, Ridgway was successful in getting the authorized strength of the 82nd and 101st increased temporarily from two to three parachute regiments and the number of battalions in the glider regiments from two to three. On January 20, 1944, the 507th and 508th Parachute Infantry Regiments were attached to the 82nd Airborne. One regiment would take the place of the 504th; the other would be used to increase the number of parachute regiments in the division to three. The 101st Airborne's 401st Glider Infantry Regiment was "temporarily" split up, with the 2nd Battalion moving to the 325th GIR, bringing its strength up to three battalions.

This was great news to Corporal Tom Porcella, with Company H, 508th. "We were given the word that the 508 was finally attached to the 82nd Airborne Division, which we were proud of. We were considered a bastard outfit. They didn't know what the hell to do with us. General Gavin really preferred to have the 504. I guess the 508, the bastard outfit was the next best thing. We were proud to be a part of the 82nd, because it had a good reputation."[27]

Shortly after joining the 82nd, while still in Ireland, the men of the 507th and 508th received some special visitors from the division. Troopers of the two untested regiments, such as Captain Briand N. Beaudin, the assistant battalion surgeon for the 3rd Battalion, 508th, were very appreciative of what these visitors brought. "Men of the 505th Parachute Infantry, veterans of the Sicily and

Italy jumps, lived with each company of the 508th for about a week and gave many helpful hints about fighting Germans."[28] As a result, the young paratroopers of both regiments were imbued with confidence from the knowledge gained from the veterans of the 505th as they began training for the upcoming invasion.

At around 9:00 a.m. on January 22, the 504th RCT followed the 3rd Infantry Division ashore on the southern end of the Anzio beachhead, landing almost without incident. However, as they were unloading, a low-flying German plane swept over the LCIs unloading the regiment and dropped a bomb that hit the LCI unloading Company G. Surprisingly, only one man was killed by this attack. Private First Class Henry E. Ferrari, an H Company trooper who came in on the G Company LCI to act as an interpreter for G Company, died of his wounds a week later. The LCIs were anchored just off the beach and had ramps on each side that were lowered so that troopers could exit the ship. After the German plane started to turn to come in for another run, Private First Class Leo M. Hart, with Company F, 504th, began scrambling down the ramp to get off of his LCI. "When I stepped off that thing I went completely underwater. I hit bottom and I followed my nose, straight ahead. The only thought I had was, 'Please keep walking straight ahead.' It was just a few steps and I was back [above the surface]."[29]

After getting ashore, the 504th RCT moved to a wooded area a short distance inland, got organized, and went into Corps reserve. Expecting swift and heavy German armored attacks once the extent of the landings became known, the Anzio invasion force was ordered to dig in on its initial objectives.

On the afternoon of January 23, the 504th was ordered to capture two bridges over the Mussolini Canal along the southern flank of the invasion beachhead. The 3rd Battalion was assigned Bridge Number 2 near the mouth of the canal near the town of Borgo Sabotini. Sergeant Louis "Lukie" Orvin, with Company I, was moving down the road toward the bridge when the Germans ambushed the column. "It was dark and they just opened fire. Lieutenant Ferrill was killed . . . he was a good officer. We jumped into the little ditches on each side of the road. Then we crawled back far enough where we could get out of the ditches and spread out to the sides. We stayed there all night.

"The next morning they sent a couple of tanks up with us. We spread across the fields on each side of the road. The tanks came up and we went on up toward the canal. We told the tanks there was a house over to our left and that we thought that there was a sniper up there. They fired a couple of rounds at the house and we didn't have any more trouble from that. We also had some artillery from the Navy that was supposed to fire some smoke. But we didn't see much smoke. They did fire some [high explosive] rounds in front of us. At first the rounds started falling behind us. I don't think we had anyone hit. Then they got the right range on it and started firing up toward the canal. We went up and took the canal [bridge]."[30]

Assisting Company I, Companies G and H on each flank poured suppressive fire into the German positions. Soon after the attack began, Company H lost its new company commander, Captain Nitz. Lieutenant Ed Sims, the executive officer, took command and kept the company moving forward in the attack. "Here for the first time, we were fighting German paratroopers and they were a formidable fighting force, but outnumbered. After several hours of hard fighting and heavy casualties, the Germans withdrew and the bridge was secured. During this action, I injured my back when I stepped backward without looking, into an open manhole. I had a difficult time standing and moving, but I made it through."[31]

The 1st Battalion was ordered to secure Bridge Number 5 farther north near where the Mussolini Canal split. Company B was in the lead and as they approached the bridge they ran into fierce opposition. The next morning, January 24, Company A supported by a platoon of tanks began a second attempt to take the bridge. After a four-hour fight the Germans were forced back across the canal and the bridge was secured.

After capturing Bridge Number 5, Sergeant Albert Clark, with Company A, ordered his squad to dig in along the canal. "We had just got dug in well when they started hitting with very heavy artillery fire and personnel attacks. We did have a tank for support for a day or so and they were called to another sector. Then we did not have any big gun support. The end of the first day of their attack, out of our [platoon of] thirty-two men, we had twenty-nine; the next night twenty-seven; the next night nineteen; then eleven; and finally down to nine men. Then we started getting a few [of our wounded] back. One day I got three men. One still had a hand in a cast. The next morning, one of them was killed by artillery fire.

"On one day, we could not get any artillery support, all we had was our 60mm mortar. We fired over four hundred rounds and were responsible for breaking up the attack."[32]

Beginning on January 24, the US 3rd Infantry Division began a drive toward Cisterna. Because the 3rd Division encountered strong resistance from the Hermann Göring Panzer Division, the 504th was ordered to make a diversionary attack to relieve the pressure. At 7:00 the next morning, the 2nd Battalion, 504th, was ordered to attack east across the Mussolini Canal to capture the town of Borgo Piave, a short distance away. The assault would commence at 1:30 p.m. the same day. Intelligence gathered indicated that the town was lightly held by low-quality troops with no tank support. The intelligence report also indicated that no enemy tanks would be able to reach the area for at least eight hours once an attack began.

The 2nd Battalion assault would be supported by three tanks and indirect fire from the 376th PFA Battalion. However, the tanks would be unable to move across the canal. The battalion's 81mm mortars and machine guns would support the attack from the bank of the canal. A rolling barrage would precede Company D in the lead, followed by Company E. Company F would remain in reserve near the canal. If at any point in the attack Company D would encounter heavy enemy resistance, Company E would automatically execute a move to the right and hit the enemy flank.

At 1:25 p.m., the 376th PFA guns opened fire, and five minutes later Company D moved forward behind the rolling barrage. As Company D moved forward the artillery concentrations were lifted and laid down farther ahead. The Germans quickly realized that the rolling barrage meant an infantry attack and began firing their own concentrations into Company D and then lifting their fire. This was intended to give the impression to Company D that the artillery fire was friendly. This ruse was successful, as Company D held up while the 376th was contacted. Orders were issued for the 376th to fire on the objective only. This left Company D almost 1,500 yards of flat, open terrain to cross without the protection of the rolling barrage. Company D quickly pushed forward, running toward the north side of the town. They were pinned down by 20mm antiaircraft fire from the town and from German positions to the north. Company E swung to the right and moved into the town.

From his position near the bank of the canal, Lieutenant William J. Sweet, Jr., the 2nd Battalion S-3, saw enemy armor moving south down the road toward Borgo Piave, with Company D, pinned down in the fields west of the road. "The enemy then counterattacked from the north and east of the town, cutting D Company off from the rest of the battalion and into two parts, and isolating E Company in the town. Five tanks and eight half-tracks mounting 20mm guns were used by the enemy, and our troops had no antitank protection at all. Our three tanks were rendered ineffective by the banks of the canal and a desire not to get on top of the banks of the canal for fear of high velocity [enemy antitank] fire. Major [Melvin] Blitch ordered F Company to pick up some antitank weapons and get D Company out of their situation. It was getting dark by the time F Company could bring any pressure to bear on the situation, as all the antitank weapons were left with the regimental supply in the rear and had to be brought forward.

"E Company was having a bad time in town. They had been hit hard twice by three medium tanks and two flak-wagons, plus about two companies of infantry. Lieutenant [Hanford] Files [Company E, CO] at last withdrew to the west side of town and set up a perimeter defense on the three roads leading towards the canal. The town was being shelled by using the 536 radio to the CP and then relaying the directions through the normal channels. By these means the companies held out until 20:20, when they left an outpost of a platoon in position and F Company covered the area where D Company had been cut in two, as the remainder of the battalion withdrew. F Company withdrew at 02:00 to their old positions on the west side of the canal.

"D Company had only twenty-eight men left when they returned and their company commander [Captain William Roe] was still missing. But the missing men from the company continued to drift in all night long, until at 08:45 the following day they had a total of forty men and officers. E Company held the outpost for the day with only an occasional exchange of artillery fire. They withdrew the evening of the 26th under cover of darkness.

"Captain Roe came in at 08:45 on the 26th with nine more men. He had gone all the way through Borgo Piave and had tried to hold the enemy from entering the town from Littoria and the northeast. He had no idea what had happened to his company when they had been hit, as he was with the point at the time. All he was concerned with was why no one had come to help him hold the enemy off.

"While our battalion had suffered heavily, the enemy had been hurt too. He had lost two dual-purpose 88mm guns, three flak-wagons, and one medium tank in the fight, and three other vehicles to mines left in the area. Three prisoners were taken and an estimated one hundred killed or wounded in the action."[33]

On the morning of January 29, another attack was scheduled for that night. The 1st and 2nd Battalion would protect the right flank of the 3rd Infantry Division during its attack northeast toward the town of Cisterna. Both battalions would move along the Mussolini Canal on their right, covering an area to the first main road on their left, a distance of about 2,000 to 3,000 yards wide. They would move in a column of battalions with the 1st Battalion leading. As they advanced, elements of the 1st Battalion would peel off to cover the canal to the right. When the 1st Battalion forces were all deployed along the canal, the 2nd Battalion would take over the advance and continue dropping elements to cover the right flank until reaching the objective, Highway 7.

That night the 2nd Battalion moved out early and into the 1st Battalion area, causing a delay in getting to the canal. Then there were not enough wooden planks to cross the west branch of the canal, causing more delay. Next an ammunition ship in the harbor area was hit and exploded, illuminating the area. It was almost daylight by the time both battalions were across the west branch of the canal.

As Company C and then Company A peeled off to cover the canal frontage to their right, Company B took the lead. Sergeant Landon Chilcutt, acting as a scout for the company, carefully approached Bridge Number 6 just after dawn. "When we got to the bridge we heard the Germans shouting and then the bridge blew. We moved on to two other bridges that we had to take."[34]

As Company B peeled off to defend the canal flank, the 2nd Battalion was ordered to take the lead and came up to join the Company B troopers on the point, who were moving quickly, hoping to get to Bridge Number 7 before the Germans blew it. The ground was very flat, with ditches that crisscrossed the area for concealment. These ditches forced the tanks to use the elevated

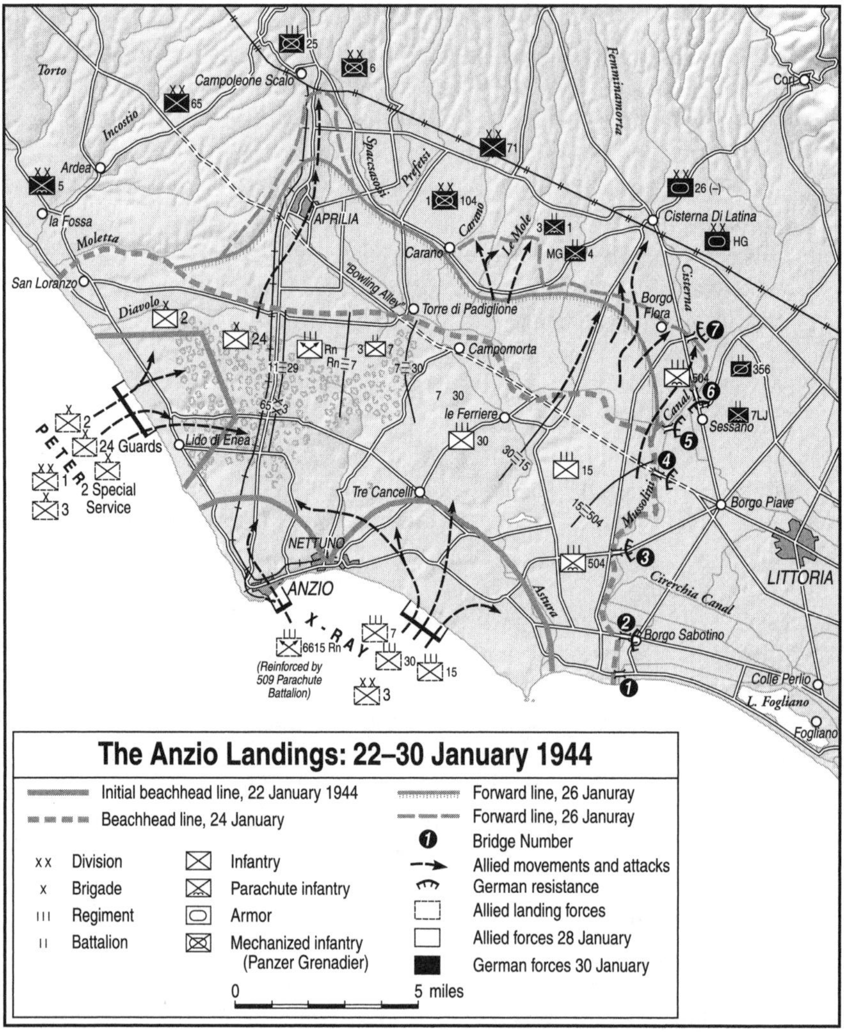

The Anzio Landings: 22–30 January 1944

roads, silhouetting them for German antitank guns positioned in the hills to the front and right flank. To the right of this open ground, the bank of the Mussolini Canal rose about ten to twelve feet. To the left the main road was elevated. Behind the 2nd Battalion was the bank of the canal that they had crossed during the night, and another canal bank was located to their front. They were boxed in with Germans afforded good observation from the hills to their right.

Lieutenant Sweet was with the 2nd Battalion Headquarters group, advancing just behind Company E and F. "The going was slow as nearly every house was defended and the enemy small arms fire from the canal banks kept the troops down low in their advance. A system was worked out whereby the troops would advance until fired on from a house or strongpoint, then the tanks would move up, blast the defenders out, to be taken by our troops. The further the advance continued the more fire was received from the right flank. At last, E Company had to be committed to clear the dike along the Mussolini Canal, north of the 1st Battalion. F Company took up the lead, using the same tactics, and advanced fairly well until they hit a strongpoint. Here the enemy did not break from the tank fire and the tanks were unable to advance or flank the position. The company had to flank, and reduce it from the east and rear.

"While F Company was doing this, the rest of the battalion was left strung out in a column along the road, and we got our first taste of the Germans' Nebelwerfer, or 'Screaming Meemies'. The entire column was shelled for about ten minutes by this fire and then hit by 88mm or antiaircraft fire. Several men from D and Headquarters Companies became casualties and the column was spread into the fields. E Company forced the Germans across Bridge Number 7 and experienced the same thing as the 1st Battalion. The Germans blew the bridge as soon as they had withdrawn across it.

"F Company reduced the [strongpoint] position and took twenty-five prisoners, then moved along the road to Fso di Cisterna. Here the Germans blew Bridge Number 8. Now it was apparent that the enemy had decided to deny us any crossings for armor in the area, so a race started for Bridge Number 9. Before D Company could get well under way, with the tanks, the Germans blew that one, leaving us with no armor crossings of the Mussolini Canal or of Fso di Cisterna."[35]

The 2nd Battalion found itself well out in front of the units on their left and with no armor support if they crossed the canal. The battalion was ordered to hold up and maintain their positions along the Mussolini Canal and the Fso di Cisterna.

On the northern side of the beachhead, the British had been attacking up the main Anzio-Albano road, and a dangerous salient was developing. By the evening of January 29, the British 1st Division had driven the Germans back, reaching the edge of Carroceto, and capturing the town of Aprilia, including a German strongpoint at the community center building, which the British referred to as "The Factory."

The same evening, the 3rd Battalion was relieved of its position on the Mussolini Canal and attached to the newly landed US 1st Armored Division, which was taking over the sector on the north side of the beachhead west of the Anzio-Albano road. The 3rd Battalion was assigned to protect the 1st Armored Division's right flank west of the highway, with the British 1st Division's sector on the eastern side. After several planned attacks by the 1st Armored were cancelled, the 3rd Battalion was detached from the division and attached to the British 24th Brigade on February 1, 1944. The British 24th Brigade meanwhile reached, but had not captured, the town of Campoleone against tough German resistance, while the 1st Armored Division cleared the railroad embankment northwest of Carroceto. The salient was now three miles deep and between a mile and a mile and a half wide.

By February 2, however, the offensive by the US 3rd Infantry Division to capture Cisterna and by the British 1st Division and 1st Armored Division to take Campoleone was spent. The 100,000 troops of the VI Corps were ordered to go over to the defensive in anticipation of a German counteroffensive. The 3rd of February was spent preparing defensive positions.

On the night of February 3–4 the Germans began a major attack to pinch off the salient in the Factory area in a double pincer assault to cut off and then destroy the entire British 3rd Brigade. One prong, west of Aprilia, drove south into the salient toward Carroceto. The other prong of the pincer pushed south to the east of Aprilia. The plan was for the two pincers to then turn east and west and drive to link up just south of Aprilia. They planned to then use Aprilia as the jumping off point for a drive south down the Anzio-Albano road all the way to the sea. The 3rd Battalion, 504th, was positioned almost precisely where the Germans planned for the two pincers to meet.

Around 11:00 p.m., the Germans infiltrated between the positions of the 3rd Brigade and began hitting the British in the rear. About 11:30 p.m. the 3rd Brigade headquarters passed through the 3rd Battalion, 504th, positions as they withdrew to avoid being overrun by the German infiltration attacks.

At around midnight on February 3–4, the Germans unleashed a massive artillery and mortar barrage on the base of the British salient to prevent reinforcement of or escape from the salient. Unknowingly, the German barrage fell largely on the 3rd Battalion positions. At about that same time Lieutenant Sims, commanding Company H, was ordered to block the Anzio-Albano highway in case the expected German attack broke through the British positions. "My company was given the mission to straddle the Albano Road north of Carreceto to help support the withdrawal of British troops. Soon after getting my company in position, British troops started passing through our lines going to the rear."[36]

The withdrawal of the British 3rd Brigade continued throughout the day, as Sims kept his men on alert for a possible enemy assault once the Germans realized the British were withdrawing. "They completed their withdrawal as darkness set in. Within the hour, a strong German force attacked our position, but we responded with devastating fire, to include heavy artillery fire, which disrupted their attack, causing them to stop and withdraw. I was sure they would try again, so I had my platoon leaders locate the British units on our flanks. I was rather disgusted to learn that they were several hundred yards behind us on an old railroad embankment. I then moved my company back to the same embankment in order to have contact on my flanks with the British. During this move my company was subjected to enemy artillery fire, and I was hit in my lower leg by a fragment. I felt the wound was not serious, so had local treatment and continued to supervise the occupation of our new position, which was accomplished before daylight on February 5, 1944.

"Shortly after daylight, the Germans increased their shelling of our position. Numerous rounds landed in my command post area causing everyone to seek shelter. I jumped into a large open slit trench next to a building, and two men came in behind me just as an explosion took place directly above the hole. The fragments came into the hole, killing the two men with me [Staff Sergeant William C. Kossman and Private First Class John A. Bahan] and I was hit in the right shoulder. The trench caved in on us and after digging out, I was taken to the hospital near Anzio. That evening the hospital was shelled by German artillery, so I located my clothes and equipment, got dressed and hitched a ride in an ambulance back to the front line and my company."[37]

On the night of February 5, the Germans began probing the defenses of the British and the 504th, looking for a vulnerable spot. Staff Sergeant Louis Orvin, with Company I, was in charge of his platoon, because almost all of the officers in the company were casualties. "I had my platoon dug in on the left flank of the Factory in a ditch perpendicular to the road. We heard a tank coming down the road, and I told the bazooka man to get ready. When we saw this vehicle it turned out to be a half-track. [The bazooka man] fired and hit the thing right at the radiator or the engine, because it burst into flames. A couple of guys jumped out and started running. I had a Thompson submachine gun and I opened fire on this guy on the right and he fell. They teach you with a Thompson submachine to fire three rounds at a time . . . quick bursts. I pulled that [trigger] one time and then I pulled it again, and I had emptied a clip.

"I went up there and walked around the half-track. There was one guy lying on the side of the road that was dead. I rolled him over and he looked like a young kid. Of course, I was just a young person myself.

"A little bit later the company commander told me to send out a patrol down the road. So I told Sergeant [George] Leoleis, 'Don't go too far. Just go down there beyond that half-track and see what you can find. Don't stay out there too long.'

"He found the other guy on the other side of the road that I had shot. Evidently I had hit him and he had died while he was running. We stayed in the holes all night long. I checked on my positions later on that night, when I heard Leoleis firing his M1. A German patrol had been coming up. He was a big strong guy. He would fire that thing and it would sound like an automatic pistol.

"I saw a man lying down on the side of the bank. Leoleis said, 'Don't bother him, he's dead.' He had been shot in the head. I don't know why he had his head up that far out of the ditch."[38]

The Germans lit the night sky with flares, hammering the British and American positions with a terrifying artillery barrage, reminiscent of World War I. The following day, February 6, was a relatively quiet day as the Germans regrouped for yet another attack. The British used the respite to reorganize, dig

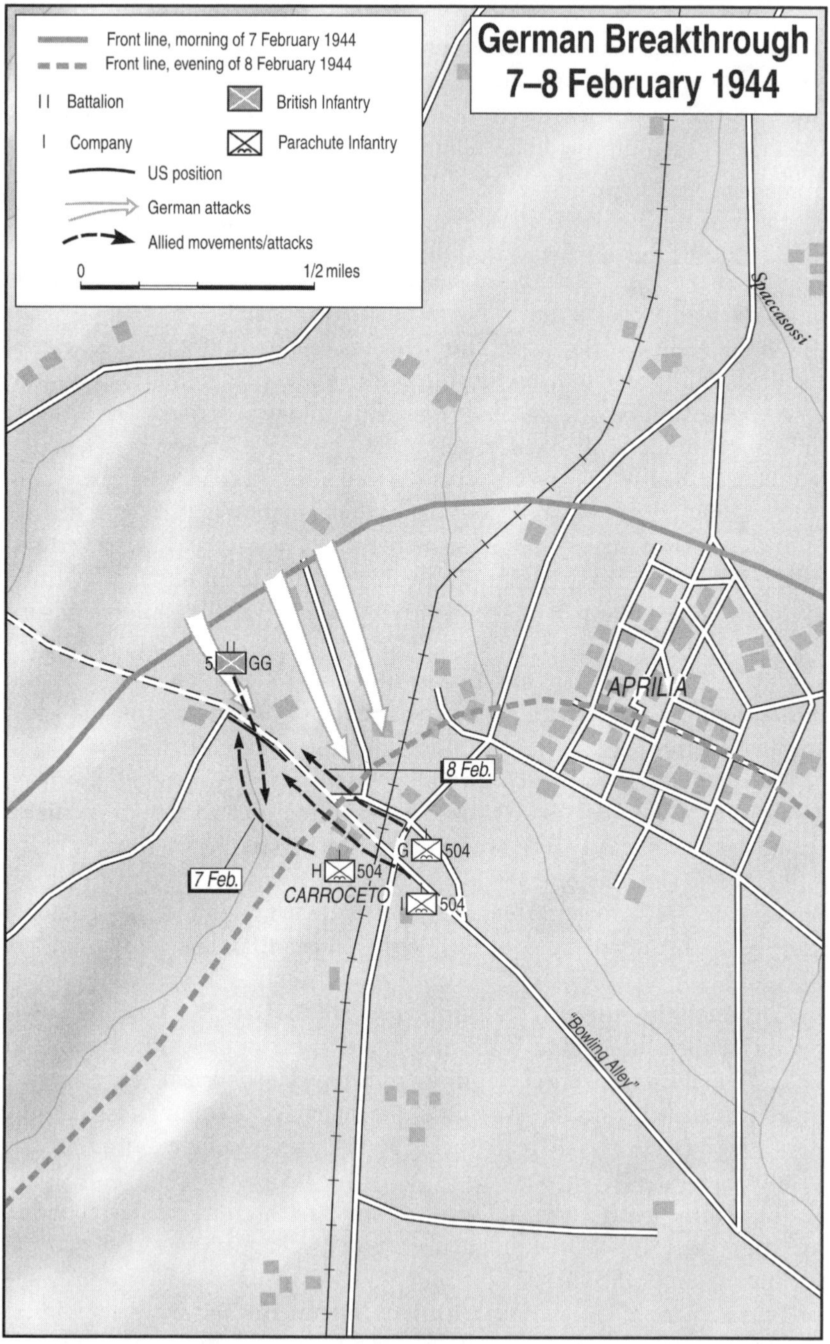
German Breakthrough
7–8 February 1944
Front line, morning of 7 February 1944
Front line, evening of 8 February 1944
II Battalion
I Company
British Infantry
Parachute Infantry
US position
German attacks
Allied movements/attacks
0
1/2 miles
Spaccasossi
5 GG
APRILIA
8 Feb.
G 504
H 504
7 Feb.
CARROCETO
I 504
"Bowling Alley"

in and strengthened their new positions. On the 7th, German artillery fire increased once again and intelligence sources warned of a renewed offensive that night.

About 7:00 p.m. on February 7, the 3rd Battalion was ordered to move south of Carroceto to act as a counterattack force. The British 1st Scots Guards replaced the battalion on the north side of the town. Shortly after arriving, Company H was ordered to move west of the overpass to help the 5th Grenadier Guards. They were only told that the Germans had broken through and were moving toward the beach, and they were to locate, engage, and stop the lead elements with a total of 2 officers and 25 men. They initially made contact with some of the British soldiers who were in full retreat. Company H continued to move forward past the British and down the slope of a hill to an old railroad embankment. The company took positions on the back side of the embankment, while the two officers, Lieutenant Jim Megellas and Lieutenant Richard LaRiviere (known as Rivers), moved forward to conduct a reconnaissance, leaving a sergeant in charge. They soon found themselves in the very midst of German infantry moving toward the railroad embankment. The Germans were shouting their locations to each other as they moved in order to maintain contact in the darkness. Megellas and Rivers moved quickly back to the railroad embankment, where their men were already engaging the German infantry.

Megellas took the entire 1st Platoon of just six men with him to try to locate friendly forces on their flanks. "I was the lead man in the patrol as we headed up the high ground to our left while the platoon sergeant, Sergeant Thomas Radika, brought up the rear, keeping the patrol together. When we reached the crest of the hill, I noticed a sharp drop on the other side: a cliff steep enough to protect our immediate left flank from an enemy attack. At this point a German machine gun opened fire from high ground across the roadbed on the silhouetted targets we presented. It was almost point blank fire. We hit the dirt and I gave the command to turn around and crawl back down the hill to the company position behind the embankment.

"Because I had started out leading the patrol, when we turned around and started going back downhill I found myself bringing up the rear. I soon caught up with Sergeant Radika going downhill. He lay motionless, his arms and legs still in a crawling position. I crawled alongside, exhorting him to get going: 'Radika, that's machine gun fire.' As I shook him I noticed that the left side of his body had been ripped open by enemy bullets. He had been killed instantly."[39]

With the cliff protecting the company's left flank, Megellas took his five remaining troopers back to the company. Megellas then led another six-man patrol that moved behind the railroad embankment to check out the area on the right flank. They followed the embankment until it intersected a road, which they crossed, and continued moving east about one hundred yards, along the base of a hill on their left. They heard Germans talking behind the hill, trying to regroup in the darkness before continuing their advance.

Megellas quickly deployed his small force at the base of the hill and waited. "As soon as we were set, the Germans, in what I estimated was a platoon-sized force, stormed over the top of the hill and straight toward us, not knowing we were positioned just below them. In the patrol, I was armed with a Thompson submachine gun; one soldier had a Browning Automatic Rifle; and the other five carried M1 rifles. We held our fire until the Germans were within close range, then we opened up with rapid fire. A large number fell with the first outburst before they could take cover and attempt to fire back. Confused and not knowing the strength and location of the force that had hit them, they retreated and took cover behind the hill."[40]

Megellas and his men reloaded and waited for the next attack, which didn't come. "We could hear the anguished cries of the wounded while their buddies were attempting to retrieve them. The Germans we fought at Anzio were highly trained, combat hardened, disciplined, and well led. The Germans at Anzio, like the troopers of the 504th, would risk their lives if need be to retrieve their dead and wounded, a mark of good troops."[41]

Megellas continued to lead his six men east, searching for any friendly forces. After about one hundred more yards, he and his men repeated the same ambush on another platoon of Germans coming down the hill toward them. The Germans fired flares attempting to locate them and dropped a mortar barrage all around them. After this ended, the patrol moved about another quarter of a mile without contacting any friendly forces. The patrol then returned to H Company, which had been heavily engaged stopping repeated assaults by German infantry during the two hours they had been gone. Megellas could spare only one man to cover the open right flank. "I placed the Browning Automatic Rifle man, Corporal John Granado, on the high ground to our right with orders to dig in and shoot anything that approached from the direction of the enemy. We placed Privates [Lawrence] Dunlop and [Sylvester] Larkin with their machine gun in the draw to our left, with the field of fire being the [rail]roadbed, in the event that the Germans attempted to storm over the road to engage us in hand-to-hand combat.

"The Germans continued an attempt to dislodge H Company from its entrenched positions with mortars and automatic fire. A few Germans were able to penetrate to the other side of the embankment from us and were lobbing grenades over the road and into our position. Meanwhile, we were lobbing grenades back at the Germans on the other side of the embankment. It was during this engagement that I suffered a flesh wound that would immobilize my left arm.

"We came through the night without further casualties while repelling every German effort to overrun our position. The break of dawn found a small force of two officers and twenty-four men still entrenched behind the roadbed and determined to hold the position against any odds."[42]

Before dawn on February 8, the 3rd Battalion was preparing a counterattack by Companies G and I to break through the German forces surrounding H Company. A little after 6:00 a.m. on February 8, Lieutenant Roy M. Hanna reported to the 3rd Battalion CP as ordered. "At the time I was in command of the battalion Machine Gun Platoon and was in support of Company G that was engaged with the enemy on another flank of the operation. The battalion commander, Lieutenant Colonel Leslie G. Freeman, relieved me of my duties and reassigned me as the company commander (temporary) of Company I. Company I had lost all of its officers (eight) and about forty percent of its enlisted personnel either killed or wounded and taken back to rear area hospitals.

"My first action was to withdraw the company to the reverse side of the railroad embankment, out of direct line of enemy fire, and had all of the men fix bayonets. This was the first and only time I had to give such an order."[43]

With Company I on the left and Company G on the right, Hanna led what was left of I Company northwest along the railroad bed to break through the German forces surrounding H Company. Staff Sergeant Louis Orvin didn't even know the name of the officer who was leading the company. "We went up this road. I was on the right hand side and I had a lieutenant that was on the left side. I had a squad behind me and he had maybe a few more men than a squad behind him. The lieutenant got up to a house on the left side of the road. He ran around a corner and got shot in the chest. He came running back and he collapsed."[44]

Lieutenant Hanna had suffered a critical wound. "It was between two ribs on the upper right side of my rib cage, into the top part of my lung, down through the lung and exited between two lower back ribs. After being shot, the right lung filled up with fluid, which stopped it from performing its normal function. Thus, because of oxygen starvation, I simply passed out."[45]

Staff Sergeant Orvin quickly took over. "I called for two men to come up behind me. One of them got right behind me and he stepped on a mine. He went up in the air and he fell down into the road. The road was cut probably six to eight feet deep at the crest of the hill.

"I told the last man to go back and get somebody with a stretcher. I wanted to get [Robert L.] Fetzer out of there. I called for our medic that was with us. I said, 'Chris, Fetzer is down there in the road. I'm going to run across this road. If they shoot at me, you don't do anything. But, if it's clear, you get down there and see if you can help him.' Well he just jumped down there.

"When I ran across the road, I rolled the lieutenant over and saw where he had been hit in the chest. I said, 'You're going to be all right. It went right through you.' But, I couldn't see where the bullet came out. I just wanted to make him feel better. I took my Thompson submachine gun and tried to spray a haystack behind the building where he had gone around the corner. I figured somebody might have been up in that haystack. But the Tommy gun wouldn't shoot. I gave all of the intermediate action. Then I threw it down and picked up his pistol.

"I had sent one man named Emmons, up ahead of us. I said, 'Emmons go down the road about a hundred or a hundred fifty yards as an outpost. If any more Germans start coming, you don't do anything but come back and let us know. Just stay down there about two minutes.'

"Emmons went down the road. As he turned around to come back, there was a German standing in the road that he had bypassed. He just ran through that German with his bayonet. He came on back.

"In the meantime, I started telling the guys we were going to withdraw. The lieutenant had regained consciousness and he got up and headed back down the road. He was a good lieutenant."[46]

At 9:00 a.m. the attack was called off until dusk, but it had managed to draw the attention of the Germans away from H Company. Meanwhile, Lieutenant Megellas awaited the next German attack. "Surrender was never an option. The Germans knew where we were, and if they wanted us they would have to come and get us. Before they did, we would take a lot of them with us."[47]

At 7:00 p.m., Companies G and I resumed the assault. Despite his terrible wound, Lieutenant Hanna continued to lead the Company I assault. However, Hanna's collapsed lung was depriving him of oxygen and when he exerted himself during the attack he passed out again. "This passing out happened probably three or four times over the next few hours,"[48]

Hanna and his Company I troopers, along with the remnants of Company G, fought their way to the high ground behind Company H and sent a runner to tell Lieutenants Rivers and Megellas to fall back while they provided overhead fire to cover the withdrawal. Lieutenant Megellas ordered his men to fall back, then moved to the exposed right flank, where he had positioned Corporal Granado with his BAR and two other men, to give them the order to withdraw. However, when Megellas arrived where he had left the men, there was no sign of them. "I made a hurried search of the area, but to no avail. The Germans had attempted to penetrate on our right, and I assumed they had become casualties defending our right flank. But because I could not find any bodies, we listed them as MIA. I later recommended Granado for, and he received, the Distinguished Service Cross."[49]

After the withdrawal of Company H was accomplished, and only then, did Lieutenant Hanna allow the medics to evacuate him. "Just after dark, our mission being completed, we received orders from Battalion Headquarters to withdraw to a more advantageous position. I got a ride to the British tent hospital, where I remained for three days. From there a trip by ship to a large general hospital in Naples where I spent the next sixty-two days."[50]

For his incredible bravery and inspiring leadership during the attacks to relieve Company H, despite being critically wounded, Lieutenant Hanna would later be awarded the Distinguished Service Cross.

The 3rd Battalion continued to hold part of the frontline positions in the critical Carroceto sector, rotating the rifle companies back as battalion reserve until relieved by British forces on February 15, 1943. By that time, the battalion consisted of about 100 men and officers. The 3rd Battalion, 504th Parachute Infantry Regiment, would be awarded a Presidential Unit Citation for the critical role it played in stopping the German breakthrough in the northern sector.

The reputation of the 504th grew among the Germans as they met these fierce warriors in mortal combat. While going through the pockets of a dead German officer looking for intelligence, a trooper found a diary and turned it over to the 504th Regimental S-2 section. They translated a passage in the diary that read, "American parachutists—devils in baggy pants—are less than one hundred meters from my outpost line. I can't sleep at night. They pop up from nowhere and we never know when or how they will strike next. Seems like the black-hearted devils are everywhere."[51]

Word of this quickly spread through the regiment. Tucker's troopers considered the term "Devils in Baggy Pants" a badge of honor and adopted it as the 504th's nickname.

CHAPTER 8

"YOU ARE ABOUT TO EMBARK UPON THE GREAT CRUSADE"[1]

While the 504th RCT fought at Anzio, in warfare reminiscent of the static trench warfare of the First World War, in Northern Ireland the 82nd Airborne Division rested, received replacements, and conducted limited training. To Lieutenant Ray Grossman, with Battery C, 456th PFA Battalion, Northern Ireland was the closest thing he had found to heaven since leaving the States. "They had whiskey, fish and chips, and people you could talk to. The mornings were cold and foggy up until two in the afternoon. We stayed in Quonset huts and tried to stay warm."[2]

Meanwhile, preparations in England were ramping up for the coming cross-channel invasion. The second airborne plan was very aggressive and called for the 82nd Airborne Division to land near St.-Sauveur-le-Vicomte to cut the western side of the Cherbourg peninsula, while the 101st Airborne Division would land near Ste.-Marie-du-Mont and open the causeways behind Utah Beach. The beach landed forces would then drive west across the peninsula to link up with the 82nd Airborne.

General Gavin was released on February 6, 1944, from his duties as the senior airborne advisor to the COSSAC staff to rejoin the division. General Ridgway assigned Gavin the responsibility for all 82nd parachute forces for the upcoming operation. Gavin immediately went to work preparing them for their missions. "I concentrated all my energies on planning, training the troops, and studying avidly the German defenses and the daily air photo coverage we were getting of our operational areas."[3]

During February, individual missions were assigned. The 505th would jump just west of St.-Sauveur-le-Vicomte and capture the town and the bridges over the Douve River, and send patrols to the south of Prairies Marécageuses. The

507th would land to the north of Hill 110 near Hills 71 and 82 and would defend against a German attack from the north. The 508th would drop astride Hill 110, consolidate its position, and move south and west to intercept German forces that would try to reinforce those on the Cotentin Peninsula.

On February 13, the 82nd Airborne Division began moving from Northern Ireland to their pre-invasion bases in England. The Division Headquarters was set up at Braunstone Park in Leicester. The 505th was billeted in Quorndon, the 325th in Scraptoft, the 80th AA Battalion at Oadby, the 320th GFA Battalion in Leicester, the 307th Airborne Engineer Battalion at Burbage, the 319th GFA Battalion near Market Harborough, and Batteries C and D of the 456th PFA Battalion at Husbands Bosworth. By the 10th of March the last units of the division, the 507th and 508th, had arrived at their new bases of Tollerton Hall and Wollaton Park respectively, at Nottingham, England.

The Division G-4, Major Bennie Zinn, described England as "some of the most beautiful country I have ever seen. We liked the old English villages and cities, the ivy covered walls, the moss covered stone fences, the bay windows in the houses, the parks, the forests, the snow covered hills, the people. We saw bombed cities, which for the first time made me fully realize how much the British had been 'taking.'

"All ages had their hands set to the task of winning the war. The women did chores that astounded us; hauling freight, working in factories, doing heavy labor, driving trucks, manning AA guns, working in railroad yards, flying planes, etc. We soon found that the women and children are friendly indeed, but the average man is rather 'stiff' and not too friendly; they have too much reserve for Yanks."[4]

Shortly after his arrival in England, Zinn and the division staff attended a top-secret briefing on the coming invasion. "We got the approximate dates, the location, the general method of attack about 19 February and it was then up to us as individual staff officers. Training was set up to be exactly like we were to execute it in France: the ground was selected and the problems began. Day after day and night after night we went over various situations. The members of the staff were getting all the details worked out, the instructions written, the supplies ordered and checked, the coordination set out. Of course, I had a wonderful group to assist in the G-4 tasks; Captain Walter B. Caughran, Captain William B. Noel, Captain Shelby White, Captain Al Ireland, W.O. Howard Goule, Master Sergeant Darrell Morton, Staff Sergeant Gene More, Staff Sergeant Sippel, Corporal Gryga, Private First Class Dzubak, and Private First Class Bob Stabb.

"Fred [Lieutenant Colonel Schellhammer, G-1] and I collaborated in getting into operation, camps for the entire division. We installed Red Cross Clubs in every camp and helped to get the Clubmobile Group going. The Clubmobile Group consisted of very fine American girls: Elma Ernst, Mariana Schallabarger, Mary Moore, and Charlotte."[5]

• • •

In Italy, the 504th received a large group of badly needed replacements to fill its depleted ranks on March 4. Private First Class James Ward was assigned to Company H. "My first night there was in a farmhouse between the lines (no-man's-land). The shelling was tremendous . . . an awful way to spend your first day on the line. I was glad to leave that farmhouse.

"My first combat experience began while on a ten-man patrol just beyond the Mussolini Canal. Big Bob Harris [six feet four inches tall], with his BAR, was number one in line. I was right behind Bob and Ray Walker was in the middle of the line. We were moving along a ditch parallel to a farm road when a Jerry machine gun opened fire. This gun was directly across the road from me, probably fifteen or twenty feet away, and firing to my rear. I hit the ground and almost immediately a potato masher struck me on my right leg. Several seconds later the second grenade landed a few feet away. I didn't have any luck finding either of the grenades, which I intended to throw back. It didn't take long either to realize that the grenades were duds or maybe landing in six inches of water caused them not to explode. In a few seconds I threw a grenade which landed exactly as planned, right in the midst of them. I could hear them shouting, scrambling around trying to find it . . . must have been three or four of them. I was looking at any moment for that grenade to come back my way. That was the longest five seconds I had ever known.

"We sent out patrols almost every night. It took a while to get used to the dead Germans which we had to look at until we were released several weeks later.

"I first met Chaplain Delbert Kuehl when Ray Walker and I were dug in on the Mussolini Canal, manning a .30-caliber light machine gun. On this particular day, shortly before dusk we observed a soldier moving in our direction. He was carrying an M1. When he arrived at our position he said, 'We're going to have a prayer meeting.' No one will ever know how much it meant to have our Chaplain there with us. You'd never know where or when Chaplain Kuehl would show up. It seemed like he was always around when you needed him most.

"It rained almost every day in the spring at Anzio. Ray Walker and I usually kept our machine gun covered with a rain coat, but this particular day we left the gun uncovered and walked down to a farmhouse nearby where we saw smoke coming from the chimney. Thought we might thaw out for a while. Lieutenant Rivers charged in the farmhouse and screamed, 'Who in the hell is on that machine gun up there?'

"Ray and I said we were. I never knew a man could get that angry. He said, 'You two SOBs get that gun down here, field strip it and I'll be back in ten minutes to check it.' I think we did it in five minutes. We were taught that your weapon comes first and should have known better."[6]

• • •

Improving weather conditions in England during March allowed the division to begin a tough training regimen. As the training for the invasion got underway, it became apparent that Lieutenant Colonel Herbert F. Batcheller was not the right officer to command the 505th. On March 21, Batcheller was relieved and sent to the 508th as the commander of the 1st Battalion. On March 22, Lieutenant Colonel William E. Ekman, the executive officer of the 508th, took command of the 505th.

Ekman certainly had his work cut out for him. Batcheller had allowed discipline to decline while the regiment was in Northern Ireland. Now it would be up to an officer not known to the rank and file troopers of the 505th to restore that discipline. Ekman assembled the regiment a short time after taking command to introduce himself and communicate his expectations of the officers and men. His speech began ignominiously when he told them that it was an honor to take command of the 508th. He quickly corrected himself, but it was too late. A chorus of catcalls, boos, whistles, and laughs cascaded from the packed crowd.

Nevertheless, Ekman took it in stride and delivered a fine speech discussing the discipline problems: AWOLs, race trouble, improper saluting, disobedience of orders, stealing, and venereal disease. He told the officers and men that he couldn't keep them from doing the wrong things, but he could make it damned hard on the ones who were caught. He indicated that he would make their stay in the camp more enjoyable by providing more entertainment, such as movies, a game room, donuts, and a reading room. His demeanor was one of a reasonable and fair man that had high standards that he expected them to meet. Most of the men and officers accepted Ekman's changes. Over the next couple of weeks, Ekman dealt with the few troublemakers effectively. He used a highly effective form of persuasion on those few problem troopers: telling them that they would be shipped to a leg unit. This quickly achieved the desired results, convincing any of the fence-setters to also comply. The respect for Lieutenant Colonel Ekman began to grow among the officers and men of the 505th.

After sixty-one days at Anzio, a tired, decimated 504th RCT was relieved on March 23, leaving the beachhead the next day for Naples. They would spend a few weeks in Naples resting before leaving for England.

There was a call for volunteers in each of the three parachute regiments of the 82nd Airborne Division to form a pathfinder team for each battalion. A large group of men stepped forward, from which each regiment handpicked 6 officers and 54 men. One of those selected was Sergeant James Elmo Jones, with Company B, 505th. "We were taken from our companies and put on detached service with the 9th Troop Carrier Command stationed at North

Witham near Grantham, where we did all of our practice jumps learning to operate the equipment.

"We usually jumped fifteen men to a team. We used seven for the lights, one for the ADF [Automatic Direction Finder], and one for the Eureka radio, plus some additional men to guard the perimeter to keep the enemy from slipping up on us and killing us while we were trying to operate the equipment.

"We were put into a barbed wire enclosure with guards walking the outside perimeter. We were not allowed to go on pass, go into towns. They treated us royally inside that compound. There was always a keg of beer in the corner of the compound. The food was absolutely excellent; steak, eggs, and everything that we hadn't had all during the war. We remained in this compound for approximately six weeks and during that time had some very important visitors . . . General Eisenhower, General Matthew B. Ridgway, General Bradley, and of course General Gavin, along with a lot of British dignitaries.

"I think the unique part of the whole situation was that we had rooms that had mats on the floor that you could walk on as if you were walking over the terrain [of the intended drop area]. It had every bridge, road, most of the houses, railroads, etc. clearly to scale on these mats, although there were no names of towns and not enough of the seashore showing to give us a clue as to where we might be jumping. We only knew that it would not be long until we left that compound."[7]

Glider-borne troops like Lieutenant James E. Baugh, with Headquarters Battery of the 80th AA Battalion, practiced loading, flying, landing, and unloading their gliders as often as C-47 and glider transport were available. "We would load on the Horsa gliders, the men would be strapped in and the vehicles would be lashed to the floor of the glider. They would take us aloft for about thirty minutes covering the whole Midlands area before detaching our towline so that we maneuvered to a landing. The pilots of these gliders were professionally trained. The officer in the copilot's seat was usually one of us who had some knowledge on how to land the contraption. Also, it was practiced by pulling two Horsa gliders with one C-47. Occasionally though, there were accidents, but surprisingly few casualties happened during our practice runs.

"Our training schedule at Oadby became increasingly more intense. Road marches of twenty-five miles were fairly common. As spring approached, outside maneuvers became more prevalent. There would be a regimental combat team in the field with batteries of the 80th Antitank elements attached. A large maneuver took place for several days in the Nottingham Forest, which I presume, had to be His Majesty's historic reservation. After every maneuver we would have a critique. These critiques would cover mostly the logistics. Communications was a big item in any operation and most especially of ours."[8]

Captain Roy E. Creek, commanding Company E, 507th, felt that the training for the upcoming invasion would prepare his men for any eventuality. "The training emphasized principles peculiar to airborne units such as speed and initiation of combat immediately upon landing; retention of initiative until the mission is accomplished; recognition of isolation as a normal battlefield condition; readiness of all units to attack or defend in all directions at any time; improvisation of weapons and equipment; use of enemy weapons and defenses; and preparedness to conquer or die."[9]

The Operations Sergeant for Regimental Headquarters of the 507th was Stefan Kramar. "When we would get back to camp after an exercise, the normal procedure was to clean our equipment, because there was an inspection shortly after we got back. This was to be sure all the weapons were clean, everything in top shape, and nothing had been lost or thrown away. Everything had to be up to snuff."[10]

Even the veteran 505th trained around the clock. Sergeant William Blank with Company G noticed that "the training was intensified; the order to move out at any time during the night was a constant practice. While in Quorndon we were taken to Sherwood Forest to go through the British Commando obstacle course. A number of practice jumps were made."[11]

The training honed the paratroopers and glider-troopers of the division to a razor's edge. Almost all of the night jumps were coupled with field problems, such as the mock capture of a bridge, a hill, or fortified position. Individual field problems were designed to simulate the mission of a particular unit in the invasion, although the members of the unit weren't given any of the specifics of where and when. Lieutenant Henry B. "Hank" LeFebvre was the platoon leader of the 3rd Platoon, Company A, 508th. "We got our first indication of what the 3rd Platoon of A Company was to accomplish somewhere in Europe. We found we were to blow up a bridge over a small river to keep the Germans from using it. We didn't know where the bridge was located, but we had the construction details as to type, length, and construction materials. From the time we arrived in Nottingham we always had an engineer platoon attached to our platoon for training. The training, of course, was always done at night. We would go out on our [training] problem and cover a bridge while the attached engineer platoon would place their charges and simulate blowing the bridge."[12]

On April 22, the 504th Regimental Combat Team arrived in England after its battle at Anzio. Lieutenant Carl Mauro had joined Company E as a replacement during the fighting at Anzio in early March. "The wharves of Liverpool, where we docked, were a beautiful sight to the battle-weary veterans. The red roof tops of the Liverpudlian homes and buildings shone brightly in the spring sunshine. We were entering another world, different from Naples, Anzio, Sicily, and North Africa. We were entering a domain more like America."[13]

The ranks of the regiment were depleted from the terrible casualties of the Italian campaigns. General Gavin visited the 504th shortly after their arrival and felt that with the replacements available in England, the 504th could be brought up to strength in order to participate in the Normandy jump. Colonel

Tucker and many of the 504th officers and men wanted to get in on what they all knew would be an historic invasion.

General Gavin approached General Ridgway with the proposal of substituting the veteran 504th for either of the untested 507th or 508th Regiments. However, Ridgway decided to leave the 504th out of the invasion plans and hold them in England as division reserve. "They were so badly battered, so riddled with casualties from their battles in Italy, they could not be made ready for combat in time to jump with us."[14]

This angered and disappointed both Gavin and Tucker. Gavin felt that "the 504th was one of the very best and would have made a tremendous difference to the division."[15]

The planning and preparations being made for the invasion were absolutely staggering. Loading tables and manifests for the aircraft had to be compiled. Intelligence reports were continually updated with the latest information. Supply calculations had to be made, and arrangements for aerial resupply coordinated. Arrangements for buses to carry the parachute and glider elements to the airfields had to be completed. Documents, map overlays, and sand tables required for the briefings that would be conducted prior to the invasion had to be created. Tech Sergeant Stefan Kramar with Regimental Headquarters, 507th, had been a commercial artist before the war. "Part of my job was to prepare the battle plan [map] overlays that would indicate the mission of the 82nd, and specifically the 507th. The overlay showed the division boundary; regimental boundary; drop zones; landing zones; command posts for the division, regiment, battalion, and special units; patrol lines; objectives; and what was to be seized and held, destroyed; and any other information vital to the operation.

"We also had a contour map that was reproduced, indicating the high and low areas of the land, rivers, marshes, roads, buildings, railroads, bridges, and other information about the area of operation. I had graduated from the Wisconsin Academy of Art, and my years of training to be an artist proved to be invaluable in working on the maps.

"It was normal to make sand tables in preparation for a drop so the men in the companies, platoons, and squads could be briefed on exactly what they were to do. Normally, we would have one sand table for each battalion, and in turn the companies would brief their squads and platoons. S-2, the Intelligence part of the unit, had the job to complete the sand tables, and made available so all the troopers would be briefed as to their mission. We tried to do this as thoroughly as possible, and of course, we had many talented people in our unit. One of the talented men in our unit had worked on sets in Hollywood for the movies, and what he could do with plaster was almost unbelievable.

"As a matter of fact, he managed to avoid a lot of bed checks because he actually made a plaster cast of his head, painted it, and attached it on top of a stuffed pair of fatigues, covered it with a blanket. When the OD [on duty] officer would come in for bed check at midnight, it was obvious that he was in bed sleeping! The truth was he had a girlfriend in town, and managed to stay out quite a bit longer than most of us were allowed to.

"He said to me, 'It would be nice if we could make a sand table, and be able to get one down to each individual company.'

"I said, 'We just do not have that much time because we have so many other things to accomplish.'

"He told me then, 'Sergeant, I worked on these sets in Hollywood, and we built amazing things. I think if I made one master table, and got it approved as to its accuracy, I could make multiple casts of the original.'

" 'How could you do that?' I asked him.

" 'Its a simple technical method. First, I would make the original out of clay, pour plaster over the original, reinforce it with gauze and stiff wire, and we would have what we called, in our business, a mother mould. Then I would cover the mould with green liquid soap as a separator, pour the plaster into it, again reinforcing the cast with gauze and wire, lift off the cast, and have a perfect duplicate of the original model. When it was dry, we would paint it.'

"I asked him how many we could cast from this mother mould, and he informed me he thought we could cast one for each company without it taking as long as making sand tables for just the battalions. It sounded good to me. We purchased the materials of clay, paint, plaster, and the other things not available through the Army supply. Using a slush fund called the Company Fund, we paid for any materials we needed to get the job done. I obtained permission for him to go to town, where he purchased the number of sacks of plaster he needed, the clay, gauze, paints, and miscellaneous items, and he came up with a beautiful sand table made of clay. The colonel, headquarters staff, and the commanders checked it for its accuracy. When it was completely approved, he started making the casts with the plaster. Now, each company would have its own sand table, which meant the briefing could be much more concentrated with less chance of mistakes.

"I got the battle plan overlays completed and checked and had them reproduced in as many copies as necessary. Every company commander and platoon leader needed an overlay to study. I went over the lines of the overlay with a Ditto pencil. The Ditto pencil was water soluble, and it would deposit a purple line on the paper. We would then transfer the drawing to a sheet of gelatin. The gelatin would be slightly damp, and the lines would transfer to the gelatin, and in this manner, we made our reproductions. We would lay a sheet of paper over the gelatin, rub it down, peel it off, and the image would be transferred onto the paper. You couldn't make many copies. The best I ever got out of a gelatin sheet was fifteen or twenty. Also included with the overlays was the contour map. All copies were numbered, and we knew exactly how many copies were printed. A log was kept so we would know where each copy was, and the number on it. It was registered in the log, and each officer or NCO had to sign for it. It was very important for security reasons that none of this information got out of the building. We were not allowed to discuss this outside the building with *anybody*! The building and the grounds were guarded very heavily with a machine gun at each corner. We could not get into the building without being identified by an officer who was on duty at all times. We enlisted men, who would report to the building each morning, many times worked far into the night, and often we just slept in the building instead of going back to the barracks tent.

"We were warned about going into town on a pass, and drinking, and getting involved with some girl. Who was to know that anyone you talked to was sympathetic to the German cause."[16]

In early May, Lieutenant Jack Isaacs, with Company G, 505th, knew that the date for the greatest amphibious and airborne invasion in history must be getting close. "We intensified our small unit training. We began to study French phrases, most of which didn't stick with us. We started studying sand tables and aerial photos of our intended objective, the location of which was unknown.

"The aerial photos were quite revealing, indicating the Germans on our intended target had prepared foxholes of their own. My platoon's objective was to seize those foxholes and use them to defend against a counterattack, which would probably come once we were on the ground."[17]

The daily aerial reconnaissance photos began to reflect ominous signs of enemy activity on Hill 110, the drop zone for the 508th. A quarry located on the western slope of the hill began to show signs of German heavy weapons emplacements. Then on the lower slopes of the hill near some wooded hedgerows, parking areas for vehicles began to appear in photos, indicating a command installation. Subsequent photos showed other areas of the lower slopes being cleared of hedgerows. Then about three weeks before the division was to move to the airfields, aerial reconnaissance photos showed black specks in a geometric pattern on the lower slopes of the hill. The number of these specks continued to grow, eventually covering over the entire hill. These were initially not identified, until photos taken in the early morning failed to show shadows. It was clear; these were holes. Shortly afterward, other photos revealed poles about eight to ten feet tall being planted in the holes. These were anti-landing obstacles, to deny the fields to glider landings. These poles were known as "Rommel's asparagus." Did the Germans know of the planned drop zones?

About a week before the division moved to the airfields, the drop zones were moved east, to areas slightly west of the Merderet River and west of Ste.-Mère-Église. This change was due to the detection of the German 91st Airlanding Division that had recently arrived on the Cotentin Peninsula. This specially trained antiairborne unit had moved into the area around Hill 110 and was headquartered at St.-Sauveur-le-Vicomte. It was working to turn all fields that were large enough for glider landings into deathtraps.

The 82nd Airborne had been just days away from unknowingly parachuting directly on top of a German division specifically trained to counter such operations.

All of the officers and men who had been involved in planning and preparations for the briefings had to create a new airborne plan. Technical Sergeant Stefan Kramar, with the Regimental Headquarters, 507th, and many others in the division worked around the clock to make the changes. "All of the preparations for the original drop had to be destroyed and cancelled. Very carefully and very thoroughly, all the paper work was burned. The papers having been numbered in our log, we could account for, and we crossed the number out as we burned each numbered piece of paper. The ashes were scattered. It would have been terrible if we would have haphazardly destroyed the secret documents. Our plaster tables were destroyed with sledgehammers, and pulverized so there was no inkling at all as to what we had planned to do. Once the demolition was completed, we immediately started over again on what was our new mission.

"Everything had to be redone, including the sand tables, overlays, supplies, battle plans, and we knew we had very little time left to accomplish this. The hours were long, and there were times I just did not bother to go back to my tent. Our meals were being sent in so we wouldn't have to waste time in the chow line. The meals came from Colonel Millett's mess, who had a reputation of setting a fine table! The meals were cooked in the CO's kitchen, and we loved it! Steak, fried chicken, roasts, pies, cakes, and all the good coffee we could drink was brought into us. I know many staff officers loved to visit our regiment so they could eat at the Colonel's mess. We could see why. Not once were we served SOS (shit on a shingle), which was really creamed beef on toast. Every once in a while they would let us go outside and stretch, and breathe some fresh air. We accomplished everything on time! Major J. T. Davis was the Operations Officer (S-3) at this time, and he was a true southern gentleman, and a joy to work for."[18]

During the intensive training that every unit had undergone, each and every man had memorized the key terrain features in the area of their drop zone and around their objective. Captain Roy Creek, the commanding officer of Company E, 507th, had confidence in his men and their ability to accomplish the assigned objective, but then everything changed. "On May 26th, closer to D-Day than anyone realized, company commanders were called into the war room where they found sand tables and map displays destroyed. Staff officers and enlisted assistants were laboriously preparing new ones. What did this mean? The answer was soon apparent. The 82nd Airborne mission had been changed. A constant study of daily aerial photographs revealed that the Germans had moved the 91st Infantry Division into the general area of St.-Sauver-le-Vicomte and were busily engaged in constructing passive and active antiairborne defenses.

"The mission of the 82nd Airborne Division, as changed, was to:

" 'Land astride the Merderet River. Seize, clear, and secure the general area within its zone. Capture Ste.-Mère-Église, seize and secure crossings of the Merderet River at La Fiere and Chef-du-Pont, and establish a bridgehead covering these two crossings. Seize and destroy the crossings of the Douve River at Beuzeville-la-Bastille and Ètienville. Protect the northwest flank of the VII Corps within the division zone and be prepared to advance west on corps order to the line of the Douve north of its junction with the Prairies Marécageuses.

" 'The 82nd Airborne Division planned to accomplish its assigned mission by dividing the division into three forces:

" 'Force 'A' to be committed before dawn of D-Day and to include the 505th, 507th, and 508th Parachute Regiments, plus necessary supporting and control elements.

" 'Force 'B' to be committed by glider before and after dawn of D-Day and [D+1] to include the 325th Glider Infantry, the bulk of the division artillery and other supporting elements of the division.

" 'Force 'C' to be committed by sea for a landing between D+2 and D+7 and to include all elements of the division not air transportable, along with attached tanks and tank destroyer units.' "[19]

By the end of May, the training ceased and the regiments of the 82nd were moved to the airfields in anticipation of the invasion. Sergeant Zane Schlemmer, a forward observer for the 81mm Mortar Platoon, Headquarters Company, 2nd Battalion, 508th, was told the regiment was moving out. "We boarded a group of ancient English buses with all our combat gear, and motored to the airports. Our battalion assembled at Saltby airfield behind a barbed wire security enclosure. We then all drew combat loads of ammunition. At the time I was carrying an M1 Garand .30-caliber rifle, mainly because most of my time was to be spent with the front line companies as a forward observer. We had been informed that the German troops had been instructed to give priority to eliminating forward observers, officers, and noncommissioned officers, in that order. So, by carrying a rifle and wearing my binocular case on the back of my rifle belt, I tried to look as inconspicuous as possible."[20]

The security at the airfields was very tight. Because of the last minute change of drop zones and objectives, officers like Lieutenant L.C. Tomlinson, a platoon leader with Company D, 508th, had the additional duty of preparing the briefings for the men. "During this period, no phone calls were allowed, the letters were censored and they were not mailed until after the operation had gotten underway. We built sand tables with terrain features, roads, large houses, large buildings, towns and so forth, and began briefing our troops.

"We were receiving daily aerial photographs of our jump area and were able to watch the telephone poles being implanted in Normandy to prevent or make glider landings more difficult.

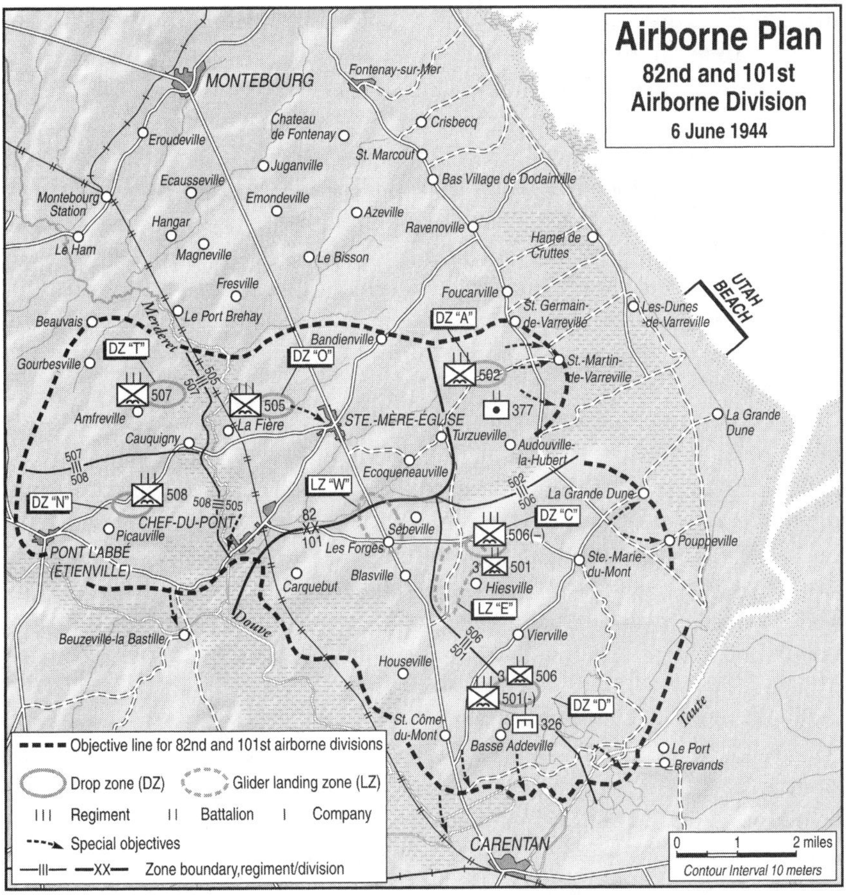

"The Air Corps was busy painting white stripes on the wings of the C-47 aircraft. The purpose of these stripes was so that planes would be recognized by our naval units in the English Channel."[21]

Shortly after arriving at the airfield, Sergeant Schlemmer attended one of the sand table briefings. "We were informed that German troops had occupied our originally planned hill and that our mission had been changed. The first session with the sand tables was without any identifying names, just the terrain with the fields, the roads, the rivers, bridges, and villages. The second session was around the same sand tables, but with English sounding names near the villages. Evansville, which in the third session became Ètienville, Port Abbey, which in the third session became Pont L'Abbe, and Pickleville, which in the third session became Picauville. At this third and final sand table session, we were informed that the invasion site was to be Normandy, France and that our objectives were to block off all German approach routes and their attempts to reach the 'Utah' invasion beach.

"We were then issued additional items, among which were silk escape maps, tiny small compasses, which we were to sew in each of our gas impregnated jump suits. We were issued 'invasion money' in several small French Franc denominations, in the event that we had to purchase anything from the French populace. We were each also issued two Benzedrine tablets to keep us awake and alert and two morphine syrettes for self-administering in the event we were wounded. We were given a small toy clicker, which we were to use for identification and communication upon landing in the pre-dawn darkness of D-Day. One click was to be answered by two clicks. Lastly, we were each issued a yellow life vest."[22]

The veteran 505th was assigned the most critical objective for D-Day of all of the parachute regiments. Lieutenant Jack Isaacs, a platoon leader in Company G, 505th, sat in the company headquarters tent while the company commander (Captain Willard "Bill" Follmer) briefed each officer in the company on the new objective for the 505th. Isaacs was told "that our intended target was the village of Ste.-Mère-Église, France. Our objective being to take and hold that village, deny the Germans the use of the roads through the area, and also prevent a counterattack if possible towards the beaches for the troops coming in there."[23]

The amount of detail given to the troopers was extraordinary. For many of the men in the 505th, this would be their third combat jump. The briefings were routine for them by now, however. As the men from Company I, 505th, gathered around a sand table, Private First Class William Tucker listened as "the briefing officer explained the mission to us, and it seemed very clear as we looked at the mock-up and aerial photographs. The principal mission of our battalion was to seize the town of Ste.-Mère-Église. One of our missions in Ste.-Mère-Église was to attack and destroy the headquarters of the German commander in the area. There weren't many questions. Everything seemed pretty clear cut, and everyone had a sense of confidence that the people higher up knew what they were doing. I had fewer fears about invading Normandy than I had sweating out some practice jumps. It was all like being part of one big machine. We felt strong and confident about what we could do, and we had no thought of failure.

"Our strength of purpose and acceptance of duties ahead were without question due to our real respect for the division's leadership. Pride in the division was above everything, without really saying so. The talk we had been given by General Ridgway probably had the most to do with it, in the sense that he had given us a feeling of unqualified involvement in a tremendous task that was grinding ahead like a juggernaut and had to be done.

"After the briefings, we had two more talks. General Gavin told us again in his quiet, businesslike way that we were well equipped, well trained, and ready to do the job with a minimum of casualties. He said that at the outset in our area we would outnumber the Germans we fought. He was low key in his comments, as always, and sort of reeked of his confidence in us.

"We had the usual dramatic speech by [Lieutenant Colonel] Krause. It had a lot of effect. The point of his speech was when he held up the American flag he always had [with him]. He said, 'This flag was the first American flag to fly over Gela, Sicily, and the first American flag to be raised over Naples. Tomorrow morning, I will be sitting in the mayor's office in Ste.-Mère-Église, and this flag will be flying over that office.' [Lieutenant Colonel] Krause's speech was stirring, because the United States flag was a powerful symbol to us of our pride, sense of duty, and determination."[24]

At the end of Lieutenant Colonel Krause's speech the battalion erupted in a massive cheer. Krause's troopers were now very much like caged tigers, just waiting to be unleashed on the Germans.

By afternoon of June 4, the paratroopers of the 82nd were spring loaded, ready to jump that night. The seaborne invasion was scheduled for the following morning, June 5. But inclement weather—rain, high winds, and rough seas—made the proposition dicey. All that Sergeant Stefan Kramar was waiting for was the word to go. "We had been fed like a dying man at his last meal. As a matter of fact, we were even asked what we might like to eat for supper on the 4th. We asked for smothered steak, and we got it, and it was very good! Smothered steak and mashed potatoes were one of our favorites. Once in a while they did get steak to cook, but we never saw it as such! It was always smothered steak. Just like we never got eggs in the shell. They were always powdered eggs; scrambled or disguised in some way. After our dinner of smothered steak, word came down that we were not going in that night because the weather was too bad. Here we were, ready to go, and all tensed up. It was decided that we needed to kill time, so in the hangar, they rigged up a big screen, and we had a musical movie . . . one of Betty Grable's. We slept on cots in the hangar after the movie.

"The next day there was a lot of uncertainty about whether or not this was the day we were going in. The date was now June 5th, which meant that D-Day would start on the 6th. It was about 2:00 in the afternoon when we got the word that we were going to go in. Poor Father John Verret must have heard more confessions that day than any other day of his life. We were settling our affairs, so if money was owed, everyone wanted to pay it back. We didn't want to go to hell for owing someone.

"Now that we were going in on the 6th, the big question came again, 'What do you want for supper tonight?' This time we asked for fried chicken. I don't know how they managed to accomplish all of this, but I'm sure they had priority."[25]

Corporal Tom Porcella, with Company H, 508th, had recently told his platoon leader that he didn't want his corporal stripes, requesting to be made a private again. Nevertheless, the men in his squad still looked up to him. Late on the afternoon of June 5, Porcella sat on his cot in the hangar waiting for orders to gear up. "Harold Wilbur came over to talk to me. He sat along side my cot and he wanted to talk. And I said, 'O.K. Harold, what do you have on your mind?'

"He said, 'Let me ask you a question.'

"I said, 'Go ahead. Shoot. What is it?'

"He said, 'Are you nervous? Are you scared?'

"I said, 'Yeah, I'm nervous. I'm scared. What the hell do you think, I'm somebody different? I'm as keyed up as everybody else.'

"He said, 'You know, Tom, I don't think I'm going to make it.'

"I said, 'Why do you talk like that?'

"He said, 'I don't know, everything has been going wrong.'

"Wilbur, a day or two before we left to go to the airfield got a 'Dear John' letter from his girl. She returned all the pictures and all the things that he sent her and gave her throughout the years. I think the ring and everything else. She had the audacity to send him the picture of the guy she married. So, this guy was really broken up and he was a really nice guy. He was a good trooper and I really felt sorry for him. He kept [saying] that he wasn't going to make it and he was going to get killed in the jump. I said, 'Harold, don't talk like that. You don't know. Let's just hope for the best.' "[26]

That evening, Private Ken Russell, a new replacement with Company F, 505th, was naturally nervous about his first combat jump. He got a plate of food from the mess serving line and looked for a place to sit. "The airforce always had good food, and they gave us what you might say was the 'Last Supper.' I recall at that 'Last Supper,' a fellow by the name of [Lee G.] Graves, who was in the company, who was a very devout, religious man. He'd always sit down at the end of the table by himself, you know. I do recall at the dinner that evening that there was something within me that wanted to be close to Graves, because he had something I didn't have. He was a devout, religious man, and I got my tray of food, and I went down, and I asked him, 'Graves, may I sit here with you?'

"He said, 'Yes.'

"I said, 'Well, may I share in your blessing?' He was aghast, because I had never done that before. None of us had. Of course, we kind of looked at him as a weirdo. I guess it was something that we sensed—danger. I didn't want to press it. But that was the first time I ever wanted to even sit close to Graves, because he would always pray."[27]

Another man in Russell's platoon who was deeply religious was Charles Blankenship. Russell admired him. "He was a devout religious fellow, nineteen years old at the time. His father was a Baptist minister. He was the only man that went to regimental headquarters and asked to take his tithe out of his meager army earnings. Blankenship, he was a nice guy. I guess he knew I was nervous. He was nervous too, but he made me feel good.

"He said to me, 'Well Russell, I'm the tough guy in the unit. I'll be around a long time. In fact, Russell, I'll tell you what I'm going to do. I'm going to raise the chickens to pick the grass off of your grave.'

"He was trying to cheer me up, I guess."[28]

At the hangar where Private Edward J. Jeziorski, with Company C, 507th, was busy checking his equipment, a radio was tuned to the German radio station that played all of the popular jazz numbers that the troopers enjoyed. "At around 8:00 p.m. someone yelled the 'Berlin Bitch' was coming on the radio. We all gathered around and sat up as she spoke. 'Good evening, 82nd Airborne Division. Tomorrow morning the blood from your guts will grease the bogey wheels on our tanks.' "[29]

Private Tom Porcella had a combat load fairly typical of most of the paratroopers. "I was wearing my combat trousers with the large pouch pockets. So, all I had to do is put on my jump jacket over the woolen shirt that I wore. The next thing that I put over the jacket was my combat belt and suspenders. The belt had pockets that you put all your ammo clips in. Attached to the belt was a shovel, a canteen filled with water, a first aid pack, a compass, and a bayonet. I believe we had about four or five hand grenades. Some of them were fragmentation grenades and the others were smoke grenades. For safety sake, we taped the handles. We had to do it because you don't know if the cotter pin would ever come out of them and it would blow you all to hell. Those grenades, I put in my lower pockets of my pants. A trench knife was securely strapped to my right boot. I put my chocolate bars in the upper jacket pockets. The gas mask was strapped to my left side. Above the gas mask I fastened the leather holster which contained a .32 Belgian pistol. Three bandoleers of ammo were slung across my chest to the left side. My rifle sling was fully extended and it also hung across my chest at an angle.

"On top of this went the main parachute. I adjusted the leg straps to fit very tightly. The reason we had it fitted real tight was because if you snapped those rings, and your leg straps were loose and went over your testicles . . . and you went out the door with all that weight . . . I don't need to tell you what would happen to the poor paratrooper. So, that's the reason we fastened the leg straps very tight while we're on the ground. We want to guarantee that they would never move while they were fitted to our legs.

"The next thing we put on was the reserve chute, which of course was attached to the main harness. Below the reserve hung a musette bag filled with three K-ration meals, a wool cap, underwear, toilet articles, vitamin pills, socks, and other things we thought were going to be important to us. Just below the musette bag, I had hanging a ten pound [Mark-4 antitank] land mine.

"To fasten all this equipment together with a belt and attaching that to the right side of the main chute proved the most difficult procedure of all. The belt must be passed through the rear of the reserve chute and attached to the left side [of the main chute]. Then, all must be adjusted so that with a quick tug, this will release the belt. This was very important, for if you could not get that out, you were in trouble all over again.

"The chinstrap of the helmet was also made to fit very tightly, because when you jump out of the plane, the initial shock of the parachute opening could push the helmet over your nose, and maybe break your nose. It could cause you a lot of facial injuries.

"I think I weighed one hundred seventy-five to one hundred seventy-eight pounds at that time. I believe with all the equipment that I was wearing plus the chute, I must have been well over three hundred pounds."[30]

One item that was issued to almost all of the paratroopers before leaving was a cheap child's toy, known as a "cricket." The cricket was made up of a couple of pieces of flat spring steel and held together by a coil spring between the two flat pieces, similar to the "A" shape and design of a clothes pin. By pinching the two separated ends of the cricket it made a "click-clack" sound. In the darkness, paratroopers could identify one another by one "click-clack," followed by two "click-clacks" from the other paratrooper. This accomplished the same type of password and response without making much noise.

Before leaving the hangar to load the planes, the troopers of Company B, 507th, were reminded one more time of their top priority upon landing in Normandy. For Private Chris Kanaras, the prophetic words stuck with him and would guide his actions on D-Day: "We were told, 'Get to the drop zone as fast as possible. Take no prisoners because they will slow you down. Avoid any possible firefights and don't carry any of our wounded, because they would slow you down. The thing is to get to the drop zone as soon as possible.' "[31]

Lieutenant Colonel Wesley T. Leeper, with the 9th Troop Carrier Command, observing the young paratroopers of the 508th as they prepared to load the C-47s for Normandy, remarked, "Never have I seen a finer group of physical specimens than the men who made up the 508th Parachute Infantry. Their faces were blackened, and their steel helmets were covered with green nets, into which had been fastened bits of green foliage. They looked like some savages I had seen in the films! Fastened to their person was more than I thought possible for one man to carry. Loaded with the 'impedimenta' these men could not stand for long, and most of them, after carefully checking to see that everything was in its proper place, lay down on the ground beside the plane which was to carry them to enemy soil. I had an opportunity to talk with some of these men before they took off, and I must say that at that moment, I was indeed proud to call myself an American . . . to know that I came from a country which produced men like these. Here was a group of young men—the flower of America—many of them, no doubt, about to face a horrible death, yet they laughed and joked about what they were going to do when 'they got home.' Many of them perhaps would never go back to America, for many soldiers prefer to have their bodies rest in the soil where their life-blood was spilled."[32]

Waiting to load up, some of the paratroopers engaged in horseplay. Private First Class Charles Miller, with Company D, 505th, and his buddy engaged in a "wrestling match while we were waiting to get on the plane to go to France. Of course, I got whipped, because he was a big guy. [Private First Class George] Rajner had been a weight lifter, in fact.

"He always said, 'If you think this is a war, you ought to see my mother-in-law and me. That's a war.' He wouldn't buy insurance, he wouldn't take the GI insurance, because he said, 'If I die, she'll get it.' "[33]

On the evening of June 5, pathfinder Private Dennis O'Loughlin, with the 2nd Battalion team, readied himself for the jump, even though he had a broken hand in a bandage. "Whether to make the jump or not with my broken hand was left up to me. They knew damned well I would jump. Told 'em if I could get that cast cut off my hand and a tight bandage put on it so I could use my fingers a little, I thought I could make it. We were hauled to a shop where they sprayed us all we wanted with green paint and handed us burnt cork to rub on our faces and hands. Then we were taken to the plane that was to take us in and lined up and had our picture taken along with the plane crew. We all got copies later."[34]

As darkness approached the pathfinders began to put on their parachutes and strap on their weapons, equipment, and special pathfinder electronic, radio, and light equipment. They then began moving to the planes to begin the loading process. The pathfinders would be the first men to land in Nazi-occupied France a few short hours away.

A group of 26 volunteers from the veteran 504th would jump on June 6 with the 507th and 508th pathfinder teams. Four volunteers from the 504th would accompany each of the six battalion pathfinder teams of the 507th and 508th and provide security on the drop zone, while the pathfinders set up the directional range finder equipment, Eureka radar beacons, and lights to mark the drop zones. Lieutenant Thomas A. Murphy, with Headquarters Company, 3rd Battalion, 504th, would jump with the 2nd Battalion, 508th team, and Lieutenant James H. Goethe, with Company A, 504th, would jump with the 3rd Battalion, 507th team.

In addition to the pathfinder team security volunteers, General Gavin took a few selected 504th officers with him for the Normandy operation. "Lieutenant Thomas Graham and Captain Willard Harrison were picked for their combat experience and reputation for toughness and courage in combat."[35] In addition, Gavin was told to take another trooper from the 504th, Lieutenant Donald Crooks, who commanded the 504th Reconnaissance Platoon. "Tucker insisted that I allow him to come along, saying he was the toughest soldier he had in the regiment—and that was saying an awful lot. This man wore a gold earring in one ear and didn't do much talking, but he had a reputation for being a very rough character indeed."[36]

The 504th Executive Officer, Lieutenant Colonel Charles Billingslea, would jump as an observer. Captain Harrison would act as Gavin's field assistant.

Following the pathfinder teams would be the 505th, with the 2nd Battalion leading, arriving on DZ "O" west of Ste.-Mère-Église at 1:15 a.m., followed by the 3rd Battalion, and the 1st Battalion. General Ridgway would jump with the 2nd Battalion. The 508th, with Gavin flying in the lead plane, would follow the 505th, with the 2nd Battalion jumping first, west of the Merderet River near Picauville on DZ "N" at 2:08 a.m., followed by the 1st Battalion, and the 3rd Battalion. The 507th would arrive last, with the 2nd Battalion in the lead, jumping west of the Merderet River near Amfreville on DZ "T" at 2:39 a.m., followed by the 3rd Battalion, and finally the 1st Battalion. Gliders carrying Tex Singleton's 80th AA Battalion's jeeps and antitank guns would arrive at 4:01 a.m. on DZ "O." Altogether, 378 planes would drop 6,418 paratroopers, with 52 Waco gliders carrying 220 antitank gun crewmen and 16 vital 57mm antitank guns.

Shortly before every man boarded his plane, he was given a letter from Allied Supreme Commander General Dwight Eisenhower that read:

> *Supreme Headquarters Allied Expeditionary Force*
>
> *Soldiers, Sailors and Airmen of the Allied Expeditionary Force!*
>
> *You are about to embark upon the Great Crusade, toward which we have striven these many months. The eyes of the world are upon you. The hopes and prayers of liberty-loving people everywhere march with you. In company with our brave Allies and brothers-in-arms on other Fronts, you will bring about the destruction of the German war machine, the elimination of Nazi tyranny over the oppressed peoples of Europe, and security for ourselves in a free world.*
>
> *Your task will not be an easy one. Your enemy is well trained, well equipped and battle-hardened. He will fight savagely.*
>
> *But this is the year 1944! Much has happened since the Nazi triumphs of 1940–41. The United Nations have inflicted upon the Germans great defeats, in open battle, man-to-man. Our air offensive has seriously reduced their strength in the air and their capacity to wage war on the ground. Our Home Fronts have given us an overwhelming superiority in weapons and munitions of war, and placed at our disposal great reserves of trained fighting men. The tide has turned! The free men of the world are marching together to Victory!*
>
> *I have full confidence in your courage, devotion to duty and skill in battle. We will accept nothing less than full Victory!*
>
> *Good luck! And let us beseech the blessing of Almighty God upon this great and noble undertaking.*
>
> *Dwight D. Eisenhower*

As Private First Class Bill Tucker, with Company I, 505th, walked to his awaiting C-47 he looked around. "Countless C-47 aircraft were all over the field. They were scattered, so it seemed impossible to count them. There were single files of bent-over men marching quietly in all directions with their parachutes to board different aircraft. A beautiful sunset was the backdrop for the scene, and you could hear the constant beat and roar of aircraft engines."[37]

Sergeant Zane Schlemmer, with Headquarters Company, 2nd Battalion, 508th, was first in line to load his plane, because he would be the last man in his stick out of the plane. He stepped up to the ladder beneath the door. "We were then pushed or hauled aboard the plane by the plane crewmen, for our individual combat loads were so bulky and heavy that it was impossible for us to get into the planes by ourselves. The moods of the various troopers ranged from nervous chatter and nervous laughter to several almost religiously quiet.

"The pilot and crewmen asked that we all cram forward as much as possible for takeoff to permit the overloaded plane to become airborne as quickly as possible. Then, in the dusk and coming darkness of the English evening at the airfield, the motors of the planes started cranking up; each coughing, then coming to life, idled, ran back, idled again, and then jockeyed into their respective takeoff positions."[38]

As his C-47 slowly rolled down the taxiway at the Spanhoe airfield, part of the seemingly endless line of planes of the mightiest airborne armada in history, Private Arthur B. "Dutch" Schultz, with Company C, 505th, sat quietly, alone with his thoughts when suddenly he heard a muffled blast. "There was a terrible explosion down the line in one of the airplanes. One of these Gammon grenades accidently went off and set the plane on fire and killed four of the troopers that were with Headquarters Company, 1st Battalion.[39] In fact, everyone was wounded or injured except [Sergeant Melvin J. Fryer]."[40] Fryer, not wanting to be left behind, found a seat on another plane carrying his company.

At airfields all over southern England, C-47s carrying the finest of American and British youth—paratroopers of the 82nd, 101st, and British 6th Airborne Divisions—taxied to the runways. Private First Class Tucker "got a good look out the window as the pilot revved the engines and held the brakes for our takeoff. What I saw was without question a scene I would carry with me always. Along each side of the runway were literally hundreds of people lined up two and three deep. United States and RAF ground personnel, British Army girls, cooks, and bakers—and no one moved. They just stared at our plane. Without moving, they seemed to offer a profound salute—and perhaps a blessing or prayer. We could feel—I know I could—the spirit of all those people with us as the pilot released the brakes and the plane surged forward."[41]

At approximately 10:30 p.m. the nine planes carrying the 82nd pathfinder teams began lifting off from their airfield at North Witham bound for Normandy.

CHAPTER 9

"ALMIGHTY GOD, OUR SONS, PRIDE OF OUR NATION, THIS DAY HAVE SET UPON A MIGHTY ENDEAVOR"[1]

As the C-47 carrying the 1st Battalion, 505th pathfinder team lifted off the runway along with the other eight planes carrying pathfinders of the 82nd Airborne Division, Sergeant James Elmo Jones looked down the aisle at the other handpicked men. "Some of the pathfinders in the plane had their faces blackened. I did not put anything on my face. I felt if I was going to die, I wanted to die looking normal.

"Since this was my third combat jump, I won't say that it was any easier, because it certainly was not. We felt that this would probably be the biggest campaign of our lives."[2]

For the men of the 507th and 508th this would be their first combat jump. And it would be made as part of the largest amphibious and airborne invasion the world had ever seen. They would be dropping into the heart of a heavily defended peninsula.

Private Tom Porcella, with Company H, 508th, and his stick boarded their assigned C-47 and got settled into their seats. Their sergeant moved up the aisle talking to each soldier in the stick, trying to reassure them. Porcella overheard "one trooper ask the sergeant if it was true that he had orders to shoot any man that refused to jump. 'That's the orders I've been given.' We had a few of the fellows that were talking, but when he said that he had the order to shoot anybody who refused to jump, the guys got kind of quiet.

"The sergeant looked out the door as the engines of the C-47s were warming up. He told us that he was watching the long formation of C-47s on the runways. The engines were just shaking the hell out of the airplane. They were revving up to full RPM

"Then, the next thing you knew we were moving. We were going down the runway. That plane was shaking, rattling, and rolling. Before you knew it, we were airborne. We seemed to gain altitude. We banked a couple of times.

"The sergeant said, 'We're in formation. We're on our way to France. It'll be some time before we reach our drop zone. So you guys just sort of relax and take it easy.' "[3]

Private Harry Reisenleiter, with Company B, 508th, saw an unforgettable sight as the planes vectored to assemble into their respective serials and later as they flew over the English Channel. "I saw something that still causes a catch in my throat. All the ships at sea, all the buildings, or anyone that could make a light without breaking their blackout codes, were blinking the three dots and a dash, for the 'V' for victory sign. They knew that the invasion was on its way, and they were wishing us well. I appreciated it and I will never forget that."[4]

With the pathfinder teams leading the way, the huge formation of 378 aircraft carrying the parachute element of the 82nd Airborne swept onward in mile upon mile of 9-plane waves arrayed in V-of-V formation. The 9-plane waves were grouped in 36- to 45-plane serials carrying a battalion. The leading serial carried the 2nd Battalion, 505th, followed by the 3rd Battalion, 505th, and then the 1st Battalion, 505th.

Captain Hubert Bass, commanding Company F, 505th, and his men were in the first nine-plane V-of-V formation, leading the main force of the 82nd Airborne Division. Bass looked at his watch; it was almost midnight. "At 23:49 hours, 5 June 1944, our flight was to rendezvous in the vicinity of Coventry, England. My thoughts while I was sitting near the plane's door were about our mission, our plans, wondering what kind of reception we would get from the Germans during the drop."[5]

Sitting near the door inside his plane, pathfinder Sergeant James Elmo Jones looked out the door at the lengthening shadows. "As it got dark when we left the coast of England, still with a long way to fly, everyone was quiet. No one was joking, no conversations were being carried on, just the constant hum of the engines. The C-47 with its door off [gave me] the ability to look out at sea and watch the water . . . watching the ships on the Channel as we flew over the top.

"In the plane, some of the men had upset stomachs because of the tension and nerves. Some men could not speak. I was so afraid that I would be the same way that I said a prayer again that I had said on the previous two combat jumps. It was simple and it was this: 'Lord thy will be done. But if I'm to die, please help me die like a man.' And then everything seemed to be OK."[6]

Looking out the door for checkpoints, Captain Bass glanced at his watch once again. "Just forty-nine minutes have passed since we left Coventry; seems like an eternity. I kept thinking of a saying I once heard. 'A coward dies many times before his death, but the valiant tastes the sting of death only once.'

"Some of the troopers in the plane had their eyes closed as if they were sleeping, others were just staring, someone would look at his watch occasionally, loosen or tighten a harness buckle. Those were brave men and [it was] a wonderful comfort to be on their team. There were several checkpoints between Coventry and the English coast. However, I was watching for the coastline, checkpoint 'Flatbush.' Then a destroyer in the Channel . . . a submarine, at which point we change our flight direction towards the Cherbourg Peninsula. Guernsey Island would be on our right.

"Lieutenant [James J.] Smith was on detached service to Division Headquarters. He was in command of our pathfinder group. Our success of hitting our drop zone depended on his group."[7]

Sergeant Zane Schlemmer, with Headquarters Company, 2nd Battalion, 508th, was the assistant jumpmaster in his stick. His position was at the end of the stick and was responsible for pushing it when they jumped. "As we reached the English Channel, it was getting dark. It seemed that as we hit the Channel, the mood changed from the chattering bravado and the stick became very quiet and almost pensive. In retrospect, it was probably the sobering thought of jumping into combat for the first time and the baptism of fire. The only lights I saw were several glows of cigarettes. From where I was, next to the cockpit bulkhead, by standing I could see past the pilot through the cockpit windshield, the blue wingtip lights of the formations stacked ahead of us in our serials."[8]

Private Eddie H. Livingston, with Company I, 504th—a member of the 2nd Battalion, 508th pathfinder team's security detail—stood in the door as the pathfinder planes crossed the west coast of the Cotentin Peninsula. "The countryside for as far as I could see, was filled with tracers and bursting shells, and aflame from fires of undetermined cause. . . . Cannon and machinegun fire raked the plane from nose to tail."[9]

Sergeant James Elmo Jones, with the 505th pathfinder team, noticed that "as we approached the drop zone, the area was obscured by low clouds. As tracer bullets from the Germans came through the clouds, you could see them light up the sky. We were all standing, and had been since we hit the coast. The equipment was extremely heavy. We were getting very tired and the only thing we wanted was to get out."[10]

Jones stood near the door waiting for the green light as the C-47 began "a shallow dive at a very high speed. Bullets were hitting the plane as if it could fall from the sky at any time. The cloud cover was still on us and the plane was still going down. We finally broke through the clouds. We were right on top of the trees. The green light came on and we jumped.

"Lieutenant [Michael C.] Chester [Company A] was the first man and I was second, behind him. On the short ride down after my parachute opened, I could hear firing all around me. I looked down and after having looked at the maps back in England, showing the countryside, I saw the trees coming up

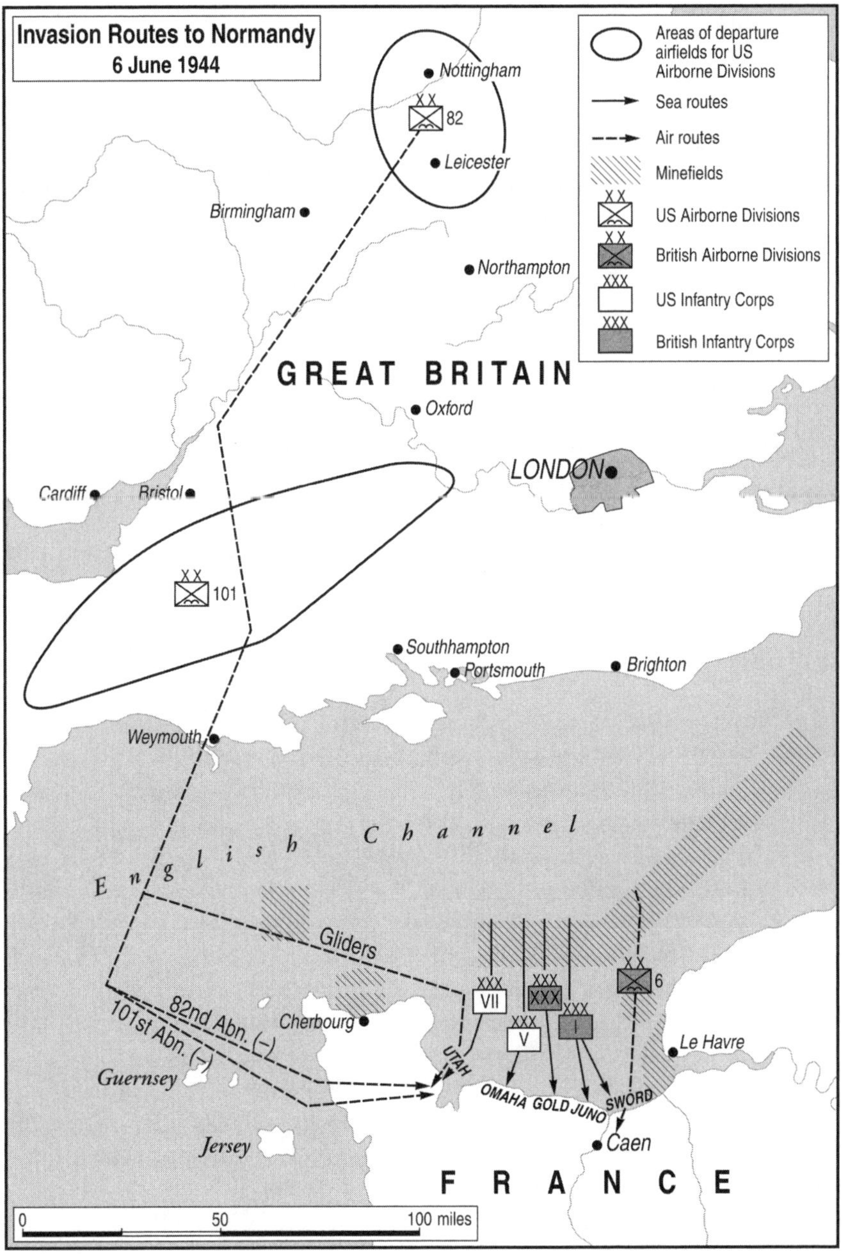

Invasion Routes to Normandy
6 June 1944
Areas of departure airfields for US Airborne Divisions
Sea routes
Air routes
Minefields
US Airborne Divisions
British Airborne Divisions
US Infantry Corps
British Infantry Corps
Nottingham
82
Leicester
Birmingham
Northampton
GREAT BRITAIN
Oxford
LONDON
Cardiff
Bristol
101
Southhampton
Portsmouth
Brighton
Weymouth
English Channel
Gliders
VII
V
I
6
82nd Abn. (–)
101st Abn. (–)
Cherbourg
Le Havre
Guernsey
Jersey
UTAH
OMAHA
GOLD
JUNO
SWORD
Caen
FRANCE
0
50
100 miles

and I honestly could see the field that we had practiced so many times looking at and landing on.

"By the time my chute opened and I could look up at the canopy, my feet hit the ground. I landed in the middle of a field. Landing was very hard. But, I had learned many jumps before to try not to tumble with so much equipment. Because it was an impossibility and almost without exception, a leg or arm would be broken. So, I simply pulled up my feet, tried to land as much as I could on the equipment, and my parachute settled over my head. And the first thing that I thought, without even trying to get out of my parachute was 'damn, I just cracked the Atlantic Wall.' "[11]

A mile southeast of the 508th DZ, Private Eddie Livingston (a veteran of Sicily and Italy and one of the 504th troopers providing security for the 507th and 508th pathfinder teams) jumped, and as soon as his chute deployed, he could feel enemy machine gun slugs hitting his canopy, while others made a snapping sound as they passed very near his head and tugged at his jumpsuit as they passed through the loose-fitting material. Landing alongside a hedgerow on the edge of a wheat field with five others, Livingston watched the other troopers very carefully and was convinced they were dead—killed during the descent. Suddenly Livingston saw a German emerge from the hedgerow. "I could hear the German approaching. Then he was standing over, me! I let him pull his rifle back, set himself for the downward plunge of the bayonet; then I tilted the muzzle of my Thompson, and let him have a clip of .45 caliber slugs in the guts, chest and face. The force and shock of the storm of slugs blew him backwards. I was flat on my back. Quickly, I reloaded the Thompson."

Landing under intense fire on the 507th DZ, Lieutenant John T. Joseph, the 507th regimental pathfinder leader, made contact only with the 3rd Battalion Eureka operator, Technician 4th Grade Paul B. Thore, and the Assistant Team Leader, 1st Lieutenant Claude V. Crooks. The three moved east in search of the light team but were unsuccessful. Lieutenant Joseph decided to abandon the search. "It was better to be sure of having one Eureka operating on time than to try to find a light or two and risk losing everything."[12]

The 82nd Airborne pathfinder teams landed on time at 1:21 a.m. The 505th Pathfinder Team was the only one dropped together on the proper drop zone. The 2nd Battalion, 505th serial, consisting of 36 C-47 aircraft leading the main force of the 82nd Airborne, were only about thirty minutes away from the designated drop zone, code named "O," when the pathfinders dropped.

Sergeant Jones and the other 505th pathfinders had to work fast. "We assembled our team within ten minutes with the exception of one man. [Pvt. Edward Devonschuk] was one of the last men in the stick to jump. We didn't know whether he was the first man killed in Normandy or what.

"We assembled the team and I got the direction of the wind and lined up the 'T' so that the seven men could go out with their lights. I took my ADF (Automatic Direction Finder), got it out of the kit, turned it on, and started assembling it. With the antenna up, it could reach (without obstructions in its way) up to fifty to seventy-five miles. I was trying to get the maximum distance with it.

"The Eureka radio was the other half of the Rebecca radio that was installed in the airplane. It was for pinpoint accuracy on dropping the troops for assembly. The ADF signal went further and the planes picked it up first. The ADF and the radar were picked up some twenty-five to thirty-five miles out over the English Channel."[13]

As the 505th serial neared the coast of France it began to descend from 1,500 feet down to 700 feet. Captain Bass could see below in the distance an unbelievable sight, "thousands of boats bobbing up and down, white foam breaking from their bows, all pointed toward France. Could they make their landings on schedule was a big question."[14]

The field where the 505th Pathfinder team had set up was now silent. Company E, 505th pathfinder Private First Class Anthony J. DeMayo crouched near a hedgerow with other pathfinders as the anxious minutes ticked by. "At this point the only sound was an occasional rattle of the equipment. We were told that it would be about thirty minutes from our drop to the drop of the main body. It felt like thirty hours. Then, off in the distance we heard the sound of the first plane motors."[15]

In the lead plane of the 82nd Airborne Division parachute element was Lieutenant Colonel Benjamin H. Vandervoort, CO of the veteran 2nd Battalion, 505th. "The mass and magnitude of the coordinated motion gave one the sensation of being part of an irresistible force that nothing could stop.

"As we came in over the Normandy coast we stood up and hooked up, ready to jump. Isolated fires were blazing on the ground below. Imagination told us they were aircraft already shot down. We ran into a cloudbank and as we came out of the clouds I could see our aircraft had begun to scatter. Flak in large volumes was coming up from Ste.-Mère-Église. Our planes were flying too high and too fast.

"I was standing in the open door ready to go—checking off the landmarks (highways, railroads, bodies of water) we had memorized during our pre-invasion briefings and studies. Suddenly the green light was turned on. I knew where we were and the signal was premature. The crew chief standing by me could communicate with the pilot over the intercom. I told him to tell them to turn 'the GD thing off' and wait and come down to the proper altitude and speed. The green light went out. We continued to fly as before."[16]

In one of the other nine planes leading the 505th, Captain Bass, the CO of Company F, was watching for the landmarks and the lights marking the drop zone as he called out the commands they all knew by heart. "Stand up and hook up! . . . Check equipment! . . . Stand in the door! I don't believe I could be heard, maybe they read my lips. Every man tightened up, pushing towards the door.

"Where was Smith's lights? I began to get worried. It was dark, clouds kept flying past, blocking vision of the ground. Our coded light was color green.

"We could pass beyond our DZ without knowing. The following planes would see us jump. We had to hit our DZ. I was determined when we crossed the second river, which was the Merderet and last reference point. To hesitate would put us within seconds of the coast. Where in the hell are those pathfinder lights."[17]

Waiting in silence on the drop zone near a hedgerow, 505th pathfinder Private First Class DeMayo and six other men got the word to move out. "At this point the other light men and I went out and turned on the lights and headed back for cover, because we surely thought this would be it, with the field lit up. But still no sound except for the sound of the planes, which were getting louder all the time."[18]

As Bass stood in the door he watched the last landmark, the Merderet River, pass beneath his plane. In the distance he could see a fire burning in Ste.-Mère-Église. "Suddenly, as if in answer to thousands of prayers, the clouds opened up and I saw lights on the ground formed in a 'T' with a green light at the bottom of the stem. Good old Smith."[19]

As the lead serial approached, German antiaircraft guns and small arms erupted with deafening explosions from 88mm and 20mm shells adding to the low roar of the engines of hundreds of C-47s. Tracers lit up the sky, as machine gun fire rose up to meet the oncoming aircraft.

As the nine planes carrying Company F and part of the 2nd Battalion Headquarters approached the lights of the drop zone, Lieutenant Colonel Vandervoort "told the crew chief to tell the pilot to pass the jump signal back to the trailing aircraft. The green light came on again and out we went."

Standing by the ADF, Sergeant Jones watched the awesome spectacle as C-47s carrying the 505th "flew directly over us and started dropping their serials right on top of the lights."[21] He saw brief glimpses of paratroopers coming out of the planes as German searchlights swept the sky and flashes of light from exploding shells momentarily illuminated the waves of aircraft moving east across the peninsula.

The plane carrying Lieutenant Colonel Vandervoort was flying too fast, and his chute opened with a tremendous shock. "It tore off my musette bag and snapped blinding flashes in front of my eyes. We were too high (perhaps 3,000 feet) and drifted away from our drop zone. As I came down I selected a small field with a clump of brush in the center and slipped my chute toward the shadows of the brush to be able to conceal myself while getting out of my harness.

"I landed on about a forty-five degree slope—hit hard and felt my ankle snap and knew at once it was broken. I got out of my chute in the shadows. I was alone—and crawled over to one corner of the hedgerows surrounding the field. The ankle hurt and I shot myself in the leg with a morphine syrette carried in our paratrooper's first-aid kit."[20]

As one planeload of paratroopers from the 2nd Platoon Mortar Squad of Company F, 505th, began to jump, it was apparent they had overshot the drop zone. With everyone anxious to exit the plane, Private Ken Russell felt his entire stick pushing for the door. "As we left the plane we had flak, machine gun fire, and everything else all the way down, because we were sitting targets."[22]

As Russell exited the plane, he saw that they were jumping right over a town where a large fire was engulfing one of the buildings near the town square. The bell in the church steeple was ringing. The French townspeople were in the square fighting the fire, using a water pump in the square to fill buckets that were passed person to person and thrown on the raging inferno. The town's German garrison was alerted and standing by, fully armed in the town square, overseeing the fire fighting. The fire lit up the entire area.

After his parachute deployed, Russell looked below and could see he was about to land on the high roof of the church, located in the middle of the town square. As Russell descended, he watched a terrifying spectacle unfold. "I saw something I never want to see in my life. I looked to my right, I saw a guy, and instantaneously, there was just an empty parachute coming down. A shell of some kind must have hit one of his Gammon grenades. He was blown away.

"I was trying to hide behind my reserve chute, because you could hear the shells hitting. We were all sitting ducks coming down.

"One guy landed in the fire. I heard him scream one time before he hit the fire. . . . I saw him land in the fire. It was heat from the fire that was drawing all these parachutes in towards the fire.

"I could feel shells hitting the parachute. When I hit the roof [of the church], a couple of my suspension lines, or maybe more, went around the church steeple and I slid off the roof. I was hanging on the edge of the roof on the right side of the church.

"[Private] John Steele came down and [his] chute covered the steeple. Sergeant John Ray, who had jumped from our plane, came down and he missed the edge of the church, he hit in front of the church. Sergeant Ray landed after we did, a split second, I would say.

"I'll never forget a red haired German soldier came around from behind the church to shoot Steele and me, who were still hanging there. As he came around, he shot Ray in the stomach. Sergeant Ray, while dying in agony, got his .45 out, and as this German soldier started turning around to us, he shot the German soldier in the back of the head and killed him. It was an agonizing death that Ray went through.

"I was scared to death. I finally got to my trench knife. It was carried down on your right jump boot. I cut my risers, threw my knife away, and fell to the ground. I looked up and I knew I couldn't do anything. I thought he [Private Steele] was dead. The only Americans that I saw there were dead, and it was our [Company F] men, you know. Most our stick were killed. Lieutenant [Harold O.] Cadish, H. T. Bryant, and Laddie Tlapa landed on telephone poles down the street. It was like they were crucified there. Charles Blankenship was in a tree. [Ernest R.] Blanchard landed in a tree, and he got so excited, he got his trench knife out to cut his risers and cut one of his fingers off and didn't know it until he was down.

"I didn't see anyone else around, so I dashed across the street and the machine gun fire was knocking up pieces of earth all around me. I ran over into a grove of trees. I wasn't completely out of town. I was the loneliest man in the world. Strange country . . . just a boy really. I should have been in high school rather than in a strange country. I think my class was graduating that night.

"There were planes still coming over bringing jumpers in. I almost ran into a flak gun in the grove of trees, shooting our men. I was scared to death. I got my Gammon grenade out, and I threw the grenade in on it. There was a huge explosion. The gun stopped firing. I ran up this field a little ways and I saw a bicycle come down the road. I knew it couldn't have been an American. I had to take care of the guy on the bicycle. I went two hundred or three hundred yards back to my left in the area where I was at, because I didn't know what else would be coming down this road. I found a guy from the 101st Airborne Division. So we went down the hedgerow and we found another guy from the 82nd. He was from the 507th, I believe. He had a broken leg. Well, we finally found several guys there.

"One of the guys said, 'Well, what are we going to do?'

"I said, 'Well, we've got to get back into Ste.-Mère-Église.' So we came back into Ste.-Mère-Église and there was [gun] fire all around the area."[23]

The combination of heavy equipment loads and some C-47s traveling faster than they should have, resulted in some troopers experiencing a terrible opening shock from their chutes deploying, blown out panels in their canopies, equipment torn off, and rough landings. Private George Jacobus, with Company E, 505th, was one such trooper. "Out the door—the worst opening shock ever. I looked at the canopy—I had blown three panels and was dropping fast. We were high—at least 1,500–1,800 feet. As the ground began to come into focus, so did a German machine gun nest on my right. There appeared to be a small building to my left. With all my strength, I pulled on the risers to go left away from the machine gun nest. I did, and slammed into the building like a ton of bricks, and on the ground, on my back. Something had hit my left eye. I knew in an instant that I had broken my left leg. It was eerie, as I lay amidst the tangled shroud lines and wriggled out of my chute. Then the pain in the left leg became a reality. It hurt like hell. Suddenly, after quite some time there was another trooper from another airborne unit. He was big enough to pick me up by the armpits and drag me over to be propped up against a tree."[24]

The plane carrying Lieutenant Roper Peddicord's Company E, 505th stick was picked up by a German searchlight. Sergeant Cullen Clark, Jr. was jumping third and could see out the door. "As soon as the searchlight picked us up and then went ahead of us, we could see the lines of tracers coming up from the ground. They looked like they were coming right in the door, but curved like a thin line of fire and hit the tail of the airplane. We were all hooked up and ready to jump, but the pilot started zigzagging and the plane engines sounded like they were going to tear off from the plane. We got away from the searchlight and Lieutenant Peddicord jumped, then we all followed him.

"Lieutenant Peddicord and I landed quite close together and I recall Lieutenant Peddicord saying, 'Clark, this makes three times we have jumped in combat and all three times we have landed close together. Now, let's start killing Germans.'

"Lieutenant Peddicord informed the planeload of men who had jumped with us, 'that the pilot apparently dropped us in the wrong spot. And all I know is that we are in France some place with German soldiers all around us, but we must find Ste.-Mère-Église and join the rest of our platoon and E Company.' "[25]

Company E, 505th platoon leader Lieutenant James J. Coyle landed without a problem. "The first man I encountered was our Battalion Commander, Lt. Col. Benjamin Vandervoort. He asked me if I had found my medical aid man, but I told him I was alone. At the time he did not mention that he was injured. But he had broken his ankle on the jump. He ordered me to continue to locate my men."[26]

Then Vandervoort took out his Very pistol and loaded it with a flare. "I then began to shoot up the green flares that were the visual assembly signal for my battalion. Troop carrying aircraft continued to pass overhead. A bundle containing ammunition came down without its chute and exploded about fifty yards in front of where I sat."[27]

Descending almost on top of that bundle was Sergeant Roy King, with Company D, 505th. "I was fascinated by the sight of the tracers flying around everywhere; when I saw a huge explosion blossom directly below me."[28] As he looked down at the explosion King suddenly saw something else flash below him. It was "a plane between me and the ground. No, it was not in trouble; I was!

"I was above the stream of airplanes that had just dropped their troopers and equipment. My immediate concern was that I could be chopped to pieces by the propellers of the oncoming planes. [I was] trying furiously to turn and face the oncoming planes in order to be able to see how to safely maneuver through them. I dropped safely through them in spite of my near hysterical struggles."[29]

As Company D, 505th trooper Private First Class Charles Miller went out the door of his C-47 he "was awed by the sight. You could just see everything. It was fantastic. It looked like a great big 4th of July celebration. The whole sky was lit up like a big show. There was Ste.-Mère-Église down below on fire."[30]

The 3rd Battalion, 505th serials flying right behind those of the 2nd Battalion now began dropping their sticks. Lieutenant Jack Isaacs was standing in the door of his C-47. This was his third combat jump. "As the 3rd Platoon leader, I had the left 'V' of three planes.

"Unfortunately, as we approached the coast we hit a rather dense fog bank, forcing some evasive action on the part of the pilots in order that they didn't run into other planes. I knew that my flight of three planes was veering to the left or the north, and that I would probably be off target.

"Breaking free of the fog, some maybe three or four miles inland. I saw no other planes. There were a few floating clouds. There was a good amount of German antiaircraft fire, both light machine gun, 20mm, and some 88mm high explosive stuff. Whether you looked north or south or east or west, you could see plenty of antiaircraft fire.

"The red light came on at approximately the right time for the drop. When the green light came on, seeing that I was over land, and it made no difference where I was over land, it was my duty to take the stick of sixteen jumpers out. This I did upon receiving the green light from the pilot.

"I landed without event. And, getting out of my equipment, of course I set out to 'roll up the stick' and find my men, any men that I could . . . take command of them and move to our objective.

"I began to hear one of those crickets, and following the sound of that cricket, I came upon a man who was badly injured. The Germans had staked out the large fields in Normandy to prevent glider landings. They had set poles in the ground, about the size of one of our own telephone poles. Not that high, but maybe ten to twelve feet off the ground. They looked like large pencils sticking in the ground. Unfortunately, this man had landed right on one of those poles and had broken his leg about midway between the knee and the hip.

"He had a severe fracture of the thigh there, was in great pain, was effectively out of the fighting, and could do nothing at all. There was no way I could take him with me. Each man carried a first aid kit, which contained morphine. I took his morphine, gave him a shot of morphine, took his rifle, put his bayonet on it, stuck it in the ground, put his helmet on top of the butt of the rifle. This was somewhat of a universal symbol that a man was out of action and certainly did not intend to fight. Then I went on about trying to find additional men."[31]

Jumping with the 3rd Battalion, 505th, were two 75mm howitzers and crews from the 456th Parachute Field Artillery. Lieutenant Clarence McKelvey, was the jumpmaster for the plane carrying one gun crew. "We had gotten the red light from the pilot, which meant for us to stand up and hook up and get ready to go. Sergeant [Joseph] Thomas and I were squatting down by the door looking at the ground, trying to pick up the pathfinder marks. We had a door bundle, and one of the men was behind the door bundle. The plan was for the door bundle [and the man] to go—then our gunner corporal would go, Corporal [James] Bates—then I would go—and the rest of the stick would go, with Sergeant Thomas clicking off the belly bundles. He would then go—the bundles going at the same time.

"When the machine gun fire hit the plane, the pilot jerked the plane over on the left side. All of us go flying on our butts. The door bundle and the man with the door bundle—they go out the door.

The 250-foot tower, Fort Benning, Georgia.
US Army photograph

Men lined up to take one of their qualifying jumps. *US Army photograph, courtesy of Weldon Grissom*

The chute deploys as a trooper makes one of his five qualifying jumps.
US Army photograph, courtesy of Weldon Grissom

Matthew B. Ridgway—US Military Academy Class of 1917.
United States Military Academy

Lieutenant Waverly Wray.
Courtesy of the 82nd Airborne Division War Memorial Museum

Lieutenant Colonel James M. Gavin—Fort Benning, Georgia.
Courtesy of Les Cruise

“40 and 8” boxcars, so-called because they were rated to carry forty men or eight horses, transport members of the 505th from Casablanca to Oujda, May 12, 1943. *Courtesy of Jerome V. Huth*

General Ridgway watches as his troopers prepare to board trains that will transport them from Fort Benning beginning on April 17, 1943, to the staging area near their port of embarkation. Note that all are wearing leggings and the standard infantry uniform, to disguise the movement of an elite airborne division from enemy spies. *US Army photograph, courtesy of the 82nd Airborne Division War Memorial Museum*

The 82nd Airborne Division disembarks from the troop ships at the harbor in Casablanca, French Morocco, May 10, 1943. *US Army photograph, courtesy of the 82nd Airborne Division War Memorial Museum*

Aerial view of the desolate bivouac near the Moroccan town of Oujda. The officers' pyramidal tents are visible at the lower left and center, while the pup tents of the enlisted men and NCOs are to the right center and upper left.
US Army photograph

In an olive grove near Kairouan, Tunisia, paratroopers of the 505th stand in line for a sparse meal, usually featuring Spam as the main dish. *Photograph by Dr. Daniel B. McIlvoy, courtesy of Mrs. Annie McIlvoy Zaya*

Typical combat load of a paratrooper. *US Army photograph, courtesy of the 82nd Airborne War Division Memorial Museum*

After his inspiring note to the officers and men of the 505th RCT, Colonel Gavin addresses the members of his stick before boarding the C-47 for Sicily, July 9, 1943. *US Army photograph, courtesy of Les Cruise*

Troopers of the 505th RCT "chute-up" and then check one another's equipment prior to loading the planes bound for Sicily. *US Army photograph, courtesy of the 82nd Airborne War Memorial Museum*

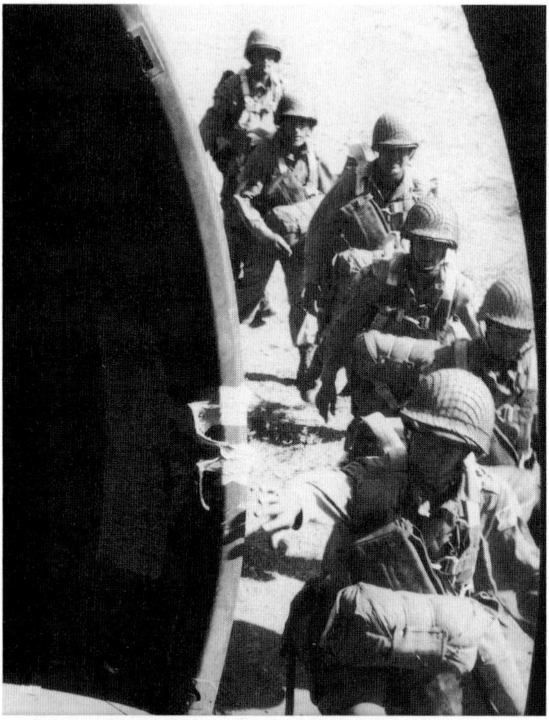

Heavily weighted paratroopers of the 505th RCT board their plane to make the first regimental-sized combat jump in US history. *US Army photograph, courtesy of the 82nd Airborne War Memorial Museum*

Paratroopers of the 505th RCT inside their C-47 destined for Sicily. *US Army photograph, courtesy of the 82nd Airborne War Memorial Museum*

Victorious troopers of the 505th pose around a knocked-out German Mark IV tank. *US Army photograph, courtesy of the 82nd Airborne War Memorial Museum*

Troopers from the 3rd Battalion, 505th, reach the crest of Biazzo Ridge. *US Army photograph, courtesy of the 82nd Airborne Division War Memorial Museum*

Troopers peer over the top of Biazzo Ridge as German infantry and tanks attack the troopers on the western slope of the ridge. *US Army photograph, courtesy of the 82nd Airborne Division War Memorial Museum*

An 81mm mortar squad with Headquarters Company, 3rd Battalion, 505th, set up on level ground just east of Biazzo Ridge. *US Army photograph, courtesy of the 82nd Airborne Division War Memorial Museum*

A Mark VI "Tiger I" tank of the Hermann Göring Panzer Division captured by the 505th. This is the tank that Lieutenant Harold H. "Swede" Swingler captured single-handedly by killing the crew with a hand grenade while they stood outside of the tank. *US Army photograph, courtesy of the 82nd Airborne War Memorial Museum*

View from the rear of the Tiger tank facing east on the road that ran through Biazzo Ridge. *US Army photograph, courtesy of the 82nd Airborne Division War Memorial Museum*

German POWs, former members of the Hermann Göring Panzer Division captured the previous day, dig graves for troopers of the 505th killed during the Battle of Biazzo Ridge, July 12, 1943. *US Army photograph, courtesy of Jerome V. Huth*

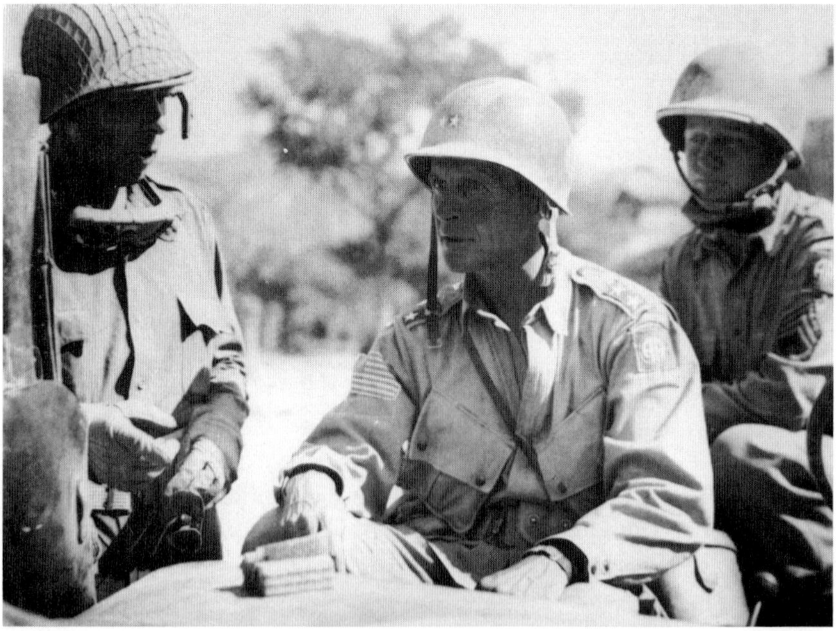

General Ridgway, sitting in the jeep (center), was not able to command either of his two parachute regimental combat teams during the first three critical days of the campaign because of badly scattered drops and the friendly fire disaster. *US Army photograph, courtesy of the 82nd Airborne Division War Memorial Museum*

C-47s sit on the tarmac ready for takeoff to drop the 504th RCT (less the 3rd Battalion) inside American lines on the Salerno beachhead. *US Army photograph, courtesy of the 82nd Airborne Division War Memorial Museum*

Eureka unit loaded into a leg bag prior to the Salerno jump. *Courtesy of Jerome V. Huth*

The 505th enters Salerno on the way to the Chiunzi Pass and, ultimately, Naples. *US Army photograph, courtesy of the 82nd Airborne Division War Memorial Museum*

Engineers of the 307th Airborne Engineer Battalion build stringers and flooring to support heavy vehicle traffic across the gap in the bridge blown by the Germans. This made it possible for the 82nd to maintain pressure on the retreating enemy. *US Army photograph, courtesy of the 82nd Airborne Division War Memorial Museum*

Troopers of the 376th Parachute Field Artillery Battalion eat Thanksgiving dinner in the mud and rain. The herculean efforts made by the officers and men of the battalion greatly assisted the 504th RCT in successfully completing its mission in the mountainous terrain on either side of the Volturno River valley. *US Army photograph, courtesy of the 82nd Airborne Division Memorial Museum*

The 504th advances through the hilly terrain near Venafro. The mules were invaluable in carrying heavy weapons, ammunition, water, food, and casualties during the fighting in the hills and mountains of Italy. *US Army photograph, courtesy of the 82nd Airborne Division War Memorial Museum*

The 504th RCT lands on the Anzio beachhead, January, 22, 1944. *US Army photograph, courtesy of the 82nd Airborne Division War Memorial Museum*

The 2nd Battalion, 504th, crosses the Mussolini Canal to make a diversionary attack, January 25, 1944. *US Army photograph, courtesy of the 82nd Airborne War Division Memorial Museum*

"When he righted the plane, we all stood up again, and the crew chief was hollering, 'Go! Go! Go!—You've got the green light!'

"I grabbed him by the chest and threw him to the back of the airplane, cussing him out a little bit saying, 'We're not over the drop zone. The pilot jerked the airplane and threw us all down.'

"By this time Corporal Bates is in the door, and Sergeant Thomas and I are in the door again looking for the marks, when the pilot jerked the plane again. Corporal Bates flew out the door—I flew out the door—head first, ass over teacups. We don't know how high we were, but I felt three things in succession—my helmet popped off my head, I felt my chute open, and I looked down and there was the ground.

"I hit the ground. We didn't have quick release chutes. So I was lying on my back, trying to get all these straps unhooked. Finally it dawned on me—I've got a trench knife on my right leg. So I get that and I'm sawing on the straps to get out, and I hear this voice saying, 'Who are you?'

"I looked up and here's this round thing sticking right in front of my forehead. It looked at the time to be about four inches in diameter. It turned out to be a .30-caliber carbine and a young boy from the 101st.

"I stammered, 'I'm an American—get that damned thing out of my face!' So he helped me out of my straps, and I stood up. About this time Corporal Bates came running across the field with my helmet—though he had lost his.

"A machine gun opened fire across the field. So the three of us started running toward the hedgerow. We dove into the hedgerow, and I got hung up with my feet dangling in the air. I had a new rubberized gas mask on my left hip and leg, and a .45 pistol on my right hip, as well as a walkie-talkie radio on which I was supposed to contact [Lieutenant] Ray Grossman once we hit the ground. I finally get down into the ditch and two things I discard—the gas mask and the radio, because I couldn't get it to work.

"We found several other guys in this ditch. We saw some buildings to our left, and we started moving down this hedgerow toward these buildings—being aware that the machine gun was to our right in the field—firing at us. We got to this little crossroads—just two dirt roads—there are two barns and two houses. When we got to the crossroads, I got out my flashlight and map, trying to figure out where we were. None of us knew.

"The machine gun opened up again. So we all hit the dirt, crawled behind the buildings—then decided that we had to do something about that machine gun or somebody was going to get hurt. It was decided that I would stay at the corner of the building with the flashlight. A couple of guys would run across the road to the back of the houses. A couple of guys would go the other way and try to sneak around behind the machine gun nest and put it out of commission. I was supposed to shine the flashlight and let them fire at me. We were getting all ready to do this when suddenly, the kid from the 101st who had helped me out of my harness, comes running up the road hollering, 'I got him!'

"Well, we had heard two explosions a little bit before that. He had gone back there and thrown a couple of grenades in behind the barricade where the machine gun nest was set up. We had no more trouble with that."[32]

Lieutenant Ray Grossman was the jumpmaster for the other Battery C gun crew assigned to drop with the 3rd Battalion, 505th. "Our pilot put that C-47 down on the deck when we hit France and then was trying to take evasive action. The green light went on, and we threw out the first door load. The pilot tipped the plane to the right and put me and the first man in the stick on the floor. When we got straightened out and jumped, the door load couldn't be found until noon the next day. We gathered up around forty troopers from all outfits and headed for Ste.-Mère-Église. I am guessing we were three miles from our DZ."[33]

The last serial of the 505th, the 1st Battalion, jumped a couple of minutes after the 3rd Battalion. In addition to his heavy combat load and M1 rifle in a Griswold case, Sergeant Harvill Lazenby, a squad leader with Company B, was carrying a double-barreled 12-gauge shotgun and a Colt .38 Special in a holster. Lazenby wanted to be able to defend himself as soon as he hit the ground. "The planes went in all directions when the flak started. We jumped around four hundred feet and we were taking a hit when we jumped. Because this was my third combat jump, I jumped with the shotgun in my hand. I landed in a sunken field alone, got out of my chute, made contact later with [Lieutenant James] Irvin, and we began to pick up guys from all units. We were between Montebourg Station and Ste.-Mère-Église."[34]

As the green light flashed on, Staff Sergeant Joseph I. O'Jibway, a platoon sergeant with Company B, went out the door. "We jumped with the plane going one hundred fifty miles per hour, five hundred feet off the ground. I lost my helmet. We hit so hard . . . the landing was sideways, I was almost knocked out. My left leg was badly injured. I came to, and all I could see was a horse and a cow in the field."[35]

The 2nd Battalion, 508th serial followed the 1st Battalion, 505th serial by five to ten minutes. General Gavin and his staff flew into Normandy with the 508th. Gavin stood in the door of the lead plane looking for landmarks as the serial flew eastward. "We had studied very carefully by the time of flight, and in my case I knew that I was to jump seven and one half minutes after crossing the coastline. More significant, however, was that after twelve minutes we went back over the English Channel. So we had to get out between that seven and a half-minute period and twelve minutes to be near where we expected to be to do our fighting.

"While we went through the fog and finally came out at about seven minutes, there was nothing to be seen except a lot of flak and small arms. However, looking ahead, there was a wide river that seemed to turn off to the west. I knew that no river on the map [was] so wide; only the Douve and if it were the Douve it was in the wrong place. So it couldn't quite be it.

"Time was going by very quickly and small arms began to come up. [At] about eight minutes the green light went on. I took one last precious look at the ground, because once you hit the ground you can only see the edge around front of you. I gave the command, 'let's go' and out we went. I landed with a pretty loud thud in an apple orchard. I got out of my equipment, made my way to the hedgerow on the edge of the field and ran into a Captain Price of my G-2 Office, who was rather slipping along the hedge on the other side."[36]

As his plane emerged from the clouds Private Tom Porcella, with Company H, 508th, heard a strange noise, as if gravel or marbles were striking something metallic. "One of troopers says, 'What the hell is that noise?' We were all looking at the sides [of the inside of the plane]. We thought, maybe something happened to the plane.

"The sergeant came to the middle of the plane and he started to talk to us, and he said, 'We're being greeted by antiaircraft fire from the Germans.' I looked out the window and you could see the stuff. You could see the shells bursting outside the plane and off in the distance you could see the machine gun fire. It looked like the bloody Fourth of July. We were lucky that our plane wasn't hit by shrapnel at all.

"No one in the plane spoke. I could feel a chill come over me, and I felt like a sitting duck. I wished we were at our drop zone. I don't know how much time went by, but all of a sudden we got the order to stand up and hook up. The silence was broken and we finally jumped up and snapped our hooks on to the wire. Then the sergeant called, 'Remember to keep your hand on the D Ring when you leave the plane. Now I want you to sound off for an equipment check.'

"Being the last man on the ship I had to reply first. I shouted, 'Seventeen OK!'

"The next man shouted, 'Sixteen OK!' And the count continued down until it was 'One OK!' which is the first man besides the sergeant.

"Then the sergeant shouted, 'Stand in the door.'

"My heart started pounding as I started saying a prayer to myself. I was so scared that my knees were shaking and just to relieve the tension, I knew I had to say something.

"So, I shouted, 'What time is it?' Somebody answered me and told me it was about 2:30. All of a sudden, I felt like I was all alone. So, I said, 'Let me say a few more prayers.' I said a couple of more Hail Mary's.

"The first man held his position in the doorway, which was the sergeant. And we all pushed up tightly against one another. We kept the pressure on the very first man.

"Then we heard, 'Are you ready?'

"All of the troopers shouted all at once, 'Yeah. Let's go.' With the roar of the engines in my ears, I was out the door and into the silence of the night. I realized I had made the jump into darkness. As the chute popped open, my head snapped forward and my feet came up. My helmet was pushed over my face. The jolt of the opening of the chute soon made everything a reality. I looked up at my chute to make sure it was OK. Then I looked down and I couldn't see anything but blackness.

"I unfastened the main belt, unsnapped my reserve and let it drop to the ground. I opened the chest strap. Now, all I had to do on the ground was to remove the leg straps and I would be free of the parachute. For a few seconds on the way down I looked around and saw the red and green flares. The brightness of the tracers flying into the sky and the sound of the machine guns firing seemed to be all around me.

"Looking up at the chute and then down at my feet, I had the shock of my life. I plunged into water. My heart was pounding and my thoughts were running a mile a minute. 'How deep is this water? Can I get free of my chute? Am I too heavy? Will the weight keep me on the bottom?' All this in a split second.

"I hit the water in a standing position and when my feet touched the bottom, I was leaning forward. I managed to straighten myself up and realized that the water was over my head and I had to jump up for air.

"The water was not as deep as I expected, so I held my breath and tried to stand. The water was just above my nose. Quickly, I stood on my toes and I was gasping for another breath of air. My heart was beating so rapidly that I thought it would burst. I pleaded, 'Oh God. Please don't let me drown in this damn water in the middle of nowhere.'

"Below the water I went and I tried to remove the leg straps. They were just too tight and wouldn't unsnap. I needed some more air, so I jumped up and as soon as my head was above water I began splashing around. I started to pray, standing on my toes with my head barely above water. My heart was beating faster.

"After a few seconds I calmed down and decided to cut the straps. 'God, my only chance is the knife. Please let it be there.' Going down into the water again, I felt for my right boot. Yes, the knife was still there. 'I'm lucky.' I slipped my hand through the loop and I tightly gripped the handle. With a fast upward motion, I removed the knife from the sheath. Quickly, I jumped up for more air and stood still for awhile, thinking, 'Now, I have a chance.' Holding the knife tighter, I went below the water. I slipped in between the leg and the strap, working the knife back and forth in an upward motion.

"Nothing happened. I was in a panic.

"I came up for another breath of air and I thought my heart was going to burst with fright. I wanted to scream for help, but I knew that would make matters worse. I told myself, 'I must think. Think! Why can't I cut the strap? My knife is razor sharp.'

"As I was gasping for air, I kept on saying Hail Mary's. It seemed an eternity before I realized I had the blade upside down. 'That's it! I'm using the back of the blade.' I touched the sharp edge and made sure it was in the upright position. Taking another gulp of air, I went down again to cut the leg straps. With a few pulls of the knife on each strap I was finally free of the chute. 'Thank God!'

"Getting rid of the chute calmed me down a little. But the weight of the musette bag and the land mine were still holding me down. With a few rapid strokes of the knife, I cut loose the land mine. Then, I unfastened the strap of the musette bag and let it fall. I adjusted the rifle and the bandoleers of ammunition to a more comfortable position. I cut away the gas mask, and removed the hand grenades from my leg pockets and put them into the lower pockets of my jacket. Reaching up, I unfastened the chinstrap of the helmet and let it fall into the water. I bent down to retrieve the musette bag. Except for the wool cap, the entire contents of the bag were disposed of, and the bag was then thrown over my head to hang behind me. I became conscious of the rifle and machine gun firing in the distance, and I was gripped with fear. All the training had not prepared me for such a landing."[37]

Lieutenant Ralph DeWeese, with Company H, 508th, also landed in the water. "I sank in the mud a good foot. Before I could get out of my chute, the wind inflated the canopy and started to drag me. My head was underwater and the chute dragged me for about three hundred yards. Several times I thought it was no use and decided to open my mouth and drown. Each time though, the wind would slack up and I'd get a chance to put my head up out of the water and catch a breath. With the last bit of energy I had, I reached down and pulled out my trench knife and cut the risers. I laid in the water for awhile and just panted, I was so exhausted."[38]

Another Company H trooper, Sergeant Dan Furlong, was the assistant jumpmaster on his C-47 carrying eighteen troopers. "The plane I was in got hit three times by an 88 and killed three and wounded four in the plane before I got out. The first one hit the wing. It took about three feet off of the tip of the wing. The next one hit right alongside the door and took the light panel off; the red, white, and green lights on the panel. And then the next one went through the floor and it blew a hole about two feet across the floor and then hit the ceiling and exploded in the plane. That's the one that killed them. It was a delayed action fuse that goes through and then blows up. It blew a hole about four feet around through the ceiling. Basically, it just about cut the plane in half. There was so much confusion in there you didn't know what was going on, because there was smoke, static lines, and parachutes all over the inside of that airplane. The lieutenant was waiting for the lights to come on and I was screaming for him to jump. The pilot was telling him to jump because he knew the lights were gone anyway. The lieutenant was probably in shock. He was standing there and the shell cut that side of the plane off right in front of him. I was at the back of the line. I was screaming for him to go, and I was pushing. So they finally got the message, I guess, and went. Three of the wounded jumped. The fourth guy who was wounded was lying on the floor. I fell with one leg in the hole in the floor and then had to crawl back out. There were static lines already hooked up and opened, and there were chutes the guys who were killed had been wearing open in the plane you had to get through to get to the door.

I was probably as scared as I ever was in my life. I thought the plane was gonna crash. I mean I didn't figure the pilot was ever gonna pull her back up again.

"But he did. He was over the top of that antiaircraft gun and he was trying to get down low, so it couldn't hit him. He went down and was heading for the treetops when I went out. The last guy out. I was probably no more than two hundred feet from the ground, if I was that far. When the chute opened it popped, and my chute popped my feet and I hit the trees. I went through the trees and I got a limb that went underneath my leg strap, came up on the side of my ear underneath my reserve chute. The limb broke and I came on through the tree and landed in a field flat on my back in a cement cow trough. It was full of water.

"The Germans were walking up the road. They could see my chute up in the tree, so they were looking for me. I could hear them running up and down the road. They had hobnail boots. They didn't see me because I was behind the hedgerow, while they were in the road. I cut my chute loose and took off."[39]

After almost drowning, Lieutenant DeWeese was lying near the edge of the flooded area, trying to catch his breath, when he saw a strange light in the distance. "Off to the west we saw what might have been a flare. It kept coming closer and soon you could see it was a plane on fire. It had been hit by flak. Just before the plane crashed, I heard the pilot gun both motors. I knew then that the crew was still in the plane. It crashed about fifty yards from where I landed and lit up the whole countryside. The Jerries fired their machine guns into the burning plane. How many were killed I don't know, but I know that no one came out alive."[40]

As Lieutenant Malcolm D. Brannen, with Headquarters Company, 3rd Battalion, 508th, descended, he dropped "through about three quarters of an apple tree. I was left hanging in the apple tree—dangling about one foot off the ground. But, I couldn't seem to get myself free of the parachute, struggle as I did. I got my trench knife and started cutting at my risers and at my leg straps. I couldn't seem to make much headway.

"Every other minute somebody would run by me on the ground and it was impossible to for me to see them to distinguish their identity. So when someone was approaching I had to quit struggling to get myself free. After they passed by I started trying to get free again. Finally my risers slipped enough to drop me the remaining foot or so to terra firma."[41]

Some planes were flying too low or very high or taking evasive actions in attempts to avoid the massive antiaircraft fire. The C-47 carrying John Taylor and a stick from Company B, 508th, was flying so low that he thought to himself, " 'We don't need a parachute for this; all you need is a step ladder.' As I recall, we weren't over two or three hundred feet in the air."[42]

Other troopers jumped from much higher than the prescribed altitude. After Sergeant Zane Schlemmer's parachute opened, he looked around at the spectacle. The entire sky was "alive with pink, orange, and red tracer bullets, which would arc up gracefully, then snap by with little tugs as they went through the parachute canopy. In the distance to the east, I could see a sizeable fire burning on the ground. This must have been Ste.-Mère-Église—although I didn't know it at the time.

"I hit in a hedgerow, coming up with very sore bruised ribs from the impact of all the equipment that I had strapped onto my body. I quickly cleared my chute harness assembly, assembled my rifle, and tucked my little revolver away.

"The moon, at that time was behind broken clouds and the reflection of the tracer bullets on these low hanging clouds created a reddish sky glow against which I could see a small lane next to the field and a small building with a tile roof. As I went from the field out into the lane, a very large orange ball of fire appeared overhead, coming in a steeply descending easterly line of flight. It looked very much like a meteor or a meteorite. But, it was accompanied by the roaring whine of two runaway, full power plane engines. Obviously, a troop carrier going down, and my immediate thoughts were of the troopers and of the crew who might still be aboard.

"I was alone. I had no idea where the hell I was, other than being in France."[43]

After Lieutenant Brannen cut himself out of his chute, he ran toward a nearby ditch to avoid machine gun fire coming from a position about one hundred yards away. As he jumped into the ditch, Brannen "could hear other men breathing and whispering the password and receiving the countersign. I found out that the men were three other paratroopers—right there in the ditch beside me—all watching that machine gun spit death to anyone in the way."[44]

Technician 5th Grade Frank Brumbaugh with Company I, 508th, landed in a field with one other trooper. Otherwise, they were alone. No other troopers had landed in their area. With the radar set turned on and working, Brumbaugh decided to check the area for Germans. "I went around the periphery of this small field, and I heard German voices on the other side at one point. I sneaked through the brush and stuff on top of the hedgerow, and I saw two German officers talking to each other, apparently unaware that we were in the field right next to them. When I saw these two German officers, in my mind's eye I saw two beautiful Lugers, which were souvenirs that I wanted very badly.

"We were ordered not to shoot unless it was totally in self defense. Since I couldn't make any noise, I tossed a white phosphorous grenade down at their feet through the hedgerow. It makes a small pop when it goes off, very little noise. It will devastate anything in the area, and it can't be put out. I got back out of the way and waited until the thing had finished burning.

"I heard small arms fire from across the hedgerow, and of course, we were with our rifles watching everything and scared to death. When the firing died down I went back to collect my Lugers. Well, both Germans were burned to death and hardly recognizable as humans. Unfortunately for the Lugers, the ammunition had exploded in the clips and blown the Lugers apart. That was not the best idea I'd ever had, but at least it got rid of Germans."[45]

Lieutenant Brannen and the small band of paratroopers he had hooked up with moved stealthily through the dark Norman countryside, attempting to find the rest of the battalion. "A corporal from the 508th acted as my scout and a private from the same company followed me. Then, two 307th Engineers brought up our rear. We came to a main road running north and south, but didn't dare stay on it, so we crossed. We found some wires running along the road—the 307th Engineers said they were communication wires, so we cut them in many pieces, covered the pieces in ditches so that the German linemen would have some work to do to restore normal communication. After following hedges north and east for a time we started due north again."[46]

Following behind the 508th serials, the troopers of the 507th began making their first combat jump. Lieutenant John T. Joseph, the 507th regimental pathfinder leader, also in charge of the 3rd Battalion Team, had managed to set up a Eureka that " 'triggered in' on the first serial ten minutes prior to scheduled arrival. When the planes came into sight it was noticed that a great amount of irregular dispersion existed in the formation. The serial flew beyond the Pathfinders and parachuted about one-half mile to the east."[47]

The drop of the leading 507th serial, composed of the 1st Battalion and some of the Regimental Headquarters, was widely scattered. The stick in the plane carrying Private Chris Kanaras with Company B had stood up and hooked up as they approached Normandy. "Once we crossed the coastline, all hell broke loose. Tracer bullets were everywhere. I was standing even with the wing of the plane and I could see all the tracers going by the wing. Only thing I could think of was when are going to get the green light and jump? At one time I could see the treetops. I was thinking, 'Man, he is too low.' Finally, he pulled up and gave us the green light and out we went. When I went out I could see the chutes being pulled from the bundles.

"The opening shock of my chute was awesome. The pilot must have been going at top speed when he gave us the green light. It had to be between three hundred and three hundred fifty feet. I hit the ground so hard I was numb for a couple of seconds. I rolled over on my stomach and I could see a big fire and explosion in the field. It must have been our bundles. It lit up the whole field I was in. A German machine gun was firing away, not too far from me. But, apparently he didn't see me because he was firing on C-47s flying low overhead.

"I reached down, got my trench knife, grabbed the suspension lines and cut them; then I ran off of the field to a ditch next to a hedgerow. I unlocked one side of my reserve chute and unbuckled the chest harness and had my rifle ready. The rest of the harness, I cut off. I was thinking, 'If the Germans were that close, there was no way I could move fast with all this equipment.' So off went the [land] mine, I kept the fuse in my pocket, off went the gas mask, the gas first aid kit, Mae West [life preserver], and my musette bag. Now I can move with my rifle, my ammunition, and grenades. I looked at my compass on my wrist and headed southeast. This is the direction of the 1st Battalion assembly area on the drop zone. Little did I know that I was nine to ten miles as the crow flies from our drop zone."[48]

In the lead plane of the 2nd Battalion, 507th serial was Lieutenant Colonel Arthur A. Maloney, the Regimental Executive Officer. "I stayed near the door (which had been removed) and attempted to keep the stick informed of our flight."[49]

Maloney got his stick up, hooked up, and through the equipment check; then moved forward to stand in the door. Jumping number five, Tech Sergeant Stefan Kramar anxiously waited in the tightly packed line of heavily laden troopers for the signal to jump. "The tracer shells looked like they were going to come right in the damn open door! Colonel Maloney was hanging onto the door with the prop wash blowing in his face. The green light went on, and the call 'Go!' was sounded."[50]

As Maloney led the stick out of the plane, his chute opened with a terrific shock. "I swung to the rear and landed flat on my back. There was no one else in the field in which I found myself. As rapidly as possible, I cut my way out of the harness and headed for the closest cover."[51]

Kramar shuffled forward, pressing toward the door as the stick jumped. "We piled out of there as fast as we could. I counted 'one thousand, two thousand,' and had not more than said two thousand, and I was in water so deep it was over my head! With all of my gear there was no way I could keep my head above water.

"As soon as I got back to the surface of the water, I pulled the release cord on my Mae West. It instantly filled up. I paddled over to what looked like a little island. I finally worked my way over to a place where I could get up on some land. I got out of my Mae West and my parachute harness, and abandoned them. With the rest of the equipment on me, I headed for the hedgerow. During the drop, my map case with all my maps of the Cotentin Peninsula that were in the map case were lost (no important information or secrets were on them)! The K-rations that I had strapped into my jumpsuit were gone. The opening shock of the chute was too much for the pockets, and they were torn out through the bottom."[52]

The next parachute serial into Normandy, the 3rd Battalion, 507th, was probably the most scattered. Some of the sticks were dropped far to the southeast. Captain Robert Rae, the CO of Service Company, 507th, landed miles to the southeast on a 101st Airborne Division drop zone. Lieutenant Francis E. "Frank" Naughton, with Headquarters Company, 3rd Battalion, 507th, was part of twelve planeloads of 507th troopers that landed even farther south, "dropped off course and widely scattered through the inundated area which extended for several miles south and southeast of Carentan. This flooded area, though interspersed with some islands of dry ground contained only a few elevated trails, and these generally meandered back into the swamp."[53]

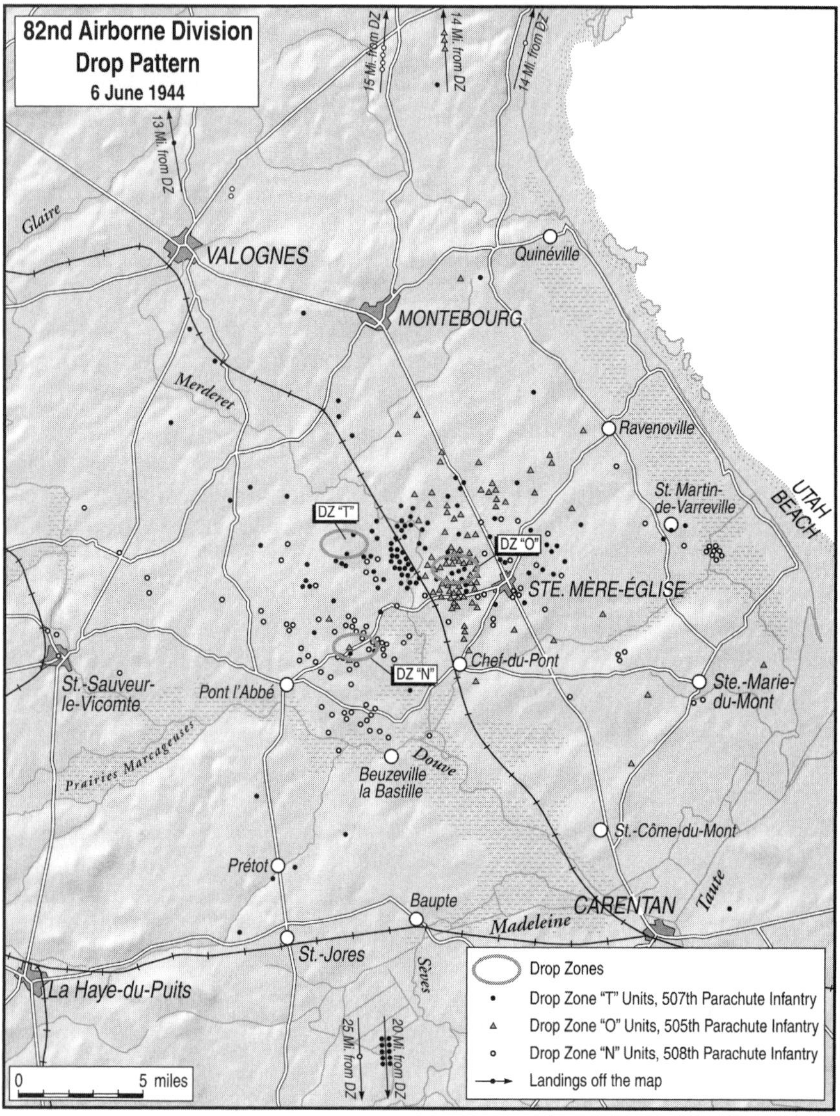

Sergeant Edward Barnes, the communications NCO for the 3rd Battalion, Headquarters Company, had a portable switchboard strapped to the front of his legs. He also jumped southeast of Carentan, near the town of Graignes. "There is no sweeter feeling than that rude jerking, letting you know your chute has opened. On the way down, I was straining to see the ground below, so I could prepare myself for the hard landing I expected, because of all the additional weight of my equipment. But to my surprise, the canopy hung up on a tree in the field, and I never had a softer landing in all my nineteen jumps. As soon as I touched ground, I unstrapped the switchboard from my legs, and started to take off my chute. As I was in the process, I heard someone approaching out of the darkness. Not knowing whether it was friend or enemy, I grabbed my carbine and spun around. In the darkness, I could see nothing, so I again started to take off the chute, and I heard the same sound of footsteps. Again, I grabbed my carbine and peered off into the darkness, but this time I could make out a figure approaching. I lay on the ground, ready to fire, trying to make out the number of men in the party, when to my amazement, it turned out to be just an old brown cow."[54]

As Lieutenant Malcolm Brannen and his small group of troopers rested in a ditch, he witnessed one of the planes carrying the 3rd Battalion, 507th, go down in flames. "I can still hear engines roaring, becoming silent, roaring again, flaming and I can still see it disappear beyond yonder hill—Finis—to one of ours—May God Bless."[55]

Because the paratroopers were so scattered, the headquarters of every German division on the Cotentin Peninsula were receiving reports of parachute landings. This caused the German commanders on the scene to overestimate the number of paratroopers that had been dropped. This in turn made them hesitant to strike decisively until they could get a better picture of what was happening.

Back at Drop Zone "O," the 505th was the only regiment in either the 101st or 82nd to have an accurate drop, thanks in large part to their pathfinder team and the experienced aircrews that had flown them into Sicily and Italy. The 1st Battalion got assembled and ready to move west to secure the eastern end of the La Fière Causeway. At the same time, the veteran troopers from the 2nd and 3rd Battalions began moving toward their objective—Ste.-Mère-Église.

At 9:32 a.m. British Double Summer Time the morning of June 6, 1944, the Allied Command announced the Normandy landings. It was 3:32 a.m. Eastern War Time in the US.

That night, June 6, 1944, President Franklin D. Roosevelt would speak to the nation and the world in a broadcast radio address. "Last night when I spoke with you about the fall of Rome, I knew at that moment that troops of the United States and our Allies were crossing the Channel in another and greater operation. It has come to pass with success thus far. And so, in this poignant hour, I ask you to join with me in prayer:

"Almighty God: our sons, pride of our Nation, this day have set upon a mighty endeavor, a struggle to preserve our Republic, our religion, and our civilization, and to set free a suffering humanity. Lead them straight and true; give strength to their arms, stoutness to their hearts, steadfastness in their faith. They will need Thy blessings. Their road will be long and hard. For the enemy is strong. He may hurl back our forces. Success may not come with rushing speed, but we shall return again and again; and we know that by Thy grace, and by the righteousness of our cause, our sons will triumph. . . ."[56]

CHAPTER 10

"WHEREVER YOU LAND, MAKE YOUR WAY TO STE.-MÈRE-ÉGLISE, AND TOGETHER WE WILL RAISE THIS FLAG"[1]

As the parachute regiments of the 82nd Airborne Division were landing in Normandy, 52 CG-4A gliders loaded with men, weapons, and equipment prepared to take off from Ramsbury airfield in southwest England. The glider serial consisted of Battery A and Battery B of Lieutenant Colonel Raymond E. "Tex" Singleton's 80th Airborne Antiaircraft (Antitank) Battalion, most elements of Division Headquarters, Division Artillery Headquarters, and the 82nd Airborne Signal Company.

Lieutenant Colonel Bennie Zinn, the Division G-4, and the other passengers of his glider had moved to their gliders around midnight. "Our glider was loaded and last minute instructions were given and I reviewed the entire program again. I gave last instructions about smoking, ditching in the channel, getting shot down in the wrong place, getting lost, fighting, surrendering if necessary, etcetera. We called the roll and all were present; Glider Number 9, Lieutenant Colonel W. L. Etiene [division surgeon], Lieutenant Irvin Bushman, Lieutenant Walschmidt (PI), Lieutenant Jacoby (CIC), Captain Rogers (Arty.), Lieutenant Davis (Pilot), Master Sergeant D. Morton (G-4), Master Sergeant [Charles W.] Mason (G-1), one MP, and my bodyguard. I talked to the pilot about his briefing and his plans, and we were ready to take off. We got off the ground at 01:30, circled the field one time and headed for the coast. We began to meet returning planes as we reached the coast."[2]

In Normandy, near the flooded Merderet River, Captain Roy Creek, the CO of Company E, 507th, moved cautiously through the darkness with a few men, trying to get some sort of unit organized. "Through the hedgerows we could hear voices. We couldn't tell if these were German voices or American voices.

'Flash' had been designated for the challenge instead of 'Halt.' From behind a tree came a challenge. 'Flash!'

"The immediate reply was, 'Flash, Hell! This is Colonel Maloney.' We knew we were among friends. [Lieutenant] Colonel Maloney, the 507th Executive Officer was a big powerful figure of a man, who in the days to come distinguished himself as the most fearless and effective leader that I saw in all of my combat experience. There were about fifty men present. Colonel Maloney assigned the highest ranking officer, [who] happened to be me, the job of organizing a perimeter defense, while he tried to contact someone on the only means of communication available, a very wet SCR 300 battalion radio.

"Troopers kept drifting in and our force was growing. Men came from all units of the 82nd Airborne Division and some from the 101st Airborne . . . what a hodgepodge of personnel. We knew nothing of what had happened to anyone outside our own small group. There was not tactical unity, no supporting weapons, just a group of invaders who were wondering what had happened to all of their thorough planning."[3]

After getting out of his chute, Corporal Wheatley T. "Chris" Christensen, with Company G, 505th, who had jumped last in his stick, started moving back to the west looking for the others. "My stick must have been scattered in three or four small fields. At this time we were being introduced to the Normandy hedgerows. You would pick up two or three men in this field and have to find an opening to get out. The next field you [would] have the same problem, but the opening [was] in another location. To add to this confusion, there was no set pattern to these fields. Those crickets we had been issued were now being put to good use.

"After getting to the end of the stick, I was told Lieutenant [Robert K.] Ringwald, our assistant platoon leader and jumpmaster wanted to see me. Both he and Sergeant [James R.] Yates were down and hurt bad. He had a broken back and Yates had two broken legs. We were fortunate in one respect that they were close together so we didn't have to move them very far to get them side by side. Removing their equipment and making them as comfortable as possible, after first placing their canteens and first aid kits within easy reach, I had the unpleasant duty of telling them we were going to have to leave them. This they both understood and we wished each other the best of luck. They were both good people."[4]

The surgeon for the 2nd Battalion, 505th, Captain Lyle B. Putnam, came upon his battalion commander, Lieutenant Colonel Vandervoort, about an hour after landing. "I located him near a small farmhouse. He was seated with a rain cape over him reading a map by flashlight. He recognized me and calling me close, quietly asked that I take a look at his ankle with as little demonstration as possible. His ankle was obviously broken; luckily a simple rather than a compound fracture. He insisted on replacing his jump boot, laced it tightly, formed a makeshift crutch from a stick, and moved with the outfit as an equal and a leader without complaint."[5]

Private First Class Les Cruise and his Company H, 505th stick had landed almost entirely on the drop zone. Cruise was able to quickly make his way to the Company H assembly point. "Within a short time our platoon was intact along with many from other 3rd Battalion companies. Many troopers arrived with the much needed equipment from the bundles dropped from each of the aircraft. These supplies were distributed to all to help get them to our objectives where they would give us the additional firepower that we required. I carried two containers of machine gun ammo in addition to my already heavy load.

"Along the road below I could see a group of officers talking to a Frenchman who had arrived on the scene and he was pointing out some directions, at least he was waving his arms in several directions. Perhaps no one spoke French."[6]

Sergeant William Blank, a Company G trooper, was close enough to overhear the conversation between the officers and the Frenchman. "[Lieutenant] Colonel Krause questioned him about the town [Ste.-Mère-Église] and the degree of troop strength. We went into the town expecting a fight."[7]

Cruise was waiting for orders when the word was passed down the column that the company CO wanted to see the platoon leaders up front. "Captain DeLong gathered H Company platoon officers together to pass along the orders given by [Lieutenant] Colonel Krause. The battalion, numbering over several hundred men, plus some troopers who had missed their drop zone, would move on Ste.-Mère-Église, where the glow in the sky was showing and take the town and defend it. We could hear sounds of machine gun and rifle fire all around, but nothing was from our immediate location. We had secured our area and were waiting orders to move, which came after the confrontation with the civilian who had been convinced to join our group. With the assistance of our new found friend we moved out towards Ste.-Mère-Église with G Company in the lead followed by H and I Company groups. Some groups were missing by the planeload, and we had no idea where they were, but we could not wait for them because time was very important to our mission's success.

"It was quite difficult to see where we were going in the dark surroundings as we stumbled down the embankment to the roadway and moved down the road in single file. We had trouble staying in line and following the man in front. I assumed we were heading for Ste. Mére and I hoped that the colonel knew our route. The trees and hedges screened the silhouettes of the men to my front. I was taken by surprise when [the man ahead of me] suddenly seemed to vanish, when I realized that he had turned right off the road into what appeared to be a cattle trail through the hedgerow and about three feet below the surface of the road. I damn near fell flat as I stumbled onto the trail fresh with cow manure. 'Where the hell are we going?' I murmured to myself. This path was almost like a tunnel through the brush, which was hanging low over our heads as we meandered along, staggering in the soft turf. I heard low muttering from others, but loud noises would give us away to the enemy, who must know we are in the vicinity. Just as suddenly as we had entered this path, we now began to exit onto what looked like a main road where we paused momentarily to reconnoiter, and check locations."[8]

After Tech Sergeant Ron Snyder, a Company G, 505th platoon sergeant, had landed near Ste.-Mère-Église, he worked to get the platoon assembled. "It was very dark. Bewildered cows were everywhere and confusion reigned. There were whistles and Very pistol signals and lots of hollering as we worked to sort out the thoroughly mixed up companies.

"Obviously, considerable time would be spent assembling. So Lieutenant [Travis] Orman suggested that I should take a few men and complete a secondary platoon assignment, which was to investigate a group of Quonset hut like buildings at the west edge of town and clear them of enemy soldiers. Off I went in the black night with a couple of riflemen and as we crawled through the fence to enter onto the highway, we froze in place at the sound of rapidly marching troops.

"Who were they? It sounded like German boots, but—maybe it could be English. We held our fire and let them pass. Later, I learned it was a company of the German 1058th Infantry bivouacked southwest of town.

"Just as we finished checking the building area for Germans, a huge flight of C-47s roared overhead and the enemy antiaircraft firing from the town resumed, and we watched, sickened and enraged as volumes of silver tracers ripped through the fuselages. I decided right then to go into town and silence those guns. By this time, I had picked up several stragglers and had a force of about ten men.

"We moved quickly, filing past the darkened houses that lined the street named Rue Chef-du-Pont. Enemy vehicles were roaring by on the main road ahead, and suddenly one truck braked to a stop, and troops from the back began firing wildly down the street. We sought refuge in doorways, and I ordered my men to withdraw. I feared the truck may drive down the street and shoot us like fish in a barrel. I left two riflemen to fire on the truck, to hold their attention, and with the rest of the men, I ran down a connecting street and then up a street paralleling the first street, hoping to outflank the enemy. This was always a main principle of our tactics. Never attack the strongpoint head on, but circle around and hit it from the flank. As we approached the main road, many German vehicles were still whizzing by, some with the headlights on, and the truck I was trying to outflank was gone. But through the trees on the town square, and illuminated by the dancing light and shadows from a burning house or a barn, I could see enemy soldiers loading several trucks, and against these, we directed all of our fire and drove them out of town in a hail of bullets."[9]

Because some of their sticks didn't hit the drop zone, the veteran troopers of the 3rd Battalion converged on Ste.-Mère-Église from all directions. Every trooper in the battalion probably remembered Lieutenant Colonel Krause's sendoff talk the previous evening: "Wherever you land, make your way to Ste.-Mère-Église and together we will raise this flag . . . the same one that flew over the Post Office in Naples . . . over the highest building in the town."[10]

Just as Snyder and his small group ceased firing, other groups were approaching the town from different directions. Corporal Chris Christensen was leading another group of Company G troopers, trying to find the rest of their company and the battalion. "I had seen this red glow in the sky and heard small arms from the same area, so assuming this was where the action was, and not sure at all where we were, this direction seemed the most logical. I also felt we had missed the DZ, as all the planes I heard after landing were well off to my left. We hadn't gone very far when I picked up four more men from the 2nd Platoon. I now knew [mine] wasn't the only planeload to be dropped here.

"Moving out, the going was slow, much like running an obstacle course with all those damn hedgerows. After all the training and preparations we had made back in England, not one word had been mentioned about them. After a short distance I [could] see we [were] approaching a small village, but I am still not sure what town it is. I [had] the men spread out on both sides of the road and we started moving through the town.

"Up until now, I hadn't seen a soul, but [had] this eerie feeling of being watched, so I [proceeded] very cautiously along. The farther we moved in, the smell of smoke [was] much stronger and visibility much poorer. About now, there [was] a break in the houses and we [were] approaching what looked like a village square. I halted the column and moved ahead to inspect what [turned] out to be a dead paratrooper hanging from a tree. Also, there are a couple more bodies laying close by."[11]

As this occurred, Krause and his 3rd Battalion were arriving on the outskirts of Ste.-Mère-Église. Because the Frenchman had told him that the town was lightly held, Krause decided to set up roadblocks on all roads leading into Ste.-Mère-Église before clearing the town. He ordered elements of Company G and Company H to move quietly through the town and set up roadblocks on all of the roads leading into town. After the roadblocks were set up, Company I would clear the town of Germans. As they cautiously moved down the main street, the paratroopers saw something that would shock, sadden, and enrage them.

For Sergeant William Blank with Company G, the images would live with him forever. "We saw a number of troopers who had landed in trees and on light wires, all of [whom] were dead. They had not had a chance to get out of their chutes."[12]

As Corporal Christensen was checking out the dead bodies in front of his column, Lieutenant Colonel Krause walked up to him seemingly from nowhere, startling him. Christensen was "told to take my group back down the road I had just come in on and set up a defensive position facing out, behind the last house on the right. We [were] about to move out when he [heard] a couple of my men laugh. He immediately [stopped] me and [started] to chew me out. He [complained that] the men [weren't] serious enough. When he had finished, I snapped to attention and gave him a parade ground salute, all the time, hoping there [was an] enemy sniper in the vicinity who [would] see and realize he [was] an officer and plug him between the eyes. No such luck!"[13]

After waiting enough time for the G and H Company roadblocks to get set up, Krause sent Company I through the town, going house-to-house and building-to-building to clean out the Germans. They took about 30 prisoners and killed the few who attempted to resist.

Another group of Company I troopers had overshot the drop zone and entered the town from the east. Carrying his .30-caliber machine gun, Private First Class Bill Tucker moved cautiously into Ste.-Mère-Église with his assistant gunner, Private Larry Leonard. Tucker could see signs of fighting that had occurred earlier as he neared the church in the town square. "I stopped under a large tree inside a five foot wall near the church. It was suddenly very quiet, and I felt very strange. It seemed as if something was moving close to me, and I swung the machine gun around. I didn't see anything until I looked up.

"There was a dead parachutist—caught in the tree and shot by the enemy—hanging from a tree right over my head. The soldier swayed back and forth. He had very big hands. His helmet covered most of his face. I felt shattered.

"As it began to get light, I began to look around carefully. The first thing I noticed was the body of another jumper about ten yards away in the tall grass near the gate. All he had on was his jump suit and harness. His boots were gone—who knows why? I guess he cut himself loose from his chute and equipment after being caught in the tree. He had apparently been shot down trying to get away. I got a good look at the trees that bordered the park. There were bodies or chutes of six or eight other paratroopers who had been caught in the trees and also shot by the Germans as they hung there.

"We ran from the park and across the square, in front of the church in the center of town. As I ran by a door of the church, I almost stopped when I saw an empty chute on the ground. Ten yards away, I saw the body of a German soldier. It was the first dead German I had seen in daylight in France. I would always remember his face. His skin was a little blue, and blood ran out of the corner of his mouth. His uniform looked immaculate. His rifle lay nearby with a fixed bayonet."[14]

This was undoubtedly the soldier Private Ken Russell had encountered a couple of hours earlier while hanging from the church roof, and who was shot and killed by Sergeant John Ray, with Company F, 505th. The empty parachute most likely belonged to Private Russell.

Company H had set up roadblocks on the Chef-du-Pont and La Fière roads west of Ste.-Mère-Église. Private First Class Cruise was part of a two-squad group assigned to the roadblock on the Chef-du-Pont road. "We deployed our land mines; glad to unload them from our musette bags, where we had stashed them in England about three hours ago. Three rows of mines were placed in front of our defense line and we hoped they would stop any German tanks that might try to dislodge us. We were assigned positions to the right and left of the road as well as on either side of it in the ditches and some troopers were given the areas in the fields to cover our flanks.

"Some troopers were assigned to dig in on each side of the roadblock about fifty feet behind the mines we had deployed across the road. [Norman J.] Vance, [Marshall A.] Ellis, [Francis B.] Gawan, and several others from the 1st Squad of the 1st Platoon were located there and some troopers were assigned to the left flank along the hedgerows facing away from Ste.-Mère-Église. [Doyle T.] Jones, [Robert E.] Coddington, [Glenn J.] Carpenter, [Alan D.] Beckwith, and [Gilbert L.] Gamelcy were among these. [Richard A.] Vargas, Larry Kilroy, and I were on the right flank above an embankment at the roadside and about fifty feet from the road. Slightly off to the left were men of the 2nd Squad, commanded by Sergeant Edward White with [Frederick C.] Neilsen, [Bernard A.] Cusmano, [Allen H.] Horn, [Boniface F.] Zalenski, and Davis plus others spread out towards the next roadway where they linked with other H Company squads.

"In the predawn darkness Vargas, Kilroy and I started our foxhole with one of us watching while two dug, and then we exchanged diggers until completed. We were located in front of a three foot high hedgerow that ran perpendicular to the road and we positioned ourselves so that we could cover effectively the field to our front. The hedgerow would provide some cover when we communicated with those on the road. In scanning the area I realized that we were very close to the hidden trail we had taken to arrive in our present spot. I had gotten used to the darkness, and though it was cloudy we could see shapes and outlines of things near us, but the high bank near the road obscured the men there."[15]

After landing on the western side of the flooded Merderet River, General Gavin worked to get things organized as rapidly as possible, because after daybreak concerted German counterattacks would commence against the landings. "I had remembered where the river was, so I turned, went towards it and as I approached the river bank I began to pick up one or two troopers. The water didn't seem too deep. There was a bright moonlight and one could see about. We began to get together.

"I was looking for some antitank weapons, particularly because I knew at daylight we'd have a very rough time with German armor. There were quite a few field entrenchments all along the edge of the river, apparently oriented towards a defense of the riverbank, in looking towards the amphibious landings farther away on the beaches. As we rounded up our gear and got a few people together, some wounded began to come in too, and they were a bit of a problem as usual. Then some jump injuries, who couldn't get about, had to be taken care of. Small arms fire began to increase a bit in intensity.

"In about fifteen minutes though a red light showed up on the far side of the swamp. Very shortly thereafter, a green light also appeared. If we had been operating according to plan those should have been the assembly lights of the 507th and 508th Parachute Infantry Regiments. I sent my aide, a Lieutenant Hugo Olsen across the swamp to gain contact with whoever was manning the lights. Olsen came back in about an hour and reported that there was a railroad directly across from where we were, directly to the east and that the river was passable, but that it was shoulder deep. He also ran into some of the 508th and understood that the commanding officer, Colonel Lindquist of the 508th was moving south towards La Fiere bridge. So he was moving along on schedule.

"I had at that time about one hundred to one hundred fifty troopers with me. They were scrambling to get the stuff out of the swamp. They were getting quite a bit in, but a lot of that equipment [that] hadn't been in the water that long, really wasn't much good to us. Our radios and bazookas were the most precious items that we lost. Gliders were to bring us our best antitank weapons, and those were the six-pounders as the British called them. They were the British version of the 57mm antitank gun."[16]

Shortly before 4:00 a.m. the glider serial approached the Channel Islands. The first nighttime glider assault landing in history was about to be executed. Lieutenant Colonel "Tex" Singleton was sitting in the co-pilot's seat of his glider as it approached the Norman coast. "Everything went well until we got just between the islands of Jersey and Guernsey, and then there was heavy flak. We came in a column of fours, and it was a nice formation. We ran into a cloudbank, milky in texture. We could see very little."[17]

On the ground, Sergeant James Elmo Jones operated his ADF as the 505th Pathfinder Team guided the tow planes to the vicinity of the landing zone. "Shortly after the parachute drop, we could hear additional planes coming in and could see by moonlight that they were pulling gliders. So, we gave instructions to turn on the lights again."[18]

Suddenly, Jones and the other pathfinders saw gliders cutting loose and gliding toward them to land on their field. "We were right in the middle of the field where the gliders were supposed to land. One of the problems was that we still had to continue transmitting on our equipment to bring in additional planes after the gliders came in. But, we had to try to get out of the way of the gliders landing. They were supposed to fly directly over and in line with the lights, make a one hundred eighty degree turn to the left, and come in and land at the far end of the field, so that they wouldn't inhibit the other gliders coming in behind them.

"There's never been a greater slaughter in the world than took place that night. If they came in low, they would fly into the hedgerows with trees on top.

When they would try to pull up and go over, they would stall out. With equipment and [up to] sixteen men in each one, it was the most horrible thing that a person could see. Some of the gliders landed on top of each other, soldiers that were trapped or wounded would cry and call for help all night. And the gliders just simply kept coming."[19]

The sight of the glider landings boosted Lieutenant Malcolm Brannen's confidence. "We saw C-47s after they had released gliders to their way and we saw gliders skimming earthward. 'Good!' We thought. Things are going as planned, and help and supplies are arriving all of the time. As we moved forward we came across parachute equipment, some loose, some in bundles still unopened, and a few opened with part of the load removed—part still there. From one bundle we took a bazooka and twelve rockets. We exchanged an M1 rifle which had a snapped stock—a casualty of the jump, for this bazooka."[20]

As the glider in which Lieutenant Tony J. Raibl, the division artillery communications officer, was riding came over the landing zone, it cut loose as planned. "Immediately it seemed as if the sky was full of gliders going in all directions. To avoid a mishap in the air, the pilot brought it down hard and crashed landed on the outskirts of Ste.-Mère-Église at 04:07 hours just slightly beyond the LZ. Due to the danger in the air, he had not been able to make his one hundred eighty degree turn. In smashing through a stone embankment, the glider was demolished, and five members of the party were injured to the extent that they could not be moved."[21]

A glider carrying Lieutenant Colonel Bennie Zinn, the division G-4, and other operations staff personnel was hit by antiaircraft fire as it landed. "Two men wounded, one severely . . . We got out and [dragged] Captain Rogers to a ditch where we gave him first aid and covered him with a chute."[22]

Colonel Ralph P. "Doc" Eaton, the division chief of staff, landed several miles from the landing zone. "I landed in the 101st Division Zone and was rather severely hurt in landing when my tow plane was shot down and the glider made shall we say 'a forced landing.' I have never been certain whether I was hit by machine gun fire prior to injury in the crash of the glider."[23] Colonel Eaton was pulled out of his destroyed glider and taken to 101st Airborne aid station at a French farm and lay in the stable until he was evacuated the next evening.

One glider landed close to the position where about 50 troopers had collected west of the Merderet River swamp under the command of Captain Roy Creek. "Just before daybreak, the first gliders began to come in. One landed in a flooded area about one hundred fifty yards from where we had our perimeter set up. As the men started to come out of the glider, enemy machine gun fire opened up from the hedgerow on the other side. We hadn't known they were there. Had they been there since our landing or had they just moved in? Maybe they had located our position and were attacking us when the glider distracted them. Anyway, they were there and men were being hit as they left the glider. Fire was placed in the general vicinity of the machine gun and this enabled a few men to make the hedgerow behind which we had cover."[24]

A few miles northwest of Ste.-Mère-Église, Lieutenant Jack Isaacs, with Company G, 505th, was still in the field where he had landed, having gathered about 35 men, most of whom he didn't know. "About this time, the gliders started coming into Normandy, and one of them chose this field that I had landed in to make his landing. He, with unerring accuracy managed to hit one of those anti-glider poles, demolishing the glider, of course, demolishing his load, which was a jeep and some other equipment, and injuring every member of the crew of that glider. So these people, instead of serving as reinforcements to our little group of thirty-five, in effect became a liability to us. Shortly after this, we managed to get these wounded glider men to our little French house [in the corner of the field]. We noticed a German soldier step out into the field over to the east side and approach the injured man that we had left there. He came over to him, looked him over, and then shot him. Of course, this infuriated all of our jumpers, and he didn't survive his trip back to the hedgerow for having shot this man."[25]

Moving down a country lane with three other Company H, 508th troopers, Private Tom Porcella came upon a farmhouse where a number of wounded troopers were being treated. He didn't recognize any of them. "Leaving the building, we went farther down the road. I came upon a glider that had crashed. Immediately we went to see if there were any wounded inside. To our surprise there was a medic attending the wounded in there. Except for one, all the glidermen had died in that crash. This one particular gliderman had his leg crushed and the medic was about to remove it. Those glidermen didn't have much of a chance. I hadn't seen a glider that wasn't badly damaged, which hadn't crashed. Paratroopers have a great admiration and respect for glidermen. We realized that their task was a lot tougher than ours."[26]

While the gliders were coming in, another group of paratroopers joined Gavin and the 150 or so men assembled on the western side of the flooded Merderet River. "At about 04:30, [Lieutenant] Colonel Maloney and [Lieutenant] Colonel Ostberg of the 507th with about one hundred fifty men had reported to me, and I decided to move as soon as possible to seize the west end of the La Fiere bridge. I considered it necessary to accomplish this before daylight, because of the impracticability of fighting through the swamps in the face of German automatic weapons fire."[27]

As Gavin began organizing his force to move out, he noticed a couple of gliders that had landed in the swamp. "Steps were taken to get the equipment out of them. With luck it would be a 57mm AT gun, which would come in very handy. In order to retrieve the contents of the gliders, the move south was temporarily delayed while patrols were sent to the gliders. Lieutenant [Thomas] Graham was placed in charge of these patrols. Lieutenant Graham returned in about a half-hour stating that he needed at least thirty men. One glider contained a '57' and one jeep. They had landed in a marsh and it was very difficult to extricate the gun and vehicle. Some German small arms fire was being received in the vicinity of the gliders at this time. Lieutenant Colonel Maloney was instructed to make the men available to Lieutenant Graham.

"About a half hour later, Lieutenant Graham returned and stated that he couldn't get out the equipment with the men he had, and that the German fire was increasing. I accompanied him to the hedge along the field containing the gliders where the fire was building up with considerable intensity. With some difficulty, additional men were obtained and finally either the gun or the jeep, I forget which now, was removed only to become bogged down in the swampy bottom. At my direction, Lieutenant Graham destroyed the jeep and removed part of the breech mechanism of the 57mm."[28]

Captain Alfred W. "Irish" Ireland had been given the special assignment to make sure that the division received their antitank guns. The 82nd would need to defend the road network north and west of Utah Beach and would undoubtedly face German armor moving from the vicinity of Valognes toward Ste.-Mère-Église and from the Ste.-Sauveur-le-Vicomte area. Ireland was a paratrooper, and the glider landing under fire he experienced was undoubtedly a harrowing experience. Ireland would no doubt have preferred to enter Normandy by parachute. He gained a new appreciation for what the "glider riders" endured. Upon reaching the division CP later that morning, he was asked about his trip in a glider. Captain Ireland only replied, "Those guys don't get paid enough."[29]

Yet, Captain Ireland was successful in helping to bring in the antitank guns the division needed. Gavin was pleased with the results. "Despite the difficulties, quite a few of them got in. We got six antitank guns in around Ste.-Mère-Église for the heavy fighting against armor the following morning."[30]

The gliders that brought in "Tex" Singleton's battalion had carried 16 precious 57mm antitank guns, 22 jeeps, 5 trailers, ammunition, water, and medical supplies. However, Singleton wasn't able to assemble his battalion. "Antitank guns were scattered all over the area. It seems that we landed when all the Germans were awake."[31] Nevertheless, the 4:00 a.m. landings by the gliders were largely successful despite the casualties.

From his foxhole near the mined roadblock on the Chef-du-Pont road just outside of Ste.-Mère-Église, Private First Class Les Cruise heard some noises in front of the Company H position. "One of those gliders had landed about three hundred yards from our roadblock. We could hear the noise as they were getting out and removing equipment. Over their shouting we heard the noise of a jeep motor starting, and several troopers left the confines of our position to help.

"Before they reached the landing spot, a jeep rushed down the road passing them even as they shouted a warning about our mines ahead. The occupants of the jeep were in a big hurry as we at the roadblock heard their running motor coming in our direction. Above all the noise, the distinct yells at the block of 'hit the ground' were heard clearly, and we all buried ourselves in the dirt of our foxholes. The driver must have thought our men were Germans and was not about to stop. Down the road they came full throttle.

"[There was] a deafening crescendo of explosive sounds as a number of our mines blew the jeep and its troopers into the air. All hell broke loose . . . flashing lights . . . with pieces of jeep and mine fragments raining down around us. Directly across the middle of our minefield they drove and immediately their direction became vertical, and in an arching skyward path they landed in the hedgerow beyond. We could hear the thump and bangs of falling parts all around us.

"The men had left the jeep on first impact and they had become the first casualties in our area, but they would not be the last. We had lost about three-quarters of our mines, which we had so carefully delivered, and they would be sorely needed in case the Krauts should attack. Those 'Amis' sure wrecked the hell out of our defenses. The troopers at the road surveyed the damage when all the raining of pieces had ceased and they ventured forth from their protective positions. They had to be careful lest another mine explode amid the smoldering scene. We would have to locate some more mines to fill in the voids and reinforce our tank defenses. Those of us nearby also came over to see the damage, and the smoking remains of the jeep were lying in the ditch at roadside. My first experience with sudden death [occurred] as the men were extracted from their perch and quickly moved by several medics to the rear areas."[32]

As dawn broke at about 6:30 a.m., Lieutenant Colonel Krause walked to the city hall in Ste.-Mère-Église, where he took out his old, worn flag and raised the Stars and Stripes over the first town liberated in France. At 6:50 a.m. Krause sent a runner to the 505th DZ to deliver a message to Lieutenant Colonel William E. Ekman that his 3rd Battalion had seized Ste.-Mère-Église.

Colonel Ekman had been dropped about two miles north of the drop zone and had a particularly bad landing. "I was knocked out and came to with everyone gone. It was dark, of course, and I found myself in the middle of a herd of cattle. Due to my difficulty in walking for the next several days, I am sure I landed astride a cow. I caught up with my staff about an hour later moving in the direction of our selected [CP] site."[33]

On the way, Ekman came upon Major Dave Thomas, the original 505th Regimental Surgeon, who was now with the 508th, and Major Jack Norton, the 505th Regimental S-3. Together, Ekman and Norton moved south where they made contact with the Vandervoort's 2nd Battalion, as it moved north on the N-13 highway toward its objective, Neuville-au-Plain. Colonel Ekman attempted to communicate with the 3rd Battalion by radio but was unable to establish contact. Concerned that the 3rd Battalion had been misdropped, or had been unable to capture the town, Ekman ordered Vandervoort to move south and assist the 3rd Battalion in capturing Ste.-Mère-Église or reinforce them if they controlled the town.

Although he didn't know it at the time, Vandervoort made a decision that would prove critical to the success of the invasion. "I sent the 3rd Platoon of Company D to Neuville-au-Plain to outpost the area that originally was to have been held by our entire battalion.

"When I got into Ste.-Mère-Église, an elderly French woman, noticing I was using a rifle to hobble about, went into her house and came out with an old-fashioned pair of wooden crutches and gave them to me. With these I was able to get about much better."[34]

Lieutenant Turner B. Turnbull, the platoon leader of the 3rd Platoon of Company D, moved north with his men to Neuville-au-Plain. There, Turnbull deployed most of his strength on the east side of the N-13 highway on a slight rise in elevation about 40 yards north of the hamlet. His men were positioned along a hedgerow that ran slightly northeast to southwest where they faced north and had a good field of fire for 600 yards. Lieutenant Turnbull positioned his bazooka team near a house next to the east side of the road to give them at least some concealment.

One of Lieutenant Turnbull's assistant squad leaders was Corporal Milton E. Schlesener. "We dug in along both sides of Route 13. Our mortar squad could not find their mortar, but they did find some machine guns and lots of ammo in supply bundles that were lying in the area. We had no idea to whom they belonged, but these were gathered and used. Lieutenant Michaelman [assistant platoon leader] took charge of that squad since it was off to the left and part of it in an orchard."[35]

This squad included squad leader Sergeant Robert "the Beast" Niland, Private First Class Horace H. Brown, Private John P. Slaverio, and Private Harold Dunnegan. They covered the field to the left of the highway with their machine gun.

Corporal Schlesener thought about how peaceful everything seemed that morning. "It certainly did not seem like we were at war. Farmers were starting to gather their cows. People were walking along the road. There were no planes flying around. The fields were real lush with grass. Our boots made a sucking sound as we were walking through it. There were small drainage ditches along the edges of the fields, the dirt had been thrown into the hedgerows. Do this for a number of years you get a deep bank to dig in to."[36]

Private Gerald Weed was Turner's communications NCO. He had been a sergeant back in England, but had been busted. Vandervoort had personally come to the stockade and obtained his release just prior to the invasion. Weed was carrying a heavy SCR 300 radio, a roll of wire, and field telephone. "Lieutenant Turnbull said, 'Get a telephone.' So I strung a wire for a field telephone out there and I hooked it up."[37]

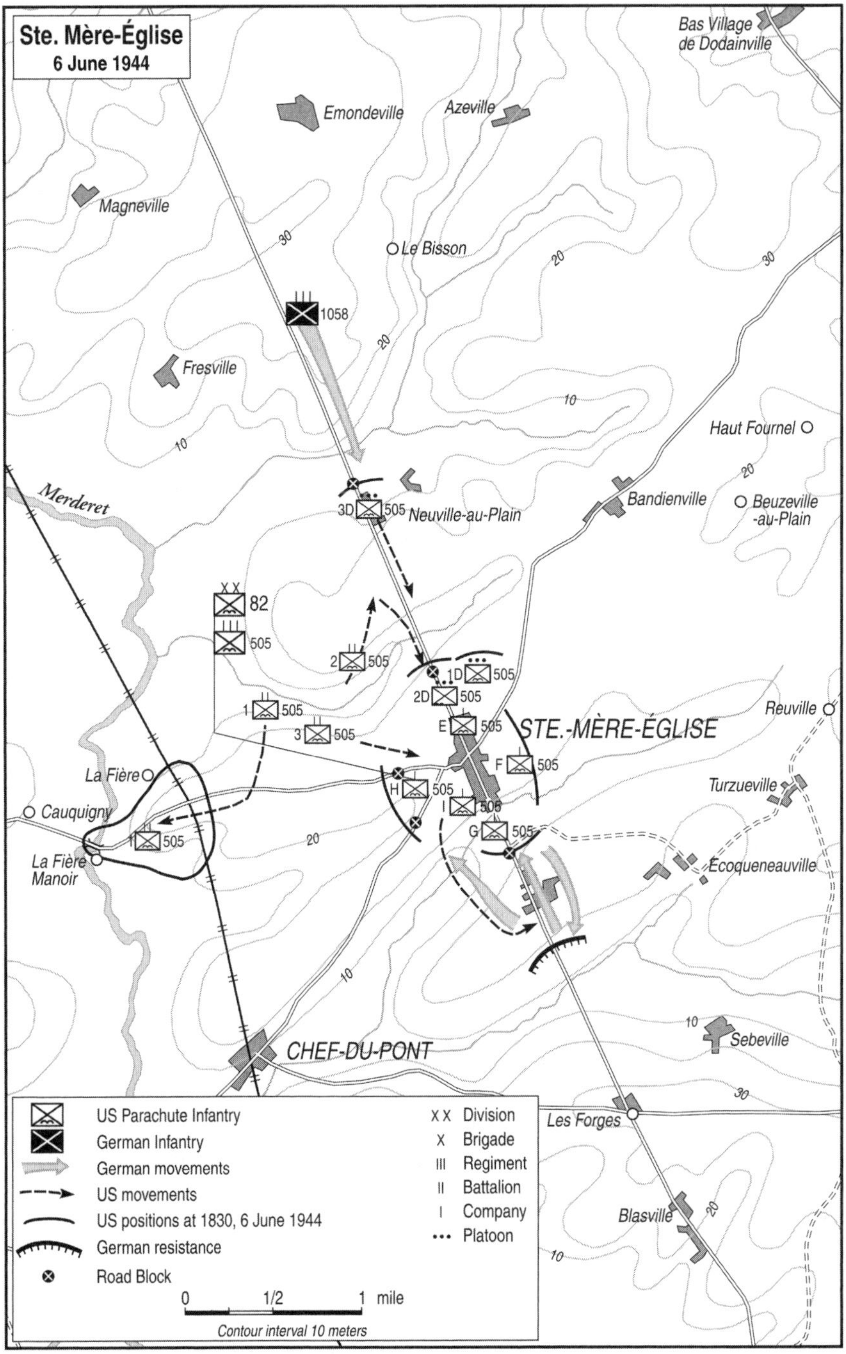

Ste. Mère-Église
6 June 1944
Bas Village de Dodainville
Emondeville
Azeville
Magneville
Le Bisson
1058
Fresville
Haut Fournel
Merderet
Bandienville
Beuzeville -au-Plain
3D 505
Neuville-au-Plain
82
505
2 505
1D 505
2D 505
1 505
3 505
E 505
STE.-MÈRE-ÉGLISE
Reuville
F 505
La Fière
H 505
Turzueville
Cauquigny
I 505
G 505
1 505
La Fière Manoir
Écoqueneauville
CHEF-DU-PONT
Sebeville
Les Forges
Blasville
US Parachute Infantry
German Infantry
German movements
US movements
US positions at 1830, 6 June 1944
German resistance
Road Block
XX Division
X Brigade
III Regiment
II Battalion
I Company
••• Platoon
0 1/2 1 mile
Contour interval 10 meters

When the 2nd Battalion entered Ste.-Mère-Église, they found it occupied by Krause's 3rd Battalion troopers. Krause and Vandervoort met and decided to divide the defense of the town, with the 2nd Battalion taking responsibility for the northern and eastern portion, while the 3rd Battalion would cover the western and southern approaches. Private W. A. "Arnold" Jones, with Company F, 505th, was assigned to the eastern part of the Ste.-Mère-Église defensive perimeter. "My machine gun was set up in the cemetery. Now, the most horrible thing I saw during the war—to the right of where we were was a grove of trees. We looked over in the trees and Charlie Blankenship, Bryant, and somebody else were hanging in the trees dead."[38]

One of the 505th chaplains was Captain George B. "Chappie" Wood. "Colonel Vandervoort asked me to do something about the men hanging dead in the trees down in the village square. There were six of them. It was affecting the morale of the men to see their buddies' lifeless bodies hanging there. I had no burial detail, so I got a detail of six men with an officer from off the front line, which was just the other side of the wall of the cemetery where we were burying the men."[39]

The men Chaplain Wood found in the cemetery were from Company F, 505th. It had been their buddies who had overshot the drop zone and had landed in the square the previous night. One of the Company F troopers chosen for the detail to cut the men down was W. A. Jones. "[Sergeant] Spencer Wurst, myself, and somebody else went over and cut them down. That was the hardest thing. Bryant was a good buddy of mine, even though he joined the regiment after we got to Quorn. He was from Fort Worth. Two of us would hold them while the third would cut them down. We cut them down, got their chutes down, and rolled them up in their chutes for Graves Registration. That has stuck with me more than anything else."[40]

Wood and the men were finishing up when they began to receive an artillery barrage. "We got five men down and into the ground when all hell broke loose, and the men were ordered back to fighting. There was much anger among the men over the killing of their buddies hanging in trees, but I explained that this was what we could expect in our kind of an outfit."[41]

Lieutenant Charles E. "Pinky" Sammon commanded the Headquarters Company, 2nd Battalion, 505th Machine Gun Platoon. "[Lieutenant] Colonel Vandervoort instructed me to set my platoon up in a defensive position one mile north and east of the town of Ste.-Mère-Église. There was no enemy activity in our area at this time, although I could hear some firing in the distance. We found the area assigned to us by the battalion commander and I established three machine gun positions, which I felt would give us good protection. I then set up a platoon command post and together with my runner took turns wrapping up in a parachute in order to get a little sleep.

"Dawn of June 6th was just breaking as I started out to check the three positions to make sure everything was in order and find out if the men needed anything in the way of equipment or food. There was at the time sporadic firing in the distance, but we had not seen or heard anything of the Germans in our area up to that point.

"As I approached the first position I called out to the corporal who was in charge—the answer came back in the form of a long burst from what was unmistakably a German machine gun and one or two machine pistols. The bullets hit the dirt at our feet and the two of us hit the ditch beside the road.

"What had happened became very clear to me at this point. The Germans had infiltrated our positions during the night and had either killed or captured the men I had placed in this position. As I lay there in the ditch with bullets whizzing over my head, I was not only scared, I was thoroughly disgusted with myself for being outsmarted by the enemy. I was worried and concerned about my men, and at the moment felt helpless to do anything about the situation. We couldn't get up without exposing ourselves to their fire, but soon discovered that as long as we stayed flat on our stomachs in the ditch, we were protected from their fire. They were set up at the junction of two irrigation ditches and were unable to depress the muzzles of their guns any further and couldn't see us due to the relative height of their position.

"I then decided that we should turn around in the ditch and attempt to crawl back to our own positions. We had gone about half way with the bullets clipping the tall grass over our head, when my runner who was now ahead of me panicked and got up to run. I tackled him just as a long burst of German fire hit all round us. From then on, I kept one hand on his foot as we continued to crawl up the ditch. We were making fairly good progress when an American machine gun began firing at us from our own positions. Since we were approaching from the direction of the enemy and were unable to stand up to identify ourselves, I could see no way out of our predicament.

"This time however, the Germans came to our rescue. The first barrage of German artillery fire came into the position and forced the American machine gunner to abandon his position just long enough for us to jump up and make a run for it. We arrived at the machine gun just as the gunner did; who by the way turned out to be one of my own men. Just for a moment I considered the irony of being killed by a machine gunner I had spent hours trying to train.

"All was confusion back in our own position. The Germans had infiltrated so well and struck so suddenly that no one knew what was going on. I managed to round up the remnants of my platoon and set up one machine gun to keep firing at the German position so they wouldn't attempt to advance further. I then had one of my men, who was armed with a carbine and rifle grenades, start firing grenades into their protected position.

"The best discovery of all however, was a mortar man from one of the rifle companies with a complete mortar and a supply of ammunition. In parachute drops, this is a rare find as often some vital part will be missing as a result of the drop. With the grenades and mortar shells falling into their position, the

Germans had no choice but to move out. They couldn't go back up the same ditch they had used to get into the position, as we had set up a machine gun to cover their return. And besides, no doubt their orders were to go forward and wipe us out.

"One by one they attempted to go over the top of their protective embankment and into the ditch I had used to retreat only an hour earlier. There were about twenty men in the position and about half of them made it into the ditch, the others were killed or wounded as they came out.

"Having become so familiar with that ditch earlier, I knew we couldn't reach them with our rifles and machine guns due to the difference in elevation of our positions. I decided the only way of reaching them was to go around on the flank and get above them and throw hand grenades into the ditch at the places I could observe the tall grass moving. We were so pinned down by artillery fire that I was unable to find anyone to go with me, and I hadn't seen hide nor hair of my runner since our narrow escape earlier. Equipment was scattered all over and I found about ten ordinary fragmentation grenades and one Gammon grenade.

"From my position on the flank, I waited until I saw the grass move. I scrambled up the side of an embankment, ran across about fifty yards of open ground, which brought me to a position right over the ditch in which the Germans were working their way into our main defenses. I got rid of the Gammon grenade and headed back to the protection of my ditch. I disappeared over the side just as a German raised up out of the ditch and fired at me with a machine pistol. I waited for a loud explosion that never came . . . my Gammon grenade had misfired.

"Since they now knew where I was, I was hesitant about going back. About this time a lieutenant from the airborne engineers came running up the road in a crouched position. He said he had three or four men with him and would like to help. We crawled up the embankment so I could show him what I was trying to do. As we cautiously poked our heads up over the top, a machine gun cut loose from the German ditch. We both slid back down the embankment. When the firing stopped I got up, but he didn't, so I rolled him over. He was shot right through the head.

"I decided to give it another try as the Germans were getting in closer all the time, which I could tell by the movement of the tall grass in the ditch, which they occupied. I pulled the pins on two grenades and started across the open area. This time they went off just as I got back to the protection of my own position.

"The firing from their position stopped, and I carefully looked over the top of the embankment. Believe it or not, a white flag was waving back and forth on the end of a tree limb. Soon a German soldier climbed up over the top carrying the white flag and started in our direction. Two or three of the dead lieutenant's men were with me and they were all for shooting him. I pointed out that he didn't have any arms and that we had to honor any attempt to surrender. He turned out to be a German doctor about thirty-five [years old] who spoke fluent English. He explained that many of their men were dead and wounded and that they would like to give up. He looked all around and seemed surprised that there were only two or three men in the position.

"I told him that we would not stop firing unless he returned and got all of the Germans to throw down their arms and to come out with their hands over their heads. He agreed to do this and after he returned, we sat there waiting for something to happen. We did not have to wait long however, as shortly after he disappeared into their position we were the recipients of the heaviest barrage of artillery and mortar fire I had experienced in the war up to that point. It was obvious that the doctor's surrender was all part of a very clever German plot. As a result, we had to abandon this position and I returned to the area where the rest of my men were entrenched. The German firing was very light now, and with ten or fifteen men we started a counterattack toward the very positions my men had been driven from at dawn. We reached the position alongside the ditch where the Germans had been holed up, and I saw that my grenades had done the job. Those that were not killed by the grenades got up to run and were cut down by machine gun fire from our main positions. There were about fifteen dead and wounded Germans lying about the position."[42]

Lieutenant Sammon and his men had just repulsed the first German attack to recapture Ste.-Mère-Église. Shortly after dawn the Germans began to heavily shell the town. Company I was in reserve, and Krause had positioned them in the town in order to be able to respond to an attack from any direction. The other rifle companies were dug in and manning roadblocks and the perimeter.

German shelling fell primarily in the town and particularly on Company I. Sergeant Bill Dunfee had come into Normandy with Company I as an extra NCO after attending a chemical warfare school after the division landed in Northern Ireland. "The enemy really socked it to us, with 88s and Screaming Meemies. The 88s were using either timed or proximity fuses, because we were receiving air bursts. The Nebelwerfers were so erratic you couldn't tell where their rockets would land. We learned in a hurry the safest place to relieve one's bladder was in the bottom of your foxhole. If Mother Nature required further relief, you were in very serious trouble. We suffered a number of casualties during this bombardment. The most gruesome being when a rocket landed amid three men in a mortar squad. They were all killed, the explosion must have detonated a Gammon grenade in one of the men's leg pocket. The secondary explosion literally blew him to bits. His head, chest, and right arm were all that remained. We learned in a hurry to cut laterally into the side of your foxhole, for a place to hide the family jewels. My musette bag received shrapnel, destroying a Gammon grenade, but not setting off the Composition 'C' contained therein."[43]

The 3rd Battalion of the German 1058th Regiment was located in wooded high ground (Hill 20) about a mile south of Ste.-Mère-Église near Fauville. At around 10:00 a.m., the Germans launched an attack from Hill 20, north on the N-13 highway toward the town with two companies of infantry and several self-propelled guns. Effective fire from a 57mm antitank gun of the 80th AA Battalion positioned at the roadblock on the south end of town stopped the self-propelled guns. The German infantry continued to advance along the hedgerows on both sides of the N-13. Private First Class Dominick DiTullio, manning a Company G outpost, almost single-handedly stopped the German infantry by ambushing the leaders, causing the force to withdraw. Company I was ordered to counterattack and throw the German assault force back. The company moved south along a hedgerow-lined dirt road that paralleled the highway west of the N-13. Sergeant Dunfee was carrying a BAR that he'd picked up during a lull in the shelling that morning. "We didn't know where we were going or why, just, 'Move out.' We hadn't gone too far before the point came under fire, killing three of the four men. Edwin Jones, the lone survivor, crawled back under our covering fire. He reported Captain [Harold H.] Swingler, [Private First Class Sam] Vanich, and [Private First Class George] Irving were dead. We had left our company executive officer in England in charge of the rear echelon, so we were leaderless."[44]

The front of the company column had turned east too soon and had entered the N-13 just in front of the positions where the German infantry had withdrawn. The point knocked out several trucks with Gammon grenades but was itself hit in the flank. Private First Class Bill Tucker took cover with the rest of the company in a ditch along the road paralleling the N-13. "We were pinned down in that ditch and couldn't even lift our heads up. No one seemed to move. We didn't know what was happening up ahead, and it was awful lying there in the ditch. The Germans were in a ditch on the other side of the road only about ten yards away to our right for a time. They threw grenades over at us. We got some firing in, but the Germans fired at us from the fields to our left. We found that [1st] Sergeant [Howard] Melvin alone had saved us from the left by covering our flank. With Captain Swingler gone, Lieutenant [Joseph W.] Vandevegt was in command of the company. Enemy firing didn't let up, and there was no choice but to move backwards in the ditch and find some place to get across the road. Just at the edge of town, we all made a dash across the road and into a sunken orchard near a house or farm.

"Larry [Leonard] and I ran into Sergeant [Charles C.] Matash, who had a bullet through his shoulder. Matash had been at the head of guys crawling in the ditch and had actually stood up in the open to draw fire so that others could get across the road. It was a dangerous move. Matash had real guts, and he later got the Silver Star for the bravery he showed."[45]

The show of force by Krause in sending Company I to attack the German forces south of town evidently convinced the German battalion commander that the town was strongly held, and no more infantry assaults were launched against Ste.-Mère-Église from the south. But they continued to shell the town with mortars, Nebelwerfers, and 88mm guns.

By midmorning, the communications and radio operator for the 3rd Platoon of Company D, 505th, Private Gerald Weed, had laid a field telephone connection from the Company D CP on the north end of Ste.-Mère-Église to Neuville-au-Plain. "I'm up on the road with Lieutenant Turnbull and I've also got a radio, beside pulling that damned telephone wire. So I have to stay right with Turnbull. We looked down the road and here comes a Frenchman riding up on a bicycle. We stop him. He could speak just enough English that we could understand him. We [could] see some guys coming up the road. We asked him and he says, 'Paratroopers with some German prisoners.' They were so far away we couldn't tell. We thought this was great."[46]

As this was occurring, Vandervoort arrived, bringing some antitank support for his blocking position on the main N-13 highway from Cherbourg. "About noon I went north to Neuville-au-Plain in a jeep with a 57mm antitank gun and gun crew. I told our 57mm antitank gun crew to go into position on the right of the road where a house offered some concealment. As we drove into Neuville-au-Plain, a French civilian passed us moving south on a bicycle. Lieutenant Turner Turnbull, the platoon leader, told me the Frenchman had just come from the north and had told them that a group of paratroopers had taken a large number of German prisoners and vehicles and were moving south on the highway and would arrive at Neuville-au-Plain shortly. As Turnbull and I walked over his position and talked, we kept watching the highway leading from the north. Shortly, a long column of foot troops appeared in the distance with vehicles scattered at intervals through their ranks. If these were prisoners, there was more than a battalion of them. We could make out the field gray of the German uniforms. On their flanks were individuals in paratrooper uniforms waving orange panels that were the recognition signal we were to have used to identify ourselves to friendly aircraft. Somehow, it looked just too good to be true. When the advancing column had closed to within about one thousand yards, I told Turnbull to have his light machine gun fire a burst into the field on the left flank of the column.

"That did it. The alleged German prisoners deployed instantly on both sides of the road and the leading vehicle, a self-propelled gun, instead of acting like the spoils of war the Frenchman said they were, opened fire on our position. Our 57mm antitank gun crew returned the fire and set fire to the leading SP [self-propelled] gun and one more that moved up behind it. A third German SP gun fired smoke shells into the road to its front to screen their position. The German infantry began to move forward on both sides of the road as their 81mm mortars started to range in on the 3rd Platoon position. I told Turnbull to delay the Germans as long as he could, then withdraw to Ste.-Mère-Église.

With that, I returned to Ste.-Mère-Église to alert my troops as to what was on the way and to check our positions to meet it."[47]

Turnbull's men opened up on the Germans as they deployed into the fields on both sides of the road. With the slight high ground and 600 yards of open ground in front of them on the east side of the road and a couple of two-story buildings on the west side, Turnbull had picked a great position from which to hold off the Germans. However, the Germans began sending men farther east and west, out of range and out of sight of the D Company troopers and their weapons. As the fighting progressed, the strength of Turnbull's platoon was slowly being whittled away, as mortar and long-range MG-42 fire took their toll.

The Germans took most of the afternoon, but by around 5:00 p.m. they threatened to get in behind Turnbull's platoon. Turnbull contacted Lieutenant Colonel Vandervoort via the field telephone to give him a report on the situation. As Vandervoort listened, he knew it was time to withdraw the platoon if possible. "The word came from Turnbull that the Germans were enveloping both flanks of his position and he couldn't hold on much longer. I sent one platoon of Company E, then in reserve, north on the left side of the highway to attack the enveloping German infantry by fire, then withdraw to their reserve position. We hoped it would help Turnbull to withdraw under the cover of this diversion."[48]

The mission was given to the 1st Platoon of Company E, led by Lieutenant Theodore L. "Ted" Peterson. "We moved quickly, but cautiously north on the west side of the highway to Neuville-au-Plain. We saw groups of the enemy on the way, who apparently did not see us, so we did not engage them. Our primary objective was to assist Lieutenant Turnbull. As we approached his approximate position, my runner and [I] crossed the road, leaving our platoon in a concealed position in a hedgerow."[49]

As this was occurring, Turnbull tried to contact Vandervoort once more. Private Weed was nearby and heard Turnbull shout over the noise of the firing and explosions. "He hollered at me and said the phone wasn't working. I traced that wire . . . I just grabbed the wire and started running with it."[50]

As Weed ran with the wire in his hand down the ditch on the east side of the highway toward Ste.-Mère-Église, almost a mile away, he kept an eye out for the enemy, who had probably cut the line. Suddenly, off to his right, Weed saw Germans moving east toward him and the highway, to Turnbull's left rear. "I saw these Germans and I don't think they saw me. When I ran out of the wire, the other piece was lying on the ground; I just kept going, because I knew the Germans had cut it. The only thing I could do was run to battalion headquarters and report what was going on."[51]

Sergeant Otis Sampson was Lieutenant Peterson's mortar squad leader and a veteran of Sicily and Italy. Sampson had his 60mm mortar set up on the left flank of the Company E platoon in some high grass. "A dirt road ran across the front of us. There was little foliage to obstruct our firing across it. Our CP was set up under a tree to our right. A lane ran directly from the position I was in up over a crest of a hill less than a hundred yards away. Here, a paratrooper lay as he had fallen, crosswise in the lane's center."[52]

Lieutenant Peterson and a couple of his men moved quickly across the highway and crept carefully toward Turnbull's position. Peterson was not sure whether they were expected. "Lieutenant Turnbull had a guard posted at the position we entered, who seemed to be expecting us. This would confirm that [Lieutenant] Colonel Vandervoort had communications with Lieutenant Turnbull, and we were expected. Lieutenant Turnbull was very calm and he had the situation well in hand, for the rough position he was in. He had about six men killed and eight or ten wounded, plus he was running low on ammunition. They were getting heavy large [caliber] mortar fire, plus machine gun and small arms fire. One particular machine gun was causing him the most trouble, and he asked us to try to knock it out. This gun was to his left front behind a farmhouse. Also, he asked us to draw fire upon ourselves, which might relieve his platoon enough to withdraw with their wounded. He said as soon as he had withdrawn, he would send a runner to give us the word.

"We moved back to our platoon and set up a line of fire on Lieutenant Turnbull's immediate left, the farmhouse with the enemy gun to our immediate front. We formed a perimeter defense with our power to the front. We commenced firing on order, firing BARs, mortar, bazooka, and small arms fire, making quite a racket. This was to reveal our position to the enemy and to try to knock out the machine gun at the farmhouse. We ceased fire shortly, and waited. All was as quiet as a church. Two scouts and I crawled and ran to the farmhouse with our platoon covering us. There was no sign of the enemy, so we fired a few bursts from our Tommy guns into the barn and house, and moved quickly back to our platoon position.

"After possibly five or ten minutes—all hell broke loose. The enemy moving west down the road near the farmhouse and to our immediate front, walked right into our hidden left flank, who were stretched out along the hedgerow so as they were practically facing east. Corporal Burke, who had already won a Silver Star for bravery, with his Tommy gun; a BAR; and three or four riflemen held their fire until the enemy was within a few feet of them. Then they opened fire. The surprised enemy took off in every direction, losing a good number of men. With that, the whole platoon opened fire with everything they had at the enemy. This included Sergeant Sampson, the greatest and most accurate mortar sergeant in the business. He fired at this close range and laid the shells down in a line right on their heads."[53]

When he heard Peterson's platoon open fire, Turnbull ordered his platoon to withdraw. The medic, Corporal James Kelly, volunteered to stay behind with the wounded. Sergeant Bob "the Beast" Niland with his Thompson, Private First Class Julius A. Sebastion with his BAR, and Corporal Raymond Smitson volunteered to cover the withdrawal.

One of the Company D troopers, Private First Class Stanley W. Kotlarz, was positioned behind a hedgerow on the west side of the highway. "The word got around that we should pull back because we were being surrounded. Shortly after that we started pulling back. We lost a guy named [Private William H.] Neuberger, he got hit in the stomach. We walked him across the road; we had to move back, and we didn't have too much time, so we put him over to one side, and I took some branches that were lying there and covered him up. Kelly stayed back with Neuberger, but he [later] died.

"In the meantime, my squad leader, Bob Niland, was going across the road to set up a defense on the other side of the road. He was just stepping over a hedgerow and they nailed him. It was a machine gun . . . an MG-42 . . . we heard the doggone thing. We could see the way he was hit . . . he was lifeless, he was bleeding, and wasn't moving. There wasn't any sense in trying to save him; cause he'd had it."[54]

As Turnbull's platoon pulled out, the fire from Sergeant Sampson's lone 60mm mortar devastated the German infantry west of the highway. "I used the mortar with direct firing from an open, high grass area, with just [Private First Class Harry G.] Pickels [the gunner] up there with me to feed the tube. We changed positions often, using various objects as sighting stakes. Our firing along with the rifles and machine gunners finally started to tell on the Krauts and their firing began to slack off. Just over the hill, the Jerries were crossing the lane one man at a time on the run. I timed the interval, and when I thought another would cross over, the tube was fed a round. And as planned, when Jerry was in the center of the lane, the shell hit, right to the fraction of a second. On the easing off of the firing, I gave a couple of the squad men a chance to use the weapon as I did, to get the feeling of what it was like under fire. I kept a close watch with my Tommy [gun].

"We had come in a little to the left of town and had met a strong force, much greater than ours. They were going to cut off Lieutenant Turnbull's platoon. As soon as the Krauts quit firing, Lieutenant Peterson, with Lieutenant [James J.] Coyle took the rifle squads and went out to find Lieutenant Turnbull and his men. We knew the Jerries had suffered in our encounter with them, but had no way of telling how bad. So far, we had not lost a man. The fight had been short and heavy."[55]

As Peterson and his men were about to cross the highway to find Lieutenant Turnbull, Peterson saw a trooper approaching. "A runner from Lieutenant Turnbull reported to me that they had successfully withdrawn their platoon. We had firepower over the enemy, and having accomplished our mission, we made a tactical withdrawal, firing as we left, and continuing part way to our lines."[56]

With the help of Peterson's platoon, Turnbull's men had shot their way out of the German trap, then conducted a fighting withdrawal. Private First Class Kotlarz was one of just sixteen from Turnbull's platoon to make it out. "We were moving pretty fast. As we were going back we'd stop and fire a few shots and then pull back."[57]

Meanwhile, at Vandervoort's CP on the north edge of Ste.-Mère-Église, Private Weed arrived, breathing heavily after running all the way from Neuville-au-Plain. "I told them what was going on. Vandervoort was propped up against a tree, and there was a naval officer that jumped in with us. They were talking and they gave me a couple of more men to go back. [Vandervoort] says, 'Go back and tell the platoon that we're going to shoot up a white flare. When they see that white flare, withdraw. They've got five minutes to withdraw before the USS *Nevada* is to lay down a barrage.' "[58]

Weed immediately took off on a run back toward Neuville-au-Plain. "Me and these two others guys [headed] down the edge of this field because we didn't want to be right on the road. So we got close enough to where we could see where the platoon was. I could see where the platoon was supposed to be, and I saw a couple of German trucks driving through there, so I knew the 3rd Platoon wasn't there anymore. About that time I saw the white flare go up."[59]

Five minutes later, Weed heard what sounded like a freight train coming, as a salvo of massive 14-inch shells arced overhead and impacted along the road in front of him. "We wanted to watch what was happening, because we could see those German trucks out there. So we just lay there and watched the whole thing. I had never heard anything like that before. Every one of those things landed within a radius of a couple of hundred yards. They were right on target. It was real effective. The Germans took off; they got the hell out of there."[60]

Lieutenant Turnbull and his fifteen troopers walked into Ste.-Mère-Église at dusk. Lieutenant Turner Turnbull's single platoon had delayed the reinforced 1058th Regiment of the 91st Airlanding Division for almost the entire afternoon, preventing them from attacking Ste.-Mère-Église and buying time for more paratroopers to filter in and strengthen the defenses of the town. Just as importantly, they had prevented a possible armored counterattack on Utah Beach. Vandervoort called it "a small unit performance that has seldom been equaled."[61]

CHAPTER 11

"THIS WAS ONE OF THE TOUGHEST DAYS OF MY LIFE"[1]

As the 2nd and 3rd Battalions of the 505th were moving to capture Ste.-Mère-Église, the 1st Battalion moved toward its objectives, the two causeways that crossed the flooded Merderet River west of Ste.-Mère-Église at La Fière and southwest at Chef-du-Pont. The causeways were chokepoints for any German force in the central part of the Cotentin Peninsula moving to attack the Utah Beach landings.

Shortly after landing, Lieutenant Jack Tallerday, with Company C, 505th, gathered six or seven of his men and began moving down a hedgerow. "It was a partial moonlight night and the hedgerow was about ten feet high, thin foliage with a bank of dirt at the base about three feet high. After going a short distance we heard, as well as observed, a group of men approaching from the opposite direction, but on the other side of the hedgerow. We stopped and I pinched my 'cricket.' We used this to indicate our presence to other men in our unit. After I pinched my cricket the second time, we heard what we thought to be a reply as the sound was similar.

"As our two groups of men approached each other, at a distance of five yards, it was quite evident by the configuration of their steel helmets that they were enemies. I believe the Germans realized this too. However, both of us, being surprised as well as frightened, continued to walk forward. As we passed, neither group spoke, and till this day why neither of our groups didn't shoot or kill the others, I don't know. It was like two ships passing in the night. You can be sure that we were more cautious during the next four hours of darkness that night, to the extent that we got into several small firefights. We shot first and asked questions later."[2]

Company A, 505th, commanded by Lieutenant John J. "Red Dog" Dolan, was assigned the key D-Day objective of seizing and defending the east end of the La Fière Causeway, including the bridge over the Merderet River. Thanks to the Troop Carrier Command, Dolan and his men had made an almost perfect drop. "We hit our drop zone right on the nose, because within twenty minutes to one-half hour, I knew our exact location. I was able to identify a 'T' intersection, dirt roads eight to ten feet wide, near our drop zone. The upper arm of which ran generally east to west, the vertical arm running north to south, to meet the road running from Ste.-Mère-Église to our objective, the bridge at the Merderet River."[3]

Company A pathfinder, Private Bob Murphy, admired Dolan. "He was an aggressive combat leader who didn't say much. But when he did converse, it was worthwhile to pay attention and follow his orders. He was one of the best; a combat out-front leader, not a follower. Dolan approached the pathfinder team. We talked about the terrain, where the railroad tracks were, the La Fière Bridge, and the east-west road, a probable location for enemy action. Lieutenant Dolan requested that Private First Class Charles Burghduff of A Company (who jumped as a pathfinder) go with the entire company, because he spoke German."[4]

After conferring with the pathfinders, Lieutenant Dolan ordered his men to deploy and move out toward their objective. "About an hour before dawn, Co. A moved out from the drop zone with about ninety percent of the men accounted for. We moved along this dirt road, the north-south arm of the 'T' intersection. Just around here, I ran into Major [James E.] McGinity [1st Battalion XO]. He moved out with us. Order of march was 1st [Platoon], Company Headquarters, 3rd, and 2nd Platoons in that order. When we reached the road running east-west from Ste.-Mère-Église, a German motorcycle passed us going toward Ste.-Mère-Église. At this time, it was still dark, but daylight was starting to break. We crossed the road and started west toward the bridge, with a hedgerow to our right between us and the road. Just about this time, contact was lost with the 1st Platoon, so the 3rd Platoon took the lead."[5]

Meanwhile, unknown to Dolan, several groups of paratroopers from all three regiments were converging on the La Fière area. T/5 William Dean, a radio operator with Company B, 508th, had landed in the flooded area of the Merderet River just north of Chef-du-Pont. "Others had landed nearby, and soon we had a small group of about six or seven and we headed north, guiding on the Paris-Cherbourg railroad right-of-way. It was past 3:00 a.m. when we got to the [road leading to the] La Fière Causeway. Here, the rigors of the preceding day and night made us first sit down, and not long after, lie down in a ditch and go to sleep. After a two hour fitful doze, we were joined by Lieutenant Homer Jones who was leading another small group of B Company men. Lieutenant Jones just an hour or so before finding us, had been named commander of Company B by

Captain [Royal] Taylor, our regular commanding officer, who had sustained a rather severe injury to his foot upon landing."[6]

Troopers that had been dropped into the flooded areas and on both sides of the Merderet River had congregated on the railroad embankment north of the La Fière Causeway. Lieutenant John H. Wisner, the S-2 of the 2nd Battalion, 507th, landed on the eastern side of the Merderet River in the flooded marsh. Wisner moved west, picking up about thirty men, mostly from the 2nd Battalion, 507th. "Upon coming to the railroad track, I noted that a large number of men had already collected on it, having worked themselves out of the swamp from both sides of the railroad.

"Before the column started moving south, I talked to a French girl in a nearby house. She showed us on a map where we were, and she told me that I could get into Amfreville by taking a road, which led off directly westward from us. I looked for the road and could not find it, and so the party moved south, having joined a body of about one hundred men under Colonel Roy E. Lindquist of the 508th. The group with Lindquist moved down toward La Fière as the advance guard of this small column. In moving in this direction, I figured that I could go via the La Fière Bridge and proceed to Amfreville to join the 507. The party got no fire during any of this time. The men moved in a double file, separated by the railroad track. Above La Fière the swamp gives off and is succeeded by a deep cut where the railroad runs under the highway from Ste.-Mère-Église. At first, I tried to send men around the flanks to cover the top of this defile. But they were so heavily burdened and so much time would be lost in sending them around that I decided to take a chance, and I moved the men right down through the cut. I started the party down the secondary road which runs east of La Fière, then decided I had better not take a chance in getting lost on an uncertain route, retraced to the railroad track, and continued on down the viaduct to the main road from Ste.-Mère-Église."[7]

Captain F. V. "Ben" Schwartzwalder, the CO of Company G, 507th, had dropped on dry ground east of the Merderet River to the northeast of La Fière. He was able to assemble about forty to fifty troopers from his company and set out to cross the causeway at La Fière. His group moved south on the railroad embankment with the other, mostly 508th troopers, led by Colonel Lindquist.

Lieutenant John W. Marr, commanding the 1st Platoon of Company G, 507th, was moving with the group south along the railroad embankment toward the La Fière to the Ste.-Mère-Église road running east and west. "Ben Schwartzwalder kept saying, 'John, we've got to get to Amfreville, that's where we're supposed to be. We can't stay on this railroad, we've got to go!'

"When we got to the Ste.-Mère-Église to Amfreville road, he said, 'This is where we've got to part company with the 508.' He put me in the lead to get up out of the railroad [cut]. We scrambled about twenty-five or thirty feet up to the overpass. We crossed the road then, after we got up there and went out into the field directly east of the Manoir down at the bridge."[8]

West of the Merderet River floodplain, Lieutenant Colonel Charles J. Timmes, CO of the 2nd Battalion, 507th, and about twenty men moved south toward the tiny village of Cauquigny, just west of the causeway. "In the hamlet of Flaux, which is across the river from La Fière, I picked up another thirty men—a platoon from D Company. I heard firing in the direction of Amfreville and figured that the battalion was attacking that village from the north and that I best take my group and move against it from the east in order to assist their mission. I thought that I was moving in on the rear and flank of an enemy force already engaged along its front. This being the assumption, I moved detachments out on both sides and began advancing them along the hedgerows. Small arms fire began to take a toll among my men, and the movement continued. I then became more aware that the situation in the village [of Amfreville] was not as I supposed it, and that I was gradually losing control of my detachment without doing any real damage to the enemy. I noted that the enemy had machine guns up high in the buildings, and that they had superior observation of my force. I therefore, began the withdrawal of my group to reorganize. As the reorganization got underway, enemy fire began to break out. I realized that these things had happened because I had gone in before I had made a sufficient reconnaissance or preparation. As the enemy began to assert themselves, I decided that I had better hold my men back. The group therefore took up a defensive position in an orchard just to the west of the river."[9]

After daybreak, General Gavin led about 300 troopers east across the river and followed the railroad embankment south toward La Fière. "It was now broad daylight. The degree of enemy buildup and his attitude made the possibility of moving down the west bank at this time appear impracticable, and I decided to move to the railroad embankment and move in the direction of La Fière. And there, pick up all who could be found from the 508, contact the 505, and attack the bridge from the east side. Orders were issued, and the movement started across the marsh."[10]

Captain Roy E. Creek, the CO of Company E, 507th, was commanding a mixed bag of about fifty paratroopers formed in a perimeter defense on the west side of the Merderet River flood plain northeast of Amfreville. "About 09:00, Lieutenant Colonel [Edwin J.] Ostberg, commander, 1st Battalion, 507 Parachute Infantry Regiment informed us that General Gavin was moving toward La Fière and that we were to follow. This meant fording the flooded area, which we had already struggled through earlier in the day. We pulled out of our position, leaving the wounded marked and as comfortable as possible and started across the marsh. As we waded in water sometimes chest deep, we were fired on by snipers, who appeared to be at long range because of the inaccuracy of their fire. But one couldn't help being concerned about the shots

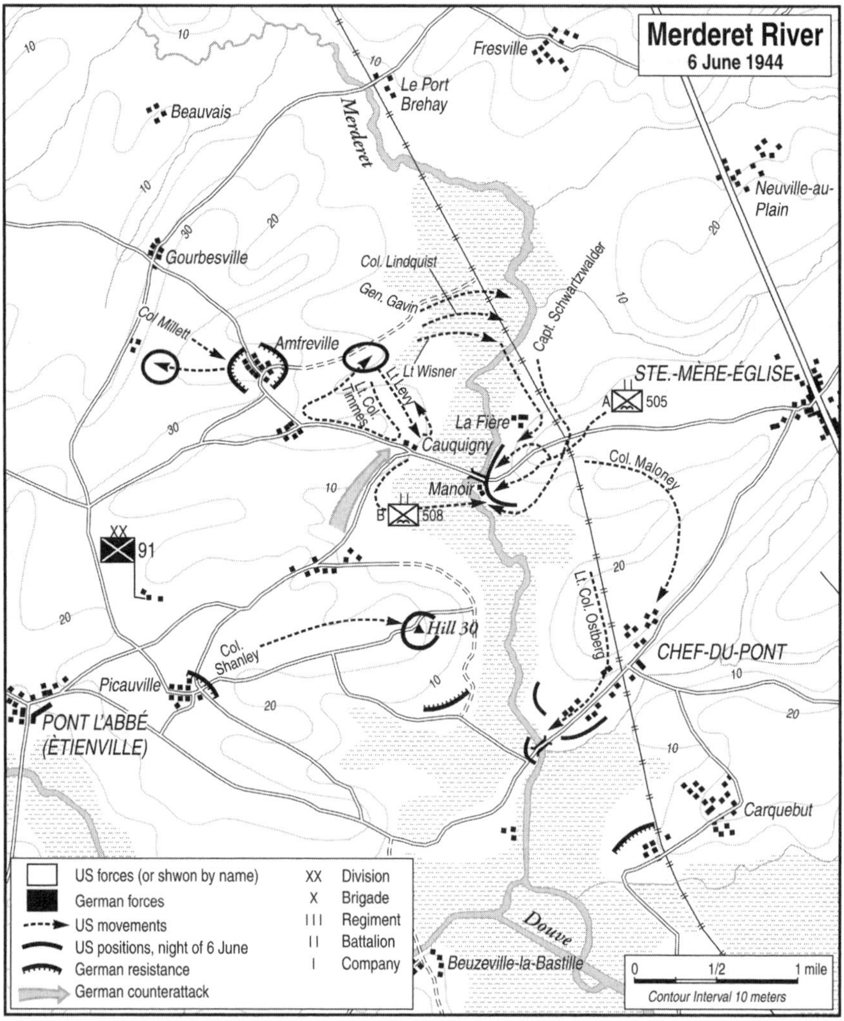

splashing water in his face. All that could be done was to keep on walking and hoping. We made it to the other side without mishap."[11]

Meanwhile, Lieutenant Dolan and his company moved along the road running west from Ste.-Mère-Église. "About seven to eight hundred yards from the bridge, we came upon a dirt road running southeasterly from the road to the bridge. Hedgerows were on either side of this road; and beyond it in the direction of the bridge, was an open, flat field, about one hundred yards deep and about seventy-five yards wide. It was here that I figured the Germans would defend if they intended a defense of the bridge. I directed Lieutenant Donald Coxon to send his scouts out."[12]

Lieutenant Coxon responded by saying, "Well, if I have to send someone out into that I'll go myself."[13]

Dolan told him he didn't have to accompany the scouts. "[Coxon] had plenty of personal courage, but he didn't have the heart to order them out without going with them."[14]

There was no other way to find out if the enemy was waiting behind the hedgerow across the field. Dolan waited with the rest of his men, looking over the top of the hedgerow as the scouts moved out into the open field. "They got about one hundred yards. A few moments later, a German machine gun opened up, killing Lieutenant Coxon and one of his scouts, [Private First Class Robert G.] Ferguson. [Coxon] was hit badly and started to come back. While he was moving along another bullet hit him in the stomach. After that, he bled to death. Second Lieutenant Robert E. McLaughlin took over the platoon."[15]

Lieutenant Dolan and the men from 3rd Platoon returned fire on the hidden German positions. Then Dolan attempted to flank the position by slipping the 3rd Platoon around the south side. "At the same time, I directed Lieutenant [George W.] Presnell to re-cross the road and attack along the northern side down to the bridge. This was done, and the 2nd Platoon didn't meet with any fire until they arrived at the bridge.

"With Major McGinity and [me] leading, a few men holding and returning frontal fire, the platoon flanked to the left. Because of the fire, we calculated that there was just one machine gun crew in our way. We cut back toward the road, travelling in a northerly direction. Major McGinity was leading and I was about three or four paces behind, and slightly to the right. There was a high, thick hedgerow to our left, and it was in here that I figured the machine gun was located. When we had traveled about two-thirds of the way up the hedgerow, they opened up on us with rifles, and at least two machine pistols. I returned the fire with my Thompson submachine gun at a point where I could see leaves in the hedgerow fluttering. Major McGinity was killed instantly. As luck would have it, there was a German foxhole to my left, which I jumped into and from where I continued to fire. I could only guess where to shoot, but I had to, as part of the 3rd Platoon was exposed to their fire."[16]

While Dolan was occupied firing at the suspected German position to his left, the "radio operator, Cpl. Frank Busa moved forward and was hit by a sniper's bullet. McLaughlin thought Busa was alive and went out to get him. But, before he could make it, he himself was hit in the upper leg. The one bullet went up through the lower part of his stomach and came out of his buttocks.

"I spotted the sniper and killed him. I then crawled to McLaughlin to give him first aid and carry him out. The lieutenant was in such excruciating pain he pleaded not to be moved.[17]

"The platoon by now was under fire from two directions; from the point where I was pinned down, and also from the direction of the bridge. I can't estimate how long we were pinned down in this fashion, but it was at least an hour."[18]

In the thick bocage country each field would become a self-contained and isolated area of action, where different units from the opposing forces could operate without the knowledge of one another until chance meetings would put them in contact with each other, often with deadly consequences. Moving west across the fields south of the main road from Ste.-Mère-Église, Lieutenant John Marr moved about 100 yards ahead of Captain Schwartzwalder's main force of Company G, 507th troopers. "We knew that was the best way to get to Amfreville was to go right down that road. A couple of scouts and I started down that field towards the Manoir. We heard these weapons firing on the north side [of the Manoir] and that was where the 505 was supposed to be. Schwartzwalder sent me around to the south of the Manoir to near the water's edge to see if we couldn't get around there. We had five people in my group and we were going down this hedgerow which was exposed to the water on one side, and the Germans opened up with a machine gun at the southeast corner of the cattle feed lot. They had a machine gun emplacement there; manned by two Germans. They opened fire, luckily high. We were within grenade distance of that machine gun when they opened up. We hit the ground and lobbed grenades, probably at least one a piece. The two Germans that were manning that gun jumped up and surrendered. But they did hit two of our people. We had to haul one out and the other was walking wounded. We went back to Schwartzwalder and told him what had happened."[19]

Right behind was Colonel Roy Lindquist's group, which attempted to move west on the road. As Lieutenant Wisner, S-2 of the 2nd Battalion, 507th, led a small group ahead of the main force, west toward the bridge, a machine gun opened up on them from down the road. "A dozen or so men in my party all hit the ditch. I sent a message back to Lindquist that I was getting fire from my front, and that I would like a patrol to knock it out. Time passed while the men rested in the ditch.

"Since nothing was happening as a result of the message, I decided to see if I could work up toward the machine gun. In the field on my right, to my surprise, I found a platoon of the 508th, and in the field on the left I found a company of the 505th. Some minutes passed and a message came up from Lindquist that he wanted me to join him for the move south."[20]

At about this time, Gavin was leading his group of about 300 troopers south on the railroad tracks. "I came upon the rear of the 1st Battalion of the 505th scattered along the edges of a small trail next to the railroad. I found out that the battalion commander, Major [Frederick] Kellam was up forward engaging a small force at the bridge. I put up a temporary command post in there and I tried to get in touch with General Ridgway. I had reports that he was then up at Ste.-Mère-Église."[21]

General Gavin then ordered about seventy-five of the men with him to execute a wide flanking movement to capture the causeway at Chef-du-Pont with an approach from the east. This force was under the command of Lieutenant Colonel Arthur A. Maloney, the 507th executive officer. A short time later, Gavin received word that the Chef-du-Pont Causeway was undefended, and he took another 75 men under the command of Lieutenant Colonel Edwin J. Ostberg, the CO of the 1st Battalion, 507th, directly to Chef-du-Pont via the railroad.

Captain Creek was one of the officers accompanying Ostberg. "General Gavin told us we should proceed south along the railroad to Chef-du-Pont where we were to seize the town and bridge across the Merderet west of the center of town. A few men who had been able to get some automatic weapons from some of the bundles that had been dropped as we jumped, were attached for this mission, and under the command of Colonel Ostberg, proceeded down the railroad toward Chef-du-Pont."[22]

After getting his force withdrawn to the orchard near the west side of the Merderet River, east of Amfreville, Lieutenant Colonel Timmes deployed them in a dug-in, perimeter defense. Timmes was aware of the importance of the La Fière Causeway, but had not received any word about who held that key ground. "I felt that I had better reconnoiter what was occurring down toward La Fière. Lieutenant Lewis Levy with D Company was sent with a patrol of seventeen men to take the bridge if possible."[23]

On their way south, the patrol ran into a group of approximately 20 men under the command of Lieutenant Joseph Kormylo, a platoon leader with Company D, 507th. "Levy came along with the group which had been sent to the bridge by Lieutenant Colonel Timmes. After talking to Levy, I sent all of my men back to Timmes' position except the machine gun crew. I attached them to Levy's group and we went on toward the church [at Cauquigny]. Levy told me that he figured that we had better try to get to the church as quickly as possible, because it was in such a position that holding it would be the strongest thing the party could do, our numbers considered.

"It was about 11:30. I could hear firing on the east bank, but it was irregular and I did not have the feeling that any important action was taking place on the other side. The group moved on down to the first hedgerow confronting the river along the west bank. As we started through the second hedgerow beyond the church, proceeding south, we drew sniper fire. The fire seemed to be coming from the east, and I had the impression that the Germans must be holding fire positions in the low land along the swamp. The fire built as we moved south and we found it unwise to proceed beyond the hedgerow north of the church, so we retraced around the hedgerows to the north, west, and then south again, and came at the church from the road which runs northwestward from the bridge.

"We got to the church without drawing fire. It was just about noontime. The men broke open their rations after setting up a fire position. The [machine] gun was set up so that it had a field of fire ranging along the western bank north of the bridge."[24]

After talking with Schwartzwalder, Lieutenant Marr moved out with his men toward the river. Marr was once again up front on the point with his scouts. "We went past where we had knocked out the machine gun to the water's edge, and came around between the last building of the Manoir and the bridge. Then after we took the Manoir, it was a very brief battle. In fact, it wasn't much of a battle at all, because the Germans in the Manoir gave up. Lindquist then told Schwartzwalder, 'I want you to move to the other end of the causeway, at the Cauquigny church.'

"So Schwartzwalder put me out in the lead again with my two scouts. He said, 'Move out, John. Let's get over to the churchyard.'

"It was about eight hundred yards across there, and it was on raised ground with water lapping up close to the roadbed.

"I had two scouts out; one was [Private] Johnnie Ward, and the other was [Private] Jim Mattingly. They were good scouts—they knew what they were doing. Ward took the lead and was about seventy-five or a hundred yards down the causeway, having crossed the bridge. Mattingly had just crossed the bridge and was standing in the middle of the road, watching Ward advance on the other side. A German in a gun emplacement on the north side of the road, with tall weeds and grass growing around it, raised up and started to draw a bead on Mattingly. I yelled at Mattingly; and Mattingly, having been looking at Ward down the road, looked to his right, swung his weapon around and shot the German. He emptied the clip in his rifle, all eight rounds. He dropped his rifle to the roadbed, fell flat, pulled out a grenade and tossed it over where that German had been standing. Four other Germans rose up and threw up their hands. Mattingly reached down and got his empty rifle and pointed it over, and five Germans directly across the road in another gun emplacement got up and threw up their hands. And now, there is Mattingly with an empty rifle, covering nine Germans. The whole thing probably took no more than fifteen seconds. I have never seen training pay off like that. He got a Silver Star for doing that."[25]

Lieutenant John Marr, Private Johnnie Ward, Private Jim Mattingly, T/5 Escobar, Corporal Lawton, and Private Mario Parletto had knocked out the machine gun defending the Manoir that had inflicted so many casualties, clearing the way for the 505 to occupy the eastern end of the causeway. Now they had knocked out the two machine guns assigned to keep anyone from crossing the causeway, allowing men to cross the river to the west, even if it was only briefly.

While this was occurring, the CO of Company A, 505th, Lieutenant Dolan, "made several attempts to move, but drew their fire. On my last attempt, I drew no fire. They obviously had pulled out. During all of this time, I could hear rifle and machine gunfire down by the bridge on the north side. This ceased about the time I returned to the rest of the 3rd Platoon, instructed the noncoms to reorganize, and to maintain their present position. I then crossed the road and located the 1st Platoon, commanded by Lieutenant [William A.] Oakley, on the north side. They were moving toward the bridge, so I instructed them to continue and dig in. I went down to the bridge and found that we had received an assist from some of the 508th Parachute Infantry. About this time, I ran into Colonel [William E.] Ekman, and sent for my 3rd Platoon to dig in on the left or south side of the bridge. The 1st was already digging in on the north side."[26]

Lieutenant Dolan thought that the Germans had been cleared from the Manoir buildings near the bridge. "But, unknown to us, there were about ten or twelve Germans holed up on the second floor of the stucco-type farmhouse. At the time they started firing, Colonel Ekman and I were casually looking the situation over."[27]

Dolan sent Lieutenant Oakley's 1st Platoon to clean out the enemy. Oakley's men circled west and approached from the southwest, where they engaged in a firefight with the Germans in the Manoir outbuildings.

The firing from the Manoir buildings had been directed at a group of troopers to the east of the main building. Lieutenant Homer Jones, a platoon leader with Company B, 508th, and about eighty troopers, mostly from Companies A and B, 508th, approached from the east, on ground that sloped down to the Manoir buildings. Jones was at the point with "[T/5] Bill Dean, [Lieutenant] George Lamm [Company A], and George's runner. Between us and the buildings was an earthen Roman wall on the side we were on. The house was built on a slope that led down from that Roman wall. We were going down in a combat formation—spread out, but we were pretty naked on the slope going down toward the building. We came under fire—automatic weapons fire as well as rifles. They were largely in a tower of the main building, the residence of the area. Bill Dean was my radio operator, and he and I headed for a tree that must have been about five inches in diameter."[28]

After finding the sparse cover of the tree, the group began returning fire. The Germans, however, were firing from small windows and protected by a thick, stone-walled building. Despite this, T/5 Dean kept up a steady fire with his carbine. "One hell of a firefight erupted during which, Point Scout [Private] John McGuire, who was just at my right elbow was shot through the head and killed. I just stared down at him, not wanting to believe what I saw. But my shock was short lived when several more volleys from the Manoir whizzed by my head."[29]

Caught on the open slope, the group was in trouble. Lieutenant Jones acted quickly, pulling out a white phosphorous grenade. "When I threw [it], that created tremendous smoke. We went back up the slope and I discovered a little sunken lane that led into the courtyard of the buildings. I started down that lane, which gave cover right up to the courtyard. I ran across the courtyard and got up to a door [on the second level] that went into the house itself. They heard me knocking on the door—there was a machine gun mounted inside the house, and they fired out right through the wood of the door, but didn't hit me. It just cut the knee of my trousers a bit. There was a lieutenant from Charlie Company named Ernie Hager and he was in the building across the lane from me, and that same burst hit his earlobe. The door had a small window about eye level, six by eight inches or so, with bars across it. There was no glass in it. I threw a hand grenade in through the window in the door, so the firing stopped.

"The house was built on a slope like a three level house, the top floor was the main floor, and on the uphill side the house would just be one story. On the downhill side there was a basement. I went down the steps on the same side of the building, into the basement of the house, [in order to go] up the stairs to get into the room where I first threw the grenade. Up above, I realized there were people. So I started firing through the floor. About this time, [Lieutenant] Lee Frigo came in. Lee was my assistant platoon leader—a pathfinder. We started shooting up through the floor together, and then they started shooting back down through the floor. Either Lee or I had thrown a grenade through the door in the back of this cellar. A first sergeant came bursting in all fired up, and went through that door with a submachine gun blazing away. There was at least one large vat of Calvados, which was spraying out all over the floor. He left to get some ammunition. There was a flight of stairs that went up to the floor above. As we were going up the stairs, somebody yelled, 'There's a white flag out.' That of course, was good news. I turned around with Lee and we went out of the house, and there were already some Germans who had come out through the door where I had initially thrown the grenade. There was a small group of Germans with their hands up and some Americans around them. Rather quickly, we were joined by Colonel William E. Ekman, the CO of the 505. I got my people together and we went across the causeway."[30]

When he received the order to move out, T/5 Dean was getting ready to eat his first meal since the previous evening. "After hastily eating a distasteful K-ration in the presence of eight or ten dead Germans, we proceeded to cross the bridge."[31]

By approximately 2:30 p.m., the Manoir and eastern end of the causeway were secure. Jones led about a company of troopers, mostly from Company B, across the causeway. Lieutenant Dolan quickly organized Company A for a possible German counterattack. "We dug in, [with] the disposition of my Company as follows: 1st Platoon on the north side of the road, the 3rd on the south and the 2nd in reserve, about four hundred yards back, so that it could also protect the rear.

"On the bridge I had three bazooka teams. Two of them were from Company A and the third was either from B or C Company. The two Company A bazookas were dug in to the left and right of the bridge. Because the road itself was the causeway type, they dug in below the level of the road. The third bazooka was over more to the south where better cover was available."[32]

Private Marcus Heim, Jr., the assistant gunner, and Private First Class Lenold Peterson were assigned to the southern shoulder of the causeway, while the other Company A bazooka team of Private First Class John Bolderson and Private Gordon Pryne were positioned on the northern shoulder. Private Heim, a new replacement, had recently been assigned as the loader. "There was a concrete telephone pole just in front of us and we dug in behind it. I do not remember how many paratroopers were around; all I saw was a machine gun set up in the Manoir house yard. On the right side down the pathway a few riflemen were placed. We carried antitank mines and bazooka rockets from the landing area. These mines were placed across the causeway about fifty feet on the other side of the bridge. There was a broken down German truck by the Manoir house, which we pushed and dragged across the bridge and placed it across the causeway."[33]

From the church at the western end of the La Fière Causeway, Lieutenant Joseph Kormylo looked through his binoculars, trying to determine who held the eastern end of the causeway. "We did not sense at that time that American forces were distributed along this shore. A little later we saw a 57mm gun on the high ground somewhat beyond the bank, and that was our first glimpse of friendly forces on the other side of the river. Just about the time Levy and I had finished setting up our position around the church, two 508 officers came up the west bank of the river with about forty men. There was a conference, and we told them that we considered this position very important, and so the 508 party joined us and set up a defensive position covering generally from the fork in the road and the ground southward from it. They had a bazooka, and so a roadblock was established near the church. While these arrangements were going forward, I noticed an intensification of activity on the east bank. Considerable mortar fire began falling among the buildings grouped beyond the bridge, and small arms fire could be heard in steadily rising volume. Men could be seen moving back and forth through the hedgerows. Levy and I were aware that our forces were engaging on the other side, and we got word up and down the line for our men to hold fire. However, I noticed there were some trigger-happy men along the right flank of our position who would periodically fire toward the other side of the river. Levy walked out into the road, took out his [field] glasses, and after looking eastward said, 'Kormylo, damn it; that's a paratrooper coming across the bridge.'

"I threw an orange smoke grenade out in the middle of the road. Immediately, we got an orange flag back from the other side of the causeway, and we then proceeded walking right down the road. We yelled back to our men to hold fire. We met [Lieutenant] Marr just to the west of the bridge. There was light sniper fire then coming from the marshes to the south of the bridge. Levy then went on over the bridge to talk to a higher commander and tell him that his detachment had secured the west bank. [He] was gone about fifteen minutes."[34]

Moving across the causeway behind Captain Schwartzwalder's group were the troopers from Company B, 508th, led by Lieutenant Jones. At the western end of the causeway they turned south and followed a road near the western edge of the Merderet River floodplain south toward Hill 30.

Lieutenant Kormylo, with Company D, 507th, waited while Lieutenant Levy crossed the causeway to find and inform a senior officer on the east side that the west end of the causeway was in American hands. "[Levy] came back and told me that he had talked to some officer of field rank and had delivered the message, and had been told that a battalion of the 505 was coming up to take the bridge over. Levy and I came on back to the west side and found that Schwartzwalder's men were beginning to take up positions around the bridgehead, although Schwartzwalder was trying to keep them in line so that he could get them moved out. Schwartzwalder, having been told where Timmes was, began to move his men northward. Most of the other 508 men who had been around the church position before Schwartzwalder crossed the bridge also moved with him, leaving only Levy, me, two 508 officers, and about eight enlisted men to man the bridgehead. About this time I had to forget about Schwartzwalder because pressure began building up against us from the south. It started with rifle fire and was joined by machine gun fire. Then I could hear tanks coming up from the distance.

"This small detachment built up along a line running directly past the church, and from this ground they faced southward toward the enemy. The [machine] gun was set so that it covered a line running across the rear of the church. The riflemen were spread out at intervals of ten to fifteen yards, and the officers took our place in the line as riflemen. The bazooka had departed with the group, which moved north. Levy, an unidentified private (later KIA), and I worked off toward our own right flank, figuring that we might swing around the left of the enemy and get in a few licks before the two forces closed. We came to an indentation in the line embankment where an opportunity was afforded for Levy to stand by and cover [the private and me] as we went on forward, hoping to get a crack at the German tanks. The tanks were already moving along the main road, and I could see their turrets above the hedgerow as they came on at a distance of about fifty yards. As they came to the intersection of the lane and the main road, the private and I saw a group of enemy riflemen moving obliquely across our front to the left, and the tanks moving in about the same direction, but coming on the inside of the riflemen. We fired a few rounds from our rifles, and then beat it back. We passed Levy and he yelled, 'Go on,' but he stayed there. We got in a ditch and started moving on back.

"The lane twisted quite a bit, thus it came about that almost immediately a German machine gun was brought forward and set up next to the road right by the lane, to fire down the line. It was defiladed to the fire of the American [machine] gun, set up along the same line to fire in the opposite direction. But the Germans had set up within five yards of Levy, where he waited in the indented embankment. Levy could hear them laughing and talking just around the corner of the embankment. He took out a grenade, pulled the pin, counted three, and gave it a little toss. It exploded between the two Germans and wounded both. He took a few steps and dispatched them with rifle fire. He then came on back and joined us, as we waited to cover his retreat.

"I thought I heard a grenade go off, and I remember that Levy came back helmetless and laughing at what had taken place. It was Levy's habit to laugh whenever things got really hot. The tanks were already up and shelling the church, and some of the riflemen had pulled back from the position. The German infantry by this time had closed right up on the road, and what remained of the American force was fighting it out, with just the edge of the hedgerow separating them. They were throwing grenades at one another, but the enemy numbers were piling up, so that it became perfectly clear that the position had no chance to hold. I saw a German come over the hedgerow at two feet distance. I emptied my carbine into him and blew the top of his head back. I thought that I saw another American up on my right. I yelled to him, 'Come on, let's go.'

"Levy, by this time, had disappeared. He was getting a closer look at the tanks. Private Orlin Stewart had been sent down to the road in front of the church to protect the bazooka man prior to [his] pulling out. Stewart stayed there. He was there when the German tanks started coming on up the road. At the road fork, he saw a tank knocked out, apparently from a bazooka hit. (There were a few independent paratroopers fighting in this area as unorganized groups.) There was a little firing after the tank was knocked out, and Stewart saw medics from both sides rush over, pick up some wounded, and begin to give them first aid. There was no firing by either side upon these aid men as they went to work.

"Two Renault tanks came up alongside the demolished tank and began to make a rush toward Stewart. Levy and Private Owen L. Garlinghouse came up along a ditch and joined him by this time. Stewart had a BAR and also had Gammon grenades. The other two men had Gammon grenades. Stewart gave them his grenade and stood ready to cover them as they threw. All three men were behind a small hedge alongside the road. They heaved the grenades as the tanks came by. There were explosions and both tanks rolled on just a little and then stopped. As the crew jumped out, the two men with Stewart heaved fragmentation grenades. Two of the Germans were hit, and Stewart shot the third man as he ran. Just at that time a big German tank moved up to the road fork with a number of infantry coming along with it. Stewart and the two others moved on north along the hedgerow. The men then withdrew. This was about the last action by Levy's small group. We got out in pretty good order, taking our machine gun and following back in collected fashion through the hedgerows to the orchard, where we rejoined Lieutenant Colonel Timmes."[35]

Lieutenant Dolan was checking the dispositions of his troopers when "Major Kellam arrived at the bridge with Captain [Dale A.] Roysdon, his S-3. He had most of his CP unit with him. I don't know whether or not a Battalion CP had ever been set up as planned, at least, I don't recall having had any communication with it. Down at the bridge now was most of Company A, about one platoon of Company B, a platoon of the division engineers (mission to blow the bridge if necessary), about half of battalion headquarters company with mortars and machine gun sections and several stray men from other regiments. The company dug in well and quickly. West of the Merderet River, was a marsh at least one thousand yards wide at its narrowest point. The road running west from the bridge could better be described as a causeway."[36]

On the western side of the river, T/5 William Dean was with the group of Company B, 508th troopers who crossed the causeway earlier, hoping to link up with the rest of the regiment on the west side of the river. "When we got to the west side of the river, we turned south toward Hill 30, and at that instant we came under heavy fire from tanks, mortars, and machine guns from our right rear. They had us in a pocket. We could not go back across the bridge!

"Straight ahead, or to the right put us in their gun sights, and to the left was the flooded swift moving river. At that point, Lieutenant [Homer] Jones yelled, 'Every man for himself.' And when the tank machine guns opened fire, Lefty Brewer and I broke for the water. An instant later, [Private Forrest V.] Brewer, my old Camp Blanding platoon sergeant lay face down in the water, dead. I swam the river back to the east shore, like a porpoise, down and up, down and up, because I was being fired at the whole way over, and beyond, since I had a ten foot bank to get over after leaving the river!"[37]

Staff Sergeant Adolph "Bud" Warnecke was leading one of the platoons of Company B, 508th troopers when they were hit by heavy German fire. "I took my platoon through a marsh. We had concealment with the tall reeds, but very little cover. I moved, took my platoon, and got to the river. At this point, a tank pulled up on the causeway approximately one thousand yards away from us. I took my men into the river, which had steep banks. We could crawl along the banks with everything covered but our heads. We were still in machine gun range. The bullets were dancing off the water and you just don't know how you could live through something like this, but we did.

"I got my platoon and got them around a bend in the river where we had cover and [were] well concealed. At this point we saw some of our own troops on a small piece of higher ground in the area. We made our way over to this area where they were. They were from another battalion. At this time I took head count and found that I had at least two men missing, one was [Private First Class Ralph] Tooley from Tennessee, and the other was [Private] Forrest Brewer from Florida. I became very fond of these two men over the past twenty months. Forrest Brewer was a professional baseball pitcher."[38]

Lieutenant Dolan heard the heavy German firing directed at the 508th troopers caught next to the west side of the flooded Merderet River. "They were gone at least an hour when we saw several of them retreating back across the marsh.

I remember that we helped several of them out of the river, which was quite shallow.

"Just about a half-hour before this attack, a 57mm antitank gun was assigned to Company A. I located this gun about one hundred fifty yards from the bridge on the road where it curves to the right as you approach the bridge. Incidentally, this was my CP and later the Battalion CP. This gave the gun excellent cover and a good field of fire.

"The machine gun fire from the Germans was very heavy by now. We didn't return their fire as there were no visible targets and our ammunition supply was limited."[39]

At approximately 4:00 p.m. Sergeant Elmo Bell, with Company C, 505th, saw German forces coming across the causeway. "This attack was led by three light tanks. These were [light] French tanks. And ahead of these tanks, there were about twelve or fifteen paratroopers who had landed on the other side of the river and been captured before they got out of their chutes. And they were marching ahead of the tanks. And the tank commander in the lead tank was standing up in the cupola directing these paratroopers to remove mines that were laying above ground, on the surface of that road and throw them [into the water].

"As they came across and came nearer and nearer to the nearest shore, I was wondering when and who was going to give the command to open fire. I knew that we had to open fire, sooner or later, and everyone was hesitant to fire because there were twelve or fifteen paratroopers ahead of the lead tank, and they were very much in harm's way. But we all knew that before the tank reached shore, that we had to take them under fire."[40]

Lieutenant Dolan was about forty yards from the bridge as the Germans came on. "The tanks were firing on us with machine guns and cannons. When the lead tank was about forty or fifty yards away from the bridge, the two Company A bazooka teams got up just like clockwork to the edge of the road. They were under the heaviest small arms fire from the other side of the causeway, and from the cannon and machine gun fire from the tanks."[41]

After getting out of the foxhole, Private Heim loaded the bazooka as they "stood behind the telephone pole so we could get a better shot at the tank. We had to hold our fire until the last minute because some of the tree branches along the causeway were blocking our view. As the lead tank started around the curve in the road the tank commander stood up in the turret to take a look and from our left the machine gun let loose a burst and killed the commander. At the same time the bazookas, 57 millimeter gun and anything else we had fired at the Germans and they in turn were shooting at us with cannons, mortars, machine gun and rifle fire."[42]

Sergeant Bell watched the tanks continue moving closer to the bridge. "When the lead tank was no more than twenty yards from the end of the bridge, the little [57mm] antitank gun fired. And whether it was by design or by accident, I don't know, but he knocked the track off the tank. The little 57[mm] was popping rounds on the front of that lead tank just as fast as they could load, but had no effect on the front armor. The lead tank was still operational except its mobility; it couldn't move. And the main gun took this little 57 under fire and killed the crew, and the machine guns were raking our defenses up and down the river."[43]

At that very moment, Company A trooper Private First Class Dave Bullington, was just about to open up with his BAR from his position in front of the hedgerow next to the river, north of the bridge. "[Sergeant Oscar L.] Queen was the first one that fired. He had the machine gun off to my right. His tracers went right in front of me. He was firing at the infantry, his tracers went right over their heads in the center of their column. He was a little high and I got him on the target, and then we let 'em have it. I don't know how many infantrymen there were; there might have been a couple hundred of them. They were all bunched up real close and made a real nice target. They were right up close to the tanks. All I remember was my BAR and Queen's machine gun. I don't know how many magazines I fired at them."[44]

Private Heim fed another rocket into the bazooka as both teams concentrated on knocking out the immobilized tank. "The first tank was hit and started to turn sideways, at the same time was swinging its turret around and firing at us. We had just moved forward around the cement telephone pole when a German round hit it and we had to jump out of the way to avoid being hit as it was falling. I was hoping that Bolderson and Pryne were also firing at the tanks, for with all that was happening in front of us, there was no time to look around to see what others were doing. We kept firing at the first tank until it was put out of action and on fire."[45]

Watching this, Dolan was awed by the courage of his two bazooka teams. "They fired and reloaded with the precision of well-oiled machinery. Watching them made it hard to believe that this was nothing but a routine drill. I don't think that either crew wasted a shot. The first tank received several direct hits. The treads were knocked off, and within a matter of minutes it was on fire."[46]

Suddenly Sergeant Bell heard the 57mm antitank gun begin firing once again, this time at the two remaining tanks as they kept up a steady fire on it with their 37mm main guns. "And they were firing as fast as they could load, but the troopers kept replacing the dead members of this little antitank gun crew. And as they were killed, they kept coming. As I recall, at least seven people were killed behind that little 57 millimeter gun."[47]

Heim continued to push rocket after rocket into the bazooka. "The second tank came up and pushed the first tank out of the way. We moved forward toward the second tank and fired at it as fast as I could load the rockets into the bazooka. We kept firing at the second tank and we hit it in the turret where the body joins it, also in the tracks and with another hit it also went up in flames. We were almost out of rockets, and the third tank was still moving. Peterson asked me to go across the road to see if Bolderson had any extra rockets. I ran across the road and with all the crossfire I still find it hard to believe I made it across in one piece. When I got to the other side I found one dead soldier, but Bolderson and Pryne were gone. Their bazooka was lying on the ground and it was damaged by what I thought were bullet holes. Not finding Bolderson or Pryne I presumed that either one or both of them were injured. I found the rockets they left and then had to return across the road to where I left Peterson. The Germans were still firing at us and I was lucky again. I returned without being hit. Peterson and myself, with the new rockets put these to use against the third tank. This was one of the toughest days of my life. Why we were not injured or killed only the good Lord knows."[48]

Dolan couldn't believe the luck of the four men. "To this day, I'll never be able to explain why all four of them were not killed. The 57mm [antitank gun] during this time was firing and eventually knocked out the last tank. The gun crew did an excellent job."[49]

Bell unexpectedly saw one of the Company C, 505th troopers leave his position. "Joseph C. Fitts ran out on to the bridge and dropped a grenade in that lead tank, and that silenced the guns on that tank. But until then, both the main gun and the machine guns had been firing constantly."[50]

The Germans were forced to flee back across the causeway, while .30-caliber bullets continued to cut them down. Faced with a possible second attack, Dolan quickly got his men resupplied. "My two bazooka crews called for more ammunition. Major Kellam ran up toward the bridge with a bag of rockets followed by Captain Roysdon. When they were within fifteen or twenty yards of the bridge, the Germans opened up with mortar fire on the bridge. Major Kellam was killed and Captain Roysdon was rendered unconscious from the concussion. He died later that day. Both of the bazookas were destroyed by the mortar fire. Lieutenant [Brock M.] Weir (Regimental Headquarters Company) and I carried Captain Roysdon back. I then took over command of the battalion, being the senior officer present."[51]

The 505th executive officer, Lieutenant Colonel Mark J. Alexander, was at the regimental CP monitoring the German attacks on the bridge and on Ste.-Mère-Église when he received word that first Major McGinity, then Major Kellam and Captain Roysdon had been killed. Alexander knew that a senior officer needed to go to the bridge area, because it was where the critical fighting was occurring at the moment. "We had been unable to make contact with Lieutenant Colonel Ekman. I talked it over with Major Norton, our S-3 at the command post and decided I should head for La Fière and the 1st Battalion defending the bridge at La Fière. I took my orderly Corporal Chick Eitelman with me. On the way, we had a scrimmage with several Germans and Chick got one through his kneecap. Chick strongly objected, but I ordered him back to headquarters where he could receive medical treatment. I proceeded to La Fière. On the way, I found a group of about forty 101st and 508th men lying in a ditch along the road. Supposedly, someone had held them in reserve. I did not know who, so I rounded them up and took them with me to La Fière.

"I found that most of A Company with Lieutenant Red Dolan were well organized and in a good situation on the right side of the road facing the Merderet River and bridge. I approved Lieutenant Dolan having moved his company back one hundred fifty yards from the intense mortar and machine gun fire along the riverbank. On the left side of the road was a mixed group of C Company, 505th men occupying a house (called the Manoir) and some 507th men under the command of a Captain [Robert D.] Rae on the ridge above the Manoir. The whole position was receiving heavy fire from the west bank around Cauquigny—mortar, machine gun, and occasionally 88mm. Through my binoculars, I spotted two German tanks screened behind the buildings in the village of Cauquigny, across the river.

"I had located one of our 57mm antitank guns, abandoned in a defilade position about seventy-five yards above the bridge and on the left side of the road. There were two holes through the shield, apparently from an earlier duel with the Renault tanks and there was no gun sight. There were six rounds of armor piercing ammunition. I put Elmo Bell and two other men on the gun. I told them that if there was another tank attack, to bore sight the gun and when they were out of ammunition, to abandon it.

"We were shelled with mortar, machine gun fire and occasional 88mm for the rest of the day. At one time in checking out our position and looking for wounded along the riverbank with medic Kelly Byars, we were caught in an exposed position and we had to lay in a foxhole for about twenty-five minutes while the Germans saturated the area with mortar fire. We had located an A Company man with a dollar sized piece of his skull blown off and still alive. We gave him a shot of morphine, but judged it would be better to come back for him after dark with a stretcher. That medic, Kelly was a real good man."[52]

Lieutenant Colonel Alexander's leadership instilled confidence in the troopers defending the bridge. Lieutenant Dolan was certainly glad to have Alexander on the scene. "Without exception, he was the finest battalion commander I ever served under."[53]

After getting the men defending the bridge reorganized, Alexander decided to report back to the division CP to inform Lieutenant Colonel Ekman and the division staff of the situation at the bridge. Alexander "headed back to the railroad junction with the dirt road just as Gavin came in from Chef-du-Pont. Seeing that we were OK at La Fière, he instructed me to take command of the position. I asked him if he wanted me on this side of the river, both sides or the other side. He instructed me to stay where we were on the east side and to hold fast, not allowing passage to the Germans. At that time he was more concerned about the situation at Chef-du-Pont."[54]

Lieutenant Gerard M. Dillon, a platoon leader with Company G, 507th, had assembled his platoon after the jump without the loss of a single man. Dillon had his men dug in at the intersection of the Ste.-Mère-Église-Amfreville road and the railroad embankment. "Just before dark, I was told by Lieutenant Eskridge, the Executive Officer of Company G and in command of the company in the absence of Captain Floyd Schwartzwalder, that I was to report to a Lieutenant Colonel Alexander from the 505th. I was informed by him that Lieutenant Colonel Timmes, who commanded the 2nd Battalion of the 507th, was in position west of the Merderet and about five hundred yards north of Cauquigny. That I was to cross the river and the inundated area and tell Colonel Timmes that General Ridgway ordered him to hold out in that position at all costs and not to surrender it.

"Two staff sergeants, whom I did not know and [who] were from other units, were assigned to accompany me. As soon as it was dusk, the three of us went to the railroad bridge across the Merderet; and after crossing it, we descended into the inundated area, which was approximately 2,000 yards wide. This area consisted of what was apparently small fields, having deep ditches dug around the perimeter of each. As a result, we would wade in the water and through this high grass, where we were in water up to our hips or shoulders for about two hundred feet, and then had to swim about fifteen feet to get across the ditches. It was slow going all the way. It took us all night to cross the inundated area."[55]

On June 6, 1944, two German regiments supported by armor had assaulted the 505th. One platoon had delayed the northern thrust for most of the day and one rifle company had stopped the attack from the west. For their outstanding courage, all four members of the two Company A bazooka teams were later awarded the Distinguished Service Cross.

CHAPTER 12

"I THINK IT'S TIME TO GET OUR WAR STARTED"[1]

During the predawn hours of June 6, 1944, individuals and small groups of paratroopers mostly from the 507th and 508th fought for survival. Widely scattered during the jump, they roamed the Norman countryside, trying to find organized units, fighting their own small wars against the enemy. It was a deadly game, where one mistake could be fatal.

In the moonlit darkness, Lieutenant Paul E. Lehman, with the 3rd Battalion, 508th, was moving with a few other paratroopers down a hedgerow-lined Norman lane. "We came across a group of five men from another battalion who were standing up in a close group talking. Immediately I went to them and strongly ordered them to scatter out into a patrol formation as to have some security and to move out at once toward their objective. No sooner had I finished my order than firing burst out nearby and we all ducked for the ground. In the darkness my chin came down on one of their bayonets, entering my throat between the chin and windpipe. The blood gushed out as if a spigot had been turned on, and Lieutenant [Briand N.] Beaudin could not stop the flow because of the type and location of the wound. Luckily he was with me, as he is the battalion surgeon, and jumped number two in the stick I jumpmastered. A facial artery directly off the jugular had been severed and each time I swallowed, it moved the artery and thus prevented the formation of a clot there."[2]

Lieutenant Beaudin took immediate action. "I was able to apply a hemostat, but with subsequent movement in the brush, the two-piece hemostat flew off, never to be found. So I applied a Carlisle dressing which was too bulky and soft to stop the flow of blood. Then, two medics, Corporal Frank Kwasnik and Private First Class Frank Ruppe, and I fanned out in different directions to locate a medical bundle, which Kwasnik did find in about thirty minutes and brought me some plasma."[3]

By the time they returned with the plasma, Lehman was barely clinging to life. "By then I was terribly weak from loss of blood and the plasma probably saved my life."[4]

As Beaudin administered the plasma, the group was still under sporadic German fire. "Unfortunately, I had no way to hook the plasma bottle up, so I had to hold it up myself with my arm extended while German snipers kept peppering me and the bottle with shots. Fortunately, they missed, and were soon routed out and killed. We then brought Lehman out with a few other wounded to a farmhouse barn. After being there an hour or so, I noticed some German soldiers coming down a nearby field towards us. I could not leave my wounded, so I waited. Soon, the open barn was raked with rifle and Schmeisser fire. I stuck my Red Cross helmet on a long pole and pushed it out the door. They stopped firing and came in to capture us."[5]

Lehman was lying on a litter when the Germans entered the building. "They searched us and then knocked on the door of the next room. When the French women didn't answer quickly enough to suit them, they threw a potato-masher grenade through the window and probably killed them instantly."[6]

Lehman, badly wounded in the throat and very weak from the loss of blood, became concerned as the German patrol prepared to move out that they might shoot him rather than be burdened with moving him. "Instead we were put out in front of them—with the doc and one of his medical aid men carrying my litter—and we were taken to their company aid station. Shortly afterwards we were evacuated by truck to a German field hospital several miles away, where we were placed in a framed barracks. The German hospital was located in what had once been a large chateau. The main building was of stone and concrete and at one time it must have been a magnificent home. Around it were many large stone barns and out-buildings to which the Germans had added five [wooden] frame barracks as additional housing for the wounded. We were well treated by the enemy medical personnel."[7]

Sergeant George Leidenheimer, also with Company B, 507th, landed near Valognes, over five miles northwest of the 507th drop zone. "When I landed I didn't see anyone. I was being fired upon by machine gun fire, so I cut my harness and put the knife back in the sheath, which I had on my boot. The firing stopped all of a sudden, so I moved in the direction of one of the hedgerows. I made it to a macadam road. I was walking along the road and I was challenged in German. So I hit the ditch alongside the road. And of course, they fired at me and I ran back about twenty yards through a gate in a stone fence.

"We were told not to fire until daylight. So I fixed the bayonet. I figured there were two Germans and if they followed me I could get them with the bayonet. They wouldn't come off the road. They just stood up on the road and looked down at the gate. I could see them; they were silhouetted. Like a dummy, I didn't kill them. Disgusted, I said, 'Well, the hell with it.' So I walked away from the gate. It was too dark for them to see me.

"I found a few of the guys. One of the kids in my platoon named Richard Guscott; he was half Indian, had crashed into a stone fence and banged up his ribs. So I hid him in the hedgerow and I said, 'Gus, I'll be back for you after while.' Well, by the time I got my guys together, got both machine guns set up, and had a whole bunch of fragmentation grenades, and plenty of ammunition, nothing was happening. So I went to get Guscott. I got about one hundred yards away and I got fired on by an MG-42. I hit the deck behind a short hedgerow and I looked where the sound came from. There was a great big open field, and two five-hundred-pound bomb craters close by, one was about thirty yards [away] and the other was about forty yards. Usually a squad of ten men will have a machine gun assigned to them. I knew there had to be a few Germans in that hole. I snapped off the safety on my Gammon grenade and I said to myself, 'Well, you had your chance and you missed. Now your ass belongs to me.'

"So I concentrated on looking at them. The next thing I heard was a noise behind me and I turned around, and you know how your helmet obscures your vision a little bit. I see a black pair of boots standing right behind me and I looked up and it was a German sergeant with a Schmeisser. The squad leader had sneaked up behind me. So what I did was leave the rifle on the ground.

"Sure enough, nine guys came out of the closest hole. When they came out, I saw the kid that fired at me with the MG-42. He was a little blonde haired blue eyed boy. I'm sure he was older, but he looked to be about fifteen years old. And he was shaking like a leaf. All of them were scared to death of me. They took the things out of my pockets that they wanted. I turned around and looked, and I could see my guys in this position with both machine guns were pointed the other way. I figured if I could just get their attention. All of the Krauts had slung their rifles over their shoulders and weren't watching me at all. This stupid kid was pointing a submachine gun at me. I was going to pop the kid and let my guys open up with the machine gun. But, they were looking the other way. The Krauts saw me looking intently over that way and they picked up the sign and they started looking that way. But, apparently they didn't see them at all. And so to fool them, I started staring off in the other direction. They brought me in to a collection point and put me in this room with about twenty-five or thirty American paratroopers."[8]

As the morning dawned over Normandy, trooper Harry Reisenleiter, with Company B, 508th, witnessed things that both frightened and infuriated him, things Reisenleiter would never forget. "The first dead paratrooper that I saw was apparently killed by a mortar round, because the fins were in the near area and it looked like a piece of the shrapnel had hit him in the back of the head. He was laid out with his hands folded and flowers between them, just like he had been laid out in a mortuary. I thought this was a very nice gesture from whoever did it for him. I'm sure it must have been one of the civilians. I also saw other troopers that were in trees that had been hung up there by their parachutes. And as they hung there, they had been shot and had their throats cut. One of the troopers had landed on the roof of a building, and his parachute was wrapped around a chimney, and he was hanging there when someone had reached out the window where he was hanging and cut his throat. Another was tied to a tree with suspension lines from his chute, and apparently he had been shot."[9]

Having been dropped far to the southeast, Sergeant Edward Barnes, the 3rd Battalion, 507th Communications Section leader, moved down lanes and roads surrounded by fields that had been flooded by the Germans, looking for any friendly face. "After I got my chute off, I started off in the direction of some small arms fire, as I did not recognize any of the landmarks that we had viewed on those sand tables back in England. By the time I got to the spot where I thought the firefight was taking place, there was silence and no one about. About an hour or so of this, I decided to lie in a ditch alongside the road, to wait for daylight so I could see just where I was headed.

"A feeling of loneliness closed in on me, as I pictured the whole German Army was trying to locate and exterminate me. At first light of dawn, I took off again, where I thought our drop zone should have been. At about 5:00 a.m., I was challenged by a voice on the other side of the hedgerow. I gave the countersign and up popped another trooper. He was in the same spot as myself, hopelessly lost.

"We continued down the road and finally ran into some more troopers, also lost. By this time we had a mighty fighting force of six troopers. In the distance we could see the outline of a church steeple. So we decided to head for the church and maybe get some information as to our whereabouts and the whereabouts of any other troopers in the area. We continued cautiously on our way toward the church, expecting any minute to be fired on by the Germans, when we heard a challenge from the ditch up the road in front of us. We gave the countersign and were told to come forward slowly. When we got to within about fifteen yards of the spot where we heard the challenge, we could see they were troopers from the 82nd Airborne. We all went up to the church in the village, which turned out to be the village of Graignes, and reported in to the commanding officer in charge, Major [Charles D.] Johnson, who was a battalion commander in the 507th Parachute Infantry Regiment. It seems the major was just as lost as the rest of us.

"After questioning some townspeople, we found we were twenty miles from our designated drop zone, which left us twenty miles farther behind the German lines. We were dropped completely off the maps we were carrying. We spent most of the day going out on patrols, harassing the enemy and rounding up lost troopers. By day's end, we had accumulated about sixty troopers. On one of our patrols, as we proceeded down the road, I could see a body lying in the roadside. As we approached, I could see it was the body of one of our airborne troopers. I rolled him over and there was a blue, round hole in the middle of his forehead. I figured he must have been dead about two hours. I don't think I can express my feeling of sorrow, as this was the first dead American soldier I had seen. I got his name and serial number from his dog-tags and turned them in to our headquarters."[10]

Staff Sergeant Donald Bosworth, with Headquarters Company, 1st Battalion, had landed in a field with six other men from his stick a couple of miles west of the 507th's DZ "T" near Orglandes. "I landed with my left leg in a foxhole, breaking my right ankle. When we got together, we saw a French farmhouse across the road and they helped me walk to it. We went to the farmhouse and knocked on the door and woke up the people. They let us in the house and hugged each one of us. They were really happy to see us. The lady in the French farmhouse was a schoolteacher and she could speak a little English. We got our maps out and they showed us exactly where we were, where Amfreville was, and what we had to do to get there.

"Because my ankle was broken and I couldn't walk, she and her husband gave us their truck. The truck was a small flatbed with two-foot sideboards and tailgate, made with 1 x 12s, giving good coverage to the men in the truck's bed. Her husband also dug up a five gallon can of gasoline he had buried in the yard and put it in the truck. Staff Sergeant A. J. Carlucci and I signed a receipt for the truck; that would enable them to collect its value from the United States. Carlucci drove and I sat in the seat beside him. On our way to Amfreville in the truck, we passed two German soldiers on bicycles going there also. The Germans were apparently gathering for breakfast. After we drove through the edge of Amfreville, we saw Americans in a field and drove through a gate to join them. It was Colonel Timmes and some of the various other groups of men."[11]

The first sergeant of Company D, 507th, Barney Q. Hopkins, had landed alone in a field west of Amfreville. "I oriented myself and headed in the direction of Amfreville. We were trained to stay off the roads, so I stayed in the field, but parallel with the road. I continued to move toward Amfreville for about forty-five minutes, wondering where everyone was. I was about twenty or twenty-five feet from the hedgerow bordering the road, when suddenly I had been challenged with the word, 'Flash.' It seemed to take me a long time to respond with 'Thunder,' but it probably was only about a five second delay, all due to my anxiety. I had been challenged by Corporal Stewart of D Company, with him was Private [Roland J.] Monfett and another D Company soldier. We discussed the situation briefly, then continued to move toward Amfreville."[12]

After daybreak, they came upon a farmhouse. Hopkins wanted to double check to make sure they headed in the proper direction to Amfreville. "I decided we should inquire. So I put myself and two men on each of the three corners of the house to serve as lookouts, and sent Monfett to the front door to find out the location of Amfreville. Monfett was about eighteen years old, a

French-Canadian and spoke French. They talked for what seemed like a long time, much longer than necessary it seemed. Then Monfett came to me and I asked, 'What did the lady say?'

"Monfett replied, 'Yes, that is the road.' I still don't understand why it took so long to say, 'Yes.'

"We continued on toward Amfreville and met four paratroopers from some other unit going in a different direction. After a short discussion, each of us headed for our assembly area. About 9:00 a.m. we met up with Colonel [George V.] Millett, who had about twenty or twenty-five men with him. They had a medium size German truck, which had some supplies and rations in it. After a brief discussion, Colonel Millett decided we should go into Amfreville. Captain [Clarence A.] Tolle [Company D, 507th] and myself, along with four or five men took the point.

"As we entered Amfreville, four or five Germans shot at us, then broke and ran to the right. Captain Tolle told me to get them, so I took two of my men and chased the Germans. We caught up with them behind a barn and they broke and ran again. I had a .30-caliber carbine, which the trigger mechanism had been converted and was made into a full automatic carbine, capable of about seven hundred rounds per minute. I shot and killed three of the Germans and my men shot and killed the other German. As I returned to Captain Tolle (my company commander), fifty yards before I reached him, he raised up and called to me. Just then a German machine gun fired and hit Captain Tolle three or four times in the chest. I ran to him and he died on my arms in a bar-ditch off the street.

"The machine gun fire had come out of a building at the end of the street with a large red cross on it. I got my men and moved to an obscure position, just across the street from the building. I told Corporal Karl [P.] Kuhn (Company D) to put a grenade in that second story window. Kuhn had a grenade launcher on his rifle. Kuhn then put one in the window, but it did not explode. I asked why. Kuhn said he forgot to pull the pin. I replied, 'Pull the pin and put another one in there.' He did and three Germans ran out of the ground floor and I shot and killed all three with my automatic carbine. I went into the building and found three paratroopers, but not my regiment, and they joined our group.

"The street turned right, and just about one hundred yards from us was a large German artillery piece, probably a 155 with a large open top vehicle hooked to pull it. I proceeded to get into the vehicle and tried to start it so we could use it against the Germans. But I was unable to start it. Then a German sniper from the tower of a building shot at me a couple of times, but missed. I put a thermite grenade over the transmission, thinking, 'I can't use it, neither can the Germans.' Thermite is very hot and will melt metal.

"I returned to Colonel Millett and he decided to withdraw, which we did. We set up a defense in a sunken road about eight hundred yards west of Amfreville. We had brought Captain Tolle's body with us. We stayed in that position about two hours. A few more paratroopers from various units joined us. By this time we had about thirty-five or forty men."[13]

After sunrise, Technician 5th Grade Frank Brumbaugh and another trooper ventured out of the small field where they had landed, looking for other paratroopers. "Every place we looked there was a parachute either on the ground, hanging in a tree, hanging on a wire or a telephone pole. The place was covered with parachutes . . . no sign of anybody around. We finally ran across a couple of guys from the 505 Parachute Infantry, later on some from the 507th, and so forth. By about 9:00 or so we had a group of about ten to twelve paratroopers, one or two from every American airborne outfit."[14]

By daylight, Private First Class William M. Sawyer, with Company D, 508th, had assembled with about twenty-five to thirty troopers. Sawyer's group attempted to fight its way to the bridge over the Douve River at Pont L'Abbe. "We tried three times to get to the bridge—the bridge we were supposed to blow."

Sawyer's group had landed near the headquarters of the German 91st Airlanding Division, and the area was thick with enemy infantry and Renault light tanks. Sawyer knew they needed to obtain antitank weapons to defend themselves from the German armor. "We looked everywhere for supplies. Every time we'd find an equipment chute, all of our bazookas were smashed."

Sawyer's group kept moving all day on June 6. "We could not find the battalion."[15]

Private David Jones, with Headquarters Company, 1st Battalion, 508th, had field stripped his M1 rifle and was cleaning it after landing in a flooded area the previous night. "Up to this time I had not fired a shot. No sooner did I get the M1 all laid out and drying nicely, someone yells, 'Tanks!' I finally got my weapon reassembled and watching those tanks rattling up that causeway towards the farmhouse that we were hiding behind gave no cause for celebration.

"Now these were French Renault tanks, probably the smallest tanks used during the entire war. But to me, they were larger than life. I remember the lead tank had its hatch open and the black-capped tank commander was exposed from the waist up, hands resting outside the turret. I can't explain why in the world I said it, but to my nearest companion I said, 'I think it's time to get our war started.' There was immediately a lot of discussion as to what the results would be if we fired on them, and the comments were not encouraging. I did fire at that tank commander with an armor piercing round that I had loaded as a number one round. It hit the turret. The black uniform disappeared, the hatch clanged shut, the tank backed off a few feet, and our group scattered to the four winds. Not only had I missed my first shot of World War II, but was now confronted with where and how to hide. All I could think of were those tank tracks running up my back as I'm lying there in the vegetable garden behind this farmhouse. The tank fired a round into the side of that farmhouse. We in our small group offered no more resistance and took off through an adjacent hedgerow."[16]

The three tanks continued east toward Beuzeville-la-Bastille with the goal of crossing the causeway at Chef-du-Pont and then onward to attack the Utah Beach landings.

By sunrise on June 6, Sergeant O. B. Hill, with Headquarters Company, 1st Battalion, 508th, was lucky to be alive. Sergeant Hill had landed five miles from his drop zone, in the floodplain of the Douve River, and almost drowned. Almost everyone in his stick had been killed or captured. His company commander, Captain Gerard A. Ruddy, was killed shortly after landing. Hill's platoon leader, Lieutenant Charles J. McElligott, was shot in the stomach and captured. Hill had almost been discovered by a passing German patrol. As he moved alone through the silence of the predawn darkness, that silence was suddenly broken. "I heard someone say, 'Flash'.

"My reply was, 'Oh shit!' I had completely forgotten the password for the moment. As it turned out, the person challenging me was Corporal William P. Brown from Detroit, one of my corporals. We compared notes and determined that we were going in the right direction. Along the way we picked up more jumpers and soon discovered that we were not the only ones who were not in the right place.

"The 508 was to destroy the bridges over the Douve River at Ètienville and Beuzeville-la-Bastille. At about 10:00 a.m. we arrived at the village of Beuzeville. This was on the Douve River, across from the town of Beuzeville-la-Bastille. We were at the bridge our unit was supposed to destroy, but we did not know that at the time.

"There was a pocket of German soldiers at this crossroad. We discovered that there was more of our group across the road from us. Together, we drove the Germans off and we crossed the road to join the others. The two groups now assembled in fields, behind a row of about seven houses along the road in Beuzeville. I located Staff Sergeant Ray Hummel from my company. We then realized that he and I were the ranking men in our group. We had no officers. We compared notes and determined that we were in Beuzeville. We could see where the two rivers came together beyond where we were. In fact, we were surrounded on two sides by floodwaters from the two rivers. In order to determine which way we should go or what we should do, Ray and I thought we should get up in one of the two story houses and see what was around us.

"We shot the lock off the back door of about the fourth house from the river. The house was occupied and the people in it were badly scared. They did not interfere. In fact, they smiled at us and gave us the run of the place. Ray and I went up the stairs just inside the back door. We were followed by Jim McMahon, who was a corporal in the wire section of my company. Ray and I went to a double window on the front of the house and were looking to see what was around us.

"We heard tanks approaching from the west and we dropped down to keep from being seen. It was three French Renault tanks that the German Army was using in that area. The center one stopped immediately under the window where we were. The top hatch opened and one of the soldiers inside stood up to look around. While he was looking, I handed Hummel a Gammon grenade and he dropped it into the tank. That tank was knocked out of action and the other two were trying to figure out what had hit it.

"We left that building and once again joined the men in the fields behind the houses;If the two tanks had pursued us, we could not have stopped them, because the heaviest weapons we had were our rifles. They did not tarry long and soon moved on their way going east from us."[17]

Even though many paratroopers were killed, wounded, and captured in those first hours; countless others were wreaking destruction, ambushing German patrols and vehicles, and taking on German forces many times their size. Company I, 508th trooper, Technician 5th Grade Frank Brumbaugh was determined to put his training to good use. "For the next two or three days we gathered up other small groups of paratroopers, all mixed together. There were no officers with us. We were trained to live and fight either alone or with one or more of our paratroop buddies.

"We accounted for quite a number of German soldiers. We had orders, for the first nine days to take no prisoners. Obviously, the reason for this was that when [we land] behind enemy lines, [we] are all by [ourselves], [and] can't afford to set up a POW compound [and] use personnel to guard prisoners. It's just totally impossible. So even though some of the Germans surrendered, or thought they were surrendering, they were disarmed and killed.

"Part of our orders were to disrupt as much communications and transport as possible. We cut telephone [and] electric wires off houses [and] poles. Anything that we could handle, we would blow up. We had quite a few blocks of C4 plastic explosive with us, and had been trained in demolitions."[18]

Shortly after landing, Private Lee Roy Wood, with Company D, 508th, began looking for a fellow paratrooper—any paratrooper. Sergeant Francis Williamson, also with D Company, 508th, had landed close by. "I was trying to get out of my chute and Wood came up on me. I told him, 'Wood, now don't you shoot me. I forgot the password.' "[19]

Wood was just glad to have found a friend. "The next guy we picked up was Lieutenant [Temple W.] Tutwiler. And then we picked up another officer. A little small guy. They called him 'Tex', but I never did know his name. Then we picked up a 505er [Private John F. Quigg]. At one time there were seven of us."[20]

The officer called "Tex" was Lieutenant Malcolm D. Brannen, with Headquarters Company, 3rd Battalion, 508th. "We ran into Lieutenant Harold Richard, A Company, 508th Parachute Infantry and his communications sergeant, Sergeant [Homer E.] Hall. It was nice being with two more of our regiment and we were glad to have met at this time.

"After a conference, we decided to ask directions at a large stone farmhouse, which was about fifty yards away. We had about twelve enlisted men and two officers in our party now. We split up and surrounded the house. Lieutenant Richard, one enlisted man, and I pounded on the door of the house. In a few seconds a very excited Frenchman came rushing out of the door. Several other occupants of the house were looking out of windows on the ground floor, as well as from windows on the upper stories of the house. In the house, the upstairs windows were alive with little kiddos, wild eyed at seeing the American uniforms instead of the usual German ones.

"By using our French guide book and maps we found out that we were between Picauville and Ètienville. Good! We were about midway between the two places and now had a definite location from which we could plan on future moves to get with our own troops. I said, 'Here comes a car—stop it.' Lieutenant Richard moved out of the doorway towards the side of the house and some of the men went to the stone wall at the end of the house. The house doors shut and I went to the road and put my hand up and yelled, 'Stop.'

"But the car came on faster. When the car went by me I ran to the other side of the road. I guess that all of us fired at the car at the same time, as a dozen or more shots rang out and I, on the far side of the road, found myself in the line of fire from the others in our group. I fell to the road and watched the car as it was hit by many shots, and saw the car crash into the stone wall and possibly the side of the house. The driver lost control of the car as he slouched in the front seat trying to avoid being hit by the bullets that filled the air around the car. The car was full of bullet holes and the windshield was shattered. I climbed upon a hedgerow six or more feet above the roadbed, and had a perfect view of the immediate situation, including the road, the house, the car, and the personnel—German, French, and American.

"The chauffeur, a German corporal, was thrown from the front seat of the car. I saw [him] trying to escape by crawling into the cellar of the house and I fired my .45 Colt pistol at him—grazing his shoulder and saw him sit down beside the house. An officer sitting on the front seat of the car was slumped onto the floor with his head and shoulders hanging out the open front door, dead.

"The other occupant of the car, who had been riding in the back seat of the Dusenberg or Mercedes Phaeton, was in the middle of the road, crawling towards a Luger pistol that had been knocked from his grasp when the car hit the stone wall and house. He looked at me as I stood on the hedge above him, and fifteen feet to his right, and as he inched closer and closer to his weapon he pleaded to me in German and also in English, 'Don't kill, don't kill.'

"I thought, 'I'm not a cold hearted killer, I'm human—but, if he gets that Luger—it is either him or me or one or more of my men.' So I shot! He was hit in the forehead and never knew it. He suffered none. The blood spurted from his forehead about six feet high, and like water in a fountain when it is shut off, it gradually subsided.

"Upon examining the personnel that we had encountered we found that we had killed a major and a major general (later learned that he was a lieutenant general) and had as a captive, a corporal, whom we made carry two brief cases that were full of official papers that we found in the car. Our intention was to turn the papers in to our headquarters when we rejoined the 508th Parachute Infantry Regiment. As we left the scene, I tore the General's hat apart, looking for further identification of name or unit to which he was assigned. I found only a name printed in it—the name was 'Falley.' "[21]

Lieutenant Brannen had just killed the commanding general of the German 91st Airlanding Division. This division was specially trained in antiairborne warfare. The loss of Lieutenant General Wilhelm Falley caused a delay in the 91st Division's reaction to the parachute and glider landings, as his staff awaited his arrival and orders, which never came.

Sunrise on June 6 found Lieutenant Ralph DeWeese, of Company H, 508th, with only three troopers. Only Private First Class Edward Polasky was from Lieutenant DeWeese's platoon. As they moved cautiously down a hedgerow-lined lane they continued to pick up more troopers. DeWeese "could hear the firing over the beach now, where the first troops were coming in. We came up to a road junction and there I saw my first Frenchmen. There were two men there and we tried to ask if they had seen any Americans. I pointed to the flag on my sleeve and pointed up and down the road. One of the Frenchmen pulled out a package of Lucky Strike cigarettes and pointed down the road. We also met Lieutenant [Victor] Grabbe and Captain [Chester E.] Graham at the road junction.

"We started working down the road where the Frenchmen said the Americans had gone. We ran into about seventy of them in a little town of Picauville. We inquired about the 3rd Battalion and one officer said he had seen Captain [Hal M.] Creary. We also contacted the machine gun platoon of the 3rd Battalion. In all, we had about two hundred men. We started marching toward Ètienville. We kept bypassing the enemy and finally set up in a field. We heard some of our weapons fire and thought it was some of our men in an attack. After sending out a patrol, we found Germans who had gotten some of our equipment and were firing our weapons."[22]

Another Company H, 508th trooper, Private Tom Porcella, became separated from his buddies and wound up with a group of paratroopers from another unit. "This group of paratroopers got the order to move single file along the hedgerow, which at that time paralleled the road. While we were proceeding alongside this hedgerow, the column stopped when we received word that someone heard a vehicle coming down the road toward us. So we wanted to know whose vehicle it was. Was it ours or was it the Germans'?

"They believed it was a German motorcyclist. The man in front of me, his name was Cantenberry says, 'I'll shoot the son of a bitch.' He raised his rifle and was waiting for the motorcyclist to come down the road. He took careful aim and waited until the cyclist was about fifty feet away and he fired a single shot. The German was suspended in midair, while the motorcycle continued to go on and crashed into the side of the road. The German soldier just lay there in the middle of the road on his back; his arms were outstretched. He looked very young. This was the first dead German I had seen since I parachuted into Normandy. We stayed in our position for awhile and we waited to see if there were anymore Germans on the way. A few minutes seemed to pass and then they gave the all clear. 'Move on.' We ran in leaps and bounds, keeping our eye on the road and on the field towards our right.

"An amazing thing was somebody was always shouting an order at us, but we never knew who the hell it was. We never knew if it was an officer or non-com, but we just followed the man in front of us and just did what we were told. After running a short distance, the column stopped again. I asked, 'Why are we stopping?'

"Someone said, 'Well, there is a road up ahead and we have to cross this road and we've got to be careful. As soon as the first man crosses, we'll get the OK to keep going.'

"So I guess one trooper decided to make his run and be the first one to cross the road. He reached the middle of the road and all we could hear was a shot that was fired and the trooper fell face down. I'll never forget; his arms were outstretched as if he was reaching for the other side. Immediately there was an exchange of machine gun fire and rifle fire. A hand signal was given to keep going. We were all moving very rapidly. Still, we didn't know where we were going and we had to leave this trooper there, right where he fell. Right in the middle of the road, all alone. It was very sad. With all of this uncertainty of not knowing where we were going, fear began to grip us. I know I was scared as hell."[23]

After landing, Major Shields Warren, the executive officer of the 1st Battalion, 508th, had assembled about two hundred men south of Drop Zone "N," and they had fought their way north, reaching a position about five hundred yards east of Picauville. That afternoon they were hit by a battalion of the 1057th Regiment of the 91st Airlanding Division, supported by Renault tanks and self-propelled guns.

Landing north of Picauville, Lieutenant Colonel Thomas J. B. Shanley, the commander of the 2nd Battalion, 508th, sent out a few men in each direction to find more men. "I had only about thirty-five men with me at dawn. At that time, I sent out more patrols and started encountering fairly heavy resistance. At approximately noon, we were heavily engaged on three sides, and I pulled out after I found that another group, larger than mine was east of us. I left behind in that place about ten men, most of whom were jump casualties."[24]

As the German battalion, which was supported by tanks, that Shanley's small group had held off all morning closed in on the tiny hamlet of Gueutteville, three troopers, despite orders to withdraw, stayed behind and covered the withdrawal, engaging the German force. Those men, Private John A. Lockwood, Private Otto K. Zwingman, and Corporal Ernest T. Roberts, all from Company D,

508th, held off the powerful German force for over two hours, buying time for Shanley and his men to pull out of Gueutteville. The three killed at least fifteen Germans and wounded many more. They were all taken prisoner, and each would later be awarded the Distinguished Service Cross.

Corporal Kenneth J. "Rock" Merritt, with the Machine Gun Platoon, Headquarters Company, 1st Battalion, 508th, had found two equipment bundles shortly after landing, illuminated by the flames from a C-47 that crashed a thousand yards away. Being alone and not knowing where he was, Merritt had taken one of the machine guns and all of the ammunition cans he could carry and had set off to find his unit. Later, Merritt had heard some noise on the other side of a hedgerow, challenged with his cricket, and given the password. "It was Lieutenant [Edgar R.] Abbott, the platoon leader of the 81mm Mortar Platoon of Headquarters Company, 1st Battalion, 508. He had with him seventeen men. By daybreak, we had assembled thirty-five men, and at 13:00 hours, on our way to join our battalion executive officer, Major Shields Warren, we ran into Captain [Jonathan E.] Adams, company commander of A Company. He had with him ten men. We now had forty-five men, including one captain, and two lieutenants. Captain Adams took command and was directed to move to Hill 30 [on the western side of the Merderet River floodplain just north of the western end of the Chef-du-Pont Causeway].

"Prior to moving out towards Hill 30, I received my first combat order. We were receiving fire from one machine gun to our right flank, and Lieutenant [Edgar R.] Abbott turned to me and said, 'Corporal, take two men with you and knock out that machine gun.' I guess it was a calm way that Lieutenant Abbott ordered me to knock out the machine gun nest, like, 'Take two men and go fill up the water cans.' Anyway, I picked a man by the name of Private [Wilbur E.] James and a former sergeant reduced to private by the name of Fairbanks to go with me. Private James knocked out the machine gun, and Fairbanks and I kept the Jerries pinned down. This was the first time we learned the little trick that the Jerries had—firing tracers three feet above the ground and then firing regular ammunition eighteen inches off the ground."[25]

As Sergeant Zane Schlemmer, with Headquarters Company, 2nd Battalion, 508th, and his group moved through the Norman hedgerow country they quickly adapted. "We came across additional troopers in the various fields waiting to ambush any German activities on the roads and lanes.

"Each of these fields seemed to be a separate battleground. Before entering, we would examine it through the hedgerows. If there were any cows, we were pleased because we could be reasonably certain that these fields, then, were not mined. Also, by watching the cows, who were by nature, quite curious animals, we could tell whether there was anyone else in that field. The cows seemed to associate people with milking, and they would stand, waiting, facing anyone in anticipation of being milked. Over all these years, I've had a place in my heart for those lovely Norman cows with the big eyes and the big udders.

"We too, became accustomed to the sound of German hob-nail boots on the Norman back roads, whereas paratrooper jump boots were rubber soled, and made a much different sound. In this way, we were able to ambush many patrols, merely by the sound on the other side of the respective hedgerows, which were too tall and too thick to see through. Also, we were able to distinguish between different rates of fire of the automatic weapons and machine pistols that identified Germans or friendlies, even without seeing them."[26]

Ordered by General Gavin on the morning of June 6 to capture the causeway over the Merderet River located just southwest of Chef-du-Pont, a force of seventy-five men led by Lieutenant Colonel Arthur Maloney made a wide flanking march to approach Chef-du Pont from the east. Shortly afterward, hearing that the causeway was undefended, Gavin personally led a second group under the command of Lieutenant Colonel Edwin J. Ostberg directly to Chef-du-Pont to seize the town immediately, as well as the causeway, if possible.

Captain Roy Creek, the CO of Company E, 507th, helped get the men up and moving south from the main road west from Ste.-Mère-Église along the railroad tracks toward Chef-du-Pont. "There were about one hundred men altogether, equipped only with what they could carry: rifles, submachine guns, three machine guns and grenades of various types, including the British Gammon grenade which packed a terrific wallop.

"At about 10:00 6 June, [Lieutenant] Colonel Ostberg and his force, comprised of men of all units of the 507 and some from the 508 had reached the railroad station of Chef-du-Pont without any opposition. The railroad station was in the center of town and the small but important bridge was a short distance southwest. A squad was sent to clear the section of town northeast of the station, which they did without incident. The remainder of the force led by Ostberg started to race through the part of the town leading to the bridge. This group was fired upon from several buildings simultaneously. Four of the men were hit and the remainder were forced to hold until the town could be systematically cleared. This took about two hours. By that time, most of the Germans had withdrawn ahead of us, apparently headed for the bridge.

"Speed seemed to be the answer. We knew the bridge must be taken before the Germans could organize their defense, so we made a semi-organized dash for it. We were too late. Two officers reached the bridge and were both shot—one toppling off the bridge and into the water; the other falling on the eastern approach. The officer toppling into the river was [Lieutenant] Colonel Ostberg. He was rescued shortly afterward by two soldiers of the 507 and lived to fight again. The other officer was dead.

"A short time later, Colonel Maloney arrived with about seventy-five more men and we set about dislodging the stubborn enemy. To appreciate the difficulties confronting us, a description of the terrain and approaches is necessary. The railroad split the town and the bridge lay to the south and west of the railroad station. Houses lined both sides of the road leading to the bridge. A short distance from the bridge on the left side of the road leading to the bridge was a large creamery, which was quite high and afforded good observation from an upstairs window. South of the creamery and on three sides of the bridge, there were obstacles, flooded areas. For practical purposes, the only approach to the bridge was the one we had chosen through Chef-du-Pont. The approaches from the west were not approaches in a military sense. They were causeways, long and straight and completely flooded on both sides. Germans were dug in on the shoulders on both sides of the road occupying foxholes dispersed at intervals of about ten yards for a long stretch leading to the bridge and beyond. No one could hope to attack successfully or withdraw along these causeways without a preponderance of supporting fires, something we did not have. Nevertheless, we were on the outskirts of Chef-du-Pont with one hundred seventy-five men.

"What are we waiting for? Let's take the bridge. Two attempts to storm the bridge proved unsuccessful. There had to be a better way. We did succeed in clearing the eastern side of the bridge, by killing about twenty-four Germans occupying positions along the shoulders of the road.

"Our own position along the edge of the road east of the bridge had become almost untenable because of rifle and direct artillery fire coming from our right flank. Just as it was beginning to look as though we might have a stalemate, Colonel Maloney was called back to La Fiere with all men available, leaving only about thirty-four men at Chef-du-Pont. Concurrent with his departure three things happened: One, direct artillery fire on our positions around the creamery reduced our strength to twenty men. Two, an observation point in the creamery noted what was estimated to be a company of Germans moving around to our left rear. And three, an officer delivered a message from General Gavin, 'Hold at all costs.' It was pretty obvious that it couldn't cost too much, but at the same time, it was doubtful we could hold something we didn't have."[27]

Lieutenant Briand Beaudin, the 3rd Battalion, 508th surgeon, who had been captured that morning, worked together with the German medical personnel at the German hospital located northwest of Ste.-Mère-Église near Orglandes to save as many patients as possible. Doctor Beaudin was limited in what he could do for the wounded. "All we had were our first aid kits. A Catholic priest who was a sergeant in the German Army and in charge of scheduling in the surgical suite in the chateau proved to be a godsend in enabling us to rush a few Americans in for definitive surgery. Private First Class [Medic Frank] Ruppe spoke fluent German, which was very helpful in many respects, not the least of which was getting us all some rations, including some ersatz tea from the German mess sergeant."[28]

Corporal Kenneth "Rock" Merritt, with Headquarters Company, 1st Battalion, 508th, moved out with forty-five other troopers toward Hill 30 at about 1:00 p.m. "Within an hour, all hell broke loose. We were pinned down from the front, the right, and the left flank. Our lead scouts were killed. We tried to counterattack, but got repulsed. We pulled back to the line of departure area, and dug in and set up a roadblock to our rear. We finally reestablished radio contact with Lieutenant Colonel Shanley on Hill 30. We tried several times to break out of our twenty acres of real estate that we were holding, but each time got pushed back. The decision was made to hold our position and the roadblock. Our location was in the vicinity of Montessy."[29]

That afternoon in a field between Ètienville and Picauville, a group of about two hundred or so 508th troopers had just finished digging in. For the first time since landing in the water the previous night, Lieutenant Ralph DeWeese, with Company H, 508th, decided to try to eat something. He had lost his musette bag in the water, which contained most of his rations. "I had some rations in my pocket and took them out and much to my disappointment they were soaking wet. I had to throw them away and that left me with no food. Everything I had was ruined."[30]

Lieutenant Barry E. Albright, with Company E, 508th, sent out by Lieutenant Colonel Shanley with a few men to round up people, found this group of troopers and led them east to Shanley's CP. After arrival of these men, Shanley received orders by radio from Colonel Roy Lindquist, CO of the 508th, to move his men to Hill 30. Shanley then relayed the order via radio to his West Point classmate, Major Shields Warren, executive officer of the 1st Battalion, 508th, who had a gathered another group of about two hundred troopers near Geutteville. The two groups joined up east of Picauville about 7:00 p.m. where they moved out, arriving at Hill 30 at approximately 2:00 a.m.

At 2:00 p.m. on June 6, the seaborne elements (Force C, known as "Howell Force") of the 82nd Airborne Division began landing on Utah Beach. Howell Force included the 456th PFA Battalion, less the two guns that parachuted with the 505th; Batteries D, E, F, and part of Headquarters, 80th AA Battalion; Headquarters and Headquarters Company, 307th Airborne Engineer Battalion; the 782nd Airborne Ordnance Maintenance Company; the 407th Airborne Quartermaster Company; the 82nd Airborne MP Company; and a Corps Medical Detachment. In addition, several units attached to the division for the invasion were part of the Howell Force: the 87th Armored Field Artillery Battalion; 899th Tank Destroyer Battalion; 3809th and 3810th Quartermaster Truck Companies; and 1st Platoon of the 603rd Quartermaster Company. And finally, Howell Force included an armored task force consisting of Company C, 746th Tank Battalion (Sherman M4 tanks); Troop B, 4th Cavalry Squadron (armored cars); and Company F of the 2nd Battalion, 401st Glider Infantry Regiment under the command of Colonel Edson D. Raff. The mission of this task force was to land as the first element of Howell Force and break through to link up with the airborne forces in order to provide a more powerful antitank defensive capability. By early evening, Colonel Raff, riding in an open jeep at the head of his force, arrived north of Les Forges, just south of Fauville, having followed elements of the 4th Infantry Division. "On arriving at forward elements of the 4th Division with the task force, I found the enemy occupying the hill [Hill 20] south of Ste.-Mère-Église five hundred yards away, with the Cannon Company of the 4th Division firing across the valley, which at 21:00 would become glider Landing Zone 'W.' Gliders, which had landed earlier, were strewn about—some of them across the valley on the enemy's wooded hill.

"It was urgent that the valley be cleared for the glider elements from England. I ordered my tanks to attack."[31]

After dismounting from the tank on which he was riding, Private First Class Lucius Young, with Company F, 401st, watched the tanks move toward Hill 20 to the north. "One of the tanks went up the road and was hit by an 88, killing the commander and wounding several of the men. A second tank tried to go up the road and it too, took a direct hit by an 88. The third tank went around to the right, but did not make it up to the field."[32]

Raff had to call off the attack to clear the landing zone. "Within an hour at least three Shermans had been knocked out and set on fire by German antitank fire."[33]

At 6:40 p.m. on June 6, 176 gliders began their journey from their airfields in England to Normandy in the largest glider mission of the war thus far. The gliders were to land at Landing Zone "W" southeast of Ste.-Mère-Église near Fauville. The gliders carried Battery C, 80th AA Battalion, with thirteen 57mm antitank guns; the 319th GFA Battalion, with their twelve 75mm pack howitzers; the 320th GFA and their short barreled 105mm howitzers; and medical personnel of the 307th Airborne Medical Battalion. In addition, the gliders carried 92 vehicles (mostly jeeps) and 107 tons of ammunition, medical supplies, water, food, mines, grenades, and other ordnance. The landings would commence at 9:00 p.m.

Southeast of Ste.-Mère-Église, Colonel Raff was desperate to divert the eminent glider landings from LZ "W," where Germans holding the wooded hill on the north side of the LZ would undoubtedly decimate the gliders if they landed there. "Despite frantic efforts to warn General Williams, Commander of 9th Troop Carrier Command of the situation on the LZ, I knew the glider lift would be on time. Colonel [James] Van Fleet, CO, 8th Infantry Regiment, 4th Division arrived on reconnaissance at the spot and I pleaded with him to make an attack to drive out the enemy force across the way. He demurred saying he had reached his forward line for the day."[34]

A short time later, Raff heard the low roar of C-47 engines in the distance to the east. "To my horror at 21:00 the glider lift came in low over the valley. Every enemy weapon opened fire on the train of C-47s and gliders. Like watching a movie in which the full plot was known, I realized that the smoking knocked out tanks were appearing as LZ markers in the evening light to the pilots in the troop carriers, so unerringly did they release the gliders over that valley."[35]

Riding in a Horsa glider, T/4 Edward R. Ryan, with Battery C, 319th GFA Battalion, "experienced ack-ack fire and saw a lot of fires on the ground, then they cut us loose. We crashed at over one hundred miles per hour in a lot less than two acres, the wings were torn off, it rolled on its side, and stopped. The pilot and co-pilot were killed instantly. There were about thirteen killed and ten escaped. The Horsa should never have been used."[36]

The glider carrying Private First Class Menno N. Christner, with Battery C, 80th AA Battalion, crash-landed and the "glider broke apart. I broke three ribs and we [were thrown from the glider and] hung in the trees . . . the pilot lying in front of the wrecked glider. He had one or both legs broken. I carried the pilot to safety. The jeep landed upside down, the co-pilot underneath. I picked the co-pilot up and carried him to safety. I heard a lot of gunfire all around and didn't know which way to go."[37]

Colonel Raff watched helplessly as the glider landings were made under intense enemy fire. "Gliders were crashing into hedgerows all around the valley. Some even landed in the enemy held woods. The British gliders made of wood completely disintegrated in the crashes. Some troop carrier aircraft then circled slowly around flying over the enemy across the valley on the way back to England. At least two were hit by fire and exploded over the enemy held hill. Men tumbled out completely stunned. It was useless to try to direct them. But out of all of this confusion units grew as individuals came together."[38]

At the causeway on the edge of Chef-du-Pont, Captain Roy Creek was holding a tenuous position with only twenty men, being shelled by a German 75mm infantry gun and mortars from the opposite bank. Creek looked up to see tow planes flying overhead after releasing their gliders to the east moments before. "As from heaven, C-47s began to appear, dropping bundles of weapons and ammunition. One bundle of 60mm mortar ammunition dropped right in our laps. Within thirty minutes, the officer who had previously delivered the 'hold at all costs' message returned with one hundred men and a 57mm gun which was pulled into position on our side of the bridge. We started firing at the enemy field piece. We didn't hit it, I am certain, but we stopped the firing and that is what we had to do in order to survive.

"At the beginning of this period of heavy shelling, I found myself exposed with no place to go. I spotted a very small brick sentry house just short of the bridge on our side. I made a dash for it and went inside and found a still burning enemy soldier, victim of a white phosphorous grenade, which apparently had been tossed in on him during earlier fighting. The house only had room for one man standing. So it became crowded with my arrival, and the other guy in there wasn't going anywhere. This coupled with the fact that the smoke and stench from the burning man caused me to make a quick decision that I would rather take my chances out in the open than risk the consequences of smoke inhalation. And besides, I reasoned that this lone house was surely an aiming point for the artillery.

"With our reinforcement, strong positions were organized to our rear and along the flooded area on either side of the road and east of the bridge. The defenses were tied in with natural obstacles on three sides of us. We opened fire with every weapon we could get into position, including our own 60mm mortar.

"On a prearranged signal, all fires lifted and ten men and one officer stormed the bridge and went into position on the western approach to guard the causeway. Five Germans made a run for it down the deathtrap causeway and immediately were shot down. That did it. The battle was over. The bridge was ours and we knew we could hold it."[39]

From their position eight hundred yards west of Amfreville, the forty or so troopers with Colonel Millett had moved four hundred yards northwest to better defensive terrain and had dug in for the night. First Sergeant Barney Hopkins, with Company D, 507th, set up a roadblock on the only road leading into their position. "We took three of our landmines and used a rope to tie them together across the road leading into our area. By dark the first night, we had our lines of defense set up. Since there had been considerable shooting in our area, the Germans sent out a half-track with machine guns mounted on it, which was spraying the hedgerows with machine gun fire. Shortly after dark—it did not get dark until about 10:00 p.m.—the Germans started coming down the road toward our area.

"We gave the situation considerable thought. If the German half-track hit one of our landmines, the Germans would know exactly where we had our defense lines. So three soldiers and I went out over to where we had our three landmines on the road as the German half-track was approaching our area. So using the rope, we pulled the mines off the road just seconds before the half-track got there. They sprayed the hedgerow where we were, but we were behind the dirt hump, so none of us were wounded, but it was a spooky feeling. The half-track went on down the road, spraying machine gun fire into the hedges, and fortunately, never did return."[40]

Late that night, Private Tom Porcella, with Company H, 508th, sat down to rest, having spent most of the day moving with, and fighting as part of, a group of paratroopers whom he didn't know. This group of troopers ended D-Day on Hill 30 west of the Merderet River. "Orders were given to dig in for the night. We were told that one man sleeps and the other man stays awake. We were also told not to smoke and keep in close contact with each other during the night. We were going to move at the crack of dawn. I remember shivering from the cold night air. My thoughts were of GI blankets and a hot cup of coffee; and thinking, how the hell did I get into this predicament? My teeth would not stop chattering and I continued thinking of England, the mess hall, the food, the hot coffee, and the warm stove. It was not possible to sleep at all. The night became colder and colder."[41]

Near midnight on June 6, found Sergeant Zane Schlemmer, with Headquarters Company, 2nd Battalion, 508th, on an outpost at the bottom of Hill 30, "bone weary, but mentally alert, dug in with a parachute; which was very, very warm, and very luxurious in my foxhole."[42]

As midnight approached, Captain Roy Creek, of Company E, 507th, who had led the fight to capture the bridge at Chef-du-Pont, finally sat down and had an opportunity to reflect on the day's events. "As with all victories in war, we shared a let down feeling. We knew it was still a long way to Berlin.

"We began to organize and improve our position and tended to such pressing things as first aid to the wounded, twenty-five in number who could not be evacuated because of a lack of any place to evacuate them. We gathered the bodies of the dead, Americans and Germans, and covered them with parachutes.

"D-Day was almost over and it had gone fast, and in a little while it would be D+1. When would the beach forces come? They should have already done so. Maybe the whole invasion had failed. After all, we knew nothing of the situation except as it existed in Chef-du-Pont, and Chef-du-Pont is a very small town.

"As I sat pondering the day's events, having been in command subsequent to Colonel Ostberg's injury, I reflected upon the details of the fighting and the bravery of every man participating in it. Some had lost their lives; some others had been seriously wounded and lay inside the creamery, perhaps wondering if they would ever be evacuated. We had done some things badly. But overall with a hodgepodge of troops from several units who had never trained together as a unit, didn't even know one another, and were engaged in their first combat, we had done okay. We captured our bridge and held it. We knew we could beat the enemy and we faced D+1 with confidence and anticipation.

"At 24:00 hours, our fears were dispelled. Reconnaissance elements of the 4th Infantry Division wheeled into our creamery yard complete with a few rations, which they shared with us. As we dug in, and made ourselves comfortable for a turn at short naps, the smell of death, which was to be with us for a long time to come, had begun to permeate the night air. It was D+1 in Normandy."[43]

CHAPTER 13

"I DON'T KNOW OF A BETTER PLACE THAN THIS TO DIE"[1]

At 2:00 a.m. on June 7, in both Normandy and back in England, most of the officers and men of the 82nd Airborne Division were busily working to prepare for that morning's combat operations. Many of them had not slept in more than thirty hours; most wouldn't sleep for another eighteen or more. At the La Fière Bridge, Sergeant William Owens, with Company A, 505th, stayed awake all night, alert for signs of German infiltration. "About 2:00 in the morning I heard a tank on the causeway and thought, 'Here we go again.' Then I heard them trying to push the disabled tank out of the way, and I knew if they succeeded, we would be through. So, I took a couple of Gammon grenades and crawled to approximately thirty to forty yards from them, as it was quite dark. The first one I threw missed and hit the disabled tank instead of the one that was trying to move it. But, the Germans didn't take any more chances, they put the tank in reverse and moved back. I threw the other grenade, but missed again."[2]

Private Edward C. "Bogie" Boccafogli, with Company B, 508th, had just arrived on Hill 30. What Boccafogli found on the hill shocked him. "It was a mess there. There were so many wounded along the ditches. They had them head to toe. I believe it was Major [Shields] Warren who took command of our battalion, because [Lieutenant] Colonel Batcheller had been killed. I found some of the men from my company, Sergeants James [W.] Smith, and Jim Kurtz; Albert Patchell, [John] Payet, and a few others who were there. That made me feel better, because we had a confused mess. We had men from the 505 PIR, we had men from the 101st Division mixed in with us."[3]

Private First Class Walter H. Barrett, with Company B, 508th, had been wounded in the thigh during the fighting withdrawal to Hill 30. The medic had refused to give him morphine, because he was concerned about Barrett being able to keep up with the group. Barrett was one of the last to arrive, around 2:00 a.m. with the help of his best friend. "Ed [Suits] assisted me by putting my right arm around his neck and his arm around my waist. With this arrangement, we were able to maneuver."[4]

By 2:00 a.m., Lieutenant Colonel Shanley had collected about four hundred troopers from every regiment of the 82nd and 101st Airborne Division, many of them wounded. All together, the troopers had only one 60mm mortar, three .30-caliber machine guns, one BAR, and one bazooka. Private First Class Frank Staples was a bazooka gunner with Company D, 508th. "I was the only one on Hill 30 with a bazooka. Someone found one and gave it to me. I wasn't all that eager to get it. I don't know why they picked on me."[5]

Making matters even worse, Staples didn't have his assistant gunner—he would have to load it himself. "Joe Lizut was supposed to be my loader when we jumped in Normandy. He came out of the plane right behind me. It was a real lonely feeling when I'd draw fire."[6]

Back in England, the troopers of the 1st Battalion, 325th; the 325th Regimental Headquarters and Headquarters Company; and Company A, 307th Airborne Engineer Battalion, were awakened at 2:00 a.m. and fed breakfast in preparation for their trip to Normandy. One hundred gliders would transport them, made up of two serials.

The first serial of fifty gliders would consist of thirty-two CG-4A gliders, flying Headquarters and Headquarters Company of the 1st Battalion, 325th, and Company A, 307th Airborne Engineer Battalion, while the three rifle companies of the 1st Battalion, 325th, would be aboard eighteen Horsa gliders, totaling 717 officers and men. In addition, the gliders would transport seventeen jeeps, three 57mm antitank guns, six 75mm pack howitzers, and twenty tons of supplies and ammunition.

The second serial of fifty gliders would transport the 325th Regimental Headquarters and Headquarters Company, including the Antitank Company with its nine 57mm antitank guns; the 82nd Reconnaissance Platoon; and part of the Division Artillery; a total of 251 officers and men. Twenty-four vehicles, two 75mm howitzers, and another one and a half tons of supplies would also be on board. All of these gliders were destined for Landing Zone "E" about two and a half miles southeast of Ste.-Mère-Église on the east side of the N-13 highway near Hiesville.

During the predawn hours on Hill 30, paratroopers were busy digging defensive positions and establishing outposts and roadblocks, all with enlisted men taking orders from NCOs and officers they hadn't served with and didn't know. Staff Sergeant George E. Christ was the communications section leader for the 2nd Battalion, 508th. "Colonel Shanley had his hands full trying to organize us, as we were from all different regiments. It was Lieutenant [Lloyd L.] Polette

[, Jr., with Company F, 508th,] who activated combat patrols and set up roadblocks at various points leading to Hill 30."[7]

At dawn on June 7, the Germans attacked Hill 30 from three sides and hit the roadblock defending the western approach to the Chef-du-Pont Causeway. The fighting was vicious, with fields and hedgerows changing hands several times as attack and counterattack swept back and forth over the contested ground. The fighting was often close and hand-to-hand.

Private First Class Harold Kulju was a radio operator with Headquarters Company, 2nd Battalion, 508th, but was manning a foxhole on the perimeter. "The Germans started setting up French 75s [75mm artillery] in the next hedgerow. We had one guy that had an .03 Springfield rifle, with a launching attachment on the muzzle, and that was our only artillery piece. He delayed the Germans somewhat, which was quite fortunate."[8]

Patrols were sent out to find equipment bundles. Private Boccafogli was a member of a couple of these patrols. "We went down through the farmhouses, behind the farmhouses, through the brush, until we got to the swamps by the Merderet River. There were twelve of us. We waded out into the water. The parachutes with the colors we knew were supply chutes. So we waded out and we started to drag them in, and the water in some places was three feet deep; some places, it was just almost over your head. One of the chutes we dragged in had a body on it. The next thing you know, we're dragging the chute in, and we're getting fired on from the other side of the swamp, quite a distance (four hundred to five hundred yards). Bullets were striking the banks all around us and in the water, and as I went underwater with my head to keep myself from getting hit, I lost my helmet. One of the fellows on the bank got a direct hit. He was killed. We had to leave his body there. We got the chute out. The bundle, when we got it back, it turned out it had anything but what we needed. It was a lot of spare parts. There was a machine gun, but there was no ammunition. Another bundle had mortar rounds, nothing but mortar rounds and land mines."[9] Unfortunately, the ten bundles that were recovered contained no rations, medical supplies, or mortars. A single .30-caliber machine gun was the only crew-served weapon found in the bundles.

After the German assault that morning was thrown back, Private Tom Porcella, with Company H, 508th, revisited one of the fields that had been the scene of some of the fiercest fighting. "I remember Sergeant [Ralph J.] Busson coming over to me and a few other troopers and asking for volunteers to go back into the field that we just left and see if we could find any wounded, because we didn't know whatever happened to those troopers over there. About eight of us volunteered to go back into this field and we volunteered to bring in the wounded. I don't know where the stretcher came from, but somebody had a stretcher. We picked it up and we went to the next field.

"We entered this field and we saw two troopers lying on the ground. I looked at this one trooper and he had his head completely blown apart, and it was unrecognizable. So I fished around and I looked for his dog-tag, and on his dog-tag

I read the name, R. W. Benson. He was from H Company. I knew R. W. Benson very well. He was one of the original paratroopers from the 3rd Battalion, and it was a terrible shock for me to see what happened to him. The only thing I hope—he died fast.

"A few feet away from him, there was a trooper lying down. He looked like something a bomb blew up; he was just butchered meat. There was blood all over the place. One leg was mangled and the other leg was sort of grotesquely underneath his body. So I tried to find out who it was, and I pulled out his dog-tag, and it was a guy named Dean, another H Company man. While I was moving him around a little bit, I heard a groan. I thought for sure he was dead, but he let out an awful groan, and he sort of threw me back for a minute and I was glad to see the guy was still alive, but I didn't know if he would ever make it. So I [went to get] the stretcher and we carefully, the best we could, put this poor trooper on the stretcher. So we had to take him back to the position where we were. Somewhere around the line, we found a place to put all these wounded troopers.

"All the troopers were laid in this field right alongside the hedgerows for as far as your eye could see. Exactly how many troopers were there, I don't know. We grabbed the stretcher and back we went to the field to see if we could find any more wounded troopers. While we were searching for troopers, I happened to notice, in the corner of the field there was a German, evidently trying to escape between the hedgerow. Some trooper shot him and he never got through the hedgerow. He was half on one side and half on the other.

"Alongside this German, there was another German; you could see that he took his boot off. Evidently, he was shot in the foot and he was attempting to put a bandage around the wound. And I'm sure that some other trooper came along and shot him while he was trying to bandage himself.

"Then we proceeded to jump over this hedgerow, down onto the road, still searching for more American paratroopers. All we saw were dead Germans all over the place. There were two Germans in the hedgerow. They were lying on their back. There was this one [dead] German, he had both hands together like he was praying and he was begging for his life; his eyes were wide open and I could visualize judging by the look on his face that he was terrified. I could imagine him saying something in German and was begging this trooper not to shoot him. His expression seemed to be frozen right on his face. It looked like fear. It looked like he was pleading for his life.

"A few feet away from him, there was another [dead] German lying on his back. He had a different look on his face. He looked like he had a sneer on his face. Who knows, he could have been cursing this trooper out. Maybe he knew the trooper killed the other German, and he figured he was going to die, but he had a sneer on his face. He also died with his eyes wide open.

"We proceeded down the road. We weren't able to find any more troopers. So we decided to go back to our positions and report to the sergeant that we hadn't seen any more.

"While walking along the hedgerow with another trooper, where the wounded were lying, a voice called out to me, 'Hey, trooper, come over here.' As I walked toward him, I asked him how he felt. He wanted to know how badly he was hit. Looking down at him, I saw all the flesh was blown away from the right side of his face. He started to cry and he was reaching for his face with a hand that was black as dirt. Quickly, I grabbed his wrist and told him not to touch his face and that he would be all right. He asked me for a cigarette and a drink of water. I didn't have any cigarettes cause I had lost everything I had [when I landed] in the water. He said he had some in his pocket. I removed one of the cigarettes, lit it for him, and I gave him the cigarette."[10]

That day, word spread among the 508th troopers of the death the previous day of one of the favorite men in the regiment, Captain Ignatius P. Maternowski. Sergeant Zane Schlemmer's reaction to the news was typical: "We learned of the death of our Catholic chaplain who had jumped with us, when the Germans grenaded a gully where he was attending our wounded. So we vowed then and there, to avenge his death with little regard for any proprieties of warfare thereafter."[11]

As the sun rose on June 7, Lieutenant Gerard Dillon, with Company G, 507th, and two staff sergeants were on the western edge of the Merderet River floodplain north of Cauquigny. They were carrying an order from General Ridgway for Lieutenant Colonel Charles Timmes, commander of the 2nd Battalion, 507th, to hold his position west of the Merderet River at all costs. They had struggled all night to navigate the flooded area. Dillon "could see the farmhouse previously pointed out to me as the position of Lieutenant Colonel Timmes. The two staff sergeants and I split up, they going to my left and to my right. I told them that from that point every man was to run as fast as he could, to try to reach the area where Colonel Timmes was, and to give him the message. The three of us then took off, and fortunately, all three of us made it.

"The Germans were then at Cauquigny and could easily have picked us off as we crossed the open fields on high ground running toward the farmhouse. But not a shot was fired at us. After we arrived at the farmhouse, a young private, having seen us cross this ground, decided he was going to go out and try and retrieve a calf that had been hit previously during the day before, so that they would have food. As soon as he stepped out of cover into the open field, he was shot by a machine gun located near Cauquigny.

"After giving the message to Colonel Timmes, the three of us who had crossed the inundated area were told by him to come into the farmhouse, which was his command post, and to take off our clothes so they could be hung before a fire to dry. In addition, he told the French lady, who was the wife of the owner of the farmhouse to cook something for us. She cooked a chicken, which the three of us ate. It was the first food I had eaten since the morning of D-Day. Not having slept for over thirty-six hours, I then went to sleep and slept until the afternoon of D+1.

Members of the 2nd Platoon Mortar Squad, Company F, 505th. Sergeant John P. Ray (left), Private First Class Philip M. Lynch (left center), Private John M. Steele (right center), and Private Vernon L. Fransisco (right) ready for an inspection. *Courtesy of the 82nd Airborne Division War Memorial Museum*

Lieutenants Harold J. Carroll (left) and Stanley Weinberg (right), Company B, 505th, prepare to assemble an equipment bundle, May 30, 1944. *Photograph by Stanley Weinberg, courtesy of Ms. Ann Weinberg*

Loading equipment bundles to the bellies of the C-47s prior to the jump. *Photograph by Stanley Weinberg, courtesy of Ms. Ann Weinberg*

Troopers with Regimental Headquarters, 505th, move to the hangar as continuing rain causes the June 4, 1944, jump to be postponed. *Courtesy of Jerome V. Huth*

C-47s, with white invasion stripes painted on the wings and fuselage, lined up ready for takeoff. *US Army photograph, courtesy of the 82nd Airborne Division War Memorial Museum*

Paratroopers of the 508th chute-up at the Saltby airfield prior to boarding their C-47s for Normandy. *US Army photograph, courtesy of the 82nd Airborne Division War Memorial Museum*

One of thirty-six troopers of the 82nd Airborne Division who drowned in the flooded Merderet and Douve Rivers in the predawn hours of June 6, 1944. *US Army photograph, courtesy of the 82nd Airborne Division War Memorial Museum*

This C-47 was shot down and crashed in the flooded area of the Merderet River. *Photograph by Joseph F. Comer, Company H, 505th, courtesy of Les Cruise*

One of the troopers killed during the predawn glider landings by Battery A, 80th Airborne Antiaircraft (Antitank) Battalion, and elements of division headquarters, June 6, 1944. *Courtesy of Jerome V. Huth*

Medics risk their lives searching for those injured in the glider landings on the morning of June 6, 1944. *Courtesy of the Silent Wings Museum*

The church at Ste.-Mère-Église, where Privates John M. Steele and Kenneth Russell hung suspended by their parachutes on the steeple and roof. They watched the troopers in their stick being shot while helpless in their harnesses. The church was the focal point for the 3rd Battalion, 505th, on the morning of June 6, 1944. *Courtesy of the 82nd Airborne Division War Memorial Museum*

Technician 5th Grade Kenneth E. Geiler, with Company H, 505th, in the protection of his foxhole, with a bazooka and a Thompson submachine gun close at hand. The shelter half lines his foxhole and provides warmth at night. Geiler was killed in action on June 24, 1944, in the Bois de Limors. *Courtesy of Les Cruise*

The effects of almost continuous shelling by artillery, dual-purpose 88mm flak guns, Nebelwerfers, and mortars of the German 1058th Regiment. This view is in Ste.-Mère-Église along the N-13 highway. *US Army photograph, courtesy of the 82nd Airborne Division War Memorial Museum*

Looking northwest, the Manoir house and outbuildings. *US Army photograph, courtesy of the 82nd Airborne Division War Memorial Museum*

Looking west, the La Fière Bridge and Causeway. The flooded Merderet River is visible to the right and left center. *Courtesy of the 82nd Airborne Division War Memorial Museum*

Initial La Fière Bridge defensive positions. *US Army photograph*

The three German tanks knocked out by Company A, 505th, bazooka teams and the 57mm antitank gun. The two tanks on the left and right are French Renaults, and the one in the middle is a Hotchkiss tank. *Still photograph extracted from US Army film, courtesy of Martin K. A. Morgan, Research Historian, National D-Day Museum*

The Chef-du-Pont area looking northwest. *US Army photograph*

The bodies of Lieutenant James A. Gayley, commander of Company A, 325th Glider Infantry Regiment, and sixteen of his men, killed in the crash of their Horsa glider near Hiesville, June 7, 1944. *US Army photograph, courtesy of the Silent Wings Museum*

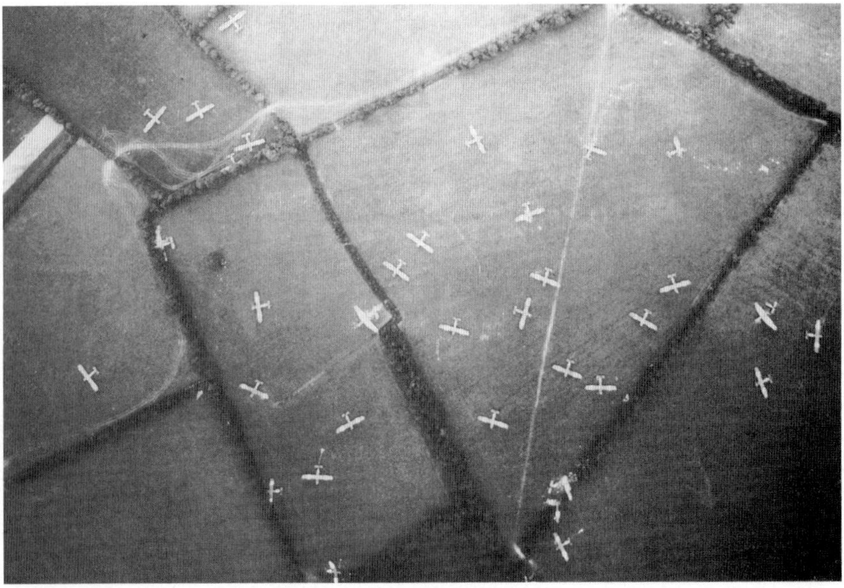

Aerial photograph of the glider landings on June 7, 1944. *US Army Air Corps photograph*

Looking south toward Ste.-Mère-Église, the German self-propelled gun singlehandedly destroyed by Private John E. Atchley is in the foreground. The destroyed self-propelled gun seen in the distance, was knocked out by a 57mm antitank gun crew from Battery A, 80th AA Battalion, firing from farther down the road. *US Army photograph, courtesy of the 82nd Airborne Division War Memorial Museum*

The hedgerows provided a ready-made defensive work with camouflage for the defender, but could be a deathtrap if outflanked, which allowed enfilading fire to be brought to bear by the attacker. *US Army photograph*

Aerial photograph of Ste.-Mère-Église looking north, taken by the 67th Tactical Reconnaissance Group on June 8, 1944. The N-13 highway runs north from the town. The lane used by Company E, 505th, to outflank the 2nd Battalion, 1058th Regiment of the 91st Air Landing Division, runs west from the highway just north of the town, while the road used by elements of the US 746th Tank Battalion to outflank the German armor runs east from the highway. *Courtesy of Robert M. Murphy*

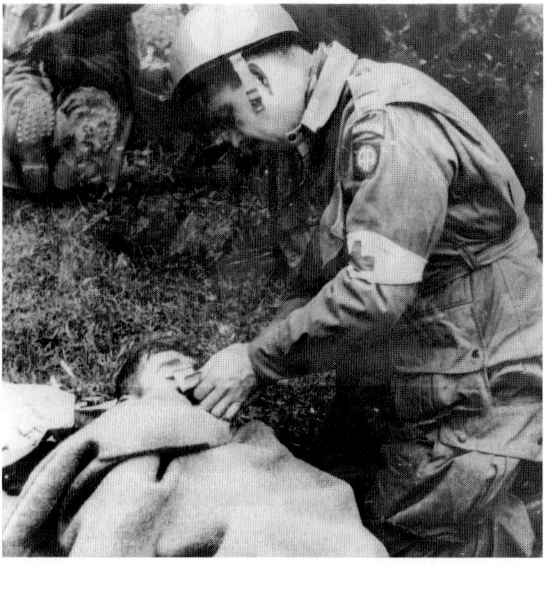

A medic with the 307th Medical Company treats the wounded of both armies, June 7, 1944. *US Army photograph, courtesy of the 82nd Airborne Division War Memorial Museum*

Jim Schaffner (left) and Gerald Arnold (right), with the 325th Glider Infantry Regiment, stand in front of the Cauquigny Church. Dead German soldiers lie by the stone wall on the right. Lieutenant Robert Rae and his Provisional Company of the 507th cleared this area. *Courtesy of Mrs. Jim Schaffner, Gerald Arnold, and the 82nd Airborne Division War Memorial Museum*

A water-cooled .30-caliber heavy machine gun manned by troopers of the 325th is sited to cover the field in front of the hedgerow. This gun was very effective at delivering devastating firepower but was heavy and not easily moved during an attack. *US Army photograph, courtesy of the 82nd Airborne Division War Memorial Museum*

An 81mm mortar crew fires in support of a mission called in by field telephone. The wires for the telephones were laid by men of the 82nd Signal Company. *US Army photograph, courtesy of the 82nd Airborne Division War Memorial Museum*

Lieutenants Briand Beaudin (left) and Paul E. Lehman (right, seriously wounded on June 6) celebrate liberation on June 16, 1944. *Courtesy of the 82nd Airborne Division War Memorial Museum*

Germans casualties of the heavy fighting against the 82nd Airborne Division during the Normandy campaign. *US Army photograph, courtesy of the 82nd Airborne Division War Memorial Museum*

Private Robert B. White checks the status of his latest victim in the deadly hedgerow fighting of Normandy. The paratroopers were at their best when engaging the enemy at close range. They were expert marksmen and had cat-quick reflexes. A near miss is visible on the right sleeve of White's jumpsuit, where a bullet made two holes but left White unharmed. *Photograph by Henry LeFebvre, courtesy of Robert B. White and Henry LeFebvre*

One of two German 75mm antitank guns defending the highway at Les Rosiers, east of St.-Sauveur-le-Vicomte, wiped out in brutal fighting by Company D, 505th, on June 15, 1944. *Photograph by Dr. Daniel B. McIlvoy, courtesy of Mrs. Annie McIlvoy Zaya*

Company E, 505th, and Headquarters Company, 2nd Battalion, 505th, move through the ruins of St.-Sauveur-le-Vicomte, devastated by a massive VII Corps artillery barrage, June 16, 1944. *US Army photograph, courtesy of the 82nd Airborne Division War Memorial Museum*

"After awakening, Lieutenant John Marr, who was the platoon leader of the 2nd Platoon of G Company and was also at the farmhouse, along with Captain Schwartzwalder, showed me the positions around the farmhouse. We also went to the road, which was to the north of the farmhouse that led to what everybody called the 'gray castle.' That was the location of a German army corps headquarters.

"On D-Day, Johnny Marr had planted antitank mines along that road to protect the position the Timmes group was defending. A German colonel was driving along the road toward the farmhouse and his vehicle struck one of the mines, killing him. Marr took from the body of the colonel, a map which showed the precise locations that were supposed to be the drop zones for the three parachute regiments of the 82nd Airborne Division. Except for occasional mortar fire, the Germans did nothing toward attacking the Timmes defensive position on D+1."[12]

The Aldermaston and Ramsbury airfields in England were a beehive of activity during the predawn hours of June 7. After eating breakfast, Lieutenant Wayne W. Pierce, the executive officer of Company B, 325th, got the company assembled, formed up into platoons, and made a check of each squad to insure that everyone was present. "Shortly after 3:00 a.m., our column of troops was moving out on a one mile march to the airstrip, where our gliders were lined up, ready for takeoff. It was still dark when we stopped under the huge wing of the British Horsa glider that would serve as our transport to Normandy. Made of plywood, the Horsa could carry thirty men with their equipment, plus a pilot and co-pilot."[13]

Lieutenant James B. Helmer, commanding the Machine Gun Platoon, Headquarters Company, 1st Battalion, 325th, with his men and their gear, prepared to board their GC-4A Waco glider. "Our heavy equipment and machine guns had been loaded the day before to save time and confusion at the last minute. Our glider load consisted of one water cooled machine gun, twelve boxes (3,000 rounds) of machine gun ammunition, six cloverleaves of extra mortar ammunition, a demolition kit containing the equivalent of twenty-five pounds of TNT, camouflage nets, spare [machine gun] barrels, spare parts kit, one gallon of water for the machine gun, an emergency five gallon can of drinking water, two collapsible rubber life rafts, and fifteen men including the pilot and co-pilot. Each man carried his gas mask and pack with shelter half, raincoat, toilet articles, one day's K-rations, two days' emergency D-rations (six concentrated chocolate bars), first aid packet, and extra cigarettes. Each man also carried his personal weapon, ammunition for it, plus two hand grenades, a trench knife or bayonet, and a life belt. The personal weapons total: One Thompson submachine gun with two hundred rounds of .45-caliber ammunition (my own), two carbines with seventy-five rounds each, and eight M1 Garand rifles with one hundred twenty-eight rounds each. I also carried a complete set of maps, both small and large scale, of the area we were to land in. The total load, including personnel, weighed approximately 4,500 pounds. Our 'safe load' in practice had always been 3,750 pounds, but the pilot assured me our load would fly OK. The main danger of an excessive load [was] the necessity of increasing the landing speed and a longer landing area.

"While the men removed their equipment and put on their life preservers, the pilot and I proceeded to fill out numerous forms listing the personnel and particulars as to the load and glider number. This 'red tape' was a nuisance, but proved to be necessary from past experience when planes or gliders had been lost and no lists had been left behind to tell them who was in them. The men removed their equipment, since if we would be cast loose and land in the channel, a man with sixty or seventy pounds of equipment on might be pulled under before he could inflate his life preserver.

"We were all finally seated with our packs, gas masks, and equipment packed over, under, and around us. However, we were number twenty-eight in the formation, so, at the rate of one takeoff per minute, we would have about a half an hour after the first plane took off. In a few minutes we saw the first plane and glider rise and start to circle off the field."[14]

It was 4:39 a.m. on June 7. From both airfields, 100 gliders began lifting off behind their tow planes and forming up for the trip across the Channel to Normandy, bringing badly needed infantry reinforcements for the hard-pressed 82nd Airborne Division.

Lieutenant Pierce took off a short time afterward. "There was a slight mist of rain in the air and the first streaks of dawn in the sky as our C-47 tow plane churned down the runway, trying to gain flying speed. The time was about 4:40 a.m. The Horsa glider, larger than the C-47 tow plane, was a heavy load for the C-47 to tow. At this moment, seated on each side of the barrel shaped Horsa, we were concerned with the takeoff. We had flown in Horsa gliders before, but never when loaded as heavily as we were this morning. In training, we did not normally carry a full basic load of ammunition. Today, we not only had our basic load, but each of us had picked up an extra hand grenade, an extra bandoleer of .30-caliber ammunition and maybe had squeezed a little something extra to eat in our pack. In addition to this, boxes of mines, extra ammunition and cans of water were tied to the floor in the center of the glider.

"Slowly, the runway dropped away and the rumble of the wheels changed to the familiar 'swoosh' of air over the plywood structure. We were airborne! On takeoff, the glider lifts off the runway before the tow plane, and in flight the glider normally flies higher than the tow plane. This is done in part to stay out of the prop blast and give a smoother ride. On this crucial morning, however, our tow plane was having trouble getting into the column for our flight to Normandy."[15]

The time seemed to pass very slowly as Lieutenant Helmer waited for his glider to take off. Then finally, "our plane lumbered out in front of us. With the sensation of being present at the opening kickoff at a football game, we watched the slack come out of the towrope, the signal man to our left drop his lighted panel, heard the plane engines roar, and we were moving down the runway. With a little sway, we took wing. In a few seconds our plane had gained its flying speed and our trust was in the plane and the towrope connecting us to it. We made our circle and in a few minutes were drawing up to our place in the formation. The men were gradually settling down for the ride ahead, and several were already falling asleep. The first part of the ride was smooth and there was little to see other than the fields below, just becoming visible in the dawn, and an overcast sky above us.

"Shortly after leaving the coast, we noticed our first fighter escort planes. This escort gradually increased to several dozen. The air was becoming gradually rougher and finally Sergeant [Archie] Bates, seated opposite me, had to relieve himself of a good breakfast eaten about two o'clock that morning. We fortunately had some empty gallon cans previously collected from the kitchen for that purpose, and needed them because several other men soon followed Bates' example. I had hoped for a smooth air trip to avoid airsickness among the men, but this was not to be. Due to the subsequent odor, I broke a rule I had laid down before we started and let the men smoke. This relieved most of the tension that automatically builds up as soon as one man gets sick. The rest of us weathered the trip, leaving the buckets for the few unfortunates."[16]

Private First Class Clinton Riddle, a radio operator and runner with Company B, 325th, was one of the men from company headquarters on Lieutenant Pierce's Horsa glider. "I sat in the front seat near the pilot. The ride was not rough and I was sitting and taking it easy. From the very front seat I had a ringside view of the Channel. It was a breathtaking experience to look out."[17]

Lieutenant Pierce was concerned about the tow plane and glider in which they were riding maintaining altitude and speed to keep up with the serial. "Standing between the pilot and co-pilot, I could see the slack in the towrope as we lost altitude, and the battle the glider 'guider' was having to keep us from becoming entangled in the one hundred yards of nylon rope connecting us to the C-47. I knew that it was only a matter of time until we would have to ditch in the water if we continued.

"After a brief conversation with the pilot, I gave the order to open the door at the rear of the glider and to start throwing out the boxes of mines, ammunition, and cans of water we had lashed to the floor. Men were alerted and were standing by in case we ditched; they would take emergency axes from the wall of the glider and cut holes in the top of our compartment to permit us to climb out on top of the fuselage and the wings. We were told the wings were full of ping-pong balls, so they would not sink.

"We were as low as three hundred feet when the first boxes were pushed out the rear door. Knowing the urgency of this action, the men moved quickly to unload our glider of this extra weight."[18]

As Riddle helped the others throw out the extra weight, he thought they might be too late. "All you could hear was a rushing of the wind as it swept past the glider, and the groaning of the men in the glider."[19]

As the weight went out the rear door, Pierce noticed that the glider began to level off. "Gradually we began to gain altitude and as we came within sight of the French coast, we forgot our immediate predicament and began to look about at the action below us. A disabled C-47 returning from its mission in Normandy ditched in the water and the crew climbed out on top of the fuselage."[20]

Riddle, however, was looking above. "The fighter planes were three layers thick overhead, and the train of C-47s and gliders reached as far as I could see."[21]

As their glider approached Utah Beach, Lieutenant Pierce got his men ready for the landing. "I returned to my seat on the bench along the wall of the glider and gave the order to secure equipment. Helmets were put on, packs were adjusted, bandoleers slung over the shoulder, and weapons were held securely. As I leaned over to pick up my pack and equipment the glider made a lurch as the pilot cut loose from the tow plane and made a steep banking turn."[22]

It was 7:00 a.m. . . .

As the glider banked, Riddle could clearly see the fields below. "It didn't take long to see that the Germans had dug holes in the fields and set posts upright and placed mines on every post. After we released from the tow plane, we were on our own. We wanted to get down as quickly as possible because of the small arms fire. Yet we must pick out a place big enough to land on the way down.

"As I raised up to look out the front, the pilot pointed towards a small garden-like spot, completely enclosed by hedge. Some with trees growing out of the hedgerows. The pilot brought the glider in low over the first hedgerow, and cut the top out of some of the trees with the wing. The glider hit the ground, bounced a time or two, then rolled to a stop. The pilot had done a great job in bringing the glider down without crashing into a hedgerow or something else."[23]

The big Horsa gliders were far too large, loaded too heavily, released too low, and going too fast for the small, hedgerow-lined Norman fields, some of the largest of which had glider landing obstacles planted in them. Private Richard D. Weese was aboard another of the Horsa gliders transporting Company B. "I was sitting near the tail with my rifle across my legs, sitting on a life raft, holding on to the ribs of the plywood glider. All of a sudden, we started to slow down. We had been cut loose from the C-47. We were told that the glider would circle twice and come in. We were too heavy and only circled once.

"I had a perfect view of the Plexiglas windshield and pilots. The right wing hit a tree and broke off, tipping the glider to a left forty-five degree angle. The glider hit the top of a hedgerow, tearing off the wheels, and hit the ground. All I could see was plywood and Plexiglas coming at me. I shut my eyes and holding on for life, my M1 left my lap. I opened my eyes and the glider had cracked open like an egg. Troopers were piling out; the only one hurt was the platoon sergeant, but not bad enough to keep him down. We all rushed out of the glider,

I found my M1 up near the cockpit, grabbed a bandoleer of ammunition, and jumped out into a ditch near the glider next to the pilot. [The glider pilot] looked at me and said, 'I'm sorry.'

"I said, 'You got us here.' Gliders were landing so close together that it was dangerous to move until all had landed."[24]

Sergeant Arthur Jacikas was aboard one of the Company C Horsa gliders. "We landed in an open field, but apparently it was armed with ground explosives, which we rolled across. The glider blew up and the front half separated from the rest of the glider. My leg was broken in two places, another soldier's collar bones were broken, and the glider pilot's nose was cut off when the front half crashed into a hedgerow."[25]

Private First Class Ray T. Burchell, with Company C, 325th, riding in another Horsa, braced for the impact as his glider tried to land in a hedgerow-lined field going far too fast. "My glider crashed landed, breaking apart, I was knocked out. When I came to, Corporal James Bristow was there. First Sergeant [Roosevelt] Harwood had broken his collarbone. The glider pilot lost one leg. He laid in a ditch next to a hedgerow. I stuffed his pant leg into the leg socket—took his .45 out of the holster. He was in a state of shock. I told him if any Germans came near him, shoot first and ask questions later. Jimmy and I took off, running."[26]

Standing just behind the pilot and co-pilot as his Horsa was cut loose, Tech Sergeant Harold Owens, with Company A, 325th, was able to easily see the terrain below. "I saw our last checkpoint was Ste.-Marie-du-Mont. I recognized the little square with the well in the middle of it from the sand table. I went back to my seat and sat down. I grabbed a hold of my seatbelt, because it wouldn't wrap around me. I held on to that and we hit the ground. We hit in one field and it bounced up over the hedgerow into the next field. Somehow that pilot got the nose of that glider headed between two big oak trees. When that thing hit the second time, the tail came off. I did a forward flip with my arms and I caught the main body of that glider. The mud, gravel, rocks, dirt and everything coming up and hitting me in the face, I just thought that it's just the way it feels to die, because I figured I was going to be killed. But it stopped. I brushed myself off and I looked up and saw all the guys all pushed forward in the front of the glider. I said, 'Just get out of here and protect this glider.' "[27]

As the Horsa gliders were crashing, the CG-4A gliders were approaching Utah Beach. Lieutenant Helmer ordered his men to prepare for landing. "I had the men throw off their life belts and buckle their safety belts for the landing. We had dropped to about one hundred feet before coming over the beach and should have had about five minutes before cutting loose. Just before giving us the signal to cut [loose], the tow plane was supposed to carry us up to about five hundred feet to pick a favorable landing field.

"However, we had just gotten our belts buckled when we got the green light from the plane and our pilot released the towrope. Things happened fast. We were too low, about three hundred feet, and going much too fast for a safe landing. The pilot spotted a field to our left and we turned sharply and dived for it. I yelled at the men to lean forward and brace themselves. I knew we were going to crash.

"Suddenly, our wheels hit and we were racing across the field at well over one hundred miles per hour. At a glance, I saw three other gliders at the far end of the field, one of them still moving. Our pilot was reaching frantically over his head for something, but the co-pilot saw him and reached up and pulled a lever. I realized that it was our parachute attached to brake our speed. At the same time, I saw a flash on the field ahead and a gush of smoke blew across in front of us. The next second, we had a violent jolt as we hit a small ridge in the field, at about the same time as our chute snapped open at the rear. Then we were through the smoke and skidding on our nose toward a marsh directly ahead. But the chute had done its work, and all at once we were not moving anymore.

"The jolt had splashed most of the contents of the buckets over the equipment on the floor, but we weren't concerned about that. The men had the two rear doors opened as well as the two forward emergency doors and we were scrambling out on all sides."[28]

The glider carrying Lieutenant Colonel Klemm Boyd, the CO of the 1st Battalion, 325th, hit the top of a hedgerow. "The speed was one hundred seventy miles per hour and we were eight feet above the ground when we hit the trees."[29]

After getting out of his wrecked CG-4A and looking about at the carnage, Major Teddy H. Sanford, executive officer of the 1st Battalion, 325th, felt bitter about what had just happened. "Many of the crashes of the gliders were a direct result of the failure of the tug pilots to give the glider pilots altitude enough to make a proper approach and come in slow. Tug pilots had been instructed to go up to seven hundred feet after crossing the beach and very few, if any, of them increased their altitude. Cutting the gliders loose at two hundred feet, traveling one hundred twenty miles per hour, in an area with such small fields doesn't give the glider pilot any opportunity at all to select the field or to make the proper approach for a landing. Under the conditions which our pilots landed in Normandy, they had no opportunity for selection of the field, or to turn to make any approach to it. It was just cut loose and land, which put a great many of our gliders into trees and resulted in rather high casualties."[30]

Ten out of the eighteen Horsa gliders were destroyed and all but one damaged. Twenty-five of the eighty-two American-built Waco gliders were destroyed, with forty-one more damaged. The 1st Battalion, 325th, suffered seventeen killed, all passengers in one of the Horsa gliders. Ninety-eight troopers were injured or wounded during the landings.

At the same time these landings were taking place, another one hundred gliders were lifting off in England, carrying the remainder of the 325th. The first serial of this mission consisted of twenty CG-4A Waco and thirty British Horsa gliders, which transported the 2nd Battalion, 325th, and the 2nd Battalion, 401st, which had been transferred from the 101st Airborne Division and attached to the 325th Glider Infantry Regiment. The second serial of fifty Waco gliders would carry Service Company, 325th, along with twenty jeeps, nine trailers, twelve extra 81mm mortars, and six tons of ammunition. The gliders in these two serials would land at LZ "W" located astride the N-13 highway southeast of Ste.-Mère-Église at Les Forges. The two serials were scheduled to land at 9:00 a.m. and 9:10 a.m. respectively.

Private First Class Lewis A. Strandburg was a member of Company E, 2nd Battalion, 401st Glider Infantry Regiment. Strandburg was assigned to one of the Horsa gliders for the journey to Normandy. "That day we were to see action for the first time . . . going from the peace of England to the war-torn and German infested fields of Normandy on a glider flight of less than two hours. The sun was just peeping over the horizon when grim, determined men marched out onto the [air]field. No one said a word, for our thoughts were elsewhere. Everyone appeared glassy-eyed and in a trance.

"We loaded into gliders and at 07:00 the first glider was lifted off the runway. It was our turn. We felt the tug of the tow plane and the glider began rolling down the runway gathering speed every second. Soon the rumbling wheels on the tarmac ceased and we were airborne.

"Looking out the ports, we could see the ground getting farther and farther away, until the buildings below looked like toy cities. We circled the field until all the remaining gliders were in the air, then set our course for Normandy."[31]

At the landing zone in Normandy, Tech Sergeant Harold Owens, with Company A, 325th, crawled out of his Horsa glider. "We gathered up what was left of our company, there weren't too many of us, because Lieutenant [Jim A.] Gayley, our company commander, and sixteen men with him were killed. We lost quite a few men in the landing. We got organized and we took up a defensive position."[32]

After landing, Lieutenant James Helmer, the commander of the Heavy Machine Gun Platoon, Headquarters Company, 1st Battalion, 325th, got his men out of their damaged CG-4A glider. "We started to unload our equipment when,—whoosh-whoosh—most of the men having heard it before in Italy, recognized the unmistakable sound of a German rocket [Nebelwerfer] battery. We dived into the edge of the swamp we had almost landed in, and as we did so, I saw two rockets go over. Then came the explosions about a hundred yards away. Several of us moved back to unload more equipment, when—whoosh-whoosh—and we hit the dirt again. We spent the next five or ten minutes shuttling our equipment from the glider to the ditch between bursts of rockets.

"We soon saw Lieutenant [Walter] Davenport, our battalion supply officer and Tech Sergeant [Alfred] Gallagher, my platoon sergeant with another squad of machine gunners. After moving a couple hundred yards down a lane, we ran into our company commander, Captain [Alex] Bishop. We got out our maps and with the aid of the troops already in the area, determined our location, about 1,500 yards in from the beach and almost five miles from our designated landing zone. Lieutenant Davenport had located two jeeps and two trailers of ammunition, which had landed nearby, so we sent some men to help him get them out of the gliders. In a little while, they brought them around and we loaded most of our equipment (eighty to ninety pounds per man) onto the jeep and headed for our previously appointed assembly area.

"I believe it was when we were getting our units organized in the assembly area that we heard that Lieutenant Jim Gayley and quite a few of his men were killed in their glider landing. I do not recall who took command of A Company after that."[33]

The executive officer of Company B, 325th, Lieutenant Wayne Pierce, finished accounting for the officers and men after getting them assembled, then began moving through Ste.-Marie-du-Mont toward their planned initial objective. "Our company had fared well, all officers were on hand and very few landing casualties were reported. We passed the bodies of several German soldiers lying in the street at Ste.-Marie-du-Mont. Other companies of the 1st Battalion joined us as we moved in an approach march formation toward Chef-du-Pont. The glider pilots with us were ecstatic; this would give them something to talk about when they got back to England.

"As we moved forward, Captain [Richard] Gibson told me that our battalion commander, Lieutenant Colonel Klemm Boyd, had been injured in the glider landing and that Major Teddy Sanford was leading the battalion.

"Things were going smoothly, we could hear occasional small arms fire and sporadic artillery. Our immediate concern was to be on the lookout for snipers hidden in trees along our route. Verbal orders came for the battalion to move to an area near La Fière, west of Ste.-Mère-Église."[34]

At the east end of the La Fière Causeway over the Merderet River, the sound of armored vehicles could be heard by the paratroopers who had held on to the little bridge the previous day. The control of the causeway was vital to both sides. The Germans needed it to attack the Utah Beach landing forces. And it was the choke point that the 82nd Airborne Division needed to stop the numerically superior German forces from crossing the river to attack those landing forces. At approximately 8:00 a.m., Sergeant William Owens, with Company A, 505th, "first heard armored vehicles coming from across the river. We let them come on."[35]

When the attack began, Lieutenant Red Dolan was checking on the 1st Platoon positions north of the bridge. "For about an hour before the attack, they increased their mortar fire to the extent that the 3rd Platoon was just about knocked out, but not quite. I was not aware of this at the time. In addition to already heavy casualties, Sergeant [Lawrence F.] Monahan, the platoon sergeant was fatally wounded. The 1st Platoon was under heavy fire also.

"The second attack was with two tanks and infantry. I was unable to estimate the size. The tanks stayed out of effective bazooka range. (We had one bazooka left.) Not hearing any fire from the 57mm, I went over to it and found it unmanned. I tried to fire it, but the crew had taken the firing mechanism. I organized five or six men behind the hedge on the southerly side of the road with Gammon grenades, and just about this time, two of the gun crew returned with the firing mechanism. They knocked out the two tanks. They were two youngsters not more than seventeen or eighteen years old, who returned on their own initiative. I recommended them for Silver Stars."[36]

Owens, although relieved to see the German tanks destroyed, knew all too well what was coming next. "They tried to get the infantry through to knock us out. All we had was small arms and 60mm mortars, but we succeeded in driving them back. The Germans pulled back on the other side, and in about a half hour or so, they began throwing 88s and 4.2 [inch] mortars at us. They really clobbered us. All our communications were knocked out. Private [William A.] Ross, with our walkie-talkie, took a direct hit with an 88.

"Then they sent the infantry again, and again we drove them back. After a little lull they started all over again. This time Lieutenant Oakley was hit. I crawled over to him and gave him a shot of morphine and tried to bandage him, but he had a hole in his back near his kidney the size of a man's fist. I offered to send a man back to try and find a medic and take him back. But he said he could make it alone.

"Sergeant [Jim] Ricci and Sergeant [William] McMurchy had already been wounded and were out of action. All this time we were under heavy artillery fire. Right after Lieutenant Oakley left, I began crawling around, getting all the ammo and grenades from the dead and wounded, for I knew then we would need every round we could get our hands on. I took stock of what weapons, ammo and men we had left. It turned out to be a good thing, for right after that the Germans hit us again. They must have received reinforcements, for the artillery shells and mortars were coming in like machine gun fire. I don't know how it was possible to live through it.

"Then their infantry came again and we gave them everything we had. The machine gun I had was so hot it quit firing. I took Private [Wesley H.] McClatchy's BAR (he had been wounded earlier) and I fired it until I ran out of ammo. I then took a machine gun that belonged to a couple of men who took a very near hit. They were killed. The gun had no tripod, so I rested it across a pile of dirt and used it. With this and one other machine gun and a 60mm mortar, we stopped them, but they had gotten to within twenty-five yards of us."[37]

Out of the corner of his eye, Company A trooper, Private First Class Dave Bullington, noticed motion coming from the hole occupied by Sergeant Oscar Queen. "He had a machine gun and he'd shake that thing and say, 'That thing is going out.'

"I said, 'Oscar that thing is just getting broken in.' I wasn't going to tell him it was going out. He said he [had] fired about 10,000 rounds through it."[38]

As the fighting raged, Private Bob Murphy, a pathfinder who had rejoined Company A for most of the fighting, noticed their medic moving under fire from one wounded man to another. "Kelly 'Moose' Byers was a fantastic, brave hero, who spent two days out in the open, under heavy fire, giving medical aid to our A Company men."[39]

Sergeant Owens sent his runner, Private Bob Murphy, to find Lieutenant Dolan to ask if they should pull back, since his platoon was almost out of ammunition and was down to around fifteen men. Murphy returned a short time later with Dolan's answer scribbled on a scrap of paper. It read, "I don't know of a better place than this to die."[40]

Murphy said that Dolan told him that they were to stay where they were. Owens accepted the order and whatever fate awaited him and his men. "I really thought we'd had it, but then they threw up a Red Cross flag and stopped firing. I quickly stood up and stopped my men. Then I sat down and cried. I had sent Corporal D. J. Franks back to find some help for us, but before he found Colonel Ekman we had fought them off. I was so glad to see him come back a little later, for I didn't really think he could get out. When they had the Red Cross flag up, I moved to where I could get a good view of the causeway. I estimated that I could see at least two hundred dead or wounded Germans scattered about. I don't know how many were in the river. It took them about two hours to get their wounded out, then they started shelling us, but not too badly, just enough to keep us on edge. They continued shelling us all day long, but it was only sporadic. They never tried to get the infantry across again after they raised the Red Cross flag."[41]

Dolan told his men to prepare for another attack, an attack that never came. "The rest of our stay at the bridge was uneventful, except for the continued mortar fire, and at the end, artillery fire which damaged the 57mm. In conclusion, we held the bridge until relieved. In Company A, alone, in those days (three in all), we had seventeen known dead and about three times that number wounded. The rest of the battalion also had heavy casualties. I recommended Sergeant Owens and my four bazooka men for the DSC. The bazooka men were awarded the DSC., but Sergeant Owens was not. This is a story in itself."[42]

As the fighting raged at the La Fière Causeway, Private First Class Lewis Strandburg, with Company E, 401st, was asleep in the Horsa glider carrying him to Normandy. "The trip across the English Channel was quite smooth. We had been given two motion sickness preventative pills before taking off, so most of us slept for a good bit of the crossing. When I awoke, the coastline of Normandy was just coming into view."[43]

Riding in one of the Horsa gliders, Private First Class Fred Kampfer, with Company G, 325th, could see tracers in the distance. "As we approached the coast, we came under heavy antiaircraft fire."[44]

As his glider approached the landing zone, Strandburg felt the glider suddenly decelerate. "Our pilot released the towrope. There was complete silence, except for the rushing wind as the glider dove earthward [and] banked slightly while our pilot selected a spot to set her down. The rush of the air diminished somewhat and shortly we could feel the ship leveling off. Suddenly, there was a terrific crash and the whole sea and earth seemed to have crushed in on us. Water, mud, equipment and pieces of the glider (what was left of it) came rushing through the fuselage. Then everything became deathly still . . . .

"I was dazed for a second or two and when I snapped out of it, I found myself sitting up to my neck in water, even though I had been seated toward the rear of the glider. All those seated in the forward section were completely submerged and had to be unbuckled from their seat belts before they could come up for air. The glider was almost completely demolished upon impact with the flooded field, except for a few feet of the tail assembly. (I had picked a good seat!)

"The pilot and co-pilot were some twenty feet out in front of the wreckage with parts of the controls still in their hands. To see the wreckage, one would have thought no one could have walked away from it alive. Fortunately, however, no one had been seriously injured. We were badly shaken up and had received a few cuts and bruises, but the flooded field had actually helped us by breaking our direct contact with the hard earth."[45]

Captain Joe Gault, the CO of Company F, 325th, and twenty-eight men of his weapons platoon and company headquarters were riding in a Horsa glider as it approached the landing zone. "Upon landing we had too much speed and went through the hedgerow into the next field. However, we went between two trees on the hedgerow and the wings folded back into the fuselage, cracking the whole glider. My runner was sitting in the floor with his head in my lap. He was instantly killed, as were the next four men sitting down from me—the mortar section leader, Sergeant Joe Dichuccio from Beckley, West Virginia and three of his section. We had a total of ten killed and nine badly injured. We attended to the wounded and turned them over to the medics. I gathered what was left of our glider load, and we were put into an orchard where the battalion assembled."[46]

Kampfer's glider experienced a similar crackup. "The size of the Horsa glider no doubt contributed to our crash into a hedgerow at about one hundred miles per hour. The pilot in our plane was killed and the co-pilot was paralyzed. Our platoon leader, Lieutenant Guy W. Gowen was killed, and many others, including myself were seriously injured. Our regimental surgeon, Captain [Louis P.] Murphy was in the area [and] tried to treat as many of the wounded and injured as possible. I was hurting from shoulder and back injuries and was given morphine for the pain. Small arms fire was heavy at times and shelling went on through the night and into the next day."[47]

Lieutenant Lee Travelstead, commanding the Heavy Machine Gun Platoon of Headquarters Company, 2nd Battalion, 401st, was in one of the American-built CG-4A gliders as it approached the landing zone. "It was eerie to see the bursts [of flak], and wonder if the next would hit us. We cut loose from that three hundred foot nylon umbilical cord that tied us to the C-47 tow plane and we plunged in a wild gyrating pattern toward one of those small, littered fields of Normandy. Landing roughly, but upright and safely, we clambered out. I bid the glider pilot good-bye. A German burp gun fired from somewhere. It was an introduction to that sound. It can never be forgotten."[48]

The two battalions suffered sixteen fatalities and seventy-four were injured or wounded during the landing. Fifteen of the sixteen deaths were aboard Horsa gliders. Sixteen of the Horsa gliders were destroyed and ten damaged out of the thirty employed. Twelve CG-4A Waco gliders were destroyed and another thirty-eight damaged out of seventy gliders. As the last of the 325th Glider Infantry Regiment landed, a German counterattack on Ste.-Mère-Église was threatening the entire lodgement.

CHAPTER 14

"COLONEL, AREN'T YOU GLAD WAVERLY'S ON OUR SIDE?"[1]

At dawn on June 7, Lieutenant Colonel Vandervoort, CO of the 2nd Battalion, 505th, was at the Battalion CP on the north side of Ste.-Mère-Église monitoring events just north of the town. "Shortly after first light 7 June, the 1st Battalion, 1058th Grenadier Regiment reinforced by elements of the Seventh Army Sturm Battalion, a specially trained counterattack unit, succeeded in driving the D Company platoon defending along the east side of the highway, back and away from the road on the north edge of the town. From the north three battalions of German infantry supported by three artillery regiments and a number of 75mm and 7.62cm self-propelled guns marched south to clear a battalion and a half of American paratroopers off Highway N-13, the main road to the landing beaches. A fourth German infantry battalion south of Ste.-Mère-Église put the paratroopers in a vise. The German Kampfgruppe operating with the usual German efficiency and ferocity powered methodically into the northern environs of Ste.-Mère-Église. A German breakthrough into the town appeared imminent."[2]

The 1st Battalion of the 1058th Regiment, 91st Airlanding Division, was on the left flank, east of the N-13 highway, while the Seventh Army Sturm Battalion and seven self-propelled guns of the 709th Antitank Battalion moved south on the highway itself. The 2nd Battalion, 1058th, advanced through the fields to the west on the right flank.

Defending the north side of the town east of the N-13 highway was a single platoon of Company D, 505th, led by Lieutenant Thomas J. "Tom" McClean. A roadblock manned by a platoon of Company D, 505th troopers commanded by Lieutenant Oliver B. "O. B." Carr, Jr., defended the N-13 highway. The sector west of the highway was held by Headquarters Company, 2nd Battalion, 505th.

Gunfire from the ferocious fighting north of Ste.-Mère-Église grew louder as the two D Company platoons held off attacking hordes of German infantry supported by self-propelled guns. Company D, despite being outnumbered by over twenty to one, gave ground grudgingly, making the Germans pay dearly for every field and hedgerow. The Sturm Battalion and the self-propelled assault guns pressed the attack to the very outskirts of Ste.-Mère-Église. A convoy of German trucks, moving south on the highway toward the north end of town, carrying infantry from the Sturm Battalion, was engaged at long range by a 57mm antitank gun under the command of Lieutenant John C. Cliff, from Battery A, 80th AA Battalion. The lead truck was hit and knocked out, which caused confusion and disrupted the convoy. A German armored car then engaged Lieutenant Cliff's gun, but his crew knocked that out as well. Next a German Sturmgeschütz (Stug III Ausf. G) self-propelled assault gun moved south toward the gun, projecting smoke canisters ahead to shroud its advance. The self-propelled gun suddenly appeared out of the smoke, advancing rapidly at close range. The assault gun got to within fifty yards of Vandervoort's CP before Cliff's gunners disabled it with two rounds. However, the vehicle's 75mm main gun continued to fire at Cliff's gunners at almost point-blank range.

Lieutenant Cliff maintained observation on the gun and gave verbal adjustments to the crew as they loaded and fired, continuing the short-range dual until they finished off the enemy inside the vehicle. Then they moved their 57mm antitank gun up to the side of the knocked-out assault gun in order to have a clear field of fire. As they were getting the gun loaded, a second self-propelled gun up the highway fired on the crew, wounding them.

With the antitank gun out of action, the self-propelled assault gun began moving toward the north end of town, projecting smoke canisters ahead to shroud its advance. Private John E. Atchley, with Company H, 505th, courageously left his cover and single-handedly manned the antitank gun. Even though Atchley had never fired an antitank gun before, he loaded and fired, missing the oncoming self-propelled gun. He single-handedly reloaded the gun and adjusted the aim as the German assault gun bore down on him. At a range of about one hundred yards, he fired the second round, knocking out the German vehicle. The other five German assault guns retreated, stopping the armored thrust at the very edge of Ste.-Mère-Église.

Lieutenant Colonel Vandervoort didn't have much in reserve to counter a German breakthrough. "D Company's reserve platoon consisted of Lieutenant Turner Turnbull (half Choctaw Indian) and sixteen survivors from Neuville-au-Plain. His platoon, first to meet the juggernaut from the north, had delayed the Germans bravely, but at a terrible sixty-percent cost in casualties. Dug in behind D Company was Company E, the battalion reserve. They had only company headquarters and two platoons. One was Lieutenant Peterson's platoon of two lieutenants and about thirty-nine troopers. The other was an improvisation of glider pilots and 101st stragglers totaling about thirty-five men and officers armed only with individual shoulder weapons.

"The situation brought 1st Lieutenant Waverly W. Wray, Executive Officer of D Company, to the 2nd Battalion, 505 Command Post early in the morning to get help. Waverly was from Batesville, Mississippi. He had acquired all of the woodsman skills as a boy. In his hands, a rifle was a precision instrument. He claimed he had 'never missed a shot in mah life that ah didn' mean to.' In his early twenties, at the peak of physical fitness and mental quickness, he had the combat 'sixth sense' of the true warrior—an indefinable intuition, which warns of danger before it appears. A veteran of Sicily and Italy, he was as experienced and skilled as an infantry soldier can get and still be alive. Personally, he walked with the Lord. Some of the troopers called him 'The Deacon' because of his deep-south religious convictions—but never to his face. He didn't drink, smoke, curse, nor chase girls. When angered, he would resort to 'John Brown.'

"He was one of a few men in the regiment whom the chaplain could count on being present at services every Sunday. A God-fearing young man of uncompromising courage, character, and professional competence; combat leadership naturally gravitated to Waverly.

"Waverly explained the situation on the D Company front. The platoon, driven off the road, had suffered casualties, but was still intact and available for action. I told him to return to his company and counterattack the flank of the encroaching Germans. In his Mississippi drawl, he said, 'Yes, Suh,' saluted, about faced, and moved out like a parade ground sergeant major.

"Back in the company area he told his injured company commander, Captain T. G. Smith what they had to do. He collected all of the grenades he could carry from the company headquarters personnel. Then armed with his M-1 rifle, an Army .45, and a silver .38 revolver stuck in his jump boot, he went on a reconnaissance to better formulate his plan of attack.

"The terrain was mixed agricultural farm fields, orchards, and pasturage bound by man-high field stone and earthen embankments. These were the renowned hedgerows of Normandy, bordered by sunken cow lanes worn by centuries of traverse. Enemies could be a few feet apart and not be aware of each other. The fields were small—few running more than one hundred fifty by three hundred yards. Infantry could cross only at great peril. The checkerboard layout of the land forced the combatants into close alignment at ideal ambush and small arms killing range. In that maze of natural fortifications, troopers and Germans exchanged fire and jockeyed for positions all along the northern environs of the town. It took real courage just to move about, much less voluntarily go alone to find the foe. Waverly knew the terrain because D Company had occupied the ground earlier.

"With utmost stealth and courage, he moved up the sunken lanes, across the orchards, through the hedgerows and ditches sprinkled with German units moving forward for their next drive to take the town. He went north about three

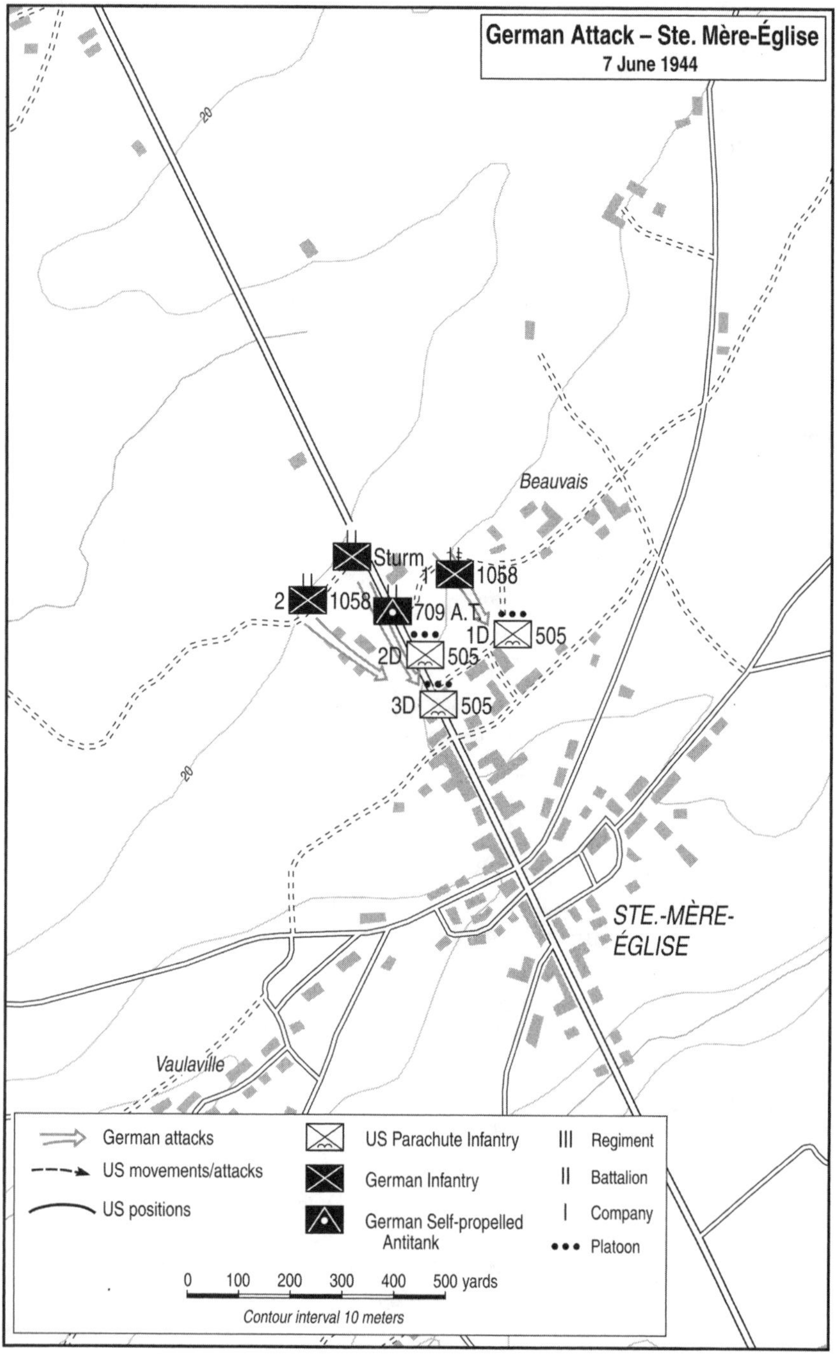
German Attack – Ste. Mère-Église
7 June 1944
20
20
Beauvais
Sturm
1
1058
2
1058
709 A.T.
1D
505
2D
505
3D
505
STE.-MÈRE-ÉGLISE
Vaulaville
German attacks
US movements/attacks
US positions
US Parachute Infantry
German Infantry
German Self-propelled Antitank
III Regiment
II Battalion
I Company
••• Platoon
0 100 200 300 400 500 yards
Contour interval 10 meters

hundred yards along the enemy left flank, then moved west a couple of hundred yards at right angles to the German axis of attack. That brought him a hedgerow or two away from the N-13."[3]

Acting as lead scout, Wray told Lieutenant Tom McClean and his 1st Platoon to follow him. McClean's platoon would make the attack on the German battalion after Wray had reconnoitered the area and determined the German dispositions. Leading his small force, Wray moved around the left flank of the German battalion and approached it from the rear.

Lieutenant Colonel Vandervoort described what happened next: "Then, moving like the deerstalker he was; he went south along a ditch until he heard guttural voices on the other side of the hedgerow. Stepping up and looking over the earthen embankment, he saw eight Germans in a sunken lane gathered around a radio. Covering them with his M1 rifle, he barked in his best command voice, 'Hande Hoch!' Most instinctively raised their hands, except one who tried to pull a P-38 pistol from the holster on his belt. Wray shot the man instantly.

"At the same time, two Germans stood up in a slit trench about one hundred yards to his left rear. With burst from Schmeisser machine pistols, they tried to take his head off—clipping two 9mm pieces out of his right ear. Momentarily disregarding the hail of bullets from behind, Wray shot the other seven men in the lane dead.

"Whirling around, he jumped back down into the ditch, loaded another eight round clip into his M1 and dropped the other two Germans across the field with a shot apiece. The eight dead Germans in the lane were the Commanding Officer and Headquarters Staff of the 1st Battalion, 1058th Grenadier Regiment."[4]

Lieutenant McClean arrived at the hedgerow across the field just in time to witness Wray's action. "My platoon was deployed along a hedgerow. I first saw Lieutenant Wray when he was approximately thirty to fifty yards to my left front. I saw him in a standing position firing down. I couldn't see who he was shooting at, as he was standing on a small rise from my position.

"I started to go to his assistance when I saw German troops approximately fifty yards to my right front. They were to Lieutenant Wray's left rear. Realizing that he did not see them as he was engaged in firing his rifle, I directed my platoon fire on the Germans."[5]

Private Frank Silanskis saw Wray disappear from view as he continued his one-man reconnaissance patrol. "The next time I saw Lieutenant Wray is when he came out of the hedgerow kicking two German prisoners. Lieutenant Wray had part of his ear and his helmet strap shot away. He was mad. He kept saying, 'John Brown Germans.' "[6]

Platoon Sergeant Paul D. Nunan, with the 1st Platoon, noticed the wound and how close Wray had come to being killed. "The bullet had struck his steel helmet almost dead center at the front rim. A quarter of an inch lower and it would certainly have gone into his forehead. Instead, the bullet was deflected and struck the hinge of his chin strap and clipped a piece of Lieutenant Wray's ear, leaving his face, neck, shoulder, and part of his uniform covered with blood."[7]

After returning to McClean's platoon, Lieutenant Wray positioned a 60mm mortar and a .30-caliber machine gun on the left flank of the German battalion, which was located in a sunken lane between two hedgerows. Lieutenant McClean's platoon was spread out along a hedgerow at the end of the lane, on the left flank of the German battalion. Wray then ordered the mortar to open fire at the far end of the lane, then adjusting the fire to walk the shells up the lane toward his position. At the same time, he had the .30-caliber machine gun open fire, shooting deadly enfilade fire into the German infantry packed into the lane.

As the mortar rounds struck overhanging tree limbs, they exploded, creating tree bursts. In order to escape the mortar shrapnel raining down on them and machine gun bullets ripping into their flank, many Germans began to spill out of the hedgerows into the fields to the front and rear of the lane. As they poured into the open, they ran right out in front of McClean's platoon, which took them under small arms and machine gun fire. It was a slaughter.

Sergeant Nunan soon saw a German major carrying a white flag move out into the field in front of the platoon's positions. Sergeant Nunan moved over the hedgerow and out into the field with Captain Smith, Lieutenant McClean, and an enlisted man to speak with the German. Nunan could see a Red Cross brassard on the German major's sleeve, signifying he was a doctor. "He spoke English well, and at the request of our Captain T. G. Smith, we agreed to a one hour truce so that the Germans be allowed to leave their medics and wounded with us, and that a wounded American glider pilot be turned over to us.

"Suddenly our men on the right flank opened fire. Captain Smith, the major, myself, and two others were still exposed in the open field. Only later did we learn the Germans on the right flank had started to withdraw as soon as the negotiations started, which caused our men on the right to open fire again. Captain Smith refused the German terms and shortly after a green flare was fired by the Germans and we began receiving fire from German 88s."[8]

Private First Class Charles Miller, a Company D trooper, heard the explosions from the high velocity antiaircraft guns begin. "They told us, 'Get the hell out of here!' And we did. But, on the way out there was a good friend of mine, Red. . . . Big Red [Corporal Kenneth W. Auther]. I thought he was taking a leak. Instead of that, his blood was coming out of his stomach, just like urine, just pouring out of him. What had happened, a medic told me later, a shell or bullet had hit the artery, that main artery, and it just burst open and he was dead in three or four minutes.

"There was nothing we could do. We're not doctors. It was awful to stand there and watch him die, but there was nothing we could do, except hold his hand, and try to make it a little bit easier for him."[9]

Meanwhile, the demoralized survivors of the German battalion fled north, exposing the left flank of the Sturm Battalion attacking straight down the N-13 highway, causing it to withdraw, and effectively halting the German attack. Shortly afterward, Lieutenant Colonel Vandervoort was informed that the German battalion east of the highway had been destroyed. "D Company moved back into their original defensive positions. Midmorning, Waverly returned to tell me the D Company area was secure. There he was—minus part of his ear. Blood had dried down his neck and the right shoulder of his jump jacket, fore and aft. I said, 'They've been getting kind of close to you haven't they, Waverly?'

"With just a grin, Waverly replied, 'Not as close as ah've been gettin' to them, Suh.' Waverly led Company D in throwing back the deepest penetration the Germans ever made into Ste.-Mère-Église, and in the process shattered the 1st/1058th."[10]

As Wray and Company D, 505th, were destroying the German battalion on the northern edge of Ste.-Mère-Église, southeast of the town the 2nd Battalion, 325th, and the 2nd Battalion, 401st, got assembled and organized, ready to move out. The 2nd Battalion, 325th, and the 325th regimental headquarters moved through Chef-du-Pont and then northeast to a bivouac location on the road, about halfway to Ste.-Mère-Église. The 2nd Battalion, 401st, was ordered to attack the town of Carquebut, southeast of Chef-du Pont.

The 1st Battalion, 325th, also began moving to their assigned bivouac location east of the La Fière Causeway at the railroad crossing. Lieutenant Wayne Pierce, with Company B, kept his men spread out in their tactical column, because they had the natural tendency to bunch up as they marched. "Our route took us along a back road, not much more than a path. A group of French people, perhaps three families, was hiding in a ditch along this road. For concealment, they had covered their hiding place with brush. They were following orders from the BBC telling them the people of Normandy to get out of the villages along the coast.

"Between Ste.-Mère-Église and La Fière, we set up positions along a railroad embankment as a reserve for Task Force A. Company B, with a full complement of five officers, was better off than any of the other companies. Captain Gibson, on orders from Sanford, sent me to serve on the battalion staff with Major Sanford. At this position, Major Sanford and I were the only two officers making up the battalion staff."[11]

Meanwhile, the 2nd Battalion, 401st, moved that afternoon to Carquebut and found it free of Germans, then advanced to Le Port where they again found no enemy.

After Company D's devastating counterattack, Ste.-Mère-Église and outlying areas were shelled mercilessly all day by German artillery and mortars. Sergeant Otis Sampson, with Company E, 505th, and his men had dug foxholes to protect themselves as much as possible against the flying shrapnel. "I figured to play it safe: I had given strict orders that no one was to leave their foxholes, for sniper firing, 88s, and mortar shelling was still coming in. Being caught above ground was asking for it. In all the hell we took during the night, not one of my men was hit.

"[Private John F.] Benoit, to stretch his legs and see what was going on during a lull in the incoming shells, left the safety of his hole and started for the roadside foliage. He was hit in the leg by mortar shrapnel just short of his destination.

" 'Hoppy' [Private Ralph F. Hopkins, Jr.], our medic, just happened to be in the ditch too, where he was to be available if needed. He patched Benoit up under fire. I kept low and watched him. I had to admire that medic. He worked calmly as he treated the wound. Finishing his work, he said to me, 'You had better dig a trench for him.'

"I answered the medic with, 'Like hell I will, let him dig his damn ditch. He had no right leaving his foxhole. I gave strict orders not to!' I was angry. I had lost a man for not obeying me. Yet, I knew how hard it was to stay in a foxhole, cramped as they were without wanting to get up and walk around some when the shelling would let up.

"Then on second thought, [I told Benoit,] 'Get on my back and I'll crawl to the CP where they have the deep trench.'

" 'No, I'll go myself!'

" 'Get the hell on my back!' I said angrily, knowing time was being wasted.

" 'No, I'll go on my own!'

" 'Go ahead if that's the way you want it, but keep low.' I watched him to see that he made it as he crawled along the hedgerow border to the CP I just couldn't help feeling pride for that Frenchman, who had brought the wound on himself and was looking for no sympathy or help."[12]

The mission of the special armored task force commanded by Colonel Edson Raff, consisting of Company C, 746th Tank Battalion, a platoon of armored cars, and Company F of the 401st, riding on the backs of the Sherman tanks, had been to break through from Utah Beach to Ste.-Mère-Église on D-Day. The force would give the 82nd Airborne Division some much needed firepower and most of all, a heavier antitank defense. However, on the morning of June 7 General Ridgway had not seen any US seaborne forces. Because of the lack of radio equipment, there had been no communication with Colonel Raff regarding the location of his force and when it might arrive.

About 10:00 a.m. some of the 505th pathfinders at Ridgway's CP were sent on a mission to bring some tanks up from the beach to the hard-pressed 505th troopers around Ste.-Mère-Église. Sergeant James Elmo Jones, with the 1st Battalion team, was one of the troopers chosen "to form a patrol and go back to the beach, contacting General [Raymond O.] Barton, the commanding general of the 4th Infantry Division, and tell him that we needed assistance, because German tanks were moving in, for him to send troops and tanks as quickly as possible to help stave off the counterattack on Ste.-Mère-Église that was obviously coming."[13]

Lieutenant James J. "J.J." Smith would lead the patrol. Sergeant Jones would be joined on the patrol by "Corporal Lewis D. Allen, Corporal Howard W. Hicks, Corporal George H. Purcell, and Private Julius A. Wyngaert. Before we left, we had to take all personal items such as billfolds, pictures, everything but our dog tags off our uniforms. We could not take any prisoners because we needed to get to the beach, which was approximately four miles away, as quickly as possible.

"We started and it seemed everywhere we went we either had to evade or kill German soldiers that were either trying to fight or trying to get away. Many of them were in our way, and we simply could not take prisoners. We finally made it to the beach. When we got there we saw the American tanks parked under trees with canopies from some American parachutes spread out for sunscreen. They were listening to the radios on the tanks as to how the invasion was coming.

"As we literally ran up, we bumped into a lieutenant colonel, and Lieutenant Smith said, 'Take me to your commanding officer.'

"The lieutenant colonel said, 'I'm the commanding officer.'

"Smith said, 'Hell, I don't mean you, I mean General Barton.'

"So, [the lieutenant colonel] put us in a jeep. He went along, and we took off to see General Barton, who was in his headquarters vehicle. We burst into his room, and he heard our story. We had not shaved, we were dirty, we probably looked terrible. But, he was very reluctant to send tanks that far away, because they had not penetrated in any way up toward the center of the peninsula. We didn't know it, but there were two or three men in the command vehicle. One of them spoke up and said, 'I think you should do it. I think you should send the tanks up.' We turned around, and there was General Lawton Collins, [the VII Corps commander] who happened to be there at the time. Within fifteen minutes, we had five tanks and we were riding on the back of them to show them the best way to get back. Five tanks on the way toward Ste.-Mère-Église."[14]

By early afternoon, when the 2nd Battalion, 8th Infantry Regiment, didn't arrive in Ste.-Mère-Église as planned, Lieutenant Colonel Krause took some of his 3rd Battalion troopers to relieve Lieutenant McClean's Company D platoon from their roadblock northeast of town. Krause ordered McClean to take his platoon on the double to the CP of the 12th Infantry, 4th Division, at St.-Martin-de-Varreville over four miles away to see if they could determine the location and status of the 8th Infantry.

As Lieutenant McClean and his men double-timed to St.-Martin-de-Varreville, they passed through the area occupied by the 1st Battalion, 8th Infantry, and somehow the two units missed each entirely.

Lieutenant McClean's platoon arrived at the CP of the 12th Infantry and was informed that the 2nd Battalion, 8th Infantry, had been held up by the Georgian Battalion defending Hill 20, and then by artillery fire interdicting their approach from the south up the N-13 highway. With this information, McClean took his platoon and double-timed back the four miles to Ste.-Mère-Église.

At about the same time, Company E, 505th platoon leader Lieutenant James J. Coyle received an order to report to the E Company command post. "I received an order from our company commander, Captain Clyde Russell to go to the beach by jeep with two men from D Company, and try to contact the 4th Infantry Division to get one of their artillery observers to Ste.-Mère-Église to give us fire support.

"I was able to reach the 4th Division as they were moving from the beach. But they had only one observer left alive and could not release him to aid us. I noticed a tank unit along the road and explained our needs to the lieutenant colonel in command. But he could not release any tanks to me without orders from his command. It was frustrating to see all those tanks not engaged while we were fighting so hard a few miles away. But there was nothing a lieutenant could do, so I returned to Ste.-Mère-Église with nothing but a bit of helpful information: The tank commander was in radio contact with tanks which were assigned to us. He told me they were on their way to Ste.-Mère-Église from a round about route through Chef-du-Pont.

"As soon as I reported to battalion headquarters upon my return, we were given an order to move into position north of Ste.-Mère-Église to prepare to attack the enemy who were closing in on the town."[15]

Unknown to General Ridgway, Colonel Raff's tanks had taken the road west to Chef-du-Pont and then the road from Chef-du-Pont northeast toward Ste.-Mère-Église, bypassing the German force near Fauville. From his position at the roadblock on the Chef-du-Pont road southwest of Ste.-Mère-Église, Sergeant William Blank, with Company G, 505th, heard the unmistakable sound of tanks. "When the first tank appeared to our front, I called for [Private Clifford L.] Dinsmore in the trench to tell me if it was one of ours. As he raised his head up, he said it was ours. A sniper shot him through the neck and he died shortly thereafter."[16]

In the early afternoon Raff's armored spearhead of the Howell Force arrived at Ridgway's CP by this circuitous route. Just behind the Howell Force tanks, Colonel James Van Fleet, commander of the 8th Infantry Regiment, 4th Division, arrived at Ridgway's command post in an armored car. He told Ridgway that his 8th Infantry was fighting its way north up the N-13 highway and would reach Ste.-Mère-Église in about an hour. Based on this, they decided to conduct a joint attack north out of Ste.-Mère-Église at 5:15 p.m. The 2nd Battalion, 8th Infantry, would attack on the left flank of Vandervoort's 2nd Battalion, 505th, which would attack north along the N-13 highway.

Around 3:30 p.m., Lieutenant Eugene Doerfler, S-2 of the 2nd Battalion, 505th, arrived at Ridgway's CP and guided two Sherman tanks from Raff's force to the battalion's positions just north of Ste.-Mère-Église.

The situation north of Ste.-Mère-Église was still critical. The almost complete destruction of the 1st Battalion, 1058th Grenadier Regiment, had temporarily relieved German pressure. However, five enemy self-propelled guns of the 709th Antitank Battalion and the Seventh Army Sturm Battalion remained north of the town astride the N-13 highway, while the 2nd Battalion, 1058th Regiment, was positioned west of the highway. The Germans continued to shell Ste.-Mère-Église and the 505th positions in preparation for a renewed attack to capture the town.

Because Captain Russell was suffering from a recurrence of malaria, Lieutenant Frank Woosley would be the acting CO of Company E for the attack. Lieutenant Woosley rounded up about twenty to twenty-five misdropped troopers of the 101st Airborne and about ten men from Company E Headquarters and formed them into a provisional platoon designated as 2nd Platoon, Company E, and assigned them to Lieutenant Coyle.

Lieutenant Coyle's platoon would attack north out of Ste.-Mère-Église west of the N-13 highway. The 1st Platoon, Company E, 505th, led by Lieutenant Ted "Pete" Peterson, would attack north right up the highway. Lieutenant McClean's Company D platoon would attack north in the fields east of the highway, if they arrived in time after double timing back from the 12th Infantry Regiment's command post. The 2nd Battalion, 8th Infantry Regiment, 4th Division, would attack north on the left flank of Coyle's provisional 2nd Platoon. The attack would commence at 5:15 p.m.

Private First Class Earl Boling was a rifleman in Peterson's platoon. "As we were hearing rumors that the beach troops would be arriving soon, we were ordered to prepare to attack. Of course, this was good airborne strategy. When one is surrounded, tired, hungry, and low on ammunition, the best possible thing to do is attack."[17]

In his foxhole behind a hedgerow, Sergeant Otis Sampson, with Company E, 505th, heard an ominous, low rumbling sound which grew louder. "It was toward the middle of the afternoon that I heard tanks coming. Thinking them to be the enemy, I waited back of the bank, as their sounds grew closer. I had several Gammon grenades laid out in front of me to do battle with them the best I could. I saw some foliage across the field being pushed inward and the front of a tank appeared and came to a halt. Its motor idled. A cocky American voice came from the man that was standing up in the turret. Our long wait was over.

"June 7th—4:00 p.m., 'Get ready to move out!' was the order we received. We moved back through the city on the same street we came in on. We came to a halt on its outskirts, on a road running west. A long stone cemented building was on our right and an orchard across the street."[18]

Near the Company D command post, Private First Class Stanley W. Kotlarz, one of the sixteen survivors of Lieutenant Turner Turnbull's platoon from the previous day's fighting at Neuville-au-Plain, got up to move forward with the platoon just as a German artillery shell exploded. "I got hit in the wrist and in the arm. A guy by the name of Brown got hit in the head. And Lieutenant Turnbull, it sheered the top of his head right off. When it hit all of us seemed to go up in the air. When I got up, I saw Brown crawling away, staggering. Turnbull was lying there with his brains peeling out of his head."[19]

The death of Lieutenant Turnbull, only a day after he and his platoon held off an entire regiment, was a tremendous blow to D Company and to the 2nd Battalion. Lieutenant Turnbull was one of those great officers that led from the front. Sergeant Floyd West described Turnbull as "more than a damn good officer, he was my friend."[20] Lieutenant Colonel Vandervoort recommended Lieutenant Turnbull for a Distinguished Service Cross, but he would later be posthumously awarded only the Silver Star.

After Lieutenant Coyle organized his provisional platoon of strays, he moved them into position just north of town. "We took up positions along a road which runs west from the main highway. It is the road which has the last house on the north edge of the town.

"Two tanks which had been attached to us arrived and they would cover our open flank as we attacked. There was heavy machine gun fire coming across the field from our front. My original order was to take my platoon across this field."[21]

However, Coyle and Woosley put their heads together and came up with a plan to skirt the open field. Lieutenant Coyle "got permission to take them north up a dirt road on the left of the field, which provided better cover and concealment."[22] It was a daring plan, which if successful would have Coyle's platoon on top of the Germans before they knew what hit them. But if the Germans spotted them coming up the road, they could trap the platoon in a confined space and could cut it to pieces with mortar and artillery fire.

Sergeant Sampson's mortar squad was assigned to support Lieutenant Peterson's 1st Platoon of Company E. Just prior to the jump off time, Sampson, "the mortar artist" was about to go to work. "Our platoon runner came back to inform me we were wanted forward. I grabbed the mortar and with the rest of the squad, I followed the runner to the front where the forward squads had sought protection in a ditch on the near side of a sparsely planted tree hedgerow. Here, I was told by either Sergeant Smith or Lieutenant Peterson, 'Give us mortar fire in that next hedgerow. They are there in force.' The hedgerow ran west from the Montebourg road [N-13]."[23]

Shortly before 5:00 p.m., the 8th Infantry Regiment had not yet arrived and would not be available to attack north on the left flank of the 2nd Battalion. Company E would have to cover it themselves. Lieutenant Woosley, Lieutenant Eugene A. Doerfler (Battalion S-2), and Lieutenant Coyle met with the commanders of the two Sherman tanks that would accompany them. They decided to use one tank and the 101st troopers and other strays of the provisional platoon to cover the left flank. Coyle, Woosley, Doerfler, and ten men from Company E headquarters would accompany the other tank and would take the front and right when they reached the intersection with the hedgerow across the field where the Germans were firing.

As the assault was about to commence, the 746th Tank Battalion taskforce that Lieutenant J. J. Smith had acquired from the 4th Infantry Division approached Ste.-Mère-Église from the east. This task force, consisting of the tank section of the Battalion Headquarters, the assault gun platoon (then M4 Shermans), and Company B, had left its bivouac area northwest of St.-Martin-de-Varreville with Smith's pathfinders riding on top of the tanks. The five Sherman tanks of the assault gun platoon and one tank from the tank section led the column, followed by the main body of Company B tanks, then the Battalion CP half-track, and finally, two more tanks bringing up the rear.

Pathfinder Sergeant James Elmo Jones, with Company B, 505th, had to jump off of the back of the tank he was riding as it rolled through Ste.-Mère-Église. "We arrived there in a very short period of time, although one was lost when it ran over a mine. The tanks never really stopped long enough to let us off, but kept attacking north [out] of Ste.-Mère-Église."[24]

It was approximately 5:00 p.m., just fifteen minutes before the scheduled attack. But the tankers of the 746th Tank Battalion, knowing nothing of the attack, just barreled right up the N-13 highway running head on into the remaining five German self-propelled assault guns and some German infantry in trucks.

Lieutenant Houston Payne was commanding the lead tank. Payne knocked out two self-propelled assault guns and a towed antitank gun before his tank was hit and he was wounded. He managed to get his tank pulled to the side of the road. Another Sherman moved past Payne's tank and continued the attack.

Just before 5:15, Vandervoort received a welcome hand from a newly arrived forward artillery observer. "The 8th Infantry field artillery observer placed a 155mm barrage two hedgerows in back of the German front line position."[25]

Peterson's Company E platoon opened up with a mortar barrage, supplied by the single 60mm mortar of Sergeant Sampson's squad. Sampson had his men working like a finely tuned engine. "Shortly before the mortar was set up and firing, one trooper came up and dropped several bags of ammunition. Each one of my men had brought me their supply. We could have never done the job without those extra rounds. We were in plain sight of the enemy and bullets were flying by. My men didn't hesitate. They tried to give us mortar gunners the protection we needed with their rifle fire. The teamwork paid off. My first rounds overshot the hedgerow. Once the range was found, we laid them in, one round in a machine gun nest, killing them all."[26]

Simultaneously, Peterson's platoon unleashed a torrent of fire from rifles, carbines, BARs, .30-caliber machine guns, and Thompson submachine guns into the points in the hedgerow across the field where Germans were spotted or suspected to be. Sampson's 60mm mortar gunner, Private First Class Harry

G. Pickels, fed the mortar while Sampson adjusted it to place rounds just behind the German-held hedgerow along its entire length.

At 5:15 p.m. Coyle's platoon and the two Sherman tanks began moving north up the lane. Woosley, Doerfler, and Coyle led the way on both sides of and just behind the lead tank. As they moved forward, the tank commander saw something up ahead and stopped the tank.

Lieutenant Woosley moved up a little way and then saw what was holding up the tank: "As we proceeded along the lane we came to a dead American soldier lying in the tank's path just short of the enemy's position. The tank commander didn't want to run over the body. I had what I consider a combat lapse and walked right in front of that tank. I lifted the body, even looked at his dog tags with sorrow for his family. I laid him in a ditch so the tank could move forward. I returned to the rear of the tank. Lieutenant Coyle told me he was amazed that I was not killed."[27] The column then continued to move forward cautiously.

As they neared the hedgerow where the German front was located, Coyle watched for any signs the Germans had the lane covered by a machine gun or worse, a self-propelled assault gun. "When we reached the intersection of another dirt road running east to the highway, we found the enemy behind the hedgerow bordering this road. We had come up on his flank and by pure chance he had left it unprotected."[28]

Lieutenant Woosley couldn't believe their luck. He immediately got the lead tank into action. "When we reached the lane that was the enemy's position, I had the tank make a ninety degree turn and fire down the sunken lane."[29]

The tank fired the .50-caliber machine gun, the 75mm main gun, and the .30-caliber coaxial machine gun, devastating the Germans packed into the narrow lane. Simultaneously, Lieutenant Coyle deployed his ten Company E troopers into perfect enfilade positions. "We poured fire up the ditch from our positions. After about fifteen minutes of firing, a white flag appeared in the ditch. I called for a cease fire, and it was with some difficulty in all the noise of battle that I was able to get our firing stopped."[30]

Sergeant Sampson began to see some Germans emerge from the front of the hedgerow. "The rifle and machine gun fire along with the mortar shelling had many of the Jerries willing to come out with white flags. To stop those men from getting killed, I stood up and yelled, 'Cease fire! Cease fire!' But the tension was too high. The Germans ran back to the protection of the hedgerow."[31]

The Germans' intentions to surrender were not all that clear to Private First Class Earl Boling. "The Germans started to surrender, then seemed to change their minds and started firing again. However, some had run into the open and at this time Lieutenant McClean's D Company platoon opened up on their flank."[32]

Even though Coyle heard the firing from Sampson's mortar and Peterson's platoon, the white flag had convinced him the Germans had had enough.

"Frank Woosley and I went up the road to accept the surrender. But before we got very far two hand grenades came over the hedgerow. He went into the ditch on one side of the road and I on the other. We thought at the time that we had stepped into a trap.

"We returned to our position and resumed fire. This time we did not cease until the enemy ran out of the ditch into the large field next to it with their hands raised. When I saw that there were over one hundred of the enemy running into the field, I went through the hedgerow with the intention of stopping them and rounding them up. But as soon as I got through the hedgerow into the ditch on their side, I was hit by machine pistol fire coming down the ditch. The Germans had not quit yet. One of my men followed me through the hedgerow and fired an unmanned German machine gun up the ditch ending any further fire from the enemy."[33]

To the east, Peterson's platoon kept up a tremendous volume of small arms fire on the hedgerow, while Sampson's mortar was lobbing shells just over the front hedgerow of the lane where the Germans sought refuge.

Sampson suddenly saw some Germans attempting to escape the rain of bullets and shrapnel hitting all over the hedgerow. "I was set up on the extreme right flank of the field. When some tried to escape in the mouth of a ditch to the right front of me, I quickly brought my mortar into play there. It paid off.

"Mortar ammunition gone, I used my Tommy gun on the escaping Jerries. I can never recall crossing the open field and going to the right of the forward hedgerow. I must have been partly across the field when I used the Tommy gun. For I was that close. I couldn't miss. The ditch was their death trap. I saw the backs of four still going. As long as the enemy had a gun in his hands, even though he was running the other way, to me it was open season on them. It was Lieutenant Packard's Tommy gun I was using. It had more than paid for his death that occurred back there on the Volturno railroad yard in Italy. It was so easy, I felt ashamed of my self and quit firing. That was the one time I felt I had bagged my quota."[34]

The Germans realized that there was little chance of escape and began emerging into the field in front of their hedgerow. The number of Germans coming out of the lane worried Woosley. "The enemy seemed to come from everywhere with raised hands until it looked like an army. I had difficulty locating enough soldiers for the guard detail. I wondered what would have happened if they knew how small a unit I had left at this point. Corporal Sam Applebee, in helping to round up the prisoners came across one officer who refused to move for him. With Appleby's own words, 'I took a bayonet and shoved it into his ass and then he moved.'

"You should have seen the happy smiles and giggles that escaped the faces of the prisoners to see their lord and master made to obey, especially from an enlisted man."[35]

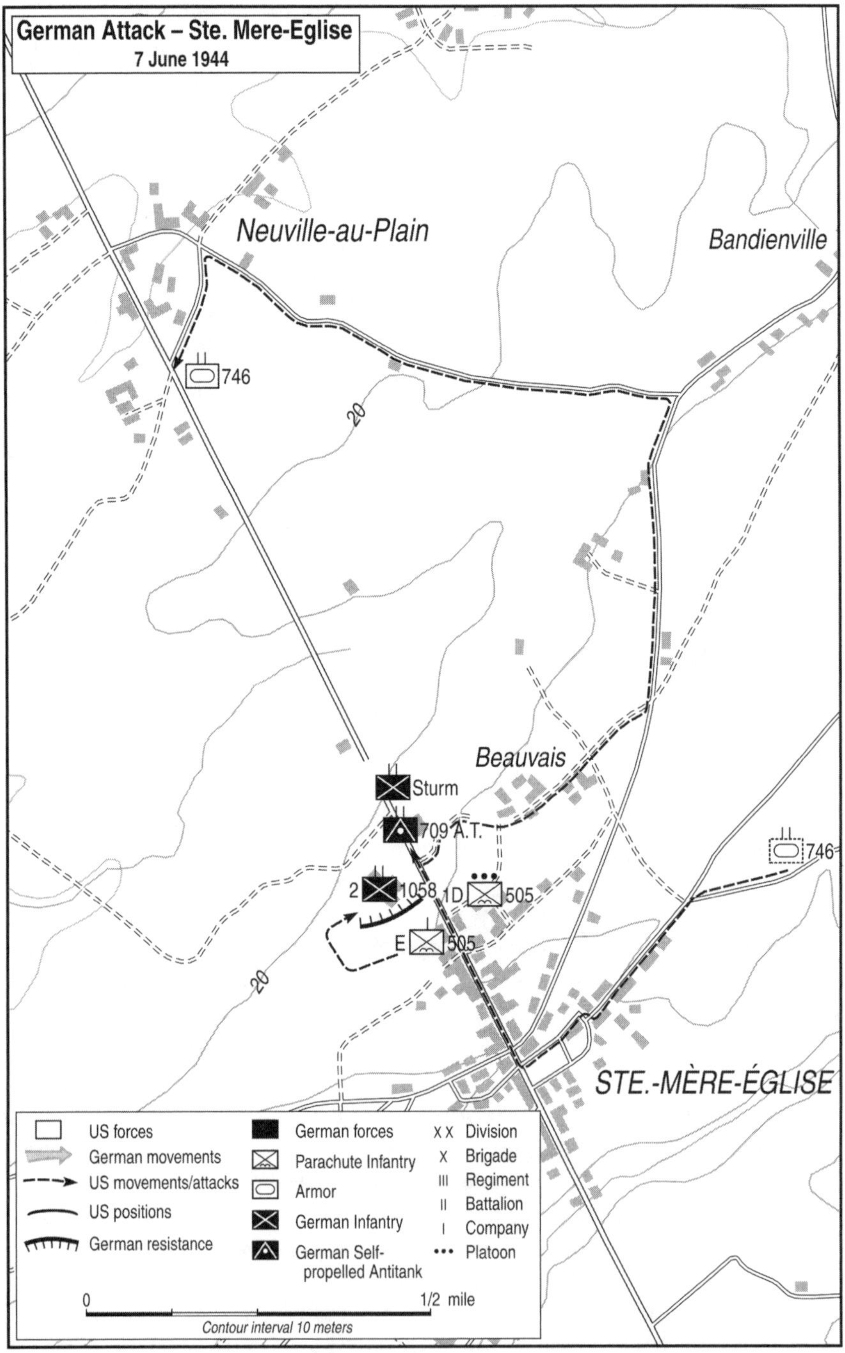
German Attack – Ste. Mere-Eglise
7 June 1944
Neuville-au-Plain
Bandienville
746
20
Beauvais
Sturm
709 A.T.
2
1058
1D
505
E
505
746
20
STE.-MÈRE-ÉGLISE
US forces
German movements
US movements/attacks
US positions
German resistance
German forces
Parachute Infantry
Armor
German Infantry
German Self-propelled Antitank
X X Division
X Brigade
III Regiment
II Battalion
I Company
••• Platoon
0
1/2 mile
Contour interval 10 meters

With the firing ceased, Sampson, for the first time, took notice of the ghastly scene in front of him. "I remember very vividly looking over the dead and wounded in the ditch and the surrounding area. One mortar shell had landed on top of the bank near the deep ditch and partly covered some of the dead and wounded with a heavy layer of dirt. Every time a wounded man breathed the soil would rise and lower. I could partly see the eyes of one man who was lying on his back. An awful scared look was in his eyes as I looked down on him. Fearing, I guessed that I would put a bayonet into him. I made no attempt at helping them.

"I looked up. No more than fifty feet from me in the open field next to the hedgerow were about fifty to sixty Germans with their hands up, standing in a group. I saw the tall form of Lieutenant McClean from D Company. He was on the other side of the road with some of his men, where more of the enemy had surrendered.

"I started from the Montebourg road and walked west on the north of the hedgerow with my men trailing. It was a double hedgerow with a sunken lane in between. Here was where Jerry had made his stand.

"One wounded German looked at my canteen and asked what sounded to me like, 'coffee.' I gave him my canteen and moved on, forgetting the incident. At the end of the field I ran into Lieutenant Coyle. He had a large group of prisoners guarded by our company headquarters men.

"He told me part of the story of his attack. 'We caught them unaware. It took twice to make them surrender and then I got hit in the rear,' he said, laying his hand on his rear cheeks.

" 'Let me take a look and see how bad it is,' I said as he lay on the ground. A bullet had almost completed its journey through both cheeks. I applied a bandage, saying, 'Lieutenant, just remember, I put your first granny rag on.' Completing the job, I said, 'Just lie here and I'll see someone picks you up.' "[36]

Coyle replied that he'd been all right before Sampson came along. "I was given first aid after the prisoners were collected and rode back on a tank to the battalion aid station in the old school in Ste.-Mère-Église. The next day I left Ste.-Mère-Église in an ambulance to return to England and hospital."[37]

After leaving Coyle, Sampson took his squad back to the N-13 highway. "On returning to the Montebourg road I was hailed by the wounded Jerry I had given my canteen to. I had forgotten all about him. He passed it back empty, but the look he gave me was one of thanks. I met Jack Hill, roaming around the area on my return to the Montebourg road. He showed me a beautiful watch, saying, 'A German officer lost his arm and I bandaged it up for him. He could speak English well. He offered me the watch and I refused it. I didn't want him to think he had to pay me. The officer said, 'You might as well have it, for it will be taken from me later.' He seemed to be a very pleasant man and showed little sign of the pain he must have been in.

"Our partial company, still minus two platoons, returned to our area in Ste.-Mère-Église without getting a man killed. We hit fast and hard, each man doing his part. The price the Germans paid for that short encounter in dead and wounded was terrific, not counting the men captured. The sight that met our eyes after that encounter was a gruesome one."[38]

The battle had been an overwhelming victory for the two platoons of Company E and the single platoon of Company D. Before he was evacuated, Coyle was given a preliminary prisoner count. "In this battle E Company, with two platoons, captured one hundred sixty-eight prisoners. I do not know the number of dead left in the ditches. Lieutenant Peterson's platoon on my right flank captured the German commander. Corporal Sam Appleby shot one German captain as he tried to escape the trap. A platoon of D Company, commanded by Lieutenant Thomas J. McClean captured a great number who tried to escape across the main highway [N-13] and ran into his position."[39]

While the paratroopers destroyed the German infantry, Lieutenant Colonel C. G. Hupfer and Major George Yeatts, with the 746th Tank Battalion, reconnoitered a route around the German flank by taking the road northeast toward Bandienville, then turning north. They skirted the open flank created by the destruction of the 1st Battalion, 1058th, that morning. Even though under observed artillery fire, they found the route open and returned to move two platoons of Company B, 746th Tank Battalion (consisting of ten Shermans), up the route around the German flank. They had orders to drive through to Neuville-au-Plain and attack the retreating German armored column.

The Company B tanks arrived at Neuville-au-Plain in time to destroy two more German self-propelled assault guns, while losing two of their own tanks. They liberated nineteen American prisoners and took about sixty German prisoners.

That evening, Private George Jacobus, a Company E, 505th trooper, who had broken his left leg upon landing, sat manning a .30-caliber machine gun. With him were fellow injured troopers Private Marvin Gilmore, with Company E, 505th, and a 508th trooper named Bill in a horse barn a few miles north of Ste.-Mère-Église. Jacobus hoped that American forces would overrun the area before the Germans discovered them. But that didn't happen. They were discovered by German survivors of the 1058th Grenadier Regiment who were retreating from the great slaughter inflicted upon them by Jacobus' own 2nd Battalion, 505th, north of Ste.-Mère-Église. "We fought our best fight with a ragtag German platoon. We ran out of ammunition and agreed among ourselves to surrender. The first face I saw was a Nazi with a machine pistol pointed straight at my face. He wanted to pull the trigger. In my best foul mouth cursing I told him where to go. In an instant a German officer appeared telling him to get out, and to inform us that he spoke perfect English. Further conversation informed us that he had worked for the New York Central Railroad for several years, had gone back to Germany in 1938, and had been taken into the army. He was a captain in rank.

"We talked—he kept ordering the young fanatical Nazi out to the road. We had slightly wounded several of his men. They had set up a defensive position on the road. His outfit had taken a bad beating at Ste.-Mère-Église and they were on their way north to [Orglandes].

"There was a flatbed truck along in an hour or so. I was literally tossed on the truck and driven away into the late afternoon, June 7th, with nothing but a hidden knife. I never saw [Private] Marvin Gilmore again. He was listed as KIA, leaving a wife and two year old son, Ronnie. It was almost dark. The truck stopped and two Germans took me off the truck and left me on the side of the road. Early the next morning an ambulance took me to a POW camp near [Orglanges], June 8th."[40]

Lieutenant Colonel Vandervoort was justifiably proud of his understrength battalion's overwhelming victories that day. "We had annihilated the 2nd Battalion, 1058th German Infantry Regiment. The 1st Battalion, same unit was completely routed. Four hundred eight prisoners were captured and counted. Thirty-six enemy vehicles and guns destroyed. Four hundred fourteen enemy dead were counted within and in front of our positions."[41]

Lieutenant John C. Cliff, with Battery A, 80th AA Battalion, would later be awarded the Silver Star for his part with his antitank gun crew in knocking out the three German vehicles that morning. For single-handedly knocking out a German self-propelled assault gun, Private John Atchley, with Company H, 505th, would be awarded the Distinguished Service Cross.

A great many German as well as American casualties resulting from the terrible fighting to the south near Ste.-Mère-Église continued to arrive at the German 91st Division Field Hospital located at a chateau near the town of Orglandes. Lieutenant Paul Lehman, with the 3rd Battalion, 508th, had suffered a punctured artery in his throat and was captured on June 6, along with his battalion surgeon, Lieutenant Briand Beaudin, and few other wounded troopers. He owed his life to Beaudin, who had kept him alive. Lehman observed the German medical staff and their American POW medical personnel working together to save all of the patients, regardless of whether they were Americans or Germans. "The Doc [Lieutenant Beaudin], of course, supervised all the medical attention that was possible with the limited facilities at hand. Through his efforts, a few of the most critical cases were operated on by the German surgeons. They were overwhelmed with cases to the point of exhaustion day and night. One operated on me the next night [June 7] and tied off the severed artery and sewed up the wound on the inside only. Every day additional wounded were brought to our building, and when I was strong enough to get up and move about, I interviewed each one for information of our troops.

"When some of my strength had been regained, I took over administration of our barracks—the serving of the meals, sterilization of water, cleaning up the building, fixing of the beds, carrying some of wounded outside during the hours of sunlight, salvage of equipment and collecting of personal effects of those who died, etc."[42]

By the late afternoon of June 7, Private Arthur B. "Dutch" Schultz, with Company C, 505th, at the La Fière bridge area, had endured almost continuous German shelling all day. "I was walking to the rear for some reason when I crossed paths with Lieutenant Colonel Mark Alexander, who had assumed command of the 1st Battalion, when a young trooper approached us and said that he had been hit. Both of us looked and couldn't see anything until he turned his back, exposing a gaping shrapnel wound. I was partially immobilized, while the colonel called for a medic and started telling this scared kid that he was going to be all right, while gently helping him sit down on the ground. What was so incongruous to me at that moment was the fact that this wounded trooper was able to walk, and the other was that this battle-tough commander showed so much tender care in the middle of all the death and destruction that was everywhere."[43]

Late in the day of June 7, the 2nd Battalion, 401st, left the village of Le Port on the northern shore of the Douve River and marched through Chef-du-Pont, then toward Ste.-Mère-Église, where they bivouacked with the 2nd Battalion, 325th, and regimental headquarters about nine hundred yards northeast of Chef-du-Pont. At 9:00 p.m. the 2nd Battalion, 325th, was attached to the 505th and moved from the bivouac area to Ste.-Mère-Église.

While fighting raged north and west of Ste.-Mère-Église, about 150 troopers, primarily from the 507th and under the command of Major Charles D. Johnson, the executive officer of the 3rd Battalion, 507th, defended the village of Graignes. They had been dropped more than twenty miles southeast of the drop zone. During the day and night of June 7, they conducted several reconnaissance patrols, which managed to avoid contact with German forces by hiding submerged in the swamp. With the help of the French in and around the town, they recovered many equipment bundles, providing an abundance of crew-served weapons and ammunition.

West of Ste.-Mère-Église, Lieutenant Wayne Pierce, the XO of Company B, 325th, reported to Major Teddy Sanford, the commander of the 1st Battalion, 325th, after Lieutenant Colonel Klemm Boyd had been injured in the crash of his glider. At the time, Lieutenant Pierce constituted the entire battalion staff, because of injuries and missing officers from the morning's glider landings. "Just before dark, General Gavin came by in a jeep, picked up Major Sanford and me and we drove with a couple of riflemen to General Ridgway's CP in a farmhouse near Ste.-Mère-Église. Here, I rested in the orchard while Gavin conferred with Ridgway, and Sanford was briefed by the division staff. After dark, probably about 11:00 p.m., we moved slowly back up the road toward where we had left the battalion. We stopped about halfway between Ridgway's CP and the battalion, moved off the road into a small field bordered by a high hedge and lay down to try to sleep."[44]

Early the next morning, Lieutenant Waverly Wray took Lieutenant Colonel Vandervoort to the site of his remarkable feat the previous day that had resulted in the destruction of the 1st Battalion, 1058th Grenadier Regiment. Vandervoort saw firsthand evidence of what he had been told. "Waverly and I went over the ground he covered the preceding morning. The dead battalion commander and seven staff corpses were still there. It had to be an eerie shock to any German visiting the place. Across the field were two dead Schmeisser armed Grenadiers—both shot in the head.

"John Rabig, Waverly's first sergeant, summed up Wray's performance the next day with the comment, 'Colonel, aren't you glad Waverly's on our side?' Waverly's unique performance set him apart as an authentic hero, but he never showed it in his demeanor. He was nominated for the Congressional Medal of Honor. The recommendation was downgraded and awarded as a DSC. Those who knew him best think of Waverly W. Wray as the 82nd Airborne Division's undiscovered World War II equivalent of Sergeant Alvin C. York. He stands tall among those who made the great invasion succeed."[45]

CHAPTER 15

"VAN, DON'T KILL THEM ALL. SAVE A FEW FOR INTERROGATION."[1]

During the night of June 7–8, through messengers and radio contact, Ridgway and Gavin were able to determine that four main groups of paratroopers were isolated west of the Merderet River. They were: the mixed force of mostly 508th troopers commanded by Lieutenant Colonel Thomas J. B. Shanley near the river on Hill 30 between the La Fière and Chef-du-Pont Causeways; Lieutenant Colonel Charles Timmes' group of mostly 2nd Battalion, 507th, in an orchard near the river north of the La Fière Causeway; about two hundred men west of Amfreville under the leadership of Colonel George V. Millett, Jr.; and another two hundred north of Amfreville under Captain Allen Taylor, the CO of Company H, 507th. The generals worked to formulate a plan to save these groups from being destroyed piecemeal. Their first order was for Captain Taylor and his group to link up with Colonel Millet's group if possible.

At 8:00 p.m. sixty-seven men and three officers moved down Hill 30 to establish a roadblock protecting the western end of the causeway that ran east to Chef-du-Pont. Maintaining this roadblock would deny the causeway to German armor and a direct route to Utah Beach. One of the three officers leading the force was Lieutenant Ralph DeWeese, with Company H, 508th. "We moved down Hill 30 and set up a defense to hold until we could contact the rest of the outfit. We hit no opposition and set up a roadblock at the road junction."[2]

The 456th PFA Battalion, less the two-gun section that had jumped with the paratroopers, began landing on Utah Beach at midnight, bringing valuable firepower to the division.

That evening, Sergeant Robert D. Shields, with Company A, 508th, left Hill 30 and courageously crossed the causeway to Chef-du-Pont, scrounged critical spare parts to fix the two SCR 300 radios with the force on Hill 30, and returned before daybreak.

Near midnight, Lieutenant Walter J. Ling, with Company B, 508th, was ordered to take a patrol from Chef-du-Pont across the causeway to contact Lieutenant Colonel Shanley on Hill 30. Sergeant Bill Call was a squad leader in the platoon. "Lieutenant Ling told me to gather up four or five guys, and I did. There were six of us in the patrol with Ling. On this route, there were Germans who had dug in on the side [of the causeway] that were dead. One in particular had been hit with a phosphorous grenade. He was half out of his hole; he was probably about six foot seven, a big guy. He was burned like a hot dog that had been left on the fire too long. He was split open, and he stunk to beat hell.

"When we got to the hill, they challenged us and I forgot the countersign. After we got to the top of the hill, Ling had us stay right there and he went to wherever Shanley had his headquarters."[3]

While Call was waiting for Ling's return, he heard a German truck approaching a farmhouse below the hill, where a French farmer and his family had been treating a few wounded 508th troopers.

Two of these wounded were Lieutenant Ralph DeWeese's Company H troopers. "The French people were very good to us and were taking excellent care of them. That night we heard some noise over around the house and a truckload of Jerries had come down to set up a roadblock at the junction. They went into the house and found Lieutenant [Donald J.] Johnson and a medic. They took them outside and shot them. They also burned the house, but the French got [Melvin H.] Pommerening and Wogan out OK. They also killed one of our men and we got about four or five of them. They loaded in a truck and took off, leaving mines and all kinds of equipment behind."[4]

A short time afterward, Ling returned and told Call to move out. "Ling wanted to get out of there before morning. It was scary as hell. But Ling got us there and he got us back."[5]

In the 505th sector, Colonel Ekman, wanting to make sure the 505th exploited the destruction of two battalions of the 1058th Regiment and keep the surviving Germans on the run north of Ste.-Mère-Église, ordered an attack to commence shortly after midnight on the morning of June 8. With the 2nd Battalion, 505th, attacking on the right and the 3rd Battalion, 505th, on the left, bounded by the Merderet River on their left flank, the 505th drove north.

As Company I, 505th, moved forward during the darkness, Sergeant Bill Dunfee was taking turns as a scout. "Attacking at night to avoid exposure in the fields between hedgerows is great, if you're not a scout. This puts horrible pressure on the scouts. We would send two scouts forward from one hedgerow to the next, [and] if all was clear, they would return and move the company forward. To be fair, we took turns; going in pairs we would rotate after two or three exposures. [Albert A.] Dusseault and I were taking our turn, when the plan misfired. We had gone to the next hedgerow and peered through, there was no sign of the enemy, so we returned and moved the platoon forward. We made it back to within a few feet of the hedgerow when the Germans opened up on us from their side with machine pistols and rifles. We hit the deck firing and started lobbing grenades over the hedgerow. They answered in kind with potato mashers. Our fragmentation grenades being superior, our side prevailed. We had one casualty, Lieutenant [Walter B.] Kroener, our acting CO; a potato masher had landed near him, blowing dirt and gravel into his face. He wasn't pretty, but wasn't seriously hurt.

"Continuing this night attack, [Richard L.] Almeida was shot through the armpit. A large artery was severed and the medics couldn't stop the flow. [He was] evacuated to the States with a useless right arm.

"Another casualty of this action was one of the new men. He was shot through the forehead giving him an instant frontal lobotomy. What amazed me was that he remained lucid, he was able to walk with help and his mental attitude could best be described as euphoric, he was however, blind. I had the eerie feeling I was talking to a dying man. I assured him he would be evacuated, and all would be well. I'm afraid my voice betrayed my concern, because he told me, 'Don't worry about me Sarge, I'm going to live, you guys may not.' I admired his guts, but had no desire to trade places."[6]

By 4:30 a.m. the 2nd Battalion, 505th, moved through Neuville-au-Plain, where they found nineteen wounded troopers, including some of Lieutenant Turnbull's platoon holding the town. Hupfer's tanks had liberated them the previous evening.

Colonel Millet's two hundred 507th troopers dug in west of Amfreville had been attacked by strong German forces several times on June 7, but had thrown back every attack. Sometime after midnight on the morning of June 8, First Sergeant Barney Hopkins, with Company D, 507th, walked the perimeter, warning the men that a large group of troopers would be joining them, so they wouldn't accidentally fire on them as they approached. "Colonel Millett had radio contact with Captain Allen Taylor (Company H) that his group was going to join us. Captain Taylor and about two hundred men came in just after dawn on D+2."[7]

Shortly after sunrise on the morning of June 8, General Gavin walked the battlefield north of Ste.-Mère-Église with Lieutenant Colonel Vandervoort, who briefed him on the previous day's fighting. When Gavin viewed the fields strewn with hundreds of German corpses he jokingly said to Vandervoort, "Van, don't kill them all. Save a few for interrogation."[8]

After delivering the order from Ridgway to Timmes to hold his position the previous morning, Lieutenant Gerard Dillon, with Company G, 507th, found himself still at the orchard on June 8. "On the morning of D+2 the Germans hit us at about seven or eight a.m. in an attempt to overrun the position. They attacked three or four times with infantry supported by mortar and artillery fire, but were repulsed each time."[9]

On the east side of the Merderet River at Chef-du-Pont the 508th sent patrols south to contact the 101st Airborne, which was supposed to be holding Carquebut and Le Port. Instead they found both towns now held by strong enemy forces. When the patrols reported back, Captain Royal Taylor, the CO of Company B, 508th, was ordered to take his force of less than one hundred men and wipe out the Germans in both towns. As Taylor's force approached Carquebut, they began receiving fire, but it was passing overhead. As they closed in, a short firefight ensued and the German force surrendered. Taylor's men killed about 15 Germans and took about 120 prisoners. Part of Taylor's men were detached to take the prisoners back to the POW cage, while Taylor led the remainder of his force to Le Port, where the Germans there also surrendered after a short fight.

Ekman's 505 troopers continued to drive north, with the 3rd Battalion moving toward the town of Grainville and the 2nd Battalion attacking on their right toward Fresville. In this hedgerow country, even a few Germans properly positioned behind hedgerows, taking advantage of every terrain feature, and using manmade objects to maximum effect, could inflict heavy casualties and stop the advance of forces many times their size, as D Company had demonstrated the previous two days.

A small hamlet surrounded a fork in an unpaved country road in the 3rd Battalion sector, with the road to the right going to Fresville and the left to Grainville. With rifle squads reduced to six or seven men apiece, Company I moved out from the crossroad along the road to Grainville. The lead platoon had one squad moving in the fields to the left of the road, with another to the right, and a third squad, led by Sergeant Felix C. Sandefur moving directly down the road. In the field to the left of the road, walking about ten yards behind Private Arthur Hile, Private First Class Bill Tucker was carrying his .30-caliber machine gun. Tucker had a couple of strays from the 508th acting as the assistant gunner and ammo bearer. "We started to attack through fields and two or three-foot deep hedgerows covered with thorns. There were also a couple of pig troughs that we went through or around.

"As we got up near the curve of the road, we heard Germans firing from the right with MG-42 machine guns. We figured Sandefur had run into it. Suddenly, they started firing in the field almost directly from our flank. That field was covered with ditches and grass between three and four feet high, so it was impossible to see anyone. Before we knew what happened, Hile had been hit through the chest and lay dead against a small hedgerow ten yards in front of us.

"My team was pinned down in tall grass by a line of Germans to our left and by a machine gun in front of us. Snipers in trees fired down on us from the hill at the right of the road."[10]

As Tucker was lying in the tall grass trying to figure out what to do, another German opened up on them, "firing a Schmeisser submachine gun at us, from less than thirty yards away in the grass. He had us pinned down so badly that we couldn't set up our gun. The only thing to do was to try to get back with the others. Since we couldn't go around the hedgerows, we had to rip our way through. I took the lead, and the two 508th men were right on my tail. I tore the hedgerow branches apart as thorns and heavy brush ripped my wrists. My hands were bleeding in no time at all."[11]

Pulling back to the hamlet at the crossroad, Company I got reorganized and made an attempt to move around the German flank, to the right of the road. Tucker, heavily laden with his .30-caliber machine gun, got ready to follow Private First Class Ray Krupinski, the squad's BAR man, who had laid down a withering covering fire to cover the withdrawal of Tucker and his two men earlier. As Tucker looked across the field they would have to cross, he knew he would be at a distinct disadvantage carrying his machine gun. "[Frederick G.] Synold was on the right of the hedgerow covering us with his machine gun. Krupinski led the way across the field. Following him came another combat engineer we liked. He had been with us before, and he liked to be with us. I followed the combat engineer by about ten yards, and Larry [Leonard] was behind me. We had all climbed over a three-board fence about four and a half feet high. Larry had just made it over when shots rang out. Our combat engineer was hit right through the head. That left the three of us prone in the open field. There was nothing we could do except pull back over the fence. We had no cover, and the Germans were on high ground above us."[12]

As Tucker ran back and began climbing over the fence, a bullet pierced his jumpsuit jacket, hitting a Bible his grandmother had given him. It was another close call.

On the western side of the Merderet River, the suffering of the wounded on Hill 30 was terrible. Sergeant Zane Schlemmer, with Headquarters Company, 2nd Battalion, 508th, was assigned to outpost duty. "I preferred the outpost, even though we would sometimes receive fire from both sides; for back in the perimeter, we had many wounded and dying. There was no way to evacuate them. It was difficult to listen to their cries and the moans, because we had no medical supplies. We had not received resupply of ammunition, equipment, food, or water. We could do without these items, but the lack of medical supplies and blood plasma was really felt by everyone."[13]

Corporal Kenneth "Rock" Merritt, with Headquarters Company, 1st Battalion, 508th, and about forty-five men were dug in at a crossroads near Montessy, a small village on the northern shore of the Douve River, south of Hill 30. "We received a call from Lieutenant Colonel Shanley on Hill 30 that they needed blood plasma real bad. We had plenty of it. It just happened to land in the area our equipment bundles did. Captain [Jonathan E.] Adams asked for volunteers—three men volunteered. They strapped blood plasma to their bodies and when night fell, they took off. The blood plasma patrol did not get through. Lieutenant [Roy W.] Murray got killed, Corporal [James E.] Green was found in a hedgerow one week later, completely dazed, due to a concussion hand grenade. Private First Class Circelli made it back to our position, his lip and chin almost shot off. He was also shot in the neck and [had] several shots in his right arm."[14]

The Germans attacked Hill 30 from three sides, while an entire battalion of German infantry supported by French tanks and Sturmgeschütz III assault guns attacked the roadblock at the western end of the Chef-du-Pont Causeway. The fighting was again ferocious, and Shanley's mixed group of paratroopers manning the roadblock were finally pushed back.

Around 4:00 p.m., one of the two waterlogged SCR 300 radios was finally working. One of the radio operators, Private First Class Harold Kulju, tried to make contact with friendly forces. "I got an answer back from three guys who were holding a bridge. They stated that they had contact with [the 508th] regiment, and that they thought that regiment would be able to contact division, and division was in contact with division artillery. So, [Lieutenant] Colonel Shanley gave me coordinates, which I forwarded to them, and we asked for artillery fire as soon as possible on these coordinates. They agreed to relay the message. We had no idea whether we were going to get any artillery support or not; whether the artillery unit would even get the message or not.

"I was lying in a slit trench facing the hedgerow where the [German] artillery was being set up, and then in front of me, in another slit trench, was a glider pilot. Suddenly, I heard this weird noise and the shells started exploding where the Germans were. The message we had sent got through, and the division artillery, hit the target dead center the very first volley. It caught the Germans out in the open, completely by surprise. Some of them had shells in their hands ready to throw into the open breeches of the French 75s. There were dead Germans all over the place when we got over there."[15]

Sergeant Schlemmer, manning an outpost, was thankful for the artillery fire, because he was running very low on ammunition. "This [artillery] fire broke up several German attacks at very critical times for us in the outpost. After one firing to break up a German attack coming up a sunken lane very near our outpost, we captured and retrieved two small German artillery cannons and some shells. These, we hauled back up to Hill 30 to turn around and use for the next attack."[16]

After dark on D+2, Lieutenant Woodrow W. Millsaps, with Company B, 508th, and Lieutenant Lloyd Polette led a thirty-man combat patrol to drive the Germans back and reestablish the roadblock at the west end of the Chef-du-Pont Causeway. In savage fighting, the patrol killed thirty Germans in close, sometimes brutal hand-to-hand combat, with no prisoners taken.

North of Ste.-Mère-Église, the 3rd Battalion, 505th, deployed G and H Companies on the right of I Company, and a night attack supported by tanks jumped off to take Grainville. Company I fixed bayonets, formed a skirmish line, and began the attack. The tanks knocked out most of the German positions, and the attack carried all the way into Grainville, which was captured around 11:00 p.m.

By the end of the fighting, Private First Class Bill Tucker, a Company I trooper, was bone tired after an advance that had lasted for twenty-three hours. "The attack pushed us right into the position we were supposed to be in earlier that day, on the curve in the road where Sandefur's squad had been. Larry [Leonard] and I settled in for the night in a six-foot square former German foxhole with straw in the bottom. The Germans had used it for a machine gun to cover the road we had tried to move down earlier. The hole was a classic machine gun nest, and the gunners must have been really experienced. They had dug firing shelves on three sides, and the fourth was blocked by an immense hedgerow corner. They had a clear field of fire for at least seventy-five yards down the road where Sandefur had come from.

"As we moved around in the dark, someone found some bodies in a ditch about twenty yards from our hole. The bodies were Sandy and all his men, lying along the ditch about five to ten yards apart. Apparently, when Sandy's squad went down the road, the German machine gunner had fired at Sandy twenty yards away in the lead."[17]

That night, in the orchard held by the 2nd Battalion, 507th, Lieutenant Gerard Dillon, with Company G, 507th, was present at the farmhouse that was acting as the command post. "On the night of D+2, we were running short of ammunition and Timmes instructed [Lieutenant John] Marr to try to find a ford across the inundated area, and to cross over to the other side where the rest of the division was [located]; and to tell them of the need for ammunition and other supplies which were then running low. His other purpose for finding the ford was that in the event it became absolutely necessary to relinquish the Timmes position it could be a line of withdrawal therefrom. Marr took one man with him, and they stumbled onto a brick roadway, which was just underneath the surface of the water and crossed the inundated area. He proceeded over it to the other side and ran into the 325th Glider Infantry Regiment.

"Informing a lieutenant colonel of that regiment about the ford, the lieutenant colonel promptly contacted General Ridgway, who ordered that battalion of the 325th to cross the ford and then to proceed to attack the Germans at Cauquigny."[18]

Ridgway ordered Colonel Millett to move his force of about four hundred twenty-five troopers from their position west of Amfreville east to join Timmes' 507th group on the western side of the Merderet River. Captain Paul F. Smith, the CO of Company F, 507th, got the troopers under his command ready and awaited the word to move out. "Just after midnight, by the light of a burning house set afire by the Germans, our force got underway with Colonel Millett and Captain Taylor leading the way and Lieutenant Roger Whiting and

I acting as the rear guard element (self appointed since apparently this function had been overlooked).

"We had ninety-six prisoners to take along and guard. The column moved out of the south end of the CP area and turned northeast toward the Amfreville-Gourbesville highway. A short time later as Lieutenant Whiting and I were patrolling the prisoner column, we heard two MG-42s firing up ahead. We moved to the head of the column where I talked to Colonel Millett. He told me that he was going to backtrack the column and try another route. I told him that Whiting and I would stay as a covering force while the column backed itself. As the column moved back, Lieutenant Whiting and I threw hand grenades and fired at the general direction of the MG-42s, distracting the attention of the gunners until the column was clear of the area. We then backtracked and eventually caught up to the column.

"When we found it, the column was halted, so we moved up the column to the location of the prisoners and sat down to rest. When the column hadn't moved in about fifteen minutes, we suspected something was wrong. We moved toward the head of the column, but when about half way to the front, we found that the front half of the column had moved off—a connecting file had fallen asleep. We were now located west of the Amfreville-Gourbesville highway.

"Suddenly I found myself in command of about one hundred fifty men and some ninety prisoners, with only a vague idea of where we were supposed to be going and of our mission when we got there. I did know however, that Colonel Millett originally was headed in the direction of the Merderet River, which was located to our east, so I decided to keep on in that direction.

"We crossed the highway and shortly thereafter met Captain [Sanford] Frank, a 507th officer, who had been with the Colonel Millett group. He said that he had missed the rear half of the column and had turned back to locate us. He thought he knew where the front part of the column was located and proceeded to lead us forward. We moved on east and slightly north, until daylight overtook us in a large square field, from which we could see the Merderet River."[19]

On the night of June 8, Lieutenant Wayne Pierce, with Company B, 325th, temporarily assigned to the 1st Battalion staff, was told of the order for an attack by the battalion. "On orders from Gavin and Lewis, Sanford made plans for our battalion to ford the Merderet River and attack the Germans holding the west bank of the river at the La Fière-Cauquigny church causeway. We were to be led across the ford of the Merderet by a 507 lieutenant [John W. Marr], who had come across the ford seeking assistance for a group of 507 men under the command of Lieutenant Colonel Timmes. These one hundred men under Timmes had been holed up at a farm and orchard since landing on D-Day.

"Sanford's plan of attack was that we proceed in a column of companies in the order of Company C, A, and B. Company C was to ford the river and turn slightly to the right and attack what we called the 'gray castle', where German troops were known to be housed. Company C was to make a show of firepower against the 'gray castle', then fall back to the farm orchard. Company A, next in line was to proceed through the orchard and then turn slightly to the left and follow a country road about one half mile to a road junction. Here they were to set up a blocking action to keep German reinforcements away from the La Fière Causeway. Company B, next in line, would pass through the orchard then turn to the left and attack toward the Cauquigny church and the La Fière Causeway. After falling back from the gray castle, Company C was to align on the right of Company B in the attack toward the causeway.

"We started moving at 11:00 p.m. along the railroad which paralleled the river. The flooded Merderet was several hundred yards wide at this point. Major Sanford went along with the lead company and I shuttled along the column to make sure that all units moved as planned."[20]

Lieutenant John Marr led the battalion across the sunken road underneath the surface of the Merderet River. "They had engineers laying this white tape going down both sides of the roadbed, for the follow-on of the column."[21]

The ford across the Merderet River north of La Fière was shallow enough that Captain Samuel F. Bassett, the battalion surgeon, was able to drive his jeep and trailer carrying medical supplies across with him. As the 1st Battalion, 325th, made their way toward Timmes' position east of Amfreville, they came under small arms fire from the gray castle to the northwest. Captain Bassett and his men "were forced to abandon our jeep and trailer in the orchard of the Jules Jean farm. We went in [to Timmes' position] on foot and set up our aid station in a shed attached to the house. The shed had stone walls and a pole ceiling, which held hay in the loft. This shed was normally used for livestock or machinery."[22]

Lieutenant Pierce was at the ford of the Merderet River, monitoring the progress of the column, when he noticed something wrong. "Standing at the turnoff spot where we were to ford the river, I realized the tail of the column had passed me; no more troops were coming along the tracks in the dark. Knowing that all units had not yet passed, I ran back along the track about one quarter mile and found the tail of the column sitting on the rails of the track resting. The man in the lead who had broken contact in the column was asleep. I shook him awake and got the men moving. We caught up with the rest of the column after we forded the river. It was a dark, black night as we forded the river. Company C made a lot of noise and drew a lot of fire in their feint on the gray castle. Company A proceeded through the orchard and moved out on the road leading to Amfreville. Company B was making the swing to the left toward Cauquigny church and the causeway as Company C came back in line. As we walked in the dark, I talked to Lieutenant Buester Johnson of

Company C. He and the men of Company C were elated. They had done a lot of shooting and felt that they put fear in the Germans. Buester said, 'They can't shoot worth shit.' Buester (or 'Rooster' as we called him) was a 'Georgia Cracker' who got along well with his men. He had joined the 325 the same day I did, in November 1942.

"Major Sanford and I along with a couple of communication men followed behind Company C in a position that we thought would put us near the center of the two attacking companies. We crossed a road that was to be one of our guiding terrain features in the attack, moved through a wheat field and came to a small orchard. Our little headquarters group took a German prisoner from the corner of this orchard. He was not a very alert outpost guard for his unit. The time was a little after 4:00 a.m., June 9. It was still so dark that you could see only a few feet in any direction."[23]

With Company B on the left moving east just north of the main road and Company C on their right crossing the fields bordering the main road on the south, the 1st Battalion, 325th, began their attack to capture the western end of the causeway.

North of the main road, Private Richard D. Weese, with Company B, could see the gleam of their bayonets reflecting the moonlight as they approached an orchard. As the company skirmish line reached the edge of the orchard, the Germans opened up with a withering fire, killing eighteen men and wounding many more. Weese continued advancing as men fell around him. "B Company moved through the orchard in the attack, made with a lot of rifle and machine gun fire from the enemy. We took up positions in a perimeter defense."[24]

Because Lieutenant Marr had already been through the area of the western end of the causeway on June 6, he was asked to accompany Company C to assist them with finding their way in the darkness.

At the same time as B Company was approaching the orchard, Company C crossed the main road that ran east and west between the causeway and Amfreville. They then fixed bayonets and spread out in a skirmish line and moved quietly east through the hedgerow-lined field next to the main road toward the causeway. They crossed through an orchard at the far end of the field and came to a sunken road. There, through a thin hedgerow, they spotted German artillery with their crews in the field on the other side. The Germans manning the guns were caught by surprise and some called out seemingly wanting to surrender, causing the Company C troopers to withhold their fire. Lieutenant Marr was with the Company C commander, Captain Dave Stokely. Marr smelled a trap. "They ran up white flags as if they wanted to surrender. But, I had already been exposed to that twice. So I indicated to the company commander, I said, 'They are not going to give up. That is a ruse to get us to expose ourselves, and then they're going to level in on us.'

"But the company commander sent this tech sergeant forward, who spoke German. He was supposed to go up and negotiate with the Germans."[25]

While this was occurring, there were a few moments of uncertainty about what to do; then the platoon in the center started to advance across the sunken road toward the Germans. Private First Class Raymond T. Burchell had an uncomfortable feeling that this was too easy as he crossed the road with the platoon. "Everything seemed to be going as planned, we were advancing, no shots had been fired, when all of a sudden, all hell broke loose. I thought we had met up with the whole German Army."[26]

The Company C platoon was caught in the sunken road, with German machine guns firing at them straight down the road from both flanks. This enfilading fire pinned down most of the company. From his position near the right flank of the C Company skirmish line, Sergeant Harry Samselle could see where most of the deadly fire was coming from. "They had a German machine gun that was upstairs in a farmhouse to our right, and they were just mowing us down. I emptied my M1 at them and I don't know what happened to them."[27]

A moment later, Samselle saw what looked like a German ammo truck coming toward them on the sunken road. He then saw Lieutenant Paul S. Kinsey, limping from a leg wound, stand up in the road to stop the truck. As the truck pulled to a stop beside him, a German in the passenger seat stuck a Schmeisser out of the window and opened up at point blank range on Lieutenant Kinsey. With lightening quickness, Kinsey grabbed the barrel of the gun, pushing it to one side, and dropped a hand grenade into the cab almost simultaneously, killing both occupants. The explosion knocked Kinsey to the ground. Samselle then saw him grab an .03 Springfield rifle. "He opened up on it, he had a rifle grenade or something. [The truck] just blew up."[28]

On the left flank of Company C, Private First Class Robert L. Swick stepped out into the middle of the road just as he looked to his left. "There was a machine gun no more than thirty feet from us and he fired on us. [Private Augustine] Mondello started talking to his mother, so I knew he was hit. The man behind me was set on fire. He must have been hit in the cartridge belt.

"I ran across this dirt road, it intersected with a black topped road. I ran across the black topped road, got into the ditch, and there was our mail orderly, [T/5 Clement L.] Gillio and a boy by the name of [Private First Class Kinard W.] Marshall. It was still dark and we could hear them moving their machine guns to fire on us across this black topped road. So Marshall threw a phosphorous grenade and when it went off it lit up all three of those [Germans] and set them on fire. Gillio said, 'Loosen my belt, loosen my belt.' I went up there and tried to loosen his belt, and he was dead."[29]

Some of the troopers tried to come to the aid of the platoon on the far side of the road, which was being fired on from three sides. Sergeant Samselle and a number of other troopers crossed the road, broke through the small hedge on the opposite side, and charged the German artillery crews. "There were seven of us crossing this wheat field and I was the only one who made it."[30]

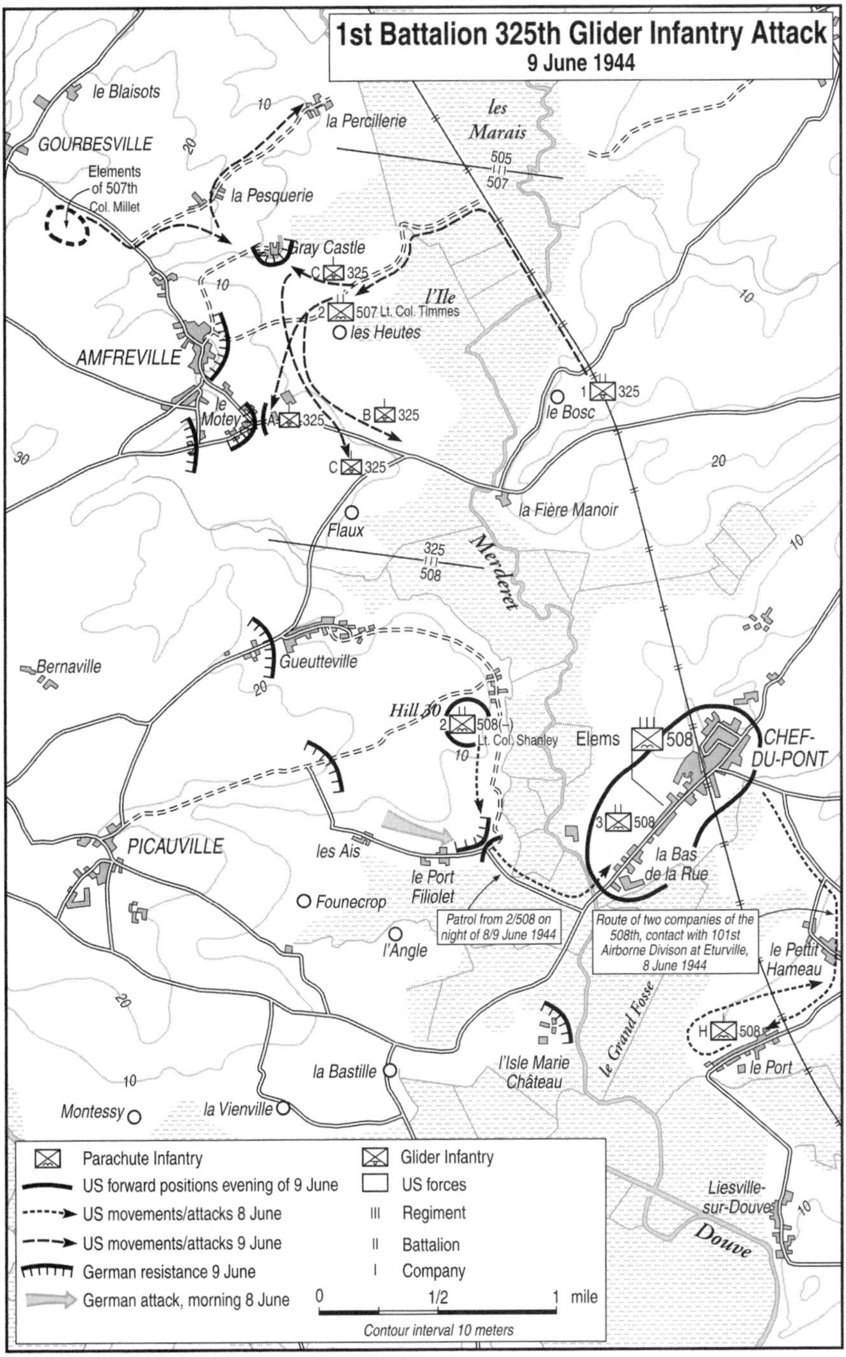
1st Battalion 325th Glider Infantry Attack
9 June 1944
le Blaisots
GOURBESVILLE
la Percillerie
les Marais
la Pesquerie
Elements of 507th Col. Millet
Gray Castle
C 325
505
507
l'Ile
2 507 Lt. Col. Timmes
les Heutes
AMFREVILLE
le Motey
A 325
B 325
C 325
1 325
le Bosc
la Fière Manoir
Flaux
325
508
Merderet
Bernaville
Gueutteville
Hill 30
2 508(–)
Lt. Col. Shanley
Elems 508
CHEF-DU-PONT
3 508
la Bas de la Rue
PICAUVILLE
les Ais
le Port Filiolet
Founecrop
l'Angle
Patrol from 2/508 on night of 8/9 June 1944
Route of two companies of the 508th, contact with 101st Airborne Divison at Eturville, 8 June 1944
le Petit Hameau
le Grand Fosse
H 508
le Port
l'Isle Marie Château
la Bastille
la Vienville
Montessy
Liesville-sur-Douve
Douve
Parachute Infantry
US forward positions evening of 9 June
US movements/attacks 8 June
US movements/attacks 9 June
German resistance 9 June
German attack, morning 8 June
Glider Infantry
US forces
III Regiment
II Battalion
I Company
0 1/2 1 mile
Contour interval 10 meters

On the far side of the road, Burchell watched some men try to make it back by running across the road, only to be cut down by machine gun fire zipping down the lane from opposite directions. "We were greatly outmanned, had walked into a trap and were taking very heavy casualties. Some of our company was surrendering, when Charlie DeGlopper stood up with his BAR blazing away, hollering to us, 'Get out! Get out! Pull back!' Charlie stood in that road, putting clip after clip into his BAR."[31]

As the six feet seven inch DeGlopper stood in the middle of the sunken road firing, the Germans concentrated their fire on him, and away from his comrades, allowing many of them to escape. DeGlopper was hit and seriously wounded, but continued to fire his BAR on full automatic. He was hit again and knocked down. He rose to his knees and continued to fire, until yet another burst struck him and killed him. He had killed and wounded a great number of Germans and had covered the withdrawal of the remnants of his platoon. Private First Class Charles N. DeGlopper would later be posthumously awarded the Congressional Medal of Honor for his courageous self-sacrifice.

Thanks to DeGlopper, Burchell was able to make it back across the road and began trying to slip away. "I was crawling back on the ground in a wheat field, a German machine gunner was cutting down the wheat above my head and it was running down my back."[32]

After the seven guys with him were cut down, Sergeant Samselle could see German infantry closing in. "That was when Captain Stokely surrendered to them. Whenever he told us to surrender, I just stuck my rifle in the ground and walked off with my hands up."[33]

As Samselle was marched at gunpoint back to the sunken road, where the Germans were rounding up prisoners, he saw his company commander, Captain David Stokely, being roughed up by the Germans. "They hit him with a rifle and broke his arm."[34]

Samselle then noticed his platoon leader lying on the ground, bleeding from multiple gunshot wounds. "We had a lieutenant [Kinsey] that was hurt pretty bad. Me and another guy picked him up and put his arms around our necks, and were carrying him. I thought he was dead and we started to lay him down, and he said, 'Don't leave me here boys.' So we picked him up and took him to a German aid station and they took care of him. Then they took us up the road and put us in a hog pen."[35]

As the Germans continued to hunt the survivors of Company C, Private First Class Robert Swick decided to leave the ditch he was in and cross the black-topped main road to get back to the field that C Company had just crossed. "I ran to the corner of that field that was no more than ten or fifteen feet [away]. I met some boy from the company. We heard small arms fire on the other end of that field. He said, 'I'll take off and you cover me.'

"I let him go—over twenty yards—nobody fired at him. So I jumped up to run to follow him. There were two German soldiers standing side by side. They both yelled, 'Halt!'

"As I was running, I turned left to see what it was, all I saw was fire coming out of those two machine pistols those guys had. I dove into that ditch again. I tried to raise up, and they fired into the hedgerow bank where I was, so I stayed down. Pretty soon, I heard some Americans talking, walking through that field coming toward me. So I raised up and hell, they were prisoners. They had German soldiers behind them. They just walked and I threw my hands up and I joined these Americans coming down. They took us to their CP."[36]

Lieutenant Wayne Pierce was with Major Sanford only about forty yards behind Company C. But because the orchard obstructed his view, Pierce was unable to determine what had become of Company C from his position. "The firefight died down to just an occasional shot and became quiet. Sanford passed the word back that it 'looks like Company C is wiped out, we had better move back.' At that, everyone in our party, except me got up and stooped over, ran back along the fence row toward the wheat field.

"I watched them go, but I was not yet convinced that Company C was finished. Small arms fire in the Company B area some distance to the left was slight to heavy. Looking back, I watched the bobbing heads of Sanford and the CP group go over a little rise in the wheat field. The prisoner was moving just as fast as his captors and appeared to be taking the same evasive action.

"There I sat, crouched on my haunches, looking and listening, very much alone. I ran to my right, past the artillery piece, across to the other side of the orchard. Running under an apple tree, my helmet was knocked off my head by a low branch. The helmet was uncomfortable to wear, but it gave you a sense of safety. I went back and picked it up, all the time expecting to get a bullet in my head. On the other side of the orchard I looked through the hedge and all about for some sign of Company C. I could hear activity along the sunken road, but could not tell if this was friend or foe. By this time it was about 6:00 a.m. and quite light. I decided that if I wanted to be around for lunch that day, I had better get moving and find some friendly troops.

"I carefully placed my dispatch case and binoculars under a bush. Then I lost no time in moving back along the orchard fence and into the wheat field. Knowing that a moving target is hard to hit, I bent over and ran. Once over the small rise in the wheat field I came upon several Company C men who told me that their company was decimated. Some men had surrendered and many were killed and wounded. With these six or eight men, I moved back to the road we had crossed when we moved up during darkness. German machine gun fire was coming sporadically down this road from the Cauquigny church area. There was a steep bank on both sides of the road where we wanted to cross. I instructed the men to go one at a time and dart across the road as fast as possible. I went last and when I hit the bank on the other side I dug into the dirt.

"Across the road we were within sight of the Jules Jean farm (Timmes' orchard). By now I had accumulated a total of twenty-four or twenty-five men, a straggler or two from Company A, [and] a few [who] had fallen back from Company B, but most were Company C. The Company C men were very demoralized. One man, Sergeant [James] Mason, was without a weapon. He told me he had gone forward to meet a German officer, thinking the German wanted to surrender. When he got close enough to see the German (it was still quite dark), the German held a pistol on him. Mason was still white as a sheet, but he got away, minus his rifle. In future action, Mason was a very good and dependable combat soldier. Another man, Sergeant Reynolds Koze, had lost his Tommy gun, but picked up an M1 rifle.

"To get some semblance of order, I organized this little band into two squads, with a sergeant in charge of each. Then I told them we were going up to help Company B. Small arms fire in the Company B area was still sporadic to heavy.

"Just as we were ready to move out, we received small arms fire from our rear, toward Amfreville. At that point, not knowing what had happened to Company A, I decided the best thing for us to do was to head for the Jules Jean farm where we could get instructions from Major Sanford. To reach the farm we had to move about one hundred fifty yards across an open field. I instructed the men to all make a dash for the farm, shooting several rounds or a clip of ammunition toward our rear (Amfreville) to give the Krauts a little distraction while we ran.

"We reached the farm buildings without a casualty. At the orchard, Major Sanford was directing the companies of the 1st Battalion into the perimeter defense the paratroopers had set up."[37]

Back in the wheat field, Lieutenant John Marr, with Company G, 507th, was with two men from the 1st Battalion, 325th, who had been laying field telephone wire behind the Company C advance. Together, they were trying to escape the killing field, crawling on their stomachs, trying to escape in the early morning light as Germans surrounded the field. As they crawled back through the wheat field, Marr suddenly heard German voices. "The Germans had displaced gunners with machine guns in behind us. So here we were, we had Germans behind us, we had Germans in front of us, and we were wondering, 'Where are we going to go?'

"We would crawl maybe two body lengths and we'd stop, then crawl two body lengths and then we'd stop. We didn't want them to see a ripple all the way through there, because we figured they would fire on us, but they never did. It was broad daylight by this time. We came to a little rise where two Germans were digging in a machine gun, right alongside that main road, so they could cover both ways up and down that road. I knew there was no way that we were going to get by those guys.

"It occurred to me that old [Lieutenant Willard] Tex Young, who was the mortar man, back in Timmes group, had collected all of the mortars that we were able to pull out of the swamp on D-Day, and he was firing them in battery.

"I said, 'Maybe we can get him on the phone.' So the wireman handed me the phone and he hooked it up to this wire. Sure enough, I was able to get old Tex, and he bracketed those people in with white phosphorous rounds. Those

Germans got up, got their gun, and ran off down the road. We were able to get back into Timmes' position that way. It was an interesting morning."[38]

Back at the German CP, Private First Class Robert Swick and the other Company C prisoners stood with their hands up, unsure of their fate. "They brought Marshall in and he was covered in blood—blood running down the side of his face, and down his right arm and chest.

"They brought one of those Volkwagen [*sic*] jeeps up and said, 'Help your comrade.'

"I stood there beside him and I said, 'Marshall, have you been hit in the arm?'

"And he said, 'Yeah.'

"So I couldn't get hold of his arm. There was no way for me to get a hold of him. So he got in by himself and he sat down.

"That [German] lieutenant said, 'Help your comrade!' and chewed me out for not helping him. A truck came and they put the six or seven of us, plus the three Germans that had been burned by that phosphorous grenade in there with us. I thought sure as hell they were going to kill us. They didn't, they just stared at us like they couldn't believe it."[39]

In the brutal fighting that morning, Company C had lost half of its strength. Every officer was killed or wounded, with the company losing a total of sixteen men killed. Lieutenant Paul S. Kinsey, who had been severely wounded, would escape from a German hospital a couple of weeks later and make his way back to American lines. He would be awarded the Distinguished Service Cross for his single-handed destruction of the German ammunition truck.

While the fighting raged around the west end of the La Fière Causeway, Captain Paul Smith, leading a force of about one hundred fifty 507th men plus German prisoners, found a field near the western shore of the Merderet River. "I decided to take up a perimeter defense of this area until we could locate the friendly troops with whom we were to make contact. Before we could occupy the entire perimeter we received intense small arms fire from the northern and eastern edges of the field. I gave orders to withdraw to the southeast keeping parallel to the river. Soon after leaving that field we encountered a small settlement of houses, from which we received heavy small arms and machine gun fire. After a quick recce I decided our best course was to go through the settlement and clean it out.

"I gave orders to that effect. This firefight lasted about an hour with roughly ten percent casualties for our force. Some of those casualties were inflicted by artillery and mortar rounds that began falling in the settlement, just as we routed the last of the Germans. Throughout this action, I was accompanied by First Sergeant Hopkins. Our force then proceeded south toward the sound of firing, which I felt sure, marked the area for which we were looking. When we had gone about six hundred yards south of the settlement, I decided we had better halt and organize ourselves into a tactical force capable of being maneuvered and to count noses.

"Accordingly we halted and took up defensive positions around a field while I began the organizing task. I simultaneously attempted to reach the Regimental CP by radio (we had one SCR 300 with very weak batteries) and since we were extremely short of ammo, First Sergeant Hopkins took a detail of POWs to salvage parachute bundles lying in the swamp bordering the river. Some of the bundles were booby-trapped, causing the loss of several prisoners, while others were lost to German machine gun fire coming from both up and down the river on our side.

"About this time I managed to reach regiment on the emergency channel. Talking to Lieutenant Colonel Maloney, acting regimental commander in the absence of Colonel Millet, I reported our position, the number of personnel available and asked for orders. A few minutes later he told me to hold position until further orders from him.

"Shortly after my conversation with Colonel Maloney, Lieutenant Colonel [Harry] Harrison from the 508th walked into our perimeter with about twenty-five or thirty men. He told me that all the original front half of our column, including Colonel Millett and Major [Ben "Red"] Pearson, had been captured that morning. He told me also that they (meaning he and the men accompanying him) had seen a large body of Germans headed our way and that our only hope of surviving was to cross the Merderet River and join friendly troops on the other side.

"I argued against such a course of action, for several reasons that I then enumerated to him. First, I had orders to remain where we were until further orders from my acting regimental commander. Second, we had our backs to the swamp and river, thereby having to defend only three sides of a field, and I felt we could defend ourselves successfully against a fairly large force. Third, we could hear the sounds of an engagement going on to our southwest, indicating that there were other American troops on our side of the river and which, I felt, were in all probability the force we initially were to have made contact with. Fourth, the Merderet River had overflowed its banks, flooding the countryside, with the result that at the point where we would have to cross, it was approximately 1,400 yards wide. Most of this was swamp and could be negotiated, but the Germans had visual command of this particular stretch of river and could annihilate our group as it crossed.

"I told Lieutenant Colonel Harrison that if he wanted to take the group he arrived with across the river, I would have no issue with his decision. He refused to take any cognizance of my arguments and informed me that he was taking over as senior officer present and for me to get four or five men and lead the way across the river. I told him that I would accede to his order only under protest, and that I wanted the order repeated in the presence of witnesses of my choosing. He agreed and repeated the order in the presence of Lieutenant Cofer and First Sergeant Hopkins.

"I then picked five men, among them First Sergeant Hopkins, and we started across. We received some fire, but fortunately none of the Americans were hit, although we did lose several prisoners. We crossed the railroad at a small station house, where I posted Lieutenant John T. Joseph and Lieutenant Horace Cofer to direct the men as they came across. We hit dry ground, where we encountered several members of the 505th PIR.

"When all were across, First Sergeant Hopkins counted heads and established a defensive position, while Lieutenant Colonel Harrison left for the Division CP, and I took our prisoners (now dwindled to twenty-six) and our wounded to the Division POW enclosure and the 505th aid station respectively."[40]

Back at the orchard occupied by Lieutenant Colonel Timmes and his men, and now joined by the survivors of the predawn attack by the 1st Battalion, 325th, Private First Class Clinton Riddle, the battalion runner, was busy digging in. "While I was digging, a shell almost dropped into my foxhole. One did drop into the hole next to me, and almost cut the soldier's arm off."[41]

Captain Samuel Bassett, the surgeon for 1st Battalion, 325th, who earlier had set up an aid station in a small shed, was working to treat the casualties resulting from the earlier fighting. "The attacking rifle companies had taken a beating in the early morning hours and found themselves overwhelmed by the Germans holding the causeway. Our shed was soon 'wall to wall' with wounded. In a lull in the fighting that morning we were able to recover our jeep and trailer, which brought us much needed medical supplies.

"As the day wore on with no way to evacuate our wounded we soon had to look for more space. I checked with Major Teddy Sanford, CO of the 1st Battalion, and asked if there was any space available in the house where he had his CP. Sanford's reaction was typical of the man and was what I expected. His answer was, 'Hell, Doc, take the whole damn house! We'll move the CP out into the field!' And he did.

"We then started to move the less serious casualties across the roadway to the house. The ground floor was soon filled, but we elected not to use the upper floor because the open windows were a choice target for rifle and machine gun fire. This set up, with casualties in two buildings had its drawbacks, for every time one of us crossed the open space between the houses he was apt to draw a round or two of enemy fire. It worked out all right however, as none were ever hit.

"We needed water in the aid station and the only source on the farm was a well with a hand pump that was located in front of the house in view and range of the German riflemen. Chaplain Henry Wall took a five gallon 'jerry' can and went out to this pump for water. The Germans were either poor marksmen or they respected his Red Cross armband, I do not know, but he brought us much needed water.

"During my service as battalion surgeon, we had only two men die in our aid station. One of them was at the Jules Jean farmhouse aid station in Normandy on 9 June 1944. We were doing a double leg amputation on this man. If we had whole blood available instead of plasma, we could have saved him."[42]

From the Jules Jean farmhouse, Lieutenant Gerard M. Dillon, with Company G, 507th, noticed the German shelling begin to slacken, followed by an assault on the orchard. "The Germans hit us about three times on the morning of D+3, but were repulsed."[43]

At 5:30 a.m. on June 9, the 505th pressed the attack north toward Montebourg Station, with the attached 2nd Battalion, 325th, attacking on the right flank of the 2nd Battalion, 505th. The 1st Battalion, 505th, followed behind in reserve, while the 3rd Battalion, 505th, guarded the crossings over the Merderet River.

The 2nd Battalion, 325th, deployed with Company E on the left, Company F on the right, and Company G following in reserve. Captain Joe Gault was leading Company F as they moved through the fields. "We soon hit hostile forces. Our losses in this operation were devastating. We reorganized the company into three rifle squads with Lieutenant [Junior R.] Woodruff commanding, and the weapons platoon under Lieutenant [Harold] Hahn.

"The first word of casualties reached us with the death of Captain Irvin Bloom [Company G commander] and the severe wounding of Captain Bob Dickerson [Company E commander]. I took a phone wire section from battalion and runners from E, F, and G Companies and put myself between the two companies coordinating the attack, with phone contact back to battalion. The radios were of no value."[44]

Medic Private First Class Edwin "Tad" Lainhart got to Captain Dickerson soon after he was wounded. "He had part of the calf of his leg shot off. A little farther along in this attack, I came upon Colonel [John H.] 'Swede' Swenson, a fearless battalion commander who wore his pistol low on his hip, like a western gunslinger. The Germans were not moving fast enough ahead of us, so Swenson ordered Company G to fix bayonets and charge. It routed the Germans, but was a costly move for Company G. I was still finding wounded three hours after the attack."[45]

In the bayonet attack, the G Company commander, Captain Irvin Bloom, was killed. Quite a few of his men were killed and wounded by German fire coming about one thousand yards to the north on some high ground on the other side of a canal, while heavy fire from a wooded area to the west hit them from the left flank.

This combat was far worse than anything Private First Class Darrell C. Dilley, with Company F, 325th, had experienced in Italy. "The Germans were hitting us with 88s and machine guns; and many of our men were going down, either killed or wounded enough, they couldn't keep going. Many of our men were calling for medics for help."[46]

For Tech Sergeant George C. Speakman, the 81mm mortar section leader of the Heavy Weapons Platoon of Company E, "June 9th was the worst day of my service life."[47]

The attack by the two battalions carried to within three hundred yards of a canal about halfway between Fresville and Montebourg Station.

CHAPTER 16

"FOLLOW ME!"[1]

As dawn broke on June 9, 1944, General Gavin, who had almost no sleep since the night of June 4, was monitoring events at his command post near the railroad overpass east of the La Fière bridge. The encircling attack by Lieutenant Colonel Teddy Sanford's 1st Battalion, 325th, had failed to take possession of the western end of the causeway. Gavin received word of the results and immediately began to make preparations for another assault. "I got the details of the failure of this attack at daylight, and by that time the situation at the bridge was becoming desperate. We could not lose a moment in forcing our way across and rescuing troops on the other side, and the German strength was obviously building steadily."[2]

General Ridgway released the 2nd Battalion, 401st, to Gavin for the assault, along with orders to seize the causeway and the western shore of the Merderet River. Ridgway also arranged for artillery support from the 155mm howitzers of the US 90th Division's, 345th FA Battalion, in addition to a company of tanks. Gavin immediately issued an attack order and sent it to Colonel Harry L. Lewis, the commanding officer of the 325th.

When Colonel Lewis received Gavin's order from his S-1, Lieutenant Vernon L. Wyant, Jr., Lewis told Wyant that an attack across that causeway was a suicide mission. Lewis and Wyant went to the Division CP, where Gavin confirmed the order to Lewis and told him that the order was to be carried out.

Colonel Lewis then reluctantly sent the attack order to Lieutenant Colonel Charles A. Carrell, the commander of the 2nd Battalion, 401st. Carrell's 2nd Battalion, 401st, had recently been transferred to the 82nd Airborne Division and was attached to the 325th as its third battalion. Upon receiving the order, Carrell felt that this attack was given to his battalion because they were new to the 82nd Airborne Division, were outsiders to the commanding officers of the 82nd, and were therefore expendable. In fact, all of the parachute infantry regiments were already fully engaged. The 325th Glider Infantry had been in reserve until the previous evening, when 1st Battalion, 325th, was sent across the Merderet River, and after having launched the unsuccessful attack earlier that morning, was now dug in with Timmes' 507th troopers in the orchard north of Cauquigny. The 2nd Battalion, 325th, had been attached to the 505th the previous evening and was at that very moment attacking toward Montebourg Station. The 2nd Battalion, 401st, was the only infantry battalion in the division available to Ridgway and Gavin for this attack.

Lieutenant Lee Travelstead was the Heavy Machine Gun Platoon leader with Headquarters Company, 2nd Battalion, 401st. "Merderet and La Fière were only names on a map when Lieutenant Colonel Carrell, our West Point battalion commander for some one and a half years, told us that we would soon attack an entrenched, reinforced German regiment that was across the Merderet causeway. As he spoke he seemed unsure in manner and speech, something foreign to his calm and stable nature. That should have been an omen.

"As I understood our orders, our battalion was to sprint across the causeway, platoon following platoon, company following company, until we reached the other side. The mission was to capture the causeway area and to attack beyond. Failure had proceeded us. It sounded like suicide. The entire span was exposed to concentrated small arms, artillery, and mortar fire.

"Since we were sort of an orphan outfit, having been taken from our own regiment and attached to the 82nd's 325th, we thought we always got the dirty work, and it looked like this time we were to go through the meat grinder so the rest could follow more safely."[3]

When Private Chester Walker, a medic with Company G, 401st, was told that the battalion was going to attack across a causeway, he wasn't particularly concerned. "What we did not know was we were going to get the baptism of fire. By not having combat experience, we had no idea what lay ahead."[4]

Seeing activity and movement on the eastern side of the Merderet River in the early morning light of June 9, the Germans began to plaster it with artillery and mortar fire.

German infantry of the 1057th Regiment occupied stone houses and barns, in addition to being dug in on the western bank of the flood plain of the Merderet River. Any assault across the long, exposed causeway would be subject to converging fire from machine guns and rifles from German positions to the north and south of the western end of the causeway. German mortars and artillery were zeroed in on the causeway and the eastern side of the river, where any attack would be launched. The defenders were backed up by tanks and self-propelled guns.

The 82nd Airborne Artillery would support the assault with the 75mm pack howitzers of the 319th Glider Field Artillery Battalion and the short-barreled

105mm howitzers of the 320th Glider Field Artillery Battalion. The 90th Infantry Division Artillery's 155mm howitzers would add their weight to the barrage and then put smoke on the causeway and western shore areas just before the attack. The commander of the 90th Division Artillery Brigadier General John M. Devine; his commander of the 345th Field Artillery, Battalion, Lieutenant Colonel Frank Norris; and Norris' executive officer, Major Lloyd Salisbury, arrived at Ridgway's command post to coordinate the barrage. Lieutenant Colonel Norris was shocked when he found out what was about to take place. "The 82nd had an appalling mission that day—to seize the Merderet crossing across that single, long causeway. Two well-defended machine guns could have denied that crossing to a regiment. Ridgway told us the plan and asked if we could help. I only had five 155mm howitzers ready right then. I told him if he could wait about an hour, I'd have all twelve of my howitzers ready. Although Ridgway had [the corps commander, General Lawton] Collins and his staff breathing down his neck, he immediately turned to Gavin and his officers and said, 'The attack is delayed.' Then he said to Gavin, 'Take these officers'—Salisbury and me—'down to the bridge and show them what you want to hit.'

"So Gavin took us down to the bridge. He had a very fine foxhole just to one side of the bridge. The German firing was hot and heavy. Gavin stood by the foxhole and said, 'You two get in there and I'll show you what we want to hit.'

"I said, 'General, that's your foxhole.'

"He said, 'You look like you need it more than I do, and besides, I want you to do the shooting.' So we got in the foxhole and Salisbury began zeroing in our batteries, using one howitzer from each. Two things about Ridgway had greatly impressed me: first his instantaneous decision to delay the attack in spite of all the high level pressure on him and second, sending a general—Gavin—to make certain his orders were carried out and that we were shown every possible courtesy."[5]

Gavin set the time for the barrage to commence at 10:30 a.m. and last for thirty minutes. A dozen Sherman tanks were lined up a couple of hundred yards east of the bridge. Gavin was depending on the barrage to keep the Germans' heads down and using speed to capture the causeway before the Germans could recover after the barrage was lifted. He believed he had done everything he could to minimize potential casualties of the men of the 2nd Battalion, 401st, in the forthcoming assault.

A little before 9:30 a.m., Gavin saw the battalion approaching the Manoir area. "I asked the battalion commander to come forward to get his orders, and at that moment he declined to go into the attack, saying that he did not feel well. He was relieved of command and another officer put in charge of the battalion."[6]

Gavin felt badly about having to take such drastic action. "Carrell had never been in combat, never been in a position like that. But I had to do it. The whole battle was hanging by a thread."[7]

Colonel Lewis was forced to name Carrell's successor on the spot. He chose the Regiment's S-2, Major Arthur W. Gardner, to lead the battalion. Lewis passed over Major Charles Moore, the battalion's executive officer, because he wanted one of the men he knew and trusted leading the battalion. But men and officers of the battalion believed Major Moore was now leading them.

Lieutenant Richard B. Johnson, a platoon leader with Company E, 401st, certainly believed that Moore was in command of the battalion. "Major Moore, in temporary command, ordered Company G, 401 to lead the attack in a column of twos, one file on each side of the causeway, and then to peel off to the left on the far shore. Company E, 401 was to follow, also in a column of twos, and to turn right to clear the north shore of the bridgehead. When Captain Charles Murphy, E Company's commander, relayed these orders to us, he included his own order that 1st Platoon, of which I was platoon leader, would lead the attack for the company. My only comment was that I would go first. I was recalling the Infantry School motto, 'Follow Me!' instead of all its texts on tactics, which prescribe that the troop commander stays behind to control and direct his men forward. It was obvious that merely telling the platoon to cross the causeway, after which I would join them, was not the thing to do under the circumstances. No tactics were involved, just a bull-like rush.

"All that Murphy could say was, 'God bless you,' while two big tears rolled down his cheeks. Lieutenant Bruce Booker, Company Executive Officer volunteered to help my Platoon Sergeant, Henry Howell (a full-blooded Indian) keep the platoon and the company following me."[8]

The plan called for Company F to follow the two leading companies and attack west through Cauquigny toward the village of Le Motey. Headquarters Company would follow Company F and establish a reserve force on the west side of the causeway.

Ever since receiving the attack order, Lieutenant Lee Travelstead had worried about getting the men of his heavily laden heavy machine platoon across that long causeway. "Spinning through my head were the thoughts that it would be dangerous enough for the riflemen and their officers who would be like moving targets in a carnival shooting gallery, and especially the 'sitting duck' predicament of my own men. They would carry, in addition to their personal weapons, their heavy machine guns, tripods, and ammunition, with each man being laden with some fifty pounds of equipment.

"While extremely visible, the riflemen could run and dodge, would be a fast moving target for aimed fire, and the rest of the fire inferno was just a matter of luck if they passed through it. My men would be a bull's eye kind of target. It did sound like a death sentence for them.

"Our officers took what the men took, and I think even more, on every level. However, I would be armed only with my Tommy gun, equipped with an old gangster-like round [drum magazine], instead of the long clip, because it carried more rounds, and my own personal .45 revolver (against regulations).

I would be carrying no fifty pounds. That made me even more reflective on the set-up.

"When I talked to my sergeants, they looked at me in disbelief. Immediately they reminded me of the loads of the men, some of which made even long, tedious marches a struggle. But run? Forget it!

"About that time I got the word that Lieutenant Colonel Carrell had been relieved. That was a shock, as I had known him so long, and thought I knew him so well. As far as I was concerned, we had no battalion commander."[9]

Lieutenant Colonel Norris, CO of the 90th Division's 345th Field Artillery Battalion, was a West Point classmate of Lieutenant Colonel Arthur A. Maloney, the executive officer of the 507th, who stood six feet four inches tall and weighed 250 pounds. Several minutes after he had finished zeroing in his 155mm guns, a German artillery shell exploded near Norris. "I looked around and there was Art Maloney, flat on his back, with a lot of blood coming out of his head. We went over and I saw his eyes start fluttering, then he was conscious. A hell of a big shell fragment had gone through his helmet and gave him a big flesh wound in the head that bled like hell, but wasn't dangerous. They took him off a few yards, propped him up against a tree, then a medic put a bandage on his head. Maloney put his helmet back on and stood up again, ready to go. Pretty terrific."[10]

General Gavin was concerned about the 2nd Battalion, 401st, being able to carry out such a difficult attack, without any previous combat experience. He called Lieutenant Colonel Maloney, the 507th executive officer, and Captain Robert D. Rae, with Service Company, 507th, who was commanding one of the three provisional companies of the 507, to join him. Rae and his company had relieved the 1st Battalion, 505th, the previous day. "General Gavin told me that my company would be used as reserve in case the glider infantry attack faltered, that we were to provide supporting fire during their attack, but that we were not to move out except on his command. He asked that I personally remain in my present position so he could locate me if necessary."[11]

Maloney called a meeting of the 507th officers present. The 507th S-2, Lieutenant John H. Wisner, listened as Maloney explained the plan. "When what he was asking for became plain, every man there turned pale. Silence.

"Then one officer spoke up, 'Colonel, it will be a slaughter! They can fire on us from three sides for five hundred yards.'

"Maloney said, 'I know, but Timmes is over there and we must go to his help.'

"Silence once more. . . . Timmes was on the other side being methodically cut to pieces by the Germans. A great deal of the regiment and even the division were embarrassed. . . . I looked carefully from face to face for a man to make a counter argument . . . no one could. No one could deny that we owed it to Timmes, no matter how thick the bullets on the causeway. I had been contemplating the Merderet for three days and I could not think of any other way to get across."[12]

Captain John Sauls, commanding Company G, 401st, led his men single file through the Manoir and behind a stone wall on the south side of the road near the bridge. The rest of the battalion followed Company G in column through the Manoir. While waiting behind the protection of the stone wall, each man now had time to think about his mortality and confront his fears of the upcoming attack. They would run across an exposed 500-yard-long causeway with Germans firing every weapon at their disposal from the front and both flanks in an attempt to stop them.

At precisely 10:30 a.m., a deafening artillery barrage began hitting the German positions on the far side. Gavin watched as shell after shell from thirty-nine artillery pieces, twelve tanks, and a platoon of 81mm mortars exploded almost continuously on the other side. "We poured everything we had right on top of the German positions. It was just hair-raising. The noise, the unbelievable shrieking of the shrapnel, the screeching of the German horses—they had a lot of horse drawn artillery—the cries of the men who were hit, the tank guns, machine guns, mortars, BARs, carbines, rifles. Soon, Germans in a bad state of shock, their faces covered with dust, and blood trickling from their mouths, began coming across the causeway with their hands up."[13]

Gavin looked at his watch—it was 10:45 a.m.; time for the 2nd Battalion, 401st, to make their charge. "They had been instructed to run as fast as they could across the causeway—I gave them the signal, and from their positions, crouching along the side of the road, they began to run."[14]

Upon seeing Gavin's signal, Captain John Sauls turned to his Company G, 401st glider troopers, who were sheltered behind a stone wall of the Manoir that fronted the river, and shouted, "Follow me!" Then he courageously led his men forward in a run across the causeway. As some of his men followed Sauls onto the road, over the bridge, and across the causeway, the Germans opened up with a tremendous amount of machine gun and rifle fire. And then shortly, mortar and artillery rounds began hitting Company G on the causeway. Men began dropping all along the column. The wounded and dead began to fill the areas on both sides of the causeway. As Company G trooper Private Melvin L. Johnson moved across a gap in the stone wall, bullets from a German machine gun covering the gap struck him in the head. The sight of Private Johnson's body caused several men to freeze, holding up the entire battalion strung out in a column behind them.

Company G medic Private Chester W. Walker was about halfway back in the company column. "Machine guns were firing from different directions and mortar shells were plastering the area. About the time I reached the entrance of the causeway, the medic with me [Raymond Michalski] took a bullet in his wrist. I helped him bandage his wrist and by that time wounded glidermen began to multiply. I encouraged anyone who could walk or crawl to get behind the stone wall where it would be safe to patch up their wounds."[15]

Brave men of the 3rd Platoon, Company B, as well as the 1st and 2nd Platoons of Company A, 307th Airborne Engineer Battalion, now moved out on the causeway and began removing mines and other debris that would impede, injure, or kill the men making the assault crossing. They tried to figure out a way to clear the causeway of the three knocked-out German tanks just west of the bridge that blocked the roadway. However, they missed picking up one of the American antitank mines lying on the causeway road near one of the knocked-out German tanks.

A Sherman tank began moving across the causeway in support of the infantry. As it went around one of the knocked-out German tanks, it struck the mine. The tank lost one of its treads and pivoted across the road, blocking it. The explosion wounded seven men in the mortar section of the Company G Weapons Platoon. Staff Sergeant George F. Myers was hit above the eye by shrapnel but continued to lead his remaining men across the causeway.

Company E was following Company G down the path next to the stone wall, when the column stopped. Lieutenant Richard B. Johnson, leading Company E's 1st Platoon, went forward to investigate. "Following G Company, I led my platoon down this lane to the river, where I found to my dismay, that the column had come to a halt.

"A paratroop captain was there, shouting, 'Get those men moving,' but even if they had been able to hear him over the thunder of outgoing and incoming artillery, I doubt if it would have helped. Nor would it have helped if I had joined in his shouting, so I took a deep breath and walked out over the bridge. Just at the crown of the bridge was a G Company man [Andrew Pavka] whom I happened to know. He was flat on his stomach and peering over the bridge, when he suddenly started to slide back down.

"I said, 'You're going the wrong way, Pavka.'

"And he replied, 'I can't help it, sir, I'm hit.'

"It was now past 10:45 and the artillery barrage was due to lift at eleven. The situation had to be stirred up, so I walked farther out on the causeway. A G Company man whom, minus his right hand, I ran in to later in an English hospital, told me, 'Lieutenant, we thought you lost your f___ing mind.'

"I found a G Company officer [Lieutenant Frank E. Amino] huddled with his men on the south bank of the causeway and asked him, 'Frank, what's the holdup?' He replied he did not know, and it was obvious that he had no intention of going forward to find out. (His caution didn't avail him, however, for he was killed a few days later.) I later learned that Lieutenant Don Wason, leader of G Company's 1st Platoon had been shot dead as he reached the west end of the causeway and that was the cause of the stoppage. Don was a fine fellow and a good friend."[16]

Miraculously, Captain Sauls, Lieutenant Wason, and about thirty of his men made it through the hail of bullets and shrapnel to the western end of the causeway. But, Lieutenant Wason was killed shortly afterward as he single-handedly took out a German machine gun and its crew that had been firing straight down the causeway toward the bridge. Lieutenant Donald B. Wason was later posthumously awarded the Distinguished Service Cross for taking out the machine gun that was the cause of so many casualties on the causeway.

Captain Sauls ordered Sergeant Wilfred L. Ericsson to lead the group to the left as ordered, to begin clearing the German positions on the riverbank south of the causeway as planned. Sauls remained at the western end of the causeway, ready to direct more of his men in the proper direction.

But, concentrated German machine gun, mortar, and artillery fire cut down those following Captain Sauls' small group. They hit the ground, seeking what little protection the shoulders on both sides of the causeway offered. Captain Sauls and his small force were now isolated and heavily outnumbered by the Germans on the western shore.

As the Company G troopers behind Captain Sauls clogged the ditches on both sides of the causeway, wounded survivors who could walk began to filter back, and the attack looked as though it would fail. Lieutenant Johnson knew that he would have to keep Company E moving or they would become pinned down and slaughtered by the incoming mortar and artillery fire. "I had no intention of letting G Company hold us up until the barrage ended, so I moved forward to the burned out tank, where I could see that nobody was using the right side of the causeway. On the spot, I decided that E Company would have to cross single file on the right. I looked back and saw only one man following me. He was a former sergeant in Company G, who had been busted to private in the marshaling area and transferred to Company E for trying to inflict on himself a sufficient wound to keep him in England. I shouted to him that I wanted E Company to start moving forward, but the noise was such that he couldn't hear me. I took a round of ammunition from a belt hanging out of the tank and scrawled a huge 'E' in the burnt paint on the side of the tank.

"He nodded and slid back, and I was shortly joined by Lieutenant [Bruce] Booker and [Anthony] Plicka, the point of my 1st Squad. I told Booker what I had in mind, and then Plicka and I took off as fast as we could go for the west bank. I was running somewhat down the north side of the causeway, in the faint hope that it would at least shelter my legs from any fire coming from the south side, when I stepped in a hole and sprawled full length in the swamp. Plicka put the butt of his rifle down to me and heaved me out of the swamp.

"A little farther on, Plicka suddenly took a swan dive forward, landing on his belly with his rifle cradled in his arms, as if he had spotted a target to fire on from a prone position. I said, 'Don't stop here, Plicka,' to which he replied in the exact same words Pavke had used, 'I can't help it, sir, I'm hit.' "[17]

Private First Class Lewis A. Strandburg, a radio operator with Company E, was burdened by his heavy SCR 300 radio. "Before we had advanced only a short distance I was forced to abandon my set and proceed as a rifleman. Each weapon had to be employed to its best advantage. The attack was a mad scramble across the bridge with many of my buddies dropping like flies all around me. We were inclined to crawl on our bellies, but the shout of 'Get up—Keep moving!' was what we heard above the din. Looking up, I saw my division commander, Major General Ridgway, and my regimental commander, Colonel Lewis, standing in the middle of the causeway urging the men forward. A lot of respect and admiration was earned by those two commanders that day and if they had not shown the guts they had, we probably would have remained on our bellies and been blown away by the enemy mortars, artillery fire, and rifle fire. In the middle of the causeway were three knocked out tanks, which had to be dragged out of the way before we could advance."[18]

General Ridgway knew that he had to keep the men moving forward. "The fire was so intense that the men were physically recoiling. We just grabbed our men and walked them out. The physical force of that fire pouring in was such that they just stopped and started back—not from cowardice at all. We just grabbed them by the shoulders and led them down into this thing and pushed them. We were right there, too. This is where your personal presence makes a hell of a lot of difference. I haven't the slightest doubt that if Gavin and I and the battalion commanders had not been there, that crossing of the causeway would not have succeeded. The men would not have gone."[19]

Witnessing this was Colonel Norris, who was directing the fire of the 90th Division's artillery from Gavin's foxhole. This was Colonel Norris' first taste of combat. "The most memorable sight that day was Ridgway, Gavin, and Maloney standing right there where it was the hottest. The point is that every soldier who hit that causeway saw every general officer, and the regimental and battalion commanders right there. It was truly an inspirational effort. And to top it all off, Ridgway, with all the problems he faced, had the courtesy to go out of his way to thank me for our artillery support."[20]

Ridgway, standing on the causeway road, seeing the attack held up by the mass of men around the wreckage of the crippled tanks, ran to help the troopers from Company A and B of the 307th Airborne Engineer Battalion. By that time they had gotten the Sherman running and were attempting to tow the three burned-out German Hotchkiss and Renault tanks off of the road. At the same time, the medics began helping the wounded back to the protection of the Manoir area. All of this served to further congest the causeway.

As Company E platoon leader Lieutenant Johnson neared the western end of the causeway, he turned to see if the rest of his platoon had followed him. "It was now eleven o'clock and the artillery barrage had turned to a few rounds of smoke. A German machine gunner north of the causeway recognized the significance of the smoke, raised his head and started firing. Most of E Company was strung out behind me, and fully exposed to his fire, but he was mostly concerned about me, his closest threat. Fortunately for me, his gun must have struck the stop at the right-hand end of its traverse arc and stopped his swing just in time. I think I could feel the breeze of those bullets passing just inches behind me. If I had been one step later, I believe he would have sawed me in half. At this point, my kidneys injected a huge dose of adrenaline into my bloodstream and I began to believe I was untouchable, could lick any number of Germans, and go all the way to Berlin.

"At the end of the causeway, I turned right to get behind that gunner, but he saw me coming, and tossed a potato masher hand grenade at me, which landed in a huge and squishy pile of farmyard manure, and sank. The books all say that in such a case one should grab the grenade and throw it back, but none of them tell you how to find it in a manure pile. To get away from the grenade, I executed what must have been a world record for the standing sideways broad jump, which landed me back in the swamp again, but a piece of the grenade sliced through my left arm.

"This time it was my turn to play with a hand grenade, but we were only about twenty feet apart, and I guessed that the German manuals also instruct one to throw a grenade back. Our grenades were timed to explode four and a half seconds after you pulled the pin and let go of the handle. Four and a half seconds were just too long for our close proximity. Accordingly, I pulled the pin, let go the handle, and counted 'one a thousand, two a thousand, here, you bastard!' and I lobbed it into his foxhole. Sure enough, he picked it up to throw it back and it exploded in his hand!"[21]

As a few Company E men arrived at the western end of the causeway, they followed Lieutenant Johnson's example and began attacking German positions fronting the river north of the causeway. Company G troopers were doing the same to the German positions firing from the hedgerow bordering the flooded area south of the causeway. German machine gun and rifle fire began to slacken somewhat. However, the mortar and artillery fire continued unabated.

Now, Captain James M. Harney led Company F, 401st, forward as the wounded from both Company G and E crawled, hobbled, and struggled back to the relative safety of the Manoir wall. A good number of Company G and E soldiers clogged the ditches on both sides of the three knocked-out German tanks, together with the lone American tank that had hit the mine, causing the Company F glidermen to pile up in the ditches behind. Captain Harney tried to lead his men through the maze of wounded and dead bodies that littered the causeway road and ditches.

Private First Class Lucius Young, with Company F, somehow made it through the mass of dead, wounded, and those taking cover in the ditches and moved as fast as he could across the causeway. "I got about three-quarters of the way over and saw smoke coming from a church steeple on my right front. I stopped and fired, and then was hit, I guess from a mortar shell. . . . My left shoulder and neck felt like a hot poker had been drawn across them."[22]

Lieutenant Lee Travelstead watched the carnage and confusion on the fire-swept causeway and waited for his turn to lead his heavy machine gun platoon across. "The rifle companies charged across the causeway. Of course, it was not one fast sprint. The dead and wounded littered the way. Some made it. Some did not. Some stopped. Some had to be prodded. Some had to be led. It is still a wonder that any made it.

"The machine gunners and I waited. Deep in my pocket, I had a small box of chocolate covered cherries that I had carried from England for some special occasion. This was it. I devoured the entire box waiting for the order to jump-off.

"It came. Was it high noon? My orders were, 'Keep your heads. Keep your equipment. Keep moving. That way we'll make it.' We moved through the fire like a mule pack train. I moved as did the human mules, steeling myself so as not to run forward. Mules doing the job of race horses is apt. It was unreal. The men—beasts of burden—could not really even defend themselves. About all I could do was lead them, and anyway, that is what combat command, at any level, is all about.

"Dead and wounded were everywhere as I moved steadily along. Then I saw General Ridgway in the causeway trying to remove a cable from the track of a tank to clear the way. It was bad enough for any of us to be there, but a two-star general? He neither looked up nor spoke, he was so intent. I looked. I said nothing.

"The other heavy weapons outfit, the mortars, led by Lieutenant [Joseph I.] Shealy was in our predicament. He was almost immediately seriously wounded. Some of our men were killed—others wounded. General Ridgway just kept working at the tank, apparently oblivious to all else."[23]

The situation was critical. Gavin, observing the confused scene, believed that the attack had stalled. He turned to Lieutenant Colonel Maloney and Captain Rae with the 507th and said, "All right, go ahead! You've got to go!"[24]

At that moment, Rae turned to his men, about ninety 507th paratroopers. "I gave the command, 'OK, let's go to the other side'—moved out on the road leading to the causeway, saw that my men were moving out on the double, then took off for the other side.

"We had many casualties crossing the causeway and constantly tried to get the glider infantry to join with us. It is unbelievable the number of men that were immobile on the shoulders of the causeway. Many were wounded, but the majority were not. Many of these soldiers were caught up in our momentum and started moving again."[25]

As he crossed with Rae, Corporal Howard R. Huebner, with Company C, 507th, saw bodies everywhere. "I remember going around one of the tanks and stepping on dead soldiers and [being] under fire from the Germans."[26]

About the same time as Rae's 507th paratroopers were making their way through the mass of men on the causeway, Ridgway and the engineers moved one of the knocked-out tanks out of the road. Ridgway now stood in the middle of the road shouting, urging the men forward. Private First Class Strandburg got to his feet and began to run. "Finally, the way was cleared and our boys poured through like water from a broken dam. We would run a few yards, hit the ground, catch our breath and make another dash. This went on for what seemed like an eternity, every minute of which, I was expecting to feel the piercing of an enemy bullet or a piece of shrapnel."[27]

Lieutenant Travelstead and his men, burdened by their heavy machine guns, tripods, and ammunition, trudged steadily toward the western end of the causeway. "Without stopping to fire, most of my men and I got across the causeway. That was the first goal—just to get on the other side alive.

"Then, we were to set up our guns to give their withering fire. I fired away at a two-story building and its windows from which we were being pinned down by heavy fire. Something happened and we moved."[28]

Captain Rae, at the head of his company, made it to the western end of the causeway without being hit. "As we arrived on the other bank, a few glider troops headed to the left as they left the causeway. I led my men to the right. There was small arms fire coming from a cemetery on the right. We cleared this area and followed a few Germans as they ran from the cemetery and church area. Things became quiet on this side of the church area, so I gathered my company from a field or orchard area and returned to the road at the causeway. We then saw two or three German prisoners heading towards the American side."[29]

As Rae and his men were destroying the Germans around the church, Lieutenant Travelstead led his heavy machine gun platoon west on the main road to a crossroads. "Then I saw Captain Harney [Company F], one of our company commanders and a close personal friend at that time and a man on whom I could rely. He was trying to organize the attack. He was, while not in fact, but in act, the battalion commander. He was taking hold of us and many paratroopers from the 507, I believe. It was not every man for himself, mainly because men need leaders; but it was every group for itself. Captain Harney was trying to do something.

"He sent me up the right fork [to the northwest] with my guns and most of my men. Along the road, in the small ditches for a little cover, we moved steadily, looking for a good place to set up the machine guns to accomplish something—not just shoot to be shooting. There was enough noise.

"Perhaps because of the exposed nature of the causeway, although I moved forward, ahead of the machine gunners, I walked in the ditches beside the road. The advance slowed.

"Suddenly, down the center of the road there came running toward me a helmetless (red-haired or curly haired, or both) paratroop lieutenant. He shouted something to the effect, 'Show ourselves; and move 'em.' I stepped with him into the middle of the road.

"To me there was one big satisfaction because there we were, paratroopers and glidermen fighting side by side, with the paratroopers, often a standoffish lot from the glidermen, willingly taking orders from me as though I were one of them. After Normandy the paratroopers and glidermen had a sense of camaraderie that had never before existed, and I would hazard a guess that much of it had to do with that day on the Merderet.

"The fire and blasts were withering. Soldiers pinned down shouted for the machine guns. Sergeant [Joseph] Sindad, who was with me, and I moved forward. His machine gun had no tripod. He had no ammunition. Without a word, he ran back through the rain of small arms fire, mortars, and artillery some one hundred fifty yards to get ammunition. Back he came with the ammunition.

"Sergeant Sindad, cocky and sure of himself, together with Sergeant [Ernest] Neinfeldt, a real solid young man, and Sergeant [Harold J.] Lowe, calm and taciturn, were all with me. I am sure there were some of the other men, such as Viera, who was always around.

"Sergeant Sindad ran forward to set his gun up at a high point, so he could rake the area. I do not know whether he had a tripod, or how he did it, but he was hard at work."[30]

Captain Harney, the CO of Company F, 401st, decided to push his men up the main road toward Le Motey to give depth to the bridgehead, instead of filling the center and joining flanks with Company E on the right and Company G, 401st, to his left. At about this time, Rae and his 507 troopers had completed the destruction of the Germans at the church, Rae also led his 507 troopers west on the main road. "I then took my men up the road leading from the causeway towards Le Motey. Just before I reached the crossroads at Cauquigny, I met a glider captain [Harney] standing with one or two enlisted men. Some small arms and machine gun fire was coming from the fields to the right and left of the road leading to Le Motey. The heaviest fighting seemed south from the crossroads. I asked him where he needed help. He said the road leading south.

"I split my force, sending half down the road leading south with Lieutenant [James D.] Orwin and another lieutenant. Lieutenant Orwin was killed during this action. I took the balance of my men and headed for Le Motey."[31]

Staff Sergeant Edward J. Jeziorski, with Company C, 507th, who had double-timed across the causeway carrying a .30-caliber light machine gun on his shoulder, took the road to the south and immediately ran into resistance. "At a road fork, a German MG-42 took us under fire. [Grover] Boyce and I set our light machine gun up on the road shoulder and knocked him out. We then continued our advance.

"We hit a field with close to two hundred black bicycles in it all scattered around . . . must have been a German mobile reserve force that we hit just as they were arriving. We knocked the hell out of them."[32]

Meanwhile, Captain Rae and the other half of his men moved up the road toward Le Motey behind Company F, 401st. "A short distance from the crossroads, I ran into a group [of Company F troopers] pinned against the embankment of a ditch by machine gun fire. I worked my way up the ditch and knocked it out with a hand grenade. We kept moving to Le Motey, the Germans were moving out now. When we reached Le Motey, a glider machine gun crew had set up two guns at a crossroads. Right after we arrived, artillery started pounding this area."[33]

Unknown to either Rae or Travelstead, US artillery had been ordered to fire on Le Motey. This was because of an assumption that any German counterattack would come down the main road through Le Motey toward the causeway. This artillery fire was meant to interdict any German movement east on the road through Le Motey.

Captain Rae and his men got to Le Motey just as Travelstead and his machine gunners began raking the retreating Germans. Travelstead was standing in the road, observing the fire of his machine guns as the artillery hit them. "Just at that moment in the attack, two paratroopers stepped beside me in the center of the road, as if to be bodyguards, and as one, we were blown into a ditch to the left of the road. I lay motionless under them waiting for them to get up. Not one moved. Then I knew they were both dead.

"Was I dead? I heard nothing. Under them, I saw nothing. I was stunned. Was that my heart that missed a beat? If so, I must be alive.

"I dug myself out from between the two dead paratroopers, who must have taken the brunt of the explosion and shrapnel, and by fate or who knows what, had saved my life. I had never seen them before. I never knew who they were.

"What was wrong? I was not dead, but the world seemed quiet. Then, I realized I was deaf.

"I reached for my Tommy gun and noticed my arm was stiffening. I saw blood oozing through my upper sleeve. I started to get up to walk and my leg was stiff. I looked down and saw blood coming through my pants leg. (Luckily I was not seriously wounded, and the deafness from the concussion wore off.)

"Heavy artillery and mortar fire was falling directly on us. It was probably zeroed in on the fork or crossroads directly to our front. It seemed to me a combination of our own and that of the enemy. I sent as runners the fastest and most dependable men available to the rear to see if they could get the barrage lifted before it killed all of us. I know I sent two men and it might have been three, and the numbers I sent was for one reason—I did not think one man would make it. Maybe none would. That was our communication set-up. There was no change from 2000 years ago.

"My top sergeant, Sergeant Dyer, raced to my aid. He, and it might have been Sergeant Lowe or [Leonard] Viera looked at me in disbelief. Sergeant Dyer, a hard-nosed Tennesseean was shaken to see me. I guess [I] looked awful. He wanted to carry me back to the aid station personally, but it was not possible because he was now in command.

"I worked my way back along the same ditches, now filled with the dead and wounded of the paratroopers, glidermen, and Germans. It was some five hundred yards to the aid station, which turned out to be the same building that I had fired into when I crossed the causeway.

"Propped up against the stone wall, I remembered then, as now, the trite phrase, that you never hear or see the one that gets you. I noticed for the first time that my wristwatch had been blown from one wrist and an ID bracelet from the other.

"I could not, and cannot forget the two paratroopers who, in a matter of seconds, almost as angels, had stepped to my side, taken the explosion and shrapnel from me and died instantly. Why?"[34]

Because Harney and his men were deployed across the main road from Le Motey to the causeway, Rae had planned to deploy his men on their right flank. But a short time later more glider infantry arrived, so Rae decided to get his 507th troopers resupplied. "We needed ammunition, this area was quiet, so I took my men and headed back to Cauquigny. When we arrived at the crossroads, they were in the process of establishing a regimental CP. Colonel Lewis was there and I believe a major, too. This was the first time I had seen a senior officer since I crossed the causeway.

"I reported to Colonel Lewis and asked if we should return to the other side of the causeway or remain with him. He told me to go stay in the orchard behind the CP and wait for further orders. I left a man on the road with instructions to send all paratroopers to the orchard. It was not long before the remains of the group I had sent south from the crossroads, reported in. It was about noon now, so we ate and rested. Except for some sporadic sniping, everything was quiet. We killed one sniper in a tree during this time.

"I received word to report to the regimental CP. If I remember correctly, it was General Gavin who told me a patrol had been sent out to contact Colonel Timmes, but they were not able to get through. He told me he wanted me to take my men and contact Colonel Timmes. We had no trouble reaching Colonel Timmes."[35]

Because Harney had pushed his force up the main road instead of tying in with Company G and Company E on each flank, dangerous gaps existed between the three companies. The withdrawal of Captain Rae's forces unknowingly amplified the problem.

As each company tried to establish a line, German pockets that had been bypassed opened up on them from the rear. Then they were hit with German artillery, mortar, and automatic weapons fire. This caused Harney to withdraw his force near Le Motey to the right in an effort to find Company E on his flank. About the same time, Company E withdrew to its left looking for forces with which to join flanks. As both companies withdrew, Harney's men ended up two hedgerows behind Captain Murphy's Company E force. Unwittingly, some men in Company E, after being fired upon from the rear, took off, causing a momentary panic, when word spread from those men that the Germans were counterattacking.

While this was taking place, Company G moved to its right looking for contact on their flank. It was at about the time that Rae and his men were moving north to contact Timmes that German artillery began to fall. Company F and Company E were subjected to an intense barrage for about an hour, followed by the sight of enemy troops moving across the fields to their front. German mortar fire was particularly heavy, in an attempt to keep the glidermen from raising their heads as the German infantry closed in. But as soon as the mortar fire lifted, the Company E and F troopers rose up behind their hedgerows and delivered a devastating torrent of fire on the oncoming German infantry, knocking them back.

Private First Class Lewis Strandburg, with Company E, 401st, a radio operator without his radio, had been fighting as an infantryman since shortly after the initial assault. "We were able to repulse the first attack, but they regrouped and attacked again. This time we had a little more difficulty, but again we were able to fight them off."[36]

As this was occurring, Captain Rae and his paratroopers were returning from their mission to contact Timmes. "When I reported back, Colonel Lewis ordered me to move forward and plug a hole in the defense line."[37]

Rae took his men west from the church to the third unimproved road, where he ordered his men to dig in along a hedgerow line running north. "We had set up a position and were digging foxholes when mortar shells started raining on us, and the sounds of a counterattack drew ominously near. We had a good position and were set up to hold it.

"I heard someone shouting, 'Rae.' It was General Gavin. He told me he wanted me to move forward. We went into Le Motey and stayed at the crossroads. We received artillery fire and small arms until midnight. We were relieved the next morning after the 90th Infantry Division passed through Le Motey."[38]

While the 2nd Battalion, 401st, and Rae's 507th troopers were battling to hold the bridgehead, Colonel Roy Lindquist, the CO of the 508th, was ordered to take one battalion and assist in expanding the bridgehead south to make contact with Shanley's troopers on Hill 30. Taking a mixed group of 508th troopers across the causeway, Lindquist moved south against almost no resistance to Hill 30. A short time before the arrival of Lindquist and the relief force, Lieutenant Colonel Louis G. Mendez had arrived on Hill 30 with ten men, after spending the last three and a half days moving east in search of friendly forces.

The next morning at 5:00 a.m., the 358th Infantry Regiment, 90th Division, crossed the Chef-du-Pont Causeway without enemy resistance and passed through the 508th lines, while the 357th Infantry passed through the 2nd Battalion, 401st lines at 5:40 a.m. as both regiments attacked west. The 1st Battalion, 325th, and the 2nd Battalion, 401st, remained in their positions acting as a reserve in the event of an enemy counterattack. The 507th assembled east of the Merderet River, while 508th, less H Company, which was guarding the southern flank of the division at Le Port, assembled on Hill 30.

On the morning of June 10, Private First Class Clinton Riddle, with Company B, 325th, returned to the small orchard where his company had been caught in a devastating crossfire of German machine guns the previous morning near Cauquigny. "One of my best friends and eighteen others lay dead in this little orchard. They were all in a line, just as they had entered the orchard in an attack. You could almost step on the bodies, from one to the others. One of the boys had his hand extended straight up in the air as though he was reaching for someone or something. He was wearing a pair of black gloves that probably somebody had sent from home."[39]

South of Hill 30 near the village of Montessy, Corporal Kenneth Merritt and about forty survivors had been holding roadblocks around a key road junction and been surrounded by German forces since the afternoon of D-Day. "We had been in combat for four days, and we only jumped with three meals. I was giving Private First Class Circelli water through a blood plasma tube. He was one of the blood plasma patrol members who got back to our position all shot up. He asked me when did I think the seaborne troops would arrive. I was thinking [of] how to answer Private First Class Circelli—I looked up and saw a 2½-ton truck, American truck, coming towards us. At that moment, I knew the seaborne [invasion force] had arrived inland. It was the Texas/Oklahoma Division—the 90th Division.

"They picked up all of our wounded and evacuated them to the rear. Captain [Jonathan] Adams moved up to Hill 30, where the 508 Regiment was now being assembled. We got our first hot meal in five days. The next three days were spent regrouping the units, issuing new weapons, and getting ready for our next mission. I was promoted to sergeant, since my section chief, Sergeant John Pavlick, got killed on the first day."[40]

By June 10 in Graignes, southeast of Carentan, Major Charles Johnson, the executive officer of the 3rd Battalion, 507th, had organized 173 officers and men from the 507th, 7 troopers from the 101st Airborne, and a glider pilot into a perimeter defense of the town, awaiting a link-up with forces coming from the beaches.

Lieutenant Francis E. "Frank" Naughton, with Headquarters Company, 3rd Battalion, 507th, was called to Major Johnson's CP and given an order to blow a bridge on the road that led south from Carentan in order to eliminate that route for their withdrawal. Naughton blew the bridge "just as the Germans were attempting to force its crossing. After the bridge was blown, a sharp firefight ensued, and the American force of about twenty-five men was able to drive a force of about the same size into the surrounding swamp."[41]

Captain Leroy David "Dave" Brummitt, the S-3 of the 3rd Battalion, 507th, and second in command at Graignes, received some ominous intelligence from one of the reconnaissance patrols. "On D+4 a German scout was killed. His

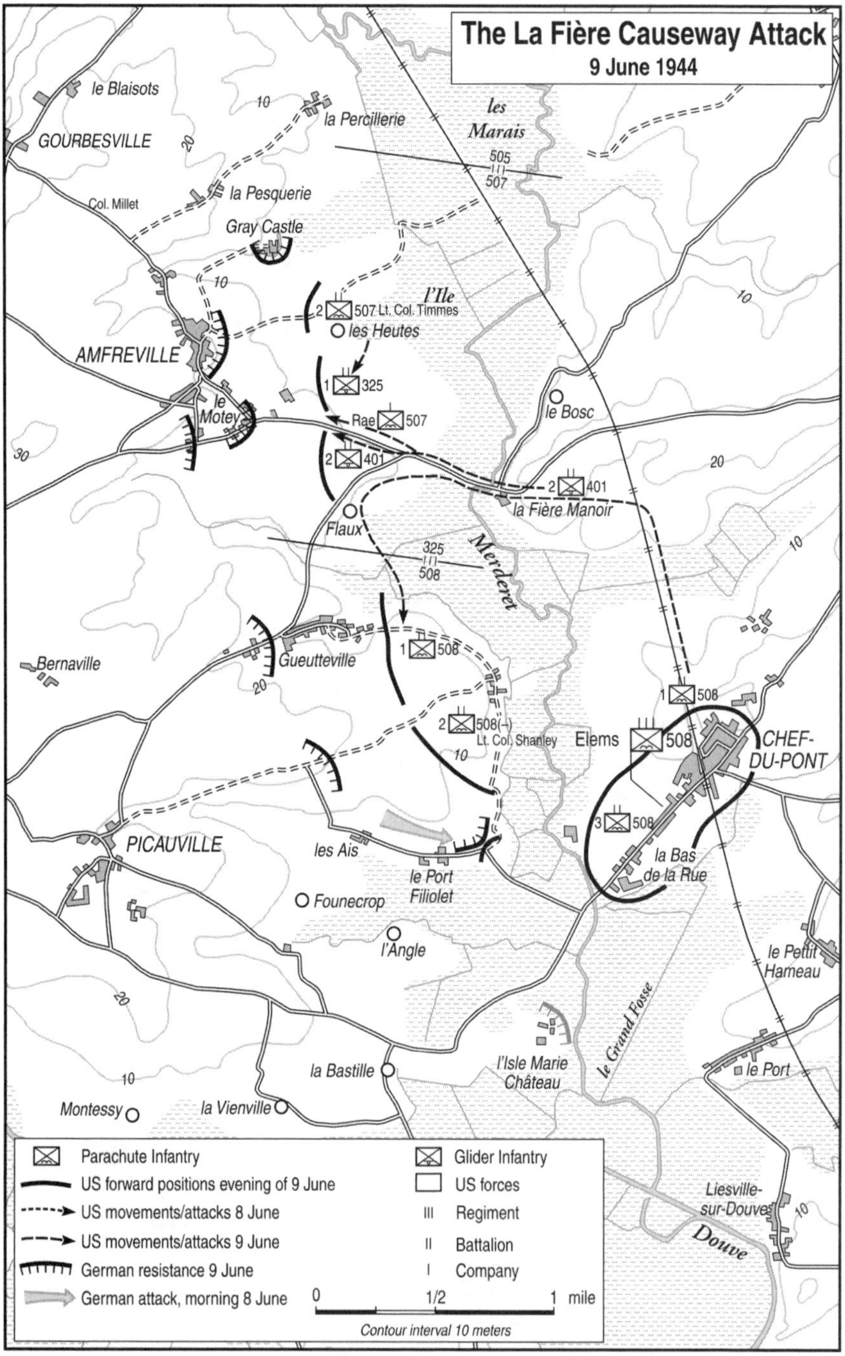

The La Fière Causeway Attack
9 June 1944
le Blaisots
GOURBESVILLE
la Percillerie
les Marais
la Pesquerie
Col. Millet
Gray Castle
l'Ile
507 Lt. Col. Timmes
les Heutes
AMFREVILLE
325
le Motey
Rae 507
401
le Bosc
la Fière Manoir
Flaux
Merderet
325
508
505
507
Bernaville
Gueutteville
508
508(–)
Lt. Col. Shanley
Elems
508
CHEF-DU-PONT
PICAUVILLE
les Ais
le Port Filiolet
Founecrop
l'Angle
la Bas de la Rue
le Petit Hameau
le Grand Fosse
l'Isle Marie Château
le Port
la Bastille
Montessy
la Vienville
Liesville-sur-Douve
Douve
Parachute Infantry
Glider Infantry
US forward positions evening of 9 June
US forces
US movements/attacks 8 June
Regiment
US movements/attacks 9 June
Battalion
German resistance 9 June
Company
German attack, morning 8 June
0 1/2 1 mile
Contour interval 10 meters

papers identified him as a member of the reconnaissance battalion of an armored division."[42] The scout was a member of the 17th SS Panzer Grenadier Division, moving north to attack the beachhead around Carentan.

At 2:00 p.m. on the tenth, the 1st and 2nd Battalions of the 505th began an assault to capture Le Ham and Montebourg Station. Lieutenant Colonel Mark Alexander was still in command of the 1st Battalion, 505th, after the deaths of Majors Kellam and McGinity on June 6. "Lieutenant Colonel Bill Ekman had requested that I give the attack order. My order was for the 1st Battalion to lead, followed closely by the 2nd Battalion. After the 1st Battalion had taken Montebourg Station, the 2nd Battalion was to take the lead, turning to the left forty-five degrees and take Le Ham."[43]

As the attack was under way, Private First Class Arthur B. "Dutch" Schultz, with Company C, 505th, noticed one of his buddies, Private First Class Raymond Gonzales, who had seen two of his closest friends killed during the first couple of days of the invasion. "He cried over their deaths and swore that he would avenge their deaths by not taking any prisoners.

"I ran by a wounded German soldier lying alongside a hedgerow. He was crying in a loud voice. I passed by him and stopped, for some unknown reason, and turned around. I saw Gonzales had put the muzzle of his rifle between the eyes of this German, while asking if he had a pistol. A moment later, Gonzales pulled the trigger. There wasn't the slightest change in his facial expression. I was both awed and appalled by what I saw. Most of me wanted to do what Gonzales had done. Along the way, I had been taught that a 'good German is a dead German.' "[44]

Everything seemed to be going as Alexander planned it. "The first part of the attack worked fine, and the 1st Battalion with a beautiful smoke screen got into and cleared Montebourg Station with minimum losses. While we were still clearing the village, Colonel Ekman, the 505th CO, came up and wanted to know what I was doing waiting on the east side of the bridge. I told him I was waiting until the battalion had cleared the village. We were standing at the northeast corner of the arching bridge over the railroad. In spite of my telling him that a German machine gun located on the road to Le Ham was firing on the bridge, he started to cross it. The Germans opened fire on him and he had to make a running jump off the rear end of the bridge. Colonel Ekman left to check on the 2nd Battalion. After we had cleared the village and the 2nd Battalion had passed through, I set up a CP about seventy-five yards east of the railroad overpass.

"The 2nd Battalion was one half hour late in following, giving the Germans time to get set on the other side of the village, and they stopped the 2nd Battalion cold just beyond the village."[45]

Private First Class Irvin W. "Turk" Seelye was advancing across open ground southwest of Montebourg Station with Company E, 505th, as the 2nd Battalion took over the attack. "Our skirmish line was spotted by the enemy

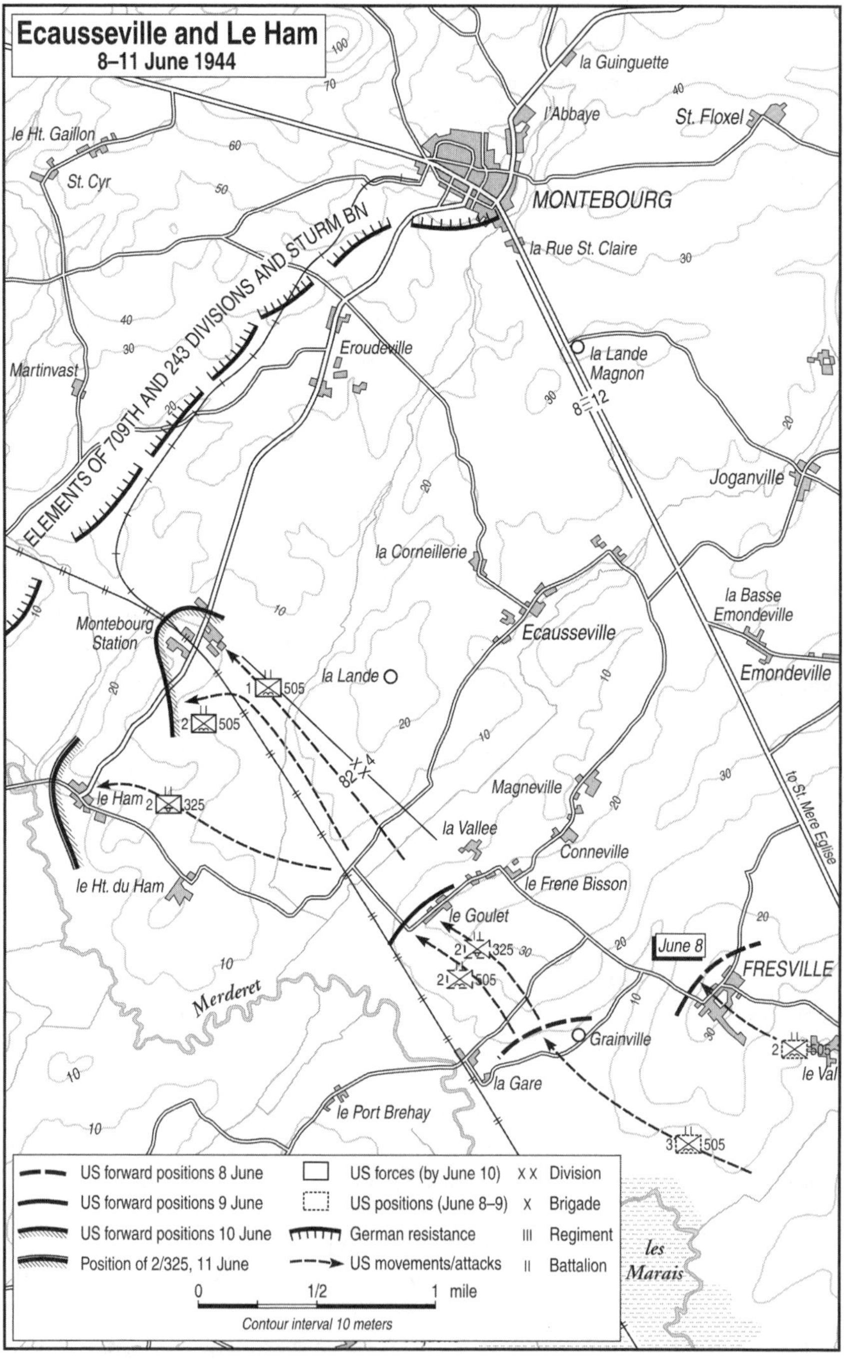
Ecausseville and Le Ham
8–11 June 1944
la Guinguette
l'Abbaye
St. Floxel
le Ht. Gaillon
St. Cyr
MONTEBOURG
la Rue St. Claire
ELEMENTS OF 709TH AND 243 DIVISIONS AND STURM BN
Eroudeville
la Lande Magnon
Martinvast
Joganville
la Corneillerie
la Basse Emondeville
Emondeville
Montebourg Station
Ecausseville
la Lande
1 505
2 505
82
Magneville
le Ham
2 325
la Vallee
Conneville
le Frene Bisson
le Ht. du Ham
le Goulet
2 325
2 505
June 8
FRESVILLE
Merderet
Grainville
2 505
le Val
la Gare
le Port Brehay
3 505
to St. Mere Eglise
les Marais
US forward positions 8 June
US forward positions 9 June
US forward positions 10 June
Position of 2/325, 11 June
US forces (by June 10)
US positions (June 8–9)
German resistance
US movements/attacks
Division
Brigade
Regiment
Battalion
0 1/2 1 mile
Contour interval 10 meters

as we crossed a railroad grade. Artillery—air bursts, were directed toward us. We passed through a lightly forested area. Corporal Ralph H. McGrew, Jr. was killed by a sniper. At about 17:00 hours, Germans were spotted up ahead. Shortly thereafter a mortar shell exploded at my side. I was blinded, [had] broken bones, and [was] bleeding. I spent the next twelve months in an Army hospital."[46]

Alexander decided to go forward to see if he could give the 2nd Battalion a hand. "In a reconnaissance with my artillery observer, I had spotted a German multiple-firing railroad gun, I think a 40mm 'pom-pom' north of the village. We brought in artillery fire on the gun and silenced it. The 1st Battalion was receiving a great deal of fire, including a lot of 'Screaming Meemies' from the north on our right flank."[47]

The 2nd Battalion, 505th, kept attacking until it reached the edge of Le Ham that night, but was ordered by Lieutenant Colonel Ekman to withdraw about 11:00 p.m. after savage fighting. Several German counterattacks during the night were repulsed.

On the morning of June 11, the 2nd Battalion, 325th, was brought up. Ekman got support from the newly arrived 456th PFA Battalion, with a fifteen-minute barrage. The 2nd Battalion, 505th, probed the German positions, while laying down a base of fire, while the 2nd Battalion, 325th, assaulted the town. Captain Joe Gault led Company F, 325th, forward into the teeth of the German-prepared fortifications east of Le Ham. "We moved out and advanced down a slight incline to a small brook. The fire was spasmodic to the brook, but accurate, and upon entering the brook, all types of enemy fire broke out and the brook was also mined with antipersonnel mines. Sergeant Forest Nipple, a squad leader from the 2nd Platoon, was hit by such a mine and died on the spot. I advanced on up the slope and noticed Sergeant Robert McCarthy had been hit in the head. He was staggering around firing his rifle up in the sky. [Lieutenant] Colonel Swenson had been hit in the stomach and was trying to get up and move on."

One of the 2nd Battalion, 325th medics, Private First Class Edwin "Tad" Lainhart, moved through the storm of lead and shrapnel to tend the wounded, falling all around him. "I found my best friend, [Private First Class] Herbert Sanderson [Company G, 325th], mortally wounded. When I came upon him the first thing he said to me was, 'Lainhart, I thought you were never coming.' In training, he would always remark when passing the medics . . . 'Lainhart, if I ever get wounded, I want you there pronto!'

"Well, I did not get there 'pronto' and due to my delay and no whole blood, Herb did not make it. On this same round, I found [Lieutenant] Colonel John Swenson propped up against a tree, wounded badly. Someone had put a bandage on him, but he was in severe pain. I looked at his wound and asked him to let me give him a shot of morphine. He replied, 'No, that would knock me out, and I need to be alert and know what is going on.'

"I rushed back to the aid station and got two litter squads. One picked up Swenson and the other went after Herb Sanderson."[48]

Intense German fire had stopped all of the rifle companies in their tracks. With Swenson and the other two rifle company commanders down, Captain Joe Gault, the CO of Company F, 325th, tried to get the 2nd Battalion reorganized and moving again. "We were pinned down by small arms fire. I looked down to my left and here came General Ridgway and his aide—standing tall. His words were, 'Captain Gault, this is not a voluntary proposition. Move your men out.'

"The fire became so severe that we had to move forward by crawling. We advanced on a machine gun that was giving us immense problems. Grenades knocked out the gun and its gunners, and one gunner was set afire by a phosphorous grenade. After knocking out the gun, we advanced on toward our objective.

"At a farm barn we captured several Germans. We regrouped and jumped off again, not far from Le Ham. Because we had been ruffled up and had lost a good many men, as we advanced the men began to run and yell. In the only charge I ever saw or participated in, we moved into Le Ham.

"Sergeant Fred A. Mason from Ridgeville, Indiana, led down a hedgerow. I was second and behind me was Sergeant Albert Kost from Weirton, West Virginia. All of F Company came rushing behind us and as we were just through town, an artillery shell landed very, very near us. Sergeant Mason was hit in the foot. Sergeant Kost, behind me was mortally hit and died screaming as I administered morphine to him. Again, I was not hit—hard to explain. We took up defensive position and came under the heaviest 88 fire of the Normandy offensive."[49]

By about 8:00 p.m. on Sunday, June 11, the 2nd Battalion, 325th, had secured Le Ham at a tremendous cost. The 2nd Battalion, 325th, which had fought valiantly, was released from attachment to the 505th and rejoined the 325th the following morning at 10:00 a.m. The 505th remained along the eastern side of the Merderet River, patrolling across the river until relieved on the evening of June 12–13.

That same Sunday morning, as the 2nd Battalion, 325th, was attacking toward Le Ham, in Graignes many of the 507th troopers were attending Mass in the local church when word came that a large German force was approaching the town. Lieutenant Frank Naughton, with Headquarters Company, 3rd Battalion, 507th, immediately grabbed his weapon and ran to check the defensive positions. "The attack was certainly not a surprise, and it was badly organized, resulting in what had to be a piecemeal effort that lacked coordination. Nevertheless, it did provide a sample of the firepower that was available to the Germans, even if in using it, they exposed themselves unnecessarily by failing to use covered approaches. The attack was short lived, about thirty minutes in all, and in truth had the effect of buoying the Americans who were then secure in the knowledge that they had inflicted heavy casualties on the enemy, while sustaining only a few casualties.

"It was about an hour before the next attack came, and it was much heavier and was supported by continuous heavy mortar fire. At one point in the battle, the perimeter was almost breached, and it was only the rapid movement of elements to meet shifting threats that the position held. Again, the Germans sustained heavy casualties. Trucks could be observed moving from collecting point to collecting point, where their dead had been piled for pick-up.

"Our mortar fire had been extremely accurate. Also, hard work in preparing machine gun positions paid off as large numbers of Germans had attempted to attack through the crossfire of two or more guns. However, our casualties had begun to mount, and the aid station was filled to overflowing.

"The lull after this second attack, an attack which had gone on for some forty minutes, was ominous. During this respite, those soldiers who were able to inch forward could observe some activity going on to their front (west and southwest) and could hear the sound of vehicular movement. This, in particular, had a disquieting effect. Once again however, the interaction with the citizens of Graignes helped prepare for the next German assault. Carrying parties, sometimes consisting of children, supplied food and water. Other citizens assisted in the redistribution of ammunition, which was running low. And, a few carefully selected citizens sallied forth, under direction of the mayor, on one pretext or another to get some idea of what the enemy was doing. At the aid station, women were assisting the battalion surgeon and his few medics cope with the demands of the wounded in the face of pitifully few medical supplies. And always, the mayor and his principal subordinates stood by to help; theirs was a calming influence on the townspeople, many of whom were in the church during the actual fighting, and so far, the church had not had a direct hit. It was during this lull that the area in an arc north and east of Graignes, comprised mostly of swampland, began to produce a threat from Germans evacuating Carentan or from positions north and west thereof. Attracted by the din of the battle in Graignes, they appeared to hesitate in their movement toward the village, especially when they were taken under fire by sniper and mortar fire. Their presence, though, served notice that this one area of withdrawal would be infested with enemy.

"This, then, was the situation that existed at dusk when what proved to be the final assault was launched. Whatever mistakes the Germans made in their preceding assaults were converted to 'lessons learned' as they now launched a truly coordinated attack. It was obvious at once that the attacking force was at least twice the size of the one that preceded it. Moreover, it had the support of both heavy mortar and 88mm antitank guns, and the fire of these weapons had a devastating effect. An early salvo destroyed the belfry of the church and succeeding salvos systematically reduced other buildings and prepared positions to shambles. With the loss of the belfry went observation for mortar fire (the mortar platoon leader and his assistant were killed) and soon the mortars were elevated to the maximum degree and the remaining rounds poured into the tubes to try to stop the attackers at the forward edge of the battle area.

"The defenders had no place to go, stayed and fought, firing every available weapon until there was no more ammunition to fire. This state of affairs came a lot sooner than expected, so numerous was the attacking force. Nevertheless, the attacker paid dearly and at every point of attack. Estimates of enemy KIA, compiled from French sources, ranged from five hundred to one thousand. One pair of machine guns caught several score of Germans in an open area and despite the reduced visibility, was able to stave off an early breech. The Germans did break through, however, and when they did, it seemed that every soldier was firing a machine pistol, albeit in most cases indiscriminately. Many were observed to be wearing black uniforms, giving substance to an early report that at least a part of the attacking force was composed of SS troops. They were numerous, so numerous in fact that it was possible for some soldiers to sink deep into their deep foxholes and literally wait until they had been overrun and then, while [*sic*] the Germans systematically destroying the town and rounding up its staunch citizens, slip into the swamp. Two squads were able to escape in this manner."[50]

Captain Dave Brummitt was the S-3 of the 3rd Battalion, 507th, and was second in command at Graignes. "As the last position was being outflanked, I ordered the crewmembers of the remaining light machine gun to withdraw to a previously designated fallback position. During the movement, both crewmembers were killed. I discarded my carbine, scooped up the machine gun (minus the damaged tripod) and the box of ammunition and leaped over a stone wall from which two troopers were giving me covering fire. As I reached their side, both were killed by small arms fire. I swung the gun around, and steadying it, fired a burst in the direction of the enemy fire. I heard no more from that sector. There was a lull in the fighting, and not having received any recent communication from Major Johnson, I moved to another firing position behind a stone wall near the church.

"Battalion Sergeant Major [Robert A.] Salewski approached me with information that 'Major Johnson gave the order to abandon the position and attempt to return individually to friendly lines. He and others in the command post have gone.' I walked over to the command post and found the report to be accurate. I did discover, however, that the Battalion S-1 (Lieutenant [Harry E.] Wagner) plus a number of other troopers were still in firing positions nearby.

"Later, it was reported that Major Johnson had been killed during the move. The battlefield was silent as I pondered this information and automatically I began an estimate of the situation. Darkness had fallen some time before and the German attack had ceased, perhaps for the night. However, they most likely would resume at daylight. Our chances of survival would be slim indeed if we continued to defend the position. A night withdrawal to my earlier recommended, march-plan assembly area, for those of us remaining, appeared to offer a chance to reach the 507th area. From the assembly area, we could move into the swamps and thereafter implement my march-plan toward the 101st Division.

"It appeared that we were the last remaining members of the 3rd Battalion Headquarters and Headquarters Company. I gave the S-1 and sergeant major an order to 'round up all the people you can find and follow me.' Still carrying the machine gun and box of ammunition, I led the way to the assembly area. Except for my having stumbled into a water-filled ditch, the march was reasonably silent and without incident. Upon arrival in the assembly area, I passed the machine gun to a trained gunner, posted sentinels, dispersed the men in hedgerows for concealment and instructed them to get some rest. In an effort to ascertain our strength, as daylight broke, I passed my pocket notebook around with instructions [for everyone] to jot down their names. Shortly thereafter, a sentinel observed another group of troopers approaching. It turned out to be a group led by Lieutenant Naughton and included Captain [Richard H.] Chapman, the Headquarters Company commander. After a discussion between Captain Chapman and myself, it was agreed that I would assume command of the entire force. The names of the new arrivals were jotted down and passed to the battalion sergeant major as an abbreviated 'morning report.' Our total strength was eighty 3rd Battalion troopers, seven 101st Division troopers, two Spaniards and perhaps a French citizen.

"Since we had no food and only the water in our canteens, a foraging party consisting [of] the two French speaking Spaniards and a French citizen was dispatched to obtain food using French Francs obtained from the officers' escape kits. Also, two small boats were obtained for use in crossing any deep water, including the canals, on our planned march the following night. The foraging party was successful. During the day, we cleaned weapons, checked remaining ammunition for redistribution and rested in concealment. Fortunately, we were not discovered by the Germans, and the few nearby French people did not reveal our presence. After nightfall, we began the march through the waist to chest-high water of the swamp. I designated one man as 'point' to lead the way, using his compass along the predesignated route, while I followed a few paces to his rear, sighting through my compass as a double check. Soon, we became confused, so I took the point, where I remained for the rest of the withdrawal. As we encountered a canal, we made use of the boats for ferrying and were able to reach our midpoint objective, a small spit, by morning nautical twilight. We still were undetected by the Germans, and again sought concealment in the hedgerows until resuming the march the following night. Without losing a man, we reached our objective on June 13, spotting a reconnaissance element of an armored cavalry unit in close proximity to the 101st Division."[51]

After the Germans captured Graignes, they massacred all of the wounded paratroopers, the battalion surgeon, and his medics, 24 in all. They also executed the two town priests and two women for helping the medical team tend to the wounded. A total of 32 of the town's citizens were killed during the fighting or were executed, and another 44 were imprisoned for collaboration. The German attack and revenge had destroyed 66 homes, partially damaged 139 more, and destroyed the church.

However, the gallant stand by those few 507th paratroopers contributed substantially to the success of the Normandy campaign, by delaying and inflicting heavy casualties upon the 17th SS Panzer Grenadier Division. Captain Frank Naughton, with Headquarters Company, 3rd Battalion, 507th, summed up their achievement this way: "For five days, the Americans were able to outwit, out maneuver, and out fight a German force that desperately needed the road network that Graignes overlooked, whether to evacuate Carentan or reinforce it."[52]

In recognition of their great courage, sacrifice, and battlefield performance, the 325th Glider Infantry Regiment would later be awarded a Presidential Unit Citation. The Headquarters and Headquarters Company of the 82nd Airborne Division were awarded a Presidential Unit Citation for their performance in the June 6–9 actions. The 507th Parachute Infantry Regiment would later be awarded a Presidential Unit Citation for holding positions west of the Merderet River, tying down large enemy forces, and for the assault crossing of the Merderet River.

CHAPTER 17

"MY GOD, MATT, CAN'T ANYTHING STOP THESE MEN?"[1]

The 508th Regimental Combat Team was formed consisting of the 508th Parachute Infantry Regiment (PIR); the 319th Glider Field Artillery (GFA) Battalion; Batteries A and B, 80th Airborne Antiaircraft (Antitank) Battalion; Company A, 307th Airborne Engineer Battalion; and a platoon of Troop B, 4th Cavalry Reconnaissance Squadron. The 508th RCT was given the mission of forcing a crossing over the Douve River to establish a bridgehead at the town Beuzeville-la-Bastille. The assault was scheduled for one minute after midnight on June 13. Engineers from Company A, 307th, would row Company F, 508th PIR, across the river in assault boats. The 319th GFA Battalion would provide supporting fire for the crossing. The remainder of the 508th would cross the river over a causeway on foot at 4:00 a.m.

On the night of June 12, Private First Class Dwayne T. Burns, with Company F, 508th, followed the man ahead of him in the column, trying not to lose contact. "Lieutenant [Hoyt T.] Goodale, who was our acting company commander, led us down to the Douve River. We waited on the bank for two hours. We had a reporter from *Life* magazine who asked us our names and where we were from. That would be something if they used our story! At midnight, we very quietly got into assault boats and started for the south bank at Beuzeville-la-Bastille. This action worried me because F Company had never seen an assault boat, much less crossed a river in one. Besides, it didn't look like much of a boat to me! I was a poor swimmer and being loaded down with combat gear was not going to enhance my chance of getting across if the Germans caught us out in the middle of the river.

"We paddled very quietly and all went well. I was surprised at how warm the water felt when my hand dipped into it. 'Just right for a Saturday night bath,'

I thought. 'Good Lord! If the wind is right, the Germans will smell us coming!' We hadn't had a bath in twelve days! While we still were a long way from the bank, we stopped paddling and slipped over the sides of the boat. The water at this point was about four feet deep, but I was glad to get out of the boat. We sloshed along for another hundred yards before reaching the bank.

"As we came out of the water, two German tanks drove up the road. I don't think they knew that we were in the area, because both were knocked out with one bazooka round each. Lieutenant Goodale then radioed back for artillery. It must have been heavier than anything we had ever used before for we could hear it coming from a long way back. It sounded like they were throwing boxcars at the Germans. We lay there, hugging the river bank as the town exploded, thanking the good Lord that it was ours coming in."[2]

During the fifteen-minute barrage, engineers from Company A, 307th, began work to repair the bridge blown by the Germans over the Douve River that had created a gap about mid-way across the causeway. Burns felt the ground shake as the artillery hitting the town sounded like one continuous explosion. "After the artillery lifted, we attacked the town. By five o'clock in the morning the regiment was across the bridge and on its way to the next objective."[3]

As Company F was wiping out the defenders in Beuzeville-la-Bastille, the 1st Battalion, 508th, crossed the causeway, turned southwest, and moved toward Cretteville. A combat patrol under the command of Lieutenant Courtney M. Weaver, Jr., led the way. As they approached the town they heard the sound of tank engines. One of the patrol's bazooka gunners, Private Robert B. White, was called up front. "There was a two story, long, house at a crossroads, the only thing there. We moved up behind it and got the bazooka loaded.

"Lieutenant [Rex G.] Combs said, 'I'll cover you.' We stepped out from the corner of that house and blasted this tank and 'Hack' [Private First Class Paul A. Haskett] had a bazooka and he went around the other side and blasted the other tank. We found out they were sitting there with the engines running and the radios on, and there was nobody in them. So we threw a white phosphorous grenade in them and moved out."[4]

The 1st Battalion moved through Cretteville about 7:45 a.m. and continued toward Coigny. The 3rd Battalion and regimental headquarters, which had crossed behind the 1st Battalion, moved south in the center of the bridgehead to Taillerfer, which it reached by 7:00 a.m. There, it formed a perimeter defense that blocked the road between Pont Auny and Hotot.

Next to cross the causeway, the rest of the 2nd Battalion pushed south on the eastern side of the regimental sector toward Baupte. Company E took the lead and were met by two tanks sent north from Baupte. Corporal Robert B. Newhart and his platoon heard the tanks approaching. "A very little tank came down a narrow wagon track between two hedgerows. We used our Gammon grenades. The crew popped out firing—we returned fire. The two crewmen died—none of us were hit."[5]

At 11:00 a.m., the 1st Battalion knocked out five French Renault tanks at Feacquetot, and at about 4:15 p.m., entered Coigny, their objective. They formed a perimeter defense. About 7:00 p.m., Companies A and B, along with two 57mm antitank guns, moved to clear the area around the town. Company A ambushed and wiped out another five Renault tanks before returning to the battalion perimeter.

As the 2nd Battalion got within a mile and a half of Baupte, they were hit by heavy machine gun and small arms fire. The battalion formed a perimeter defense and sent out patrols to try to determine the strength of the enemy. The patrols reported that the opposition consisted of an enemy battalion, supported by tanks and artillery. At 4:15 p.m., the battalion attacked, with Company F on the left, Company D on the right, and Company E following in reserve. Accompanying the battalion were two 57mm antitank guns of Battery A, 80th AA Battalion. The assault ran into fierce German resistance.

The Germans counterattacked with infantry and tanks. Staff Sergeant Richard E. Rider immediately deployed his 57mm antitank guns to stop the threat. He directed their fire while exposing himself to fire from both of the tanks and German infantry firing machine guns in support of the counterattack. When one of his guns was attacked by four Renault tanks and a Sturmgeschütz assault gun mounting a 75mm high-velocity gun, Rider took over for the gunner. While under heavy fire from the German armor, Rider quickly knocked out the first vehicle, then calmly destroyed the next two, causing the remaining tanks to pull back. Rider moved the gun to another location and when the tanks attempted to move, he ambushed both, destroying them. Staff Sergeant Richard E. Rider would later be awarded the Distinguished Service Cross for his outstanding courage and leadership.

After his company had been stopped by 20mm antiaircraft fire, Private First Class Burns got the word to take cover. Just moments later, the German positions began to get pounded by artillery, courtesy of the 319th and 320th GFA Battalions, as Burns and his buddies watched. "After an artillery barrage, good old F Company was on its way again."[6]

The 2nd Battalion infantry eventually prevailed in the fight, which lasted over an hour, destroying four 20mm antiaircraft guns and a number of machine guns, and killing a great many Germans in the process. They drove the surviving enemy back into Baupte.

As Company F moved into the outskirts, Burns found himself in a cemetery. "At first I thought that this was great luck as I made my way forward, slipping from tombstone to tombstone, until the firing got heavy and a machine gun opened up around me and I had them ricocheting off the tombstones all around me, and I had them coming at me from all directions. 'Damn! I have to get out of here,' I muttered. 'This is a hell of a place to die!'

"Using what cover I could find, I started working my way over to the edge until I came to a fence. I lay there waiting for things to quiet down. When the firing eased off I came up and over the fence in one motion, making a dash across the street and into the doorway of a building. We worked all the way through the southern part of town. Heavy fighting lasted more than an hour as we went from building to building. While F Company was fighting in the south part of town, E and D Companies were fighting in the northern part."[7]

Northeast of the town, Company D ran into a company of German infantry and several tanks defending a vehicle park. After clearing the northern part of Baupte, Company E moved out to assist Company D in wiping out the vehicle park. Bazooka teams from the two companies knocked out another ten Renault tanks, and the few remaining Germans fled, leaving about fifty vehicles behind. As Corporal Robert Newhart with Company E entered the park, he noticed a large amount of food left behind by the fleeing enemy. "We finished their food. Someone discovered a locked box. They blew it open to discover a box full of money. Pictures were taken of guys lighting cigars with money. Most of the money was burned, but most everyone kept a souvenir."[8]

After securing the town, Private First Class Burns was taking it easy. "We had been fighting all day and were getting some well deserved rest behind some of the houses in town when we heard the sound of a tank coming down the main street. Sergeant Thompson and I reacted at the same time. We both grabbed our M1s and a Gammon grenade. I went around the left side of the house, but Sergeant Thompson went through the house and got there first. Just as I reached the corner of the house, I saw Sergeant Thompson throw his grenade. I watched it spinning through the air. I saw the lanyard unwind and pull the pin. It seemed to be happening in slow motion. Then, boom! The tank stopped going forward and slid sideways, right into the side of a building. The top hatch was open and we both stood there waiting with our weapons ready. It was so quiet that I could hear my heart beating. Nobody moved inside the tank.

"Sergeant Thompson yelled, 'Cover me!' and moved toward the tank, climbed up and looked down inside. 'Come here,' he said, motioning for me. I climbed up and looked in. It was a small French tank with German markings. Inside, I saw the crew. Both of them had died from broken necks. We closed the hatch and went back behind the house to finish resting. Scratch one more tank. We dug in for the night after the fiercest action the regiment had seen. We could use a good night's rest."[9]

The 508th Regimental Combat Team made contact with the 101st Airborne Division on the causeway south of Baupte. A platoon of Company A, 307th Engineers blew the railroad bridge west of Baupte, the bridge on the causeway to Baupte, and the culvert west of Hotot.

On June 13, after resting and reorganizing since the tenth, the 507th moved to an assembly area north of Picauville, while the 325th moved to an assembly area south of the town in preparation for an attack to the west the following day. The 505th was trucked to an assembly area east of Picauville where it was to remain in division reserve. The combat-tested US 9th Infantry Division would be attacking on the right of the 507th.

That morning, Captain Roy Creek, who had landed in Normandy as the CO of Company E, 507th, was now in command of the terribly depleted 1st Battalion. "On D+7 battalion commanders were summoned by Colonel Maloney to be told that the 90th Infantry Division had hit stiff resistance and that the 507th was being ordered to pass through them, regain the initiative and press the attack toward St.-Sauveur-le-Vicomte. The attack would be in coordination with the 9th Infantry Division, a combat-experienced unit from North Africa fighting.

"As I was returning to my command post, a jeep carrying two impressive looking officers stopped me as I was walking. They were big, wearing clean uniforms and big blue scarves. I was small, wearing a dirty impregnated uniform that had been submerged in the Merderet River three times, with me in it. I was for the first time aware that I needed a change of clothing. In short, I was ashamed of my unkempt appearance in contrast to their splendor.

"The larger of the two said, 'Hey, soldier, where can I find the battalion commander of the 1st Battalion, 507th?'

"I replied, 'You've already found him, I'm it.'

"He looked at me in disbelief. He informed me of his plan of attack the next morning and parted with a warning that they were combat experienced and fresh and well rested, having just landed, and that we should move as aggressively as possible in order to stay abreast. He sure didn't want to have an exposed flank. I reassured him that we would do our best."[10]

Early on June 14, Lieutenant Gerard Dillon, a platoon leader with Company G, 507th, was briefed on the plan for the attack: "On D+8 we were ordered forward again to attack in order to cut the Cotentin Peninsula. The attack was to be on both sides of the road leading toward St.-Sauveur-le-Vicomte. The 507th led this attack. The 3rd Battalion was to the right side of the road. Company G was one of the lead companies. My platoon was the lead platoon of Company G in this attack.

"At about 9:00 a.m. [on June 14] we arrived at the point where the 90th Infantry Division had relieved the 82nd on D+4, because it had not moved since relieving the 82nd. We went into a sunken road between two hedgerows and Captain Schwartzwalder ordered all of the 60mm mortars of the company bunched together to lay fire on the next hill where the Germans were dug in.

"At about 9:30 that morning we [moved] out of the sunken road and over the hedgerow. I told all of the men in my platoon that once they got over the hedgerow to start firing as fast as they could and run as quickly as possible down into the valley between the hills and up the other hill to the next hedgerow. We did this and arrived at the next hedgerow to find that the Germans had started to retreat from our advance and had moved back up the hill.

"One of my squad sergeants and I ended up looking up at a German machine gun right above our heads at the hedgerow. We both pulled the pins on our grenades and threw them over the hedgerow, and that was the last of that gun. Then, regrouping at that hedgerow, we went up to the top of the hill, which was our company objective, where we were ordered to stop and dig into a defensive position, and await the unit that was supposed to come up on our right.

"We did that and I was given Sergeant [Reynolds J.] Bello, who was platoon sergeant of the 1st Platoon, as my assistant platoon commander. He and I occupied the same foxhole for awhile and were sitting talking to each other since nothing was happening, the Germans having moved out ahead of us toward the west.

"While we were sitting on the side of the foxhole, the Germans started shelling us with mortar fire, and a mortar shell dropped to the left rear of Sergeant Bello, knocking both him and me into the hole. Fortunately, I had my helmet on. Bello did not. Bello was killed instantly. I fell into the hole with shrapnel in my back, just to the left of my spine, and another shard went through the back of my helmet and caught me behind the right ear. The helmet is what saved me. My belt stopped the other shard of shrapnel that hit me in my back.

"I was taken to the aid station, and subsequently evacuated that night down to the beach. On the following morning I was placed aboard a Landing Ship Tank and transported back to England, to a general hospital, where the shrapnel was eventually removed."[11]

As the 507th moved forward, it met stiff German resistance but continued to attack, driving the Germans before them. The attack of the 3rd Battalion, 507th, outran the 9th Infantry Division on the right, leaving their right flank vulnerable. The 3rd Battalion was ordered to turn north toward Renouf to protect the flank. The 2nd Battalion took up the drive and kept the attack rolling. But severe resistance and strong counterattacks by enemy infantry supported by tanks, combined with the depleted state of the battalion, forced the lead to be taken by the 1st Battalion, which maintained the push toward La Bonneville.

Private Chris Kanaras and what was left of Company B, 507th, assaulted a German strongpoint along a hedgerow. "After killing several Germans, a machine gun in the corner of the hedgerow stopped us. Lieutenant [James F.] Clarke took the bazooka from Marty [Freedman] and stood up to fire at the gun, but the machine gun cut him down. He was the last of our officers.

"Then the Germans laid three mortar shells on us. Several of us were wounded. I lost part of the bridge of my nose and two small pieces of shrapnel lodged in my jaw. The third shell sent a small piece in the back of my neck. I had to ask one of the wounded where I was hit. He pointed to my nose. I felt my nose and most of it was OK, so I made the other wounded take their [sulfa] pills and led them back to the battalion aid station."[12]

Captain Roy Creek's 1st Battalion, 507th, was hit by a fierce German counterattack a couple hours after it took the lead in the attack. "By noon our ragtag outfit had been motivated to outdistance the unit on our right by 1,500 yards and was being counterattacked on our exposed flank. This forced us to hold up and deal with our flank where the attacking German unit was reinforced by tanks, small French tanks, but big to us. We managed to hold what we had with help from Lieutenant Colonel Timmes until nightfall. Artillery fire during the night took a heavier toll and though we advanced another one thousand yards or so the next morning, the resistance was getting stiffer and our losses had been heavy. I myself was commanding a battalion of just over one hundred men. About mid-morning, elements of the 505th Parachute Infantry Regiment passed through, regained the initiative and pushed on to help seal off the area to the north."[13]

By 10:00 p.m. that night, the 1st and 2nd Battalions of the 507th had reached the edge of La Bonneville and, with the help of a platoon of tanks from Company A, 746th Tank Battalion, had stopped German counterattacks that had hit them that afternoon and evening.

On the left flank of the 507th, the 2nd Battalion, 401st, led the attack west on the morning of June 14. When Private First Class Lewis Strandburg, with Company E, 401st, moved through Ètienville, he found "a town that had been completely leveled by our dive bombers and artillery. Now the enemy was putting on the finishing touches with their artillery. It was early dawn when we pushed through the town, but the going was rough and with enemy artillery landing all around us, we had to pull back and try a flanking attack. Just as we started across an open field, out of nowhere came a heavy barrage of mortar fire. We were pinned down and I found myself in a mud hole huddled up to a dead Nazi. The barrage lasted some forty-five minutes and took a heavy toll. It was here that I lost one of my closest buddies, Platoon Sergeant Frank Studant. He was one of the best liked men of the company. He was killed by a direct hit while trying to scatter his men during the barrage. We had been friends since training days at Fort Bragg. That was a particularly sad day for me and for everyone who knew him. It is hard enough to see the enemy dead along the way, but extremely hard to see one of your own get it.

"After the barrage lifted, we immediately pushed forward and were able to push the enemy back without giving them the opportunity to take up defensive positions. By dusk, we had almost reached our objective. The last couple of miles we moved up the road in single file under the cover of darkness. An amazing little incident occurred that night. It seems a squad of Germans whom we had, apparently, pocketed earlier in the day, heard us marching up the road. It was so dark that night you could hardly see your hand in front of your face, and thinking it was a squad of their own troops, fell in at the rear of the column. They didn't know they were marching with their enemy and we didn't know they were German until we reached our objective and started digging in.

Suddenly, someone spotted the Germans, but being well outnumbered, they surrendered without firing a shot. They were as surprised as we were!

"That night it rained steadily, as it did a good bit of the time we were in Normandy, and we spent a cold, miserable night in muddy foxholes."[14]

The next morning at 5:00 a.m. on June 15, the 325th attacked west toward Crosville. Private First Class Clinton Riddle, with Company B, was carrying a radio during the attack. "By 08:10 we came to the first creek and received artillery fire. Company B was the only company that made it through, [along] with two heavy machine gun sections with us. We passed around a [German] tank that held us up for a while. By sundown we had gone three miles.

"Later that night, other companies took care of the tank and remaining Germans and came up to where we were. So many snipers were in the area, supplies could not get through. We didn't have any food or water. I caught some rain water during the night in my shelter-half.

"The 1st Battalion of the 325 had been replaced by the 2nd Battalion, 401st, before taking Crosville. The 2nd Battalion, 401st, after taking Crosville was to hold the high ground beyond Crosville. They became lost in the dark and Company B and the 1st Battalion had to attack and hold the area 2nd Battalion, 401st, was assigned."[15]

Lieutenant Paul Lehman, with the 3rd Battalion, 508th, a POW since D-Day, had recovered somewhat from a severed artery in his neck. At a chateau near Orglandes that was being used as a German field hospital, Lehman was put to work as the administrator in one of the wood-frame barracks housing German and American patients. "From day to day some of our wounded were evacuated by ambulance to another German hospital to the north. From D-Day plus six, the artillery of our own forces moving in from the beaches fired on the roads just to the rear of the hospital. Many [explosions] were very close and large hunks of shrapnel fell around our building. One short round actually hit the road outside the main chateau, killing a German doctor and wounding three other men.

"It was a most trying ordeal and for about three consecutive nights we lay trembling in the [wooden] building or in the lean-tos we had built outside, as the shells whistled overhead or crashed into the adjacent fields. Another frame building constructed while we were there and not a good thirty yards away, was torn in half by a direct hit. Luckily, no one had moved into it.

"We ripped sheets in half lengthwise and laid out a big panel outside our building in the letters 'USA' so that our planes would know that American troops were in the building. All of the buildings had large red crosses painted on the roofs, and we knew that they were not the targets of the artillery, but were merely close to road networks over which the Heinies were moving supplies, men, and equipment.

"When our forces had gotten to within a mile or so, evacuation was stepped up and, with only German wounded left in the chateau, we moved into the building too, so as to have better protection. The night before our forces captured the surrounding territory we had one hundred eight men there. They tried to evacuate as many as possible before the roads were cut off.

"We stalled in every conceivable way, so as to slow the process down. They would ask for, say, walking wounded and two litter cases. So we made all the wounded get into cots and act as if they were litter cases. It turned out that they moved forty-eight that last night, when it is possible they could have taken close to a hundred.

"All the next morning [of June 16] we could see American troops passing on a road not too far away. With recapture in sight, Dr. Beaudin and I took over the hospital. The pistols of the two remaining German doctors were handed over to us, as well as the keys to various supply rooms.

"Early in the afternoon, after considerable skirmishing and firing on the other side of the chateau, our troops surrounded the hospital. [They] passed out cigarettes and rations to our [wounded patients] and it was really a happy occasion.

"Soon they moved on after making arrangements for the evacuation of the wounded on the following morning. The following day they were evacuated, the most serious cases first. Then the doctor, myself, and a number of aid men got transportation back to our unit.

"First we reported in to higher headquarters. While there newspapermen took our pictures and notes on our experiences, and said that this outfit serviced the *Washington Star* and *Post*. Personally, I received the most touching welcome by both the men and officers. Stories had circulated of how I had bled to death or died any number of ways (according to the imagination of the teller), and it had become an accepted fact. Everywhere I went, men got up to shake my hand and express their happiness at my being alive. I'll never forget it. The colonel [Lieutenant Colonel Louis G. Mendez, Jr.] then assigned me as battalion S-2."[16]

Lieutenant Colonel Mark Alexander, commanding the 1st Battalion, 505th, was given the order to pass through the 507th and continue the attack westward. "On June 15th the 1st and 2nd Battalions launched an attack to the west—objective St.-Sauveur-le-Vicomte—to speed up cutting off the peninsula and isolating Cherbourg—1st Battalion on the right, 2nd Battalion on the left. To our left was the [325th] and on our right the 9th Division.

"In leading off, the 1st Battalion had to pass through elements of the 9th Division on our right. It was a green regiment that was bogged down in a hedgerow and was getting shot to pieces by German mortar fire. Our experienced battalion drove the Germans back, and as I once said, we passed through the 9th like a dose of salts, and at the end of the day, we had progressed about halfway to the Douve River north of Crosville, where we sat down for the night.

"We had experienced only sporadic resistance, mainly from a stone walled farmhouse and buildings. We had a few casualties including Lieutenant Gerald Johnson who had suffered a round through his shoulder and a new first lieutenant replacement shot through the knee.

"We were again ahead of the 2nd Battalion, even though I had given Lieutenant Colonel Vandervoort my two tanks when he was held up by a rock walled farmhouse complex. We were again open on our right flank."[17]

Along the highway to St.-Sauveur-le-Vicomte, Company D, 505th, ran into a hornet's nest of German resistance at Les Rosiers, including two 75mm antitank guns and a 37mm antiaircraft gun. Company D trooper Private First Class David Bowman advanced under tremendous enemy fire during the "combined infantry-tank attack, which developed into the most heated battle in which I participated in Normandy. We were moving forward under constant artillery and small arms fire. The resistance was so heavy that we could move forward only in spurts. We'd hit the ground, open fire, get up, rush forward a short distance, and hit the ground again. A few men were hit during these movements. Some just lay there; others limped to the rear. Tanks were on our left flank, and I heard the rumble of some to our right.

"After moving forward some distance, our unit was halted and [William R. "Rebel"] Haynes and I were instructed to direct fire so it would complement that from the machine gunners to our right, Private Donald MacPhee and Private First Class Thomas Byrd.

"The enemy fire from small arms, tanks, and artillery was heavy. After an indeterminable passage of time, I heard Byrd shouting, 'MacPhee!' 'MacPhee!' (I later learned that both had been killed around that time.) Shortly after this unfortunate incident, Haynes was hit and went to the rear.

"We continued our advance . . . but for some distance we endured the sight of burning tanks and their hapless crews. One would see tankers, mostly German, I believe, but also many Americans, draped over the turrets, burning atop their burning tanks. Evidently, no quarter was given by either side, as would be expected under these conditions. When the tanks were disabled and the surviving crew attempted to abandon them, the enemy would mercilessly cut the men down."[18]

Fire from the German high velocity guns was terrible. As Corporal Wilton Johnson with the Machine Gun Platoon of Headquarters Company, 2nd Battalion, 505th, was working his way up the highway looking for a place to set up his machine gun, he was struck down by shrapnel in the back from an aerial burst. "Private Elmer Pack, who was in my squad, pushed a rag in my back to stop the bleeding and probably saved my life."[19]

Vandervoort took the two tanks from Company A, 746th Tank Battalion, and with a platoon from D Company worked around to the flank of the German position as their heads were kept down by the fire from the 2nd Battalion 81mm mortars. The Company D platoon and the tanks overran and wiped out the Germans manning the position. By 7:00 p.m., the 2nd Battalion reached the creek north of Crosville, which the 1st Battalion had reached earlier.

The 507th relieved the 508th south of the Douve River around Baupte, Cretteville, and Coigny the next morning at 4:15 a.m. The 508th crossed the Douve and moved to a position northwest of Ètienville, with the 3rd Battalion, 508th, relieving the 3rd Battalion, 505th, at Crosville by 9:00 a.m. The 325th reached the Douve River southeast of St.-Sauveur-le-Vicomte about 10:00 a.m., then began cleaning up pockets of resistance that had been bypassed and sending patrols across the river.

Before sunrise, Lieutenant Colonel Alexander ordered the 1st Battalion, 505th, to attack again with the objective of capturing St.-Sauveur-le-Vicomte. "We launched our attack at dawn, had stiff resistance from an 88 gun position, but by 14:00 hours, we had reached the road paralleling the Douve River and were again ahead of the 2nd Battalion on our left. I could hear fighting on the main road to the southeast. The 9th on our right was far behind.

"I set up a defensive position on the river road, defending from the northeast and southwest. We had no more than taken up our defense than a German command car with four occupants drove right into us from the north along the river road. Our men shot them to pieces. I don't know how it happened, but a German artillery major survived the incident.

"Some Frenchman on a bicycle saw the action, turned around and pedaled madly back northeast on the river road. I'm sure he informed the Germans of our position. Shortly thereafter, I spotted German tanks on a road junction about three quarters of a mile to the northeast on the river road. I had my artillery observer bring down a concentration of fire. When the smoke cleared, the tanks had gone and I saw no further German action in that area."[20]

Meanwhile at midday, Vandervoort, with his 2nd Battalion, 505th, reached the high ground on the Douve River southeast of St.-Sauveur-le-Vicomte. He entered a chateau overlooking the town, where from an upper story window, he looked northwest into the town. He was astounded by what he saw. On the main highway running north and south through St.-Sauveur-le-Vicomte, thousands of German troops and horse-drawn heavy equipment were moving south, attempting to escape before the peninsula was cut. Vandervoort immediately got on the radio and reached Major Jack Norton, the 505th's S-3. He told Norton what he was seeing, but terminated the conversation before providing the coordinates. Major Norton deduced the location and quickly got word to Colonel Ekman, who in turn contacted General Ridgway to arrange bringing artillery fire to bear upon the enemy concentration. As it happened, Ridgway had General Omar Bradley with him when he received word and decided to take Bradley with him to watch the impending fireworks.

Every available artillery piece in the VII Corps within range and not firing in support of another unit was alerted. Using a forward observer, who was accompanying Vandervoort, a massive TOT (time-on-target) barrage was arranged. Artillery batteries would fire at slightly different times depending upon the distance from the target and velocity of the shells being fired so that all of the rounds fired would arrive at the target at the same time. As the precise moment approached, the air filled with a low roar, which reached a crescendo as hundreds of artillery shells converged on the highway in St.-Sauveur-le-Vicomte. A couple of seconds later, almost the entire town was engulfed in near simultaneous explosions. After calling in a slight adjustment to the fire, a second TOT barrage destroyed those German troops, vehicles, and horses not hit in the first barrage.

Vandervoort's 81mm mortars even got into the act. One of the ammo bearers was Private First Class James V. Rodier. "I could see a self-propelled gun being knocked out in the town. There was other artillery coming from the same direction our mortars were firing. I do not know what kind of guns the enemy was using, but they were getting the worst of the deal."[21]

As the second barrage lifted, Vandervoort ordered his battalion to cross the bomb damaged bridge over the Douve River and capture St.-Sauveur-le-Vicomte. Company F would lead the assault and, upon crossing the bridge, would circle the town to the north and block the road running west from the town, while Company D following them would circle the town and cut the road leading south, and Company E would move straight through the town.

With his squad leading, Sergeant Spencer Wurst, with Company F, moved through a ditch beside the main road leading into town, waiting for the inevitable German fire to hit them. "The Germans had taken position on the other side of the river to our left and right front, on slightly higher ground. They let us get almost fully deployed along that open road before they opened up. We hit the dirt as the shells skimmed the top of the roadbed, passing over our heads by two or three feet."[22]

Staying down in the ditch would only result in high casualties; Wurst knew they had to move—and move now. "The best we could do was get the hell out of there as fast as possible. We had to jump up and run across the bridge. The instant before we made our dash, [John P.] Corti, a BAR man in my squad, was severely wounded. He had been in a prone position close to a cement power pole, which was hit by one of the shells. As we made our rush, we couldn't stop, but the medic did."[23]

As Wurst and his men closed on the partially destroyed bridge, the German fire intensified. "We were taking considerable small arms fire, which was particularly deadly in our situation. The Germans had us in sight and were firing rifles and machine guns directly on us.

"About a hundred fifty yards from the bridge, we were also taken under very heavy direct artillery fire. This was a minimum of 75mm, and probably larger, most likely from self-propelled guns. These were HE—high explosive shells, not antitank."[24]

As Vandervoort's men crossed the bridge and the Germans poured fire across the river in a vain attempt to stop them, Bradley turned to Ridgway and said, "My God, Matt, can't anything stop these men?"[25]

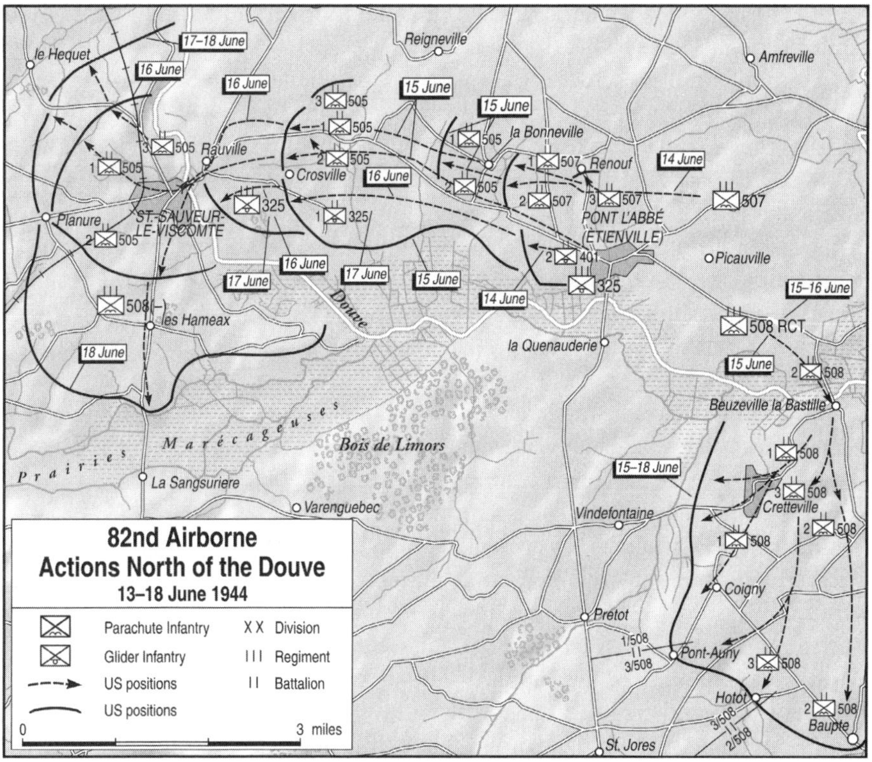

Ridgway replied, "I would rather have a platoon of those men than a battalion of regular infantry."[26]

Sergeant Paul Nunan, with Company D, got his men across the river, where they turned left and began working around the town. "They sent my platoon around to the left and we were going back into hedgerows. I had a man out in front of the platoon and he was down in the roadway. All of a sudden, he jumped back into the corner of this hedgerow and he said, 'There's a German out there, and he jumped into the hedgerow.'

"I told the people right up front against the hedgerow, 'OK everybody stay down until I give the word and then everybody stand up and open up against that hedgerow that's along the road.' I had a guy named Norman Pritchard, who either didn't hear what I said or didn't care, so he stood up all by himself. A shot rang out and he had been drilled right through the heart. I told our guys to fire into the other hedgerow that was parallel to the road. [Private First Class] Pritchard keeled over and after we had doused the area with small arms fire, I went up to him and saw he had taken one bullet. I thought of shooting him with the morphine syrette. I put it in his arm, and it stayed in a lump.

And I realized he was dead. I've reviewed that in my mind I don't know how many times."[27]

From high ground on the eastern side of the Douve, Staff Sergeant Russell W. Brown, a 60mm mortar squad leader with Company F, was firing in support of the crossing when he heard the sound of planes and looked up. "Some P-47s tried to skip bomb the bridge while our men were still crossing. They missed, turned around, and tried again, but missed again."[28]

The 82nd Airborne Division had moved past the bomb line that ran along the Douve River for that day. None of the planners believed the division would be able to cross the Douve until the following day. From his position west of the river, Sergeant Wurst saw orange smoke rising, a signal to the Air Corps that friendly forces were present. "From a distance, I could see Colonel Vandervoort, who had crossed shortly after we did, standing out in an opening with a huge orange blanket or panel. He was waving it like mad, standing there with orange smoke everywhere, trying to deter the planes. The bombs missed the bridge, but the planes also made some strafing runs."[29]

As the 2nd Battalion was crossing the bridge, Lieutenant Colonel Alexander left a platoon to block the road running parallel to the eastern side of the river and started his battalion along that road toward the bridge. Alexander, his radioman, and his orderly moved out ahead of the battalion, arriving at the bridge just as the last of the 2nd Battalion troopers had crossed. When Alexander arrived at the bridge he met Lieutenant Colonel Ekman and General Ridgway. "Ekman ordered me to bring up the 1st Battalion. I told him they were already on their way and the lead elements began arriving as I spoke. I directed them to speed up the crossing behind the 2nd Battalion."[30]

The troopers from Company F kept out of the built-up areas as they moved around the north side of town. Sergeant Wurst and his squad were still leading the company. Wurst and Corporal Bill Hodge were acting as scouts when they spotted three Germans walking, one right behind the other, along a hedgerow perpendicular to their advance, unaware of their presence. Wurst aimed and fired, hitting one of the Germans, and then drew a bead on a second. "Just as I was about to shoot, Bill opened up with his .45-caliber Tommy gun. One instant the German was in my sights, and the next he was flat on the ground. He must have been hit by a number of the .45 slugs, because he went down very fast. The other German threw his hands up in surrender, and we approached him after an intense visual search of the surrounding area. Bill and I moved up to where the bodies were lying, and Lieutenant Carroll came up with a few others from the platoon. One of the Germans was dead, and three or four of our men gathered around to watch the other one die.

"This is one of the few times I actually saw at close range the result of my own fire, or that of my squad. I thought the German was suffering terribly, and without thinking, I asked the lieutenant whether I should finish him off. Much to his credit, he absolutely refused. The sight of that man lying there slowly dying lingers in my mind to this day. He has been the subject of many nightmares over the years. I hesitate to think what kind of dreams I'd have now, if I'd put the man out of his misery."[31]

Company F fired on German traffic on the main highway running into town from the north, scattering them. They continued their advance until they reached the road that ran west from the town and set up a roadblock on it to prevent Germans from using it as an avenue of retreat. Company D, likewise, cut the road leading south from St.-Sauveur-le-Vicomte.

The 1st Battalion, 505th, moved across the bridge and began helping Company E, 505th, clear the town, which had been almost totally destroyed by US artillery fire. Late that afternoon, the 3rd Battalion, 505th, arrived in St.-Sauveur-le-Vicomte, after being relieved by the 3rd Battalion, 508th.

Lieutenant Jack Isaacs, now commanding Company G, 505th, was the fourth company commander for G Company so far in the Normandy campaign. "We were directed to attack through the town, secure the high ground to the west of town, and the battalion lined up to do this with I Company on the right and G Company on the left. We launched our attack without any reconnaissance, very little information about what we might encounter. We were fiercely opposed by several German machine gun positions."[32]

Both companies advanced under this heavy fire toward a railroad embankment where the Germans were dug in and making their stand. Company G guided on the road to their right, with Company I moving on the other side of the road, which crossed the railroad embankment via an underpass.

As Company I moved toward the embankment, Sergeant Bill Dunfee could see a German tank, sitting hull-down in the underpass waiting for them. "There was a woods on my right across the tracks. I knew if we got into the woods the tank couldn't get at us. There were some P-51s flying above us, so we signaled to them and pointed out the tank. Two P-51s came down for a look-see; the dirty birds bombed and strafed us. 'Murphy's Law' continued to prevail. The tank just sat there for another ten minutes, and finally backed away."[33]

Despite German machine gun, small arms, and mortar fire, both companies reached the embankment, with the Germans just yards away, dug in on the other side. Sergeant Bill Blank, with Company G, decided to take a quick look to see if the Germans might be pulling out. "I raised my head to look across and as I did, a German directly opposite raised up and we looked each other in the eye and ducked down. The German threw several of those blue grenades at me, but they rolled to the bottom of the embankment and exploded without harm. When I raised up again, I caught him coming up with my Tommy gun. They had a small tank just up the road aimed at the underpass. He was firing down the road at anything that moved. Fortunately, he only had armor piercing shells and they didn't cause any damage until Colonel

Krause tried to roll out a 75mm pack howitzer to fire back, which resulted in the loss of the gun and the crew. The tank made an attempt to drive through the underpass."[34]

As it did, a G Company bazooka team waited in ambush on each side of the underpass, with only three rockets. As the tank came through, Private First Class Bill G. Hahnen fired two rockets damaging the tank, which backed out of the underpass. A German counterattack with four other tanks was repulsed, with Hahnen knocking out one of them with his last rocket.

As Company G continued the attack, Lieutenant Isaacs saw both of his remaining platoon leaders get hit. "Lieutenant [William F.] Mastrangelo was wounded while we were trying to cross the railroad embankment during the day at St.-Saveur-le-Vicomte. Night fell, and we continued to attack in the dark. And while [I was] talking to Lieutenant [Travis] Orman, he was killed. All other officers had been wounded, captured, or missing. So, I found myself as the sole officer left in Company G. We had started with eight. We were now down to one."[35]

Around 10:00 p.m., the 1st and 2nd Battalions of the 508th arrived in St.-Saveur-le-Vicomte and expanded the bridgehead south of the town, moving down both sides of the highway that led south to La Haye-du-Puits.

During the night, Isaacs kept Company G, 505th, moving forward with the help of his NCOs, who were now leading the remnants of the company's platoons. "My noncommissioned officers were quite equal to the task and we continued to attack. The attack continued all night long, dawn finding us actually having worked our way behind the enemy positions. I had only seventeen men left, the others having been lost or strayed or casualties. But, we were in a strategic position alongside the road running west of St.-Saveur-le-Vicomte. We were actually two hundred or three hundred yards ahead of Company I, and when our position became known to the Germans, they started to withdraw from in front of Company I. Company I was delivering frontal fire, and we caused a great many casualties among the retreating Germans.

"Also, at point blank range, in this position, we observed an 88mm gun being towed down the road toward us; it was accompanied by two or three other vehicles, and approximately twenty to twenty-five men. With my seventeen men lying just alongside the road in the hedgerow, when this group approached, the rapid fire that we were able to deliver as a complete surprise to them, wiped out everybody on the German side. We knocked out the tow vehicle, the 88, the two or three vehicles accompanying it, and this further dislodged the Germans who were still attempting to defend themselves against Company I, and it became a rather serious route.

"I entered Normandy as a twenty-one year old platoon leader, and in ten days was a forty-two year old company commander."[36]

The following morning, the 507th continued to hold its sector south of the Douve, while the 325th was relieved and moved southeast of Ètienville in preparation for a crossing of the Douve the following night. The 505th consolidated and expanded the bridgehead west and north, while the 508th did the same to the south and west. The 47th Infantry of the 9th Infantry Division passed through the bridgehead and attacked to the west to cut the peninsula.

At 11:50 p.m. on June 18, the 2nd Battalion, 325th, at Pont l'Abbe began crossing the Douve River in assault boats rowed by engineers from Company A, 307th. A diversion west of the crossing by a squad of the Intelligence & Reconnaissance (I&R) Platoon, led by Sergeant Clarence Rohrbacher, drew the attention of Germans defending the southern side of the river. Company E was given the objective of clearing the town of La Quenauderie upon crossing. Sitting in one of the Company E boats, Private Rudy A. Stinnett tried to make as little noise as possible. "As we neared the far shore, Sergeant Mike Colella, our squad leader from East Palestine, Ohio, ordered us to fix bayonets.

"The village of La Quenauderie was only a short distance from where we crossed the river. As we approached the village, Sergeant Colella told us to halt and crouch down while he surveyed the buildings ahead of us. In the tenseness of the situation, one man in the squad jabbed the man ahead of him in the neck with his bare bayonet. Quick first aid was given and we started our move into the village."[37]

Just before entering the town, as prearranged, the 320th GFA Battalion and attached artillery units fired a barrage of 510 rounds, lasting 15 minutes, that struck La Quenauderie. Company E and G, on each side of the road, waited to move into the town. Company F would follow in reserve.

As the barrage lifted, Private Stinnett moved out with Company E. "The Germans had not expected our night river crossing, so we took them by surprise. Some of them were having a drinking party in a cafe. A short firefight erupted. Two small French tanks manned by German soldiers chugged down the village street to join the fight. These were disabled with Gammon grenades and bazooka fire. Company E captured about fifty prisoners and killed or wounded several others who tried to get away.

"We set up a company front on the outskirts of the village facing south toward La Haye-du-Puits. We dug in and tried to get some rest. With the south end of the bridge across the Douve River at Pont l'Abbe now secure by our action, the 1st Battalion, 325th, and 2nd Battalion, 401st, started across [the causeway]. Engineers went first and marked a footpath through the tangled girders with tape, then under harassing mortar and artillery fire, the balance of the regiment made the crossing. The crossing was completed without serious incident by daylight."[38]

As the 2nd Battalion, 325th, was closing in on La Quenauderie, the 1st Battalion, 507th, crossed the bridge west of Cretteville and attacked toward Vindefontaine just after midnight. The battalion was now commanded by Major Ben "Red" Pearson. Pearson had been captured with Colonel Millett and had escaped and made his way back through enemy-held territory to rejoin the 507th.

Almost everyone in the rifle companies had been fighting with very little sleep since landing on June 6. Lieutenant Robert H. Parks, with Company C, 507th, moved his men up to the bridge, waiting for the attack to commence. "I sent two men up the river on a recon mission. I was sitting half asleep when I caught movement in the corner of my eye and swung my weapon to cover what looked like two Germans. Luckily, before I pulled the trigger, I remembered my two guys. I came close to firing on them. I still get the shakes."[39]

At fifteen minutes after midnight the assault began. Corporal Howard R. Huebner, a machine gunner with Company C, 507th, had miraculously survived the assault across the La Fière Causeway ten days earlier. "We walked through water for about a quarter to a half mile and made an attack on Vindefontaine. My assistant got killed in front of me, opening a gate into another field. There was a German machine gun zeroed in on us. I put my machine gun in a tree notch and took the German machine gunner out. He was in a church steeple."[40]

The fighting for the town was savage. Staff Sergeant Ed Jeziorski was firing his .30-caliber machine gun almost continuously to cover the advance of the rifle squads. "My LMG [light machine gun] got very hot and quit working until I poured my canteen of water over the receiver."[41]

By 7:30 a.m., Vindefontaine was in the hands of the 507th, but the remainder of the day was spent wiping out snipers and isolated pockets of resistance.

As Private Rudy Stinnett and some of the men in his squad were sleeping in their foxholes on the southern edge of La Quenauderie, his squad leader came around waking them up. "After daybreak, Sergeant Colella came by and said he wanted five men from his squad (1st Squad, 3rd Platoon) to go on a patrol to skirt the area to see if any stray Germans might be hiding in the surrounding woods. This patrol was made up of Sergeant Colella; John Runge, a big German boy from College Point, New York; John Semperger from Sharpsville, Pennsylvania; Mansell (Red) Stone from Manchester, Kentucky; and me, Rudy Stinnett. I cannot recall the name of the other man on this patrol.

"We had been out about thirty minutes when some of the men wanted to take a smoke break. We had stopped a few minutes next to a hedgerow when we heard German voices on the other side of the hedge and a few yards ahead of us. We all sprang into action. John Runge jumped on the mound of dirt that held the hedgerow and opened fire with his BAR. The rest of us spread out and fired through the hedge brush. Near us was an opening in the hedge where a small dirt farm road came down to a livestock watering hole.

"A German soldier came into my view on this road with his rifle pointed at me. I got off one quick round in his direction with my M1 and at the same time yelled for him to surrender. In my haste, I noticed that I hit him in the forearm, but his rifle was still pointed menacingly in my direction. I also noticed that the next round had jammed the bolt in my M1.

"Threatening with my now useless M1, I again yelled at the German to drop his rifle. This he did, and I breathed a prayer as I quickly pulled the bolt back on my rifle to eject the stuck round and reload. We moved in and saw that we had destroyed a German machine gun squad and captured one prisoner.

"With the prisoner, we returned to our company position for further orders. Facing the German with my rifle jammed was a very close call. I have always thanked God for sparing me at that moment."[42]

At 5:00 a.m., the 3rd Battalion, 508th, crossed the Douve River in assault boats and was attached to the 325th. By 7:30 a.m., the 1st Battalion, 325th, and the 2nd Battalion, 401st, passed through the 2nd Battalion, 325th, positions and pushed the bridgehead west to the edge of the Bois de Limors forest, with their right flank at Le Hau de Haut and their left flank just north of La Danguerie. After making the crossing, the 3rd Battalion, 508th, was ordered to move south through Vindefontaine and seize Pretot. At 2:00 p.m., the 3rd Battalion, 508th, moved through the 507th positions at Vindefontaine and proceeded to Pretot.

The battalion met a German strongpoint about nine hundred yards south of Vindefontaine, which was bypassed, but it encountered almost continual machine gun and sniper fire as it neared Pretot. The battalion halted about six hundred yards northeast of the town and formed an all-around defense for the night.

The afternoon of the nineteenth, the 505th was relieved around St.-Sauveur-le-Vicomte and trucked to a position inside the bridgehead established by the 325th. The division artillery, the 80th AA Battalion, and other division troops moved across the causeway to positions within the bridgehead.

That night, Lieutenant Ralph DeWeese, with Company H, 508th, checked on his men to make sure they had half of the platoon awake while the other half slept. DeWeese then returned to his slit trench and tried to get a little sleep. "At about one o'clock that night I was called over to the CP and given information we were going to attack the town the next morning. We were to be ready to pull out at 4:30 and I didn't wake up until then, so we were about half an hour late. We moved into position in a large field just at the bottom of the hill. At the point we stretched out in a long skirmish line and waited for the attack. Artillery was to fall on the town ten minutes before we attacked. Six o'clock was H hour and we started to attack. The Jerries opened up with machine guns and caused quite a few casualties. One of my men was hit in the head, but not bad. His name was Felig and he had been in the platoon a short time.

"We advanced across an open field and finally I could see one of the machine guns that was causing all the trouble. Luck was with us again, because if it had been covering the field we were coming across, it would have gotten each and every one of us."[43]

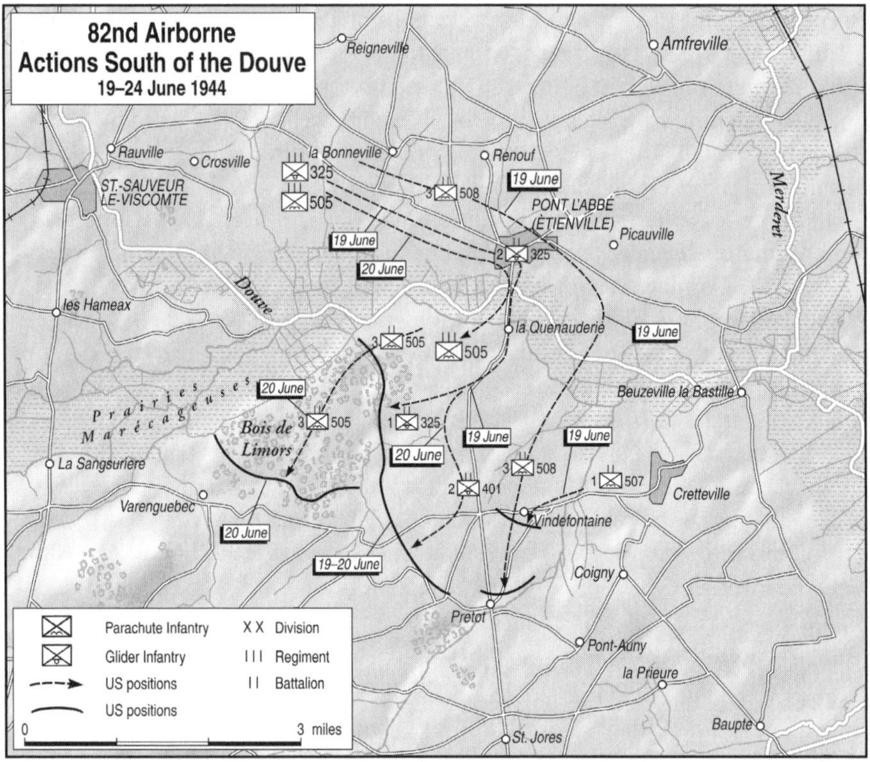

At one point the German artillery and mortar fire, coupled with the crossfire that German machine guns were delivering, had the battalion pinned down and suffering a lot of casualties. The battalion commander, Lieutenant Colonel Louis G. Mendez, crawled up to a position in front of his men, then jumped to his feet and personally led his men forward under the withering fire. The sight of Mendez leading them forward inspired the battalion to resume the attack and charge into the town, where they routed the Germans defending it. Lieutenant Colonel Mendez would later be awarded the Distinguished Service Cross for his valor and leadership under fire.

The battalion cleaned out the town, but particularly accurate German artillery and mortar fire from the high ground to the east and south inflicted more casualties. At 4:00 p.m., the 3rd Battalion was ordered to move to high ground just west of the town, where they were relieved that night at 11:30 p.m., by the 1st Battalion, 507th.

The 3rd Battalion, 505th, attacked through the Bois de Limors on the twentieth against light opposition and dug in along the western edge of the forest. The next morning, Lieutenant DeWeese was leading his men down a road going back to the position they had occupied before the assault. "As we passed down the road, we saw the body of a dead officer. It was Lieutenant [Gene H.] Williams. He was the youngest officer in the battalion and one of the best liked fellows. We all felt bad about this and a couple of days later a telegram came stating that he was the proud father of twin boys."[44]

Lieutenant Paul Lehman, the 3rd Battalion S-2, was shocked when he received the news. "Sure was a pitiful case, which affected all of us on the staff very deeply. One thing is certain, that the difference between life and death is almost one hundred percent a matter of luck, as far as being in the combat zone is concerned."[45]

CHAPTER 18

"RESOURCEFUL AND COURAGEOUS IN THE ATTACK, RESOLUTE IN THE DEFENSE, THEY FOUGHT SUPERBLY"[1]

One of the worst storms in the last fifty years struck the English Channel from June 19–21, damaging and sinking some of the Allies' small ships and destroying the Mulberry harbor on Omaha Beach that brought much of the ammunition, rations, equipment, vehicles, guns, and men to Normandy. The supply tonnage arriving in Normandy at the onset of the storm was only 73 percent of the planned target. The storm reduced that to 57 percent. This dire situation forced the Allied commanders to accelerate the capture of the port of Cherbourg to replace the Mulberry harbor that was lost. Therefore, priority to available supplies was given to the VII Corps' drive north on the Cotentin Peninsula to seize Cherbourg.

The 82nd Airborne Division consolidated its bridgehead south of the Douve River beginning on June 21. The division carried out aggressive patrolling while it reorganized and prepared for the next attack. Unlike the infantry and armored divisions, the airborne divisions were not receiving replacements. The strength of the division's rifle companies had been severely depleted by almost continuous combat for two weeks. During the period from June 21 through July 2, the weather was marked by overcast skies and rain. For most of the men, who were living in foxholes, the mud, waterlogged holes, wet clothing, and shortage of rations made life miserable.

Sergeant Zane Schlemmer, a forward observer with the 81mm mortar platoon of the 2nd Battalion, 508th, was rotated in and out of the Bois de Limors forest during those twelve cold, rainy days. "Bois de Limors was dark, cold, and rainy—everything was damp or wet. Somehow, the cooks did get hot coffee up to us—but it was the only warmth there. Our jumpsuits were gas impregnated, which helped keep the rain out, but any that got in also stayed inside our clothes."[2]

During this period, the Germans took advantage of the respite to fortify their positions, lay minefields and booby traps, dig alternate fighting positions, zero in their artillery and mortars on likely routes of approach, and reorganize their forces.

From June 26–29, Lieutenant Stanley Weinberg, with Company B, 505th, who had temporarily been transferred to Company C, voluntarily led three different patrols deep into the German positions to gather intelligence regarding troop dispositions and where their heavy weapons were positioned. With Weinberg on these patrols were Staff Sergeant Herman R. "Zeke" Zeitner (Company C) and Sergeant Charles L. Burghduff (Company A), both of whom spoke fluent German; Sergeant Clyde E. Hein; Privates First Class Stanley Gurski, Wilbert Ward, and Fred C. Cunningham, all from Company C; and Private Luis Mendieta from the Regimental S-2 Section. The patrols came under heavy fire, in one instance caught in the open and pinned down. Weinberg, who was Jewish refused to surrender and they were eventually able to escape. The patrol gathered much information and took several prisoners, who would provide valuable intelligence, which would pay huge dividends in the coming attack.

Lieutenant Gus L. Sanders, with Company C, 505th, was a great admirer of Weinberg and other Jewish officers with whom he served. "We had very few Jews in our outfit, but those we did have were very much soldiers; very tough and salty, showing lots of ingenuity, and loads of guts. They all were real 'He-men' and very tough."[3]

On July 2, orders were issued for an attack the following day. At 6:30 a.m. on July 3, the division would attack southwest toward La Haye-du-Puits, their objective being the high ground northeast of the town. On the right flank, the 2nd Battalion, 505th, would lead, followed by the 1st and 3rd Battalions in a column of battalions, moving out of the Bois de Limors at 3:00 a.m. to the line of departure, a crossing over a creek that ran south through the village of Varenquebec. At that point, the 1st Battalion would move up and attack on the right of the 2nd Battalion, with the 3rd Battalion mopping up. The 505th's objectives were to seize the northern slope and crest of Hill 131 and cut the highway from St.-Sauveur-le-Vicomte to La Haye-du-Puits. The US 79th Infantry Division would be on the right flank of the 505th. The 508th was ordered to attack from the Bois de Limors in the center of the division sector toward its objective, the southern slope of Hill 131, with the 2nd Battalion on the right, the 3rd Battalion on the left, and the 1st Battalion following in reserve. The 325th on the left flank would attack toward its objective, Hill 95, on the western end of the La Poterie ridgeline, with the 2nd Battalion attacking on the right, the 1st Battalion on the left, and the 2nd Battalion, 401st, in reserve, following the leading elements. The 2nd Battalion, 507th, would fill a gap between the 508th and the 325th, with the 1st Battalion, 507th, following, and the 3rd Battalion, 507th, screening the left rear of the division attack. The 90th Division would attack on the left flank of the 325th.

When Colonel Ekman received the attack order for the 505th, he told Gavin of an opportunity that would capitalize on the information gained by the patrols led by Weinberg. Ekman told Gavin, "One of the battalion commanders [Major William J. Hagan] reported that one of his patrols had found a flank route to the enemy rear, and that he could move his entire battalion to the enemy rear and roll up the enemy with little risk and small casualties."[4]

Gavin replied, "No, too risky. If the battalion gets caught enroute stretched out on the flank, it could be disastrous."[5]

After a few moments Ekman asked Gavin, "How about if I send a reinforced platoon to see if we could turn the enemy flank. Gavin looked at me very closely for a few seconds, nodded his head, and said, 'Okay!' then walked away."[6]

Before dawn, Sergeant Zane Schlemmer, with the 2nd Battalion, 508th, moved up to the line of departure on the edge of the Bois de Limors forest, which was held by the 1st Battalion, 508th. "We all knew the importance of capturing Hill 131—the highest in that part of Normandy. We could not see Hill 131 because of low hanging rain clouds. These clouds also meant that we would not have the promised air support for our attack; but it also meant that if we could not see the hill, neither could the Germans up there see us down below!

"At dawn our supporting artillery and mortars started pounding the German line and rear areas. Since we had to start the advance attack through the defense line of the 1st Battalion, there were not enough foxholes for protection at the starting edge of Bois de Limors; and the German counterartillery and mortars started shelling us. Private Paul Winger of E Company was from my little hometown and his wife worked with my father. The German counterbarrage killed him that morning (not far from me), so I was troubled about how I was going to address his death, for she was a very nice girl."[7]

Private Dwayne Burns, with Company F, 508th, had made it through the Normandy campaign thus far without a scratch. He wondered how long his luck would hold. "Elements of the 2nd and 3rd Battalions were to form the assault wave and as always it seemed, F Company was up front. As we moved toward the hill a halt was called. While we were waiting for word to move up, we started getting hit with artillery fire. The area we were in had trees cut down and logs were lying in rows. We dove in between the logs as the first round came in. The two troopers on my right were both killed by a tree burst. And there I lay, just twelve inches away. Lady luck was sure looking after me!"[8]

At 6:30 a.m., the decimated rifle companies once more moved forward to assault prepared German positions. On the right flank, the 505th began their attack, with 2nd Battalion attacking on the left, and as Ekman had asked, "one platoon, *reinforced with the rest of the battalion*"[9] on the right. The 1st Battalion, 505th, followed a route scouted by the Weinberg patrols that brought them to the rear of the German main line of resistance, where they struck it from behind. The primary obstacles for both the 1st and 2nd Battalions were mines, booby traps, and mortar and artillery fire. Shortly before 10:00 a.m., both battalions

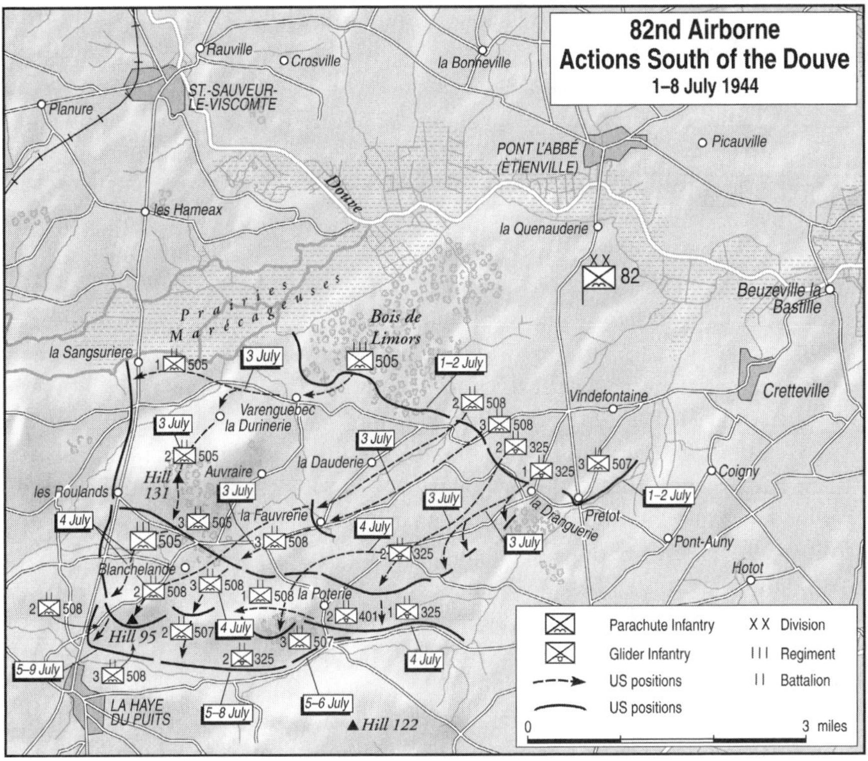

reached Phase Line "B," where the 2nd Battalion wheeled left, then assaulted and captured the northern slope and crest of Hill 131 as the 1st Battalion continued west to the highway from St.-Sauveur-le-Vicomte to La Haye-du-Puits.

In the center, the 508th ran into heavy German opposition. As a forward observer, Sergeant Schlemmer with the 2nd Battalion, 508th, had a critical job, that of coordinating the fire of the artillery and his battalion's 81mm mortars to support the attack. "I was up front with the attacking company commanders, so that if close mortar fire was needed, we could radio to the mortar positions to request it, then adjust it. We NCOs and officers each had a white sheet of paper map showing the hedgerows, orchards, fields, roads, the few farms and houses (obviously reproduced from aerial photographs) so that we could plan our advance; but it did not contain any elevations. As we advanced the paper got wetter, dirtier, and more unreadable. It was very important to have this map however, because our supporting artillery had a similar map and would tell us via radio the number of shells that they would fire into the hedgerow in front of us. We could then count the shells landing and immediately rush that hedgerow before the Germans could recover, and the artillery would lift their fire to the next hedgerow. It was the only way that an attack could be successful in that bocage country.

"Shortly after the attack started out of the Bois de Limors, off to my left I saw our battalion commander, Lieutenant Colonel Tom Shanley, who was up front with the troopers, go through a hedgerow opening, hit a booby trap tripwire and he was wounded by the explosion.

"Then, as we advanced through the various fields and orchards, I saw a movement to my left rear. I turned and saw two young Germans running and jumping into a foxhole. I fired two shots in their direction and called in German, three times to 'come out with your hands up' . . . but no response from them. So I took out one of my thermite grenades, which burns very hot, and bowled it into their foxhole and continued my advance. I am certain that they could not have survived the thermite grenade.

"We then came to a country road crossing a small stream. There, the Germans had downed and mined several trees across the road, as a roadblock. We radioed this information back so that an armored bulldozer could clear it for follow-up armor to advance up the hill behind us."[10]

Lieutenant Colonel Mark Alexander, who had been transferred on June 16 from the 505th to the 508th as the regimental executive officer, "heard over my radio that Lieutenant Colonel Shanley, leading the 2nd Battalion, had tripped a 'Bouncing Betty' [mine] and caught a ball in the back of his neck. The loss of Shanley was critical, leaving only inexperienced Captain Bill Simonds to lead the battalion. I requested and received permission from Colonel Lindquist to go forward and lead the battalion.

"I immediately went forward to the 2nd Battalion, which was involved in cleaning up a German defensive position. The battalion was unorganized and doing some looting of the captured Germans and their position. I sent Lieutenant Colonel Shanley back to the medics and proceeded to get the battalion reorganized and moving toward our objective for the day."[11]

As the attack was renewed by the 2nd Battalion, 508th, Sergeant Schlemmer found himself navigating through a quagmire in the fields. "The rain lessened, but it was very wet and muddy in the fields. I do not recall seeing any houses during our advance attack, though the map showed several—such was the hedgerow country.

"In one field I was flattened, under intense German machine gun fire, which kept hitting some cow manure several inches from my face. . . . I was pleased that the bullets were not hitting me. The cow manure kept splattering all over me and there was nothing I could do to move, but just lie there and take it with hope against hope the gunner would not adjust his fire.

"Both our 2nd and 3rd Battalions spearheaded the attack up the hill, with the 1st Battalion mopping up behind us. Sometime later, Lieutenant Rex Combs, of A Company, 1st Battalion, came across a hedgerow, which he climbed up on and discovered a field full of Germans hiding there. Single-handedly, he sprayed the field with two clips of his Thompson submachine gun, then took the remaining living Germans prisoner—forty-two of them! Rex was awarded the Silver Star for this action.

"Advancing up toward the woods on the top of Hill 131, we waited for the artillery to pound the next hedgerow with six rounds; then the five of us rushed it. It was then that the timing went wrong—for instead of raising the artillery fire to the next hedgerow, our artillery repeated and pounded us. One shell tore the front of the sole of my jump boot off and blew me into the hedgerow. The second shell then wounded me in the left arm and knocked me down again. All five of us were wounded in this barrage and the calls for 'medic!' rang out. My wound bled a great deal, but did not hurt as much as it was a numbing, aching feeling. It came as a shock and a surprise, for I never thought it would happen to me, but rather to the others. The medics finally got to me after the more seriously wounded were cared for. I then had to find a radioman to get a forward observer up to take my place in the advance."[12]

On the left flank, the 325th attacked toward Hill 95 on the La Poterie ridgeline. But because the 90th Division was held up, the 1st Battalion on the regiment's left flank came under fire from German positions in the 90th Division's sector. Private First Class Clinton Riddle, with Company B, had miraculously survived some of the most severe combat in the Normandy campaign without being wounded. "We started that morning at 07:00. It was raining cats and dogs. I was company runner for Captain Gibson. We were up front leading the attack. We had to move fast. The tracers were really flying—they were so thick sometimes it seemed like you had to stop long enough for them to zip. The Germans started to lob mortar shells in on us. One landed in our Company CP group. A whole squad was knocked out, including our radioman, Stephan Kralj. This left us with about sixty men of the one hundred fifty-five we started with. I had to take over to help operate the company radio. We advanced until we struck some tanks. We gave everything we had, which wasn't much.

"Our commander was wounded. This was the third since we started. We bypassed the tanks and drove on until night. The units to the right and left closed in, putting the Germans' backs to the wall. All three companies of the battalion were hit heavily. Company B had forty-five men left."[13]

On the right flank, the 505th made good progress despite German artillery and mortar fire, along with minefields and booby traps impeding the advance. Near the bottom of Hill 131, a private in the 2nd Battalion, 505th, found a German field telephone wire that ran from the top of the hill to frontline German positions to coordinate artillery fire. The ingenious private suggested that they follow the line, since no mines or booby traps would be planted along the path of the line. The 2nd Battalion advanced up the hill along this path and surprised the Germans occupying the observation post on the crest of Hill 131. After a brief firefight, the eighteen Germans manning the post were captured.

The 1st Battalion, 505th, moved west and cut the highway between St.-Sauveur-le-Vicomte and La Haye-du-Puits. By 12:30 p.m., the regiment had captured both of its objectives.

Cleaning out pockets of bypassed Germans, the 3rd Battalion, 505th, encountered more resistance than the two assaulting battalions, but was able to join the 2nd Battalion on Hill 131 in the early afternoon.

Because heavy counterattacks by German forces on the open left flank of the 325th were seriously delaying its advance, at approximately 4:00 p.m., orders were issued changing the objective of the 325th from Hill 95 to the eastern end of the La Poterie ridgeline and the town of La Poterie. The 508th was ordered to turn and attack south to capture the former objective of the 325th, while the 505th was ordered to capture the remainder of Hill 131, which the 3rd Battalion did by attacking from the crest down the southern slope.

On the left, the 2nd Battalion, 325th, pushed toward the eastern part of the La Poterie hill mass against tough opposition. Private First Class Darrell C. Dilley, with Company F, 325th, came under heavy machine gun and mortar fire as his company advanced. "We were getting hit pretty hard and losing men. Then we were able to get going with the help of some tanks and artillery fire. We finally moved on and the Germans were forced on back."[14]

As Private First Class Raymond T. Burchell, with Company C, 325th, fought his way toward the town of La Poterie, the German opposition increased. "This was very heavily defended by Germans. We would attack, then they counterattacked. Most of the time it was raining; we had a hard time getting in and out of hedgerows as we were slipping in the mud. It was a seesaw battle for quite awhile. We did manage to get some patrols into town."[15]

After getting the 2nd Battalion, 508th, into positions for the night, Lieutenant Colonel Mark Alexander decided to conduct a personal reconnaissance for the attack set for the following morning. "I found that there was an open valley about one quarter mile across and between us and the Germans. I moved to the left forward edge of a wooded area, crawled behind a stone wall, pulled a rock out of the wall and with my field glasses spotted two German gun positions on Hill 95.

"About that time, one of our men came walking up to my position. I called for him to get down as the Germans could see him. He kept coming and then ran like hell when the Germans put an 88 round into the wall just ahead of him. I never learned who the soldier was. I don't think he wanted me to know.

"As soon as darkness closed in, I left my observation post and returned to the battalion which was located on the back slope of a small rise in the land. I talked on a field telephone with Colonel Lindquist and told him that for the attack next morning I was going to move the battalion into a tree covered ridge leading to Hill 95 and not have to cross the open valley and be subject to direct fire from the German guns on Hill 95.

"I had no more than hung the phone back on the tree than the Germans lucked out. They put a round of 81mm mortar into the top of the tree. I think

I heard it coming, but took a dive too late. I was hit in the back by two shell fragments. It felt like someone stuck a fence post in my back and all I could do was lie there and cuss and think, 'Of all the times they were shooting at me and missed. They finally lobbed one over the hill in the dark and got me.'

"Doctor Montgomery and the medics got to me right away, taped my chest tight, closing the wound so that I would not have a blow hole and collapsed lung. They called regiment for a jeep and put me in the front seat with the driver. On the way to the hospital, we stopped briefly at regimental CP and I had a few words with Colonel Lindquist, but I could not talk very well.

"When we arrived at the field hospital, it was in a ground fog. I put my foot down to dismount from the jeep, saw two orderlies coming with a stretcher and I can only remember falling to the ground.

"The next thing I remember, two doctors were trying to take an X-ray of my chest. I was bare from my waist up, but still wearing my pants. I had the shakes and could not hold still for the X-ray.

"When I came to after surgery, Major General Ridgway was sitting on a stool by my cot holding my hand. He was talking to me, but I do not remember what he said, as I was only semiconscious.

"The next time I awakened, Father [Matthew J.] Connelly was bending over me praying. I remember telling him that I was not Catholic. He told me to just be quiet, that he was taking care of things. When I came to again, the nurse came to me, looked at my dog-tags and said your dog-tags only say you are a Christian, but you are a Catholic now, for Father Connelly just gave you the last rites."[16]

By nightfall on July 3, the 82nd Airborne Division had made huge progress on the right. It had advanced over three miles and was dug in and occupying Hill 131. It had cut the highway from St.-Sauveur-le-Vicomte into La Haye-du-Puits and was dug in at the foot of Hill 95 in the center. On the left, the division had fought almost into the town of La Poterie on the eastern edge of the ridgeline. The time for the division to attack the next morning, July 4, was set at 8:00 a.m.

To assist the badly depleted 508th, the 1st and 3rd Battalions of the 505th were ordered to capture the northern slope of Hill 95. As Sergeant Bill Blank and his squad of Company G, 505th troopers approached the foot of the slope, they began taking fire from the Germans on the hill above. "One machine gun crew set up in the corner of a hedgerow and was quickly knocked out by a German machine gun on the hill. [Private Merrill M.] Marty Scherzer, our medic, went out to take care of them and was killed by the same gun. The killing of our medic made us pretty mad, and three of us decided to find the machine gun and put it out of action. [James C. "Fritz"] Fritts, [Roy L.] Pynson, and I started crawling up a hedgerow where we thought the gun might be. Fritz decided not to go any further, so Pynson and I continued on. After a short way, we heard some noises from the other side of the hedgerow. Not knowing for sure whether they were Germans, we decided to fire a shot over their heads to see if we could draw some fire. They responded with a couple of egg-shaped grenades, which rolled down the hill and exploded. We knew we had found them. I tried to unload a clip of Tommy gun ammo into their position, but the gun jammed. Pynson and I made a hasty withdrawal to our mortar position where we proceeded to lay in a heavy concentration of mortar fire."[17]

By noon, the 1st and 3rd Battalions of the 505th had driven the Germans from the northern slope of Hill 95. The 2nd Battalion, 508th, attacked through the 505th positions and captured the crest of Hill 95 about twenty minutes later, and in the process, captured a number of enemy prisoners. Private Dwayne Burns, with Company F, 508th, was ordered to take one of these groups to the POW cage. "F Company had captured a machine gun emplacement, and Woody and I were given the job of taking the prisoners to the rear. We marched the four of them down the road until we found the regiment that was in reserve and they said they would take them off our hands. We were glad to get rid of the Germans and get back to our own company.

"As we came back into our company area we jumped into a trench about waist deep and sat down to rest. We were completely worn out. I took one end that had some tree limbs over it and was sound asleep in minutes. Later, I awoke when cold water started running down the back of my neck. It was raining again. I looked at Woody at the other end of the ditch. He was sitting there soaking wet. His head was back and his mouth was wide open, but he was sound asleep. 'You son of a gun,' I thought, 'If you're lucky, you will drown and get out of all this mess.'

"Later that afternoon I had to go back to the rear area and took the same road. There in the ditch were the same four Germans that we had turned over that morning. They were dead. I thought I was going to be sick. Someone had used a machete on their heads. Why! Why like this? Why them? These poor slobs were just pawns in the game of war, the low man on the totem pole. Just like me they had dreams, desires, ambitions, and maybe a wife or a sweetheart back home. Now they lay in the ditch with their brains oozing out into the mud. I wondered how long it would be before it was my turn to be lying in some dirty weed-choked ditch as my life slipped away. 'Oh Lord,' I thought, 'I'm going to be sick! How do you get used to looking at things like that? What is this war doing to us when we can do this to another human being?'

"I asked some of the men why they had killed the prisoners. They explained that it was the same machine gun crew who shot down their medic while he was trying to help our wounded. They demanded an eye for an eye."[18]

At 2:00 p.m., the Germans counterattacked and forced the 2nd Battalion, 508th, off of the crest of Hill 95. The 2nd Battalion fought until midnight before retaking the crest.

As the attack on Hill 95 was commencing, the 3rd Battalion, 508th, attacked southwest across open ground in front of the high point in the center of the ridgeline. As Lieutenant Colonel Mendez was leading the remnants of his battalion forward under heavy fire, his S-2, Lieutenant Paul Lehman, approached with a message. Lehman had survived a severed artery in his throat on D-Day, was captured, and then freed on June 16. As he spoke to Mendez, Lehman was hit by German machine gun fire and wounded.

Mendez immediately put Lehman over his shoulder and began carrying him to safety. "I was trying to weave back and forth so the machine gun would miss us. I was carrying him over my shoulders—he was a one hundred ninety-five pounder.

"I can still hear the thud and I thought I had been hit. It didn't hurt me though—it was Paul being hit again. So I was taking a dead man off of combat, and that was the biggest cry I'd ever had."[19] The news of Lehman's death, after everything he had survived, was deeply felt by the entire battalion.

Lieutenant Ralph DeWeese, with Company H, was ahead of the rest of the 3rd Battalion as it made the assault. "We knew there would be plenty of fireworks when we attacked the hill. I was given the mission to form three points and lead the attack for the company: one on the right, one on the left, and one in the center. I stayed with the one in the center.

"Word came around that they were going to lay artillery fire on the enemy position and we would advance under it. Man! What a terrific barrage that turned out to be. We started to advance and had to go across an open field. The Germans opened up with machine guns and mowed the men down like flies. I heard someone yell from the rear to keep going, because if the artillery lifted, they would get us all. We kept going and finally halted when word was passed up that no one was following us. Sergeant [William A.] Medford, our operations sergeant, had been killed. Two of my men dragged Sergeant [Dwayne W.] Morris out of the field under fire and brought him to cover along a hedgerow. They were Private [James H.] Daugherty and Corporal [Henning] Olson.

"At this time we had taken cover along a little hedgerow and were holding up. There were thirty-three of us in all, and I was the only officer. I sent two men back a little way to see if they could contact anyone. They came back and said there was no one in the rear. Couldn't imagine what had happened to the battalion. Thought maybe they had all been killed. I looked around at the men and they had that look on their faces as if to say, 'You're in command, what are you going to do to get us out of here?' We were isolated and couldn't go forward, because the Germans had machine guns set up there. We couldn't go to the rear or the left because that was also covered by machine guns. Later, we found out the Jerries had the whole area covered by thirty machine guns, so you can imagine the tough spot we were in.

"I thought about going to the right, and just then the Germans started pouring in timed artillery fire. It was a terrific barrage and pulverized the ground. I knew we had to do something quick because the Jerries would soon start firing mortars and would have gotten us all. Finally, I told the men to follow and I started going down a [ditch by a] hedgerow that was full of water. We didn't mind getting in the water because we knew we had to get out and do it quickly. All along the hedgerow was a solid line of dead and wounded of the 2nd Battalion that had gone through there. As I went along, the wounded kept cautioning me to stay down, because most of the men were in the same position when they were hit. We started crawling on our stomachs then. I stopped to talk to one wounded man, and he asked me if I would cut some weeds that were preventing him from stretching his legs. I cut them and helped him to straighten out his leg. Word was passed up to hurry, because they were laying mortar fire. Guess we got out just in time. We kept going a good distance, about two miles I would say, and came out on a road where there were some of our tank destroyers. I knew we were safe then. Checked up on the men and found we had only lost one man. His name was [Private First Class Theodore Q.] Svendsen, and he was hit in the neck when he turned around to follow me out. He died instantly, the men told me.

"As yet I didn't have any idea what had happened to the rest of the battalion. I found out where the regiment CP was and inquired there. They told me the battalion had to withdraw and were back in the position we had left from. That was really news to me. I got the troops and took them back to the area. The company was surely glad to see us, because before we got there, they only had fourteen in the company. Lieutenant [William J.] Garry explained they had lost contact and he couldn't give us the order to withdraw. Must say that is one Fourth of July I'll never forget. We were certainly lucky to get out of that mess."[20]

East of the attack of the 3rd Battalion, 508th, the 1st Battalion, 508th, attacked south to take the ridge at the town of La Poterie. At dawn that morning, Sergeant Bill Call, a squad leader with Company B, 508th, was dug in with his men awaiting orders. "Lieutenant [Walter J.] Ling was called back to get the order of attack and he came back and gave it to [Staff Sergeant Harold J.] Brogan, and the squad leaders. The attack was to take this hill. We had maybe 1,500 yards to go and every thirty or forty yards you had a hedgerow to go over or go through. One of the platoons was to be on our left flank and one on our right flank.

"We headed out and Sergeant Brogan, who was a hell of a good leader and a great soldier, had us cutting holes through the hedgerows instead of going over the hedgerows. We were firing and receiving no fire. We were using walking fire. We started going through and over these hedgerows. Brogan would climb on top of them and would wave us through and we kept going.

"[Corporal Robert L.] Bobby Stutt had hurt his knee on the jump and kind of walked with a great limp. So, I was chopping the holes and going through, and [then] he would crawl through the holes. We got to this hedgerow and I am chopping the hole, and he pushed me and said, 'I'm going through this one.' He pushed me on my tail and I said, 'You son of a gun!' I crawled through the hole after him.

"I just got on my feet on the other side of the hedgerow and that's when I saw the rifle fire on our left flank. I saw this tracer hit him in the shoulder. When I got to him, I rolled him over and I didn't recognize him. His face was black . . . I am sure the heart exploded, because he was dead when I turned him over. His mouth was gaping back and forth. He died instantly, he went down like a . . .

"We were all out in this open field. Then Brogan got shot through the gut. This German rifle fire and the sniper were taking us one by one. This sniper was taking his time and picking one off at a time. We were all in the open, the whole platoon. When we got to the next hedgerow facing towards the hill, we discovered the fire was only coming from the left flank. [Lieutenant Ling] came up to me and said, 'Sergeant, I'm going back to the company and see what's going on.'

"The other platoon should have been on our left flank, and one on our right. You know, I didn't know what in the hell to do. Brogan is shot through the gut in the middle of the field. [The sniper] is picking us off.

"So, [Lieutenant Ling] takes off running to the rear. I got the guys and I said, 'Over to the other hedgerow on the right flank,' so we would be facing that left flank and we would have that hedgerow as protection. Then they started zeroing in with the 88.

"We were at the base of the hill. It was no big hill. We were starting to dig slit trenches to get some cover. Every so often the 88 would zero in. [Private Paul E.] Owens was up on a tree that had been knocked down. He was extended up in the air there. . . . I don't know what the hell good he was doing there. I said, 'Come on, get over here and start digging.' They got Owens, with the 88 . . . picked the top of his head off . . . killed right away.

"[Private First Class Alphonse A.] Caplik was near him. Al had a grenade in his pocket of his jump pants. One of the pieces of the shrapnel hit his leg and set the powder on fire in the grenade. And God, he was screaming and hollering. I pulled him down off the little pine where he was at and ripped his pocket open with my jump knife. And God, the thing is fuming and the blisters started to come up on his leg. So, we got rid of the grenade. I said, 'Can you make it back?'

"He said, 'Yeah.' So he started crawling back towards the rear.

"Mickey Nichols was hit in the forehead with the shrapnel from that 88, and was bleeding like a stuck hog.

"Brogan was the last one lying out there. It's July 4th, and it's about one hundred degrees in the sun. He was out there in the middle of that field for maybe an hour and a half. [Private First Class] Clyde Moline and [Corporal] Jack Gunter came up to me and said, 'Sergeant, we want to go out and get Brogan,' who was lying in the middle of this field. When I picked my head up and looked over the hedgerow, our medic, Ditwiler was out there and he's trying to wrap a bandage around his gut. That damned sniper shot him in the wrist where he was bandaging him and he came crawling back. I sent him to the rear. The hand was paralyzed and I never saw him after that.

"I said to the guys, 'You just saw what happened to Ditwiler.'

"Well, they wanted to do it. I said, 'OK, we'll try to give you some covering fire.' But there was nothing to fire at.

"So they went out, they brought him back, and they got him to the hedgerow on the other side of right where I was digging. That damned 88 landed right in that area and it killed Jack immediately. Clyde hopped over on top of me and he said, 'Oh God, Jack is dead. Gunter is dead.'

"I said, What about Brogan?'

"He said, 'I guess he's all right.' So I went back over [the hedgerow] with Clyde and we lifted Brogan over and Jack Gunter, he was dead . . . he was gone. I am waiting for Ling to get back, to give me some sort of direction. You know you're never supposed to retreat. I don't [know] what the hell good we were doing up there getting shot at.

"This Lieutenant Smith crawled up and wanted to survey the situation. I said, 'God, look at it here. We're defenseless here and all we've got are M1s.'

"He said, 'Just hold your position, and I'm going to send a medic back up with some plasma for Brogan.' Well, he did. The medic came up and put the bottle up. And that damned sniper shot that bottle as soon as it was exposed. We had to take the needle out of Brogan. God, the guy was suffering, but he was very brave, he didn't say much.

"First Sergeant Jim Smith came up to report that they were going to shell this hill. We had to get some cover. We had these slit trenches dug, but not enough of them, however. Jimmy Smith took one, and we had a few minutes before they were going to start the barrage.

"Jim and I exchanged prayers . . . there is a Catholic prayer to the Blessed Virgin called 'The Memorare.' Jim had in his helmet, a prayer, 'The Lord Is My Shepherd.' I said, 'Why don't we trade and read each other's.'

"They started the barrage and it only lasted maybe five or ten minutes. They bombarded the hill in front of us. They traversed up the hill, then back down the hill, back up the hill, and down the hill. I have never experienced anything like that. I can see why the Germans when the artillery barrage hit them would be shaking and give up in a hurry.

"I laid on top of Brogan to give him a little protection. The impact would lift me right off of the top of Brogan . . . and Sergeant Smith, the same way in his hole. We were bouncing from the concussion.

"The problem was on our left flank. I couldn't figure out what the hell they were doing? There was nobody on that hill. I don't how it got screwed up, with the wounded going back and explaining where the fire was coming from.

"Brogan asked for a drink of water. He had a hole in his gut like [the size of] a volleyball. You could see his guts. We were advised in our training to never give anybody who had a stomach wound a drink of water, because it was an avenue for an infection. It would travel through their whole system. I gave him a drink of water. I didn't give him much. It running right out through the hole. He begged for more. And I didn't give him more. . . . I wish I would have.

"It didn't get dark there until about 10:30 at night. We've been there in that situation since about 7:00 that morning. I had no authority to pull back, but we did. About 8:30 that night, Smitty and I got Brogan on a half-shelter and started dragging him and lifting him over these hedgerows. And when we got back to the company area, which was about four hundred yards or so, my first question to Lieutenant Smith was, 'Where's Lieutenant Ling?'

"He said, 'He's not here.'

"I said, 'Where is he, Lieutenant?'

" 'I don't know.'

"They had sent him back to the rear. He had some sort of nervous breakdown. I could have killed the son of a bitch. I found out after getting the instructions he was supposed to have, that he took us four hundred yards farther than we were supposed to go. There's nothing as bad as someone sitting on your flank picking you off one by one, especially when you can't see where the fire is coming from.

"When we got back, Brogan was taken to a medical tent. They put him in it. That was the last I saw of Brogan. [Technician 5th Grade] Bill Dean told me that he saw Brogan on the hood of a jeep that night, and he was dead. Brogan and I were both Catholic. He was a Canuck."[21]

Extremely heavy German automatic weapons, mortar, and artillery fire had stopped both the 1st and 3rd Battalions of the 508th, throwing back their attempts to assault the ridgeline during daylight.

East of the 508th sector, the 1st Battalion, 325th, and the 2nd Battalion, 401st, attacked again toward the town of La Poterie at 8:00 a.m., after an extensive artillery barrage on the town and surrounding area. As Private First Class Ray Burchell, with Company C, 325th, watched the barrage, he made "a remark about us having a real good Fourth of July with all the heavy shelling."[22]

As they began the assault, Burchell encountered something completely new and deadly. "There was very stiff resistance, we could only advance a few feet at a time. We got fired on with wooden machine gun bullets. They would explode in the air like firecrackers if they did not hit you. If [you were] hit, they shattered . . . the wound was full of wood splinters. These bullets had a purple tip. It was the only sector we ran into them. A dud 88 shell came into our field, spun like a top and went through a man on the opposite corner of the field from me. You could throw a cat through this man's stomach."[23]

At approximately 8:00 p.m., the 3rd Battalion, 507th, moved out and seized the eastern hill mass of the La Poterie ridgeline and by midnight had tied in with units on either side. The 2nd Battalion, 507th, attacked at 10:00 p.m., between the positions of 2nd and 3rd Battalions of the 508th and attacked the highest hill in the center of the ridgeline. The battalion circled the hill during the early hours of July 5, against considerable machine gun and artillery fire, and assaulted it from behind, capturing it before daylight.

The night of the fourth, Sergeant Schlemmer, with Headquarters Company, 2nd Battalion, 508th, wounded in the arm by American artillery shrapnel the day before, had been evacuated from Hill 131 to Utah Beach. "The 4th of July found me aboard an LST hospital ship, bound for an English field hospital. They had to cut off my dirty, bloody, stinking jumpsuit, which I had worn continuously for the past twenty-nine days without a bath. I insisted that they let me keep my jump boots on when they operated on my wounds, for they were my most prized possession.

"I marveled at the incredible luxuries of the Navy. Clean blankets, a white sheet, canned peaches, white bread, fruit juice, and real coffee—all of which were foreign and forgotten by us in those Norman hedgerows in which we had endured."[24]

The attacks by the 82nd Airborne on July 4, resulted in over five hundred enemy killed and over seven hundred captured. But the division had suffered heavily as well, as courageous officers and men attacked a well-armed foe, dug in on high ground.

On July 5, most of the division dug in and consolidated its positions overlooking La Haye-du-Puits. However, what was left of the 325th made an assault to capture the town of La Poterie and the reverse slope of the eastern portion of the La Poterie ridgeline. Private First Class Clinton Riddle, with Company B, moved forward with what little remained of his company under extremely heavy fire. "We started the attack about noon and it lasted until five in the afternoon. When we moved into La Poterie, the Germans counterattacked with tanks and infantry. Our tanks came forward and the Germans were driven from the area. We then reached our objective. The regiment had linked up with the 90th Division."[25]

That day, the division's artillery fired almost three thousand rounds in providing tremendous assistance in breaking up enemy counterattacks on the 507th positions on the La Poterie hill mass. While defending the hills, Lieutenant Louis Levy, with Company D, was killed and Lieutenant John Marr, with Company G, was wounded.

On the 6th and 7th of July, the division maintained its positions occupying the high ground northeast of La Haye-du-Puits. In the 507th sector, Captain Roy Creek, now the executive officer of the 1st Battalion, 507th, received news that two of the regiment's most courageous officers had been hit. "In the last action in which we would engage the enemy in Normandy, both Major [Ben "Red"] Pearson and Lieutenant Colonel [Arthur] Maloney were wounded. This happened at almost the same instant while the two of them were together, reconnoitering the area for a difficult, involved reinforcing maneuver. This was during the heavy fighting on La Poterie Ridge, near La Haye-du-Puits. They were evacuated; Major Pearson was shot through the face, but not seriously wounded. Lieutenant Colonel Maloney was seriously wounded and would not return. This was a great loss to the regiment, one that would impact deeply on every man that knew him."[26]

The 8th Infantry Division passed through the 82nd positions on July 8 to attack La Haye-du-Puits. The same day, the division was placed in corps reserve and all attached units were released from attachment. Over the next two days, the division pulled back a couple of miles and assembled.

On July 8, Private First Class Riddle was pulled back with the other survivors of the 325th. "We moved to [the] corps reserve assembly at Le Comterie. We had showers and clean clothing. We went to church services on the 9th. Clean on the outside and now clean on the inside!

"We were issued jump boots. The paratroopers said what was left [of the 325th] had earned the right to wear them. We had only forty-two men in Company B, 325th Glider Infantry."[27]

Private First Class Darrell Dilley's reaction to being issued jump boots was typical. "The feeling of receiving jump boots was very welcome and we were very happy as we felt like we deserved them, since we were doing the same as the paratroopers, who were a great bunch of guys."[28]

On July 1, glider flight pay was authorized, giving the enlisted men an extra fifty dollars and the officers an additional one hundred dollars per month. At last, the glider troopers felt they were being treated equally with the paratroopers.

By July 10, the jump suit worn by Private Mark Rupaner, with Company B, 505th, was in tatters after going through so many hedgerows and getting sleeves, pant legs, and jackets caught on thorns, bushes, and trees. "We were stripped of all of our clothes and then new clothes and a new gun was [*sic*] issued to us."[29]

But the next step in the process was perhaps the most memorable for those who were present, such as Lieutenant Dean McCandless, with Headquarters Company, 1st Battalion, 505th. "An engineer unit set up showers for us—after which, I felt wonderfully clean and about ten pounds lighter."[30]

The 10th of July was Lieutenant Ralph DeWeese's birthday. "The only celebration I had was a field shower and the news we were going to the beach the next day. The 507th was close by, so I went over to see if by chance Lieutenant [Max D.] Clark was there. He and I went through [Civilian Conservation Corps] together and were the best of friends. Much to my disappointment, I found he had been killed.

"On the 11th, we got new uniforms and got all set to move to the beach. Must say that was a grand and glorious feeling after being in the front lines thirty-three days and wearing the same clothes all that time.

"When we left the east area and were coming to the beach, we passed the 82nd Division Cemetery. It was well situated and had a large English glider at the entrance. It was located at Ste.-Mère-Église. To pass by and see all those white crosses, and I must say they stretched almost as far as you could see, it gave one a strange feeling and felt as if I had a big lump in my throat. I wanted so much to visit it and see where some of my men were buried, but I couldn't."[31]

On July 11, the entire division moved down to Utah Beach, where they waited to load onto seventeen LSTs for the trip to England. It was at this point that, when many of the troopers saw just how few of them were left from their units, they realized the extent of the losses. As he was standing with his company, Private First Class Ray Burchell, with Company C, 325th, watched a new infantry unit coming ashore. "One soldier said to me, 'What company is this?'

"I said, 'Company, your ass! This is a battalion!' I thought he was going to die as he turned so white."[32]

It was almost surreal as the waiting troopers listened to popular swing music playing over loudspeakers. It was bittersweet for Private First Class Clinton Riddle, with Company B, 325th—so few of his comrades were present, but he and the other survivors were going back to England. "The companies were so small standing around on the beach, they looked like platoons instead of companies. I enjoyed the music over the PA system."[33]

Lieutenant DeWeese along with fifty-five other survivors from Company H, 508th, and their gear were loaded on LST 310 for the journey to England. "We had an awfully nice trip across the channel, and the food and quarters were great. Maybe you think it wasn't a grand sight when we saw England again. We landed at Southampton and took a train back to Nottingham. When we got back to camp, hot chow was awaiting us, and our bedrolls."[34]

Only 1,072 officers and men from the 325th, 1,119 from the 505th, 995 from the 507th, and 939 from the 508th had loaded on to the LSTs. The casualties in the Normandy campaign had been horrendous. The division had gone into Normandy with 11,770 men and officers. Total casualties were 5,436, a 46 percent rate. The division suffered the loss of 1,142 killed or dead of wounds, 2,373 wounded, and 840 missing or captured. A total of 377 were evacuated sick, and 704 men were evacuated injured.

The percentage of losses in the infantry regiments was even more appalling, with the three parachute infantry regiments suffering 55 percent and the glider infantry regiment incurring a 58 percent casualty rate. Casualties among the officers in the infantry regiments were even higher. One regimental commander had been captured (Millett, 507th) and one was relieved because of combat fatigue, later diagnosed as cancer (Lewis, 325th). Of the twelve battalion commanders who went into Normandy on June 6, two had been killed (Batcheller, 1st Battalion, 508th, and Kellam, 1st Battalion, 505th); five had been wounded (Krause, 3rd Battalion, 505th; Ostberg, 1st Battalion, 507th; Shanley, 2nd Battalion, 508th; Swenson, 2nd Battalion, 325th; Timmes; 2nd Battalion, 507th); three had been injured (Boyd, 1st Battalion, 325th; Kuhn, 3rd Battalion, 507th; Vandervoort, 2nd Battalion, 505th); and one relieved (Carrell, 2nd

Battalion, 401st). Of the battalion commanders, only Lieutenant Colonel Louis Mendez had made it through the campaign without a wound or injury serious enough to be reportable. The loss among company commanders and platoon leaders was almost as bad. Over two-thirds of all lieutenants in the infantry regiments were casualties, with a far higher percentage if those serving as staff officers are eliminated from the calculation.

However, the troopers of the 82nd Airborne Division inflicted even greater casualties on the German Army. The men of the division were too busy defeating the Germans to stop and count casualties. The division officially reported enemy losses in major battles only at an estimated 1,500, with 2,189 captured. Enemy equipment included sixty-two tanks, two light reconnaissance vehicles, twenty-four antitank guns, fourteen antiaircraft guns, three self-propelled guns, and three artillery field pieces destroyed. The German 91st Airlanding Division and the 265th Division were essentially destroyed as fighting units at the hands of the paratroopers and glidermen. In reality, the casualties inflicted on the German Army were far higher, but accurate counts or even estimates were not kept because the division had neither the time nor the manpower to maintain such counts.

General Ridgway and General Gavin were very proud of the division's performance in Normandy. Gavin felt that the accolades for the victory in Normandy belonged to the enlisted men, noncommissioned officers, and officers who had sacrificed so much: "The troopers had been splendid; resourceful and courageous in the attack, resolute in the defense, they fought superbly."[35]

Chapter 1 "Fierce Individualists"

1. W. Forrest Dawson, Saga of the All American, 1946.
2. Ross S. Carter, *Those Devils In Baggy Pants*, Buccaneer Books, Inc., 1976, Preface.
3. Russell McConnell, interview with author.
4. Otis L. Sampson, "Time Out For Combat," p. 6.
5. Ibid.
6. Charles Miller, oral history, courtesy of the Eisenhower Center.
7. Ibid.
8. James Elmo Jones, oral history, courtesy of the Eisenhower Center.
9. Arthur B. Schultz, oral history, courtesy of the Eisenhower Center.
10. Bill Welsh, "Medic Chet," *Erie Morning News*, January 31, 1995.
11. W. A. Jones, interview with author.
12. D. Zane Schlemmer, oral history, courtesy of the Eisenhower Center.
13. William Katzenstein, "Revenge is Mine," courtesy of William Katzenstein.
14. William R. Hays, Jr., "A Paratrooper in WWII," courtesy of the William R. Hays, Jr. family, pp. 1–2.
15. James Megellas, *All The Way To Berlin*, Ballantine Publishing Group, 2003, p. 2.
16. Ibid., pp. 6–7.
17. Ibid., p. 9.
18. Briand N. Beaudin, oral history, courtesy of the Eisenhower Center.
19. James Elmo Jones, oral history.
20. W. A. Jones, interview.
21. Ibid.
22. William T. Dunfee, "Parachute Infantry Training—Fort Benning, Georgia—July 1942," courtesy of William T. Dunfee.
23. Hays, "A Paratrooper in WWII," pp. 2–3.
24. Tom W. Porcella, oral history, courtesy of the Eisenhower Center.
25. Hays, "A Paratrooper in WWII," p. 3.
26. W. A. Jones, interview.
27. Dunfee, "Parachute Infantry Training."
28. Miller, oral history.
29. Hays, "A Paratrooper in WWII," p. 3–4."
30. Miller, oral history.
31. Matthew B. Ridgway and Harold H. Martin, *Soldier: The Memoirs of Matthew B. Ridgway*, Greenwood Press, 1956, pp. 32–34.
32. Ibid., p. 35.
33. Omar N. Bradley and Clay Blair, *A General's Life*, Simon and Schuster, 1983, p. 104.
34. Ridgway and Martin, *Soldier*, pp. 51–52.
35. James M. Gavin, *On To Berlin*, Viking Press, 1978, pp. 1–2.
36. David Thomas letter to Al Ireland, Sept. 6, 1997, courtesy of the 82nd Airborne Division War Memorial Museum.
37. Bradley and Blair, *A General's Life*, p. 101.
38. Gavin, *On To Berlin*, pp. 2–3.
39. Ibid., p. 3.
40. Ibid., pp. 3–4.
41. Thomas to Ireland, Sept. 6, 1997.
42. Brigadier General Walter F. Winton, Jr., (U.S. Army Retired), written account.
43. Sampson, "Time Out For Combat," p. 15.
44. Ibid., pp. 16–18, 20–21.

45. Frank P. Woosley memoirs, courtesy of Frank P. Woosley.
46. Clay Blair, *Ridgway's Paratroopers*, Dial Press, 1985, p. 44.
47. Ross Pippin, "A Paratrooper's Story: My World War II Experiences as told to Gary Shaffer," courtesy of Ross Pippin and Gary Shaffer, p. 3.
48. James Elmo Jones, oral history.
49. Bill Bishop, interview with author.
50. William L. Blank memoirs, courtesy of the 82nd Airborne Division War Memorial Museum.
51. Sampson, "Time Out For Combat," p. 21.
52. Ibid.
53. Blank, memoirs.
54. Bennie Zinn, "Travels of Bennie Zinn, World War II, 1940–1945," courtesy of Bennie Zinn, Jr.

Chapter 2 "Ready"

1. Bennie Zinn, "Travels of Bennie Zinn, World War II, 1940–1945," courtesy of Bennie Zinn, Jr.
2. Mark Rupaner, response to author's questionnaire.
3. Dave Bullington, interview with author.
4. Rupaner, questionnaire.
5. Harvill Lazenby, response to author's questionnaire.
6. Bullington, interview.
7. William L. Blank memoirs, courtesy of the 82nd Airborne Division War Memorial Museum.
8. James Elmo Jones, oral history, courtesy of the Eisenhower Center.
9. Zinn, "Travels of Bennie Zinn."
10. Blank, memoirs.
11. Zinn, "Travels of Bennie Zinn."
12. Dean McCandless, "Remembering the Army," courtesy of Dean McCandless, p. 5.
13. T. Moffatt Burriss, *Strike And Hold*, Brassey's, 2000, pp. 29–30.
14. Zinn, "Travels of Bennie Zinn."
15. Burriss, *Strike And Hold*, pp. 29–30.
16. Zinn, "Travels of Bennie Zinn."
17. Blank, memoirs.
18. W. A. Jones, interview with author.
19. Russell McConnell, interview with author.
20. William H. Tucker, *Parachute Soldier*, International Airborne Books, 2nd ed., 1994, p. 12.
21. Matthew B. Ridgway and Harold H. Martin, *Soldier: The Memoirs of Matthew B. Ridgway*, Greenwood Press, 1956, p. 65.
22. The James M. Gavin Papers, Personal Diaries, Box 8—Folder "Diary Passages, Apr–Dec—1943," courtesy of the U.S. Army Military History Institute.
23. Rueben H. Tucker, as quoted from William B. Breuer, *Drop Zone Sicily*, Presidio Press, 1983, p. 3.
24. Zinn, "Travels of Bennie Zinn."
25. Harold Owens, oral history, courtesy of Harold Owens.
26. Zinn, "Travels of Bennie Zinn."
27. Tucker, *Parachute Soldier*, p. 10.
28. McConnell, interview.
29. Daniel B. McIlvoy memoirs, courtesy of Mrs. Annie McIlvoy Zaya, p. 3.
30. Ibid., p. 2.
31. Pat Reid, "Chow," courtesy of the 82nd Airborne Division War Memorial Museum, p. 3.
32. Howard C. Goodson, interview with author.

33. McIlvoy, memoirs, p. 3.
34. James M. Gavin, *On To Berlin*, Viking Press, 1978, p. 9.
35. The James M. Gavin Papers, "Diary Passages, Apr–Dec—1943."
36. McCandless, "Remembering the Army," p. 5.
37. Bullington, interview.
38. James J. Coyle, written account in "Echoes of the Warriors," compiled and edited by George Jacobus, 1992, p. 59.
39. Ridgway and Martin, *Soldier*, pp. 65–66.
40. Coyle, written account, "Echoes of the Warriors," p. 59.
41. Ridgway and Martin, *Soldier*, p. 66.
42. W. A. Jones, interview.
43. Ridgway and Martin, *Soldier*, pp. 66–68
44. Mark J. Alexander, "Personal Memories of Sicily," courtesy of Mark J. Alexander, p. 1.
45. Willard Follmer, interview with author.
46. Ibid.
47. Ibid.
48. Ibid.
49. Ibid.
50. Ibid.
51. Ibid.
52. Sampson, "Time Out For Combat," p. 54.
53. Ibid.
54. Goodson, interview.
55. William T. Dunfee, "Sicily Invasion—Operation Husky—July 9–10, 1943," courtesy of William T. Dunfee, p. 4.
56. McConnell, interview.
57. Ridgway and Martin, *Soldier*, pp. 66, 68.

Chapter 3 "Destroy Him Wherever Found"

1. Colonel James Gavin, as quoted in Allen L. Langdon, "*Ready: The History of the 505th, 82nd Airborne Division*," Western Newspaper Publishing Co., 1986, p. 17.
2. W. A. Jones, interview with author.
3. William T. Dunfee, "Sicily Invasion—Operation Husky—July 9–10, 1943," courtesy of William T. Dunfee, p. 4.
4. Omar N. Bradley and Clay Blair, *A General's Life*, Simon and Schuster, 1983, pp. 175–176.
5. Major Edwin M. Sayre, "The Operations of Company A 505th Parachute Infantry (82nd Airborne Division) Airborne Landings In Sicily 9–24 July 1943 (Sicily Campaign) (Personal Experience of a Company Commander)," Infantry School, 1947, courtesy of the Donovan Research Library, Fort Benning, Georgia, p. 9.
6. Otis L. Sampson, "Time Out For Combat," pp. 2–3.
7. Dunfee, "Sicily Invasion," p. 4.
8. Sayre, "Operations of Company A 505th Parachute Infantry," p. 10.
9. Roy M. Hanna, response to author's questionnaire.
10. Shelby R. Hord, interview with author.
11. "82nd Airborne Division In Sicily And Italy, Part II—Sicily," courtesy of the 82nd Airborne Division War Memorial Museum, p. 34.
12. Ibid.
13. Ibid.
14. Ibid.
15. Ibid.
16. Dunfee, "Sicily Invasion," pp. 4–5.
17. Willard Follmer, interview with author.
18. Howard C. Goodson, interview with author.

19. Sayre, "Operations of Company A 505th Parachute Infantry," p. 9.
20. Dave Bullington, interview with author.
21. Robert Gillette, "The Sicily Campaign: A Personal Story of Sicily," p. 1.
22. Ibid., pp. 1–2.
23. Mark J. Alexander, "Personal Memories of Sicily," courtesy of Mark J. Alexander, p. 2.
24. Ibid.
25. Sayre, "Operations of Company A 505th Parachute Infantry," pp. 9–11.
26. Gillette, "The Sicily Campaign," p. 2.
27. Sayre, "Operations of Company A 505th Parachute Infantry," p. 11.
28. Bullington, interview.
29. Sayre, "Operations of Company A 505th Parachute Infantry," p. 11.
30. Bullington, interview.
31. Sayre, "Operations of Company A 505th Parachute Infantry," pp. 11–12.
32. Bullington, interview.
33. Sayre, "Operations of Company A 505th Parachute Infantry," pp. 12–13.
34. Tim Dyas, written account, courtesy of Tim Dyas.
35. James M. Gavin, *On To Berlin*, Viking Press, 1978, p. 26.
36. Ibid.
37. Dean McCandless, "Remembering the Army," courtesy of Dean McCandless, p. 6.
38. Ibid.
39. Elmo E. Bell and The University of Southern Mississippi Center for Oral History and Cultural Heritage, *An Oral History with Brigadier General Elmo Edwin Bell: A Saga of a Survivor*, The University of Southern Mississippi, 2003, pp. 76–77.
40. Ibid., pp. 77–78.
41. "82nd Airborne Division In Sicily And Italy, Part II—Sicily," p. 35.
42. Ibid., p. 36.
43. McCandless, "Remembering the Army," p. 6.
44. Sayre, "Operations of Company A 505th Parachute Infantry," pp. 13–14.
45. Ibid., p. 14.
46. Alexander, "Sicily," p. 3.
47. Lieutenant John D. Sprinkle would be posthumously awarded the Distinguished Service Cross for his bravery in the assault of the pillbox complex.
48. Alexander, "Sicily," p. 3.
49. Ray Grossman, response to author's questionnaire.
50. Hord, interview.
51. Ibid.
52. Ibid.
53. Ibid.
54. Follmer, interview.
55. Sayre, "Operations of Company A 505th Parachute Infantry," pp. 14–16.
56. Hord, interview.
57. Ibid.
58. Ibid.

Chapter 4 "We Had a Long Way to Go Yet, and Some of the Men Would Accompany Us No More"

1. Frank Miale, written account, courtesy of Frank Miale.
2. "82nd Airborne Division In Sicily And Italy, Part II—Sicily," courtesy of the 82nd Airborne Division War Memorial Museum, p. 25.
3. Ibid.
4. James M. Gavin, *On To Berlin*, Viking Press, 1978, p. 29.
5. Bill Bishop, interview with author.
6. Gavin, *On To Berlin*, p. 29.

7. Bishop, interview.
8. Russell McConnell, interview with author.
9. Bishop, interview.
10. McConnell, interview.
11. Robert Fielder, written account, courtesy of Robert Fielder.
12. Cloid Wigle, written account, courtesy of Cloid Wigle.
13. Wigle, written account.
14. Ibid.
15. Bishop interview.
16. McConnell interview.
17. Pat Reid, "Chow," courtesy of the 82nd Airborne Division War Memorial Museum, p. 5.
18. Fielder, written account.
19. Wigle, written account.
20. Gavin, *On To Berlin*, pp. 29–30
21. Ibid., p. 30.
22. Ibid.
23. Ray Grossman, response to author's questionnaire.
24. Gavin, *On To Berlin*, p. 32.
25. Ray Grossman, written account.
26. Ibid.
27. Private First Class Murray Goldman, sworn statement, May 16, 1945.
28. Colonel Arthur L. Kelly, Principal Interviewer, "Interview with Daniel B. McIlvoy," March 25, 1988, American Military Veterans Oral History Project, 2000, University of Kentucky.
29. Goldman, sworn statement.
30. Fielder, written account.
31. "82nd Airborne Division In Sicily And Italy, Part II—Sicily," p. 26.
32. Ibid.
33. Gavin, *On To Berlin*, pp. 30–32.
34. Jerry Huth, interview with author.
35. Miale, written account.
36. Huth, interview.
37. James Rightley, response to author's questionnaire.
38. "82nd Airborne Division In Sicily And Italy, Part II—Sicily," p. 26.
39. Miale, written account.
40. Dean McCandless, "Remembering the Army," courtesy of Dean McCandless, pp. 7–8.
41. Lieutenant John S. Thompson, "Individual Report on Operation Husky," courtesy of the 82nd Airborne Division War Memorial Museum.
42. "82nd Airborne Division in Sicily and Italy, Part II—Sicily," p. 7.
43. Ibid., pp. 7–8.
44. Ibid., p. 9.
45. Thompson, "Operation Husky."
46. Mark J. Alexander, "Personal Memories of Sicily," courtesy of Mark J. Alexander, p. 4.
47. Edward J. Sims, "Enclosure 1 To Army Service Experience Questionnaire For Edward J. Sims, Sicily ," U.S. Army Military History Institute, courtesy of Edward J. Sims, pp. 1–2.
48. "82nd Airborne Division in Sicily and Italy, Part II—Sicily," p. 8.
49. Ibid., p. 10.
50. Sims, "Enclosure 1," pp. 1–2.
51. Thompson, "Operation Husky."
52. Major Edwin M. Sayre, "The Operations of Company A 505th Parachute Infantry (82nd Airborne Division) Airborne Landings in Sicily 9–24 July 1943 (Sicily Campaign) (Personal Experience of a Company Commander)," Infantry School, 1947, courtesy of

the Donovan Research Library, Fort Benning, Georgia, p. 17.
53 McCandless, "Remembering the Army," pp. 7–8.
54. Sayre, "Operations of Company A 505th," p. 17.
55. Shelby R. Hord, interview.
56. "82nd Airborne Division in Sicily and Italy, Part II—Sicily," p. 13.
57. Fredrick W. Randall, written account, courtesy of Wheatley T. Christensen.
58. McConnell, interview.
59. Fielder, written account.
60. "82nd Airborne Division In Sicily And Italy, Part II—Sicily," p. 36.
61. Thompson, "Operation Husky."
62. Sayre, "Operations of Company A 505th," pp. 17–18.
63. "82nd Airborne Division In Sicily And Italy, Part II—Sicily," p. 36.
64. Sims, "Enclosure 1," p. 2.
65. Ibid.
66. William T. Dunfee, "Sicily Invasion—Operation Husky—July 9–10, 1943," courtesy of William T. Dunfee, p. 9.
67. Ibid.
68. William L. Blank memoirs, courtesy of the 82nd Airborne Division War Memorial Museum.
69. Dunfee, "Sicily Invasion," pp. 9–10.
70. Kurt Student, Nuremburg Trials.

Chapter 5 "Retreat Hell!—Send Me My 3rd Battalion!"

1. "Report of the 504th Parachute Infantry Combat Team in Operation Avalanche," courtesy of the 82nd Airborne Division War Memorial Museum.
2. Jerry Huth, interview with author.
3. Mark J. Alexander, "Italy—1943," courtesy of Mark J. Alexander, p. 1.
4. Bennie Zinn, "Travels of Bennie Zinn, World War II, 1940–1945," courtesy of Bennie Zinn, Jr.
5. Alexander, "Italy," p. 1.
6. "The 82nd Airborne Division In Sicily And Italy, Part III—Italy, Section IV," courtesy of the 82nd Airborne Division War Memorial Museum, p. 62.
7. "The 82nd Airborne Division In Sicily And Italy, Part III—Italy, Section III," p. 56.
8. Ibid., p. 57.
9. Ibid.
10. Joe Watts, as quoted in, Patrick K. O'Donnell, *Beyond Valor*, The Free Press, 2001, p. 66
11. Alexander, "Italy," p. 1.
12. Edward J. Sims, "Enclosure 2 To Army Service Experience Questionnaire For Edward J. Sims, Italy," U.S. Army Military History Institute, courtesy of Edward J. Sims, pp. 1–2.
13. Captain John Norton, "Pathfinder Operations—Italy 14–15 Sept. 1943," courtesy of Lieutenant General (U.S. Army Retired) John Norton.
14. Sims, "Enclosure 2," pp. 1–2.
15. James M. Gavin, *On To Berlin*, Viking Press, 1978, p. 65.
16. Matthew B. Ridgway and Harold H. Martin, *Soldier: The Memoirs of Matthew B. Ridgway*, Greenwood Press, 1956, pp. 84–85.
17. "Unit Journal of the 2nd Battalion, 504th Parachute Infantry, 82nd Airborne Division," courtesy of the 82nd Airborne Division War Memorial Museum, p. 21.
18. Ibid.
19. Reneau Breard, interview with author.
20. Major John S. Lekson, "The Operations of the 1st Battalion, 504th Parachute Infantry (82nd Airborne Division) in the Capture of Altavilla, Italy, 13 September–19 September 1943, (Naples-Foggia Campaign), (Personal Experience of a Battalion

Operations Officer)," Infantry School, 1947–1948, courtesy of the Donovan Research Library, Fort Benning, Georgia, p. 8.

21 "The 82nd Airborne Division In Sicily And Italy, Part III—Italy, Section I," p. 49.
22. Ibid.
23. Lekson, Operations of the 1st Battalion, 504th Parachute Infantry, p. 8.
24. Ibid., p. 9.
25. "Unit Journal of the 2nd Battalion, 504th Parachute Infantry," p. 21.
26. Norton, "Pathfinder Operations."
27. Ibid.
28. William Sullivan, as quoted in O'Donnell, *Beyond Valor*, p. 70.
29. Mike Colella, response to author's questionnaire.
30. George Speakman, response to author's questionnaire.
31. Major Robert L. Dickerson, "The Operations of Company E, 325th Glider Infantry (82nd Airborne Division) in the Battle of Mount Saint Angelo, 18–20 September 1943, (Naples-Foggia Campaign), (Personal Experience of a Company Commander)," Infantry School, 1947–1948, courtesy of the Donovan Research Library, Fort Benning, Georgia, p. 5.
32 Ibid., pp. 5–6.
33. Ibid., p. 6.
34. Ibid.
35. Lekson, "Operations of the 1st Battalion, 504th Parachute Infantry," p. 11.
36. Ibid., p. 15.
37. "Unit Journal of the 2nd Battalion, 504th Parachute Infantry," p. 22.
38. First Lieutenant Otto W. Huebner, "The Operations of Company A, 504th Parachute Infantry (82nd Airborne Division) in the Defense of Hill 424 near Altavilla, Italy, 17 September–19 September 1943, (Naples-Foggia Campaign), (Personal Experience of the Company Operations Sergeant and Acting First Sergeant)," Infantry School, 1948–1949, courtesy of the Donovan Research Library, Fort Benning, Georgia, pp. 10–11.
39 Dickerson, "Operations of Company E, 325th Glider Infantry," pp. 5–7.
40. Huebner, "The Operations of Company A, 504th Parachute Infantry," pp. 11–12
41. Richard Tregaskis, *Invasion Diary*, Random House, 1944, pp. 116–117.
42. Lekson, "Operations of the 1st Battalion, 504th Parachute Infantry," pp. 17–19.
43. Tregaskis, *Invasion Diary*, pp. 118, 120.
44. Huebner, "Operations of Company A, 504th Parachute Infantry," pp. 11–13.
45. Lekson, "Operations of the 1st Battalion, 504th Parachute Infantry," pp. 23–24.
46. "Unit Journal of the 2nd Battalion, 504th Parachute Infantry," p. 22.
47. Ross S. Carter, *Those Devils In Baggy Pants*, Buccaneer Books, Inc., 1976, p. 38.
48. Ibid., p. 41. The 504 was called the Legion by some of its troopers.
49. Huebner, "Operations of Company A, 504th Parachute Infantry," pp. 13–14.
50. Lekson, "Operations of the 1st Battalion, 504th Parachute Infantry," pp. 27–29.
51. "Unit Journal of the 2nd Battalion, 504th Parachute Infantry," p. 22.
52. Huebner, "Operations of Company A, 504th Parachute Infantry," pp. 14–15.
53. Reneau Breard, interview.
54. Huebner, "Operations of Company A, 504th Parachute Infantry," pp. 15–18.
55. Albert Clark, response to author's questionnaire.
56. Huebner, "Operations of Company A, 504th Parachute Infantry," pp. 18–20.
57. Lekson, "Operations of the 1st Battalion, 504th Parachute Infantry," p. 30.
58. Huebner, "Operations of Company A, 504th Parachute Infantry," pp. 20–22.
59. "Unit Journal of the 2nd Battalion, 504th Parachute Infantry," p. 22.
60. Lekson, "Operations of the 1st Battalion, 504th Parachute Infantry," pp. 34–35.
61. Huebner, "Operations of Company A, 504th Parachute Infantry," pp. 22–25.
62. Breard, interview.
63. Huebner, "Operations of Company A, 504th Parachute Infantry," p. 25.
64. Breard, interview.
65. Huebner, "Operations of Company A, 504th Parachute Infantry," p. 25.

66. "Unit Journal of the 2nd Battalion, 504th Parachute Infantry," p. 22.
67. "Report of the 504th Parachute Infantry Combat Team in Operation Avalanche."

Chapter 6 "Wait Until a Triumphant Entry Is Organized"

1. James M. Gavin, *On To Berlin*, Viking Press, 1978, p. 71
2. Major Robert L. Dickerson, "The Operations of Company E, 325th Glider Infantry (82nd Airborne Division) in the Battle of Mount Saint Angelo, 18–20 September 1943, (Naples-Foggia Campaign), (Personal Experience of a Company Commander)," Infantry School, 1947–1948, courtesy of the Donovan Research Library, Fort Benning, Georgia, p. 11.
3. Ibid., p. 9.
4. Ibid., p. 13.
5. Mike Colella, response to author's questionnaire.
6. Dickerson, "Operations of Company E, 325th Glider Infantry," p. 14.
7. Daniel Clark, response to author's questionnaire.
8. Andrew A. Devorak, response to author's questionnaire.
9. Darrell C. Dilley, response to author's questionnaire.
10. Dickerson, "Operations of Company E, 325th Glider Infantry," pp. 18–20.
11. Edwin Lainhart, "Recollections of My Experiences in World War II Medical Detachment, 325th Glider Infantry Regiment 82nd Airborne Division," pp. 4–5.
12. Dickerson, "Operations of Company E, 325th Glider Infantry," pp. 20–22.
13. Edward J. Sims, "Enclosure 2 To Army Service Experience Questionnaire For Edward J. Sims, Italy," U.S. Army Military History Institute, courtesy of Edward J. Sims, p. 2.
14. Clay Blair, *Ridgway's Paratroopers*, Dial Press, 1985, p. 191.
15. Robert Tallon, as quoted in T. Moffatt Burriss, *Strike And Hold*, Brassey's, 2000, pp. 55–56.
16. Burriss, *Strike and Hold*, p. 56.
17. Robert Tallon, as quoted in Burriss, *Strike and Hold*, p. 56.
18. Burriss, *Strike and Hold*, p. 56.
19. James B. Helmer, "Story of the 82nd Airborne Division and the 325th Glider Infantry Regiment," courtesy of Kathy Stepzinski, p. 2.
20. Clinton E. Riddle, response to author's questionnaire.
21. Gavin, *On To Berlin*, pp. 71–72.
22. Matthew B. Ridgway and Harold H. Martin, *Soldier: The Memoirs of Matthew B. Ridgway*, Greenwood Press, 1956, pp. 87–88.
23. Gavin, *On To Berlin*, pp. 72–73.
24. William L. Blank memoirs, courtesy of the 82nd Airborne Division War Memorial Museum.
25. Blank, memoirs.
26. Mark J. Alexander, "Italy—1943," courtesy of Mark J. Alexander, pp. 2–3.
27. Spencer F. Wurst, unpublished manuscript, p. 200.
28. Alexander, "Italy," p. 3.
29. Wurst, manuscript, pp. 201–202.
30. Alexander, "Italy," p. 3.
31. Wurst, manuscript, p. 206.
32. Julius Axman, as quoted in Otis L. Sampson, "Time Out For Combat," pp. 131–132.
33. Edward Carpus, as quoted in Otis L. Sampson, "Time Out For Combat," p. 133.
34. Earl W. Boling, written account in "Echoes of the Warriors," compiled and edited by George Jacobus, 1992, p. 109.
35. John W. Keller, written account in "Echoes of the Warriors," 1992, p. 191.
36. Julius Axman, as quoted in Sampson, "Time Out For Combat," p. 132.
37. Sampson, "Time Out For Combat," pp. 119–122.
38. Jack Francis, as quoted in Otis L. Sampson, "Time Out For Combat," p. 133.

39. Talton W. Long, as quoted in Otis L. Sampson, "Time Out For Combat," pp. 138–139.
40. Sampson, "Time Out For Combat," p. 124.
41. Talton W. Long, as quoted in Sampson, "Time Out For Combat," p. 139.
42. Alexander, "Italy," p. 5.
43. Ridgway and Martin, *Soldier*, pp. 89–90.
44. James Rightley, response to author's questionnaire.
45. Frank Miale, written account, courtesy of Frank Miale.
46. Reneau Breard, interview with author.
47. Gavin, *On To Berlin*, pp. 73–74.
48. Sims, "Enclosure 2," p. 2.
49. "Unit Journal of the 2nd Battalion, 504th Parachute Infantry, 82nd Airborne Division," courtesy of the 82nd Airborne Division War Memorial Museum, p. 34.
50. Sims, "Enclosure 2," p. 3.
51. Shelby R. Hord, interview with author.
52. Sims, "Enclosure 2," p. 3.
53. Francis W. McLane, "Francis W. McLane a.k.a. "Mac" World War II, Journal," courtesy of Francis W. McLane, p. 10.
54. Sims, "Enclosure 2," p. 3.
55. McLane, "World War II, Journal," p. 10.
56. Sims, "Enclosure 2," p. 3.
57. McLane, "World War II, Journal," p. 11.
58. Ross S. Carter, *Those Devils In Baggy Pants*, Buccaneer Books, Inc., 1976, p. 67.
59. McLane, "World War II, Journal," p. 11.
60. Carter, *Those Devils In Baggy Pants*, p. 67.
61. McLane, "World War II, Journal," p. 11.
62. Carter, *Those Devils In Baggy Pants*, pp. 69–70.
63. The James M. Gavin Papers, Personal Diaries, Box 8—Folder, "Diary Passages, Apr–Dec—1943," U.S. Army Military History Institute.
64. Blank, memoirs.
65. Gavin Papers, "Diary Passages, Apr–Dec—1943."
66. Ibid.
67. Sims, "Enclosure 2," p. 3.

Chapter 7 "Devils in Baggy Pants"

1. Ross S. Carter, *Those Devils In Baggy Pants*, Buccaneer Books, 1976, p. 74.
2. James Megellas, *All The Way To Berlin*, Ballantine Publishing Group, 2003, p. 28.
3. Ibid., pp. 28–29.
4. Francis W. McLane, "Francis W. McLane a.k.a. "Mac" World War II, Journal," courtesy of Francis McLane, p. 14.
5. "Unit Journal of the 2nd Battalion, 504th Parachute Infantry, 82nd Airborne Division," courtesy of the 82nd Airborne Division War Memorial Museum, p. 44.
6. Reneau Breard, interview with author.
7. McLane, "World War II, Journal," p. 14.
8. Ibid., p. 14.
9. Breard, interview.
10. McLane, "World War II, Journal," pp. 14–15.
11. Joseph W. Lyons, response to author's questionnaire.
12. "Unit Journal of the 2nd Battalion, 504th Parachute Infantry," pp. 45–46.
13. Ibid., p. 46.
14. Delbert Kuehl, as quoted in T. Moffatt Burriss, *Strike and Hold*, Brassey's, 2000, p. 59.
15. "Unit Journal of the 2nd Battalion, 504th Parachute Infantry," p. 46.
16. Megellas, *All The Way To Berlin*, p. 34.
17. Ibid.
18. William B. Breuer, *Geronimo!*, St. Martin's Press, 1989, p. 157.

19. Breard, interview.
20. Ibid.
21. Russell T. Long, "My Life in the Service, The Diary of Cpl. Russell T. Long," courtesy of Jan Bos.
22. Breard, interview.
23. Shelby R. Hord, interview with author.
24. Harry L. Reisenleiter, oral history, courtesy of the Eisenhower Center.
25. James M. Gavin, *On To Berlin*, Viking Press, 1978, pp. 83–86, 88.
26. D. Zane Schlemmer, oral history, courtesy of the Eisenhower Center.
27. Tom W. Porcella, oral history, courtesy of the Eisenhower Center.
28. Briand N. Beaudin, oral history, courtesy of the Eisenhower Center.
29. Leo M. Hart, interview with the author.
30. Louis Orvin, interview with the author.
31. Edward J. Sims, "Enclosure 2 To Army Service Experience Questionnaire For Edward J. Sims, Italy," U.S. Army Military History Institute, courtesy of Edward J. Sims, pp. 3–4.
32. Albert Clark, response to author's questionnaire.
33. Captain William J. Sweet, Jr., "Operations of the 2nd Battalion, 504th Parachute Infantry Regiment (82nd Airborne Division) on the Anzio Beachhead, 22 January–23 March 1944, (Anzio Campaign), (Personal Experience of a Battalion Operations Officer and Company Commander)," Infantry School, 1947–1948, courtesy of the Donovan Research Library, Fort Benning, Georgia, pp. 6–10.
34. Landon Chilcutt, response to author's questionnaire.
35. Sweet, Operations of the 2nd Battalion, 504th," pp. 13–14.
36. Sims, "Enclosure 2," p. 4.
37. Ibid.
38. Orvin, interview.
39. Megellas, *All The Way To Berlin*, p. 61.
40. Ibid., p. 62.
41. Ibid.
42. Ibid., pp. 63–64.
43. Roy M. Hanna, written account, courtesy of the 82nd Airborne Division War Memorial Museum.
44. Orvin, interview.
45. Hanna, written account.
46. Orvin, interview.
47. Megellas, *All The Way To Berlin*, pp. 64–65.
48. Hanna, written account.
49. Megellas, *All The Way To Berlin*, p. 67.
50. Hanna, written account.
51. *The Devils In Baggy Pants, Combat Record of the 504th Parachute Infantry Regiment April 1943–July 1945*, compiled by Lieutenant William D. Mandle and Private First Class David H. Whittier, Draeger Freres, Paris, 1945.

Chapter 8 "You Are About to Embark Upon the Great Crusade"

1. General Dwight D. Eisenhower, "Letter to Allied Soldiers, Sailors, and Airmen," 1944.
2. Ray Grossman, response to author's questionnaire.
3. James M. Gavin, *On To Berlin*, Viking Press, 1978, p. 90.
4. Bennie Zinn, "The Travels of Bennie Zinn, World War II, 1940–1945," courtesy of Bennie Zinn, Jr.
5. Ibid.
6. James L. Ward, response to author's questionnaire and written account.
7. James Elmo Jones, oral history, courtesy of the Eisenhower Center.
8. James Emory Baugh, *From Skies of Blue*, Universe, 2003, pp. 109, 111, 112.
9. Roy E. Creek, oral history, courtesy of the Eisenhower Center.

10. Stefan Kramar, "Self Portrait," p. 9.
11. William L. Blank, memoirs, courtesy of the 82nd Airborne Division War Memorial Museum.
12. Henry B. LeFebvre, written account, courtesy of Henry B. LeFebvre.
13. Carl Mauro, written account, courtesy of Carl Mauro.
14. Matthew B. Ridgway and Harold H. Martin, *Soldier: The Memoirs of Matthew B. Ridgway*, Greenwood Press, 1956, p. 92.
15. Clay Blair, *Ridgway's Paratroopers*, Dial Press, 1985, p. 242.
16. Kramar, "Self Portrait," pp. 13–17, 120.
17. Jack R. Isaacs, oral history, courtesy of the Eisenhower Center.
18. Kramar, "Self Portrait," pp. 20–21.
19. Creek, oral history.
20. D. Zane Schlemmer, oral history, courtesy of the Eisenhower Center.
21. L. C. Tomlinson, oral history, courtesy of the Eisenhower Center.
22. Schlemmer, oral history.
23. Isaacs, oral history.
24. William H. Tucker, *Parachute Soldier*, International Airborne Books, 2nd ed., 1994, pp. 29–30.
25. Kramar, "Self Portrait," pp. 23–25.
26. Tom W. Porcella, oral history, courtesy of the Eisenhower Center.
27. Kenneth Russell, oral history, courtesy of the Eisenhower Center.
28. Ibid.
29. Edward J. Jeziorski, oral history, courtesy of the Eisenhower Center.
30. Porcella, oral history.
31. Chris Kanaras, oral history, courtesy of the Eisenhower Center.
32. Wesley T. Leeper, written account, courtesy of the Eisenhower Center.
33. Charles Miller, oral history, courtesy of the Eisenhower Center.
34. Dennis G. O'Loughlin, "Fierce Individualists—U.S. Paratroopers in WWII," 1977, courtesy of Frank P. Woosley, pp. 187, 188, 189.
35. Gavin, *On To Berlin*, p. 103.
36. Ibid.
37. Tucker, *Parachute Soldier*, p. 31.
38. Schlemmer, oral history.
39. Those killed were Private First Class Robert L. Leaky, Private Pete Vah, Corporal Kenneth A. Vaught, and Private Eddie O. Meelberg (who died later that night).
40. Arthur B. Schultz oral history, courtesy of the Eisenhower Center.
41. Tucker, *Parachute Soldier*, pp. 31–32.

Chapter 9 "Almighty God, Our Sons, Pride of Our Nation, This Day Have Set Upon a Mighty Endeavor"

1. Franklin D. Roosevelt, President's D-Day Prayer, June 6, 1944, Washington D.C., Audio Recordings, Tape # RLxA-1 74-1:1 75-5(1) RL 454, Franklin D. Roosevelt Library Digital Archives.
2. James Elmo Jones, oral history, courtesy of the Eisenhower Center.
3. Tom W. Porcella, oral history, courtesy of the Eisenhower Center.
4. Harry L. Reisenleiter, oral history, courtesy of the Eisenhower Center.
5. Hubert S. Bass letter to Cornelius Ryan, March 20, 1959, courtesy of the Cornelius Ryan Collection, Alden Library, Ohio University.
6. James Elmo Jones, oral history.
7. Bass to Ryan, March 20, 1959.
8. D. Zane Schlemmer, oral history, courtesy of the Eisenhower Center.
9. J. Frank Brumbaugh, oral history, courtesy of the Eisenhower Center.
10. James Elmo Jones, oral history.
11. Ibid.
12. Brumbaugh, oral history.
13. James Elmo Jones, oral history.

14. Bass to Ryan, March 20, 1959.
15. Anthony J. DeMayo, written account, courtesy of the Cornelius Ryan Collection, Alden Library, Ohio University, p. 4.
16. Benjamin H. Vandervoort, written account, courtesy of the Cornelius Ryan Collection, Alden Library, Ohio University, p. 1.
17. Bass to Ryan, March 20, 1959.
18. DeMayo, written account, p. 4.
19. Bass to Ryan, March 20, 1959.
20. Vandervoort, written account, p. 1.
21. James Elmo Jones, oral history.
22. Kenneth Russell, oral history, courtesy of the Eisenhower Center.
23. Ibid.
24. George Jacobus, written account in "Echoes of the Warriors," compiled and edited by George Jacobus, 1992, pp. 239–240.
25. Cullen Clark, written account, courtesy of the Ryan Collection, Alden Library, Ohio University, pp. 2–3.
26. James J. Coyle, written account in "Echoes of the Warriors," p. 261.
27. Vandervoort, written account, p. 2.
28. Roy King, written account, courtesy of Roy King.
29. Ibid.
30. Charles Miller, oral history, courtesy of the Eisenhower Center.
31. Jack R. Isaacs, oral history, courtesy of the Eisenhower Center.
32. Clarence McKelvey, as quoted in "456th Parachute Field Artillery History," Starlyn R. Jorgensen, pp. 109–111.
33. Ray Grossman, as quoted in "456th Parachute Field Artillery History," Starlyn R. Jorgensen, p. 109.
34. Harvill Lazenby, response to author's questionnaire.
35. Joseph I. O'Jibway, response to author's questionnaire.
36. James M. Gavin, written account, courtesy of the Ryan Collection, Alden Library, Ohio University, pp. 2–3.
37. Tom W. Porcella, oral history, courtesy of the Eisenhower Center.
38. Lieutenant Ralph E. DeWeese, diary, courtesy of the 82nd Airborne Division War Memorial Museum.
39. Dan Furlong, oral history, courtesy of the Eisenhower Center.
40. DeWeese, diary.
41. Malcolm D. Brannen, written account, courtesy of the 82nd Airborne Division War Memorial Museum, pp. 6–7.
42. John R. Taylor, oral history, courtesy of the Eisenhower Center.
43. Schlemmer, oral history.
44. Brannen, written account, p. 7.
45. Brumbaugh, oral history.
46. Brannen, written account, p. 7.
47. Captain John T. Joseph, "The Operations of a Regimental Pathfinder Unit, 507th Parachute Infantry Regiment (82nd Airborne Division) in Normandy, France 6 June 1944, (Normandy Campaign), (Personal Experience of a Regimental Pathfinder Leader)," Infantry School, 1947–1948, courtesy of the Donovan Research Library, Fort Benning, Georgia, p. 15.
48. Chris Kanaras, oral history, courtesy of the Eisenhower Center.
49. Arthur A. Maloney, questionnaire, Attachment A, courtesy of the Ryan Collection, Alden Library, Ohio University.
50. Stefan Kramar, "Self Portrait," p. 40.
51. Arthur A. Maloney questionnaire, Attachment B, courtesy of the Ryan Collection, Alden Library, Ohio University.
52. Kramar, "Self Portrait," pp. 40, 42, 44–45.
53. Francis E. Naughton, "Narrative, Interaction of United States Forces and French Citizens during the Battle of Graignes, 6–12 June, 1944," courtesy of Francis E.

Naughton.

54. Edward Barnes, oral history, courtesy of the Eisenhower Center.
55. Brannen, written account, p. 7.
56. Roosevelt, D-Day Prayer, June 6, 1944.

Chapter 10 "Wherever You Land, Make Your Way to Ste.-Mère-Église, and Together We Will Raise This Flag"

1. Lieutenant Colonel Edward C. Krause, as quoted in Allen L. Langdon, "*Ready: The History of the 505th, 82nd Airborne Division,*" Western Newspaper Publishing Co., 1986, p. 44.
2. Bennie Zinn, "Travels of Bennie Zinn, World War II, 1940–1945," courtesy of Bennie Zinn, Jr.
3. Roy E. Creek, oral history, courtesy of the Eisenhower Center.
4. Wheatley T. Christensen, "Normandy," courtesy of Wheatley T. Christensen.
5. Lyle B. Putnam questionnaire, courtesy of the Cornelius Ryan Collection, Alden Library, Ohio University, p. 2.
6. Leslie P. Cruise, written account, courtesy of Leslie P. Cruise.
7. William L. Blank, memoirs, courtesy of the 82nd Airborne Division War Memorial Museum.
8. Cruise, written account.
9. Ronald Snyder, oral history, courtesy of the Eisenhower Center.
10. Langdon, *Ready*, p. 44.
11. Christensen, "Normandy."
12. Blank, memoirs.
13. Christensen, "Normandy."
14. William H. Tucker, *Parachute Soldier*, International Airborne Books, 2nd ed., 1994, p. 38.
15. Cruise, written account.
16. James M. Gavin interview, courtesy of the Cornelius Ryan Collection, Alden Library, Ohio University, pp. 3–4.
17. Lieutenant Colonel Raymond Singleton, "Debriefing Conference—Operation Neptune," 13 August 1944, courtesy of the 82nd Airborne Division War Memorial Museum, p. 12.
18. James Elmo Jones, oral history, courtesy of the Eisenhower Center.
19. Ibid.
20. Malcolm D. Brannen, written account, courtesy of the 82nd Airborne Division War Memorial Museum, pp. 7–8.
21. Captain Tony J. Raibl, "The Operations Of The 82nd Airborne Division Artillery (82nd Airborne Division) In The Airborne Landings Near Ste.-Mère-Église, France 6–8 June 1944, (Normandy Campaign), (Personal Experience of a Division Artillery Communications Officer)," Infantry School, 1948–1949, courtesy of the Donovan Research Library, Fort Benning, Georgia, pp. 21–22.
22. Zinn, "Travels of Bennie Zinn."
23. Ralph P. Eaton questionnaire, courtesy of the Cornelius Ryan Collection, Alden Library, Ohio University, pp. 2–3.
24. Creek, oral history.
25. Jack R. Isaacs, oral history, courtesy of the Eisenhower Center.
26. Tom W. Porcella, oral history, courtesy of the Eisenhower Center.
27. General James M. Gavin, as quoted in "Debriefing Conference—Operation Neptune," 13 August 1944, courtesy of the 82nd Airborne Division War Memorial Museum, p. 13.
28. Ibid., pp. 13–14.
29. Langdon, *Ready*, p. 56, footnote.
30. Gavin interview, Cornelius Ryan Collection, p. 5.
31. Singleton, "Debriefing Conference—Operation Neptune," p. 12.

32. Cruise, written account.
33. William E. Ekman questionnaire, courtesy of the Cornelius Ryan Collection, Alden Library, Ohio University, p. 2
34. Benjamin H. Vandervoort, written account, courtesy of the Cornelius Ryan Collection, Alden Library, Ohio University, p. 1.
35. Milton E. Schlesener letter to Frank Vanderbilt, courtesy of Mrs. Frankie James.
36. Ibid.
37. Gerald Weed, interview with author.
38. W. A. Jones, interview with author.
39. George B. Wood questionnaire, courtesy of the Cornelius Ryan Collection, Alden Library, Ohio University, p. 3.
40. W. A. Jones, interview.
41. George B. Wood questionnaire, p. 3.
42. Charles E. Sammon letter to Cornelius Ryan, March 21, 1959, courtesy of the Cornelius Ryan Collection, Alden Library, Ohio University.
43. William T. Dunfee, "Normandy, The Cotentin Peninsula," courtesy of William T. Dunfee, p. 4.
44. Ibid.
45. Tucker, *Parachute Soldier*, pp. 40–41.
46. Weed, interview.
47. Benjamin H. Vandervoort, written account, courtesy of the Cornelius Ryan Collection, Alden Library, Ohio University, pp. 1–2.
48. Ibid., p. 2.
49. Ted Peterson letter to Cornelius Ryan, March 22, 1959, courtesy of the Cornelius Ryan Collection, Alden Library, Ohio University.
50. Weed, interview.
51. Ibid.
52. Otis L. Sampson, "Time Out For Combat," courtesy of Otis L. Sampson, p. 205.
53. Peterson to Ryan, March 22, 1959.
54. Stanley W. Kotlarz, interview with author.
55. Sampson, "Time Out For Combat," p. 206.
56. Peterson to Ryan, March 22, 1959.
57. Kotlarz, interview.
58. Weed, interview.
59. Peterson to Ryan, March 22, 1959.
60. Weed, interview.
61. Vandervoort, written account, Cornelius Ryan Collection, p. 2.

Chapter 11 "This Was One of the Toughest Days of My Life"

1. Marcus Heim Jr., "D-Day, June 6, 1944," courtesy of Mrs. Marcus Heim, p. 2.
2. Jack Tallerday questionnaire, courtesy of the Cornelius Ryan Collection, Alden Library, Ohio University, p. 4.
3. John J. Dolan letter to James M. Gavin, March 15, 1959, courtesy of the Cornelius Ryan Collection, Alden Library, Ohio University.
4. Robert M. Murphy, *No Better Place To Die*, Critical Hit, 1999, pp. 20–21.
5. Dolan to Gavin, March 15, 1959.
6. William Dean, oral history, courtesy of the Eisenhower Center.
7. "Operation of the 507th Regiment Following Drop," courtesy of the 82nd Airborne Division War Memorial Museum, pp. 3–4.
8. John Marr, oral account, courtesy of Albert Parker and Jerry Newton.
9. "507–2 On D-Day And Immediately After," courtesy of the 82nd Airborne Division War Memorial Museum, pp. 3–4.
10. General James M. Gavin, as quoted in "Debriefing Conference—Operation Neptune," 13 August 1944, p. 14.
11. Roy E. Creek, oral history, courtesy of the Eisenhower Center.
12. Dolan to Gavin, March 15, 1959.
13. Murphy, *No Better Place To Die*, p. 22.

14. Ibid.
15. Ibid.
16. Dolan to Gavin, March 15, 1959.
17. Murphy, *No Better Place To Die*, p. 22.
18. Dolan to Gavin, March 15, 1959.
19. Marr, oral account.
20. "Operation of the 507th Regiment Following Drop," p. 4.
21. James M. Gavin interview, courtesy of the Cornelius Ryan Collection, Alden Library, Ohio University, p. 5.
22. Creek, oral history.
23. "507–2 On D-Day and Immediately After," p. 4.
24. "Levy's Group, (A Statement by Lieutenant Joseph Kormylo, of D Company who was with Levy)," courtesy of the 82nd Airborne Division War Memorial Museum.
25. Marr, oral account.
26. Dolan to Gavin, March 15, 1959.
27. Ibid.
28. Homer Jones, interview with author.
29. William Dean, oral history, courtesy of the Eisenhower Center.
30. Homer Jones, interview.
31. Dean, oral history.
32. Dolan to Gavin, March 15, 1959.
33. Heim, "D-Day, June 6, 1944," p. 1.
34. "Levy's Group, Statement by Lieutenant Joseph Kormylo."
35. Ibid.
36. Dolan to Gavin, March 15, 1959.
37. Dean, oral history.
38. Adolph Warnecke, oral history, courtesy of the Eisenhower Center.
39. Dolan to Gavin, March 15, 1959.
40. Elmo E. Bell and The University of Southern Mississippi Center for Oral History and Cultural Heritage, *An Oral History with Brigadier General Elmo Edwin Bell: A Saga of a Survivor,* 2003, p. 148.
41. Dolan to Gavin, March 15, 1959.
42. Heim, "D-Day, June 6, 1944," p. 1.
43. Bell, *Oral History*, p. 149.
44. Dave Bullington, interview with author.
45. Heim, "D-Day, June 6, 1944," p. 2.
46. Dolan to Gavin, March 15, 1959.
47. Bell, *Oral History*, p. 149.
48. Heim, "D-Day, June 6, 1944," p. 2.
49. Dolan to Gavin, March 15, 1959.
50. Bell, *Oral History*, p. 149.
51. Dolan to Gavin, March 15, 1959.
52. Mark J. Alexander, "Thirty-four Days in Normandy in 1944," courtesy of Mark J. Alexander, pp. 3–4.
53. Dolan to Gavin, March 15, 1959.
54. Alexander, "Normandy," p. 3.
55. Gerard M. Dillon, oral history, courtesy of the Eisenhower Center.

Chapter 12 "I Think It's Time to Get Our War Started"

1. David Jones, oral history, courtesy of the Eisenhower Center.
2. Paul E. Lehman, letter to mother, June 28, 1944, courtesy of the 82nd Airborne Division War Memorial Museum.
3. Briand N. Beaudin, oral history, courtesy of the Eisenhower Center.
4. Lehman to mother, June 28, 1944.
5. Beaudin, oral history.
6. Lehman, letter.

7. Ibid.
8. George Leidenheimer, oral history, courtesy of the Eisenhower Center.
9. Harry L. Reisenleiter, oral history, courtesy of the Eisenhower Center.
10. Edward Barnes, oral history, courtesy of the Eisenhower Center.
11. Donald Bosworth, oral history, courtesy of the Eisenhower Center.
12. Barney Q. Hopkins, written account, courtesy of Barney Q. Hopkins.
13. Ibid.
14. J. Frank Brumbaugh, oral history, courtesy of the Eisenhower Center.
15. Ibid.
16. David Jones, oral history.
17. O. B. Hill, oral history, courtesy of the Eisenhower Center.
18. Brumbaugh, oral history.
19. Francis Williamson, written account, courtesy of Kristine Nymoen.
20. Lee Roy Wood, written account, courtesy of Kristine Nymoen.
21. Malcolm D. Brannen, written account, courtesy of the 82nd Airborne Division War Memorial Museum.
22. Lieutenant Ralph E. DeWeese, diary, courtesy of the 82nd Airborne Division War Memorial Museum.
23. Tom W. Porcella, oral history, courtesy of the Eisenhower Center.
24. Lieutenant Colonel Thomas J. B. Shanley, as quoted in "Debriefing Conference—Operation Neptune," 13 August 1944, courtesy of the 82nd Airborne Division War Memorial Museum.
25. Kenneth J. Merritt, oral history, courtesy of the Eisenhower Center.
26. D. Zane Schlemmer, oral history, courtesy of the Eisenhower Center.
27. Roy E. Creek oral history, courtesy of the Eisenhower Center.
28. Beaudin, oral history.
29. Merritt, oral history.
30. DeWeese, diary.
31. Edson D. Raff, questionnaire, courtesy of the Cornelius Ryan Collection, Alden Library, Ohio University.
32. Lucius Young, "Remembering My Days in the Service," courtesy of Lucius Young, p. 1.
33. Raff, questionnaire.
34. Ibid.
35. Ibid.
36. Edward R. Ryan, response to author's questionnaire.
37. Menno N. Christner, response to author's questionnaire.
38. Raff, questionnaire.
39. Creek, oral history.
40. Hopkins, written account.
41. Porcella, oral history.
42. Schlemmer, oral history.
43. Creek, oral history.

Chapter 13 "I Don't Know of a Better Place Than This to Die"

1. Lieutenant John J. Dolan, as quoted in Robert M. Murphy, *No Better Place To Die*, Critical Hit, 1999, p. 54.
2. William D. Owens, written account, courtesy of the Cornelius Ryan Collection, Alden Library, Ohio University.
3. Edward C. Boccafogli, oral history, courtesy of the Eisenhower Center.
4. Walter H. Barrett, *My Story, Every Soldier Has A Story*, published by the author, 2004, pp. 37–38.
5. Frank Staples oral account, courtesy of Kristine Nymoen.
6. Ibid.
7. George E. Christ, "D-Day, June 6, 1944, One Soldier's Story," courtesy of D. Zane Schlemmer.

8. Harold Canyon (a.k.a. Harold Kulju), oral history, courtesy of the Eisenhower Center.
9. Boccafogli, oral history.
10. Tom W. Porcella, oral history, courtesy of the Eisenhower Center.
11. D. Zane Schlemmer, oral history, courtesy of the Eisenhower Center.
12. Gerard M. Dillon, oral history, courtesy of the Eisenhower Center.
13. Wayne Pierce, "Normandy! Let's Go! My First 60 Hours!" courtesy of Wayne Pierce, p. 3.
14. James B. Helmer, "Story of the 82nd Airborne Division and the 325th Glider Infantry Regiment," courtesy of Kathy Stepzinski, pp. 3–4.
15. Pierce, "Normandy!" p. 3.
16. Helmer, "325th Glider Infantry Regiment," pp. 4–5.
17. Clinton E. Riddle, oral history, courtesy of the Eisenhower Center.
18. Pierce, "Normandy!" pp. 3–4.
19. Riddle, oral history.
20. Pierce, "Normandy!" p. 4.
21. Riddle, oral history.
22. Pierce, "Normandy!" p. 4.
23. Riddle, oral history.
24. Richard D. Weese, response to author's questionnaire.
25. Arthur Jacikas, response to author's questionnaire.
26. Raymond T. Burchell, response to author's questionnaire.
27. Harold Owens, oral history.
28. Helmer, "325th Glider Infantry Regiment," p. 5.
29. Lieutenant Colonel Klemm Boyd, as quoted in "Debriefing Conference—Operation Neptune," 13 August 1944, courtesy of the 82nd Airborne Division War Memorial Museum.
30. Major Teddy Sanford, as quoted in "Debriefing Conference—Operation Neptune," 13 August 1944, courtesy of the 82nd Airborne Division War Memorial Museum.
31. Lewis A. Strandburg, written account, courtesy of Lewis A. Strandburg.
32. Harold Owens, oral history, courtesy of Harold Owens.
33. Helmer, "325th Glider Infantry Regiment," pp. 5–6.
34. Pierce, "Normandy!" pp. 5–6.
35. William D. Owens, written account.
36. John J. Dolan letter to James M. Gavin, March 15, 1959, courtesy of Cornelius Ryan Collection, Alden Library, Ohio University.
37. William D. Owens, written account.
38. Dave Bullington, interview with author.
39. Robert M. Murphy, response to author's questionnaire.
40. Robert M. Murphy, *No Better Place To Die*, p. 54.
41. William D. Owens, written account.
42. Dolan to Gavin, March 15, 1959.
43. Lewis A. Strandburg, written account, courtesy of Lewis A. Strandburg.
44. Fred Kampfer, response to author's questionnaire.
45. Strandburg, written account.
46. Joe Gault, "F Company 325th Glider Infantry," courtesy of Joe Gault, p. 6.
47. Kampfer, questionnaire.
48. Lee C. Travelstead, "LCT's Adventures in Normandy, June 1944," courtesy of Lee C. Travelstead, pp.1–2.

Chapter 14 "Colonel, Aren't You Glad Waverly's on Our Side"

1. John Rabig, as quoted in, Benjamin H. Vandervoort, "Waverly Wray, Ste.-Mère-Église, Normandy—June 7, 1944," p. 4, courtesy of Lieutenant General Jack Norton.
2. Ibid., p. 1.
3. Ibid., pp. 1–2.
4. Ibid., pp. 2–3.

5. Thomas J. McClean, sworn statement supporting Medal of Honor resubmission for Waverly Wray, March 1, 1984, courtesy of Lieutenant General Jack Norton.
6. Frank Silanskis, sworn statement supporting Medal of Honor resubmission for Waverly Wray, March 5, 1984, courtesy of Lieutenant General Jack Norton.
7. Paul D. Nunan, sworn statement supporting Medal of Honor resubmission for Waverly Wray, March 2, 1984, courtesy of Lieutenant General Jack Norton.
8. Ibid.
9. Charles Miller, oral history, courtesy of the Eisenhower Center.
10. Vandervoort, "Waverly Wray," pp. 3–4.
11. Wayne Pierce, "Normandy! Let's Go! My First 60 Hours!" courtesy of Wayne Pierce, p. 6.
12. Otis L. Sampson, "Time Out For Combat," pp. 211–212.
13. James Elmo Jones, oral history, courtesy of the Eisenhower Center.
14. Ibid.
15. James J. Coyle, written account in "Echoes of the Warriors," compiled and edited by George Jacobus, 1992, p. 263.
16. William L. Blank, memoirs, courtesy of the 82nd Airborne Division War Memorial Museum.
17. Earl W. Boling, written account, in "Echoes of the Warriors," p. 125.
18. Sampson, "Time Out For Combat," p. 213.
19. Stanley W. Kotlarz, interview with author.
20. Floyd West, Jr., letter to Mr. Walter J. Turnbull, Jr., April 14, 1947, courtesy of Mrs. Frankie James.
21. Coyle, in "Echoes of the Warriors," p. 263.
22. Ibid., p. 263.
23. Sampson, "Time Out For Combat," p. 215.
24. James Elmo Jones, oral history.
25. Benjamin H. Vandervoort, written account, courtesy of the Cornelius Ryan Collection, Alden Library, Ohio University, p. 6.
26. Sampson, "Time Out For Combat," pp. 215–216.
27. Ibid., p. 224.
28. Coyle, in "Echoes of the Warriors," p. 263.
29. Frank P. Woosley, as quoted in Otis L. Sampson, "Time Out For Combat," p. 224.
30. Coyle, in "Echoes of the Warriors," pp. 263–264.
31. Sampson, "Time Out For Combat," p. 215.
32. Boling, in "Echoes of the Warriors," p. 125.
33. Coyle, in "Echoes of the Warriors," pp. 263–264.
34. Sampson, "Time Out For Combat," pp. 215–216.
35. Ibid., p. 224.
36. Ibid., pp. 215–218.
37. Coyle, in "Echoes of the Warriors," p. 264.
38. Sampson, "Time Out For Combat," pp. 218–219.
39. Coyle, in "Echoes of the Warriors," p. 264.
40. George Jacobus, written account in "Echoes of the Warriors," p. 241.
41. Benjamin H. Vandervoort, written account, p. 6.
42. Paul E. Lehman, letter to mother, June 28, 1944, courtesy of the 82nd Airborne Division War Memorial Museum.
43. Arthur B. Schultz, "Normandy Campaign, From 7 June–15 June 1944," courtesy of Arthur B. Schultz, pp. 2–3.
44. Wayne Pierce, "Normandy!" p. 6.
45. Vandervoort, "Waverly Wray," pp. 3–4.

Chapter 15 "Van, Don't Kill Them All. Save a Few for Interrogation."

1. General James M. Gavin, as quoted in Allen L. Langdon, "*Ready: The History of the 505th, 82nd Airborne Division*," Western Newspaper Publishing Company, 1986, p. 64.

2. Lieutenant Ralph E. DeWeese, diary, courtesy of the 82nd Airborne Division War Memorial Museum.
3. William Call, interview with author.
4. DeWeese, diary.
5. Call, interview.
6. William T. Dunfee, "Normandy, The Cotentin Peninsula," courtesy of William T. Dunfee, pp. 6–7.
7. Barney Q. Hopkins, written account, courtesy of Barney Q. Hopkins.
8. Gavin, as quoted in Langdon, *Ready*, p. 64.
9. Gerard M. Dillon, oral history, courtesy of the Eisenhower Center.
10. William H. Tucker, *Parachute Soldier*, International Airborne Books, 2nd ed., 1994, p. 47.
11. Ibid.
12. Ibid., p. 48.
13. D. Zane Schlemmer, oral history, courtesy of the Eisenhower Center.
14. Kenneth J. Merritt, oral history, courtesy of the Eisenhower Center.
15. Harold Canyon (a.k.a. Harold Kulju), oral history, courtesy of the Eisenhower Center.
16. Schlemmer, oral history.
17. Tucker, *Parachute Soldier*, p. 49.
18. Dillon, oral history.
19. Captain Paul F. Smith, "Personal Experience of Captain Paul F. Smith during the Assault Phase of the Invasion of Normandy, France, June 6, 1944," courtesy of Paul F. Smith.
20. Wayne Pierce, "Normandy! Let's Go! My First 60 Hours!" pp. 7–8.
21. John W. Marr, oral account, courtesy of Albert Parker and Jerry Newton.
22. Samuel F. Bassett, "The Glider War," p. 1.
23. Pierce, "Normandy!" pp. 8–9.
24. Richard D. Weese, response to author's questionnaire.
25. Marr, oral account.
26. Raymond T. Burchell, response to author's questionnaire.
27. Harry Samselle, interview with author.
28. Ibid.
29. Robert L. Swick, interview with author.
30. Samselle, interview.
31. Pierce, "Normandy!" p. 9.
32. Burchell, questionnaire.
33. Samselle, interview.
34. Ibid.
35. Ibid.
36. Swick, interview.
37. Pierce, "Normandy!" pp. 9–11.
38. Marr, oral account.
39. Swick, interview.
40. Smith, "Personal Experience."
41. Clinton E. Riddle, oral history, courtesy of the Eisenhower Center.
42. Bassett, "The Glider War," pp. 1–2.
43. Dillon, oral history.
44. Joe Gault, "Company F 325th Glider Infantry," courtesy of Joe Gault, pp. 6–7.
45. Edwin Lainhart, "Recollections of My Experiences in World War II, Medical Detachment, 325th Glider Infantry Regiment, 82nd Airborne Division," courtesy of Wayne Pierce, p. 7.
46. Darrell C. Dilley, response to author's questionnaire.
47. George Speakman, response to author's questionnaire.

Chapter 16 "Follow Me!"

1. Captain John Sauls, as quoted in William B. Breuer, *Geronimo!* St. Martin's Press, 1989, p. 255.
2. James M. Gavin, *On To Berlin*, Viking Press, 1978, p. 116.
3. Lee C. Travelstead, "LCT's Adventures in Normandy, June 1944," courtesy of Lee C. Travelstead, p. 2.
4. Chester Walker, response to author's questionnaire.
5. Frank Norris, as quoted in Clay Blair, *Ridgway's Paratroopers*, Dial Press, 1985, pp. 319–320.
6. Gavin, *On To Berlin*, p. 116.
7. James M. Gavin, as quoted in Blair, *Ridgway's Paratroopers*, p. 322.
8. Richard B. Johnson, "Richard B. Johnson's Adventures in Normandy," courtesy of Wayne Pierce, p. 8.
9. Travelstead, "LCT's Adventures in Normandy, June 1944," p. 2.
10. Frank Norris, as quoted in Blair, *Ridgway's Paratroopers*, p. 320.
11. Robert D. Rae, letter to Mogens Warrer, July 29, 1971, courtesy of Albert N. Parker.
12. John H. Wisner, as quoted in Blair, *Ridgway's Paratroopers*, p. 321.
13. James M. Gavin, as quoted in as quoted in Blair, *Ridgway's Paratroopers*, p. 321.
14. Gavin, *On To Berlin*, p. 117.
15. Walker, questionnaire.
16. Johnson, "Richard B. Johnson's Adventures in Normandy," p. 9.
17. Ibid., pp. 9–10.
18. Lewis A. Strandburg, "World War II, My Life in the Service," courtesy of Lewis A. Strandburg, p. 8.
19. Matthew B. Ridgway, oral history, Part 2, U.S. Army Military History Institute, p. 18.
20. Frank Norris, as quoted in Blair, *Ridgway's Paratroopers*, p. 323.
21. Johnson, "Richard B. Johnson's Adventures in Normandy," pp. 10–11.
22. Lucius Young, "Remembering My Days in the Service," courtesy of Lucius Young, p. 2
23. Travelstead, "LCT's Adventures in Normandy, June 1944," pp. 3–4.
24. S. L. A. Marshall, "Regimental Unit Study Number 4," U.S. Army Center of Military History, Historical Manuscripts Collection, File Number 8-3.1 BB 4, p. 31.
25. Rae to Warrer, July 29, 1971.
26. Howard R. Huebner, response to author's questionnaire.
27. Strandburg, "World War II, My Life in the Service," p. 8.
28. Travelstead, "LCT's Adventures in Normandy, June 1944," p. 5.
29. Rae to Warrer, July 29, 1971.
30. Travelstead, "LCT's Adventures in Normandy, June 1944," pp. 5–6.
31. Rae to Mogens Warrer, July 29, 1971.
32. Edward J. Jeziorski, response to author's questionnaire.
33. Rae to Warrer, July 29, 1971.
34. Travelstead, "LCT's Adventures in Normandy, June 1944," pp. 5–8.
35. Rae to Warrer, July 29, 1971.
36. Strandburg, "World War II, My Life in the Service," p. 8.
37. Rae to Warrer, July 29, 1971.
38. Ibid.
39. Clinton E. Riddle, oral history, courtesy of the Eisenhower Center.
40. Kenneth J. Merritt, oral history, courtesy of the Eisenhower Center.
41. Francis E. Naughton, "Narrative—Interaction of United States Forces and French Citizens During the Battles of Graignes, 6–12 June, 1944," courtesy of Francis E. Naughton, p. 3.
42. David Brummitt, "Experiences of Captain Leroy David Brummitt During the Allied Invasion of Normandy, France, June 6, 1944," courtesy of Paul F. Smith, p. 3.
43. Mark J. Alexander, "Thirty-four days in Normandy in 1944," courtesy of Mark J. Alexander, p. 4.
44. Arthur B. Schultz, "The General and the Private," courtesy of Arthur B. Schultz, p. 15.

45. Alexander, "Normandy," p. 4.
46. I. W. Seelye, response to author's questionnaire.
47. Alexander, "Normandy," pp. 4–5.
48. Edwin Lainhart, "Recollections of My Experiences in World War II, Medical Detachment, 325th Glider Infantry Regiment, 82nd Airborne Division," courtesy of Wayne Pierce, pp. 7–8.
49. Joe Gault, "Company F 325th Glider Infantry," courtesy of Joe Gault, pp. 6–7.
50. Naughton, "Narrative," pp. 4–6.
51. Brummitt, "Experiences of Captain Leroy David Brummitt," p. 3.
52. Francis E. Naughton, "Summary—Interaction of United States Forces and French Citizens During the Battle of Graignes, 6–12 June 1944," courtesy of Francis E. Naughton, p. 2.

Chapter 17 "My God, Matt, Can't Anything Stop These Men?"

1. General Omar N. Bradley, as quoted in Allen L. Langdon, "*Ready: The History of the 505th, 82nd Airborne Division,*" Western Newspaper Publishing Co., 1986, p. 80.
2. Dwayne T. Burns, unpublished memoirs, courtesy of Dwayne T. Burns, pp. 83–84.
3. Ibid., p. 84.
4. Robert B. White, interview with author.
5. Robert B. Newhart, response to author's questionnaire.
6. Burns, memoirs, p. 84.
7. Ibid., pp. 84–85.
8. Newhart, questionnaire.
9. Burns, memoirs, pp. 85–86.
10. Roy E. Creek, written account, courtesy of Roy E. Creek.
11. Gerard M. Dillon, oral history, courtesy of the Eisenhower Center.
12. Chris Kanaras, letter to author, courtesy of Chris Kanaras.
13. Creek, written account.
14. Lewis A. Strandburg, "World War II, My Life in the Service," courtesy of Lewis A. Strandburg, pp. 9–10.
15. Clinton E. Riddle, response to author's questionnaire.
16. Paul E. Lehman, letter to mother, June 28, 1944, courtesy of the 82nd Airborne Division War Memorial Museum.
17. Mark J. Alexander, "Thirty-four Days in Normandy in 1944," courtesy of Mark J. Alexander, pp. 5–6.
18. David Bowman, response to author's questionnaire.
19. Wilton Johnson, response to author's questionnaire.
20. Alexander, "Normandy," pp. 5–6.
21. James V. Rodier, response to author's questionnaire.
22. Spencer F. Wurst, *Descending from the Clouds*, Casemate Publishing, 2004, p. 242.
23. Ibid., pp. 242–243.
24. Ibid., p. 242.
25. Langdon, *Ready*, p. 80.
26. Ibid.
27. Paul D. Nunan, interview with author.
28. Russell W. Brown, response to author's questionnaire.
29. Wurst, *Descending from the Clouds*, p. 244.
30. Alexander, "Normandy," p. 6.
31. Wurst, *Descending from the Clouds*, p. 246.
32. Jack R. Isaacs, oral history, courtesy of the Eisenhower Center.
33. William T. Dunfee, "Normandy, The Cotentin Peninsula." courtesy of William T. Dunfee, p. 7.
34. William L. Blank, memoirs, courtesy of 82nd Airborne Division War Memorial Museum.
35. Isaacs, oral history.

36. Ibid.
37. Rudy A. Stinnett, "Crossing the Douve," courtesy of Wayne Pierce.
38. Ibid.
39. Robert H. Parks, response to author's questionnaire.
40. Howard R. Huebner, response to author's questionnaire.
41. Edward J. Jeziorski, response to author's questionnaire.
42. Stinnett, "Crossing the Douve."
43. Lieutenant Ralph E. DeWeese, diary, courtesy of the 82nd Airborne Division War Memorial Museum.
44. Ibid.
45. Lehman to mother, June 28, 1944.

Chapter 18 "Resourceful and Courageous in the Attack, Resolute in the Defense, They Fought Superbly."

1. James M. Gavin, *On To Berlin*, Viking Press 1978, p. 120.
2. D. Zane Schlemmer, "Bois de Limors to Hill 131, Normandy, France," courtesy of D. Zane Schlemmer, pp. 1–2.
3. Gus L. Sanders, questionnaire, courtesy of the Cornelius Ryan Collection, Alden Library, Ohio University.
4. William E. Ekman, interview with Mike Ekman, courtesy of Mike Ekman.
6. Ibid.
7. Ibid.
8. Schlemmer, "Bois de Limors to Hill 131," pp. 1–2.
9. Dwayne T. Burns, memoirs, courtesy of the Eisenhower Center.
10. Ekman, interview.
11. Schlemmer, "Bois de Limors to Hill 131," pp. 1–2.
12. Mark J. Alexander, "Thirty-four Days in Normandy in 1944," courtesy of Mark J. Alexander, p. 8.
13. Schlemmer, "Bois de Limors to Hill 131," pp. 1–2.
14. Clinton E. Riddle, response to author's questionnaire.
15. Darrell C. Dilley, response to author's questionnaire.
16. Raymond T. Burchell, response to author's questionnaire.
17. Alexander, "Normandy," pp. 8–9.
18. William L. Blank, memoirs, courtesy of the 82nd Airborne Division War Memorial Museum.
19. Burns, memoirs.
20. Louis G. Mendez, as quoted in Patrick K. O'Donnell, *Beyond Valor*, The Free Press, 2001, p. 173.
21. Lieutenant Ralph E. DeWeese, diary, courtesy of the 82nd Airborne Division War Memorial Museum.
22. William Call, interview with author.
23. Burchell, questionnaire.
24. Ibid.
25. Schlemmer, oral history.
26. Riddle, questionnaire.
27. Roy E. Creek, written account, courtesy of Roy E. Creek.
28. Riddle, questionnaire.
29. Dilley, questionnaire.
30. Mark Rupaner, response to author's questionnaire.
31. Dean McCandless, response to author's questionnaire.
32. DeWeese, diary.
33. Burchell, questionnaire.
34. Riddle, questionnaire.
35. DeWeese, diary.
35. Gavin, *On To Berlin*, p. 120.

BIBLIOGRAPHY

Published Sources

Books:

Ambrose, Stephen. *Citizen Soldiers.* New York: Simon and Schuster, 1997.

Barrett, Walter H. *My Story, Every Soldier Has A Story.* n.p.: published by the author, 2004.

Baugh, James Emory. *From Skies of Blue.* Lincoln, Nebr.: iUniverse, 2003.

Bell, Elmo, and The University of Southern Mississippi Center for Oral History and Cultural Heritage. *An Oral History with Brigadier General Elmo Edwin Bell: A Saga of a Survivor.* Hattiesburg: The University of Southern Mississippi, 2003.

Blair, Clay. *Ridgway's Paratroopers.* N.Y.: Dial Press, 1985.

Boroughs, Zig. *The Devil's Tale.* n.p.: Zig Boroughs (privately published), 1992.

Bradley, Omar N., and Clay Blair. *A General's Life.* New York: Simon and Schuster, 1983.

Breuer, William B. *Drop Zone Sicily.* Novato, Calif.: Presidio Press, 1983.

———. *Geronimo!.* N.Y.: St. Martin's Press, 1989.

Burriss, T. Moffatt. *Strike And Hold.* Dulles, Va.: Brassey's, 2000.

Carter, Ross S. *Those Devils In Baggy Pants.* Cutchogue, N.Y.: Buccaneer Books, 1976.

Dawson, W. Forrest, ed. *Saga of the All American.* Atlanta: Albert Love Enterprises, 1946.

Dougdale, J. *Panzer Divisions, Panzergrenadier Divisions, Panzer Brigades of the Army and Waffen SS in the West, Autumn 1944–Februray 1945, Ardennes and Nordwind.* Alberton, South Africa: Galago Publishing, 2000.

Gavin, James M. *On To Berlin.* N.Y.: Viking Press, 1978.

Goldstein, Elliott. *On The Job Training, The Battle of Parker's Crossroads.* n.p.: Elliott Goldstein, n.d.

Kershaw, Robert J. *It Never Snows in September.* Rockville Center, N.Y.: Sarpedon, 2001.

Langdon, Allen. *Ready.* Indianapolis: Western Newspaper Publishing Co., 1986.

Leoleis, George. *Medals.* N.Y.: Carlton Press, 1990.

Lord, William G. II. *History of the 508th Parachute Infantry Regiment.* Washington, D.C.: Infantry Journal Press, 1948.

MacDonald, Charles B. *A Time for Trumpets.* N.Y.: William Morrow, Quill, 1985.

———. *The U.S. Army in World War II: The Siegfried Line Campaign.* Washington, D.C.: Office of the Chief of Military History, 1963.

Mandle, Lieutenant William D., and Private First Class David H. Whittier. (compiled by) *The Devils In Baggy Pants, Combat Record of the 504th Parachute Infantry Regiment April 1943–July 1945.* Paris: Draeger Freres, 1945.

Margry, Karel, ed. *Operation Market-Garden Then and Now.* London: Battle of Britain International Limited, 2002.

Marshall, S. L. A. *Night Drop.* Boston: Little, Brown and Co., 1962.

Masters, Charles J. *Glidermen of Neptune.* Carbondale: Southern Illinois University Press, 1995.

Megellas, James. *All The Way To Berlin.* N.Y.: Ballantine Publishing Group, Presidio Press, 2003.

Murphy, Robert M. *No Better Place To Die.* Croton Falls, N.Y.: Critical Hit, 1999.

O'Donnell, Patrick K. *Beyond Valor.* N.Y.: The Free Press, 2001.

Orfalea, Gregory. *Messengers of the Lost Battalion.* N.Y.: The Free Press, 1997.

Pallud, Jean Paul. *Battle of the Bulge Then and Now*. London: Battle of Britain International Limited, 1999.
Parker. Danny S. *Battle of the Bulge*. Conshohocken, Pa.: Combined Publishing, 1999.
Pierce, Wayne. *Let's Go!* n.p.: Professional Press, 1997.
Richlak, Jerry L. Sr. *Glide to Glory*. Chesterland, Ohio: Cedar House, 2002.
Ridgway, Matthew B., and Harold H. Martin. *Soldier: The Memoirs of Matthew B. Ridgway*. Westport, Conn.: Greenwood Press, 1956.
Ruggero, Ed. *Combat Jump*. N.Y.: Harper Collins, 2003.
Ruppenthal, Major Roland G. *Utah Beach to Cherbourg*. Washington, D.C.: US Army Center of Military History, 1994.
Ryan, Cornelius. *A Bridge Too Far*. N.Y.: Simon and Schuster, 1974.
Saunders, Tim. *Nijmegen*. Barnsley, South Yorkshire, UK: Leo Cooper, 2001.
Tregaskis, Richard. *Invasion Diary*. N.Y.: Random House, 1944.
Tucker, William H. *D Day: Thirty Five Days In Normandy*. Harwichport, Miss.: International Airborne Books, 2002.
———. *Parachute Soldier*. Harwichport, Miss.: International Airborne Books, 1994.
———. *Rendezvous at Rochelinval*. Harwichport, Miss.: International Airborne Books, 1999.
Warren, Dr. John C. *Airborne Operations in World War II, European Theater—USAF Historical Studies: No. 97*. Manhattan, Kans.: Sunflower University Press, MA/AH Publishing, 1956.
Wills, Deryk. *Put On Your Boots And Parachutes!* Oadby, Leicester, UK: Deryk Wills, 1992.
Wurst, Spencer F. *Descending from the Clouds*. Havertown, Pa.: Casemate Publishing, 2004.

Articles:
Gellhorn, Martha. "Rough and Tumble." *Colliers—The American Weekly*, December 2, 1944, p. 114.
Welsh, Bill. "Medic Chet." *Erie Morning News*, January 31, 1995.

Unpublished Sources

Unpublished written sources noted in this book, including diaries, sworn statements, letters, written accounts, memoirs, manuscripts, maps, photographs, questionnaires, US military documents, after action reports, studies, monographs, statements, and combat interviews are found in the author's collection and among the collections of the following organizations:
82nd Airborne Division War Memorial Museum, Fort Bragg, North Carolina.
Cornelius Ryan Collection, Alden Library, Ohio University, Athens, Ohio.
Donovan Research Library, Fort Benning, Georgia.
Silent Wings Museum, Lubbock, Texas.
US Army Center of Military History, Fort McNair, D.C.
US Army Military History Institute, Carlisle Barracks, Pennsylvania.
Taped interviews, oral histories, and interview and oral history transcripts noted in this book are found in the author's collection and among the collections of the following organizations:
American Military Veterans Oral History Project, 2000, University of Kentucky, Lexington, Kentucky.
Eisenhower Center, New Orleans, Louisiana.
Franklin D. Roosevelt Library, Digital Archives, Hyde Park, N.Y.

Internet Sources

508th Parachute Infantry Regiment Association, Roll of Honor, Personal Accounts, and Post War Deaths of 508th Parachute Infantry Regiment veterans, http://508pir.org/

Bowditch, Captain John III. "Anzio Beachhead 22 January–25 May 1944." US Army Center of Military History, 1990,
http://www.army.mil/cmh-pg/books/wwii/anziobeach/anzio-fm.htm

Cole, Hugh M. "The Ardennes: Battle of the Bulge." US Army Center of Military History, 1990, http://www.army.mil/cmh-pg/books/wwii/7-8/7-8_cont.htm

Fifth Army Historical Section, "Fifth Army at the Winter Line 15 November 1943–15 January 1944." US Army Center of Military History, 1990, http://www.army.mil/cmh-pg/books/wwii/winterline/winter-fm.htm

———, "From the Volturno to the Winter Line 6 October–15 November 1943." US Army Center of Military History, 1990, http://www.army.mil/cmh-pg/books/wwii/volturno/volturno-fm.htm

———, "Salerno: American Operations From the Beaches to the Volturno 9 September–6 October 1943." US Army Center of Military History, 1990, http://www.army.mil/cmh-pg/books/wwii/salerno/sal-fm.htm

Gatens, John, 589th FAB, A Battery, written account, http://www.indianamilitary.org/106ID/Units/589FA/GatensJohn_589A.htm

Michetti, Marino M., written account, Veterans of the Battle of the Bulge, http://home.cfl.rr.com/vbob18/MICHETTI.htm.

Research of the armored strength of the Hermann Göring Panzer Division during the Sicily Campaign, http://www.feldgrau.net/phpBB2/index.php

Research of the composition of German units in the Cotentin Peninsula at the beginning of the Normandy invasion, http://web.telia.com/~u18313395/normandy/gerob/infdiv/91id.html

Roll of Honor of 82nd Airborne Division, http://www.ww2airborne.us/division/82_overview.html

Unit History of the US 746th Tank Battalion in Normandy, http://www.geocities.com/viajero43081/history.htm

INDEX